ARMAGEDDON,
OIL
AND
TERROR

What the Bible says about the future

TYNDALE HOUSE PUBLISHERS, INC., CAROL STREAM, ILLINOIS

ARMAGEDDON, OIL

AND

TERROR

WHAT THE BIBLE SAYS ABOUT THE FUTURE

JOHN F. WALVOORD

WITH MARK HITCHCOCK

Visit Tyndale's exciting Web site at www.tyndale.com

Visit the author's Web site at www.walvoord.com

TYNDALE and Tyndale's quill logo are registered trademarks of Tyndale House Publishers, Inc.

Armageddon, Oil, and Terror: What the Bible Says about the Future

Designed by Stephen Vosloo

Previously published in 1974 and 1990 as *Armageddon, Oil and the Middle East Crisis* by Zondervan under ISBN 0-310-53921-8.

First published as *Armageddon, Oil, and Terror* by Tyndale House Publishers, Inc., in 2007.

Library of Congress Cataloging-in-Publication Data

Walvoord, John F.
  Armageddon, oil, and terror: what the Bible says about the future / John F. Walvoord with Mark Hitchcock.
    p. cm.
  Rev. ed. of Armageddon, oil, and the Middle East crisis. Rev. ed. c1990.
  Includes bibliographical references.
  ISBN-13: 978-1-4143-1610-9 (hc: alk. paper)
  ISBN-10: 1-4143-1610-0 (hc : alk. paper)
  ISBN-13: 978-1-4143-1582-9 (sc : alk. paper)
  ISBN-10: 1-4143-1582-1 (sc : alk. paper)
  1. Bible—Prophecies. 2. Middle East—Politics and government—1945- 3. World politics—1945-4. Armageddon.
5. Civilization, Western. 6. Petroleum industry and trade—Middle East. I. Hitchcock, Mark.
II. Walvoord, John F. Armageddon, oil, and the Middle East crisis. III. Title
  BS649.N45W34 2007
  236'.9—dc22   2006102644

Printed in the United States of America

13 12 11 10 09 08 07
 7 6 5 4 3 2 1

Contents

Preface

DR. JOHN F. WALVOORD WAS NOT A PROPHET. But most would agree that he knew more about the prophecies of the Bible than any man who lived in the last century. During his long life he dedicated himself to the study of biblical prophecy in the original languages and the cultural context of the day in which the prophets spoke.

Dr. Walvoord was widely recognized as the "dean" of Bible prophecy scholars and teachers in the twentieth century. He taught thousands of seminary students at Dallas Theological Seminary, wrote and contributed to more than thirty books, traveled extensively, and spoke to audiences around the world. His contribution to the church's understanding of what the Bible says will happen in the end times is inestimable.

In the late 1930s Dr. Walvoord declared that the Jews would return to their ancient homeland and Israel would become a new and powerful Jewish state. In the mid-1940s he repeatedly wrote that the Jews would be restored to Israel.[1] His interpretation of prophecy led him to believe that Israel had to become a state amid its enemies—no matter what the odds. He insisted Israel had to be established and survive or end-time prophecies could not be fulfilled. His literal interpretation proved to be correct. The state of Israel was established in 1948. And Israel has miraculously survived one attack after another.

Over a period of five decades, Dr. Walvoord wrote numerous books and articles on topics related to the end times. Time and time again, he sketched out lists of end-time events that became headlines years after he put them in writing. While all of his works are important and valuable, in terms of popular impact, one of his books stands alone: *Armageddon, Oil and the Middle East Crisis.*

This classic book on end-time prophecy was originally published in 1974. The outline of events he had taught throughout the previous decades came alive in the wake of the 1973 Yom Kippur War in Israel and the subsequent Arab oil embargo against the United States. Dr. Walvoord seized upon the interest in world events at that time as a unique opportunity to show how these events pointed toward the Bible's scenario for the end times.

The book, with very minor revision, was rereleased sixteen years later in 1990 in light of the Persian Gulf War. Dr. Walvoord often commented how even after sixteen years the prophetic interpretations in the book remained rock solid and required no major changes. The revised book hit the *New York Times* best-seller list and sold millions of copies. It has been translated into ten languages and is still studied throughout the world.

Dr. Walvoord was perhaps less shocked by the events that occurred on September 11, 2001, than many of his contemporaries. He had predicted the rise of Islamic terrorism. He had predicted that terrorism and access to oil would be at the center of end-time events that would rock the world.

Before his death on December 20, 2002, Dr. Walvoord told many of his students that he believed the rise of militant Islam and the war on terror might be the final piece to the prophetic puzzle. It does seem that a kind of prophetic "shift of gears" occurred on 9/11 when world attention was riveted on the Middle East.

Our post-9/11 world seems to be on a downhill collision course. Terrorism has made the world increasingly dangerous. Some say we are already in World War III. Security, safety, and peace are the top priorities on everyone's agenda. There is an almost desperate yearning for peace and safety. Israel's struggle with Hamas and Hezbollah is now a centerpiece in the war on terror, which could lead to a nuclear confrontation between Israel and Iran. Add to all this the fact that the world's thirst for Middle Eastern oil shows no signs of diminishing.

The providential presence of crude oil in the Middle East and record prices for this resource have riveted world attention on the Middle East. The security and continued prosperity of the United States and Western Europe are vitally linked to the uninterrupted flow of Middle Eastern oil.

Much has transpired in the sixteen-plus years since the release of the second version of Dr. Walvoord's classic best seller. That is why the two of us—one his son, the other his student—have collaborated to revise and update this Bible prophecy classic for another generation. It reveals once again the timeless echo of Bible prophecy as history appears to move rapidly to the last events predicted to occur before the end of the age. Once again, it points another generation of readers to the relationship between prophecies in the Bible and the headlines and events we see around us.

Great care has been taken not to change any of the core material or views of Dr. Walvoord, and some additional material has been drawn from his other works and conversations during the last two years of his life. As you can see, the original title has been changed to reflect Dr. Walvoord's belief that terrorism is an essential element that is setting the stage for the end-time scenario presented in Scripture. In chapter 1 we discuss a biblical view of prophecy. In each of the next twelve chapters, we examine a specific event—either occurring now or that will unfold in the months and years ahead—that points to the end times. In chapters 14 and 15, we explain why believers in Christ can have hope, even during today's tumultuous times.

Whether you have read Dr. Walvoord's original work and are anxious to read this update or are totally new to this material, we invite you to examine for yourself the incredible correspondence between events in our world today and God's prophetic outline found in Scripture.

—JOHN E. WALVOORD

—MARK HITCHCOCK

CHAPTER 1

WHY PROPHECY?

It's very difficult to prophesy, especially about the future.
CHINESE PROVERB

*My interest is in the future, because I'm going
to spend the rest of my life there.*
CHARLES F. KETTERING

HAVE YOU EVER DRIVEN DOWN a strange dark road in a blinding rainstorm? Every minute you wish you could see beyond the edge of the headlights to see what's ahead. If only you could know what was coming next—could intuitively know what's out there or predict what you'll find at the next bend in the road. We long to see ahead, to know, perhaps to avert disaster.

Can someone see what's ahead by intuition or a special gift? Can a prophet know the future because the path of our lives is part of a larger drama scripted ahead of time? This is what the prophets of the Bible claim. Can we know where we are in that pattern of events foretold by prophets, written in Scripture, or seen in apocalyptic visions of the future? That is what we'll explore in this book.

In the uncertain storm of the days in which we live, all of us yearn to see beyond the headlights—but can we?

THE TIME BOMB IN OUR POCKET

The terrorist bomb on a bus in Israel has jumped into everyman's life— the World Trade Center, the Pentagon, a subway in London, a train in Madrid, a hotel in paradise. No one is safe anywhere.

Four planes are hijacked. The World Trade Center is destroyed and the Pentagon attacked. The entire United States economy is thrown into a recession.

Hurricane Katrina hits the coast. Refineries stop. Ports are blocked. The price of gas soars. Oil companies report record profits. The economic cement of our lives is not cement at all.

These recent events have underscored a reality most Americans would rather ignore: We have vulnerabilities. One of the greatest is our dependence on foreign oil. The wheels of transportation that make capitalism possible depend on this oil—gas, diesel fuel, high-octane jet fuel. If the wheels stop, the economy will shatter. The supply line stretches across the world to Saudi Arabia, Iraq, Iran, and the Middle East.

New industrial nations are exploding. The rocket of economic growth in China and throughout Asia demands more and more oil. The world barely has enough to supply present demand. The clash of economic engines demands more oil when supplies are nearing the breaking point. In this decade, economic growth alone will cause an "oil break point."

In 2001, Osama bin Laden plotted to overthrow the monarchy in Saudi Arabia and take over the oil the West needs so desperately. Then he could demand any price. Demand anything.[1] In 2006, terrorists attempted to attack the heart of the Saudi Arabian oil and gas industry, the Abqaiq processing facility. Al-Qaeda claimed responsibility for the failed attack. The *New York Times* called it the first attack on Saudi Arabia's oil infrastructure.[2] In one day the story disappeared from the news.

Do these events signal what the future holds? What will happen when Islamic terrorists are willing to ignite chaos in the Middle East to destroy the Great Satan of the West? Is it possible to protect every wellhead, pipeline, processing facility, and tanker? Who will stop the sabotage, the trucks laden with explosives, the handheld rockets, the dirty bombs?

Terrorism exposes another vulnerability. The terrorist arsenal has been building for decades. Iran has purchased and supplied Russian and Chinese weaponry, which has passed through Syria into Lebanon. Before the Thirty-Four-Day War between Israel and Hezbollah in the summer of 2006, the militant organization's arsenal included approximately 13,000 rockets and medium-range missiles. Israel was surprised at the state-of-the-art weapons used by the terrorist organization. During that one clash, Hezbollah fired approximately 4,000 short- and medium-range missiles into northern Israel.

Many still believe that weapons and high explosives stored in Iraq were carried out by the truckload before American troops arrived in March 2003—and that much of these are returning in the hands of terrorists. Tons of sophisticated explosives from a wide variety of sources are now in the hands of terrorists around the globe.

Missiles, nuclear warheads, and enriched uranium from the former Soviet Union have been bought and sold around the world to the highest bidder. In the late 1980s Abdul Qadeer Khan, the renegade Pakistani nuclear engineer, sold uranium enrichment technology to Libya, North Korea, and Iran. Although Libya has given up its nuclear program, it is now clear that both Iran and North Korea have used these designs to further their nuclear programs. North Korea has the bomb and is working to perfect the means to deliver a nuclear warhead as far as the United States.[3] Public statements by Iranian president Mahmoud Ahmadinejad have led intelligence sources to believe that Iran will be able to construct powerful atomic bombs in the very near future.

Iran is hotly pursuing its nuclear program and has publicly declared its intent to obliterate Israel. Iran is fully aware that Israel might launch a preemptive strike on its nuclear production facilities, and it has financed and provided training for Hezbollah to amass thousands of rockets and build a terrorist army. In the summer of 2006 Hezbollah proved it could mount a sizeable threat to Israel's security.

By arming a proxy army in Lebanon, Iran is adding another dangerous card to the game. If Israel orders an air strike against Iran, Iran can immediately order Hezbollah to strike northern Israel from the ground and with rockets from the air. Many believe it will be difficult for Israel to launch a sustained air war in both Iran and Lebanon at the same time. As Hezbollah continues to grow in Lebanon, how can Israel threaten Iran with air strikes when its northern cities are not secure?

What's the next move? Will the United States or Israel launch a preemptive strike against Iran? Will the Israeli-Arab conflict go nuclear? Will Iran unleash nuclear jihad?

While Iraq's program to develop chemical and biological weapons under Saddam Hussein was not as sophisticated or successful as early intelligence estimates indicated, much of what was started there is now in the hands of terrorist organizations. Chemical and biological weapons are being developed in every corner of the world. Terrorists around the world download the knowledge necessary to create biological agents every day from Web sites that supply the critical information. Chemical and bacteriological warfare may be as big a threat to large populations as nuclear devices or even conventional nuclear warheads.

THE IMPENDING CRISIS

The rapidly increasing tempo of change in modern life has given the entire world a sense of impending crisis. Oil and terror, the two greatest issues facing the world today, are both centralized in the same part of the world—the Middle East. Since the oil and the terrorists are in the same location, it's easy to envision terrorist attacks that could damage or interrupt world oil production. The world crises at the top of almost everyone's list are the war on terror and maintaining an uninterrupted flow of oil.

The Middle East became the center of attention during the Gulf War in 1990–1991 and made many wonder whether that conflict was to be the final war of prophetic fulfillment. Although it soon became clear that it was not Armageddon, the entire world focused on the tense situation in the Middle East. The invasions of Afghanistan in 2001 and Iraq in 2003 seem only to have added fuel to the terrorist fire. The Middle East is a powder keg that could explode at any time.

How long can world tensions be kept in check? How long can the struggle between the West and Islamic terrorism be kept from becoming a global bloodbath? The ingenuity of man has devised means of human destruction that would have seemed incredible to a previous generation. With terrorist tactics ranging from dirty bombs and suitcase-sized nuclear devices to anthrax and smallpox used as weapons of mass destruction (WMDs), the world appears to be moving toward a gigantic crisis. Can it be that the prophets of doom are right? Is the world racing toward Armageddon, the end of Western civilization?

THE VOICE OF THE PROPHETS

As alarming as these events are, they really are not surprising in light of the Bible's end-time prophecies. For centuries, people of religious faith have considered the message of true prophets to be God's revelation of His plan for human history. The Old Testament books record the lives and works of many great prophets—Moses, Isaiah, Jeremiah, Ezekiel, Daniel, Hosea, Joel, Micah, and others. These men predicted future events in vivid detail, including the rise and fall of every major world empire that left its mark on the Middle East. Some of their predictions came true within their lifetimes. Now it appears that many of their astounding prophecies could be fulfilled at any time.

Jesus Himself claimed to be a prophet and quoted from Moses, Isaiah, Daniel, and Jeremiah—many times adding interpretive comments and detailed predictions of His own. His words have been confirmed by the test of time. Jesus' prediction of the fall of Jerusalem (Luke 21:20-24) was so vivid that the early church in Jerusalem was able to escape almost certain destruction by fleeing the city before Titus destroyed it in AD 70. As then, so now, crucial predictions about Jerusalem and the nation of Israel are, in fact, the key to understanding a carefully predicted chain of events that will mark the last days of our civilization.

Jesus predicted the persecution of the church, the fall of Jerusalem with the destruction of the Temple, the scattering of the Jews into all nations, and the amazing survival and growth of the church. Along with the Old Testament prophets, He saw a time when Israel would be reestablished as a nation (see Matthew 19:28; Matthew 24:15-20; and Acts 1:6-7). All this has been realized in history. But He also warned those who understood the Old Testament prophets to watch Jerusalem and the Middle East for signs of the approaching end of world civilization, the end of the "period of the Gentiles," also referred to in some

The Period of the Gentiles

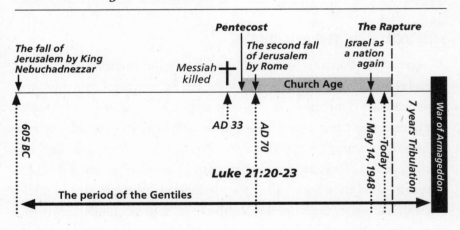

They will be killed by the sword or sent away as captives to all the nations of the world. And Jerusalem will be trampled down by the Gentiles until the period of the Gentiles comes to an end. (Luke 21:24)

translations as the times of the Gentiles. The Jews, He said, "will be killed by the sword or sent away as captives to all the nations of the world. And Jerusalem will be trampled down by the Gentiles until the period of the Gentiles comes to an end" (Luke 21:24).

Over five million Jews are now back in the land, the largest movement of Jews in history—far more than the two million who left Egypt for the Promised Land under Moses. Jerusalem, the city of dispute and negotiation, was won in 1967, only to become the object of a diplomatic tug-of-war. What is the future of the Holy City? If the period of the Gentiles is, in fact, nearing an end, what will happen next? What are the final events of world history as "the period of the Gentiles comes to an end"? Is there a sure word about tomorrow? Is this a word of hope or a warning of doom?

THE SEARCH FOR ANSWERS

Modern man is asking questions about the future as never before. They are solemn questions; they are searching questions. The Bible is certainly the best place to look for answers. Many of the biblical prophecies cited in this book are coming true before our very eyes. Even the most skeptical person can put these prophecies to the test by noting the literal, precise fulfillment of past prophecies.

For this reason, biblical prophecy is being discussed more than ever before. In these prophecies it is possible to probe for clues to find where we are in God's program and the predicted events that may occur in our lifetime. Prophecies, which in the past were sometimes brushed aside as incredible, are now being studied again.

The study of prophecy has been plagued by two extremes. The one extreme is to disregard prophecy or to interpret it in a nonliteral sense. About half of the prophecies in the Bible have been fulfilled. Studying these passages makes it clear that when prophecy in the Bible was fulfilled, it was fulfilled literally. The demonstrated pattern of fulfillment to date contradicts the skeptics' theories that prophecy should be considered metaphorically.

Another extreme, however, is to take prophecies out of context and interpret them to fit every headline. One prophecy isolated and out of context should not be used to interpret headlines or set dates for future events. The careful student of prophecy attempts to put all unfulfilled prophecies together into a chronology of events that is true to their literal meaning. Careful interpretation of prophecy reveals a chronology of events the Bible predicts will set the stage for the final act of world history.

As students of the Bible observe proper interpretation principles, they are becoming increasingly aware of a remarkable correspondence between the obvious trend of world events and what the Bible predicted millenia ago. In fact, 28 percent of the Bible was prophetic at the time it was written. Not surprisingly, then, people in all walks of life and of all religious faiths are asking the question—what does the Bible say the future holds?

NO VAGUE AND GENERAL PREDICTIONS

Unlike the self-proclaimed prophets of today, Jesus and the biblical prophets did not peddle vague and general predictions that could be adjusted to any situation. The prophecies recorded in the Bible are detailed and intricately interwoven. Although interpretation of minor points may vary, the overall picture is frighteningly clear.

The Bible does not simply speak of a final destructive world war but of a whole series of carefully timed events that are like signposts on the road to Armageddon.

Armageddon has come to describe anyone's worst fear of the end of the world. The prophets have described it more specifically as the final suicidal war of a desperate world struggle centered in the Middle East. It will be the final act in a terrifying series of events that are very much related to today's headlines. This final, history-shattering war will occur (1) on schedule, (2) at a specific time, and (3) in its predicted location.

The name *Armageddon* actually comes from a Hebrew word meaning "the Mount of Megiddo," a small mountain located in northern Israel at the end of a broad valley. This valley has been the scene of many military conflicts in the past and will be the focal point of this great future conflict.

The Bible clearly spells out the key events that will precede this last great conflict. The final countdown will involve years rather than days. Even before the countdown, the Bible predicts a number of preliminary moves, which will shape the political, economic, and religious climate necessary for end-time events. These preparatory steps are now falling into place in rapid succession. As these moves are completed, a more specific timetable of events can begin. The final countdown involves a brief period of preparation with the last seven years clearly delineated. The last half of these seven years will be three and a half years of unparalleled disaster and war, climaxing at Armageddon. Though we'll examine each of these events in greater detail later in the book, they are summarized below:

1. **Revival of the Roman Empire.** Prior to these last seven years, a group of ten leaders, or what we might call the "Group of Ten," will rise from Europe, as indicated by the ten horns of Daniel 7:7-8 and the similar description of the end-time government in Revelation 13:1. This alliance or confederacy of ten leaders and the nations they represent constitutes a revival of the Roman Empire and the beginning of the final stage of the fourth beast in Daniel 7.

   These countries will include European countries and possibly nations in western Asia and northern Africa. This Group of Ten will control the nations and geographic areas from the ancient Roman Empire. The Group of Ten will rise to power because the West will desperately need to guarantee the peace and security of the Middle East. This will temporarily be accomplished in a seven-year covenant of peace and protection with Israel. Without a forced peace, disruption of the West's oil supply and an escalation in terrorism will threaten to bring Western civilization to its knees.

2. **Israel's survival is threatened.** The reestablishment of the nation of Israel in the Middle East was necessary to start the Armageddon calendar. Almost since its birth, however, Israel has been threatened with extinction. Nonetheless, prophecy seems to indicate that Israel will not be destroyed by war. Instead, Israel will eventually be betrayed and forced to accept an outside settlement at the peace table. The Middle East oil blackmail and new economic and political alignments in the Middle East will eventually rob both the United States and Russia of a determining voice in the final settlement.

3. **True believers disappear.** The world will be traumatized by the fulfillment of what theologians call the rapture of the church—the sudden removal of every Christian from the world (1 Thessalonians 4:13-18). This will fulfill the promise of Christ to His disciples when He said, "I will come and get you, so that you will always be with me where I am" (John 14:3). At that time, Christians who have died will be resurrected, and every true Christian living in the world will be suddenly removed to heaven without experiencing death.

   The disappearance of millions of Christians will deepen the religious confusion, already evident in the current cultural obsession over the supernatural and mystical phenomena. The organized church with every true Christian removed will fall into the hands of political opportunists.

4. **Power is centralized in one man.** From the many negotiators and leaders involved in the Middle East, one new international leader will emerge from Europe to superimpose a peace settlement on Israel and the more militant Muslims and to assure the West's sup-

ply of oil. This will bring an era of false peace, a move toward disarmament, and a major push for a new world economic system. These first three and a half years will be the calm before the storm as the new leader consolidates his power.

The last three and a half years will include a series of almost inconceivable catastrophes. Just before this period begins, Russia and a group of Islamic allies will attempt a final bid for power in the Middle East, but their armies will be supernaturally destroyed (Ezekiel 38–39). The balance of power will swing decisively to the world's new strongman. As Satan's man of the hour, he will then attempt to destroy Israel, now disarmed and at peace. In the fashion of the Babylonian and Roman emperors, he will deify himself and command the worship of the world.

5. **A series of natural disasters shake the world's foundations.** The world will begin to come apart at the seams—worse than any ecologist's nightmare. Acts of man, resulting in thousands of martyrs, and acts of God will combine to cause great disturbances in the world and universe. Stars will fall and planets will run off course, causing chaotic changes in climate (Revelation 6:12-14; 16:8-9). Unnatural heat and cold, flooding, and other disasters will wipe out much of the food production of the world (Revelation 6:6-8). Great famines will cause millions to perish (Matthew 24:7). Strange new epidemics will sweep the world, killing millions. As the period draws to a close, earthquakes will level the great cities of the world, and geological upheavals will cause mountains and islands to disappear in the seas (Revelation 16:17-21). Disaster after disaster will reduce the world population in the course of a few years to a fraction of its present billions.

6. **The march to Armageddon.** Topping even these disasters will come a world war of unprecedented proportions. Hundreds of millions of men will be involved in a gigantic world power

struggle centered in the Holy Land (Revelation 16:13-16). The area will become the scene of the greatest war of history. Great armies from the south will pour into the battle arena (Daniel 11:40) and other great armies from the north will descend on Israel (Daniel 11:41). Climaxing the struggle will be millions of men from the Orient and China who will cross the Euphrates River and join the fray (Daniel 11:44; Revelation 9:13-16; 16:12). Locked in this deadly struggle, millions will perish in the greatest war of all history. This is what the Bible describes as Armageddon.

Before the war is finally resolved and the victor determined, Jesus Christ will come back in power and glory from heaven. His coming, accompanied by millions of angels and raptured Christians, is described in graphic terms in Revelation 19. Coming as the King of kings and judge of the world, He will destroy the contending armies and bring in His own kingdom of peace and righteousness on earth.

As incredible as these prophecies are, even now the world is moving toward these events. The nations are taking their predicted places. The escalating crisis in the Middle East is a buildup to the start of the Tribulation. Ancient prophecies are being fulfilled. The world is rushing toward Armageddon!

THE FINAL ACT

Sometimes life feels like entering a dark theater and realizing you are coming in near the end of a play with several acts. We didn't write it. We didn't ask to be thrust into the play. We can be certain this drama is nearing the last act. Even though we did not see the beginning we can look back and see the plot and direction of the play. But even then, how can we be sure when the next act will start?

The prophets talked a lot about the last act. All we can do is look for the events that set up the last act. If they occur now, we can be fairly certain the last act is just ahead. When the curtain comes down on this scene, will the next act be the last? To be sure, we need to know what will happen on the world stage to set up the last act. What are the events, the characters, and the plot that will bring the play of world history to its predicted climax? Will we be wise enough to see it coming? Will we be ready? In the coming chapters, we will examine some of the events that are either already unfolding or that we know will occur based on biblical prophecy. We'll examine the first event in chapter 2, which shines the prophetic spotlight squarely on the Middle East.

See how today's headlines relate to this chapter at http://www.prophecyhotline.com.

CHAPTER 2

OIL BECOMES THE ULTIMATE WEAPON

EVENT #1: The Middle East becomes the center of a desperate struggle for oil as demand exceeds supply, prices soar, and industrialized nations fight for economic survival.

> Oil depletion is arguably the most serious crisis ever to face industrialized society.
>
> PAUL ROBERTS, *THE END OF OIL*

> When, and in precisely what form, we will experience the next great energy shock cannot be foreseen. Perhaps it will be triggered by a coup d'etat. . . . Or it might be a major act of terrorism, or a catastrophic climate event. Whatever the case, our existing energy system, already stretched to its limits, will not be able to absorb a major blow.
>
> MICHAEL T. KLARE, *BLOOD AND OIL*

IMAGINE THE DAY THE PRICE of oil triples. The news of the hour may be a hurricane or earthquake that has wiped out ports and refineries, a terrorist attack on the energy infrastructure in Saudi Arabia, wells on fire in Iraq, the sinking of supertankers in the Strait of Hormuz, or a nuclear interchange in the Middle East.

Like the events of 9/11 or news of any disaster, people around the world watch in shock. Few who watch the initial news reports can imagine how one or two simple catastrophes will change the world forever. The real shock is not the event—it is the domino effect when the oil break point occurs.

Most people rush to the closest gas or petrol station. Some of these businesses have handwritten "sold out" signs on the pumps. Many have broken windows. Others have lines of cars and trucks blocks long. In the panic many people wait in line with tanks half full of gas. Gas containers disappear from stores. When people begin to hoard, it makes matters worse. Countries also begin to hoard. One by one the industrial powers of the world announce the need to build massive strategic petroleum reserves. New restrictions and taxes on energy immediately become a priority of every government.

Overnight, a black market in heating oil, gas, and diesel fuel springs up. People begin worrying about the next winter. How will they heat their homes? How can they afford higher utility bills? Will their savings last that long?

The economic effects on transportation are obvious. Commuters who depend on automobiles cannot get to work. Airlines cancel flights and apply for government subsidies. Truckers refuse to load freight until prices stabilize. Ports back up as the transportation chain breaks down. Ships with cargo form long lines at sea waiting to come into port.

Those who can get to their jobs face an uncertain future. Businesses and factories that use transportation to supply just-in-time inventory come to a halt. Even assembly lines that keep running cannot ship products and equipment to their customers.

People begin to hoard everything. Stores close when present inventories are wiped out. Governments call out the military to establish order.

Yes, these scenes are easy to imagine. It is difficult to know how the oil break point would affect you and your family. But it's too late to pretend it cannot happen. If the supply of oil—or the energy infrastructure that refines and distributes oil—hits the breaking point, the economy of the United States and other industrial giants will desta-bilize. Third World countries struggling for survival will be destroyed by a disruption in the price and availability of oil. The break point will come when demand suddenly exceeds supply. Oil futures on the com-modity markets will spike. Nations will rush to hoard more strategic reserves. The high cost of petroleum products alone will cause the wheels of Western economic growth to grind to a halt. The world will be changed forever on that day.

CRUDE AWAKENING

In the fall of 1973, a group of Arab nations staged a Pearl Harbor–like attack on Israel on Yom Kippur (Day of Atonement), the most holy day of Judaism. Israel was able to ward off the invaders with the sup-port of several Western nations and maintain control of the strategic Golan Heights in the north, territory that Egypt and Syria had hoped to capture.

One of the important results of the war in 1973 was the coming together of Arab nations as never before. Although the unity was mani-fested partially in the military conflict, it became increasingly evident that the Arab world's bid for power was going to be based on its control of the major oil resources. In a new show of unity, the Arab world, on October 17, 1973, reduced its production of oil below the previous norm and attempted to embargo nations that favored Israel, principally the United States and the Netherlands.

The price of oil quadrupled to twelve dollars a barrel. The grim prospect of having insufficient fuel for homes, industry, and the military sent shock waves around the world. Those who lived through that time can still remember the long, winding lines at gas stations and the result-ing panic. A new war was in progress, an economic war of tremendous implications. For the first time in centuries, the Middle East became a major consideration in every international event.

In the 1970s the rapid increase in consumption of energy through-out the world brought warnings of an impending crisis. By then, oil had proven to be cheaper and easier to use than coal. Much of the United States' electricity, especially in the East, depended upon energy derived from oil. Ecologists had opposed the use of coal, particularly the lower grades that were economically feasible, because of air pollution. At that time nuclear power was opposed by just about everyone.

The continued increase in automobile travel, especially in the United States, led to a rising demand for oil for which there was no suitable substitute. Any reduction in oil supplies would inevitably affect automobile travel and with it the total automobile industry. The prospect of limited supplies of gasoline threatened the lifestyle as well as the economic prosperity of the United States. Europe and Japan were even more dependent on oil from outside sources, and the threat of limited oil produced panic unprecedented since the days of World War I. A whole new alignment of international power was underway, and no one could accurately predict the future.

Fast-forward to the twenty-first century. The United States continues to consume more and more oil each year. Americans use about 21 million barrels of oil a day, or 25 percent of the oil produced in the world. If present trends continue, U.S. consumption is expected to rise to 27 million barrels a day by 2020, and U.S. oil demand will expand 34 percent by 2030.[1]

China's accelerating economy has an insatiable thirst for oil. World demand shows no signs of slowing, while supply and production have remained static. No new refinery has been built in the United States since 1976, meaning the nation cannot count on much growth in its domestic production of oil.

The razor-thin margin between world supply and demand became apparent in August 2005 when hurricanes Katrina and Rita hit the Gulf Coast and sent shock waves through the world oil market. For the first time, gas prices shot up thirty cents a gallon to a national average of over three dollars a gallon. In 2006, gas prices went above three dollars a gallon several times before settling down. When they did, oil dropped out of the news.

But crude oil is a finite resource, and the rate of consumption is continuing to rise dramatically. Even though experts estimate that there is a forty-year supply, calculated at current consumption rates, the supply of cheap oil is dwindling, and the United States is still dependent on imports from hostile and potentially unstable nations.

While opinions on the time line vary, experts agree that the world's addiction to oil is "hastening a day of reckoning."[2] World oil demand hit 86 million barrels a day in 2006 and continues to grow at about two million barrels a day every year. Peter Tertzakian, chief energy economist at a leading energy investment firm, puts this in perspective. "Sometime in 2006, mankind's thirst for oil will have crossed the milestone of 86 million barrels per day, which translates to a staggering one thousand barrels a second!"[3]

When will the world no longer have access to affordable oil? According to a report in *National Geographic*: "It could be 5 years from now or 30: No one knows for sure, and geologists and economists are embroiled in debate about just when the 'oil peak' will be upon us. But few doubt that it is coming. 'In our lifetime,' says 46-year-old economist Robert K. Kaufmann of Boston University, 'we will have to deal with a peak in the supply of cheap oil.' The peak will be a watershed moment, making the change from an increasing supply of cheap oil to a dwindling supply of expensive oil."[4]

The peak in oil production outside the Middle East has already happened, and some industry observers believe the worldwide oil production peak will happen in 2016.[5] By as soon as 2010, the pressure for world consumption will push toward 95 million barrels a day. If present trends continue unchecked, projected world oil consumption in 2020 could rise to about 120 million barrels a day—up 60 percent from 1999. But where will the oil come from, and at what price?

THE VITAL ROLE OF MIDDLE EAST OIL

On the basis of proven oil reserves, the Arab world is in a good position to control oil production and blackmail other nations. The Middle

Oil Reserves by Country

COUNTRY	PROVED RESERVES (BILLION BARRELS)
1. Saudi Arabia	266.8
2. Canada	178.8
3. Iran	132.5
4. Iraq	115.0
5. Kuwait	104.0
6. United Arab Emirates	97.8
7. Venezuela	79.7
8. Russia	60.0
9. Libya	39.1
10. Nigeria	35.9
11. United States	21.8
12. China	18.3
13. Qatar	15.2
14. Mexico	12.9
15. Algeria	11.4
World Total	**1,292.5**

SOURCE: U.S. Energy Information Administration, "World Proved Reserves of Oil and Natural Gas, Most Recent Estimates" (posted October 5, 2006), based on information from *Oil & Gas Journal*, January 1, 2006.

East/Persian Gulf has about 60 percent of the known oil reserves of the world lying beneath its desert sands.

In addition, the countries of the Middle East have sophisticated handling and processing facilities that have been developed by the major Western oil companies. In rapid succession these facilities were nationalized. A few national leaders now control not only a major portion of the world's oil reserves but some of the most advanced production and processing facilities in the world. Without a continued supply of Middle Eastern oil, the industrial giants of the West simply do not have the energy they need for industrial production, transportation, electricity, and heat.

Of all the nations of the world, the United States is the largest consumer of crude oil, using one-fourth (about 20 million barrels a day) of the total production of the world. Still, the United States has taken no decisive action in the face of Arab threats. The nation managed to survive the 1973 embargo through a variety of indirect maneuvers, including increased imports from Iran. It also has made no advances in curbing increasing demand for oil or creating public policy that will lead to energy self-sufficiency.

THE PROBLEM THAT WON'T GO AWAY

The crisis of 1973 is history, but what was a passing problem may soon draw the Western world into a confrontation from which there is no escape. When the Arab nations first demonstrated their control over the world's oil in 1973, their first step was to restrict oil output and delivery. The cutbacks were linked to a demand for Israel's complete withdrawal from all lands that it had occupied by war, including the restoration of Jerusalem, or at least a portion of it, to the Arabs. Led by King Faisal of Saudi Arabia, the Arabs threatened to restrict the shipment of oil to the entire world and embargo oil to selected nations like the United States. Along with the restrictions on the amount of oil delivered were shocking increases in the price of oil.

In short-term results, the Arab oil blackmail in 1973 proved that Europe, Japan, and the smaller emerging industrial nations were more vulnerable to political manipulation than the United States and Russia, and this scenario continues today. The impact in Europe was felt immediately, and citizens quickly turned down their thermostats and restricted their automobile use. As the price of oil went up, so did the prices of almost everything else.

Japan was forced to pay increasing billions for oil imports, resulting in a temporary decline in its economy and increasing inflation. Within a year the inflation rates doubled in many countries, including Italy, France, Belgium, and Great Britain. Great Britain braced itself for the worst economic days since the 1930s, muddling through until reduction of consumption and North Sea oil production began to solve some of Britain's economic woes.

But the price of Persian Gulf crude oil did not decrease after the crisis of 1973–1974. In retrospect the prices seem low by today's standards. But higher oil prices and the continued pressure for price increases began to quietly erode the economic stability of the Western world. The Arab oil blackmail had begun the fastest transfer of money in history. A few Middle Eastern countries were accumulating more wealth more quickly than even the conquistadors when they seized the gold of the Incas. And the final price would not be exacted in gold alone, but in the political and economic reshaping of the world.

Europe Hedges Its Bets

In reaction to the energy crisis in 1973, energy policy changed across Europe. The European community generally saw the need both to reduce consumption and to impose taxes on gasoline to raise significant revenue.

High taxes on gasoline limited consumption and encouraged use of public transportation and the development of alternative energy sources. France pursued a policy to use nuclear reactors to supply much of its electrical power. By 2007, conservation was a way of life in Europe, and the price per gallon of gas was more than twice the cost in the United States. Prices above six dollars a gallon were the rule, and increases caused much less concern than in the United States.

Countries with high taxes on gasoline include Japan, Great Britain, Norway, Poland, Turkey, and South Korea. This shift took more than two decades to accomplish. Gasoline in Brazil is still more expensive than in the United States, but nearly all of the country's 34,000 gas stations offer ethanol as a flex-fuel at attractive prices. One reason Brazil has been able to convert to ethanol so quickly is because it's an ideal geographical location for growing sugar cane, a much more energy-rich feeding stock than corn, which the United States uses for its ethanol production.[6]

Like the rest of the world, Europe still needs fossil fuels and cannot live without them. Because the price of fuel is set in dollars, the strength of the euro holds down the price of oil as long as prices do not rapidly escalate. But if the underlying cost of oil doubles or triples, most countries will be pushed to the edge of economic disaster.

The United States Bets on Cheap Oil

Immediately after the energy crisis in 1973, the entire world began to increase oil discovery and production with new determination. The rise in oil prices suddenly made costly exploration and production methods worth the risk. But moves toward stimulating increased production or extensive exploration soon faltered in the United States as politicians debated and disagreed over energy policy decisions. Self-sufficiency seemed only a political slogan.

The initial drilling boom in the mid-1970s, combined with prior discoveries in Prudhoe Bay, Alaska, lifted U.S. production only 4 percent from 1979 to 1985. Then production began falling again. In 1985 the United States imported less than 30 percent of its oil. In the mid-1990s imported oil broke the 50 percent mark for the first time. By 2005–2006, the number reached 60 percent.[7] The gap between oil consumption and production continues to widen. Clearly, the United

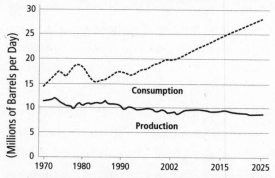

U.S. Dependence on Imported Oil

SOURCE: U.S. Energy Information Administration, "Annual Energy Outlook with Projections to 2025 - Market Trends - Oil and Natural Gas," Figure 99, http://www.eia.doe.gov/oiaf/archive/aeo04/gas.html (accessed December 12, 2006).

States is no longer one of the world's great producers of oil. To reverse the decline would require gigantic new reserves several times larger than Prudhoe Bay.

Of all the major oil importers, the United States had seemed to be in the best position to develop self-sufficiency at the time of the Arab oil embargo. Yet as time passed, the country was unable to move forward with a decisive energy program. The American public continued to believe that a cheap and plentiful supply of oil was their birthright.

As prices began to rise in 2005, the public outcry was directed at the oil companies, which seemed to be reaping exorbitantly high profits. ExxonMobil had a record $36.1 billion profit in 2005 and gave its chairman a $400 million retirement deal. It was estimated that 2006 profits for ExxonMobil would soar to about $40 billion.[8] As prices rose even more rapidly in 2006, however, that anger seemed aimed at the government.

That isn't surprising. When any major problem confronts a society, the first reaction is generally anger, resignation, and wishful thinking. It takes much longer to develop a society's will to change and embrace lifestyle changes. The price of oil was lowered by increases in production before and during the elections in 2006. The public outcry focused on the war and overlooked the issue of energy self-sufficiency. But the problems of oil and war are inextricably linked.

Breaking the dependence on foreign oil will not be easy—and may take decades. Increased exploration and development cannot solve the problem without painful conservation and a switch to alternative fuels.

THINKING OUTSIDE THE BARREL

In 2005 the United States consumed about seven billion barrels of oil and the equivalent of eleven billion barrels of oil in the form of coal, natural gas, uranium, and hydroelectric power. The United States is rich in coal—with the equivalent of one trillion barrels of oil.[9]

Uranium is abundantly available for nuclear power. Heavy oil sup-

Oil Consumption *(Barrels per Day)*

1. United States	20,030,000
2. European Union	14,590,000
3. China	6,391,000
4. Japan	5,578,000
5. Russia	2,800,000
6. Germany	2,677,000
7. India	2,320,000
8. Canada	2,300,000
9. South Korea	2,061,000
10. France	2,060,000
11. Italy	1,874,000
12. Saudi Arabia	1,775,000
13. Mexico	1,752,000
14. United Kingdom	1,722,000
15. Brazil	1,610,000
World Total	**80,100,000**

SOURCE: Central Intelligence Agency, *The World Factbook 2006*

plies in the form of tar sands in Alberta, Canada, far exceed the oil reserves of Saudi Arabia. But coal, uranium, or tar sands will not solve the immediate problem. Energy equivalence on paper is not gasoline in the tank.

The problem is America's continued dependence on light crude oil. Approximately 40 percent of the fuel the United States consumes is oil—used primarily for cars, trucks, trains, and airplanes. The nation consumes 43 percent of the world's motor gasoline. Without it, the transportation system of the entire U.S. economy would collapse. Addiction to this specific form of energy means that the United States cannot dodge the bullet if anything suddenly disrupts the supply of light crude oil from the Middle East.

Given the increasing volatility of the Middle East, the United States must carefully consider all possible alternatives. One of America's other primary sources of foreign oil is Venezuela, but prospects for a continuing, productive relationship are uncertain—at best. As Venezuela continues to struggle with its own political discontent, the South American country's president, Hugo Chavez, openly criticizes the "imperialist policies" of the United States. Now representing the Venezuelan-owned, mega-oil-producer Citgo, Chavez has traveled numerous times to Iran and is closely allied with Iranian president Mahmoud Ahmadinejad. Chavez has signed a series of energy accords with Iran, including a two-billion-dollar investment fund to finance special projects. If a regional conflict breaks out in the Middle East, particularly involving Iran, the danger looms that Venezuela will use oil as a weapon and carry out threats to cut off the United States' supply.

For decades visionaries have dreamed of hydrogen as the ultimate replacement for petroleum for cars and trucks. But this cannot happen without decades of research and development. It would mean new energy production, new cars, and entirely new fueling stations. Even a trillion dollar investment in a switch to hydrogen would take decades to implement.

A lead article in *Fortune* magazine on the future of fuel announced, "Stop dreaming about hydrogen. Ethanol is the answer to the energy dilemma. It's clean and green and runs in today's cars. And in a generation, it could replace gas."[10]

For transportation, biofuels are the most likely replacement for fossil fuels. Today's gas stations can handle a mix of up to 85 percent ethanol and 15 percent gasoline. "Flex-fuel" vehicles or "E85" vehicles would allow conventional automobiles to burn either gasoline, ethanol, or both. Ethanol produces less energy per gallon than gasoline—it takes about 30 percent more ethanol per mile than gasoline—but it's one answer to the United States' dependence on light crude oil. And ethanol could be delivered using the current infrastructure of gas stations across America.

But a rapid transition to use cornstarch ethanol for all transportation in America is simply not possible at current consumption levels. Some critics believe that producing fuel from crops consumes more energy than it produces. In 2006 American production of ethanol consumed 14 percent of the country's corn production while providing little relief from the country's dependence on fossil fuels.[11] To divert more of the country's food supply to ethanol would create serious shortages in the world food supply and still would not meet the demand. It takes eleven acres of land to grow enough corn to power one car with ethanol for one year (ten thousand miles). That's the same amount of land required to feed seven people for one year.

David Pimentel of Cornell University notes that if we decided to run all our cars on ethanol we would need to cover 97 percent of our land with corn. Of course, ethanol could be used simply to supplement our gasoline needs, not totally replace them. But it doesn't appear to be an immediate answer to the problem.[12] According to reporter Adam Wilmoth, "Some maintain that even if the entire grain production of the United States were converted to ethanol, it would only equate to a 16 percent reduction in petroleum usage."[13]

The position of the U.S. Energy Department is that the development of cellulose-based ethanol will be necessary to significantly cut our dependence on gasoline. Cellulose comes from the walls of plant cells and can be extracted from cornstalks, grasses, tree bark—things that are abundant and that would not disrupt the world's food supply. The U.S. Congress passed a comprehensive energy bill on July 29, 2005, that mandated the use of 250 million gallons of cellulosic ethanol a year by 2013. The engineering and production problems to do this have not yet been solved.

Can biofuels replace gasoline in time to prevent a major conflict in the Middle East? The 250 million gallons of ethanol mandated to be produced in 2013 would amount to less than the equivalent of two days supply of gasoline consumed in the United States.

The Natural Resources Defense Council has charted a future in which biofuels will slowly replace gasoline as technology makes transportation more efficient. The group advocates aggressive government investment in research, development, and deployment, noting that "the private sector is unlikely to invest on the scale or at the speed that we need if we are to wean ourselves from oil." [14]

Even if it does so, from 2010 to 2020 biofuels will replace only a fraction of the consumption of oil. It will still take from 2020 to 2035 to replace more than half of the petroleum used for transportation. The Department of Energy predicts that it will take until at least 2030 for ethanol to put a 30 percent dent in America's gasoline consumption. [15]

All the available research on alternative energy sources to replace gasoline comes to the same conclusion. *Fortune* says, "In a generation, it [ethanol] could replace gas."[16] It will take time—at least a decade, more likely two decades—and an extraordinary change in the U.S. culture to make this happen. Even at lower consumption rates, alternative energy sources for transportation for Great Britain and Europe will be equally difficult to achieve in a short time frame. The Council on Foreign Relations said that U.S. energy independence is impossible for "at least several decades" and "unachievable for the foreseeable future."[17] Until then, what happens in the Middle East may still throw the West into panic and cause severe economic hardship.

New energy sources to replace oil lost to natural disasters, terrorism, war, or a nuclear exchange in the Middle East are at least ten to twenty years away. For now, the West has no alternative but to defend its supply of oil at any cost.

That means, for the foreseeable future, oil will power the global economy. The question remains—does the United States have the will to reduce its dependence on foreign oil? Is it possible that America will allow its economic future to be destroyed by international events it cannot control?

In the first decade of the twenty-first century, dependence on Middle Eastern oil is increasing at the same time terrorism, the threat of nuclear weapons, and instability are rising in the Middle East. This volatile combination of terrorism, weapons of mass destruction, and the coming break point in oil supply is an explosive mix that could threaten to push the entire civilized world into chaos.

WHOM CAN ISRAEL TRUST?

From Israel's standpoint, the situation is decidedly an unhappy one. If the United States is weakened by a new energy crisis, will it continue its unilateral support of Israel?

How long will America continue to defend Israel's interests when the United States itself so desperately needs oil from the Persian Gulf? The nation became deeply committed to the defense of Saudi Arabia and Kuwait during the first Iraq war. The second Iraq war once again revealed the United States' determination to control events in the region. But can the military intervention of the United States really stop the disintegration of the balance of power in the region? With the growing problems in Iraq and Afghanistan, how long will the United States be willing to commit its military forces in the region? Will it have the political and economic will to stop the proliferation of nuclear weapons in hostile countries like Iran?

The Middle Eastern countries supply oil, but they also supply the money needed for industrial investment and to finance government deficits. They're awash in oil money. As purchasers of vast amounts of military hardware, machinery, and technology, they can choose to buy or not to buy from any particular country. These wealthy nations can choose to shift vast amounts of money from dollars to euros. They can invest in, or pull all their investments from, any country they choose. In terms of money alone, the other Arab countries and Iran have a vast amount of investable income that can be moved from bank to bank or country to country—which could play havoc with world currencies and world trade.

In long-term results, the Arab countries and Iran have been able to consolidate both wealth and power. The cost to the world, and especially to Israel, will not just be calculated in petrodollars. These new realities are forcing a closer relationship between key European countries and some of the most powerful countries in the Middle East. Russia has forged an economic and political alliance with Iran. China and India are becoming huge consumers of oil. China will deal with anyone, even outlaw states, that can supply its growing need for oil. The enormity of the coming energy crisis will seize the attention of the entire world.

THE UNITED STATES TO USE "ANY MEANS NECESSARY"

In the wake of the 1973 oil embargo and the 1979 Iranian hostage crisis, the Persian Gulf region rose to the very top of the U.S. security agenda—a place it has occupied ever since. President Jimmy Carter announced an important policy change in 1980. In his State of the Union address on January 23, 1980, he said that access to the Persian Gulf was a vital national interest. He declared that to protect that interest the United States was prepared to use "any means necessary, including military force." The policy became known as the Carter Doctrine.

In August 1990 President George H. W. Bush and defense secretary Dick Cheney put the Carter Doctrine into action. On August 2, 1990, Saddam Hussein sent Iraqi troops into neighboring Kuwait. This move immediately alarmed the United States over fear that Iraq might try to move into Saudi Arabia, thereby controlling almost half of the world's proven oil reserves (the total oil reserves of Iraq, Kuwait, and Saudi Arabia).

The primary U.S. concerns in the early days of the Iraqi invasion of Kuwait were oil and the fate of Saudi Arabia. In a nationally televised address on August 8, 1990, the president announced that the United States would use military force to repel the invasion, and the main motivation he gave for the use of military force was America's energy needs. He said, "Our country now imports nearly half the oil it consumes and could face a major threat to its economic independence. . . . The sovereign independence of Saudi Arabia is of vital interest to the United States."

Appearing before the Senate Armed Services Committee on September 11, 1990, Secretary of Defense Cheney said, "Once [Saddam] acquired Kuwait and deployed an army as large as the one he possesses, he would be in a position to be able to dictate the future of world-wide energy policy, and that [would give] him a stranglehold on our economy."

While other justifications for the war, such as liberating Kuwait, were given, experts agree that the Gulf War in 1990–1991 was the first war in world history almost entirely about oil. But while the Gulf War was the first war over oil, it won't be the last.

Unless there are drastic changes in U.S. consumption, by 2030 the United States will import twice as much oil as it did in 1996, and since most of that oil comes from the Middle East, U.S. actions to protect these interests will increase as well. Most of Europe and Japan are more dependent on imports than the United States. They too must protect their future supply of energy from the Middle East to protect their economic interests. The Middle East/Persian Gulf will continue to be the focus of the world.

THE INVASION OF IRAQ

Why was the world surprised when the United States invaded Iraq in 2003? No matter what the excuse, it is evident that the nation is willing to pay almost any price to control events in the Middle East. History books will have to settle the issue of whether the war began because of hard evidence that Saddam was building weapons of mass destruction or simply to establish military control of the region and the flow of oil to the West.

In fact, the entire region is now less stable than it was before the invasion. The American-led war in Iraq has cost more than $200 billion and continues to inflict a high cost in human lives because of thousands of military and civilian casualties. Radical Islamic terrorism has been given a new justification to hate the great Satan of the West and a convenient place to begin the battle. Iran has been emboldened by the U.S. distraction in Iraq and is flexing its muscles in a dramatic bid for regional supremacy. Iran is also seizing the opportunity to fuel terror in Iraq—stoking the Sunni–Shiite division.

The fiction that one superpower like America can occupy a country, restore order, and secure the export of oil to the West is now gone. In short, occupying forces cannot protect the wellheads and pipelines from sabotage. And they cannot stop the kidnapping and killing of civilian workers. In *The End of Oil*, Paul Roberts notes:

> *In fact, the greatest casualty of the Iraq war may be the very idea of energy security.*
>
> *But with the continuing fiasco in Iraq, it is now clear that even the most powerful military entity in world history cannot stabilize a country at will or "make it" produce oil simply by sending in soldiers and tanks. In other words, since the Iraq invasion, the oil market now understands that the United States cannot guarantee the security of oil supplies . . . for itself or for anyone else. That new and chilling knowledge, as much as anything else, explains the high price of oil.*[18]

Whether out of fear of weapons of mass destruction or simply concern that the region will ignite and tensions in the region will spin out of control, the United States once again has attempted to control events in the Middle East with American troops.

THE TERRIBLE DILEMMA FACING THE UNITED STATES

The United States finds itself in a very difficult position as the only superpower in the world. Its economic and military power is dependent on oil from the Middle East and OPEC nations, so it has made several pledges related to this region:

1. The United States has promised to protect the State of Israel and has supplied Israel with the most sophisticated weapons and equipment available.

2. The United States has proven it will protect its vital interests in the Middle East by "any means necessary, including military force."

3. The United States has pledged to attack any nation that openly supports terrorism and did so in Afghanistan.

4. The United States has pledged to control weapons of mass destruction anywhere they are a threat to Israel or the United States.

This situation will only get more difficult, and the cost to protect America's interests in the Middle East will increase dramatically. Europe is also a major stakeholder in this crisis. In a severe crisis it does not appear that the United States alone can solve this problem. The West must create new alliances to protect its interests. Unstable prices or the loss of the oil supply could destroy the economic fiber of the West. The Middle East and the Persian Gulf will continue to be the focus of world attention, and any major crisis that engulfs the region will bring an international cry for peace.

END-TIME PROPHECY IN THE MAKING

The Bible predicts that a new alignment of nations will emerge to control events in the Middle East (see Daniel 9:27; 11:40-45). A coalition of ten world leaders will consolidate the power of the West into an iron fist. Until very recently there has not been a threat to the Western world that could cause such a shift in the balance of power. But Europe's industrialized nations must have a secure, guaranteed flow of oil and security from the social disruption of Islamic terror imported from the Middle East. The political and economic implications to the world would be no less than those occurring when the Roman Empire combined many nations into one political and economic unity to dominate the world and enforce the *Pax Romana* (Roman Peace).

The Middle East is about to explode and drag the world into one of the most difficult and terrifying conflicts in world history. The time between the cycles of violence in the Middle East crisis is shortening. The bloodshed over oil and power has just begun. Deep-seated passions, religious fanaticism, and poverty fuel suicidal terrorism. Countries in the region will not be able to resolve this crisis on their own.

Terrorism, instability, and the threat of a disruption in oil have created a greater need for peace than any international situation since the Cold War. Outside nations must protect their interests and stop the bloodshed. The prophets of the Old Testament predicted just such a situation. From a biblical standpoint this is the most dramatic evidence that the world is now headed down the road to Armageddon.

The Prophetic Destiny of the Middle East

Civilization began in the Middle East with the creation of Adam and Eve. It was there that the great empires of the past rose and fell—Egypt, Assyria, Babylon, Medo-Persia, Greece, and Rome.

It will be in the Middle East that the future world government will have its center of political and economic power. The enigma of how the underdeveloped Middle East could once again become the center of world history has suddenly been solved by the world's economic dependence on oil and the worldwide need to stop Islamic terrorism. Already strategic geographically as the hub of three continents, the Middle East is destined to be the center of a world struggle for wealth and power so great that it will engulf the entire world in a gigantic battle centered in the valley of Meggido—also known as Armageddon.

The Coming Crisis—How Far Away?

The coming crisis in the Middle East is looming. Western civilization would be brought to its knees by a sudden disruption in the supply of oil. Whether by terror, nuclear exchange, or a bidding war for oil—it could happen suddenly and without warning. The world's need for carbon-based fuel is rapidly approaching the breaking point. The Middle

East is the only place where that thirst can be quenched. Alternative fuel for transportation worldwide is ten to twenty years away. If the Middle East is to rise to power, now is its hour of opportunity. If Islamic terrorism is to attain its goals, it must act soon.

See how today's headlines relate to this chapter at http://www.prophecyhotline.com.

CHAPTER 3

TERRORISM REACHES EVERYONE

EVENT #2: Islamic terrorism fueled by hatred of the West and Israel pushes the world to the brink of total chaos.

> To achieve such sweeping change, bin Laden espouses a strategy that turns on one premise: The believers must attack World Infidelity, in the form of the United States and its allies, head-on. . . . The concomitant requirement for such a strategy is that violence against the United States has to be catastrophic. . . . The killing must be on a grand scale.
>
> DANIEL BENJAMIN AND STEVEN SIMON, *THE NEXT ATTACK*

> The world today is a more dangerous place than at any time in history.
>
> BILL O'REILLY, *THE O'REILLY FACTOR*

THE EVENTS OF 9/11 STRUCK to the very core of the American way of life and national psyche. For the first time in their history, Americans no longer felt safe and invulnerable to attack on U.S. soil.

In the wake of the tragedy, we have all become familiar with the Homeland Security Advisory System. The color-coded graphic contains five levels that grade the perceived risk of terrorist attack. The five levels are: low, guarded, elevated, high, and severe. The threat of a terrorist attack is a new aspect of everyday life in America. But even now we hardly notice. For most people it really does not seem to matter much whether the threat is low or high.

Suicide attacks, insurrections, and riots have kept world attention on this gathering threat. Terror dominates the headlines. But violence always seems to erupt somewhere else. The wishful thinking is that the trouble will always be "over there."

Israel is definitely in the center of the terror bull's-eye. From the beginning of the Al-Aqsa Intifada (uprising) in September 2000, over one thousand Israelis (mostly civilians) have been killed by terrorists. More than four thousand Palestinians have died as well. And the attacks

 ## A Brief History of the Worldwide Islamic Terror Network

Al-Qaeda means "the base" in Arabic. It was founded in Afghanistan in 1979 by Osama bin Laden. When most people think of Al-Qaeda they only think of 9/11; however, there have been about a dozen major Al-Qaeda attacks worldwide since 9/11.

Hamas is an acronym of the Arabic *Harakat al-Muqawama al-Islamiya,* which means "Islamic Resistance Movement." The word *Hamas* corresponds to an Arabic word meaning "enthusiasm." Hamas was founded in the Gaza Strip in 1987 for the express purpose of eliminating Israel. It is funded by Iran, Palestinian expatriates, and private benefactors in other Arab states. Hamas is responsible for over one hundred homicide bombings in Israel. In January 2006, Hamas won a surprise victory over the Fatah Party in the Palestinian parliamentary elections, taking 76 of the 132 seats.

Hezbollah, which means "Party of God," was founded in 1982 by followers of Iranian cleric Ayatollah Khomeini as an arm of Iran with the chief purpose of destroying Israel and as a means to create an Islamic republic in Lebanon. It is funded and armed by Iran through Syria. Estimates of Iranian support for Hezbollah range from $100 to $300 million per year. Hezbollah has funded and aided Al-Qaeda. Hezbollah was responsible for the bombing of the U.S. Embassy in Beirut in 1983 that killed 63 people and the truck bomb that destroyed the U.S. Marine barracks in Lebanon in 1983 that killed 241 U.S. soldiers.

continue. Hamas, an avowed terrorist organization that refuses even to recognize Israel's right to exist, is now in control of the Palestinian Authority. Hezbollah has gained stature in the Muslim world after squaring off with Israel for thirty-four days in the summer of 2006. It is now firmly embedded to Israel's north in Lebanon.

Increasingly, the United States is being attacked for its support of Israel. This has much more far-reaching implications for our lives than we have imagined. Islamic terror and its threat to the peace and security of the West could be a key signpost on the road to the end times.

TERROR COMES TO AMERICA

Terrorism, fueled by fanatical Islamic ideology, has reared its ugly head over and over again in the last twenty-five years. For the United States it began with the Iranian hostage crisis in 1979. The next attack occurred when Hezbollah bombed the U.S. Embassy in Beirut in 1983, killing 63 people. Then on October 23, 1983—also in Beirut—a truck bomb slammed into a U.S. Marine barracks, killing 241 U.S. soldiers.

Islamic terror first came to American soil on February 26, 1993, when a truck bomb was exploded in the World Trade Center in New York City. This was a dreadful portent of the rising threat to America and the world. But few realized the ominous nature of that event at that time.

On September 11, 2001, the entire world was awakened suddenly to the awfulness of the new global threat—a threat unlike anything the world has ever seen. Feeding on hate for the West and Israel, a well-organized network of Islamic radicals had begun its open warfare with the United States. This was the first stunning attack that gripped the nation, but it was only the portent of many more.

TERROR IS EVERYWHERE

Islamic terrorists hit Bali, Indonesia, on October 12, 2002, killing 202.

On the eve of national elections, four trains in Madrid, Spain, were hit on March 11, 2004. The attacks altered elections in Spain and led to the country's withdrawal from the war in Iraq.

Terror struck Great Britain on July 7, 2005, when four bombs in central London were detonated in a span of fifty-six minutes, killing 37 and injuring 700. It was the worst attack in London since the blitz of World War II.

For at least eleven consecutive nights in late 2005, France endured riots that spread to 300 French cities. The rioters, who mainly targeted vehicles, were primarily youths born of Arab and African immigrants in poor suburbs. About 5,000 cars were torched—1,400 on one night (November 6) alone. France's far-right political party, the National Front, emerged stronger than ever after the civil unrest.

Muslim fury erupted all over the world as angry rioters demonstrated for days in February 2006 over a cartoon in a Danish newspaper that depicted the prophet Mohammad as a terrorist. Iran and Syria did all they could to fan the flames. Riots broke out in places such as Pakistan, India, Indonesia, Norway, and Thailand. This proved that any incident can provoke protests, riots, and terrorist attacks around the world, thanks to instant worldwide news and the Internet.

It's clear that Islamic extremism and terror have gone global. Part of the frustration with terror is that it lurks in the shadows. It relies on stealth to commit its dastardly deeds. It uses the Internet to spread the ideology and tactics of terrorism to every corner of the world. Nameless, faceless terrorists patiently and painstakingly weave their web of destruction in secret. With an enemy like this, conventional military strength is often of little use. The world faces a totally unconventional enemy that aims to push Western civilization back into the Dark Ages.

While many members of Al-Qaeda and other terrorist cells have been captured or killed, for the most part terrorists are hard to find and sometimes almost impossible to root out. Osama bin Laden orchestrated the 9/11 attacks in September 2001 and disappeared into hiding while continuing to release murderous messages of encouragement to his followers. For every terrorist that is killed or captured, several more are easily recruited from refugee camps, mosques, or the disenfranchised Muslim minority across Europe.

WMDS AND TERROR

How serious is the threat of worldwide terror? Could it really spread to everyone? Could the whole world feel its fury?

It took only three years for the United States to build the world's first atom bomb. The Soviets went nuclear in the 1940s, the Chinese in the late 1960s, India in the 1970s, and Pakistan in the 1990s. All of these countries set off nuclear tests to prove they had achieved their objective. Even before North Korea conducted a nuclear test in 2006, it was widely assumed that it had created as many as ten nuclear weapons.

And where is Iran on the road to achieving its nuclear objectives? It took Pakistan and North Korea roughly a decade to get enough material for their first nuclear devices. Iran has been pushing to go nuclear for two decades. For more than a decade it has played a game of nuclear hide-and-seek with the International Atomic Energy Agency.

Intelligence sources have long believed that Abdul Qadeer Khan, who is credited with developing Pakistan's nuclear bomb, sold both the design and actual P-2 centrifuges needed to create enriched uranium to Libya, North Korea, and Iran. Khan sold Libya a complete Chinese-made bomb design and most likely sold the same design to Iran.[1] It is difficult to determine who is now in possession of this type of sensitive information.

Still the world was startled when Iran's president, Mahmoud Ahmadinejad, announced in April 2006 that Iran was already conducting research on the P-2 centrifuge that would quadruple its ability to enrich uranium. In August 2006 intelligence sources predicted that Iran would have hundreds of P-2 centrifuges by 2007.[2] Centrifuges of advanced design are necessary to produce concentrations of uranium's rare component, uranium 235. Although Ahmadinejad's claim may have been an exaggeration, it certainly raised serious concerns.

Uranium must be enriched to levels close to 90 percent for use in atomic bombs. The world is not sure how or when Iran will assemble its first atomic bomb. Estimates vary, but most informed sources believe that Iran will build its first atomic bomb sometime within the next three to five years unless the program is disrupted by an attack from outside Iran. And, of course, Iran could speed this timetable dramatically by purchasing an atomic weapon from North Korea.[3]

Beginning in 2004, the Senate Foreign Relations Committee, chaired by Indiana senator Richard Lugar, surveyed analysts around the world to assess the potential threat from weapons of mass destruction. After the study was complete, Senator Lugar released this statement: "The bottom line is this: For the foreseeable future, the United States and other nations will face an existential threat from the intersection of terrorism and weapons of mass destruction."[4]

After polling eighty-five nonproliferation and national security experts, the authors of this report estimated the risk of attack by weapons of mass destruction to be as high as 70 percent by the year 2015. Most of the experts said they expect one or two new countries to acquire nuclear weapons by 2010 and as many as five by 2015.

The report from the survey also contained these findings:

- The most significant risk of a WMD attack was from a radiological weapon, the so-called "dirty bomb," in which radioactive material is put into a conventional explosive device.
- The threat that a dirty bomb will be detonated and affect a major portion of a city by 2015 was judged to be 40 percent.
- The next highest risk was an attack with a chemical or biological weapon.
- The risk of attack with conventional nuclear weapons was judged to be 16.4 percent by 2010 and 29.2 percent by 2015.[5]

TERROR AND THE TIME OF THE END

The combination of radical Islam and terror is the great new threat to the world. But what are the prophetic implications of this new menace?

The rise of Islamic terror seems to be setting the stage for the end times in at least four important ways. Let's consider each of them briefly:

1. **Time is running out.** The predictions in the Senate Foreign Relations Committee report are sobering and ominous, especially in a post 9/11 world where Iran's nuclear threat adds to the already gathering storm. A dark shadow hangs over our world. It seems like the coming of Christ could be very near. Why? Stop and think about it. End-time events predicted by the prophets of the Bible have never been so easy to imagine or so consistent with the movement of world history.

   The Bible predicts that God—not man—will bring the period of the Gentiles to an abrupt halt during the Battle of Armageddon when Christ returns to judge the world. God, not man, will control the events that lead to the reign of Christ on earth, when the Jewish people will finally be ushered into their hour of glory and peace predicted by the prophets. The lion will lie down with the lamb. The earth will be saved for the predicted millennial reign of Christ. According to the Scriptures, at the end of that reign, God, not man, will dismantle the earth and create a new heaven and new earth.

   If rogue nations or terrorists begin to use WMDs, the whole world will be thrown into chaos and confusion. Just think what would happen if one of these weapons, even a dirty bomb, was detonated in a major city in the United States or Europe. While something this catastrophic could happen to destabilize the world before the Rapture of the church, it seems much more likely that these kinds of international convulsions will be part of the post-Rapture scenario that catapults the Group of Ten and eventually the Antichrist to world power.

   Of course, God could delay or turn back the timetable for these end-time events. He could prevent terrorists or rogue nations from getting their hands on WMDs and pushing the world to the brink of chaos. But right now it looks like the stage is set for end-time events to begin, though no one on earth knows the day or the hour of Christ's coming.

2. **The nations are in place for the predicted invasion of Israel.** The rise of Islamic terror is setting the stage for the events in Ezekiel 38–39. These chapters prophesy an invasion of Israel in the end times by a vast coalition of nations, all of whom are Islamic today except Russia. Israel has said that a new "axis of terror"—Iran, Syria, and the Hamas-run Palestinian government—is sowing the seeds of the first world war of the twenty-first century. The rise of Islam, and especially radical Islamic terrorism, strikingly foreshadows Ezekiel's great prophecy. More details about this incredible prophecy will be presented in detail in chapter 7.

3. **The conditions are in place for the world to accept peace at any price.** The world is more at risk today for nuclear detonations, biological warfare, and chemical warfare than ever before. Pakistan and India have the bomb. So do China and North Korea. Iran is working feverishly to join the "nuclear club." It's only a matter of time until rogue states, terrorists, or fanatics get their hands on these weapons of mass destruction. The unrest in key Islamic nations could easily erupt into an explosive call for widespread jihad, or holy war.

Moreover, the Middle East is the only region in the world whose reserves are large enough to meet rising U.S. and international demands for oil. This deadly combination of oil and terror in the Middle East leaves the West especially vulnerable.

In this climate of terror and uncertainty, the world yearns for some way to make the unrest stop. People the world over are clamoring for peace. People are also yearning for safety. The world has become obsessed with security. We have never felt more unsafe, more exposed, more vulnerable, than we do right now. We want safety: safety for ourselves, safety for our children, safety from a nuclear nightmare, safety from terrorist bombings, safety from bioterrorism, safety from chemical warfare. People will naturally begin to search for someone who can make sense out of it all—someone, anyone, who can bring peace when the world is on the brink of disaster.

Of course, this longing is nothing new. But with the rise of fanatics and war by stealth—the sudden, unexpected strike of terrorism—the cry for peace and safety has become a worldwide cadence. As terror and disruption of the supply of oil collide, the world will be willing to pay any price for peace in the Middle East. This is just the scenario that will catapult a leader to the world stage to consolidate power and promise peace to a world on the brink of disaster.

4. Globalism would allow one man to declare himself world ruler. The scourge of global terror has served to bring the world together. After the flood of the earth recorded in Genesis, the Bible says that all the people of the world congregated at one location under the leadership of one man, Nimrod, to build a great tower to the heavens (Genesis 10:8-10; 11:1-9). The whole world was one community in global rebellion against its Creator. God came down and confounded the language of man, dispersing the rebel race over the face of the earth.

Ever since that time, Satan has tried in vain to again bring the world under the control of one man through whom he could rule the world. The pharaohs, Nebuchadnezzar, Alexander the Great, the caesars, Napoleon, Hitler, and Stalin have entered and left the stage of world history.

The Bible predicts that in the end times the world will once again come together in a one-world economy, government, and religion to shake its collective fist in the face of the Creator. The Antichrist will lead this global union against God (Revelation 13:3-18).

Until recently it would have been impossible for one world ruler to instantaneously communicate with the entire world and control the world economy. But all that has changed dramatically. The 1990s have been called the decade of globalization. Incredible developments occurred that advanced globalization at warp speed. Here are just a few of the main contributors.

- The end of the Cold War
- The creation of the World Trade Organization
- The advance of the Internet
- The creation of CNN and instant global news
- The need for global cooperation on environmental issues
- The threat of terror worldwide
- The global need for oil

The world that seemed so large, expansive, and hopelessly fragmented only a few decades ago now seems small and interconnected.

In the face of the terror threat, nations can no longer afford to go it alone. Those in the West, especially, must rely on one another. Isolation is a thing of the past. International cooperation is necessary to share critical intelligence and surveillance information to stop the advance of terrorism.

Worldwide terror is bringing the world together. The Antichrist will take advantage of this opportunity created by fear and will seize control of the global network of nations to rule the world.

TRUE PEACE IS COMING

God will allow even that which is evil to advance His prophetic program. The false peace offered by the Antichrist will be shattered, followed by the catastrophic judgments that end the period of the Gentiles. God, not man, will bring true peace to earth. It's hard to imagine world peace in these troubled times. But it is coming. There will be real, permanent, universal peace when, and only when, the Prince of Peace comes to rule over the earth.

 See how today's headlines relate to this chapter at
http://www.prophecyhotline.com.

CHAPTER 4

ISRAEL: GROUND ZERO FOR THE END TIMES

EVENT #3: Israel aggressively defends itself in a sea of enemies—bringing the world to the brink of World War III.

> The Jewish people have unchallengeable, eternal, historic right to the Land of Israel, the inheritance of their forefathers.
>
> FORMER ISRAELI PRIME MINISTER MENACHEM BEGIN

> Israel is exceptionally strong and knows how to defend itself.
>
> FORMER ISRAELI PRIME MINISTER SHIMON PERES

ON ANCIENT MAPS ISRAEL WAS often placed at the center, signifying that it was at the center of man's activity. While Israel is no longer in the middle of the world map, it still occupies the center place in world headlines. Stop and think about it. It's very difficult to pick up a newspaper or news magazine, or watch a cable news program, and not read or hear something about Israel. Notice this the next time you read the paper or listen to the world headlines on the evening news. Israel is everywhere. There's the Israeli-Palestinian quagmire, terrorist attacks, peace talks, land for peace, the Gaza pullout, the war with Hezbollah and Hamas, and critical elections. And this is nothing new. It's been this way for at least thirty years.

Israel is the nation at the center—the center of politics, terrorism, the peace talks, and jihadist hatred.

Have you ever wondered why? Why is Israel so important? Why all the fuss over a Middle Eastern nation that's no bigger than New Jersey? The reason goes all the way back to Abraham and reaches forward to the end of time.

Israel. It's the key. History proclaims its past. Headlines proclaim its present. Prophecy proclaims its future.[1]

THE HORIZONTAL VIEW OF PROPHECY

The promises and prophecies pertaining to Israel are intricately interwoven throughout the entire Bible. Some involve general promises, but most involve specific and detailed glimpses into the future. When the prophets described future events, it was as if they were looking horizontally at distant mountain peaks. They described these peaks of history in vivid detail but often had little understanding of the vast valleys of time that separated the events they described.[2]

The "Mountain Peaks" of Prophecy

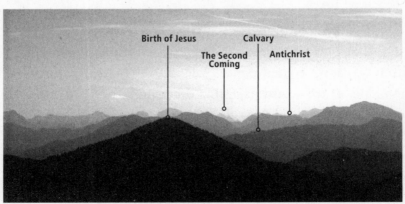

Many of the prophecies about Israel are especially confusing unless they are carefully fitted together and compared to the history of the Jewish people and the Land of Promise. Jerusalem has been destroyed many times. Three times the Jews have been scattered from the land—and three times they have returned. The prophecies of their scattering and return must be compared to the actual historical facts. It is important to ask what prophecies have been fulfilled and which can be expected to be fulfilled in the future. Many ancient prophecies that have not yet taken place may well occur within our lifetime. The prophecies in the Bible make it clear that Israel's past, present, and future are key to what will happen next in the world.

Prophetic Questions about the Promised Land

When the biblical promises and prophecies speak of the Promised Land, do they describe an actual land with geographic boundaries? Is this literal or figurative language? If the promise of the land pertains to an actual geographic location, have the Jews ever possessed it? Does the land really belong to them?

If the land was promised and prophesied as a reward for obedience, is it possible that disobedience and unbelief have caused the promise to be withdrawn? Is the promise restated in the New Testament? Are there conditions to that promise?

The answer to these important questions requires a further investigation into the specifics of the promises and prophecies about Israel. These specifics must then be compared to the actual history of the Jewish people and the Land of Promise.

To really understand the present and its deep-seated issues and struggles in the Middle East, we have to go all the way back to the days of Abraham and the promises God made to him. To see into the future we have to look back to the past.

Abram, the Man of Destiny

In the twentieth century, the world witnessed one of the greatest miracles of history—the restoration of an ancient people to the land of their fathers after centuries of being scattered among every nation of the world. The story of Israel's return, stirring as it is, has deep roots that reach back four thousand years to the city of Ur of the Chaldees, an ancient city in Mesopotamia located not far from Babylon. It was there that Abram, a man of destiny, lived in a city of advanced culture. To Abram came the command to leave the land of his fathers and go to a land God would show him.

The story of Abram begins in Genesis 11:27 and ends with his death in Genesis 25:8. In a book that devotes only three chapters to describing the origin of the world, fourteen chapters are devoted to the life of Abram.

In partial obedience to God's command to go to a new land, Abram left his home and became a tent dweller, moving about seven hundred miles to the northwest to Haran, where he lived until his father died. Then another pilgrimage, this time about five hundred miles to the southwest, brought him to the Land of Promise. It was there that Abram lived and died.

To Abram, a man of destiny, God gave great promises. He promised Abram would become the father of a great nation, that he would become famous and be a blessing to others (Genesis 12:2). Additionally, God promised that all the families of the earth would be blessed through Abram. History has recorded the literal fulfillment of these promises. The name Abram, later changed to Abraham, meaning "father of nations," has been a great name, revered alike by Jew, Christian, and Muslim. Not only the Jewish people but the whole Arab world descended from Abraham.

As promised, God has given Abraham so many descendants that, like dust or the stars in the night sky, they could not be counted (Genesis 13:16; 15:5). Through Abraham came the prophets, the writers of the Scriptures of the Old and New Testaments, and Jesus Christ—the Son of Abraham, the Son of David. Those who have blessed the descendants of Abraham have been blessed; those who have cursed the sons of Abraham have been cursed (Genesis 12:3). The judgments of God have fallen upon Israel's oppressors—Egypt, Assyria, Babylon, Rome, and in more modern times, Spain, Germany, and Russia. The final judgments will come when the period of the Gentiles ends.

The Promise of the Land

In the center of God's promises to Abraham was the promise to give his descendants a land. The whole drama of Abraham's life revolved around his willingness to leave Ur of the Chaldees to go to a new Land of Promise. The promise did not simply involve spiritual blessing; the lifelong pilgrimage of Abraham was a necessary part of the fulfillment of the promise for a land.

In Genesis 15 the confirmation of the promise is stated in no uncertain terms. Abraham's faith in leaving his home to receive this land was rewarded with a detailed explanation of the promise. The biblical narrative presents the description of the land in definite terms with clear geographic boundaries, and it even indicates the peoples who inhabited the land at that time: "So the LORD made a covenant with Abram that day and said, 'I have given this land to your descendants, all the way from the border of Egypt to the great Euphrates River—the land now occupied by the Kenites, Kenizzites, Kadmonites, Hittites, Perizzites, Rephaites, Amorites, Canaanites, Girgashites, and Jebusites'" (Genesis 15:18-21).

This biblical account clearly referred to a specific geographical land, not some general blessing or a promise of heaven. The continued revelation of God to Abram elaborated the promise again as recorded in Genesis 17. Here Abram's name was changed to Abraham because of the promise that he would be the father of many nations.

The promise of the land is tied to the promise of a continuing heritage: "I will confirm my covenant with you and your descendants after you, from generation to generation. This is the everlasting covenant: I will always be your God and the God of your descendants after you. And I will give the entire land of Canaan, where you now live as a foreigner, to you and your descendants. It will be their possession forever, and I will be their God" (Genesis 17:7-8).

The meaning to Abraham and the early readers of Scripture is evident. The land promised was Israel, stretching from the Sinai Desert north and east to the Euphrates River. This would include all the holdings of present-day Israel, Lebanon, and the West Bank of Jordan, plus substantial portions of Syria, Iraq, and Saudi Arabia. And remarkably, as described in Genesis 17, the covenant was described as an everlasting covenant, and the land of Canaan promised as an everlasting possession.

In light of the raging controversy over who owns the land of Israel, it's important to remember that the only specific piece of land on this earth that God ever promised to any people was the land of Israel, described in Genesis 15, to the Jewish people.

While God promised the land to Abraham, he never possessed it. He was one hundred years old when God miraculously enabled him to have a son, Isaac, to fulfill His promises. But even after the birth of Isaac, Abraham did not possess the land, except for the small portion that he bought as a burial plot for Sarah. Instead, God plainly told him that his descendants for hundreds of years would not possess the land. They would, in fact, be strangers in a foreign land, where they would be oppressed as slaves. After four generations they could return to the land when the sin of the Amorites had run its course (Genesis 15:13-16).

History records that the Jewish people have been exiled from their land on three major occasions in the past and that they have been supernaturally restored to their land by God each time. The chart below gives a very concise overview of Israel's past departures and providential returns.

The Israelites' Departures and Returns

DEPARTURES	RETURNS
First Departure: Egypt	First Return: Under Moses
Second Departure: 10 northern tribes by Assyria in 722 BC; 2 southern tribes by Babylon in 605–586 BC.	Second Return: Under Zerubbabel (538 BC), Ezra (458 BC), and Nehemiah (444 BC)
Third Departure: Romans in AD 70	Third Return: Began in 1871 and continues today

Prophetic Hope for a Last Return

With each of the first two departures, there was a glorious return. But what about the third departure? Jesus clearly predicted that the magnificent Temple of His lifetime would be completely demolished so that not one stone would be left on top of another (Matthew 24:2). The fate of Jerusalem and the Jewish people was understood to take a drastic turn for the worse within the lifetime of the generation that heard His message. And, of course, the prophecy of Jesus was literally fulfilled in AD 70 when the Roman army under the emperor Titus destroyed Jerusalem and the Temple. But the nagging questions remained: Was Israel finished? Were the promises to be set aside?

The apostle Paul, himself an Israelite, struggled with these very questions. His conclusion was simply an emphatic *no!* "I ask, then, has God rejected his own people, the nation of Israel? Of course not!" (Romans 11:1).

Would there be a fulfillment of the everlasting covenant to possess the land, a land with clear geographic boundaries promised as an everlasting possession? The writer of the book of Hebrews reviewed the promises to Abraham. Were they conditioned on Israel's obedience, thereby nullified because of Israel's disbelief? No, they were not. The final outcome was immutable, unchangeable. For example, there was God's promise to Abraham.

Since there was no one greater to swear by, God took an oath in his own name.... God also bound himself with an oath, so that those who received the promise could be perfectly sure that he would never change his mind. So God has given both his promise and his oath. These two things are unchangeable because it is impossible for God to lie. Therefore, we who have fled to him for refuge can have great confidence as we hold to the hope that lies before us. This hope is a strong and trustworthy anchor for our souls. It leads us through the curtain into God's inner sanctuary. (Hebrews 6:13, 17-19)

The succinct and straightforward testimony of both the Old and New Testaments points to a final return to the land promised. This hope of restoration has sustained the Jews through nineteen hundred years of struggle. Christians who have understood the clear prophetic witness of the Bible have expected it to happen for hundreds of years, even when the odds were overwhelmingly against it. Some of the key events leading to this prophecy's fulfillment are described below.

Scattered persecutions. The centuries that followed AD 70 were tragic for Jews. Afflicted by persecutions of incredible severity, their total number at one time shrank to approximately one million. Hated by professing Christians and non-Christians alike, they were driven from land to land, never finding rest or prosperity except for brief periods of time.

From all outward appearances, Israel's future was hopeless. In the seventh century the Arabs took possession of Israel's ancient land. In the twelfth century the Christian crusaders were established in Israel for a brief time but were finally defeated by Saladin in 1187. The Ottoman Turks took over in 1517 and continued their control over the Promised Land until Turkey was defeated in World War I. A dramatic turn of events began in 1917 when General Allenby conquered Jerusalem, and the British occupation of Palestine (Israel) began.

Beginnings of the third return. The return of Jews to the land was beset by many problems, although as early as 1871 a few Jews had managed to return to the land, and about twenty-five thousand Jews had settled there by 1881. The idea of the Jews repossessing their ancient land was not stated in any formal way, however, until it was adopted in the first Zionist congress, called in 1897 by Theodor Herzl. The goal of reclaiming the land of Palestine as a home for the wandering Jews, although seemingly an idealistic dream, brought the light of hope to Jewish eyes around the world.

The Balfour Declaration of 1917. The progress was painfully slow. By 1914 the number of Jews in the land had reached only eighty thousand. During World War I, to gain support of Jews for the war effort, the British foreign secretary, Arthur J. Balfour, issued the Balfour Declaration on November 2, 1917. This declaration indicated approval of Israel's goal: "His Majesty's Government views with favor the establishment in Palestine of a national home for the Jewish people." Pressure from the Arab world, which would have no part in establishing a home for Israel, and the desire of Britain to maintain friendship with the Arab nations, prevented any fulfillment of this promise. Little progress had been made when World War II broke out in 1939. By that time, however, four hundred thousand Jews had managed to find their way into the country in spite of severe restrictions on Jewish immigration and laws that did not allow Jews to possess real estate.

The state of Israel established in 1948. Many anti-Semitic historical revisionists, such as Iran's president, Mahmoud Ahmadinejad, deny that the Jewish Holocaust ever occurred. However, World War II, which resulted in the terrible massacre of millions of Jews under Nazi tyranny, created a favorable attitude and worldwide sympathy for the Jewish people. Certainly there should be some place where the wandering Jew could have a home. Although an Arab League was formed in 1945 to oppose Jewish expansion, the United Nations created a home for Jews in Palestine after World War II with the approval of the United States and Russia. The directive stated that Palestine should be divided into a Jewish state and an Arab state, and five thousand square miles were assigned to the infant state of Israel.

Israeli-Arab War, 1948–1949. On May 14, 1948, when British control ended, Israel became an independent state for the first time in hundreds of years. The population of the new nation included six hundred and fifty thousand Jews and many hundreds of thousands of Arabs. The settlement, however, was quite unacceptable to the Arab world. Israel was attacked on all sides by Egypt, Jordan, Iraq, Syria, Lebanon, and Saudi Arabia. Israel's defense was heroic, and the armies of her opponents were disorganized. Although thousands of Israelis fell in battle, by the time a truce was arranged on January 7, 1949, Israel had extended her area of possession from five thousand square miles to eight thousand square miles, including much of the Negev, the great desert to the south. Israel's history from that date to this has been one of unending trouble, recurring warfare, ongoing attempts at peace, but gradual strengthening of the nation.

Israel's Time Line from 1948

1948	The state of Israel declares its independence and is attacked by five Arab nations.
1949	Jerusalem is divided into two parts (New City under Jewish rule; Old City under Jordanian rule).
1956	Israel, Great Britain, and France capture the Sinai from Egypt.
1964	The PLO is established.
1967	In the Six-Day War (June 6–11), Israel defeats Egypt, Syria, and Jordan and gains control of all Jerusalem, the Golan Heights, the West Bank of the Jordan River and the Gaza Strip.
1973	On Yom Kippur (Day of Atonement) Egypt and Syria launch a surprise attack against Israel, but Israel turns them back.
1979	Israel and Egypt sign the Camp David Accords, in which Israel agrees to return the Sinai Peninsula to Egypt in exchange for peace.
1982	Israel invades Lebanon in what was known as Operation Peace of Galilee.
1987–1993	The first Intifada (Palestinian uprising) erupts in the West Bank and Gaza Strip.
1991	During the first Gulf War, Israel is hit by Iraqi Scud missiles.
1993	The Oslo Accords are signed. Israeli prime minister Yitzhak Rabin and PLO chairman Yasser Arafat shake hands at the White House.
2000	Israel withdraws from Lebanon. The second Intifada erupts in September when Ariel Sharon visits the Temple Mount.
2003	The United States presents the "Road Map" for peace in the Middle East.
2005	Israel pulls out of all twenty-one settlements in the Gaza Strip.
2006	Israel wages a bloody 34-day war against Hezbollah for the return of kidnapped soldiers (while also trying to secure the release of a soldier abducted by Hamas just a few weeks before Hezbollah's provocation).

HAVE THE PROPHECIES BEEN FULFILLED?

From the time of the promise to Abraham to the present hour, the prophecies about Israel's total possession and blessing in the land have not yet been fulfilled. The pulse of Jewish history, with three successive departures from and three returns to their Promised Land, has been a dramatic one. The most dramatic events, however, are still ahead. Is the present return of Israel the beginning of the last and ultimate regathering of Israel? Is this one more in a series of current events preparing the way for the end of the period of the Gentiles? As non-Jewish nations jockey into position for their last moments of glory and judgment, the stage is set for the final end-time events predicted as the end of the period of the Gentiles. Then and only then will Israel finally experience all that has been promised and hoped for since the time of Abraham.

The year 2006 appears to have been a key turning point in the regathering of the Jewish people to their homeland. In 2006, for the first time in about 1,900 years, Israel became home to the largest Jewish community in the world, surpassing even the Jewish population in the United States. From a population of about 650,000 when the Jewish state was founded in 1948, the Jewish population of Israel grew to more than 5.3 million in 2006. It is expected to grow to more than 6 million by 2020. The restoration of the Jewish state and return of all twelve tribes to Israel are necessary preconditions for the events of the end times to be fulfilled.

But the return of the Jews to Israel has been no easy road to glory. Negotiations for peace in the Middle East have not produced a lasting peace. The doves and peacemakers in Israel will eventually lead their country into a peace that will compromise their security in the hope of economic prosperity. It is sad to forecast that a nation that defended herself so bravely for fifty years will be lulled into a false peace with international guarantees that will be of no help in the final hour the Bible describes as "such a time of terror. It will be a time of trouble for my people Israel" (Jeremiah 30:7).

The outline of prophecy is self-evident. After their initial return, the Jews will go through a period of false peace, an international betrayal, and a bloodbath of astounding proportions. Without the direct intervention of God, both Israel and the Jewish people would be completely destroyed.

The Old Testament prophet Jeremiah describes the time of trouble for Israel in vivid terms. This is the last three and a half years of the seven-year tribulation period leading to the final battle—the Battle of Armageddon. It will begin when the false peace with Israel is broken by the new leader of the Group of Ten.

This period of history is often called "the great tribulation" and a time of "greater anguish than at any time since world began" (Revelation 7:14; Matthew 24:21). It is detailed in the book of Revelation as a specific time ending the period of the Gentiles. Israel, Jerusalem, and the Temple rebuilt during the peace will be "turned over to the nations. They will trample the holy city for 42 months" (Revelation 11:2).

After promising the Israelites' return, Jeremiah warned, "This is what the LORD says: 'I hear cries of fear; there is terror and no peace. Now let me ask you a question: Do men give birth to babies? Then why do they stand there, ashen-faced, hands pressed against their sides like a woman in labor? In all history there has never been such a time of terror. It will be a time of trouble for my people Israel. Yet in the end they will be saved! 'For in that day,' says the LORD of Heaven's Armies, 'I will break the yoke from their necks and snap their chains. Foreigners will no longer be their masters. For my people will serve the LORD their God and their king descended from David—the king I will raise up for them'" (Jeremiah 30:5-9).

A NEW KINGDOM WILL COMPLETE THE RETURN

The final return will not be completed until Christ returns to intervene as judge of the nations and the promised King to restore David's throne. The prophecies concerning the return, so dramatically begun in our history, will not be completed until all living Jews (drastically reduced in number during the Great Tribulation) are finally established in the Promised Land for a millennium of both peace and prosperity. Many of the Old Testament prophets, such as Ezekiel, Isaiah, Daniel, and Micah, echoed similar visions of this period.

Jeremiah prophesied the judgment that would fall on the non-

Jewish nations and then reported the message from the God of Israel in these words:

> But I will gather together the remnant of my flock from the countries where I have driven them. I will bring them back to their own sheepfold, and they will be fruitful and increase in number. Then I will appoint responsible shepherds who will care for them, and they will never be afraid again. Not a single one will be lost or missing. I, the LORD have spoken! "For the time is coming," says the LORD, "when I will raise up a righteous descendant from King David's line. He will be a King who rules with wisdom. He will do what is just and right throughout the land. And this will be his name: 'The LORD Is Our Righteousness.' In that day Judah will be saved, and Israel will live in safety. (Jeremiah 23:3-6)

Ezekiel's prophecy makes it clear that this will finally be accomplished immediately after a period of judgment and that the completion of the return will bring every living Jew into the land: "Then my people will know that I am the LORD their God, because I sent them away to exile and brought them home again. I will leave none of my people behind" (Ezekiel 39:28).

The present return of Israel to the land sets the stage for an important series of end-time events. Prophecies clearly predicted that Israel would be reestablished as a nation before the end of the period of the Gentiles. But non-Jewish nations were described as still in control of the destiny of Israel during a final hour of judgment and suffering. Jesus predicted, "They will be killed by the sword or sent away as captives to all the nations of the world. And Jerusalem will be trampled down by the Gentiles until the period of the Gentiles comes to an end" (Luke 21:24).

The next dramatic moves will involve the continued struggle for control of Jerusalem and the return of a portion of the land to the Palestinian Arabs as already witnessed in the Israeli withdrawal from Gaza in 2005. This struggle will become increasingly explosive because of the five million Palestinians dispossessed. Many have been forced to live as refugees and exiles in surrounding Arab states. Palestinian guerilla groups spawned from the refugee camps have pursued a strategy of terror and have made it difficult for moderate Arabs to negotiate compromise solutions.

Arab leaders have managed an uneasy alliance with the Palestinians that has often exploded in violence. In October 1974 the Arab summit conference at Rabat offered a solution for the sake of unity. The occupied West Bank of the Jordan was to become an independent Palestinian state run by the Palestine Liberation Organization (PLO). A government in exile was to be formed by early 1975 to prepare for negotiation with Israel.

The West Bank was originally conquered in the War of 1967 and, from Israel's point of view, is a legitimate possession of Israel. Israel continued to plant new settlements and the Palestinians continued to resist. Much of the world, however, including the United States, is putting pressure on Israel to turn the West Bank and the Gaza strip into an independent Palestinian state separate from Israel. This is the gist of the so-called "Road Map" for peace. However, the road map was tattered and torn after the stunning victory by Hamas in the Palestinian parliamentary election in January 2006. Initial exit polling indicated that the ruling Fatah Party had secured a fairly safe majority. But the next morning the world awoke to the stunning news that the Islamic terrorist group Hamas had won a landslide victory, securing 76 of 132 seats in the parliamentary elections. Fatah, the party of Palestinian Authority president Mahmoud Abbas, claimed a mere 43 seats.

TERRORISM AND THE NEED FOR PEACE

Hamas's support from Arab states and Iran will continue to be a thorn in Israel's side and create the ever-present threat of a terrorist war of attrition, by which they attempt to slowly wear down the Israelis through constant friction and harassment. Israel's economic resources are consumed and combatants and civilians are killed with no clear gains or victory. Cease-fires and peace negotiations are only attempts to gain advantage and continue the conflict.

Reaction around the world to the Hamas victory was swift and severe. America has said that it will not deal with Hamas unless they change their charter, which boldly calls for the destruction of Israel. Western nations threatened to cut off financial support to the Palestinian Authority as long as Hamas is in power, so Iran soon pledged $50 million to the Hamas-led government in Palestine.

On June 25, 2006, Hamas terrorists, using a system of tunnels, attacked an Israeli military outpost. They killed two soldiers, wounded three others, and kidnapped a sixth Israeli soldier. This sparked a fierce response from Israel. Then, on July 12, Hezbollah terrorists, in an almost identical attack, came across Israel's northern border from Lebanon, killing several Israeli soldiers and kidnapping two others. This second attack erupted into a thirty-four-day war during which Israel hit Hezbollah targets in southern Lebanon and was pummeled day after day by thousands of rockets and missiles supplied by Iran.

When one connects the dots, in fact, it's clear that Iran was behind these attacks. Iran is currently enriching uranium and threatening to annihilate Israel. If Iran obtains nuclear weapons, the missiles landing on Israel in the future could be armed with nuclear warheads. Israel's fierce reaction to the kidnapping of the two soldiers by Hezbollah could have been motivated by Israel's knowledge that a preemptive strike against Iran's nuclear facilities is inevitable. Weakening Hezbollah may have been an important first step in Israel's overall strategy for dealing with its greatest threat—Iran.

Terrorists now openly control the Palestinian government. Hamas, Hezbollah, terrorist attacks, reprisals, or Iran's nuclear ambitions could easily push the Middle East into open warfare. As moderate Arabs and European allies consolidate wealth and power, a forced settlement may be the only solution. New leaders will emerge to promise just such a peace. Israel's willingness in August 2006 to turn over southern Lebanon to a European-led peacekeeping force could easily be a prelude or first step in Israel's acceptance of a treaty that guarantees peace. With the threat of escalating terror and a disruption of the West's oil supply, the pressure for a "superimposed peace" will lead to the formation of the most vicious world empire of all time.

See how today's headlines relate to this chapter at
http://www.prophecyhotline.com.

CHAPTER 5

THE DECLINE AND FALL OF AMERICA

EVENT #4: American power and influence in the Middle East fade as the United States retreats to deal with the energy crisis and problems at home.

The average age of the world's greatest civilizations from the beginning of history has been about 200 years. During those 200 years, these nations always progressed through the following sequence:

> From bondage to spiritual faith;
> From spiritual faith to great courage;
> From courage to liberty;
> From liberty to abundance;
> From abundance to complacency;
> From complacency to apathy;
> From apathy to dependence;
> From dependence back into bondage.

COMMONLY ATTRIBUTED TO ALEXANDER FRASER TYTLER

I think that a lot of [Americans] are carrying around in their heads, unarticulated and even in some cases unnoticed, a sense that the wheels are coming off the trolley and the trolley off the tracks. . . . That our pollsters are preoccupied with "right track" and "wrong track" but missing the number of people who think the answer to "How are things going in America?" is "Off the tracks and hurtling forward, toward an unknown destination."

PEGGY NOONAN, OCTOBER 27, 2005

65

WHAT IS THE PLACE OF America in end-time prophecy? In the last one hundred years, the United States has become one of the most powerful and influential nations in all of history. Following the breakup of the Soviet Union, it became the only superpower in the world. Does the Bible have anything to say about the future of the United States?

The ancient prophets were primarily concerned with the Holy Land and its immediate neighbors. For this reason, it's not surprising that geographic areas remote from this center of biblical interest do not figure largely in prophecy and may not be mentioned at all. No specific mention of the United States or any other country in North or South America can be found in the Bible. Also, none of the rather obscure references to distant lands can be taken specifically as a reference to the United States. Therefore, any final, conclusive answer to the question of America's role in the end times is impossible. The prophetic timetable does point to some general conclusions about the role of the United States in end-time events, however.

THE WORLD SITUATION AT THE END TIME

The Bible provides an outline of major stages after the Rapture of the church: (1) a period of preparation, (2) the peace treaty that begins the seven-year tribulation period, and (3) the rise of the Antichrist, who will declare himself world ruler and break the peace treaty, beginning the time of Jacob's trouble. This will usher in the terrible judgments of the last three and a half years of the period of the Gentiles.

1. **Preparation.** Immediately after the Rapture there will be a
   period of preparation in which a group of ten world leaders will
   consolidate the power of the West and will emerge on the world
   stage. This ruling group or oligarchy will unite the European and
   Mediterranean countries into a new revived and powerful Western
   coalition like the Roman Empire. This is the iron fist that will stop
   the chaos.

2. The peace treaty. At the conclusion of this period of preparation, "a ruler will arise" (Daniel 9:26), the head of the Group of Ten, and will make a seven-year covenant with Israel (Daniel 9:27). This treaty will introduce a period of protection and peace for Israel by the leader who will later declare himself world ruler. The "small horn" of Daniel 7:8 will be revealed as the coming world dictator who will take over the power consolidated by the Group of Ten. This marks the beginning of what is generally described as the last week of Daniel's seventy weeks of years—the seven-year tribulation period.

3. The world dictator. The world leader will break his covenant with Israel after three and a half years. He will declare himself world dictator and assume the prerogatives of deity. He will declare himself god and will use the new demonic world religion to fool many. These rapid-fire events will usher in the Great Tribulation with its corresponding period of persecution for Israel. This three-and-a-half-year period will end with the gathering of rebelling armies moving toward Israel to begin the Battle of Armageddon.

Although the Scriptures do not give any clear word concerning the role of the United States in relation to the revived Roman Empire, it is clear this will be a consolidation of the power of the West. Unlike the coalitions led by the United States, this coalition will be led by others—the Group of Ten.

It is very likely that the United States will be in some form of alliance with this coalition whose power is centered in Europe and the Middle East. Most citizens of the United States of America have come from Europe, and their sympathies would more naturally be with a European alliance than with Russia or countries in eastern Asia. It may even be that the United States will provide large support for the Group of Ten as it will seem to be opposed to Iran, Russia, Asia, and Africa.

Actually a balance of power in the world may exist at that time that's very similar to the present world situation; namely, Europe and America may be in formal alliance with Israel in opposition to the radical Islamic countries of the Middle East, as well as Russia and China. Based on geographic, religious, and economic factors, such an alliance of powers seems a natural sequence of the polarization of nations in a tug-of-war over the Middle East and its resources.

NO LONGER A SUPERPOWER

What is perfectly clear is that the world dictator will lead the only superpower in the world by the middle of the great tribulation period (Revelation 13:7). Even if the United States has an alliance with the revived Roman Empire, something will have happened to the United States' role as the world's policeman. It will simply drop out as a superpower. The end-time events do not include America as the great international superpower it was at the beginning of the twenty-first century.

But what could reduce America to a subordinate role as ten Western leaders consolidate the West's political, economic, and military power? What kind of event could bring America to her knees? At least four possibilities, which fit the current world situation, could occur alone or in a fatal combination.

1. **Terrorist attack**. First, some maintain that the total absence of any scriptural reference to America in the end time is evidence that the United States will have been crippled by a nuclear attack, weapons of mass destruction, or some other major catastrophe. If that were the case the United States would no longer be a major player in international affairs. In the post-9/11 world the detonation of a dirty bomb, nuclear device, or biological weapon on U.S. soil is a dreaded yet distinct possibility. Such an attack could kill millions of people, cripple the economy, and reduce the United States to a second-rate power overnight.

2. The "break point" in oil. The second event that could demote the United States from superpower status would be reaching the break point in oil. Such a break point will be reached when the oil crisis finally peaks and the entire world energy complex scrambles to rebalance itself, stake out energy claims, and adjust to the new situation. According to some experts, this point may be reached in the next decade. If the United States is still dependent on imported oil when this occurs, America will enter the uncharted waters of a new era of uncertainty and volatility.[1]

Iran, the world's fourth leading exporter of oil, has promised the United States "harm and pain" if it takes any serious action against Iran's nuclear ambitions. Part of this harm and pain might come in reduced oil exports that could strangle the West with a dramatic rise in oil prices. Though America does not import any oil from Iran, any substantial reduction in the world's oil supply anywhere in the world will cause the price of oil to escalate dramatically on world markets.

If the oil break point is reached without sufficient preparation, U.S. national security would be compromised. The U.S. military machine runs on oil—lots of oil. Without it, America cannot exert its power on the world stage. In this scenario, all available fuel would have to be conserved and diverted to protect our nation. Strategic energy reserves would quickly dry up if the oil supply from the Middle East were disrupted. If oil from the Middle East stopped abruptly, trucks that transport necessary food, medicines, and the necessities of life would compete for meager resources. Nonmilitary aircraft would immediately face severe cutbacks in aviation fuel. Normal commercial traffic would come to a screeching halt. The U.S. economy would go into full cardiac arrest.

The world is entering the long dark tunnel of a new energy era. Only God knows what's at the end of the tunnel for our world and for America. The unquenchable thirst for oil may lead to America's downfall.

3. **A fall from within.** Third, history records how many great nations have risen to unusual power and influence only to decline because of internal corruption, compromise, and a collapse of political will. It may well be that the United States today is at the zenith of its power much as Babylon was in the sixth century BC prior to its sudden downfall at the hands of the Medes and the Persians (Daniel 5).

Any realistic survey of moral conditions in the world today would justify a judgment of God on any nation, including the United States. The long-suffering God has offered unusual benefits to the United States, both in political and religious freedom and economic blessing. But it could be argued that America has squandered its birthright and that judgment is long overdue. The question no longer is whether America deserves judgment, but rather why divine judgment has been so long withheld from a wasteful nation that is blessed so abundantly.

A partial answer to this question may be that the United States has been a major source of Christian testimony in the world. Although the United States represents only about 5 percent of the total world population, in the last century many of the missionaries and much of the money spent on world evangelism have come from America. God's major purpose in this present age is to call people to faith in Christ and to have the gospel preached to all nations. The prosperity America has enjoyed is God's blessing and is intended to be used in spreading Christianity to the ends of the earth.

Another important reason for delay in divine judgment upon America is the Abrahamic promise concerning his seed, "I will bless those who bless you and curse those who treat you with contempt" (Genesis 12:3). For the most part, the United States has been a defender of the Jewish people. In America, descendants of Abraham have enjoyed religious freedom and the opportunity to create wealth. Judgment on other nations has frequently been preceded by anti-Semitism and open hostility or persecution of the Jewish people. In the United States, Jewish people have enjoyed opportunity and freedom from persecution. The political influence of both the Jewish and evangelical communities has guaranteed that the United States remains a staunch ally of the nation of Israel.

4. **The Rapture reason.** The fourth possible explanation for America's absence in the end times is the Rapture of the church. It's clear that if Christ came for His church and all true Christians were taken out of this world, America would be weakened and perilously crippled. While America is not the Christian nation many people envision, America has more believers in Jesus Christ per capita than any other nation.[2] If the Rapture was to happen today, the true church would suddenly be gone, and America would experience a significant loss of leaders and citizens in all walks of life. The Rapture of the church would seriously disrupt the U.S. economy, government, and military forces.

Moreover, when the Rapture occurs, America's missionary endeavors will come to an abrupt halt. It is very likely that America will immediately withdraw her support of Israel. The drastically changed situation could alter God's material and political blessing upon the United States. If God's purpose for the United States is to build His church, evangelize the world, and protect Israel, America may no longer be the fortunate recipient of God's blessing or protection after the Rapture.

In all probability the decline of the United States will result from the impact of not one but several events that combine to make the

United States withdraw from the role of superpower and world police-man. The U.S. intervention in Afghanistan and Iraq has proven that playing the role of world policeman is a difficult, bloody, and impossible task.

When the United States abandons its unilateral role as the most dominant power in the world, the balance of power will shift quickly to Europe and the Middle East. One or more of the possible scenarios described above could seriously weaken the U.S. economy and turn America's attention to itself and provoke a national mood of isolationism in world affairs.

AMERICA'S TIME IS SHORT

Although any conclusion about the role of America in the end times is necessarily tentative, the scriptural evidence is sufficient to conclude that America in that day will not be a superpower and apparently will not figure largely in either the political, economic, or religious leadership of the world.

Yet in view of the imminent return of the Lord, Christians in the United States—and around the world—should remember that the cause of evangelism is urgent. If prophecy has any one message for this generation, it's that time and opportunity are short. Impending world conditions soon may close the door for further witness in many areas. What is true of America is true for the evangelical church throughout the world. The prophetic timetable serves to emphasize the importance of the present task of spreading the gospel, beginning at Jerusalem and to the uttermost parts of the world.

The destiny of nations is in the hands of the omnipotent God. Every nation is "under God." History is moving inexorably to its prophesied consummation as the nations of the world take their places to act out the drama of predicted end-time events. The divine program in all its detail will be fulfilled. The world will rush to judgment. The Son of God will reign in Zion. The nations will bow at His feet. Ultimately the present earth will be replaced with a new heaven and a new earth in which the new Jerusalem will be the home of the redeemed of all ages. The elect of all nations will continue throughout eternity to worship and adore the infinite triune God whose majesty, wisdom, and power will be unquestioned. In that eternal day, God's love and grace will be supremely revealed in those among all nations who have been redeemed by the blood of the Lamb.

See how today's headlines relate to this chapter at **http://www.prophecyhotline.com.**

CHAPTER 6

THE NEW
PAX ROMANA

EVENT #5: To save Western civilization from total collapse, the "Group of Ten" world leaders create an iron fist to stop the chaos and assure the supply of oil to the West.

Any peace, even the most inequitable, should be preferred to the most righteous war.

CICERO

We must build a kind of United States of Europe.

WINSTON CHURCHILL

At the dawn of the twenty-first century, a geopolitical revolution of historic dimensions is under way across the Atlantic: the unification of Europe. Twenty-five nations have joined together—with another dozen or so on the waiting list—to build a common economy, government, and culture. Europe is a more integrated place today than at any time since the Roman Empire.

T. R. REID, *THE UNITED STATES OF EUROPE*

NO MATTER HOW ONE LOOKS at it, the world today is a more dangerous place than at any time in history. Nuclear weapons in the wrong hands could wreak catastrophic, apocalyptic havoc. Terror attacks threaten to cut the oil supply line to Western nations that depend on Middle East oil for the survival of their economies. Michael Klare, an expert in global politics, observes, "Regional conflict, civil war, insurgency, terrorism—these are the most persistent and widespread threats to the global flow of petroleum in the early twenty-first century."[1]

How long can the world tolerate this explosive situation with hostages, terrorist attacks, the escalating Middle East crisis, the proliferation of nuclear weapons, disrupted oil supplies, and the daily threat of war?

The only real solution is a peace treaty that settles disputes, disarms the antagonists, and provides absolute guarantees. In short, a peace treaty backed up by force. A powerful leader will seize world attention by such an offer when the world is on the brink of chaos. He will give the world what it wants. He will bring terror under control, guarantee the flow of oil, and temporarily diffuse the time bomb in the Middle East.

PEACE AND THE FINAL COUNTDOWN

A peace settlement in the Middle East is one of the most important events predicted for the end times. The signing of this peace treaty will start the final seven-year countdown leading to Armageddon and introduce the new world leader who will be destined to become world dictator—the infamous Antichrist.

According to Daniel 9:27, the last seven years leading up to the second coming of Christ will begin with just such a peace settlement. The same passage describes a covenant to be made between the nation of Israel and the ruler who will rise to power (Daniel 9:26), who is related to the Roman Empire and the people who destroyed Jerusalem in AD 70. While the details of the covenant are not given, it will be an attempt to settle the Arab-Israeli controversy that has focused world attention on the Middle East. It will promise to stop terrorism and stabilize the world economy. It may take the form of a forced peace settlement in which Israel returns the land conquered through war in exchange for strong international guarantees for Israel's safety and abundance.

Scriptures describe a world situation not unlike what we have today preceding such a peace settlement. First there will be an alignment of ten leaders who emerge to protect the interests of the West. In Daniel 7:7 and 7:24 this is symbolized by ten horns on a beast that represents the last world empire, the Roman Empire in its final and revised form. Many interpreters of biblical prophecy have felt that the European Union will be a fulfillment of this predicted alignment of nations. The European Union is the preliminary form or at least the forerunner of this ten-leader group. The final power block initially led by the Group of Ten will constitute the revived Roman Empire, which will have the economic and political power necessary to control Europe. The final leader to emerge must eventually be able to seize control of three of the ten leaders and create a consolidation of power very much like the Roman Empire of the past (Daniel 7:8).

THE MARCH OF EMPIRES

About 2,500 years ago the Jewish prophet Daniel was given a panoramic revelation by God that revealed the sweep of world history from Daniel's day all the way up to the second coming of Jesus back to planet earth. His timeless prophecy is as relevant today as the day it was written. Events we see happening today strikingly foreshadow his ancient message.

Daniel wrote most of his great prophecy in the middle of the sixth century BC, near the end of the seventy-year Jewish exile in Babylon. During this time of discipline by God, He knew that His people would have all kinds of questions. They were no doubt asking questions such as—Is God finished with us? Will God be faithful to His covenant with Abraham to give us the land of Israel forever? Will the Kingdom promised to David ever be realized? Will the Messiah ever come to rule and reign over the earth?

In Daniel 2 and 7 God encouraged His people and answered their questions by giving them an overview of the course of world history. God wanted them to know that His promises were sure and that He would keep His Word—that the promised Kingdom would eventually come to Israel. However, God also wanted them to know that the Kingdom would not come immediately. Before the King and His Kingdom would come, four great world empires would rule over Israel in succession. With the benefit of twenty-twenty hindsight we now know that these four empires were Babylon, Medo-Persia, Greece, and Rome.

In Daniel 2 these four empires are pictured as four metals in a great statue that King Nebuchadnezzar saw in a dream. In Daniel 7 these same world empires are pictured as four great wild beasts rising up out of the Mediterranean Sea.

Up to this point almost everyone is in general agreement about the meaning of Nebuchadnezzar's dream in Daniel 2 and Daniel's night vision in Daniel 7. But in Daniel 2 the final form of the Roman Empire is pictured by the feet of iron and baked clay and the ten toes on the image. Likewise in Daniel 7, the final phase of the Roman Empire is depicted by the ten horns on the terrifying beast. These ten toes and ten horns are identified as ten kings (Daniel 2:44; 7:24). Yet we know from history that the Roman Empire never existed in a ten-king form as required by both Daniel 2 and 7.

Moreover, there is a complete, sudden destruction of the great image in Daniel 2 and the beast in Daniel 7. But the Roman Empire gradually deteriorated and declined until the western part of the empire fell in AD 476 and the eastern leg was cut off in AD 1453. A more gradual process could hardly be imagined. With its slow decline, the Roman Empire left unfulfilled the sudden destruction of the feet of the image and the ten-horn stage of the beast in Daniel 7:7.

INTERPRETING THE FUTURE IN LIGHT OF THE PAST

The principal reason for believing in the revival of the ancient Roman Empire is the simple fact that prophecy requires it. Prophecies dealing

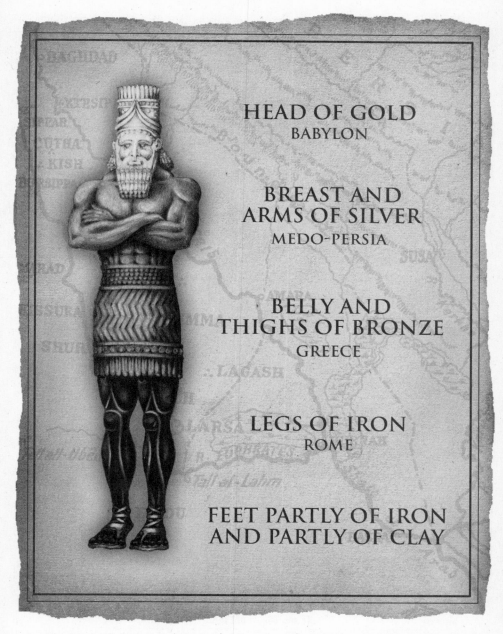

HEAD OF GOLD
BABYLON

BREAST AND
ARMS OF SILVER
MEDO-PERSIA

BELLY AND
THIGHS OF BRONZE
GREECE

LEGS OF IRON
ROME

FEET PARTLY OF IRON
AND PARTLY OF CLAY

with the final phase of this empire have not been literally fulfilled like the prophecies of the first three world empires. To those who believe the Bible, the prophecies of the future are just as authentic as the prophecies already fulfilled in the history of past world empires. One must conclude that a revival of the ancient Roman Empire in the form anticipated in the unfulfilled prophecies of Daniel is yet to appear on the stage of world history.

The future form of the Roman Empire according to Daniel will emerge prior to the coming of Christ to rule and reign over the earth. This future manifestation will take the form of a coalition or confederation of ten world leaders (symbolized by the ten toes in Daniel 2 and the ten horns in Daniel 7) that will encompass the same basic geographical territory as the original or historical Roman Empire.

In presenting these two forms of the Roman Empire, Daniel skips over many centuries from historical Rome immediately to end-time prophecy. This kind of "prophetic skip" is consistent with a principle found in much of Old Testament prophecy: Often the writer describes events that were prophetically fulfilled in Israel's exile or the first coming of Christ and then moves almost immediately from those details into end-time prophecy, describing the Great Tribulation and millennial reign of Christ. (See, for example, Isaiah 9:6-7; Daniel 9:26-27; Zechariah 9:9-10; Malachi 3:1-3.)

The end-time ten-king form of the Roman Empire is pictured in Daniel 2 as the ten toes on the great metallic image and in Daniel 7 as ten horns on the fourth or terrible beast. The chart below shows the parallels between Daniel 2 and 7, especially in the final phase of the Roman Empire.

Comparison of Daniel 2 and Daniel 7

WORLD EMPIRE	DANIEL 2	DANIEL 7
Babylon	Head of Gold	Lion
Medo-Persia	Chest and Arms of Silver	Bear
Greece	Belly and Thighs of Bronze	Leopard
Rome	Legs of Iron	Terrifying Beast
Revived Rome	Ten Toes	Ten Horns
Empire of the Antichrist		Little Horn

THREE FUTURE STAGES OF THE ROMAN EMPIRE

It appears that the future, revived Roman Empire will go through three stages. First, a group of ten kings or some form of a ruling oligarchy within the ancient Roman Empire will appear, described here as the Group of Ten. This will mark the first phase of its revival. Second, a strong man will emerge who will consolidate these ten nations into a united empire and probably extend its borders in various directions. Third, there is the final stage of the revived Roman Empire when, by declaration or edict, its power extends to the entire earth. The Antichrist will simply declare he is ruler of the world in the power vacuum created by the destruction of the armies of Gog and Magog described in Ezekiel 38–39. The final or third stage may be in a state of partial disintegration at the time of the second coming of Christ since it appears that there is warfare and rebellion against the new, self-declared world ruler at the end of the Great Tribulation.

It's probable that the revived Roman Empire will include nations from Europe and possibly even from northern Africa and some nations from western Asia, since the revived Roman Empire to some extent is viewed as including the three preceding empires that were largely Asiatic. As the Holy Land is the center of biblical interest, it would only be natural for the empire to include this area, especially when one considers that the Holy Land became a part of the area of influence of the Roman Empire as demonstrated in the treaty with Israel (Daniel 9:27) and in the later warfare described as being in this area (Ezekiel 38–39; Daniel 11:40-45; Zechariah 14:1-3).

Although the specific identity of the ten kings, or world leaders, can't be determined at this time, there has been much speculation concerning the materials that form the toes of the image described in Daniel 2:41-43. They are described as being partly of iron and partly of pottery or dried clay. In the prophecy attention is called to the fact that iron does not mix with the clay and therefore that the feet of the image are the weakest portion of the entire structure. According to Daniel 2:41-43, "The feet and toes you saw were a combination of iron and baked clay, showing that this kingdom will be divided. Like iron mixed with clay, it will have some of the strength of iron. But while some parts of it will be as strong as iron, other parts will be as weak as clay. This mixture of iron and clay also shows that these kingdoms will try to strengthen themselves by forming alliances with each other through intermarriage. But they will not hold together, just as iron and clay do not mix."

It is clear that since the legs of iron represent the strength of the ancient Roman Empire, the clay must in some sense denote the idea of political weakness or instability. The best interpretation is that the clay mixed with iron represents the diverse racial, religious, or political elements that are included in the confines of this final revived Roman Empire that contribute to its ultimate downfall. This view is supported by the fact that the revived Roman Empire, when it does reach its world stage, will immediately begin to encounter difficulties that result in the final world conflict, which is underway when Christ returns.

This mention of iron and clay, or inherent strength and weakness at the same time, is reflected in the European Union (EU) today. The EU has great economic and political clout, but its diversity in culture, language, and politics is also ever present. One can easily see how the EU could become the feet and toes of iron and clay.

E-UNIFICATION OF THE ROMAN EMPIRE

It appears that the revived Roman Empire described by Daniel is beginning to take shape. The reunification of the Roman Empire began officially in 1957 with a treaty appropriately named "The Treaty (or Treaties) of Rome." This treaty was signed on March 25, 1957, on Capitoline Hill, which is one of the famous Seven Hills of Rome. Gradually, yet steadily since then, the nations of Europe have come together one by one. Amazingly, this amalgamation of nations has taken only about fifty years.

The addition of ten new nations to the EU on May 1, 2004, brought the total number of members to twenty-five. These nations brought

75 million people into the EU, expanding the population of the EU to 450 million people and surpassing North America as the world's biggest economic zone. On January 1, 2007, two more nations, Romania and Bulgaria, were admitted to the European Union.

At least two key events in the twentieth century provided the necessary impetus for the reuniting of Europe, which was the core of the historical Roman Empire. First, there were two world wars. For centuries the nations of Europe fought one another again and again. But in the aftermath of World War II, a dramatic change occurred. Instead of building up for the next great armed conflict as they had done for centuries, they decided to come together in a coalition of nations that was originally called the Common Market. For the first time in 1,600 years the necessary preconditions for a reunited, revived Roman Empire predicted by Daniel were in place. This situation establishes, at least on the surface, a peaceful relationship between these major countries. This is a necessary prelude to the revival of the Roman Empire as prophesied in the Bible.

Second, the dissolution of the Soviet Union paved the way for the rise of the revived Roman Empire. The eight Eastern European nations that joined the EU in 2004 could never have joined it as long as the Soviet bloc was still in power. So, the fall of the Soviet empire in 1991 was another necessary development that set the stage for the revival of the Roman Empire.

Economic self-interest, national security, and the threat of international terrorism in Europe and the Middle East point to the necessity for an alliance of nations to bring peace and economic prosperity to the region. Changes necessary to make the situation conform to the prophetic anticipation of Daniel could take place rapidly in the present world scene.

BACK TOGETHER AGAIN

The Roman Empire that had ceased to exist for 1,600 years appears to be coming back together before our eyes. The EU today has a 732-member parliament; a parliament building in Strasbourg, France; a presidency that rotates among the member nations every six months; a supreme court; committees; and one currency that has been approved by thirteen of the twenty-seven member nations and is currently in circulation. The EU allows unrestricted travel for citizens among member nations, and it is presently working toward a unified military and criminal justice system.

What has developed in Europe during the last fifty years looks strikingly similar to what the Bible predicts for the end times. The basic governmental and economic components are in place for some kind of ten-ruler group or committee to come on the scene in the EU and ascend to power. And the next step will be for one man to rise to ultimate power in that group and take over as the strongman to rule the world. That man will be the Antichrist, and he will rule over the final form of the Roman Empire and ultimately the whole world.

While the current EU is not the final, ultimate fulfillment of the biblical prophecies, the events in Europe today seem to be the necessary prelude to the reunited Roman Empire prophesied by Daniel over 2,500 years ago.

The stage is set for a new alignment of power similar to the revived Roman Empire, which will promise peace to a world disrupted by catastrophe and on the brink of chaos.

HOW MUCH LONGER?

What form will the coming peace settlement take? In view of the many surprises in the Middle East, it is hazardous to guess the precise form of such a final peace settlement. It is also difficult to predict what catastrophic events will make this forced peace necessary. Will it be the economic chaos created by the oil breaking point with soaring prices and disruption of supply? Will it be a new outbreak of all-out war with chemical weapons or use of tactical nuclear weapons? Will it be a sudden escalation in the Middle East crisis? Whatever the reason, the world must be in danger of self-destruction or Israel and the nations of the world would not surrender power to the new leaders of the revived Roman Empire.

Whatever the precipitating events or the form of the peace agreement, ultimately it must give Israel security from attack and freedom from the constant state of military defense. It is very possible that an international peacekeeping force and secure boundaries may be guaranteed by the new and powerful Group of Ten. A general disarmament in the area may also be part of the agreement. In the aftermath of Israel's indecisive war with Hezbollah, Israel was willing to allow a peacekeeping force, led by EU forces, to guarantee the security of its northern border. Israel's agreement to have a U.N. peacekeeping force control southern Lebanon could be a prelude to its willingness to give over more and more of its security to the West.

The key issue in negotiations will be the city of Jerusalem itself, which Israel prizes more than any other possession. Undoubtedly there will be a strong attempt to maintain Jerusalem as an international city, with free access not only for Jews, but for Christians and Muslims as well. The Temple area may be internationalized, and Israel's territorial conquests will be greatly reduced.

With the rise of radical Islamic terrorism and the changing role of the United States as the sole supporting force behind Israel's continuity as a nation, it seems that any settlement that does not deal with Jerusalem will not satisfy the Arab world.

How soon will such a peace settlement come? No one can predict. But come it must—here the Scriptures are emphatic. There will be a treaty between the new world leader and Israel (Daniel 9:27) that will permit Israel to continue and to renew her religious ceremonies, including the building of a Jewish Temple and the reactivation of Jewish sacrifices. All of this was anticipated in the prophecies of Daniel 9:27 and 12:11 and was implied in the prophecy of Christ Himself relating to the stopping of the sacrifices when the treaty is broken (Matthew 24:15).

Made to Be Broken

How will Hamas, Hezbollah, other Islamic extremists, and Iran ever negotiate a settlement of any kind when they do not recognize Israel's right to exist? After the Israel-Hezbollah war in the summer of 2006, we can see how the Middle East situation can rapidly deteriorate, requiring a strong military presence to restore order. Or perhaps a peace settlement will be accepted by these nations to give them a temporary position of advantage in preparation for a possible later war with Israel.

Unfortunately, the final peace will only be a temporary consolidation of the world leaders' military and economic power—it will be a peace made to be broken. The peace settlement prophesied in Scripture will be a bid for world recognition by the new leader of the revived Roman Empire. The peace will be observed for only three and a half years and will be a major stepping-stone in his rise to world power. The peace settlement will be destined to be broken, bringing devastating consequences for the world and terrible persecution for Israel. This breaking of the treaty will commence what Christ described as "greater anguish than at any time since the world began. And it will never be so great again" (Matthew 24:21). Jeremiah referred to this period as "a time of trouble for my people Israel" (Jeremiah 30:7).

Waiting for the Prince of Peace

The final persecution of Jews during their time of trouble will awaken Israel's understanding about what has taken place. All the hopes and illusions of the past will be stripped away. This clear fulfillment of prophecy will lead to the startling realization that the first coming of the Messiah is past and that His second coming is near. In the anguish of the last three and a half years of the time of horror, Jewish believers from this period will cling to the hope of Christ's second coming. Jesus prophesied that He would not come again until Israel would say, "Blessings on the one who comes in the name of the LORD!" (Matthew 23:39).

See how today's headlines relate to this chapter at
http://www.prophecyhotline.com.

CHAPTER 7

THE RUSSIAN-ISLAMIC INVASION OF ISRAEL

EVENT #6: In response to the "Group of Ten," a new alliance of Islamic nations and Russia challenges the West, attacks Israel, and is destroyed.

> Would it be a difficult military option? Sure, it would be a difficult military option. But you cannot remove it from the table. I think we could have Armageddon.
>
> SENATOR JOHN MCCAIN, *MEET THE PRESS*, APRIL 2, 2006

> "CNN has received unconfirmed reports that Russian and coalition forces in Lebanon are beginning to advance toward the Israeli border. Israel radio is reporting that a column of some five hundred Russian and Iranian battle tanks is heading south from Beirut and is expected to link up with another two thousand tanks positioned just east of Tyre and Sidon." . . . He knew the prophecy cold by now. He knew what was coming next. The judgment of Russia. The destruction of radical Islam. The realignment of nations and fortunes, unprecedented in human history.
>
> JOEL ROSENBERG, *THE EZEKIEL OPTION* (A NOVEL)

ONE OF THE GREAT EVENTS of the end times is an invasion of Israel by a vast horde of nations from every direction. This invasion, which is known as the Battle of Gog and Magog, is graphically described in Ezekiel 38–39. Taken literally, it predicts a last days invasion of Israel from every direction by a vast horde of nations and God's direct, supernatural intervention to annihilate the invaders. Events in our world today strikingly foreshadow this coming invasion. These nations, which will not be a part of the Group of Ten, will act independently of the world dictator.

To help us gain a clear understanding of Ezekiel 38–39—two riveting chapters—and how current events point toward their fulfillment, we will use the standard questions of journalism: who, where, when, why, what, and how.

THE PARTICIPANTS (EZEKIEL 38:1-7): WHO?

The prophecy of the battle of Gog and Magog begins with a list of ten proper names in Ezekiel 38:1-7, or what we might call God's Most Wanted List:

> And the word of the LORD came to me saying, "Son of man, set your face toward Gog of the land of Magog, the prince of Rosh, Meshech and Tubal, and prophesy against him and say, 'Thus says the Lord GOD, "Behold, I am against you, O Gog, prince of Rosh, Meshech and Tubal. I will turn you about and put hooks into your jaws, and I will bring you out, and all your army, horses and horsemen, all of them splendidly attired, a great company with buckler and shield, all of them wielding swords; Persia, Ethiopia and Put with them, all of them with shield and helmet; Gomer with all its troops; Beth-togarmah from the remote parts of the north with all its troops— many peoples with you. Be prepared, and prepare yourself, you and all your companies that are assembled about you, and be a guard for them." (Ezekiel 38:1-7, NASB)

The name *Gog*, which occurs eleven times in Ezekiel 38–39, is a name or title of the leader of the invasion. It is clear that Gog is an individual since he is directly addressed several times by God (38:14; 39:1) and since he is called a prince and ruler (38:2; 39:1, NASB). The Group of Ten's bold move to consolidate absolute power over the Middle East will result in a disastrous countermove by Gog, the military leader of a coalition of Islamic nations and Russia.

The other nine proper names in Ezekiel 38:1-7 are specific geographical locations: Magog, Rosh, Meshech, Tubal, Persia, Cush (often translated as Ethiopia), Put, Gomer, and Beth-togarmah. None of the place names in Ezekiel 38:1-7 exist on any modern map. Ezekiel used ancient place names that were familiar to the people of his day. While the names of these geographical locations have changed many times throughout history and may change again, the geographical territory remains the same. Regardless of what names they may carry at the time of this invasion, it is these specific geographical areas that will be involved. Each of these ancient geographical locations from Ezekiel's day will be briefly examined, and the modern counterpart will be identified.[1]

Magog

The Jewish historian Josephus reported that the ancient Scythians inhabited the land of Magog.[2] These northern nomadic tribes inhabited land from Central Asia across the southern steppes of modern Russia. Magog today probably represents the former underbelly of the Soviet Union: Kazakhstan, Kyrgyzstan, Uzbekistan, Turkmenistan, and Tajikistan. Afghanistan could also be part of this territory. Each of these nations is dominated by Islam. Their combined population is in excess of ninety million.

Rosh

Bible scholars have often identified Rosh with Russia. But this conclusion has not been unanimous. There are two key issues that must be resolved to properly interpret Rosh in Ezekiel 38–39: (1) Is Rosh a common noun or a name? and (2) Does Rosh have any relation to Russia?

The first point that must be considered is whether the word *Rosh* in

Ezekiel 38:2-3 and 39:1 (NASB) is a proper name or simply a common noun. The word *rosh* in Hebrew simply means head, top, summit, or chief. It is a very common word that appears over six hundred times in the Old Testament.

Many translations render *rosh* as a common noun and translate it as the word *chief*. The King James Version, Revised Standard Version, English Standard Version, New American Bible, New Living Translation, and the New International Version all adopt this translation. However, the Jerusalem Bible, New English Bible, and New American Standard Bible all translate *Rosh* as a proper name indicating a geographical location.

The weight of evidence favors taking *Rosh* as a proper name in Ezekiel 38–39. There are five arguments that favor this view. First, the eminent Hebrew scholars C. F. Keil and Wilhelm Gesenius both hold that the better translation of *Rosh* in Ezekiel 38:2-3 and 39:1 is as a proper noun referring to a specific geographical location.[3]

Second, the Septuagint, which is the Greek translation of the Old Testament, translates *Rosh* as the proper name *Ros*. This is especially significant because the Septuagint was translated only three centuries after Ezekiel was written (obviously much closer to the original than any modern translation). The mistranslation of *Rosh* in many modern translations as an adjective can be traced to the Latin *Vulgate* of Jerome.[4]

Third, in their articles on *Rosh*, many Bible dictionaries and encyclopedias support taking it as a proper name in Ezekiel 38. Here are a few examples: *New Bible Dictionary, Wycliffe Bible Dictionary,* and *International Standard Bible Encyclopedia.*

Fourth, *Rosh* is mentioned the first time in Ezekiel 38:2 and then repeated in Ezekiel 38:3 and 39:1. If *Rosh* were simply a title, it would be dropped in these two places because when titles are repeated in Hebrew they are generally abbreviated.

Fifth, the most impressive evidence in favor of taking *Rosh* as a proper name is simply that this translation is the most accurate. G. A. Cooke translates Ezekiel 38:2, "the chief of Rosh, Meshech and Tubal."

He calls this "the most natural way of rendering the Hebrew."[5] The evidence of biblical scholarship implies that *Rosh* should be understood as a proper name, the name of a specific geographical area.

Having established that *Rosh* should be taken as a proper name of a geographical area, the next task is to determine what geographical location it refers to.

There are three key reasons for understanding Rosh in Ezekiel 38–39 as a reference to Russia. First, linguistically, there is evidence that *Rosh* is Russia. The great Hebrew scholar Wilhelm Gesenius noted in the nineteenth century that "Rosh is undoubtedly the Russians."[6]

Second, historically, there is substantial evidence that in Ezekiel's day there was a group of people known variously as Rash, Reshu, or Ros who lived in what today is southern Russia.[7]

Third, geographically, Ezekiel 38–39 emphasizes repeatedly that at least part of this invading force will come from the "distant north" (NLT) or the "remote parts of the north" (NASB). Biblical directions are usually given in reference to Israel, which on God's compass is the center of the earth (Ezekiel 38:12). If you draw a line directly north from Israel, the land that is most remote or distant to the north is Russia. Therefore, it seems very likely that Russia will be the leader of the Gog coalition.

Meshech and Tubal

Meshech and Tubal are normally mentioned together in Scripture. In his notes in *The Scofield Study Bible* for Ezekiel 38:2, C. I. Scofield identified Meshech and Tubal as the Russian cities of Moscow and Tobolsk. Scofield wrote, "That the primary reference is to the northern (European) powers, headed up by Russia, all agree. . . . The reference to Meshech and Tubal (Moscow and Tobolsk) is a clear mark of identification."

While the names do sound alike, this is not a proper method of identification. Meshech and Tubal are mentioned two other times in Ezekiel. In Ezekiel 27:13 they are mentioned as trading partners with ancient Tyre. In Ezekiel 32:26 their recent defeat is recorded. It is highly unlikely that ancient Tyre (modern Lebanon) was trading with Moscow and the Siberian city of Tobolsk. The preferred identification is that Meshech and Tubal are the ancient Moschoi and Tibarenoi in Greek writings or Tabal and Musku in Assyrian inscriptions. The ancient locations are in present-day Turkey. This is best understood as a reference to modern Turkey, an Islamic country. Current trends in Turkey appear to be moving the nation away from Europe back toward Russia and other Islamic nations.

Persia

The words *Persia*, *Persian*, or *Persians* are found thirty-five times in the Old Testament. In Ezekiel 38:5, Persia is best understood as modern-day Iran. The ancient land of Persia became the modern nation of Iran in March 1935, and then the name was changed to the Islamic Republic of Iran in 1979. Iran's present population is sixty-eight million. Iran's regime is the world's number one sponsor of terror. Iran is making its bid for regional supremacy at the same time it is pursuing nuclear weapons. The Iranian president has declared that Israel "must be wiped off the map." Clearly, modern Iran is a country hostile to Israel and the West. (It is even more of a threat to Israel because of the end-time beliefs of its president, an issue we'll examine in greater depth later in this chapter.)

Ethiopia (Cush)

The Hebrew word *Cush* in Ezekiel 38:5 is often translated Ethiopia in modern versions. Ancient Cush was called Kusu by the Assyrians and Babylonians, Kos or Kas by the Egyptians, and Nubia by the Greeks. Secular history locates Cush directly south of ancient Egypt extending down past the modern city of Khartoum, which is the capital of modern Sudan. Thus, modern Sudan inhabits the ancient land of Cush. Sudan is a hard-line Islamic nation that supported Iraq in the Gulf War and harbored Osama bin Laden from 1991 to 1996. It is not surprising that this part of Africa would be hostile to the West and could easily join in an attack on Israel.

Libya (Put)

Some ancient sources indicate that *Put* or *Phut* was a North African nation—with references documented in the Hebrew text footnotes in the New Living Translation for a number of passages, including Jeremiah 46:9 and Ezekiel 27:10; 30:5. The Babylonian Chronicles, a series of tablets recording ancient Babylonian history, indicate that Putu was the "distant" land west of Egypt, which would become modern-day Libya. The Septuagint, which was the Greek translation of the Old Testament, renders the word *Put* as Libues. Modern Libya is an Islamic nation that has been under the rule of Colonel Mu'ammar al-Gadhafi since 1969. Libya's recent attempt to placate the West does not change its allegiance to Islamic extremism and hatred of Israel.

Gomer

Gomer has often been identified by Bible teachers as Germany, or more particularly East Germany before the fall of communism. This identification is superficial and not the literal meaning of the word in its cultural and historic context.

Gomer is probably a reference to the ancient Cimmerians or *Kimmerioi*. Ancient history identifies biblical Gomer with the Akkadian Gi-mir-ra-a and the Armenian Gamir. Beginning in the eighth century BC the Cimmerians occupied territory in Anatolia, which is modern Turkey. Josephus noted that the Gomerites were identified with the Galatians who inhabited what today is central Turkey.[8] Turkey is an Islamic nation with deepening ties with Russia. Turkey's natural allegiance is not to the EU but to her Muslim neighbors. Turkey has a formidable military presence on the northern border of Iraq near the conflict that will emerge over the West's attempt to control the Middle East.

Beth-togarmah

The Hebrew word *beth* means "house," so Beth-togarmah means the "house of Togarmah." In Ezekiel 27:14, Togarmah is described as a nation that traded horses and mules with ancient Tyre. Ezekiel 38:6

states that the armies of Beth-togarmah will join in, too, from the distant north. Ancient Togarmah was also known as Til-garamu (Assyrian) or Tegarma (Hittite), and its territory is in modern Turkey, which is north of Israel. Again, Turkey is identified as part of this group of nations that attack Israel to challenge the Group of Ten.

Mapping the End Times

All the nations that will participate in the battle of Gog and Magog can be seen in the map below.

Based on these identifications, Ezekiel 38–39 predicts an invasion of the land of Israel in the last days by a vast confederation of nations from north of the Black and Caspian Seas, extending down to modern Iran in the east, as far as modern Libya to the west, and down to Sudan in the south. Therefore, Russia will have at least five key allies: Turkey, Iran, Libya, Sudan, and the Islamic nations of the former Soviet Union. Amazingly, all of these nations are Muslim nations, and Iran,

Battle of Gog and Magog

Libya, and Sudan are three of Israel's most ardent opponents. Many of these nations are hotbeds of militant Islam and are either forming or strengthening their ties with each other. This list of nations reads like the Who's Who of this week's newspaper. It does not require a very active imagination to envision these nations openly challenging the West and conspiring together to invade Israel in the near future.

THE PERIOD (EZEKIEL 38:8): WHEN?

One of the principal questions one could ask about this battle is: When is the battle going to occur? Clearly, it has not occurred in the past. But could it happen soon? What indications do we have in Ezekiel 38—39 about the timing of this invasion? Several opinions have been offered by capable Bible scholars on this point, and there has been considerable disagreement. Some have felt that the battle will take place before the Rapture; others believe it will take place in connection with the Battle of Armageddon at the end of the Great Tribulation. Some find it at the end of the Millennium, since there is a reference to Gog and Magog in Revelation 20:8.

It won't be possible to consider all these views in detail, but we're given some hints that suggest when this battle will take place. One of the clues given is that the battle will take place at a time when Israel has been regathered into its ancient land and is dwelling securely and at rest. There aren't too many times when Israel is at rest in God's prophetic program. The Jews have been scattered and persecuted over the face of the earth, and not even in the future will Israel have many periods of rest.

Certainly Israel is not at rest today. Israel is an armed camp, living under a truce with its Arab neighbors. Its enemies would drive every Israelite into the Mediterranean Sea and kill them if they could. The reason that they do not is because, humanly speaking, Israel has a good army that is more than a match for its neighbors. Today an armed truce and a no-man's-land separate Israel from its enemies.

Every young Israeli man is required to have three years of military training and every young woman two years of military training. While the women are trained for jobs that are not necessarily combatant, they also learn to use weapons, so that if they need to fight, they can. After military training, many of these young people are settled in villages near the border, where they can serve a double purpose—following their occupation, whatever it is, and serving as guards for the border of Israel. Israel's current state of unrest does not correspond to Ezekiel's prophecy. If Russia should invade the Middle East today, it would not be a fulfillment of this portion of Scripture. That has to take place when Israel is at rest.

One point at which Israel will be at rest is in the millennial kingdom. But we are told expressly that in the millennial kingdom there will be no war (Isaiah 2:4), and only when the rebellion occurs at the end of the Millennium when Satan is let loose (Revelation 20:7-9) does war break out. Certainly Israel is not going to be at rest under these circumstances either, once Satan is let loose.

Some have suggested that Israel will be at rest in the period of the Great Tribulation just before the second coming of Christ and that the prophecy of Russia will be fulfilled at that time. However, in the time of the Great Tribulation Israel will not be at rest, for Christ told them to flee to the mountains to escape their persecutors. Therefore the invasion described by Ezekiel could not be a part of the Battle of Armageddon at the end of the Great Tribulation.

There is only one period in the future that clearly fits this description of Ezekiel, and that is the first half of Daniel's seventieth week of God's program for Israel (Daniel 9:27). After the church has been raptured and saints have been raised from the dead and the living saints have been caught up to be with the Lord, a Group of Ten world leaders will lead a coalition of countries similar to the former Roman Empire. Out of the Group of Ten will come a strongman who will become its dictator (discussed in previous chapters). Daniel 9:26 states that "a ruler will arise." He will enter into a seven-year treaty of protection and peace with the people of Israel (Daniel 9:27).

Under that covenant, Israel will be able to relax, for their Gentile enemies will have become their friends, apparently guaranteeing their borders and promising them peace. Therefore, it seems clear that the battle will come when Israel has been lulled into the false security of the peace agreement signed by the leader of the revived Roman Empire. This peace treaty will be signed by the leader representing the combined economic and military power of the Western coalition. With these international guarantees, Israel will turn her energies toward increased wealth rather than defense—only to have the peace treaty shattered in less than four years.

Nevertheless, the first three and a half years of the Great Tribulation is the one time when a regathered Israel will be at rest and secure. Apparently Russia and her Islamic allies will invade the land of Israel during that period, possibly toward its close, and the Scripture will then be fulfilled.

THE PURPOSE (EZEKIEL 38:9-12): WHY?

The fourth key issue that is addressed in Ezekiel 38–39 is the purpose of this invasion. Both the human and the divine purpose for the invasion are given. The invading force will have four main goals:

1. Acquire more territory (38:8)
2. Amass wealth (38:12)
3. Destroy the people of Israel (38:11, 16)
4. Confront and challenge the Antichrist or the West who will be Israel's ally as a result of the treaty in Daniel 9:27. The divine purpose in allowing this invasion is expressed in Ezekiel 38:14-16. Through the attack God will be sanctified in the eyes of the nations.

THE PROCEEDINGS (EZEKIEL 38:13–39:20): WHAT?

Beginning in Ezekiel 38:13 and continuing through Ezekiel 39:20, the focus is on the fate of the invaders and the aftermath of the invasion. When these nations invade the land of Israel, it will look like the biggest mismatch in history. It will make the invasions of Israel in 1967 and

1973 by the Arab nations pale in comparison. When Russia assembles this last-days' strike force, it will look like Israel is finished. But God is in control of the entire situation. He will mount up in His fury to destroy these godless invaders. "But this is what the Sovereign LORD says: When Gog invades the land of Israel, my fury will boil over! In my jealousy and blazing anger, I promise a mighty shaking in the land of Israel on that day" (Ezekiel 38:18-19).

God will intervene to rescue His helpless people and will use four means to destroy Russia and her allies. The four means of destruction are listed in Ezekiel 38:19-22: a devastating earthquake; soldiers turning swords against each other; disease; and a cataclysmic combination of torrential rain, hailstones, fire, and burning sulphur. The famous Six Day War occurred in Israel in June 1967. This will be the "One Day War" or even the "One Hour War" when God supernaturally destroys this Russian-Islamic horde.

There are four key events that occur in the aftermath of this invasion:

1. **The Birds and the Beasts (Ezekiel 39:4-5, 17-20; Revelation 19:17-18).** The carnage that results from this slaughter will provide a great feast for the birds of the air and the beasts of the field. God refers to the carnage as "My sacrificial feast" and "My banquet table," to which He invites the birds and the beasts as His guests.

2. **The Burying of the Dead for Seven Months (Ezekiel 39:11-12, 14-16).** Clean-up squads will be assembled to go through the land. They will set up markers wherever they see a human bone. When the gravediggers come behind them they will see the markers and take the remains to the Valley of Gog's Hordes for burial. The cleansing will be so extensive that a town will be established in the valley at the gravesites to aid those who are cleansing the land. The name of the town will be Hamonah (horde).

3. The Burning of the Weapons for Seven Years (Ezekiel 39:9-10).
The burning of weapons (spears, bows, and arrows) for seven
years has led some to wonder if the nations will regress to using
primitive weapons in the end times. Others maintain that Ezekiel
used ancient weapons that were familiar in his day to describe
and anticipate modern weapons. We are not in a position today
to settle this problem with any finality. Whatever the explanation,
the most sensible interpretation is that the passage refers to actual
weapons pressed into use because of the peculiar circumstances of
that day.

Because Ezekiel 39:9 mentions the weapons will be burned for
seven years, many place this invasion before the seven-year tribulation period. Yet as has been mentioned, Ezekiel 38 makes it clear that
Israel will be at peace when this invasion occurs, and it is difficult to
picture Israel living peacefully before the Rapture. Of course, this
means the burning of weapons will continue for the first few years
of the millennial reign of Christ after His second coming. This will be
part of the ongoing cleansing of the land after Christ establishes His
Kingdom on earth.

4. The Blessing of Salvation (Ezekiel 39:22). In the midst of His
wrath and fury, God will also pour out His grace and mercy
(39:22). God will use the awesome display of His power against
Russia and her allies to bring many—both Jews and Gentiles—to
salvation. Many of those who turn to the true God as a result of
this demonstration of His power will undoubtedly be among the
vast group of the redeemed in Revelation 7:9-14.

THE PROPHETIC SIGNIFICANCE: HOW?

The final question to consider is how the world stage today is being
set for the fulfillment of this incredible prophecy. What are some
of the key developments we are witnessing today that point toward
this invasion? What recent or current developments correspond with

Ezekiel's prophecy? There are eight major events in the last sixty years that point toward the fulfillment of Ezekiel's prophecy.

Israel Will Be Regathered

First, for the events of Ezekiel 38–39 to be fulfilled Israel must be regathered to her land in unbelief. Ezekiel 38 follows the famous dry bones vision in Ezekiel 37 that pictures the physical restoration of Judah and Israel to the land followed by her spiritual restoration to the Lord. In Ezekiel 37 the restoration occurs in stages. It begins with restoration to the land in unbelief. Unbelieving Israel's initial regathering is further confirmed by the fact that only after the battle of Gog and Magog do many in Israel turn to the Lord (Ezekiel 39:22).

As we saw in chapter 4, Israel's regathering in unbelief has occurred dramatically in stages beginning in 1871 and continuing up to the present day. Thus, what we see happening before our eyes, the restored unbelieving Jewish state, is a necessary precondition for Ezekiel's prophecy to be fulfilled.

Israel Must Possess the Mountains of Israel

Second, according to Ezekiel 39:2-4, Israel must possess the "mountains of Israel" when this invasion occurs. God tells the future invaders: "I will turn you around and drive you toward the mountains of Israel, bringing you from the distant north. I will knock the bow from your left hand and the arrows from your right hand, and I will leave you helpless. You and your army and your allies will all die on the mountains. I will feed you to the vultures and wild animals." The famous Six Day War in Israel in 1967 helped set the stage for this to be fulfilled. Before the Six Day War all of the mountains of Israel, with the exception of a small strip of West Jerusalem, were entirely in the hands of the Jordanian Arabs. Only since 1967 have the mountains *of* Israel been *in* Israel, thus setting the stage for the fulfillment of this prophecy.

Israel Must Be at Peace

Third, according to Ezekiel 38, Israel must be "at rest" and "living securely" when this invasion occurs. The drive for peace in the Middle East has consumed Western diplomats and dominated world news. From the Oslo Accords to the Road Map for Peace, brokering a peace agreement between Israel and her neighbors is one of the major international priorities. A peaceful solution to the Israeli-Palestinian crisis is integrally linked to stability in the Middle East and Persian Gulf. The ongoing quest for Middle East peace points toward the peace treaty in Daniel 9:27 and the period of security in Ezekiel 38.

Russia Reclaims Its Lost Glory

Fourth, one of the most significant international developments in the last fifty years, one that is a necessary prerequisite for this invasion, is the remarkable rise of Russia to a place of world prominence. Along with the United States, Russia (previously the Soviet Union) has been one of the world's great military powers. Although some hopeful signs of democracy appeared in Russia after the dissolution of the Soviet Union in 1991, there are growing fears that Russia today is regressing back to her old totalitarian, autocratic ways. Russian president Vladimir Putin and many of the key leaders in his government served as officers in the KGB. Putin has made numerous moves to centralize authority. Experts maintain that Russia's oil wealth is allowing Putin to take the country back toward autocracy without any public outcry.[9]

Russia has a vital interest in the Middle East and Persian Gulf. This is her neighborhood. Some control over this area is vital to Russia's national security. Moreover, since the fall of the Soviet empire, the great Russian bear has been like a mother bear robbed of her cubs. The fall of her empire brought national humiliation. In April 2005, during his annual state of the nation address, Putin declared that the collapse of the Soviet Union was "the greatest geopolitical catastrophe" of the century.[10] He seems to long for the good old days of the U.S.S.R. For Russia, an invasion of Israel with an Islamic coalition would be an opportunity for her to reclaim her lost glory and assert control over the Middle East.

Ezekiel 38:1-5 lists "Rosh" (Russia) and "Persia" (Iran) as allies against Israel in the end times. This prophecy was written almost 2,600 years ago and yet reads like today's headlines. The Russian-Iranian alliance is becoming cozier all the time. Here are just a couple of troubling examples of this emerging partnership: Russia sold Iran a nuclear reactor and later sold twenty-nine of its most advanced missile systems to the radical regime for a pricey one billion dollars. These missiles would be used against U.S. or Israeli planes should they attempt to take out Iran's nuclear facilities. Furthermore, Russia consistently obstructs any meaningful U.N. sanctions against Iran for its nuclear program.

Hatred of Israel Will Increase

Fifth, the rise of pandemic Islamic fundamentalism with its virulent anti-Semitism and hatred of the restored Jewish state provides a powerful motivation for this invasion. While Islam is and always has been a religion of violence and terror, the modern rise of the Islamic terrorist state began in early 1979 in Iran when the Shah was ousted by the Ayatollah Khomeini. Iran has exported this terror movement to neighboring Islamic nations. Of course, Ezekiel does not mention Islam or terrorism as a driving force behind this invasion since Islam did not exist until the seventh century AD. However, today all the geographical areas other than Russia that he identified as participants in this invasion are identifiable Islamic nations (Central Asia, Libya, Sudan, Iran, and Turkey). This sets the stage for the final jihad into Israel depicted in Ezekiel's prophecy. For these Islamic allies the Gog and Magog invasion will be an opening to drive Israel into the sea and lure the West into a final clash of civilizations since Israel will be protected by her covenant with the Antichrist.

Iran Becomes a Key Player

Sixth, Iran (Persia) is a key player on the world scene today as required by Ezekiel 38:5. Clearly, Iran is public enemy number one today in the

West and in Israel. As home to radical jihadists and a supporter of terror groups around the world, Iran cannot be allowed to possess nuclear weapons. This is unthinkable. Therefore, we can expect a great deal of focus on Iran in the near future. And all of this is greatly exacerbated and complicated by the fact that Iran has about 10 percent of the world's proven oil reserves. Uncertainty over the situation in Iran is part of the reason that oil prices neared an all-time high during the week of August 8–12, 2005, closing at over sixty-five dollars a barrel.

To make matters even worse, in June 2005 the Iranian people elected the hard-liner Mahmoud Ahmadinejad as their new president.[11] He is the former mayor of Tehran and a former Revolutionary Guard commander. On October 26, 2005, he said flat out that Israel should be "wiped off the map" and that "anyone who signs a treaty which [recognizes] the entity of Israel means he has signed the surrender of the Muslim world." He further called for Iranians "to riot against Zionists [Israel] and unbelievers" in a nationwide demonstration on Friday, October 28, 2005, during al-Quds—or Jerusalem—Day. Ahmadinejad participated in the large demonstration himself along with others who backed his call for the destruction of the Jewish state. The marchers carried placards that read, "Death to Israel, death to America." Iran's new president has also stated that the Holocaust never occurred and that the Jewish state should be relocated to Europe. All of this inflammatory rhetoric comes at a time when the United Nations is cautiously dealing with Iran about sanctions over its resumption of its nuclear program. Needless to say, tensions in the region are mounting. Iran is awash in oil money and is earnestly seeking nuclear weapons.

On January 9, 2006, Iran broke the seals that International Atomic Energy Agency (IAEA) inspectors had placed on two nuclear plants, the Uranium Conversion Facility in Isfahan and the centrifuge plant at Natanz. Iran then restarted its nuclear program, breaking a two-and-a-half-year moratorium.[12]

On April 11, 2006, another key milestone in the Iran crisis was reached. At that time Ahmadinejad made several announcements:

I am officially announcing that Iran has joined the group of countries which have nuclear technology.

At this historical juncture, I announce, in shadow of the Mahdi, the lord of time—may we hasten his return—through the sacrifices of our scientists and our devoted youth and the prayers of our brave people, we have mastered the nuclear fuel cycle on a laboratory scale. And we have enriched uranium to the necessary level for nuclear power generation.

I formally declare that Iran has joined the club of nuclear countries.[13]

Ahmadinejad has made a number of anti-Semitic statements:

No doubt the new wave [of attacks] in Palestine will soon wipe off this disgraceful blot [Israel] from the face of the Islamic world.[14]

Israel must be wiped off the map. . . . The establishment of a Zionist regime was a move by the world oppressor against the Islamic world. . . . The skirmishes in the occupied land are part of the war of destiny. The outcome of hundreds of years of war will be defined in Palestinian land.

Although the main solution is for the elimination of the Zionist regime, at this stage an immediate cease-fire must be implemented.

A new Middle East will prevail without the existence of Israel.

Are they human beings? . . . They [Zionists] are a group of bloodthirsty savages putting all other criminals to shame.

Israel is destined for destruction and will soon disappear . . . a contradiction to nature, we foresee its rapid disappearance and destruction.

The Zionists and their protectors are the most detested people in all of humanity, and the hatred is increasing every day.

The occupying regime of Palestine has actually pushed the button of its own destruction by launching a new round of invasion and barbaric onslaught on Lebanon.[15]

At a meeting in April 2006, he made more inflammatory comments. He said that Palestine "will soon be freed." He referred to Israel as a "constant threat" and "permanent threat to the Middle East" and said the Middle East will "soon be liberated." In one of his most revealing statements, the Iranian president said, "The Zionist regime is an injustice and by its very nature a permanent threat. Whether you like it or not, the Zionist regime is heading toward annihilation. The Zionist regime is a rotten, dried tree that will be eliminated by one storm."[16] Could this be a threat of a nuclear attack against Israel? What could annihilate Israel by one storm other than a nuclear bomb?

Ahmadinejad's government, along with Syria, is the primary supporter of Hezbollah and Hamas. In late 2006, Iran pledged $120 million to the Hamas-led Palestinian government.[17] This "aid" will certainly be used to buy weapons and prepare for an attack against Israel.

Ahmadinejad's fanatical hatred of Israel is permeating the news media in Iran. An editorial titled "Preparations for the Great War" appeared in *Resalat*, one of Iran's daily newspapers. The editorial said, "The great war is ahead of us, [and will break out] perhaps tomorrow, or in another few days, or in a few months, or even in a few years. For the first time in the 60 years of its disgraceful life, the Zionist regime—the West's beloved in the Middle East—tasted the taste of defeat, and the citizens of this regime trembled at the menace of Hizbullah's missiles. . . .The nation of Muslims must prepare for the great war, so as to completely wipe out the Zionist regime, and remove this cancerous growth. Like the Imam (Ayatollah) Khomeini said: 'Israel must collapse.'"[18]

Another conservative Iranian newspaper, *Keyhan,* printed this bellicose statement, "Hizbullah destroyed at least half of Israel in the Lebanon war. . . . Now only half the path (to its destruction) remains.

. . . Just as in one 33-day [sic] war more than 50 percent of Israel was destroyed, and the hope of its supporters for the continued life of this regime was broken, it is likely that in the next battle, the second half will also collapse."[19]

Ahmadinejad and the Apocalypse

Not only does Ahmadinejad make provocative statements, but he is motivated by an end-of-days messianism that feeds his warped sense of divine destiny. He believes the apocalypse will occur in his own lifetime, and his statements suggest that he believes his destiny is to bring about the end times and usher in the coming of the Islamic messiah.

As a Shiite Muslim, Iran's president is deeply committed to an Islamic messianic figure known as the Mahdi (Arabic for "rightly guided one"), sometimes referred to as the Hidden Imam (leader). He seeks to bring apocalypse upon the world and is fixated on what is known in Islam as Mahdaviat—quite simply, this is the desire to help prepare for the Mahdi.

Ahmadinejad appears to believes he is invincible. He declares, "I have a connection with God, since God said infidels will have no way to harm believers. . . . We have [only] one step before we attain the summit of nuclear technology. . . . The West will not dare to attack us."[20]

Reporter Anton La Guardia, writing for the online British news source telegraph.co.uk, points out that all Muslims expect a divine savior, the Mahdi, to appear in the earth's final days. Ahmadinejad and his cabinet are rumored to have signed a contract pledging to work for his return. La Guardia says Muslims believe that the Mahdi's "return will be preceded by cosmic chaos, war and bloodshed. After a cataclysmic confrontation with evil and darkness, the Mahdi will lead the world to an era of universal peace."

He adds, "Mr. Ahmadinejad appears to believe that these events are close at hand and that ordinary mortals can influence the divine time-table. The prospect of such a man obtaining nuclear weapons is worrying. The unspoken question is this: is Mr. Ahmadinejad now tempting a

Islamic Beliefs about the Mahdi

1. Islam's primary awaited savior

2. Descendant of Muhammad

3. Caliph and Imam of Muslims worldwide

4. Unparalleled political, military, and religious world leader

5. Revealed after a period of great turmoil and suffering on earth

6. Establishes justice throughout the world

7. Leads a revolution to establish a new world order

8. Will go to war against all nations who oppose him

9. Makes a seven-year peace treaty with a Jew of priestly lineage

10. Conquers Israel for Islam and leads final battle against the Jews

11. Rules for seven years in Jerusalem

12. Causes Islam to be the only religion on earth

13. Discovers biblical manuscripts that convince Jews to convert

14. Brings the Ark of the Covenant from the Sea of Galilee to Jerusalem

15. Has the power from Allah over wind, rain, and crops

16. Will possess and distribute great wealth

17. Face will shine like a star and will be loved by all

* Randall Price, "The 'Second Coming' of Islam," *World of the Bible News and Views* 8, no.1 (Summer 2006): 3. Used with permission.

clash with the West because he feels safe in the belief of the imminent return of the Hidden Imam? Worse, might he be trying to provoke chaos in the hope of hastening his reappearance?"[21]

Iran is dominated by Shiite Islam, whose spiritual leaders, called Imams, are bloodline relatives of the prophet Ali, Muhammad's cousin. There is a prophecy in Islam about the coming of the Twelfth Imam— Muhammad al-Mahdi. The Twelver sect believes he was born in AD 868 and disappeared in AD 874 into the cave of the great mosque of Samarra (in modern Iraq) without leaving any descendants. They teach that the Twelfth Imam was still active and communicated by messengers until AD 941 when all communication and contact with this world was cut off.[22]

According to Islamic teaching, he will return near the end of the world to rule the earth for seven years and bring about the final judgment and end of the world.[23] This seven-year rule for the Mahdi is interesting because the Bible predicts that the Antichrist or false messiah will dominate the earth for seven years, ruling the entire world for the final half of the seven-year period. It's possible that the Islamic expectation of a messiah who will rule for seven years could set them up to initially accept such a leader who will make a seven-year peace treaty according to Daniel 9:27.

Ahmadinejad's view of the end times is also influenced by his close ties with the messianic Hojatieh society, led by Ayatollah Mesbah Yazdi. Twelvers believe that until the Twelfth Imam returns, every true Muslim must put himself under the authority of a holy man known as an ayatollah, who is able to mediate salvation. This spiritual leader often appears with the new president in public. The Hojatieh believe that only great tribulation, increased violence, and conflict will bring about his coming. The "creation of chaos on earth," they believe, can speed up the Imam's return. For Ahmadinejad, an all-out war with the West would be an open invitation for the return of the Mahdi.[24]

The president's apocalyptic view is so strongly ingrained that he fired Iran's most experienced diplomats and many other officials who don't share his view of the coming apocalyptic conflict, replacing them with fellow zealots.[25] On November 16, 2005, in a speech in Tehran to senior clerics, Ahmadinejad said that the primary mission of his regime was to "pave the path for the glorious reappearance of the Imam Mahdi (May God Hasten His Reappearance)."[26]

Ahmadinejad gave a speech at the United Nations in September 2005 that many were expecting to be diplomatic. But they were shocked when he spoke in apocalyptic terms and ended the speech with a messianic appeal to God to "hasten the emergence of your last repository, the Promised One, that perfect and pure human being, the one that will fill this world with justice and peace."

Ahmadinejad provided his own account of the U.N. address and his otherworldly experience:

> One of our group told me that when I started to say "In the name of God the almighty and merciful," he saw a light around me, and I was placed inside this aura. I felt it myself. I felt the atmosphere suddenly change, and for those 27 or 28 minutes, the leaders of the world did not blink. . . . And they were rapt. It seemed as if a hand was holding them there and had opened their eyes to receive the message from the Islamic republic.[27]

This account is reminiscent of Hitler's mesmerizing, satanic speeches to the German people. German chancellor Angela Merkel has openly compared the Iranian president to Adolf Hitler. Yet reporter Anton La Guardia offers a different interpretation of the reason for the audience's reaction:

> Western officials said the real reason for any open-eyed stares from delegates was that "they couldn't believe what they were hearing from Ahmadinejad." Their sneaking suspicion is that he relishes a clash with the West in the conviction that it would rekindle the spirit of the Islamic revolution and speed up the arrival of the Hidden Imam.[28]

Mortimer Zuckerman warns the West to be aware of the Iranian president's real intentions: "His foreign policy ambition is an Islamic government for the whole world, under the leadership of the Mahdi, the absent Imam of the Shiites—code language for the export of radical Islam. And he casts himself as Hitler reincarnated, calling for Israel to be 'wiped off the map.' Who can think that Iran poses no threat to world peace? History tells us that when madmen call for genocide, they usually mean it."[29]

Turkey Aligns with Islamic Neighbors

The seventh event necessary before the battle of Gog and Magog occurs is this: Turkey must be willing to join the coalition of nations against Israel. For years, this seemed highly unlikely, since Turkey has made every attempt to become part of the European Union. With great fanfare on October 3, 2005, the European Union launched formal negotiations in Brussels to discuss Turkey's admittance to membership in the European club. Several months earlier European leaders had decided to open talks to consider Turkey's admission to the EU. Even the possibility of this merger was hailed as the meeting of East and West.

However, it now appears certain that the EU will reject Turkey's bid for admission. Both France and the Netherlands rejected the proposed EU constitution, and one of their main objections was the notion of enlargement, especially admitting Turkey to the EU. Support for Turkish accession among the fifteen EU countries that have been members the longest is only at 32 percent. However, the EU does not want to alienate the Turks; thus, the EU appears to be stringing Turkey along for geopolitics. There are five key reasons the EU will reject Turkey:

1. *It is a Muslim country.* Islam phobia is on the rise in Europe. This feeling will be heightened in light of terrorist attacks on European soil.
2. *It is too big.* With 70 million people, Turkey would be the second largest EU nation, behind Germany.
3. *It is agrarian.* The EU supports farmers with huge subsidies.
4. *It is poor.* Turkey's gross domestic product per capita is only 27 percent of the national average.
5. *It has enemies.* Turkey faces two historic enemies within the EU: Greece and Cyprus.[30]

These developments are interesting, because the Bible predicts in Ezekiel 38 that Turkey will be part of a massive Russian-led invasion of Israel in the end times. The main countries that will participate in this invasion are Russia, Iran, Libya, Sudan, Central Asian nations, and Turkey. At present the government of Vladimir Putin in Russia is gaining greater control and appears to be moving back toward the days of communist dictatorship. Iran, Libya, Sudan, and the nations of Central Asia are all predominantly Islamic, and it is not too difficult to see them all joining in for one last jihad against Israel. As Turkey moved more and more toward the West, it appeared highly unlikely that she would ally herself with a Russian-Islamic coalition against Israel. But that seems to be changing. Turkey's admission to the EU now seems hopeless. And when Turkey is rejected by the West, she will have to look elsewhere to bolster her strategic ambitions.

The AKP (Justice and Development party) of Prime Minister Recep Tayyip Erdogan is an avowedly secular party, but with Islamic roots. It poses a difficult challenge to Turkey's eighty-year-old secularism, founded by Mustafa Ataturk. It seems clear that the AKP wants to move the country and its foreign policy in a more Islamic direction. In recent months, Erdogan has reached out to some very unsavory characters in Turkey's neighborhood. He visited President Bashar Assad of Syria in early 2005 and traveled to Iran to meet with the Iranian mullahs.

Erdogan's chief adviser, Ahmet Davutoglu, is the driving force behind Turkey's foreign policy changes. He is now contending that Turkey has an historic opportunity to be a leader in the Muslim world. He also believes that her geographic position requires improved relations with Russia. Earlier this year, overcoming decades of enmity, Turkey signed a trade pact with Russia. At the same time Turkey is being rebuffed by Europe and is warming relations with Russia, anti-Semitism in Turkey has been growing. According to a recent article, "At any bookstore in Istanbul or Ankara you will find prominently displayed Adolph Hitler's *Mein Kampf*, a popular seller these days."[31]

While there may be many twists and turns in Turkey and other nations of the world before the Rapture occurs, what is occurring right now appears to be moving Turkey back toward Russia and the Muslim world just as one would expect if the battle of Gog and Magog is near.

Saudi Arabia Aligns with the West

Eighth, Ezekiel 38:13 (NASB) mentions "Sheba and Dedan and the merchants of Tarshish" as lodging a lame protest against the Gog and Magog invasion of Israel. There is general agreement that Sheba and Dedan inhabited northern Arabia, or what today is Saudi Arabia.

Ezekiel 38:13 indicates that Saudi Arabia and its Western allies will object to this invasion by Russia and an Islamic horde. Although Saudi Arabia is no great friend of the West, she is the one Islamic nation that consistently serves her own self-interest by conveniently allying herself with Western nations. Thus, the mention of a protest by Sheba, Dedan, and Tarshish corresponds with current developments.

Events in our world today indicate that the great Battle of Gog and Magog in Ezekiel 38–39 could be very near. All of the necessary antecedents for the fulfillment of this prophecy are in place or are moving in that direction. The Jewish people have been regathered to their land in unbelief, the Middle East peace process is front and center in international diplomacy, and the invaders in Ezekiel 38 are identifiable nations who have both the desire and the potential to fulfill the Gog prophecy.

The remarkable correspondence between world events and what Ezekiel predicted is another indication that the coming of the Lord could be very soon.

RUSSIA'S LOSS—THE ANTICHRIST'S GAIN

As will be discussed in the next chapter, Russia's attack on Israel will not simply be an attack on Israel alone, but it will be a challenge to the peace and protection promised by the new leader of the Western coalition. By this time the emergence of the powerful new alignment of Europe and the Middle East will have seriously limited Russia's role in the world. The attack by Russia will be a desperate attempt to recoup her position as a world power with influence over the Middle East.

The attack on Israel will transpire as a direct confrontation between

RUSSIA'S INVASION OF ISRAEL
AS DESCRIBED IN EZEKIEL 38–39

BEGINNING OF THE LAST SEVEN YEARS OF THE PERIOD OF THE GENTILES

BATTLE OF ARMAGEDDON AND THE SECOND COMING OF CHRIST

① PEACE TREATY
(signed by leader
guaranteeing Israel's
security)

② RUSSIAN INVASION
(to challenge the new
leader's control and
growing power)

**③ INVADERS
DESTROYED**
(supernatural destruction
of those reaching Israel)

**ISRAEL AT PEACE
AND DECEIVED**

**ISRAEL PERSECUTED
AND LOOKING FOR
THE MESSIAH**

**FIRST 3½ YEARS
OF END TIMES**

**GREAT TRIBULATION
3½ YEARS**

**④ ABOMINATION
OF DESOLATION**
(new leader breaks the
peace and desecrates the
Temple, declaring himself
world ruler and "God")

⑤ WORLD REVOLT
(world revolts against
the world ruler and sends
armies to the Middle East)

Russia and her Islamic allies and the new leader of the Western coalition. With the United States in isolation, the balance of power in the world will have shifted so that the revived Roman Empire is on one side and Russia and her allies are on the other. Because of this, the destruction of the Russian army becomes tremendously significant.

Once this occurs during the Battle of Gog and Magog, the balance of power will fall dramatically into the hands of the new world leader that emerges from the Group of Ten. This greatly changed world situation will position him as the most powerful and charismatic ruler in the world, setting the stage for the apocalyptic events that will soon follow.

The threat of Russian intervention in the Middle East is real. Her current financial diplomacy in the Middle East will not be sufficient to give her a major role in determining the area's future. Her eventual bid for power will be a military disaster. In the end, Russia and her unwitting allies will reap a terrible judgment from God for their blasphemy, terror, and hostility toward Israel. Like many nations before, they will feel the curse of God—promised to all those who curse His chosen people.

 See how today's headlines relate to this chapter at
http://www.prophecyhotline.com.

CHAPTER 8

THE COMING WORLD DICTATOR: "THE WORLD IS MINE, AND I AM GOD"

EVENT #7: One leader seizes power by uniting the military and economic powers of the West—declaring himself world ruler.

When the Jews return to Zion, and
A comet rips the sky,
And the Holy Roman Empire rises
Then you and I must die.

From the eternal sea he rises,
Creating armies on either shore;
Turning man against his brother
'Till man exists no more.

THE OMEN (1976)

IN THE HISTORY OF THE world many a great man has dreamed of someday having the world at his feet. In the Middle East many great nations have risen and fallen. Egypt was a powerful nation in the Middle East fifteen hundred years before Christ—followed by Assyria with her capital at Nineveh. Nebuchadnezzar, the great king of Babylon, carved out an expansive empire that included most of western Asia.

About three hundred years before Christ, Alexander the Great and his armies swept as far east as India and for a brief time ruled all of western Asia, northern Africa, and southeast Europe. At the time of Christ the Roman Caesars had subdued southern Europe, northern Africa, and western Asia to form the greatest empire ever known in history. In more modern times, Napoleon dreamed of world conquest only to have his dreams shattered at Waterloo. In the twentieth century Hitler dreamed of someday having the world at his feet.

But none of these men ever really conquered the entire world. The military conquerors of the ancient world at best conquered portions of Europe, North Africa, and western Asia, but no world ruler has ever controlled all of the three major continents related to the Middle East, much less the nations of the Western Hemisphere: North America, Central America, and South America. Until our generation, a universal world government wasn't really possible.

The advances of modern technology in communication, transportation, and the weapons of war have suddenly shrunk our world. A missile can reach any part of the world in less than thirty minutes. Television, radio, and the Internet provide instant communication. A world where men could once live in relative isolation is now geographically one. Every major event, whether it is an oil embargo, the development of a new nuclear weapon, or the threat of starvation, is now covered by international television that brings distant events into the homes of people around the world. Men and nations can no longer live in isolation.

During and following World War I, for the first time, steps were taken to form an international body to prevent further world wars. The resulting League of Nations, however, was unsuccessful. With Congress already disillusioned by the practical results of World War I, the United States was not ready for such a role in world affairs. The idea of world government seemed unnecessary for a country oceans away from problems in Europe and Asia. But the earth was growing smaller, and America's isolation could not last for long. In 1941, the United States once again was drawn into a world war. The attack on Pearl Harbor marked the end of America's attempt to ignore her responsibilities in a shrinking world.

By the end of World War II, a frightening new dimension had been added to the need for a world government. Although the war itself was devastating and extended throughout more of the world than any previous war had, it ended with the atomic holocaust of Hiroshima and Nagasaki, Japan. With the advent of the atomic bomb, no nation or people would ever be safe again. The destructive capabilities of war had increased to a degree never before considered possible.

Nuclear destruction threatened not only military forces but entire cities and civilian populations. Now a war of days or weeks could destroy the entire world. The time had come for a new international world organization.

WORLD GOVERNMENT—MAN'S LAST HOPE

A shared global fear of a major conflict involving atomic weaponry gave birth to the United Nations in 1946. Though it included only a portion of the world's nations at first, the United Nations soon grew to include most of them. With the admission of China, all the major nations and most of the smaller nations became part of this international structure. But the United Nations lacked the power and authority to prevent war. Throughout history, its weakness has been demonstrated again and again. Its failure to solve the conflict in Southeast Asia and its continued inability to prevent conflict in the Middle East has demonstrated that the United Nations is not the final answer.

Still, some form of universal government seems the only hope for a world that could easily destroy itself. The problems facing the world—terrorism, nuclear war, overpopulation, starvation, pollution, and economic instability—are international problems. Even terrorist groups like Al-Qaeda and Hezbollah now threaten the delicate web of international interdependence. New economic challenges face the world. There simply will not be enough oil to fuel the economies of the West, India, and China. The international distribution of resources and the control of currencies will soon necessitate regulation by some type of world agency. The United Nations, the Common Market, and the World Bank are only the beginning of a quest for some solution to the world's increasing problems.

Many international leaders and intellectuals believe that a strong and effective world government is the only hope for the survival of man on this planet. For instance, at the United Nations in December 1988, Mikhail Gorbachev said, "Further global progress is now possible only through a quest for universal consensus in the movement towards a new world order."[1] As these attitudes are increasingly expressed in our time, it is important to ask what the Bible says on this subject. As a matter of fact, the prophets anticipated just such a state of affairs in the world as the end times approach.

DANIEL'S PROPHECY OF WORLD EMPIRES

The prophets may never have realized the modern reasons for a world government, but they did predict that history would end in one central government that would attempt to encompass the entire world. The Bible not only predicted the rise and fall of history's strongest world empires, but with prophetic accuracy has described the events that will lead to a final world government before the second coming of Christ.

As we have already seen in chapter 6, the prophet Daniel, for instance, described the series of developments that will bring the entire earth to a final world government, which will reach its climax when Christ returns to judge the nations and set up His Kingdom on earth (Daniel 7). Daniel predicted with accuracy the progression of preceding world empires. The first empire described by Daniel was that of Babylon, which conquered Jerusalem when Daniel was a teenager. As a prophet during the Babylonian exile, Daniel predicted the fall of the Babylonian empire and the rise of the Medes and the Persians, which he witnessed during his lifetime. But most important, Daniel revealed a prophetic list of all the world empires that would rise and fall before the second coming of Christ. Daniel's prophecy offers a complete outline of the history of world empires written before these empires existed. This outline is so essential to the understanding of the future of the nations that Jesus related His predictions to events in Daniel's prophecy.

Daniel's outline of world empires included the empire of Greece and the Roman Empire. Daniel also anticipated a final stage to the Roman Empire that has not yet come to fruition. It is this final world empire and its world dictator that will push the world toward Armageddon. In that final clash of nations, the history of empires built by conquest will be ended forever by the second coming of Christ. Empires and governments created by men will be replaced by the direct rule of God on earth—a final millennium of peace, righteousness, and prosperity before history ends in a new heaven and a new earth.

Daniel named the empires of Babylon, the Medes and the Persians, and of Alexander the Great in his prophecies. After the decline and fall of the Greek city-states, the next empire to arise was that of Rome, which came into power in the centuries preceding the coming of Christ. This fourth empire was not named by Daniel but was described as "terrifying, dreadful, and very strong. It devoured and crushed its victims with huge iron teeth and trampled their remains beneath its feet. It was different from any of the other beasts, and it had ten horns" (Daniel 7:7). The armies of Rome crushed all opposition and extended the iron control of the Caesars over all of southern Europe, western Asia, and North Africa. But Daniel also observed that in the last stage of the empire the iron would be mixed with baked clay, implying that the fourth kingdom would be vulnerable to sudden destruction, just as pottery can easily be shattered (Daniel 2:41-45).

According to Daniel's prophecy, this fourth empire of the Caesars, although seemingly destroyed, is not actually dead and gone. A final form of the last empire is destined to emerge when ten leaders from nations originally in the Roman Empire emerge from a new union of Europe and Mediterranean nations (Daniel 7:7).

Daniel's vision of this stage of the Roman Empire involves a beast, symbolically representing the Roman Empire, with the ten horns on the beast representing ten kings yet to rise on the stage of world history. The interpretation of the prophecy was directly given to Daniel, as recorded in Daniel 7:23-24: "This fourth beast is the fourth world power that will rule the earth. It will be different from all the others. It will devour the whole world, trampling and crushing everything in its path. Its ten horns are ten kings who will rule that empire."

The first phase of Rome's rise to power and the empire's division and decline are now ancient history. But the final phase of the fourth kingdom has not yet occurred. This has led students of biblical prophecy to expect a new concentration of power to emerge in Europe and the Mediterranean. The fourth world empire will be revived as a final prelude to Armageddon and the second coming of Christ.

The first movements toward the revival of the fourth empire are in today's headlines as Europe moves toward the revival of the Roman Empire. This will set the stage for the emergence of the new world dictator.

THE COMING DICTATOR'S FIRST MOVE

A new world dictator will first reveal himself in the role of a peacemaker in the Middle East. This event will take place during the first stage of the revived Roman Empire, the fourth world empire described by Daniel. Symbolically the new world leader is depicted as "another small horn" who will emerge from the ten-leader oligarchy controlling the political and military power of the West (Daniel 7:8). Daniel described his vision of the new world ruler's rise to power in these words: "As I was looking at the horns, suddenly another small horn appeared among them. Three of the first horns were torn out by the roots to make room for it. This little horn had eyes like human eyes and a mouth that was boasting arrogantly" (Daniel 7:8).

The Group of Ten that consolidates the power and wealth of the Middle East will soon come under the control of this new leader. Bible expositors have concluded that this emerging ruler will first of all subdue three of the original ten leaders and then take control of the entire coalition. The leaders will yield control of the new European Union to this new strong man of the hour.

Daniel identified this man as the one who eventually will become the final world dictator, the Antichrist described in Revelation. He is described as different from the other ten leaders, speaking out against God, persecuting believers in God, and growing in power until he controls the entire world for a period of forty-two months.

The interpretation given to Daniel is, "Then another king will arise, different from the other ten, who will subdue three of them. He will defy the Most High and oppress the holy people of the Most High. He will try to change their sacred festivals and laws, and they will be placed under his control for a time, times, and half a time" (Daniel 7:24-25).

The time period of his absolute rule can be calculated as a year, plus two years, plus half a year—three and a half years (Daniel 12:11; Revelation 13:5).

UNDERSTANDING DANIEL'S SEVENTY WEEKS

Daniel's prophecy provides the key to the entire drama of the last days. The new world leader will cause a series of world-shattering events, which are described in detail by Daniel and the writer of the book of Revelation. Jesus identified this man as the final military conqueror who will invade Jerusalem and desecrate the Temple, "'the abomination that causes desolation,' spoken of through the prophet Daniel" (Matthew 24:15, NIV).

In Daniel 9:24-27 the prophet recorded a revelation of seventy "sevens" of years, which totals 490 years, in which great events would take place in relation to Jerusalem and the Jewish people. The first two major time segments involved 483 years, or sixty-nine "sevens." The word translated *week* (KJV) actually means "seven" and refers to years, not days. We know that this refers to years for two main reasons.

Daniel's Seventy Weeks

(Daniel 9:24-27)

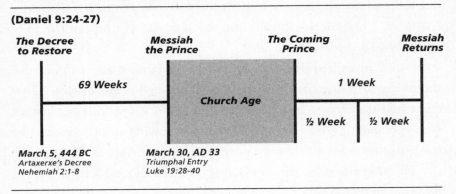

First, nothing of any significance happened within a 490-day period after Daniel's prophecy. Second, according to Daniel 9:2, Daniel was already thinking in terms of years in the same context. This period was described by Daniel in these words: "Know and understand this: From the issuing of the decree to restore and rebuild Jerusalem until the Anointed One, the ruler, comes, there will be seven 'sevens,' and sixty-two 'sevens.' It will be rebuilt with streets and a trench, but in times of trouble. After the sixty-two 'sevens,' the Anointed One will be cut off and will have nothing. The people of the ruler who will come will destroy the city and the sanctuary. The end will come like a flood: War will continue until the end, and desolations have been decreed" (Daniel 9:25-26, NIV).

The first time segment of Daniel's seventy weeks began with the decree to restore and rebuild Jerusalem, the decree given to Nehemiah on March 5, 444 BC. The first seven weeks, or forty-nine years, marked the time needed to rebuild Jerusalem. The second segment of sixty-two weeks of years (434 years) marked the time that would pass until the Messiah was cut off. Adding these two segments reveals the amazing accuracy of Daniel's prophecy; the 483 years ended on March 30, AD 33, just before Jesus was rejected by the nation of Israel and crucified.[2]

But one week of seven years is still left unfulfilled. Daniel 9:26 predicts "a ruler will arise whose armies will destroy the city and the

Temple," referring to the Roman army of that day, which did come and destroy the city and the Temple in AD 70. But for the future ruler of the revived Roman Empire, his prophetic destiny during the last seven years awaits. The new leader of the revived Roman Empire will seize control of the nations led by an oligarchy of ten world leaders. With that power consolidated, he will then make his next decisive move. He will negotiate a peace covenant, guaranteeing Israel's security and bringing peace to the Middle East. According to Daniel, this important move will begin the last seven years of the predicted 490 years. It will be, in fact, the last seven years of world history before Armageddon and the second coming of Christ.

"He will confirm a covenant with many for one 'seven.' In the middle of the 'seven' he will put an end to sacrifice and offering. And on a wing of the temple he will set up an abomination that causes desolation, until the end that is decreed is poured out on him" (Daniel 9:27, NIV).

The world leader will move from a tactic of peace to a tactic of crushing power. As dictator of the revived Roman Empire, he will make peace with Israel, and he will keep his covenant during the first three and a half years of his rule. In the middle of the seven years, however, he will break his agreement. As noted in the previous chapter, this very possibly will coincide with Russia's attempt to invade Israel and Russia's mysterious annihilation. With the world balance of power dramatically in his favor and the world dazzled by the defeat of Russia and her Islamic allies, the Antichrist will show his true colors. He will declare himself world dictator and move to crush all opposition.

FORTY-TWO MONTHS OF HORROR

The prophets throughout the Bible have described the last years before the second coming of Christ as a time of great trouble. This is the time when the last world dictator will "devour the whole world, trampling and crushing everything in its path" (Daniel 7:23). Jesus described this time as one of "greater anguish than at any time since the world began.

And it will never be so great again. In fact, unless that time of calamity is shortened, not a single person will survive. But it will be shortened for the sake of God's chosen ones" (Matthew 24:21-22).

This is the same period and the same ruler described in Revelation 13. Revelation 13:5 tells us he will be given power and authority to reign for forty-two months. Revelation 13:7 reveals: "And the beast was allowed to wage war against God's holy people and to conquer them. And he was given authority to rule over every tribe and people and language and nation." Satan's man of destiny will have forty-two months of power as the world dictator. In the process of this rule, God will bring His terrible judgments on a wicked, Christ-rejecting world.

The prophetic calendar has been announced for centuries. The die is cast. The Middle East will return to the center of the international stage. The ten world leaders will emerge to consolidate the power lost by the fall of Rome. The future world dictator will await the right moment to upset three of these leaders and seize control of the Group of Ten, thereby controlling all the nations in the new European Union.

For three and a half years he will masquerade as a prince of peace, the savior of the world. For the next three and a half years he will use satanic wonders and power to declare himself god and ruthlessly crush all opposition.

Near the end of that period the nations of the world will field armies to challenge him. Gripped in a dramatic world war, the armies will converge to begin the suicidal Battle of Armageddon, as described in chapter 13.

TOOLS OF WORLD DOMINATION EXIST TODAY

It is most significant that in the twenty-first century not only does a need for a world government exist, but the tools for establishing such a government are now in our hands. Today the electronic media, especially use of television via satellite, is a tremendous tool that allows instant communication with the entire earth. CNN now reaches almost every corner of the world. Access to the Internet and satellite cell phones reach around the globe.

Missile warfare is also a tremendous tool to enforce world rule. Missiles can be fired and guided by GPS to almost any spot in the world in less than thirty minutes. A ruler with nuclear submarines and missiles at his disposal could threaten any portion of the world—blackmailing it into submission with the threat of extinction. No previous ruler in the history of the world has had such fearful weapons to enforce his rule.

In the field of economics, the Bible predicts that the world ruler will have absolute control of the economy, and no one will buy or sell without his permission (Revelation 13:17). Today, with the advent of electronic funds transfer, electronic banking, and widespread use of debit and credit cards, this is literally possible for the first time in world history. Large transfers of cash are already controlled by the government. Hundreds of millions of dollars move by wire every day in the international banking system. Credit and debit card transactions are verified in real time by phone, cell phone, and Internet access. At first the government control of the banking system might simply be a move to control the money used to finance terrorism or criminal activity. It is hard to imagine how international terrorism could be stopped without it.

Every person and business would have an account on the approved and government-controlled network. Everyone would be required to have a permanent identification number. Employers could only pay employees by electronic transfer of funds. All mortgages and utility bills—in fact, the sale or purchase of anything—would require such an account. When a person wanted to make a purchase, the store would simply check the person's account electronically and then subtract his or her purchases instantly by connecting to the system by phone or Internet.

In such a scenario currency and barter would be outlawed. The banks would recall all currency and simply issue credits to electronic accounts. If a world ruler chose to use such a system instead of money, no one could buy or sell unless the government provided an approved number, bar code, or mark. The government would have absolute economic control.

In our modern world all forms of representative and democratic governments will continue to be plagued by overwhelming problems. These will tend to undermine efforts at strong and resolute world leadership. As both domestic and international problems increase, the world will look for a new leader to act decisively to end the turmoil precipitated by events in the Middle East crisis and the threats to the world's oil supply. Both the need and the tools for the control of the world by one strong ruler exist today. The increasing availability of nuclear weapons, the propaganda power of the world media, and the blackmail power of international economic agreements and embargoes will make it possible for a world dictator to seize control of the world in a way that would have been impossible in any previous generation.

In an amazing way, the necessary ingredients for a world government are present for the first time in the history of civilization. The time may not be far away when such a government, foretold in Scripture, will have its accurate and complete fulfillment.

See how today's headlines relate to this chapter at http://www.prophecyhotline.com.

CHAPTER 9

THE FINAL HOLOCAUST

EVENT #8: The world ruler breaks his peace with Israel, destroys the Temple in Jerusalem, and attempts to exterminate the Jewish people.

> I am worried by the growing anti-Semitism and anti-Zionism in the world.
>
> STEVEN SPIELBERG

BY ANY STANDARD THE JEWISH people have suffered more abuse and mistreatment than any group of people in human history. They have been the world's scapegoat. Stereotypes abound. And the virulent virus of anti-Semitism shows no signs of dying. In recent years it has simply mutated into a new strain. There's a powerful resurgence of anti-Semitism worldwide, especially in Europe, where it's being fueled by a growing population of Arab immigrants.

One outgrowth of anti-Semitism in recent years is a strange case of historical revisionism. As incredible as it may seem, some today are questioning if the Jewish Holocaust at the hands of the Nazis even occurred. Iranian president Mahmoud Ahmadinejad recently stated that the entire Jewish Holocaust is probably a myth, or if it did occur, it was greatly exaggerated.[1] Most of the world was appalled when he addressed a government-sponsored conference for Holocaust deniers and white supremacists that met in Tehran in December 2006. Afterward, he welcomed participants in his office, saying, "The Zionist regime will disappear soon." According to the *New York Times*, he "also suggested that the work of the government-sponsored conference—billed as a chance for 'both sides' on the Holocaust to be heard—should continue with the formation of a committee to determine whether the mass killings by Nazis of Jews and others really happened."[2]

THE NEW ANTI-SEMITISM

A new term has arisen in recent years to describe the modern rise in anti-Semitism. It's been termed "the new anti-Semitism." But what is the new anti-Semitism? How is it different from the old form?

The old anti-Semitism was hatred for the Jewish people and a desire to eradicate them. The new anti-Semitism is opposition to the very existence of a state for the Jewish people. It's a denial of Israel's right to exist and a desire to eradicate the Jewish state. Jews everywhere are now being held responsible for the military policies of the Israeli government. Jews and the existence of the state of Israel are being blamed for everything from terrorism to the threat of nuclear war in the Middle East.

The new anti-Semitism is interesting in light of Bible prophecy, which tells us that in the end times Israel will be hated by the nations of the earth. The Bible presents the coming tribulation period as a time of mounting opposition against Israel climaxing in an attack by all the nations of the earth.

Zechariah 12:2-3 says, "I will make Jerusalem like an intoxicating drink that makes the nearby nations stagger when they send their armies to besiege Jerusalem and Judah. On that day I will make Jerusalem an immovable rock. All the nations will gather against it to try to move it, but they will only hurt themselves."

In other words, while many nations will relish the idea of conquering Jerusalem, those who try to possess her will face disaster. Israel will be a heavy jagged stone that will cut to pieces those who try to remove her from her place. The frustration and hatred toward Israel in our world today are obvious. But what is behind all the animosity?

WHY THE WORLD HATES ISRAEL

Israel has been threatened repeatedly, particularly since the birth of the modern nation in 1948.[3] Scripture, particularly Revelation 12, reveals that the real source of opposition against Israel is Satan. As the enemy of the Jews and Jesus, their Messiah, he is the original source of anti-Semitism.

Satan has been on a mission to destroy the Jewish people and prevent the Messiah's coming ever since God promised Abraham that the Messiah would come through his line. Satan instigated several unsuccessful attempts to eradicate the Jewish people. First, Haman tried to wipe out the Jews in the days of Esther in about 480 BC. Next, the Syrian monarch Antiochus Epiphanes tried to destroy them in about 165 BC.

When those plans failed, Satan plotted to kill Christ. Satan tried to destroy Him right after His birth through the evil of King Herod (Matthew 2:16-18). When this failed, he inspired the Jewish and Roman leaders to kill the Son of God. However, he could not foresee the resurrection of Christ.

Now Satan is working on yet another plan. Once again, he is seeking ways to destroy the Jewish people over whom the Messiah is to rule. He made his greatest attempt to destroy the Jewish people under the Third Reich, when Adolph Hitler sent six million Jews to their death.

In the end times, the Antichrist will begin his career by acting like he is the great friend of Israel, but in the Great Tribulation he will slaughter the Jews mercilessly (Daniel 7:25; 8:24; 11:44). The Antichrist will be totally empowered, controlled, and motivated by Satan, so his persecution of Israel must be an expression of Satan's hatred for Israel (Revelation 13:4).

ISRAEL LETS DOWN HER GUARD

As a result of the coming peace treaty with the Antichrist, Israel will exhibit a new sense of security and lay down her weapons. For almost three and half years, peace for Israel will stand firm. But this era of peace and productivity will end when the coalition of nations described in Ezekiel 38 makes its final move into Israel. As we saw in chapter 7, this strike force will include Russia and her Islamic allies. In one of the great miracles of all history, God will supernaturally annihilate these invaders.

Apparently, the Antichrist will rise up during this time of mayhem and chaos to seize global control and position himself as the world's omnipotent ruler. His first order of business will be to secure Israel and the Middle East. In one of the great double-crosses of all time, the Antichrist will break his peace treaty with Israel at the midpoint of the seven-year agreement. The Antichrist will then attempt to finish what Hitler started. His goal will be nothing short of genocide, and he will almost succeed. Zechariah 13:8 says that two-thirds of the people of Israel will die and one-third will be left in the land.

THE COMING TIME OF TROUBLE FOR THE PEOPLE OF ISRAEL

Many end-time prophecies were given to Israel concerning a coming "time of trouble for my people Israel" or what's commonly called the "time of Jacob's trouble" (Jeremiah 30:7, KJV).

The first place this time of future tribulation is prophesied in the Bible is in Deuteronomy 4:30: "In the distant future, when you are suffering all these things, you will finally return to the LORD your God and listen to what he tells you." In Scripture this time of trouble is related to the end times when Israel will be regathered to her ancient land. The prophet Jeremiah records: "For the time is coming when I will restore the fortunes of my people of Israel and Judah. I will bring them home to this land that I gave to their ancestors, and they will possess it again. I, the LORD, have spoken!" (Jeremiah 30:3).

The Top 10 Prophecies of Israel's Future

1. Israel will be regathered and formed into a nation (Isaiah 43:5-6; Jeremiah 30:3; Ezekiel 34:11-13; 36:34; 37:1-14; Romans 11:25-27). Preparation for this began in May 1948 and continues to the present.

2. The Antichrist will make a seven-year treaty with Israel (Daniel 9:27).

3. The Jewish people will rebuild the Temple in Jerusalem (Matthew 24:15).

4. Russia and her Islamic allies will invade the nation of Israel when she is at peace (Ezekiel 38–39).

5. The Antichrist will invade Israel and desecrate the Temple (Matthew 24:15-20; 2 Thessalonians 2:4).

6. Many Jews will flee into the wilderness (Revelation 12:13-17).

7. During the Tribulation, two-thirds of the Jews will perish (Zechariah 13:8).

8. The armies of the world will gather in northern Israel at Megiddo (Revelation 16:12-16).

9. Jerusalem will be attacked and taken (Zechariah 12:1-9; 14:1-2).

10. Jesus Christ will return from heaven to defeat the armies of the world gathered in Israel, and many Jews will turn to Jesus as their Messiah (Zechariah 12:10; Revelation 19:19-21).

Immediately after this prediction of Israel's return is the description of her time of trouble. Israel is described as a woman experiencing the pains of childbirth. Her day of trouble is described in graphic terms in Jeremiah 30:7: "In all history there has never been such a time of terror. It will be a time of trouble for my people Israel. Yet in the end they will be saved!" On the basis of this promise, the progression or sequence of events as they relate to Israel in the end times will be her regathering, her time of trouble, and finally her time of deliverance when Christ returns.

We see the same basic order of events in Daniel's description of this future period. Key sections of Daniel's prophecy have already been explained, and Daniel 11:40-45, which contains an important description of events at the end of the period, will be explained in chapter 13. The prophet's concluding description of this period is given in Daniel 12:1: "At that time Michael, the archangel who stands guard over your nation, will arise. Then there will be a time of anguish greater than any since nations first came into existence. But at that time every one of your people whose name is written in the book will be rescued." The verses that immediately follow indicate that this will occur directly before the second coming of Christ.

This great time of trouble for Israel will be the period just before the second coming of Christ to the earth. In Daniel 7:25 and 12:7 it is described as extending for "time, times, and half a time," or three and a half years. This is in keeping with other prophecies of Daniel, such as Daniel 9:27, where it is described as half of a seven-year period. Revelation 12:6 speaks of the period as 1,260 days, or forty-two months (Revelation 13:5). Brief though it may be, this three-and-a-half-year period of great horror will include the most awful times of catastrophe and destruction that Israel and the entire world have ever known. Many other passages in the Old Testament give additional descriptions, such as Daniel 7:7-8 and the explanation of it in Daniel 7:19-27. The Great Tribulation, according to Scripture, will be followed by a time of glorious restoration for the Jewish people (see Joel 2:28-32; 3:17-21; Zephaniah 3:14-18; Zechariah 13:8–14:21). The Old Testament as a whole bears a clear witness to this climactic period of trouble that is unprecedented in the entire history of the world but especially for the Jewish people. The current problems facing Israel and the Jewish people are only the beginning of this great time of trouble yet ahead.

GOD IS IN CONTROL

It's painful to discuss the second holocaust that the Jewish people will endure in the final years of this age. However, the good news is that God will use this terrible disaster to bring the Jewish people to faith in Jesus as their Messiah. God will put them in the vice of judgment, and as a result, many of the Jewish people will call out to Him for deliverance and salvation. Isaiah 64:1 records their future call to the Lord for rescue: "Oh, that you would burst from the heavens and come down! How the mountains would quake in your presence!" Even at His second coming, many of the Jewish people will look upon the pierced Messiah and receive Him as Savior (Zechariah 12:10).

Terrible times are ahead for Israel. But in the end God promises that millions of Jews will be saved. We can already see how the stage is being set for the fulfillment of these amazing prophecies.

 See how today's headlines relate to this chapter at http://www.prophecyhotline.com.

CHAPTER 10

IRAQ: THE NEW BABYLON
ECONOMIC CENTER OF WORLD POWER

EVENT #9: The world ruler makes Iraq the new commercial and economic center of his world rule.

"The logistics alone are incredible, the cost, the . . . everything."
"What?"
"He wants to move the U.N."
"Move it?"
"Where?"
"It sounds stupid."
"Everything sounds stupid these days," Bailey said.
"He wants to move it to Babylon."
"You're not serious."
"He is."
"I hear they've been renovating that city for years. Millions of dollars invested in making it, what, New Babylon?"
"Billions. . . ."
"Within a year the United Nations headquarters will move to New Babylon."

TIM LAHAYE AND JERRY JENKINS,
LEFT BEHIND (A NOVEL)

WE ARE ALL PAINFULLY AWARE that Iraq has dominated U.S. foreign policy. The bloodshed and struggle over Iraq continues unabated.

It all started in 1990. Beginning in that year with the attack of Kuwait, Saddam Hussein became the world's public enemy number one. From that time until his capture, he did everything he could to harass and hinder Israel and the West, especially the United States.

The events during the first Gulf War in the early 1990s did not fulfill any specific biblical prophecies. But the subsequent invasion of Iraq and U.S. attempts to rebuild the city of Baghdad have created a scenario that requires reexamination of prophecy about the region. Does the rise of Iraq to world prominence have any significance for understanding end-time prophecy?[1]

BABYLON: CITY OF MAN

Jerusalem is the city that appears most often in the pages of the Bible. Jerusalem is mentioned just over 800 times. It is first named in Genesis 14 and last mentioned in Revelation 21. Jerusalem is consistently pictured in the Bible in a positive light. It is the city of God.

What many people may not realize is that the second most-mentioned city in the Bible is Babylon. The ancient city is located on the Euphrates River in modern Iraq near the Persian Gulf. Babylon is mentioned about 290 times in the Bible.

Babylon first appears in Genesis 10–11 and last appears in Revelation 17–18. Throughout the Bible, in contrast to Jerusalem, Babylon is pictured as man's city. It is consistently portrayed as a place of rebellion and pride. It was the first city built after the Flood. It was founded and ruled over by the world's first dictator, a man named Nimrod. It was the location of the famous Tower of Babel. From its inception Babylon was both a literal city and the false religious system that emanated from it. According to Revelation 17:5, "A mysterious name was written on her forehead: 'Babylon the Great, Mother of All Prostitutes and Obscenities in the World.'" Babylon, then, from its beginning is both a city and a system.

In Genesis 14, both Jerusalem (ancient Salem) and Babylon (ancient Shinar) are mentioned. They are total opposites. In this chapter, Babylon attacks Sodom and carries away its citizens, including Abraham's nephew Lot. When Abraham gets the news, he pursues Lot's captors and rescues his nephew. Melchizedek, the king of Salem, then comes out to bless Abraham.

From this point on in the Bible, we have what one might call "a tale of two cities." It's Jerusalem, God's city, versus Babylon, man's city. The story of these two cities takes us from the beginning to the end. It begins in Genesis and ends in Revelation.

In Revelation 17–18 Babylon is finally destroyed by God. In the final climax of world history, in Revelation 21, the New Jerusalem comes down out of heaven from God as the capital city of the new heaven and new earth and the eternal abode of God and His people.

That's a thumbnail sketch of the story of Babylon and Jerusalem from beginning to end. The basic lesson is simply this: Man's city falls, but God's city remains. Babylon is destroyed forever, but the heavenly city, the New Jerusalem, descends from heaven to endure forever.

With this basic blueprint in mind, let's take a closer look at a few of the details the Bible gives us about Babylon's history and destiny.

"FALLEN, FALLEN IS BABYLON THE GREAT!"

Most of the references in the Bible to Babylon concern the Babylonian empire that ruled the world of that day from 605–539 BC. King Nebuchadnezzar was the great leader of this empire. He invaded Judah three times. In the first invasion (605 BC), Daniel was taken captive. The second time the Babylonians came was in 597 when Ezekiel was carried away. Finally, in 586 Nebuchadnezzar's forces came and destroyed the great Temple of Solomon in Jerusalem.

Many of the prophets, including Isaiah, Jeremiah, Ezekiel, and Habakkuk, wrote about the Babylonians. This evil empire was the great menacing lion kingdom of sixth century BC (Jeremiah 4:7; Daniel 7:4).

The prophets warned Judah to repent or else God would send the Babylonians as an instrument of His discipline. However, once the Babylonians had come and destroyed the Temple, the message turned from one of judgment on Judah to hope for the future. Part of this message of comfort and hope was that God would repay Babylon for her sins. This message was intended to give God's people comfort, encouragement, and hope.

The Bible gives a detailed description of the destruction of Babylon in three key Old Testament passages: Isaiah 13; Isaiah 46–47; and Jeremiah 50–51.

Isaiah's Prophecy of Babylon's Final Destruction

Isaiah 13:4-5 says, "Hear the noise on the mountains! Listen, as the vast armies march! It is the noise and shouting of many nations. The LORD of Heaven's Armies has called this army together. They come from distant countries, from beyond the farthest horizons. They are the LORD's weapons to carry out his anger. With them he will destroy the whole land."

Isaiah continues in 13:10-13:

> The heavens will be black above them;
>   the stars will give no light.
> The sun will be dark when it rises,
>   and the moon will provide no light.
> "I, the LORD, will punish the world for its evil
>   and the wicked for their sin.
> I will crush the arrogance of the proud
>   and humble the pride of the mighty.
> I will make people scarcer than gold—
>   more rare than the fine gold of Ophir.
> For I will shake the heavens.
>   The earth will move from its place
> when the LORD of Heaven's Armies displays his wrath
>   in the day of his fierce anger."

In this chapter it appears that the prophet is looking down the corridors of time to the far destruction of Babylon in the end times since nothing like this happened to Babylon in the past. Jesus even referred to Isaiah 13:10 in Matthew 24:29 when He described the stellar signs that will accompany His second coming to earth.

The prophet also seems to refer to the far view, that is, the destruction of Babylon in relation to the second coming of Christ, in Isaiah 13:20-22, which says,

> *Babylon will never be inhabited again.*
> *It will remain empty for generation after generation.*
> *Nomads will refuse to camp there,*
> *and shepherds will not bed down their sheep.*
> *Desert animals will move into the ruined city,*
> *and the houses will be haunted by howling creatures.*
> *Owls will live among the ruins,*
> *and wild goats will go there to dance.*
> *Hyenas will howl in its fortresses,*
> *and jackals will make dens in its luxurious palaces.*
> *Babylon's days are numbered;*
> *its time of destruction will soon arrive.*

Isaiah 13:19 even says that when Babylon is finally destroyed it will be like Sodom and Gomorrah. "Babylon, the most glorious of kingdoms, the flower of Chaldean pride, will be devastated like Sodom and Gomorrah when God destroyed them."

As far as the historic fulfillment of these verses is concerned, it is obvious from both Scripture and history that these verses have not been literally fulfilled. The city of Babylon has never been destroyed suddenly and cataclysmically like Isaiah 13 describes. Babylon continued to flourish after the Medes conquered it under the leadership of Cyrus. When the Persians under King Cyrus conquered Babylon in 539 BC the city wasn't even destroyed. Though its glory dwindled, especially after the control of the Medes and Persians ended in 323 BC, the city continued in some form or substance until AD 1000 and did not experience a sudden, cataclysmic termination such as is anticipated in this prophecy.

Since nothing like this ever happened to the city of Babylon in its long and storied history, and since the Bible is God's Word and must be literally fulfilled, then we must conclude that it's a future event. And there's only one time in man's history when all this will occur: at the end of the future tribulation period in conjunction with the second coming of Jesus Christ.

Armageddon Brings Babylon's Destruction

Isaiah 14 seems to further confirm that the city's ultimate destruction is related to the second advent of Christ and the Day of the Lord. The satanic power behind Babylon, addressed as "Lucifer, son of the morning" (Isaiah 14:12, NKJV), is portrayed both in his original rebellion against God and in his ultimate judgment. The destruction of Babylon is related to the time of final restoration for the Jewish people (Isaiah 14:1-3) and the judgment upon the rulers of the nations (Isaiah 14:4-7).

The final Old Testament prophecy about Babylon is found in Zechariah 5:5-11. This prophecy also indicates that Babylon will be rebuilt in the end times.

In Zechariah 5, the prophet Zechariah sees a vision of a basket that is full of wickedness, personified as a woman. A heavy lid is put on the basket to keep the evil in check. God doesn't want the wickedness to get out. As Zechariah sees the basket being carried away, he asks where the basket is being taken. The angel replies, "To the land of Babylonia, where they will build a temple for the basket. And when the temple is ready, they will set the basket there on its pedestal" (5:11).

When Zechariah wrote these words, the Babylonian empire had already been conquered by the Medo-Persians about twenty-five years earlier. And there is no event after Zechariah's prophecy that could be legitimately seen as the fulfillment of this prophecy. So what does this mean? It means that Zechariah's prophecy is still in the future. It means that someday, when the necessary preparations have been made, wickedness again will be focused in the land of Babylon. Wickedness will rear its ugly head in the place of its origin—Babylon.

The Bible indicates that history will come full circle in the end times and that Babylon will be the headquarters for the final world ruler, the Antichrist (Revelation 17–18). The city of Babylon has never been completely destroyed as the Bible predicts in such passages as Isaiah 13 and Jeremiah 50–51. These texts indicate that Babylon will be wiped out like Sodom and Gomorrah, that no brick from the city will ever be used again, that no one will ever live there, and that the city will never be rebuilt. For these passages to be literally fulfilled, Babylon must be rebuilt to all its former glory and destroyed once and for all at the end of the time of great horror.

BABYLON IN THE END TIMES

In the final mention of Babylon in Revelation 17–18, the city of man is symbolized by a seductive harlot riding on the back of the Antichrist, who is symbolized by a wild beast. This connection between Babylon and the Beast, or the Antichrist, indicates that the two will be closely allied. Babylon in the end times, like Babylon in the beginning, will be both a false religious system and a literal city on the Euphrates River that will serve as an economic and commercial capital for the Antichrist.

Revelation 17 seems to focus on the religious aspect of Babylon, while Revelation 18 focuses on the city's political and economic characteristics. Revelation 17 depicts the destruction of the Babylonian false religious system by the Antichrist and his henchmen at the midpoint of the seven-year Tribulation.

The New Superchurch

This false religious system is probably a kind of "superchurch" or world church that will pull together people of various religious backgrounds into one great ecclesiastical alliance. It will probably be centered in the restored, rebuilt city of Babylon.

Even now, we see hints of what this may be like, as a number of people in the church deny some of the central tenets of the faith. This is not surprising, given the movement toward a world church within Protestant Christianity during the last century. When the World Council of Churches was organized in Amsterdam in 1948, one of its aims was to bring all branches of Christianity, including Protestant, Roman Catholic, and Eastern Orthodox churches, under one organization. In the process, strict adherence to biblical doctrine and orthodox theology was sacrificed for organizational unity. Church leaders weren't engaged in minor disputes over some fine point of theology but over the central doctrine of Jesus Christ—who He was and what He did when He died upon the cross.

Disputes in theology are not new, and departures from strict adherence to biblical truth have occurred throughout the centuries, beginning in the days of the apostles (see 2 Peter 1:1-2; 2 Peter 3:3-4; 2 Timothy 4:2-4). In the past century, however, changes in theology have been more rapid and more devastating to biblical faith than ever before. The belief that the Bible is the Word of God has been abandoned by many within the church.

The Disappearance of True Believers

Yet the Bible makes clear that the situation will be far worse in the end times. The Holy Spirit, who now restrains evil in the world and who indwells the church, will be taken away at the time of the Rapture. In other words, the Spirit's restraining influence through the Church will be removed (2 Thessalonians 2:6-7). Obviously the removal of every Christian in the world who is indwelt by the Spirit will release a flood tide of evil such as the world has never seen. It will allow the immediate takeover of the world church by those completely devoid of Christian faith and will allow other forces of evil a free hand in human history.

Fear and panic will accompany the disappearance of true believers from the earth at the time of the Rapture (1 Thessalonians 4:13-18). This will amplify the world's desire for a strong religious organization to bring order from that religious chaos. With millions of people disappearing, natural disasters, a rapid rise in demonic power, and false prophets performing signs and wonders, the world will be grasping for something that is secure. In desperation the masses will turn to the world church for help.

Without the redeeming presence of true believers, people from all kinds of religious background or no religious background will combine into a powerful religious and political institution. This superchurch will have power to put to death those who resist its demands for adherence (Revelation 17:6). The new world church will be in alliance with the political powers of the reunited Roman Empire. This combined effort will prepare the way for a new government with absolute power over the entire world. This unholy alliance is portrayed symbolically in Revelation 17, which describes a wicked harlot riding a scarlet-colored beast.

False Religion and False Peace

For centuries expositors have recognized the harlot as the symbol of false religion and the scarlet beast as representing the political power of the revived Roman Empire in the end times. While their alliance will bring a temporary stability to the world, it will also create a blasphemous religious system that will lead the world to new depths of immorality and departure from true faith in God.

One of the fruits of their combined power will be the forced peace with Israel. While there will be some show of religious tolerance in permitting the revival of Judaism, it will be short-lived and will continue only as long as the peace treaty is observed. In other parts of the world, persecution and martyrdom will follow the extending power of the combined political and ecclesiastical alliance. But the final form of world religion will emerge later.

The Group of Ten and the Antichrist will use this false religious system as long as it serves their interests. However, at the midpoint of the Tribulation, the Antichrist and the Group of Ten will no longer need the power and help of the superchurch. The Antichrist will destroy this false religious system and replace it with his own ecclesiastical apostasy, the final form of religious wickedness, the worship of himself (Revelation 17:16-17).

"After All This"

Revelation 18 begins with the words "After all this" ("And after these things" in the King James Version). This indicates that Revelation 18 records events that will follow the fall of the religious harlot or super-church during the middle of the Tribulation. Revelation 18 focuses on the political and economic system centered in Babylon that will reach its zenith under the rule of the Antichrist.

The description of the sins of Babylon as "piled as high as heaven" (Revelation 18:5) is an unmistakable allusion back to the Tower of Babel, whose bricks were piled up toward heaven (Genesis 11:5-9). This marked the beginning of the pride, selfishness, and greed associated with the ancient political and economic world capital in Babylon. When the Antichrist makes Babylon his capital, the city will seem invincible. But the sin of this city will be piled up, and God will bring the Antichrist's enemies against the city to burn her with fire.

Revelation 18 prophesies the final destruction of the city of Babylon just before the second coming of Jesus Christ in Revelation 19:11-21. When Babylon falls suddenly and unexpectedly, the leaders and merchants of the world will marvel and be terrified at the destruction of the great city (Revelation 18:9-19). Babylon's fall will be a dreaded omen of the total unraveling of the Antichrist's world empire. It is significant that the final destruction on earth before Jesus returns will be the razing of Babylon, man's city.

BABYLON BACK IN THE NEWS

Four key factors indicate that Babylon could quickly become the city described in end-time prophecy:

First, Saddam Hussein began renovating the ancient city while in power. While the rebuilding is far from complete, the fact that it even began is intriguing. During Operation Iraqi Freedom and for several years after, American troops were stationed in the city of Babylon in a place appropriately named "Camp Babylon." Many military ceremonies were held there.

Fifty miles to the north, the United States has begun a massive project to build and staff a fortress-like embassy complex beside the Tigris River in Baghdad. The embassy, known as "Embassy Baghdad," is the largest of its kind in the world—the size of Vatican City, with a population of 5,500. The embassy complex covers 104 acres and includes 21 buildings. It dwarfs U.S. embassies elsewhere that typically cover about 10 acres. The Baghdad embassy has its own defense force and self-contained power and water.

USA Today provided this description of "Embassy Baghdad":

> *The massive new embassy, being built on the banks of the Tigris River, is designed to be entirely self-sufficient and won't be dependent on Iraq's unreliable public utilities.*
>
> *The 104-acre complex—the size of about 80 football fields—will include two office buildings, one of them designed for future use as a school, six apartment buildings, a gym, a pool, a food court, and its own power generation and water-treatment plants. The average Baghdad home has electricity only four hours a day, according to Bowen's office. The current U.S. Embassy in Iraq has nearly 1,000 Americans working there, more than at any other U.S. embassy.[2]*

Some worry that this massive symbol of U.S. presence in Iraq sends the wrong signal to the Iraqi people. But could it be that Embassy Baghdad is another key step toward the rise of Babylon?

Saddam Hussein compared himself to Nebuchadnezzar and began rebuilding Babylon. The United States has focused the resources of the wealthiest and most powerful country in the world on the task. The construction of this massive embassy in Baghdad could signal the beginning of a long-term Western presence in Iraq. Embassy Baghdad could easily be a first step for other Western powers to join in to rebuild a "New Babylon," preparing the city for its role in end-time events.

Second, Iraq sits on the fourth largest known crude oil reserves in the world (estimated at 115 billion barrels, compared to Saudi Arabia with about 266 billion barrels). However, some believe that Iraq may have as much as 300 billion barrels or 30 percent of the known reserves in the world. Iraq's actual oil reserves are still unknown since, according to the U.S. Energy Information Administration, 90 percent of Iraq's regions are unexplored. No one really knows how much oil Iraq has. Consider this. There are only 2,000 wells in all of Iraq compared with one million in Texas alone.[3] Just next door to Iraq, tiny Kuwait has 10 percent of the proven oil reserves.

The ousting of Saddam from power has resulted in a lifting of the sanctions and limitations on Iraqi oil sales. In the years ahead, one could expect that billions of dollars, euros, and yen will flood into Iraq. Western companies are salivating over Iraq's petroleum potential. Oil experts believe that with improved, modernized infrastructure, Iraq could easily pump out four million barrels a day. And this number could skyrocket if more reserves are discovered.[4] Future oil revenues and attempts to rebuild and stabilize Iraq by the United States and the West point to the rebuilding of Babylon as a major economic center for the Middle East.

Third, due to the war there, Iraq has become and continues to be a major focal point in the Middle East and Persian Gulf. With mounting casualties and the growing sense that the United States and its allies are stuck in a quagmire, many are now wondering if the war there will ever end. The answer is yes, at some time, because the Bible predicts that Babylon will become a world headquarters for the Antichrist. We don't know when or how it will finally grind to a halt, but as the war there continues to drag on, the United States will be forced to step up pressure on the Iraqis to get their government on track. If some degree of stability and security can be achieved, other nations will move quickly to Iraq to get a piece of this developing, oil-rich nation.

Fourth, the symbolic and strategic reasons for the Antichrist locating a capital city in Babylon would be powerful. What better place for the Antichrist to locate a major economic center than Babylon? It's in the geographical center of the Persian Gulf area surrounded by rich oil reserves. It's not far from Iraq's borders with Iran, Kuwait, and Saudi Arabia, affording a strategic location between these four oil-rich nations. Also, as the oil reserves of other Middle Eastern nations are being drained by millions of barrels a day, Iraq's vast reserves are hardly being touched. Iraq's huge oil reserves are sitting on the sidelines in the world's scramble for energy. In the next decade, as Iraq's oil potential is explored and ready to come online, Iraq could be poised to emerge as *the* oil giant. It could also be this buried treasure that leads the Antichrist to put his headquarters in Babylon so he can control the vast oil reserves of the world. [5]

Babylon also has symbolic significance. It was the ancient capital of King Nebuchadnezzar. It is the place where Alexander the Great died in 323 BC, and he had intended to make it his eastern capital.

The symbolism of such a move would be significant. The Antichrist will put his eastern capital in Babylon and control the main oil fields of the world. Just like Alexander the Great, the Antichrist will attempt to show his power over the world economy by making Babylon the center of his world rule.

While we don't know exactly how Babylon will be rebuilt or what will motivate men to carry out this task, the Bible says it will occur. And current events seem to indicate that it could be soon.

ANOTHER PIECE OF THE PUZZLE

Knowing what the Bible says about Babylon in the end times, we shouldn't be surprised by the rise of Iraq. This rise could serve as a perfect prelude for the building of Babylon in the near future. It's interesting that Iraq has come out of relative obscurity in the past twenty years to play a significant role in the world. The rise of Iraq to world prominence and the ongoing conflict are not accidents. The staggering oil wealth of Iraq is not just a stroke of good fortune. The resurgence of Iraq, the efforts that have already been made to restore and rebuild Babylon, and the rich oil reserves available to finance the rebuilding of the city all make the picture the Bible paints for Babylon in the end times very realistic.

Iraq occupies a pivotal role in the world today and in God's prophetic program. The headlines about Iraq are another part of the rapidly developing matrix of events in the Middle East that are setting the stage for the final end-time events predicted in God's Word.

See how today's headlines relate to this chapter at http://www.prophecyhotline.com.

CHAPTER 11

CHINA FLEXES ITS AWESOME POWER

EVENT #10: The dragon of Asia, starved for oil and economic growth, challenges the world ruler's control of the Middle East.

China's explosive growth could be the dominant event of this century. Never before has a country risen as fast as China is doing.
STAPLETON ROY, FORMER U.S. AMBASSADOR TO CHINA

ONE OF THE COLOSSAL DEVELOPMENTS of the twenty-first century is the political and military awakening of Asia—especially China. The great nations of Asia east of the Euphrates River, slumbering for centuries, are now beginning to stir and become a major factor in the international, socioeconomic, and political dynamics. The immensity of their geography and population make their development especially significant.

The People's Republic of China, with a population of 1.3 billion, is flexing its muscles around the globe. And most of this has taken place in the last twenty-five years. China's economic growth and power are rapidly accelerating. Even if there were no Scripture hinting at the place of China in end-time events, it would only be natural to expect them to be part of the worldwide scene in the end times.

THE CHINESE CENTURY

The June 20, 2005, cover story in *U.S. News & World Report* is titled: "The China Challenge." The article notes that China's economy is growing faster than that of any other nation in modern history. Soon it will become the world's second-largest purchaser of oil and leading buyer of cars, computers, and appliances. "Perhaps more important," the article continues, "China today is infused with a profound sense of destiny, a steely determination to regain primacy in world affairs. The rest of the world is just beginning to digest what that might mean."[1] *Time* also ran a cover story on this nation, called "China: Dawn of a New Dynasty," in January 2007. Reporter Michael Elliott writes: "China is aiming to become the world's greatest power."[2]

Consider these statistics on China's phenomenal rate of growth drawn from the two articles:

- China's economy is growing at a staggering 10 percent per year.
- China's economy will become the second largest in the world by 2020 (surpassing Japan and behind only the United States).
- China has sixteen of the world's most polluted cities.
- An estimated two million people in China have a net worth of at least forty million dollars.
- In 2003 China had 269 million cell phone users; there will be 500 million in 2008.
- China's military budget is the third largest in the world. China has cash for missiles, satellites, and other advanced weapons.
- Military spending has increased 300 percent in the last decade.
- China still regards Taiwan as a renegade province.
- Chinese nationalism is on the rise. The Chinese want to reclaim the grandeur of their past.
- The trade gap between China and the United States is growing by 25 percent per year. Last year Americans spent $162 billion more on Chinese products than the Chinese spent on U.S. products.

The 2006 *Quadrennial Defense Review* released by the Pentagon described China as possessing "the greatest potential to compete militarily with the United States and field disruptive military technologies that over time offset traditional U.S. military advantages."[3] In fact, the anticipated growth of China's influence has already led many to dub this "the Chinese century." Undoubtedly, China will be a key international player to reckon with in the years ahead.

"CHINDIA"

Another country experiencing exponential growth is India. Some experts have coined a new term to denote this new combined world power—*Chindia*. Together, China and India have a combined population of 2.3 billion! Experts predict a mega boom there that will dwarf anything one can imagine. According to an article posted at Bloomberg.com, "The combined gross domestic production of China and India may be $16 trillion a year by 2020. . . . The two nations may account for 17 percent of world GDP by then, up from 7 percent now."[4] A 5 percent increase in anything there, such as cars or cell phones, is the equivalent of a 40 percent increase in the United States simply because they have eight times as many people.[5]

One expert says that, "Chindia will be the main event—almost the only show on the planet—for perhaps the rest of your life."[6]

The combined Chinese and Indian economies will have staggering global effects.

FUELING THE DRAGON

One of the most dramatic results of the rise of China is its influence on world oil markets. China is already the world's second largest consumer of oil, and its consumption increases by 7.5 percent a year, seven times faster than the United States. By 2010 China will have ninety times more cars than it had in 1990. At the current rate of growth, China's thirst for oil will increase by 150 percent by 2020. China's oil imports doubled from 2000 to 2005. If China's oil imports keep rising at the current rate, its oil demand by 2025 would be 21 million barrels a day, matching current U.S. consumption.[7] By 2030, it's projected that the number of cars in China will surpass that in the United States. What does this mean?

China has no long-standing strategic interests in the Middle East, but China is quickly cultivating ties with Saudi Arabia. In light of its exploding economy and need for oil, the Chinese are now scouring the earth for black gold.

China has entered into a series of agreements with Venezuela, which is America's fourth largest oil supplier, to give China a greater share of Venezuelan oil. Chinese state-owned companies are also seeking ambitious deals in Canada, which is another key U.S. supplier. China's third largest oil producer even made an ill-fated, hostile bid for the American oil company Unocal in 2005. The China Petrochemical Corporation has made a deal with Iran worth $100 billion to develop Iran's Yadavaran oil fields.

China is doing all it can to curry favor with Iran and keep the oil flowing. China holds one of the five permanent seats on the United Nations Security Council, and the Chinese have consistently obstructed any meaningful sanctions against Iran for its nuclear ambitions. Also, in the 1990s, China began selling sophisticated missiles to Iran, and Iran has passed these missiles on to Hezbollah. During Israel's war with Hezbollah in the summer of 2006, the Israeli warship *Hanit* was hit by an Iranian-made variant of a Chinese antiship missile.

Clearly, China is actively pursuing every opportunity to secure her energy resources for the future. Chinese officials already know what's finally beginning to dawn on everyone else—China's growing appetite for oil will be insatiable as her economy explodes. Here's one more fact about China's impact on the world oil market. At present about 58 percent of China's oil imports come from the Middle East, but by 2015 about 70 percent of her oil must come from that region.

All this will have a dramatic impact in at least three ways. First, China will continue to expand and siphon off more and more of the available crude from Iran, Russia, and the world market. Second, it will further concentrate the United States' and Europe's attention on the Middle East, as they will become more dependent than ever on oil from key allies in the Middle East. And third, because of its rapid growth, China will inevitably be forced to compete directly with the West for the oil in the Middle East.

DANIEL'S PROPHECY OF AN INVASION FROM THE EAST

The meteoric rise of China from a backward communist nation to an economic and military juggernaut appears to fit in with the biblical alignment of nations in the end times. The Bible predicts that world power will be divided into four main geographical regions. This alignment of nations is described by the directions on the compass in relation to the nation of Israel. To the north is Russia, along with Turkey and Iran. The southern region includes the modern Islamic nations of Egypt, Libya, and Sudan. The western region contains the kingdom of the Antichrist—centered in the reunited Roman Empire. The nations east of the Euphrates River invade the Middle East in the end times (Revelation 16:12-14).

Students of Bible prophecy have long believed that China would be the leader of this great eastern power. What we see happening there today is staggering. The transformation is radical and accelerating. One could easily see how this great rising power will be the final great kingdom standing to challenge the power of the Antichrist. Prophecies in Daniel 11, along with Revelation 9 and 16, paint a vivid picture of what is expected to happen right before the Battle of Armageddon.

In Daniel's prophecy of "the time of the end" beginning in Daniel 11:35, a king is pictured in the Mediterranean who engages in a military conflict with the king of the south, the king of the north, and a military force from the east. This king, who by this point will have assumed the role of a world dictator, is the head of the revived Roman Empire. In the latter part of the Great Tribulation, just prior to the second coming of Christ, major portions of the world will rebel against him. This explains the military conflict with armies pushing against him from the south, the north, and the east.

The prophecy in Daniel 11:44 says, "But then news from the east and the north will alarm him, and he will set out in great anger to destroy and obliterate many." Although we aren't given every detail, it appears that this news concerns a military invasion from the Far East. This is probably the first word of trouble in the Far East related to the Antichrist's worldwide empire and comes as an added blow to the insurrection in the north and the south.

But the conflict with the armies of the north and south is not completely resolved as the armies from the east join the melee. At the time of the second coming of Christ a great war is underway in which the armies are deployed over much of the Holy Land with the valley of Armageddon as its focal point.

This passage in Daniel, however, explains that nations from the east will have a place in the great world conflict of the end times.

The 200 Million Man March

Two important passages in Revelation, namely 9:13-21 and 16:12-16, also suggest that one of the large armies employed in the final world conflict will be a military force of great power from China. The first hint of this is found in Revelation 9, where the apostle John says:

> Then the sixth angel blew his trumpet, and I heard a voice speaking from the four horns of the gold altar that stands in the presence of God. And the voice said to the sixth angel who held the trumpet, "Release the four angels who are bound at the great Euphrates River." Then the four angels who had been prepared for this hour and day and month and year were turned loose to kill one-third of all the people on earth. I heard the size of their army, which was 200 million mounted troops. (Revelation 9:13-16)

The passage goes on to describe the character of this army and the fact that one-third of the world's population was killed in the resulting military struggle.

Although all of the details are not entirely clear, the most reasonable explanation of this prophecy, related as it is to the great Euphrates River that forms the eastern boundary of the ancient Roman Empire, is that the army comes from the Far East and crosses the Euphrates River in order to participate in the struggle that is going on in the land of Israel. The statement that it is "prepared for this hour and day and month and year were turned loose to kill one-third of all the people on earth" means simply that special angels had been prepared to unleash an army for the day of battle that follows.

The most staggering statistic is the fact that the number of the army is declared to be two hundred million. Never in the history of the human race until now has there been an army of this size. The total number of men under arms in World War II on both sides of the conflict combined was never more than fifty million. Therefore, many have been tempted to spiritualize the number or to regard the army as demonic rather than human. The statistics of two hundred million horsemen must have been especially astounding to the apostle John, for at that time the total world population did not exceed this number.

With the advent of the twenty-first century, an army of two hundred million men from the east becomes increasingly possible. For the first time in history such an army is plausible. If such an army is to be raised up, it would be natural to conclude that it would come from China and possibly India, the great population centers of the world. It's fascinating that China alone claims to have more than two hundred million men and women fit for military service, the figure mentioned in Revelation 9:16.[8]

Although their militia includes the home guard, which under present circumstances would not be thrown into a battle such as the one in Revelation, it at least introduces the possibility that the number should be taken literally. If so, this is an imposing statistic of the power and influence of China in the final world war. The deadly character of the army is revealed in their slaughter of one-third of the world's population, a figure mentioned in Revelation 9:15 and again in Revelation 9:18.

A third biblical reference related to China in the end times is found in the sixth bowl judgment described in Revelation 16:12, which says, "Then the sixth angel poured out his bowl on the great Euphrates River, and it dried up so that the kings from the east could march their armies toward the west without hindrance." Revelation 16:14 (NIV) reveals that this movement is part of a worldwide gathering of "the kings of the whole world" in order that they might participate in "the battle on the great day of God Almighty." According to Revelation 16:16, the geographical focal point of the gathering is Armageddon (Mount Megiddo in northern Israel).

The most simple and suitable explanation for understanding "the kings from the east" (Revelation 16:12) is to take the passage literally. The Euphrates River then becomes the geographic boundary of the ancient Roman Empire. The kings of the east are kings from the east or "of the sun rising"; that is, monarchs who originate in the Far East. The battle that ensues is therefore a genuine military conflict.

The interpretation of Revelation 16:12, if taken literally, provides an important piece of information concerning the final world conflict. According to this verse, the invasion from the east starts by an act of God in drying up the Euphrates River. This miraculous drying up of the Euphrates River permits easy access for the descent of the tremendous army of two hundred million men from China upon the land of Israel. This act of God will allow the army to cross the dry riverbed just as the children of Israel were able to walk on dry land when they reached the Red Sea and the Jordan River.

From the standpoint of Scripture, the Euphrates is one of the important rivers of the world. The first reference is found in Genesis 2:10-14, where it is mentioned as one of the four rivers having its source in the Garden of Eden. The Euphrates River is mentioned a total of nineteen times in the Old Testament and twice in the New Testament. In Genesis 15:18 it is described as the eastern boundary of the land promised to Israel. An army, therefore, that crosses the Euphrates River from the east to the west invades the Promised Land.

The Euphrates River has long been an important geographic barrier, and in the ancient world it was second to none in importance. Its total length is some seventeen hundred miles, and it is the main river of southwestern Asia, dividing the land geographically much as the Mississippi River divides North America. Not only from the standpoint of prophecy, but historically, geographically, and biblically the Euphrates River is the most important in the ancient world. To take the Revelation 16 passage literally makes perfect sense.

It makes sense to interpret the phrase "the kings of the east" literally as well. After all, one could reasonably expect that nations from the Far East would be involved in a world war culminating in the oil-rich Middle East. Thus, identifying the kings of the east with China, and possibly other nations such as India, fits the biblical evidence.

China's Middle East Move

One final question concerning China: Why would China, and possibly other nations such as India, move into Israel in the end times? The Bible never says specifically why the kings of the east make their move, but it appears that China's final great invasion is against the Roman ruler or the Antichrist. As we have already seen, in the end times the Antichrist will establish his headquarters in Babylon right in the middle of the world's great oil producers (Saudi Arabia, Iraq, Iran, and Kuwait).

By strategically positioning himself in this location, the Antichrist will exercise domination over the Middle East and its oil reserves. By controlling this part of the world, he could easily strangle other nations into submission by means of oil blackmail.

With this picture in mind, one can easily imagine what will happen. As the Great Tribulation lurches to its climax, China and other nations east of the Euphrates will tire of the Antichrist's control of the world's oil supply and will decide to make their final move for survival. They will have no other choice. Oil will be the lifeblood of their civilization.

As this advancing horde drives westward, they will capture and destroy Babylon as recorded in Revelation 18. By this act, they will destroy the Antichrist's great city and secure control over the oil supply they desperately covet. By this time the Antichrist will have retreated to Israel, so the great eastern army will advance to Israel for the final showdown of east versus west. The horrific clash of armies comes at Armageddon in northern Israel. During the final act of this drama Christ will interrupt this conflict with His second coming to earth. He will destroy the Antichrist and all the armies gathered at Armageddon (Revelation 19:11-21).

China intends to dominate the world in the twenty-first century. Its rapid economic growth requires more and more oil and inevitably puts it in competition with the West. It is not surprising that the Antichrist's bid to dominate the world from Babylon will inevitably be challenged by the nations east of the Euphrates River. In China, as in other parts of the world, the stage is being set for the final drama in which the kings of the east will fulfill their important role in end-time events.

See how today's headlines relate to this chapter at http://www.prophecyhotline.com.

CHAPTER 12

NATURAL DISASTERS, DISEASE, AND FAMINE REACH EVERYONE

EVENT #11: Billions die in the worst series of disasters in the history of the world.

If you look over behind me, that's a tornado. Yes! A twister in Los Angeles. It's one of many tornadoes that are destroying our city. There's another one! That's the Los Angeles skyline! It's unbelievable! It's huge! I've never seen anything like that.

THE DAY AFTER TOMORROW (2004)

MANY SIGNS TODAY POINT TO imminent, worldwide catastrophe. Even the most casual observers seem to be taking note of the actual and potential disasters the world faces. In one generation mankind has moved from apparent self-sufficiency to a feeling of impotence in the face of mounting world problems. In addition to fears about nuclear arsenals, dirty bombs, terrorists, and increasing pollution, in the twenty-first century natural disasters such as tsunamis, earthquakes, and hurricanes of unparalleled magnitude are occurring with frightening regularity. Add to this the real threat of an imminent, worldwide plague that could wipe out millions. It is easy to imagine how terrible disasters could accelerate in frequency and converge on the globe at the same time. People everywhere are wondering if these events could be signs of the times. Does the Bible have anything to say about natural disasters and deadly plagues in the end times?

HURRICANES, TSUNAMIS, AND EARTHQUAKES

Even people with little or no interest in Bible prophecy are suddenly wondering if all the natural disasters in the world signal that we are getting near "closing time." On December 26, 2004, Asia experienced an unparalleled tsunami, the worst natural disaster in recorded human history. The catastrophe left at least 200,000 dead and millions homeless. Then only a few months later in August 2005, the U.S. Gulf Coast was ravaged by Hurricane Katrina, the worst natural disaster in U.S. history, which wiped out a major American city. Katrina was followed quickly by Hurricane Rita, which also wreaked havoc along the Gulf Coast.

On October 8, 2005, a 7.6 magnitude earthquake—the same intensity as the 1906 San Francisco earthquake—rattled Pakistan, killing about 75,000 and injuring over 100,000. The tremor left 3.3 million people homeless and directly affected the lives of four million people.

Jesus Himself predicted that this present age would be marked by upheavals in nature and terrible plagues (Matthew 24:7; Luke 21:11). These are general signs, which mark the entire course of the present age between the two comings of Christ. However, like birth pangs, they will relentlessly grow in intensity and frequency in wave after wave of crippling contractions, indicating that the end of the age is approaching (Matthew 24:8; 1 Thessalonians 5:3).

What we are witnessing today gives a frightening preview of what's coming during the end times when these disasters intensify and go global.

PANDEMIC SUPERFLU

The recent spate of new diseases is nothing short of alarming. There have been so many new diseases emerging, it's difficult to keep up with them all. There's Ebola, West Nile virus, Lyme disease, mad cow disease, SARS, and Asia's newest threat—bird flu. The human death toll from the Asia bird flu is still not significant, but U.N. officials warn that the outbreak is far from over. The disease has killed people in nine countries, including Azerbaijan, Cambodia, Indonesia, China, Vietnam, and Thailand. But it is being battled in Japan, Laos, Pakistan, South Korea, Malaysia, and Russia. The specific strain of bird flu in Taiwan and Pakistan is different from the one in the other countries.

All of these new diseases come on the heels of the AIDS virus, one of the most destructive plagues the world has ever seen. Over 25 million people have died of AIDS since 1981, and 3.1 million died in 2005 alone. And just think, in the 1970s scientists believed they had basically conquered these kinds of diseases. The sudden and continuing outbreak of new diseases is astounding.

Jesus warned that worldwide plagues would portend His return to planet earth. In Luke 21:11 Jesus said, "There will be great earthquakes, and there will be famines and plagues in many lands, and there will be terrifying things and great miraculous signs from heaven."

There are growing concerns that a flu virus similar to the 1918 virus will move from birds to the human population and cause cataclysmic destruction. In the article "Flu Hope, or Horror?" editorialist Charles Krauthammer reports that the 1918 Spanish flu virus that caused a horrible pandemic was recreated by scientists recently. This virus was a bird flu. Krauthammer notes that "when the re-created virus was given to mice in heavily quarantined laboratories in Atlanta it killed the mice more quickly than any other flu virus ever tested."[1]

National Geographic's October 2005 cover article was titled "The Next Killer Flu: Can We Stop It?" It predicts, "Sooner or later a deadly virus that can jump from birds to people will sweep the globe." The article adds that the world is overdue for a flu pandemic. A new flu virus

161

spread throughout the world's population three times in the twentieth century.

In 1918–1919 the "Spanish" flu killed an estimated 50 to 100 million people. *National Geographic* says that the virus "swept the globe in 1918 and early 1919. Except for a few Pacific Islanders, everyone on Earth was exposed to the disease, and half got sick."[2] Just think about that. Everyone on the earth was exposed to the disease. And that was long before jet air travel and the age of globalism. Second, the Asian flu, a mixture of bird and human viruses originating in southern China, killed one million people in 1957. Finally, the Hong Kong flu (also a mixture of bird and human viruses that killed about 750,000 people) struck in 1968.

What will happen in the twenty-first century? The article says that the H5N1 virus that is killing poultry and a few people in Asia could be the next global pandemic if it gains the ability to quickly spread from person to person. Incredibly, it is estimated that deaths from such a widespread pandemic could range from a conservative "7.4 million to an apocalyptic 180 million to 360 million." Yes, you read it correctly—180 to 360 *million*.

According to experts a virus today would move twice as fast as the earlier major flu outbreaks due to rapid means of travel. This quick spread of the virus would severely limit the ability of officials to halt its transmission with a vaccine. Even during the pandemic in 1968 that lasted 342 days, the flu moved more slowly.

The world is ripe for the kind of global scourge predicted in the Bible for the end times. Jesus forecasted sweeping plagues that would wreak havoc all over the world during the last days (Luke 21:11). The apostle John predicted that the fourth seal judgment, which will include plagues or pestilence along with other disasters, will wipe out 25 percent of the world's population. "Its rider was named Death, and his companion was the Grave. These two were given authority over one-fourth of the earth, to kill with the sword and famine and disease and wild animals" (Revelation 6:8).

No one can say for sure that any plagues or pandemics we currently see on the horizon are the ones predicted by Jesus or John. But we can say that globalism, rapid means of travel, and dense urban populations have paved the way for this kind of devastation to sweep the globe, leaving carnage in its wake.

FAMINE AND STARVATION

Another massive problem is starvation. Famine and starvation are caused by several factors: overpopulation, flawed domestic policies or institutional failure, and war. One of the obvious causes of famine in our world is overpopulation or overconcentration of people in certain areas.

Overpopulation is becoming a real problem, especially as people become more and more concentrated in urban settings. Consider the statistics on the exploding world population in the chart below:

World Population Growth

ESTIMATE	YEAR
1 billion	1804
2 billion	1927
3 billion	1959
4 billion	1974
5 billion	1986
6 billion	October 12, 1999

From 1900 to 2000 world population increased from 1.6 billion to 6.1 billion. World population in 2006 is estimated at about 6.6 billion.

Population growth in the United States and Western Europe has tended to slow in recent years, but in other portions of the world the population explosion continues. The world population increases at the dizzying rate of about eighty million people every year. Additionally, cities in urban areas gain about sixty million people every year. Social planners have warned that unless drastic changes are made in the birth rate, the need for food alone could cause a worldwide catastrophe in the next decade. It is only a matter of time before the number of people in the world exceeds the capacity of world food production and distribution. This will result in the starvation of millions of people.

The world food crisis greatly accelerated during the economic problems of the 1970s. In the 1980s the food crisis continued in various parts of the world, with millions of people dying of starvation. The energy problems of the Third World have contributed to the situation. The high cost of oil has reduced the supply of petroleum-based fertilizers and has made them too expensive for most underdeveloped countries. Droughts, storms, floods, and changes in climate have ravaged crops around the world as well.

Another real problem is that economic, structural, and political upheaval creates distribution problems so that even in places where crops normally would have been sufficient to feed the population, they were not available to meet people's needs. As natural disasters, civil war, and terrorism increase, the institutional structures to combat famine will be severely curtailed. Tensions will increase between the nations who have food and those that struggle with hunger. All the attendant ills of pestilence and disease present insuperable problems for the coming generation in underdeveloped countries.

CHRIST'S PROPHECY OF THE GREAT TRIBULATION

The Olivet discourse (Matthew 24–25) was Christ's answer to the disciples' question concerning the end of the age and described this same period. The Lord Jesus spared no words in describing the awfulness of the period. According to Matthew 24:15 (NIV), it will begin with "'the abomination that causes desolation,' spoken of through the prophet Daniel"; that is, the desecration of the Temple that Israel will build in the last days and the stopping of the renewed Jewish sacrifices and ceremonies. This will signal the beginning of the awful period.

Christ advised those in Judea at that time to flee to the mountains (Matthew 24:16). He advised them not to return to their houses to gather up anything, but to flee with utmost speed. It will be a time of great trial and trouble for those with small children. He instructed them to pray that their flight would not be in the winter, when the cold weather would make it more difficult, nor on the Sabbath, when Jews normally do not journey and their detection would be easier.

Christ concluded in Matthew 24:21-22 (NIV): "For then there will be great distress, unequaled from the beginning of the world until now—and never to be equaled again. If those days had not been cut short, no one would survive, but for the sake of the elect those days will be shortened." Here the same terminology is used as in Daniel 12:1, where the period is called "a time of distress such as has not happened from the beginning of nations until then" (NIV). Like Jeremiah and Daniel, Jesus calls that period unprecedented—there has never been a time like it in the history of the world, and there never will be another time like it.

Christ describes the days of tribulation as being so severe that if they were not "cut short," meaning "cut off" or "terminated," by His second coming, no one would survive the awfulness of the period, and all would perish. It is "for the sake of the elect" that Christ will come to terminate this period after three and a half years and deliver those who have put their trust in Him. By "the elect" He may have meant Israel as the chosen people, or both Jews and Gentiles who come to Christ in salvation during this awful period. They are the chosen ones, chosen for deliverance at the end of the period, and they will be delivered.

According to Romans 11:26: "And so all Israel will be saved. As the Scriptures say, 'The one who rescues will come from Jerusalem, and he will turn Israel away from ungodliness.'" Israel as a nation will be delivered from her persecutors, and although subject to searching judgment as described in Ezekiel 20:34-38, those who are judged worthy will enter into the blessedness of the millennial kingdom. Those survivors who will have turned to God during the Great Tribulation will become the parents and grandparents of new generations that will populate the earth during Christ's reign on earth. A similar judgment for Gentiles is described in Matthew 25:31-46, where the sheep are ushered into the Kingdom and the goats, representing the unsaved, are put to death. During the last three and a half years of the tribulation period, in spite of terrible disasters and persecution, God will miraculously provide for the survival of His people.

DETAILS IN THE BOOK OF REVELATION

The most detailed description of the Great Tribulation is found in the book of Revelation, beginning in chapter 6 and continuing throughout much of the book. In chapter 16 an unparalleled account is given of the terrible catastrophes and destruction of human life that will occur at the end of the period of chaos. The overall sequence of events in the period is described as the breaking of seven seals. As recorded in Revelation 4 and 5, in his vision of heaven John sees a scroll sealed on its edges with seven seals. When the scroll is unrolled, the first seal is broken, then the second, and in succession, all the seals through the seventh. These introduce events and situations that describe this general period.

In Revelation 6–19, there are seven seal judgments (Revelation 6–8), seven trumpet judgments (Revelation 8–9), and seven bowl judgments (Revelation 15–16). These series of judgments will be poured out successively during the Tribulation and will bring terrible disaster to everyone.

Seven Seals of Horror

The first seal portrays a terrible and satanic world government that will rule during the period of the Great Tribulation. This is described in more detail in Revelation 13. The second seal describes war, for the greatest war of all history will occur near the close of the period. The third describes famine, the result of both war and the catastrophes that will overtake the earth. The fourth seal describes death, for one-fourth of the world's population will be killed by war, hunger, disease, or wild animals.

Isn't it interesting that many of the new killer viruses that threaten to wipe out millions originate in animals or "the wild beasts of the earth"? A group of international scientists have concluded that the HIV virus that causes AIDS can be traced to African monkeys. The deadly Ebola virus, found in humans and primates, may be carried by fruit bats. The Nipah virus in Malaysia killed over one hundred people when it jumped from pigs to humans. So far, it has not jumped from human to human, but if it did, the death toll could be unimaginable. And the deadly bird flu that threatens a world pandemic comes from various kinds of birds. These may be the kinds of deadly diseases that wipe out billions.

The fifth seal reveals the extensive persecution of the period, for many who put their trust in Christ will seal their testimony with their own blood. The sixth seal describes the coming ecological nightmare. Stars will fall from heaven, and there will be disturbances in the seasons and cycles of nature. The sun will become black, and the moon will become as blood through the haze of destruction. Great earthquakes will move across the earth. Revelation 6 summarizes the entire period as a time when "the wrath of the Lamb" will be poured out on the earth—a time of divine judgment (Revelation 6:16).

Seven Seal Judgments

First Seal (Revelation 6:1-2)	White Horse: Antichrist
Second Seal (Revelation 6:3-4)	Red Horse: War
Third Seal (Revelation 6:5-6)	Black Horse: Famine
Fourth Seal (Revelation 6:7-8)	Pale Horse: Death and Hell
Fifth Seal (Revelation 6:9-11)	Martyrs in Heaven
Sixth Seal (Revelation 6:12-17)	Universal Upheaval and Devastation
Seventh Seal (Revelation 8:1-2)	The Seven Trumpets

Seven Trumpets of Disaster

The seven seals, however, are only the introduction—the general description of the period. When the apostle John sees the seventh seal on the scroll opened, the seven angels who stand before God are given seven trumpets that depict specific catastrophes, many of which will destroy large portions of the earth. Great disturbances will affect nature and change climates. A third part of the earth will be consumed by fire—either by a direct act of God or by God's use of other means, such as nuclear disaster or a disturbance of the earth's orbit around the sun. A third part of the sea will become as blood, and a third part of sea life will be destroyed. As the trumpets continue to sound, one catastrophe after another will afflict the earth. Demon possession will be common, as described in Revelation 9, and the torment of those afflicted with demons will be like the torment of one bitten by a scorpion.

The sixth trumpet signals the advance of a great army from Asia numbering two hundred million (Revelation 9:16). This will be a massive movement of men across the continent, probably led by China (see chapter 11). As startling as its size, so, too, will be its power to kill men. It will "kill one-third of all the people on earth" (Revelation 9:15). This apparently will be a human slaughter in addition to that mentioned in Revelation 6:8. The book of Revelation makes very clear that the combined catastrophes of this period will destroy more than half of the world's population.

Seven Last Bowls of Wrath

With the sounding of the seventh trumpet, a new series of catastrophes is revealed, as recorded in Revelation 16. These are the vials or

Seven Trumpet Judgments

First Trumpet (Revelation 8:7)	Bloody Hail and Fire: One-Third of Vegetation Destroyed
Second Trumpet (Revelation 8:8-9)	Fireball from Heaven: One-Third of Oceans Polluted
Third Trumpet (Revelation 8:10-11)	Falling Star: One-Third of Fresh Water Polluted
Fourth Trumpet (Revelation 8:12)	Darkness: One-Third of Sun, Moon, and Stars Darkened
Fifth Trumpet (Revelation 9:1-12)	Demonic Invasion: Possession and Torment
Sixth Trumpet (Revelation 9:13-21)	Two-Hundred-Million-Man Army: One-Third of Mankind Killed
Seventh Trumpet (Revelation 11:15-19)	The Kingdom: The Announcement of Christ's Reign

the bowls of the wrath of God. The symbolism is of a full bowl containing a judgment from God that will be poured out on the earth. As these successive bowls are poured out, great catastrophes will afflict the earth. Men's bodies will be covered with sores and afflicted with terrible pain; all life in the sea will die; the rivers and fountains of water will become as blood; unnatural heat will scorch the earth as the heavens are disturbed in their normal course. The sun will eventually be blackened, resulting in increasing darkness, changes in climate, and destruction of plant life.

The disasters poured out from the bowls of wrath are clearly described as the result of God's direct judgment. These judgments can be interpreted as supernatural acts of God, but some could also be interpreted as the consequences of a nuclear war that God allows. Nuclear war would cause tremendous loss of life, disturbance of the earth's orbit, and disruption of nature's cycles. The cumulative effects of nuclear war would cause human suffering from painful radiation burns and poisoning of water and food by radiation. Even a limited nuclear exchange could precipitate a series of earthquakes and geological activity that would continue a chain of destruction throughout the world.

Unusual demon activity will follow the pouring out of the sixth vial, which will dry up the Euphrates River and will further prepare the way for the great army from the East headed for Armageddon. The final judgment, described as the seventh bowl of the wrath of God, will occur during World War III, as the armies of the earth converge on the Middle East for the final desperate Battle of Armageddon. The entire earth will literally be shaken, its great cities will be destroyed, and the contour of the earth will be changed. Islands will disappear; mountains will be leveled.

This will be the final hour of divine judgment on a world that has rejected the Messiah and refused to let Christ reign over it. This war and series of plagues will leave a wake of almost unbelievable destruction of human life and property. It will be exactly what Christ

Seven Bowl Judgments

First Bowl (Revelation 16:2)	Upon the Earth: Sores on the Worshippers of the Antichrist
Second Bowl (Revelation 16:3)	Upon the Seas: Turned to Blood
Third Bowl (Revelation 16:4-7)	Upon the Fresh Water: Turned to Blood
Fourth Bowl (Revelation 16:8-9)	Upon the Sun: Intense, Scorching Heat
Fifth Bowl (Revelation 16:10-11)	Upon the Antichrist's Kingdom: Darkness and Pain
Sixth Bowl (Revelation 16:12-16)	Upon the River Euphrates: Preparation for Armageddon
Seventh Bowl (Revelation 16:17-21)	Upon the Air: Earthquakes and Hail

predicted—a time of trouble so great that if it were not terminated by His own second coming to the earth, no human life would survive. But this time of trouble will only be the background for God's final dealings with men. It will set the stage for the Battle of Armageddon and the judgments that will come when Jesus Christ returns.

 See how today's headlines relate to this chapter at *http://www.prophecyhotline.com.*

CHAPTER 13

THE LAST SUICIDAL BATTLE OF WORLD WAR III

EVENT #12: The armies of the world clash in the huge Valley of Meggido (Armageddon) in the final battle of World War III that begins just before the return of Jesus to planet earth.

I turn back to your prophets in the Old Testament and the signs foretelling Armageddon, and I find myself wondering if we are the generation that is going to see that come about. I don't know if you have noted any of those prophecies lately, but, believe me, they describe the times we are going through.

PRESIDENT RONALD REAGAN (1983)

There is no doubt that global events are preparing the way for the final war of history—the great Armageddon!

BILLY GRAHAM, *TILL ARMAGEDDON*

PEOPLE EVERYWHERE SEEM TO HAVE a sense that the world is moving rapidly toward some great crisis, possibly even a great finale. I'm sure you've felt this way yourself sometimes in light of all the danger, uncertainty, and instability the world faces. Statistics bear this out.

Here's a brief sample of what Americans believe about the book of Revelation and the end times.

> 59 percent believe that the prophecies in Revelation are going to come true.
>
> Nearly 25 percent believe that the Bible predicted the September 11 attack.
>
> 35 percent are paying more attention to how news events might relate to the end of the world.
>
> 17 percent believe the end of the world will happen in their lifetime.[1]

It seems clear that the collective sense of angst about our world and where it's headed is building. We all wonder how much longer until the lid blows off.

THE BLUEPRINT OF WORLD WAR III

Students of the Bible realize that prophecy provides a blueprint of the steps that will lead up to the final Great War, or what we might call World War III. It all begins with the rise of the final world ruler.

Proclamation of a New World Government

Ironically, the Antichrist will commence his world government by proclamation. Using his consolidated position of power in the Middle East, he will promise a new day of peace and prosperity for all who recognize his leadership. His message will be carried by television, radio, and Internet to the entire world in one day. The brilliant leader who enforced peace in the Middle East will seem to be the answer for a troubled world. His promise is a world government that will end all conflicts and bring plenty to the earth.

This man's absolute control of the world will give him power such as no man has ever had in human history. His brilliance as a leader will be superhuman, for he will be dominated and directed by Satan himself. But during his three-and-a-half-year rule, he will ruthlessly crush all opposition. His true character is indicated by the titles given to him in Scripture. He is described as "the beast" (Revelation 13:1-4), and Satan is described in his true character as "the great dragon" (Revelation 12:9; 13:4). This period of world history will be the culmination of Satan's dream to be like God, to control the world, to be the object of worship and adoration, and to secure the absolute obedience of all men.

The Rush to Judgment

The new world dictator's blasphemy, disregard of God, hatred of the people of God, and murder of countless believers in Christ will bring down the terrible divine judgments described in Revelation 6–18. Catastrophe after catastrophe will follow as the Great Tribulation unfolds.

The world will become increasingly discontented with the leadership of this world dictator who promised to bring them peace and plenty but instead brings the world one massive catastrophe after another. The wonders and miracles he will perform and his demands to be worshipped as God will only lead to the need for more oppression and persecution of dissenters. In spite of the tremendous power placed in the hands of the world dictator, he will be unable to control the situation. Major segments of the world will begin to rebel against him. Eventually they will converge in the Middle East to fight it out for international power.

The Outbreak of World War III

The prophet Daniel gave a graphic picture of this situation. After introducing the world ruler in Daniel 11:36-39 as an absolute ruler who will claim to be God, the prophet explained that the armies of the world will rise up in rebellion against him. According to Daniel 11:40, "Then at the time of the end, the king of the south will attack the king of the north. The king of the north will storm out with chariots, charioteers, and a vast navy. He will invade various lands and sweep through them like a flood."

Revolt from the South and North

Daniel's prophecy also described a great army from Africa, including not only Egypt but other countries of that continent. This army, probably numbering in the millions, will attack the Middle East from the south. At the same time Russia and the other armies to the north will mobilize another powerful military force to descend on the Holy Land and challenge the world dictator. Although Russia will have had a severe setback about four years earlier in the prophetic sequence of events, she apparently will have been able to recoup her losses enough to put another army in the field. The first battles of World War III will be confused as the armies move back and forth with varied success and failures. Apparently the world ruler will be able to crush some of the first attempts at revolt and gain some preliminary victories, especially in the south, and he will be able to drive back the invasion from Egypt and Africa.

China Makes Her Move

But even as the world dictator appears to gain control of the situation, a report will come of the advancing army from the east (Daniel 11:44). To contend with this advancing horde of two hundred million (Revelation 9:16), he will be forced to divert a major portion of his military strength to defend himself. Then further tidings will come of another army advancing from the north. At this point the greatest war of all history, involving hundreds of millions of people, will be set in motion, with the land of Israel as the major battleground. But this will be more than just another world war, for it will play a special role in preparing the world for the next series of prophetic events.

Satan's Battle Plan

According to Revelation 16:13-14, the armies of the world will gather by demonic influence. The world ruler, who was established and aided

174

in his control of the entire world by the power of Satan, now will be attacked by armies that have been inspired to come to battle by demons sent forth from Satan.

In Revelation 16:13-14 (NIV), John writes: "Then I saw three evil spirits that looked like frogs; they came out of the mouth of the dragon, out of the mouth of the beast and out of the mouth of the false prophet. They are spirits of demons performing miraculous signs, and they go out to the kings of the whole world, to gather them for the battle on the great day of God Almighty." The unclean spirits, symbolized by frogs, represent demons who are Satan's messengers. They proceed out of the mouth of the dragon, the beast, and the false prophet—the evil trinity that is controlling the world.

The Satanic Trinity

Satan's program is always one of substitution. As Christians in their faith have a triune God—the Father, the Son, and the Holy Spirit—so the forces of evil will represent themselves as triune, with the dragon, or Satan, corresponding to God the Father; the beast corresponding to Christ as the King of kings and Lord of lords; and the false prophet corresponding to the Holy Spirit. Just as the task of the Holy Spirit is to cause all men to worship Christ and the Father, so the false prophet will cause men to worship the beast and the dragon. Proceeding from this evil trinity, the demons will go forth, supporting their work with satanic miracles. This demonic sorcery will deceive the kings of the earth into joining the world rebellion with the prospect of gaining world power.

The Battle of the Great Day of God

According to Scripture, the demons will "gather them for battle against the Lord on that great judgment day of God the Almighty" (Revelation 16:14, NIV). Why will Satan organize a world war to disrupt his world kingdom? Satan's desperate strategy will be much more important than his control of the world through the world dictator. Although from their point of view they are gathered to fight it out for world power, the armies of the world will actually be assembled by Satan in anticipation of the second coming of Christ. The entire armed might of the world will be assembled in the Middle East, ready to contend with the power of Christ as He returns from heaven. As subsequent events make clear, the movement will be completely futile and hopeless. The armies of the world are by no means equipped to fight the armies of heaven. Still Satan will assemble the nations for this final hour, and in fact, the nations will choose to side with Satan and oppose the second coming of Christ. It will be the best that Satan can do. These events will give the nations their choice and allow Satan his desperate bid to oppose Christ's second coming.

Armageddon

The world's armies will confront each other, gathered "to a place with the Hebrew name *Armageddon*" (Revelation 16:16). Armageddon is the Hebrew expression formed from the word *har*, meaning "mountain," and *Megiddo*, referring to a location in northern Israel. Mount Megiddo is a small mountain located near the Mediterranean Sea, overlooking a valley that stretches out to the east. This broad valley, some fourteen miles wide and twenty miles long, apparently will be the focal point for the marshaling of the armies for the final battle of World War III. Although much too small to contain the millions of men who will be involved, it will be the geographic focal point of the final world war and catastrophe popularly referred to as the Battle of Armageddon. Actually, the armies will be deployed for several hundred miles in every possible direction—north, south, and east.

As the armies of the world move toward the final Battle of Armageddon, the world war that has erupted will have already claimed millions of casualties. Scripture gives only a meager description of the major movements and battles involved. As the armies converge on the Valley of Armageddon, the world will be shaken by the last divine judgment of the series, described as the seventh bowl of wrath.

The apostle John explained the scene in these words:

And the demonic spirits gathered all the rulers and their armies to a place with the Hebrew name Armageddon. *Then the seventh angel poured out his bowl into the air. And a mighty shout came from the throne in the Temple, saying, "It is finished!" Then the thunder crashed and rolled, and lightning flashed. And a great earthquake struck—the worst since people were placed on the earth. The great city of Babylon split into three sections, and the cities of many nations fell into heaps of rubble. So God remembered all of Babylon's sins, and he made her drink the cup that was filled with the wine of his fierce wrath. And every island disappeared, and all the mountains were leveled. There was a terrible hailstorm, and hailstones weighing seventy-five pounds fell from the sky onto the people below. They cursed God because of the terrible plague of the hailstorm. (Revelation 16:16-21)*

To Curse God and Die

The armies of the world will be used as Satan's pawns for this final hour of victory. The revolt against the world dictator will cause the nations to assemble in the Middle East. The crescendo of wars and destruction will increase until the entire world is on the brink of oblivion. Rather than humble themselves, the leaders of the world will be ready to curse God and die (Revelation 16:9, 11, 21). The final showdown between God and the nations will be ready to occur.

The prophets revealed that all these events will be the preparation for the great climax of history in the second coming of Christ, the establishment of His Kingdom on earth, and the judgment of wicked men who would not have Christ reign over them.

The Rider on the White Horse:
From Manger to Power and Glory

In His first coming to earth, Jesus Christ was born in a stable, relatively unnoticed by the world. Announced by John the Baptist, He came as the servant and Savior described by the Old Testament prophets (Isaiah 42:1-4; 53:1-12). He lived in a time of comparative peace when the Roman Empire controlled Israel. He was tried and convicted in

Jerusalem. At the request of the Jewish leaders, He was nailed to a cross by Roman soldiers. Israel rejected the suffering Messiah who came as a servant. After His resurrection and appearance to many, He ascended into heaven from the Mount of Olives near Jerusalem.

The second coming of Jesus Christ to the earth will be no quiet manger scene. It will be the most dramatic and shattering event in the entire history of the universe. His coming in power and glory will seize the attention of the entire world. The revived Roman Empire will have expanded to a world empire with the world dictator's proclamation forty-two months earlier. After about three years the world empire will be torn by rebellion, resulting in a terrible world war, described in Daniel 11:40-45; Revelation 16:14-16; and Revelation 19:11-21. Millions of people will already have been killed in the previous fighting and disasters. Great armies from the north, south, and east will have reached the Middle East, with major contingents gathered in the Valley of Armageddon. Jerusalem, formerly a key city of the world dictator's rule, will be under attack, with house-to-house fighting (Zechariah 14:2). The entire world will then be stopped in awe by the final convulsive shaking of the earth (the last bowl of wrath, Revelation 16:17-21) and the dazzling appearance of the Son of Man descending from heaven with all His saints (Revelation 19:11-16).

In the New Testament the doctrine of the Second Coming is one of the major revelations of prophetic truth. It is estimated that one out of every twenty-five verses in the New Testament refers either to the Rapture of the church or Christ's second coming to set up His Kingdom. Christ Himself described His coming graphically as a glorious event, comparable to lightning coming out of the east and shining to the west (Matthew 24:27). He described His coming as the climax to the Tribulation:

> *Immediately after the anguish of those days, the sun will be darkened, the moon will give no light, the stars will fall from the sky, and the powers in the heavens will be shaken. And then at last, the sign that the Son of Man is*

coming will appear in the heavens, and there will be deep mourning among all the peoples of the earth. And they will see the Son of Man coming on the clouds of heaven with power and great glory. (Matthew 24:29-30)

Many other references to this event are found in the Gospels (Matthew 19:28; 23:39; Mark 13:24-37; Luke 12:35-48; 17:22-37; 18:8; 21:25-28).

Even on the occasion of Christ's departure from earth, the angels reaffirmed the doctrine of the Second Coming, addressing the disciples: "Men of Galilee, . . . why are you standing here staring into heaven? Jesus has been taken from you into heaven, but someday, he will return from heaven in the same way you saw him go!" (Acts 1:11). There are many other references to this event throughout the remainder of the New Testament (see Acts 15:16-18; Romans 11:25-27; 1 Corinthians 11:26; 2 Thessalonians 1:7-10; 2 Peter 3:3-4; Jude 1:14-15).

An Awesome Spectacle

The most detailed description of the Second Coming is found in the book of Revelation itself, which was named for the fact that Christ will reveal Himself to an awestruck world at His second coming. Revelation 1:7 states: "Look! He comes with the clouds of heaven. And everyone will see him—even those who pierced him. And all the nations of the world will mourn for him. Yes! Amen!"

The most graphic picture of all, however, is found in Revelation 19:11-21. As a climax to the Battle of Armageddon, the heavens will break open with the glory of God, fulfilling the prediction of Christ that His coming will be like the lightning shining from the east to the west. As revealed in other Scriptures, the heavens will have been darkened by earlier judgments from God (Matthew 24:29), but at that moment an unearthly, brilliant light will spread itself across the heavens, startling the entire earth.

As contending armies pause in their conflict, the heavens will open, and Christ will begin the majestic procession from heaven to earth. The words of this prophecy are the most dramatic to be found anywhere in world literature.

> *Then I saw heaven opened, and a white horse was standing there. Its rider was named Faithful and True, for he judges fairly and wages a righteous war. His eyes were like flames of fire, and on his head were many crowns. A name was written on him that no one understood except himself. He wore a robe dipped in blood, and his title was the Word of God. The armies of heaven, dressed in the finest of pure white linen, followed him on white horses. From his mouth came a sharp sword to strike down the nations. He will rule them with an iron rod. He will release the fierce wrath of God, the Almighty, like juice flowing from a winepress. On his robe at his thigh was written this title: King of all kings and Lord of all lords. (Revelation 19:11-16)*

This spectacle will certainly be an awesome one—millions of men and angels reflecting the glory of God and led by Christ astride a white horse, the symbol of a conqueror.

The world will first cringe in fear before this spectacle, but then the armies on both sides of the great world war will forget their differences and attempt to unite and fight the armies from heaven. This rebellion, inspired and organized by Satan (Revelation 16:13-14), will be a futile, suicidal effort to resist God. Revelation 19:15 describes the judgment that follows.

The sharp sword that goes out of the mouth of Christ is apparently a symbolic revelation of the command that will be issued. All the wicked hosts will be destroyed. The verses that follow reveal that the birds of the air will be invited to feast upon the flesh of the kings, mighty men, and horses slain in this great and catastrophic judgment (Revelation 19:17-18). The beast—that is, the world ruler—and the false prophet associated with him will be captured alive. According to Revelation 19:20, these two will be cast directly into a "fiery lake of burning sulfur."

The prophet Zechariah gives additional insight into the events related to the Battle of Armageddon. On the very day of the second coming of

Christ there will be house-to-house fighting in Jerusalem (Zechariah 14:2). The prophet also describes the dramatic geological upheaval that will occur when Christ finally sets foot on the Mount of Olives.

> *I will gather all the nations to fight against Jerusalem. The city will be taken, the houses looted, and the women raped. Half the population will be taken into captivity, and the rest will be left among the ruins of the city. Then the LORD will go out to fight against those nations, as he has fought in times past. On that day his feet will stand on the Mount of Olives, east of Jerusalem. And the Mount of Olives will split apart, making a wide valley running from east to west. Half the mountain will move toward the north and half toward the south. (Zechariah 14:2-4)*

The second coming of Christ will bring an abrupt halt to the final world war and the wave of destruction that will have almost destroyed the earth. His coming will also end the period of the Gentiles, during which Gentile nations determined the destiny of Jerusalem and oppressed the people of Israel.

CHRIST'S TRIUMPHANT RETURN

A complete understanding of the characteristics and background of Christ's second coming is crucial for every student of prophecy. The descriptions given in Scripture allow a sharp contrast to be made between Christ's second coming to earth and His earlier Rapture of the church. They allow us to make the following observations about His return. It will be:

A personal return. The second coming of Christ will be a personal return. The same Jesus Christ who was born of a virgin, who died on the cross, who rose again, and who ascended into heaven will soon come back bodily to the earthly sphere to exert His power and sovereignty in the world. It is quite clear that it will be a bodily return, not merely the spiritual presence of Christ. Zechariah 14:4 refers to the fact that "on that day his feet will stand on the Mount of Olives, east of Jerusalem." As the feet of Christ left the Mount of Olives in His ascension, so they will return, this time to demonstrate His omnipotent power.

A visible and glorious return. The return of Christ will be a visible and glorious return. According to Scripture, everyone will see Him (Matthew 24:30; Revelation 1:7). The second coming of Christ will not take place in a moment, as is true of the Rapture of the church. Christ's return will be a spectacular and majestic procession from heaven to earth that will take many hours. During this period, the movement of the procession and the earth's continued rotation will permit the entire world to witness the event. The ultimate destination of the procession will be to Israel, leading to the destruction of the armies assembled for the Battle of Armageddon and Christ's final descent to Mount Zion.

A return with the heavenly host. According to Scripture, a huge body of heavenly hosts, described as the armies of heaven, will accompany Christ in His second coming (Jude 1:14). Believers who were raptured at the beginning of the tribulation period, who are in heaven with the Lord as promised in John 14:1-4, will return to the earth as part of this vast company. Angels also will join Christ in this great procession from heaven to earth (Matthew 25:31).

A return that shakes the earth. After the armies of the world are already gathered for battle at Armageddon, the final bowl of wrath, described in Revelation 16:17-21, will be poured out, resulting in flashes of lightning, thunder, rumblings, and a severe earthquake. Cities will collapse, islands sink, and mountains disappear. Huge hailstones, each weighing seventy-five pounds, will fall from heaven. Then, after His procession from heaven and His destruction of the opposing armies, Christ's feet will touch the Mount of Olives outside Jerusalem. At that moment the mountain will be divided, and where the Mount of Olives stands today, a great valley will stretch out into the Jordan Valley below. This is only one of the tremendous changes that will take place in the topography of the Holy Land as a precursor to Christ's reign. Christ's second coming will drastically change the geography of the earth.

A return to judge the nations. In showing the majestic sovereignty of God in human history, the second Psalm gave this description of the world situation at the second coming of Christ: "The kings of the earth prepare for battle; the rulers plot together against the LORD and against his anointed one. 'Let us break their chains,' they cry, 'and free ourselves from slavery to God'" (Psalm 2:2-3).

The rebellion of the nations will draw a derisive laugh from the Lord. "But the one who rules in heaven laughs. The Lord scoffs at them. Then in anger he rebukes them, terrifying them with his fierce fury" (Psalm 2:4-5). Prophets throughout the Old Testament have pointed to a time when God will speak forth in righteous judgment on the earth. His final purpose is revealed in Psalm 2:6: "I have placed my chosen king on the throne in Jerusalem, on my holy mountain." At His second coming, Christ will claim possession of the nations as His inheritance. His judgments will be absolute, for as the psalmist predicted: "You will break them with an iron rod and smash them like clay pots" (Psalm 2:9). In light of this predicted judgment and the return of Christ, those who heard were instructed to serve the Lord and worship Him (Psalm 2:10-12). God promised to send His Son at the appointed time to reign over the earth and to begin His absolute rule of peace and justice. And so it will be that the rulers and their armies who resist Christ's return will be killed in a mass carnage. The rebels who are killed in the Battle of Armageddon will remain in their common grave until the final resurrection and judgment at the end of the thousand-year reign of Christ (Revelation 19:17-21).

A return to rule from Zion. The purpose of Christ's return to the Mount of Olives will be to establish Jerusalem as the capital of His new world kingdom. The law will once more go forth from Zion (Isaiah 2:3). Christ's return will save Jerusalem and the nation of Israel from complete annihilation. This direct intervention of God in saving Israel and returning Jews from all nations was predicted as early as the promise recorded in Deuteronomy 30:3: "Then the LORD your God will restore your fortunes. He will have mercy on you and gather you back from all the nations where he has scattered you."

Christ Coming to Judge and Rule

A multitude of Old Testament passages develop the same theme of a final kingdom of justice, righteousness, and peace to be established in Jerusalem. In Psalm 24 the gates of Jerusalem are urged to open and welcome the coming King. Psalm 72, in the form of a prayer, describes the reign of the coming King and the blessing and peace that will follow. In this final kingdom all kings will bow down before Him and the nations will serve Him (Psalm 72:11). Psalm 96 declares that His coming will be for judgment: "For he is coming! He is coming to judge the earth" (Psalm 96:13). Psalm 110 predicts that at the coming of Christ His enemies will be made His footstool, and He will reign in the midst of His enemies. It will be a time when Christ "will punish the nations and fill their lands with corpses; he will shatter heads over the whole earth" (Psalm 110:6).

The Major and Minor Prophets also address Christ's second coming. According to Isaiah 9:6, the child to be born will be the Mighty God and the Prince of Peace. When He comes, "His government and its peace will never end. He will rule with fairness and justice from the throne of his ancestor David for all eternity. The passionate commitment of the LORD of Heaven's Armies will make this happen!" (Isaiah 9:7). The entire eleventh chapter of Isaiah describes the coming of Christ and His judgment and righteous rule of the earth. Many other passages give a glowing description of the glorious kingdom of Christ on earth.

The Second Coming itself is pictured in Daniel 7:13-14: "As my vision continued that night, I saw someone like a son of man coming with the clouds of heaven. He approached the Ancient One and was led into his presence. He was given authority, honor, and sovereignty over all the nations of the world, so that people of every race and nation and language would obey him. His rule is eternal—it will never end. His kingdom will never be destroyed."

In a similar way Daniel 2:44 predicts that at His coming, Christ will establish His reign on the earth. "During the reigns of those kings, the God of heaven will set up a kingdom that will never be destroyed or conquered. It will crush all these kingdoms into nothingness, and it will stand forever."

Living Jews Regathered and Judged

The annihilation of the armies that resist Christ's return will be God's judgment on the nations. After the final carnage of the Battle of Armageddon, the surviving people of the world will be judged one by one. All living Jews, the surviving nation of Israel, will be brought home again, because God will leave none of His people behind (Ezekiel 39:28). Each one will face God as his judge, and none will escape this judgment. The rebels who have not accepted Christ as their Messiah prior to the Second Coming will be put to death (Ezekiel 20:38). The remaining believing Jews who have survived the persecution will be the first citizens of Christ's new Kingdom on earth. Their hour of persecution will be finished forever, and they will receive all the blessings that have been promised to the children of Israel since the time of Abraham (Jeremiah 31:31-34; Romans 11:26-27).

Other Survivors Face Judgment

The judgment of the non-Jews who survive the tribulation period is described in Matthew 25:31-46. According to this Scripture, Christ will gather all the Gentile population of the earth to appear before His newly established throne in Jerusalem. In this judgment, individuals will fall into one of two classes—the sheep or the goats. Christ as King will invite the sheep to enter into His Kingdom. They are the ones who will have aided the Jews during their intense persecution. They will have visited them in prison, clothed them when naked, fed them when hungry, and hidden them from their tormentors.

The greatest demonstration of true faith in God during this period of intense anti-Semitism will be action taken to help the suffering Jews. While these works in themselves will not be the basis of salvation, even in this period, to befriend a Jew during this time will be unmistakable evidence of true faith in Christ and an understanding of the Scriptures.

Accordingly, these believers will be known by their works in a difficult time, but like the believers of all ages, they will be saved solely by faith in God through the gracious death and redemption of Jesus Christ.

By contrast, unbelievers will be exposed by a revelation of their selfish cruelty toward the Jews during the Great Tribulation. These individuals, described as goats, will be cast into everlasting fire. Just as unbelieving Jews will be judged, so, too, unbelieving Gentiles will be judged.

The remaining population of the earth, still in their mortal bodies, will then enter the millennial kingdom of Christ's reign on earth. The Kingdom will begin with all unbelievers removed from the earth. As young children mature and new babies are born during the coming thousand-year reign, each of them will also have his or her moment to believe or rebel. But at the beginning of the period the rebels will have been completely purged, and the world will enter a new era of peace to rebuild and replenish the earth.

From Disaster to Utopia

A utopian world will follow the colossal failure of man's attempt to control human history. Three judgments will have purged the world of all who have not believed in Jesus Christ. The armies of the world will have been destroyed on the battlefields of the Middle East. Unbelieving Jews will have been judged and killed. In the judgment of the sheep and goats, unbelieving non-Jews will also have been purged from the earth. The entire adult population of the earth that remains will have experienced regeneration through faith in Christ.

Believers of the past will also have a part in Christ's reign of righteousness. The individuals who placed their faith in Christ during the centuries of the church age will be taken from the earth just before the end times begin. As explained in the next chapter, at the moment of the Rapture, the dead in Christ will be raised, and the living will be taken from the earth. In new, resurrected bodies they will join Christ in the heavens to be saved from the time of judgment on the earth. Believers who died during Old Testament times or during the time of Tribulation

Summary of Unfulfilled Prophecy

Rapture of the church	1 Corinthians 15:51-58; 1 Thessalonians 4:13-18
Revival of Roman Empire under ten leaders	Daniel 7:7, 24; Revelation 13:1; 17:3, 12-13
Rise of European dictator	Daniel 7:8; Revelation 13:1-8
Peace treaty with Israel signed seven years before second coming of Christ to establish His Kingdom on earth	Daniel 9:27
False world religion established	Revelation 17:1-15
Russia and her Islamic allies attack Israel about four years before second coming of Christ	Ezekiel 38–39
Peace treaty with Israel broken: world government, world economic system, world atheistic religion begins, three and a half years before second coming of Christ	Daniel 7:23; Revelation 13:5-8, 15-17; 17:16-17
Martyrdom of many Christians and Jews	Revelation 7:9-17; 13:15
Three crashing waves of catastrophic divine judgments poured out on the earth	Revelation 6–18
World war breaks out in Middle East: Battle of Armageddon	Daniel 11:40-45; Revelation 9:13-21; 16:12-16
Second coming of Christ	Matthew 24:27-31; Revelation 19:11-21
Judgment of the wicked	Ezekiel 20:33-38; Matthew 25:31-46; Jude 1:14-15; Revelation 19:15-21; 20:1-4
Satan bound	Revelation 20:1-3
Resurrection of Old Testament and Tribulation saints	Daniel 12:2; Revelation 20:4
Millennial kingdom begins	Revelation 20:5-6
Rebellion at end of the Millennium	Revelation 20:7-10
Resurrection and judgment of the wicked and Satan: Great White Throne Judgment	Revelation 20:11-15
Eternity begins: new heaven, new earth, new Jerusalem	Revelation 21–22

will be raised and given new, resurrected bodies at the time of Christ's second coming. This entire company of saints from the past will be present to observe and help administer the new Kingdom on earth.

In a dramatic turn of events, the King of kings and Lord of lords will have seized direct control of human history. A world formerly dominated by Satan and evil men will now be ruled in righteousness and equity. A world torn with war and disaster will enjoy a thousand years of peace. The surviving population of the earth will enter a golden age, when man's intelligence and best energies will be used to rebuild the world and live for the glory of God. Satan will be bound; evil will be directly and swiftly judged by God Himself. Nature will be released from bondage in this balanced and peaceful world where the lion will lie down with the calf (Isaiah 11:6).

THE QUESTION FOR THIS GENERATION

The series of crises in the Middle East during this generation is only the beginning of a series of events that will lead inevitably to the second coming of Christ. The first important series of prophetic events in our day came when Israel returned to her land and proved to the world that she would not be driven into the sea. The second series of prophetic events began when Europe and the world suddenly realized their common enemy in terrorism and their crippling dependence on Arab oil. Traditional power alignments have now been shaken, and a new coalition of European nations is emerging. As these events continue, the countdown to Armageddon could begin at any time. Our generation may well witness the stirring events described in the dramatic prophecies of the Old and New Testaments.

A pointed question is pertinent to each of us in this generation: Are we ready for the coming of the Lord?

 See how today's headlines relate to this chapter at http://www.prophecyhotline.com.

A PROMISE TO REMEMBER

The Rapture: The act of Christ's raising up to heaven all living true believers.

TIME, JULY 1, 2002

WHILE MANY DRAMATIC PROPHECIES AWAIT fulfillment at the end of the age, none is more important or heartwarming than a simple promise Christ made to His disciples. On the night before His crucifixion as He gathered with them in the upper room, Christ warned them that He was going to leave and that they could not follow Him. One of them was going to betray Him; another would deny Him. The disciples were deeply troubled.

In this tense atmosphere, Christ spoke the memorable words recorded in John 14:1-3: "Don't let your hearts be troubled. Trust in God, and trust also in me. There is more than enough room in my Father's home. If this were not so, would I have told you that I am going to prepare a place for you? When everything is ready, I will come and get you, so that you will always be with me where I am."

HOW THE NEW PROMISE DIFFERS
FROM THE SECOND COMING

This coming, often referred to as the Rapture of the church, was dramatically different from events Christ had announced in the Olivet discourse as recorded in Matthew 24. There He had predicted many events preceding His return to the earth. This will be a time of great tribulation, beginning with the desecration of the Jewish Temple and including a period of intense persecution for the people of Israel. This time of trouble will climax dramatically with the glorious appearing of Christ to set up His Kingdom.

But the promise Jesus made to the disciples in the upper room involved an entirely separate event—the coming of Christ to meet believers in the air, the Rapture of the church.

The promise of the Rapture added a new dimension to the disciples' expectations. Jesus was returning to heaven to prepare a place for them. He would return to receive them to Himself, taking them where He was in the Father's house. This was a promise of removal from earth and entrance into heaven. He mentioned no signs preceding and no tremendous prophecies that needed to be fulfilled before it happened. It was to be an imminent hope, an expectation each day after He left them.

Some Bible interpreters attempt to associate this coming of Christ for believers with His second coming to earth with the heavenly hosts from heaven to set up His kingdom (Revelation 19). But many other interpreters who have carefully studied this and other passages assert that Christ's coming for His own was predicted as an entirely separate event that will precede rather than follow other major end-time events.

Believers today can cling to the same hope that Christ promised His troubled disciples. It would be natural to be troubled if Scripture did not show that believers in this age won't face inevitable martyrdom in the Great Tribulation. Christians today need not fear the catastrophic days about to overcome the world. Instead, they have the imminent hope of Christ's return and their being joined to the Lord to enjoy His presence forever.

Years after the first announcement of this promise by Christ, the apostle Paul gave the Thessalonian church additional details on this precious hope, which he received through divine revelation (1 Thessalonians 4:13-18). He described this coming of Christ for His own as a truth that God wanted the Thessalonians to know and understand.

According to Acts 17:1-9, Paul, Silas, and Timothy preached the gospel in Thessalonica for three Sabbath days, with the result that "many God-fearing Greek men and quite a few prominent women" believed. But unbelieving Jews opposed Paul's ministry and threatened his life, so Paul and his companions left secretly by night to avoid being killed. Sometime later Paul sent Timothy back to see how the Thessalonians were getting along. Timothy's report to Paul gave a glowing testimony for Christ. Everyone in the region was talking about this Jesus of Nazareth who died and rose again to be the Savior of those who trusted in Him.

But Timothy also brought back theological questions that he could not answer, and one of them apparently related to the subject of the Lord's return. The Thessalonians believed that their loved ones who had died would be raised, but they wondered whether they would be raised before or after the coming of Christ for those still living. This question reveals that Paul had already taught them about the coming of the Lord for them. For these believers, the Rapture, the catching up of the church (1 Thessalonians 4:17), was an imminent hope, an event that would occur before the tremendous end-time judgments of God prophesied in the Old Testament. They simply wanted to know if their dead loved ones would be raptured with them.

In reply, Paul assured the Thessalonians that God did not want them to be ignorant about this truth or to sorrow like unbelievers who had no hope. He went on to assure them of the certainty of their hope in 1 Thessalonians 4:14: "For since we believe that Jesus died and was raised to life again, we also believe that when Jesus returns, God will bring back with him the believers who have died." This hope of Christ's return for the living and the dead was just as certain as were the facts of the death and resurrection of Christ, in which they had put their trust.

But what did Paul mean when he said that "God will bring back with him the believers who have died"? This is related to the truth found in 2 Corinthians that when Christians die their souls go immediately to heaven and we "would rather be away from these earthly bodies, for then we will be at home with the Lord" (2 Corinthians 5:8). Paul's answer to the Thessalonians was direct and easy to understand. When Christ comes from heaven to meet believers, He will bring these souls with Him. Their bodies will be raised from the grave at the Rapture, and their souls will reenter their resurrection bodies.

Paul then described the event:

> We tell you this directly from the Lord: We who are still living when the Lord returns will not meet him ahead of those who have died. For the Lord himself will come down from heaven with a commanding shout, with the voice of the archangel, and with the trumpet call of God. First, the Christians who have died will rise from their graves. Then, together with them, we who are still alive and remain on the earth will be caught up in the clouds to meet the Lord in the air. Then we will be with the Lord forever. (1 Thessalonians 4:15-17)

This new truth, not revealed in the Old Testament, was given to Paul "directly from the Lord" (1 Thessalonians 4:15). Those living at the time of the Lord's return will not go before the resurrection of the bodies of believers who have died.

Paul describes the scene this way: The Lord will descend from heaven with a shout, literally a shout of command. Christ will order the resurrection of the dead and the translation of the living.

This promise is in keeping with what Christ announced to His disciples while on earth when He said: "Don't be so surprised! Indeed, the time is coming when all the dead in their graves will hear the voice of God's Son, and they will rise again. Those who have done good will rise to experience eternal life, and those who have continued in evil will rise to experience judgment" (John 5:28-29).

Although the Rapture will be a partial fulfillment of His promise of the resurrection of the dead, since it involves only the resurrection of the Christians who have died in this age, it will be the Lord speaking with authority when He gives the shout of command. This will be accompanied by the voice of Michael the archangel (1 Thessalonians 4:16; Jude 1:9) and signaled "when the last trumpet is blown" or "the trumpet sounds" (1 Corinthians 15:52). It will be the final call for Christians, those who have heard the call of the gospel and responded in faith. They will have heard the call to service and yielded their hearts

A Comparison of the Rapture and the Return
(Christ's Second Coming)

THE RAPTURE	THE RETURN
Christ comes in the air (1 Thessalonians 4:16-17)	Christ comes to the earth (Zechariah 14:4)
Christ comes for his saints (1 Thessalonians 4:16-17)	Christ comes with his saints (1 Thessalonians 3:13; Jude 1:14)
Christ claims His bride	Christ comes with His bride
Not in the Old Testament (1 Corinthians 15:51)	Predicted often in the Old Testament
Imminent; no signs beforehand (1 Corinthians 15:52)	Many signs beforehand (Matthew 24:4-29)
A time of blessing and comfort (1 Thessalonians 4:18)	A time of destruction and judgment (2 Thessalonians 2:8-12)
Involves believers only (John 14:1-3; 1 Corinthians 15:51-55; 1 Thessalonians 4:13-18)	Involves Israel and the Gentile nations (Matthew 24:1–25:46)
Will occur in a moment; only Christ's own will see His advent (1 Corinthians 15:51-52)	Will be visible to the entire world (Matthew 24:27; Revelation 1:7)
Tribulation begins	Millennium begins
Christ comes as the bright morning star (Revelation 22:16)	Christ comes as the Sun of Righteousness (Malachi 4:2)

and lives to the Lord. This will be the end of their earthly pilgrimage and the beginning of eternity in the presence of the Lord.

A REUNION IN THE AIR

What a moment that will be! For the first time, believers in Christ will see the One whom, having not seen, they have loved (1 Peter 1:8). And what a reunion it will be for Christians who have been separated by death! Families will be reunited and friends will see each other again. Their joy at being in each other's presence will be increased by the fact that they will never be separated again. They shall be forever with the Lord.

In light of this marvelous promise, Paul tells the Thessalonians: "So encourage each other with these words" (1 Thessalonians 4:18). Such comfort would be impossible if believers first had to pass through the traumatic events of the Great Tribulation, which few would survive.

Some years later Paul added further light on this important subject when writing to the Corinthian church. After fourteen chapters of correcting them in various doctrinal and moral matters, in chapter 15 he set forth the great doctrines of the faith. He proclaimed again the gospel that Christ had died for their sins. The resurrection of Christ, he reasoned, is the basis for our hope for the resurrection of our own bodies from the dead. Our present bodies, which are destined for the grave, must necessarily be renewed and made over into heavenly bodies suited for spiritual experience and service in the presence of the Lord. Accordingly, in God's plan the normal course is birth, life, death, and resurrection for those who put their trust in Him.

At the close of the chapter, however, the apostle declared a mystery, a truth hidden in the Old Testament but revealed in the New Testament (Colossians 1:26). The new revelation was that there will be a grand exception to the normal rule of life, death, and resurrection. He declared: "But let me reveal to you a wonderful secret. We will not all die, but we will all be transformed! It will happen in a moment, in the blink of an eye, when the last trumpet is blown. For when the trumpet sounds, those who have died will be raised to live forever. And we who are living will also be transformed" (1 Corinthians 15:51-52).

Christians living on the earth at the time of the Lord's return will need to have their bodies transformed just as much as those who have died and been buried. As Paul pointed out, their bodies will be corruptible—subject to decay, age, and all the ills of this life. The bodies of Christians are mortal, that is, subject to death.

As Paul reasoned elsewhere (Ephesians 2:1-3; Philippians 3:21), men's bodies are also sinful, not suited for the holy presence of the Lord. A dramatic transformation is necessary, described here as a change to a body that will never grow old and will never die.

As Paul expressed it in 1 Corinthians 15:53: "For our dying bodies must be transformed into bodies that will never die; our mortal bodies must be transformed into immortal bodies." When this is accomplished at the time of the coming of Christ for His own, "Death is swallowed up in victory" (1 Corinthians 15:54).

THE RAPTURE MUST OCCUR BEFORE OTHER END-TIME EVENTS

By contrast, the many passages that deal with the second coming of Christ to set up His Kingdom never mention the translation of living saints, although they do describe the resurrection of martyred dead.

The reason is that saints who have lived through the horrific events will not be translated when Christ comes to set up His Kingdom but rather will be ushered into the millennial reign of Christ in their natural bodies. They will need to lead normal lives, plant crops, build houses, bear children, and repopulate the earth. Such would be impossible if all saints were translated and given heavenly bodies at the time of the introduction of the Kingdom. This is one important reason that the Rapture must take place earlier in the order of events before end-time troubles overtake the world.

Between the time when the church is caught up to heaven and Christ returns in triumph to set up His Kingdom, enough time must pass for a new body of believers, both Jews and Gentiles, to come to Christ and be saved. During the tribulation period of seven years, those living will have a final chance to believe and demonstrate their faith. Those who do will be the ones to populate the millennial earth. Those who have been translated and resurrected earlier at the Rapture will be in their resurrected, perfect bodies and will join Christ in His reign.

LIVING IN EXPECTATION

Paul assured the Corinthian church, just as he had the Thessalonians, of the wonderful hope of Christ's imminent return. Once again, he made no mention of any preceding events. As in other passages, the Day of the Lord, the age in which God deals directly with human sin, will begin immediately after the Rapture, as indicated in 1 Thessalonians 5. The fact that the Day of the Lord begins then makes clear that the church will not go through the judgments of the Day of the Lord and will not suffer the wrath of God, which will be poured out on unbelievers at that time (1 Thessalonians 5:9). These first-century Christians were challenged to live in expectation of Christ's coming, when the dead in Christ will be raised and living Christians translated. This blessed hope (Titus 2:13, NIV), this purifying hope (1 John 3:2-3, NIV), and this comforting hope (1 Thessalonians 4:18, NIV) should thrill the heart of every true believer in Christ. Especially in these momentous days, we should be alert to the challenge of being ready for the coming of the Lord.

See how today's headlines relate to this chapter at http://www.prophecyhotline.com.

CHAPTER 15

SCANNING THE HORIZON

Now learn a lesson from the fig tree. When its branches
bud and its leaves begin to sprout, you know that summer
is near. In the same way, when you see all these things,
you can know his return is very near, right at the door.

JESUS CHRIST, MATTHEW 24:32-33

AS TODAY'S HEADLINES REPORT CURRENT developments in the
Middle East, serious students of prophecy expect the next dramatic
and important event to be the Rapture of all true believers. Skeptics
have been quick to point out that though the return of Christ has been
the hope of every generation since the time of the apostles, the promise has not been fulfilled. The apostle Paul clearly hoped that Jesus
would return in his lifetime and taught the early church to watch for
the Lord's return at any time. Likewise, the members of the early
church in Thessalonica believed that Christ might come in their lifetimes, and they were comforted by the expectation of being joined to

their deceased loved ones. But the centuries passed and the event has not taken place.

WHY HAS CHRIST DELAYED HIS COMING?

Why has Christ not already fulfilled His promise to come and receive His own unto Himself? From the human point of view, it may appear that Christ has delayed His return. Yet Scriptures make it plain that, from the divine standpoint, God is never late. In fact, when it comes to the fulfillment of biblical prophecy, delays are not unexpected. It has always been preceded by centuries of history that moved with sovereign precision to allow predicted events to occur exactly as promised, complete to the very last detail. For instance, Christ's first coming was also anticipated for thousands of years before it occurred, yet it took centuries for the earth to be prepared for His coming. During this time, the Greek language was developed and adopted throughout the Western world. This prepared the way for the New Testament to be written in a precise and widely used language.

Also, the Roman Empire was established and brought comparative peace in the Middle East. Jewish life and worship in Israel were ready for the Messiah's coming. John the Baptist came to announce the Messiah's coming and call the nation to repentance. The *Pax Romana* (the Peace of Rome) had opened international trade and communication, making it possible for first-century Christians to spread the gospel message throughout the entire Roman Empire and eventually the world.

The prophecies of Christ's first coming were fulfilled in a day carefully prepared by a sovereign God. The prophecies of Christ's return for believers and eventual second coming will be fulfilled in this way—in God's perfect timing.

But there is also a warm and personal reason why Christ has not returned. As the apostle Peter explains: "The Lord isn't really being slow about his promise, as some people think. No, he is being patient for your sake. He does not want anyone to be destroyed, but wants everyone to repent" (2 Peter 3:9). The delay of Christ's return to the earth for His own comes from a heart of love. A God of compassion is still waiting for many to hear the gospel and respond in belief. The delay is for us, so that we can respond in faith and carry this message to others.

The Scriptures indicate that God will not wait forever. Christ Himself used an illustration concerning His coming to establish His kingdom. He compared His coming to the times of Noah. When Noah built the ark in obedience to God's command, more than one hundred years elapsed before the Flood. Noah attempted to warn his generation, but they scoffed at his message and laughed at his efforts to build the ark. The day came, however, when the ark was finished and the animals went into the ark. Observers could have seen Noah and his family entering the ark. And then God shut the door (Matthew 24:37-39). Then it was too late! Those outside the ark perished in the flood that followed.

While Christ used this illustration in reference to His second coming, the same illustration can be applied to His coming for His church at the Rapture. God is patient and waits far beyond what human patience endures, but the time will eventually come when God will act.

Therefore, we have a special burden as well as a special privilege. Those who have confidently received Jesus Christ as Savior have the hope that they may at any moment be called to join Christ in the heavens. For those who have not responded in faith, the same moment will mark the beginning of a series of catastrophic events that will bring God's judgment on the world in which we live.

The burden of our generation is to make God's message of salvation clear in a time of confusion. Living faith brings happiness and meaning into our day-to-day existence. It also provides hope in a world that is rushing to judgment. Each of us must be sure that we have understood and responded to God's message of salvation.

The seriousness is that the time is short. Everyone must decide what they will do with Him. Jesus Christ was God who stepped out of eternity into time; was born of a virgin; lived a sinless life; and was rejected by His generation. He came to die on the cross for the sins of the world and rose the third day with a new resurrected body.

Christ ascended into heaven and will return to take those who believe in Him to Himself. All that is required of each and every one of us is that we accept His sacrifice by faith and invite Him into our lives. That begins a walk of faith that never ends. When He returns all those who have accepted Him as Savior will be taken out of this world. The Rapture is the first event in the unfolding of the end-time events described in this book.

Jesus died for you on the cross to purchase a pardon for your sins. All that God requires is for you to receive this pardon by faith and accept Christ as your personal Savior. "But to all who believed him and accepted him, he gave the right to become children of God" (John 1:12).

Once we understand this message we must lovingly communicate this urgent message to our families, friends, and everyone we can. The headlines are screaming that the time is short. The communication of this message is especially important in this generation that may witness the final hour of God's judgment on the world.

When the Rapture of the church was explained, no signs were ever given indicating the specific expectation of this event. Instead, believers in Christ were asked to look for His coming and to anticipate that it could occur at any time. This attitude characterized the early church and has been the hope of the church from the first century until now. But since there are no signs for the Rapture itself, what are the legitimate grounds for believing that the Rapture could be especially near for this generation?

The answer is not found in any prophetic events predicted before the Rapture but in understanding the events that will follow the Rapture. Just as history was prepared for Christ's first coming, in a similar way history is preparing for the events leading up to His second coming. Previous chapters in this book have explained the amazing historical developments that seem to be precursors to the predicted events that will occur soon after the Rapture.

THE THREE MAJOR DIVISIONS OF PROPHECY

Many different places, players, and events fill their own unique roles in the drama of the ages. This book has focused on twelve of these crucial events related to the end times.

To make it easier to grasp and discern where we are today in God's prophetic program, the major signs related to the end times are divided into three main categories: prophecies about the church, prophecies about the nations, and prophecies concerning Israel (1 Corinthians 10:32).

The prophecies that relate to the future of the church explain events and trends that will occur in the true church, as the body of believers, or in the organized church as an institution. Prophecies about the church as an institution often involve those who are only professing Christians. The Bible has much to say about this professing or organized church and the religious climate of the end of the age. These prophecies reveal the role of the superchurch and the False Prophet during the Tribulation period (Revelation 17:1-18) and the final rule of the Antichrist who will demand worship as God during the final years of the Tribulation.

The rise and fall of nations has been important to prophecies in both the Old and New Testaments. Of special interest today are prophecies that describe the international situation in the final years of history before Armageddon. These prophecies have a remarkable similarity to what we observe in the world today and, as such, constitute a warning of the approaching coming of the Lord.

Prophecies about Israel, and especially Jerusalem, provide important reference points for all of prophecy as well. The most significant prophetic event of the twentieth century was the restoration of the people of Israel to their land. All the prophecies of the end of the age indicate that at that time the Jews will be back in their land, precisely the situation in which they find themselves today.

Added to this situation is the worldwide expectation for a world government, which, according to Scriptures, will occur three and a half years before the Second Coming. Likewise, world religion, anticipated in Revelation 17, has already taken form in the world church movement which, after the Rapture, will be devoid of any true Christians.

These major situations that are true now, and that were not true seventy-five years ago, point to the conclusion that the Rapture itself may be very near. All areas of prophecy combine in the united testimony that history is preparing our generation for the end of the age.

In each area of prophecy a chronological checklist of important prophetic events can be compiled. In each list, in regard to the church, the nations, or Israel, the events of history clearly indicate that the world is poised and ready for the Rapture of the church and the beginning of the countdown to Armageddon.

A Prophetic Checklist for the Church

When all the predicted events relating to the church are placed in chronological order, it is evident that the world has already been carefully prepared for Christ's return. This checklist includes the major prophetic events in the order of their predicted fulfillment.

1. The rise of world communism made possible the worldwide spread of atheism.

2. Liberalism undermines the spiritual vitality of the church in Europe and eventually America.

3. The movement toward a superchurch begins with the ecumenical movement.

4. Apostasy and open denial of biblical truth are evident in the church.

5. Moral chaos becomes more and more evident because of the complete departure from Christian morality.

6. The sweep of spiritism, the occult, and belief in demons begins to prepare the world for Satan's final hour.

7. Jerusalem becomes a center of religious controversy for Arabs and Christians, while Jews of the world plan to make the city an active center for Judaism.

8. True believers will disappear from the earth to join Christ in heaven at the Rapture of the church.

9. The restraint of evil by the Holy Spirit will end.

10. The superchurch will combine major religions as a tool for the false prophet who aids the Antichrist's rise to world power.

11. The Antichrist will destroy the superchurch and demand worship as a deified world dictator.

12. Believers of this period will suffer intense persecution and be martyred by the thousands.

13. Christ will return to earth with Christians who have been in heaven during the Tribulation and end the rule of the nations at the Battle of Armageddon.

A Prophetic Checklist for the Nations

The prophetic events related to the nations can be compiled chronologically. Consider how the following list of significant world events—past, present, and future—shows that the world is being dramatically prepared for end-time events.

1. The establishment of the United Nations began a serious first step toward world government.

2. The rebuilding of Europe after World War II made a revival of the Roman Empire possible.

3. Israel was reestablished as a nation.

4. Russia rose to world power and became the ally of the Islamic world.

5. The Common Market and World Bank showed the need for some international regulation of the world economy.

6. China rose to world power and developed the capacity to field an army of two hundred million as predicted in prophecy.

7. The Middle East became the most significant trouble spot in the world.

8. The oil blackmail awakened the world to the new concentration of wealth and power in the Middle East.

9. The Iron Curtain fell, removing the final barrier to the revival of the Roman Empire.

10. The world clamors for peace because of the continued disruption caused by the high price of oil, terrorist incidents, and the confused military situation in the Middle East.

11. Ten leaders (the Group of Ten) will emerge from a European coalition—beginning the last stage of the prophetic fourth world empire.

12. In a dramatic power play, a new European leader will uproot three leaders of the coalition and take control of the powerful ten-leader group.

13. The new European leader will negotiate a "final" peace settlement in the Middle East (broken three and a half years later).

14. Russia and her Islamic allies will attempt an invasion of Israel but will be miraculously destroyed.

15. The European leader will proclaim himself world dictator, break his peace settlement with Israel, and declare himself to be God.

16. The new world dictator will desecrate the Temple in Jerusalem.

17. The terrible judgments of the Great Tribulation will be poured out on the nations of the world.

18. Worldwide rebellion will threaten the world dictator's rule as armies from throughout the world converge on the Middle East for World War III.

19. Christ will return to earth with His armies from heaven.

20. The armies of the world will unite to resist Christ's coming and will be destroyed in the Battle of Armageddon.

21. Christ will establish His millennial reign on earth, ending the period of the Gentiles.

A Prophetic Checklist for Israel

Although Israel's future cannot be separated from the wider sweep of history, prophecies about the Jewish people and the nation have their own distinct order of predicted events. In this prophetic checklist, as in the others, the events already in motion suggest the final countdown to Armageddon may already have begun.

1. The intense suffering and persecution of Jews throughout the world led to pressure for a national home in Israel.

2. Jews returned to the land, and Israel was reestablished as a nation in 1948.

3. The infant nation survived against overwhelming odds.

4. Russia emerged as an important enemy of Israel, but the United States came to the aid of Israel.

5. Israel's heroic survival and growing strength made it an established nation, recognized throughout the world.

6. Israel's military accomplishments were overshadowed by the Arabs' ability to wage a diplomatic war by controlling much of the world's oil reserves.

7. The Arab position is strengthened by their growing wealth and by alliances between Europe and key Arab countries.

8. The increasing isolation of the United States and Russia's growing alliance with nations in the Middle East make it more and more difficult for Israel to negotiate an acceptable peace settlement.

9. After a long struggle, Israel will be forced to accept a compromise peace guaranteed by the new leader of the European coalition.

10. The Jewish people will celebrate what appears to be a lasting and final peace settlement.

11. During three and a half years of peace, Judaism will be revived and traditional sacrifices and ceremonies be reinstituted in the rebuilt Temple in Jerusalem.

12. Russia and her Islamic allies will attempt to invade Israel but will be mysteriously destroyed.

13. The newly proclaimed world dictator will desecrate the Temple in Jerusalem and begin a period of intense persecution of Jews.

14. Many Jews will recognize the unfolding of prophetic events and declare their faith in Christ as the Messiah of Israel.

15. In the massacre of Jews and Christians who resist the world dictator, some witnesses will be divinely preserved to carry the gospel message throughout the world.

16. Christ will return to earth, welcomed by believing Jews as their Messiah and deliverer.

17. Christ's thousand-year reign on earth from the throne of David will finally fulfill the prophetic promises to the nations of Israel.

A COMPELLING SEQUENCE OF EVENTS

The earlier chapters of this book present the overall prophetic message about the future as it relates to history and today's headlines. Although prophecies about the church, the nations, and Israel are often presented in separate sections of biblical revelation, they are intricately related to each other in the unfolding of history. Israel obviously had to be reestablished as a nation in Palestine before many of these end-time events could begin. The coming leader of the European Union could hardly gain recognition by negotiation of a peace covenant with Israel if Israel did not exist or if there were no Middle East crisis. Without the economic necessity of oil and the fall of the Iron Curtain, European countries could hardly be expected to unite and take an active role in the Middle East crisis.

Many students of prophecy believe that Israel has now completed the first step in her restoration and fight for survival. Currently more Jews live in Israel than any other country in the world, yet they still do not live in peace with their neighbors. The Bible predicts that lasting peace will not come in the Middle East until a new world leader emerges from the Group of Ten leaders who begin the revival of the Roman Empire.

The signing of that peace settlement is the second step in Israel's prophetic calendar, and it will mark the beginning of the last seven years before Armageddon. These last seven years will be a time when evil is unrestrained and God's judgment is poured out on the world. The third step in Israel's restoration will begin when her peace treaty is broken. The fourth and final step will begin with the return of Christ and Israel's deliverance.

For those who believe in Christ, Israel's present situation is tremendously significant. If the next stage in Israel's restoration cannot come until the church is removed, the coming of Christ for His followers must occur soon. As the Middle East crisis continues, powerful alliances will emerge between European and Arab countries. But the coming world dictator cannot make his decisive move until the church is removed. Only then will Satan have a free hand to manipulate history using the forces of evil. For these reasons, informed Christians expect that the coming of the Lord is the next important event on the prophetic calendar.

THE FINAL STAGE IS SET

The world today is like a stage being set for a great drama. The major actors are already in the wings waiting for their moment in history. The main stage props are already in place. The prophetic play could begin at any time. The Middle East now occupies the attention of the world leaders. Those who control the tremendous oil reserves of the area have great political and economic power. The meteoric rise of Islamic fundamentalism, the election of Hamas to power in Palestine, the presence of Hezbollah in Lebanon, and Iran's determination to destroy Israel have lit the fuse to an already explosive situation. Israel desperately needs the covenant of peace promised in prophecy. Old friendships may change as European nations seek new alliances and agreements to protect themselves in a changing world situation. The Middle East will continue to be the focal point of international relationships.

Russia is poised to the north of the Holy Land for entry in the end-time conflict. China is now a military power great enough to field an army as large as that described in the book of Revelation. Each nation is ready to play out its role in the final hours of history.

Our present world is well prepared for the beginning of the prophetic drama that will lead to Armageddon. Since the stage is set for this dramatic climax of the age, it must mean that Christ's coming for His own is very near. If there ever was an hour when men should consider their personal relationship to Jesus Christ, it is today. God is saying to this generation: "Prepare for the coming of the Lord."

See how today's headlines relate to this chapter at http://www.prophecyhotline.com.

Acknowledgments

THIS BOOK BECAME A PROJECT with a life of its own—through the vision and dedicated work of many people. If my father were still alive, I know he would affirm everything in the book. It faithfully represents his vision and understanding of what the Scriptures teach about the future. Many hearts and minds joined together to make this happen.

Before my father died he confirmed the outline of prophecy that had been his life's work. He asked me to put together a revised and expanded edition of *Armageddon, Oil and the Middle East Crisis*. He suggested the title *Armageddon, Oil, and Terror* and outlined the strategy and concepts presented in this work. Although I had written the previous editions of the book with his guidance, I realized I needed someone with special knowledge and talent to help fulfill my father's larger vision for this new work.

A total stranger called me a couple of years after my father's death and asked the question, "It's been fourteen years since the last edition of *Armageddon*; isn't it time to publish it again with everything that is happening in the world?" The caller, an author and avid student of prophecy, then went on to explain how events unfolding in the news were exactly what my father outlined in the previous editions of the book.

The caller, Dr. Mark Hitchcock, had already authored more than a dozen books on Bible prophecy. He had known and admired my father. They became friends when Mark was a student at Dallas Theological Seminary. His study of the Scriptures confirmed every detail of biblical prophecy my father had taught.

I asked Dr. Hitchcock to work with me as writer and researcher for this edition. We worked as a team for more than two years to complete this book. In the process I discovered Dr. Hitchcock to be a wise and godly man who understands what the Scriptures teach about the future. We spent many hours discussing the key points in the book—and always arrived at the same conclusions. His contribution to this edition and to my father's legacy has been immense. He has been like a brother to me in this project.

As the manuscript was being completed, John Van Diest became a champion for the book. John is a friend and had studied under my father. He understood exactly why this book had to be published. His excitement and passion were contagious.

Doug Knox, at Tyndale House Publishers, embraced our vision and helped us put together an amazing team to publish this book. Jan Long Harris joined in to shape the direction of the book. I have greatly appreciated her friendship, gracious spirit, and thorough oversight as she led the team inside Tyndale.

Kim Miller became much more than our editor. She took the time to familiarize herself with the complexities of end-time prophecy. Many of her suggestions and insights were incorporated into the book. Mark Hitchcock and I both believe the book was greatly enhanced by her remarkable editorial work.

Many others at Tyndale have contributed to the launch of this book. Their dedication and vision helped take this important book to a new generation of readers.

But most of all, I appreciated the support and understanding of Mark Taylor, president of Tyndale House Publishers. His father, Ken Taylor, and my father were friends during their lifetime. Mark instantly understood what I was trying to accomplish with the book. He understands what it means to secure a father's legacy. His leadership has secured his father's legacy and has made Tyndale the amazing publisher it is today.

My thanks to everyone on the team.

—John E. Walvoord

I AM DEEPLY GRATEFUL FOR the opportunity John gave me to be part of this project. I loved his father, learned a great deal from him, and held him in highest esteem. Working on this book has been one of the major highlights of my life and ministry. One of the unexpected blessings to come out of this project is that John and I have developed a friendship that I will always treasure.

—Mark Hitchcock

Endnotes

Preface

1. John F. Walvoord, "Is the Seventieth Week of Daniel Future?" *Bibliotheca Sacra* 101 (January–March 1944), 30–49; "Is the Church the Israel of God?" *Bibliotheca Sacra* 101 (October–December 1944), 403–416; "The Fulfillment of the Abrahamic Covenant," *Bibliotheca Sacra* 102 (January–March 1945), 27–36; "The Fulfillment of the Davidic Covenant," *Bibliotheca Sacra* 102 (April–June 1945), 153–166; "Israel's Blindness," *Bibliotheca Sacra* 102 (July–September 1945), 280–290; "Israel's Restoration," *Bibliotheca Sacra* 102 (October–December 1945), 405–416.

CHAPTER 1
Why Prophecy?

1. Strategic Issues Research Institute, *Strategic Issues Today*, 18 October 2001.
2. "2 Hurt by Saudi Bomb Die," *New York Times*, 26 February 2006.
3. Michael Hirsh, Melinda Liu, and George Wehrfritz, "We Are a Nuclear Power," *Newsweek*, 23 October 2006, 36.

CHAPTER 2
Oil Becomes the Ultimate Weapon

1. PBS, "Charting the World's Oil," see http://www.pbs.org/frontlineworld/stories/colombia/images/map. swf. See also Robert Samuelson, "An Oil Habit America Cannot Break," *Washington Post*, 18 October 2006, A21.
2. Tim Appenzeller, "The End of Cheap Oil," *National Geographic*, June 2004, 88. For another intriguing analysis of this situation, see Matthew Simmons, "Shock to the System: The Impending Global Energy Supply Crisis," *Harvard International Review* (Fall 2006).
3. Peter Tertzakian, *A Thousand Barrels a Second* (New York: McGraw-Hill, 2006), 3.
4. Appenzeller, "The End of Cheap Oil," 88.
5. Ibid., 90.
6. Adam Lashinsky and Nelson D. Schwartz, "How to Beat the High Cost of Gasoline. Forever!" *Fortune*, 6 February 2006, 74, 80.

7. Energy Information Administration, *Monthly Energy Review*, July 2006, table 1.7.
8. Paul Tharp, "Oil Prices Pump Up ExxonMobil Profits," *New York Post*, 27 October 2006; http://www.nypost.com/seven/10272006/business/oil_prices_pump_up_exxonmobil_profits_business_paul_tharp.htm (accessed December 12, 2006).
9. Peter Huber and Mark Mills, "Getting Over Oil," *Digital Power Group Commentary*, September 2005, http://www.digitalpowergroup.com/downloads/Commentary-Sept05.htm (accessed December 14, 2006). See also "American-Made Energy Freedom Act," http://www.house.gov/nunes/documents/AMEF_TP.pdf (accessed December 14, 2006).
10. Lashinsky and Schwartz, "How to Beat the High Cost of Gasoline," 74.
11. Ibid., 87.
12. David Pimentel, "Limits of Biomass Utilization," *Encyclopedia of Physical Sciences and Technology* (Academic Press, 2001); findings cited at http://www.healthandenergy.com/ethanol.htm (accessed December 12, 2006). To read the U.S. Department of Energy's rebuttal to some of his claims, see http://www.eere.energy.gov/afdc/altfuel/eth_energy_bal.html.
13. Adam Wilmoth, "Is Ethanol Sector Growing Too Fast?" *Daily Oklahoman*, 5 January 2007.
14. Nathanael Greene and Yerina Mugica, "Bringing Biofuels to the Pump," issue paper from the Natural Resources Defense Council, July 2005, 2.
15. Lashinsky and Schwartz, "How to Beat the High Cost of Gasoline," 75.
16. Ibid.
17. Council on Foreign Relations, *National Security Consequences of U.S. Oil Dependency*, Independent Task Force Report No. 58, released October 12, 2006.
18. Paul Roberts, *The End of Oil* (New York: Mariner Books, 2005), 337.

CHAPTER 3

Terrorism Reaches Everyone

1. William J. Broad and David E. Sanger, "New Worry Rises on Iranian Claim of Nuclear Steps," *New York Times*, 17 April 2006. See also Carnegie Endowment for International Peace, *A. Q. Khan Nuclear Chronology*, Issue Brief 8, no. 8, September 7, 2005, see http://www.carnegieendowment.org/static/npp/Khan_Chronology.pdf (accessed December 12, 2006). See also Kenneth R. Timmerman, *Countdown to Crisis: The Coming Nuclear Showdown with Iran*, updated ed. (2005; repr., New York: Three Rivers Press, 2006), 263–264.
2. The Nuclear Threat Initiative provides a summary of Iran's nuclear capabilities at http://www.nti.org/e_research/profiles/Iran/1825_6279.html.
3. Rown Scarborough, "U.S. Military Sees Iran's Nuke Bomb 5 Years Away," *Washington Times*, 31 August 2006.
4. The Lugar Letter, July 2005; see http://www.lugar.senate.gov/newsletter/2005/july.html (accessed December 12, 2006).
5. CBS News, "Experts Warn of Future WMD Attack," June 22, 2005, http://www.cbsnews.com/stories/2005/06/22/world/main703465.shtml?CMP=ILC-SearchStories (accessed December 12, 2006).

CHAPTER 4

Israel: Ground Zero for the End Times

1. Thomas Ice and Timothy Demy, *The Truth about Jerusalem in Bible Prophecy* (Eugene, Ore.: Harvest House Publishers, 1996), 8.
2. Clarence Larkin, an American pastor, introduced this concept in the early twentieth century in his book *Dispensational Truth (or God's Plan or Purpose in the Ages)*.

CHAPTER 5
The Decline and Fall of America

1. Peter Tertzakian, *A Thousand Barrels a Second* (New York: McGraw-Hill, 2006), xii–xiii.
2. According to a 2002 ABC News/BeliefNet Poll, 83 percent of Americans identify themselves as Christians. Another 13 percent say they have no religion. Just 4 percent describe themselves as Jewish, Muslim, Buddhist, or another religion. That compares to only 33 percent of the world at large who identify themselves as Christians. See a summary of this poll at http://abcnews.go.com/sections/us/ DailyNews/beliefnet_poll_010718.html (accessed December 14, 2006). See also Patrick Johnstone, *Operation World*, 4th Edition (Grand Rapids, Mich.: Zondervan, 1987), 34.

CHAPTER 6
The New *Pax Romana*

1. Michael T. Klare, *Blood and Oil* (New York: Henry Holt and Company, 2004), 146.

CHAPTER 7
The Russian–Islamic Invasion of Israel

1. For more on the Ezekiel 38–39 prophecy, with special focus on the role of modern-day Iran, see Mark Hitchcock's book *Iran: The Coming Crisis* (Sisters, Ore.: Multnomah, 2006), 160–166.
2. Josephus, *Antiquities of the Jews* 1.6.1.
3. C. F. Keil, *Ezekiel, Daniel, Commentary on the Old Testament*, trans. James Martin (Grand Rapids: Eerdmans Publishing Company, 1982), 159. Wilhelm Gesenius, *Gesenius' Hebrew-Chaldee Lexicon to the Old Testament Scriptures* (Grand Rapids: Eerdmans Publishing Company, 1949), 752.
4. Clyde E. Billington Jr., "The Rosh People in History and Prophecy, Part 2," *Michigan Theological Journal* 3 (1992): 54–61.
5. G. A. Cooke, *A Critical and Exegetical Commentary on the Book of Ezekiel*, ICC, ed. S. R. Driver, A. Plummer, and C. A. Briggs (Edinburgh: T. & T. Clark, 1936), 408–9. John Taylor agrees. He says, "If a place-name *Rosh* could be vouched for, RV's *prince of Rosh, Meshech, and Tubal* would be the best translation." See John B. Taylor, *Ezekiel: An Introduction & Commentary*, Tyndale Old Testament Commentaries, gen. ed. D. J. Wiseman (Downers Grove, Ill.: InterVarsity Press, 1969), 244. Since it appears that there was a place in Ezekiel's day known as Rosh, this is the superior translation. For an extensive, thorough presentation of the grammatical and philological support for taking Rosh as a place name, see James D. Price, "Rosh: An Ancient Land Known to Ezekiel," *Grace Theological Journal* 6 (1985): 67–89.
6. Gesenius died in 1842. See *Gesenius' Hebrew-Chaldee Lexicon*.
7. Clyde E. Billington Jr. "The Rosh People in History and Prophecy, Part 2)," *Michigan Theological Journal* 3 (1992): 145–46; Billington, "The Rosh People in History and Prophecy, Part 3)," *Michigan Theological Journal* 4 (1993): 59, 61; James D. Price, "Rosh: An Ancient People Known to Ezekiel," *Grace Theological Journal* 6 (1985): 71–73; Jon Mark Ruthven, *The Prophecy That Is Shaping History* (Fairfax, Va.: Xulon Press, 2003).
8. Josephus, *Antiquities* 1.6.1.
9. Adrian Blomfield, "Putin Is Returning Russia to a State of Tyranny," November 22, 2006, telegraph.co.uk, http://www.telegraph.co.uk/opinion/main.jhtml?xml=/opinion/2006/11/22/do2205.xml (accessed December 13, 2006). Ethan S. Burger, "The Price of Russia's 'Dictatorship of Law,'" *Christian Science Monitor*, 12 October 2006. Political scientist Arnold Beichman has dubbed Putin "Stalin lite."
10. "Putin Deplores Collapse of USSR," BBC News, April 25, 2005, http://news.bbc.co.uk/2/hi/europe/4480745.stm (accessed December 13, 2006).

11. You can find additional details on Ahmadinejad's background and beliefs in Mark Hitchcock's book *Iran: The Coming Crisis* (Sisters, Ore.: Multnomah, 2006), 68–80.

12. Kenneth R. Timmerman, *Countdown to Crisis: The Coming Nuclear Showdown with Iran*, updated ed. (2005; repr., New York: Three Rivers Press, 2006), 331.

13. The first and third statements were reported in Ali Akbar Dareini, "Iran Hits Milestone in Nuclear Technology," Associated Press, 11 April 2006. PBS's *NewsHour* reported the second in its segment "Iran Nuclear Program Defies UN," which aired on April 11, 2006, http://www.pbs.org/newshour/bb/middle_east/jan-june06/iran_4-11.html (accessed December 14, 2006).

14. The Press Association, "Iran President: Wipe Israel Off Map," October 27, 2005, http://news.scotsman.com/latest.cfm?id=2152412005 (accessed December 13, 2006).

15. The Anti-Defamation League has compiled an extensive list of Ahmadinejad statements. See http://www.adl.org/main_Anti_Semitism_International/ahmadinejad_words.htm.

16. Ibid.

17. Agence France-Presse, "Iran Increases Palestinian Aid to 120 Million Dollars," http://www.iranpress-news.com/english/source/017682.html (accessed December 13, 2006).

18. Yaakov Lappin, "Iranian Paper: Great War to Wipe Out Israel Coming, *Ynetnews*, 15 November 2006, http://www.ynetnews.com/articles/0,2340,L-3328416,00.html (accessed December 13, 2006).

19. Ibid.

20. The Middle East Media Research Institute, "Iran President Ahmadinejad: 'I Have a Connection with God . . . ,'" Special Dispatch Series—No. 1328, 19 October 2006, http://memri.org/bin/articles.cgi? Page=archives&Area=sd&ID=SP132806 (accessed December 13, 2006).

21. Anton La Guardia, "'Divine Mission' Driving Iran's New Leader," telegraph.co.uk, 14 January 2006, http://www.telegraph.co.uk/news/main.jhtml?xml=/news/2006/01/14/wiran14.xml&sSheet=/news/2006/01/14/ixworld.html (accessed December 13, 2006).

22. Ellen Knickmeyer and K. I. Ibrahim, "Bombing Shatters Mosque in Iraq," *Washington Post*, 23 February 2006, http://www.washingtonpost.com/wp-dyn/content/article/2006/02/22/AR2006022200454.html (accessed December 14, 2006).

23. Timmerman, *Countdown to Crisis*, 325.

24. Ibid., 326–327.

25. Arnaud de Borchgrave, "The Apocalyptic Vision of Iranian President Ahmadinejad," NewsMax.com, 9 February 2006, http://www.newsmax.com/archives/articles/2006/2/8/154740.shtml (accessed December 13, 2006).

26. Ibid.

27. Daniel Pipes, "The Mystical Menace of Mahmoud Ahmadinejad," *New York Sun*, 10 January 2006, http://www.danielpipes.org/article/3258 (accessed December 13, 2006).

28. La Guardia, "'Divine Mission' Driving Iran's New Leader."

29. Mortimer B. Zuckerman, "Moscow's Mad Gamble," *U.S. News & World Report*, 30 January 2006, 1.

30. *Enhanced Global Intelligence Brief*, September 30, 2005.

31. Gerard Baker, "Let's Not Talk Turkey: Guess Who Won't Be Joining the European Union Anytime Soon," *The Weekly Standard*, 29 August 2005.

CHAPTER 8

The Coming World Dictator: "The World Is Mine, and I Am God"

1. See http://www.freedomdomain.com/nwoquote.htm.

2. Harold H. Hoehner, *Chronological Aspects of the Life of Christ* (Grand Rapids, Mich.: Zondervan, 1977), 115–140. The chart on page 122 is adapted from page 139 of this book.

CHAPTER 9

The Final Holocaust

1. CNN.com, "Iranian Leader: Holocaust a Myth," 14 December 2005, http://www.cnn.com/2005/WORLD/meast/12/14/iran.israel (accessed December 13, 2006).
2. Nazila Fathi, "Israel Fading, Iran's Leader Tells Deniers of Holocaust," *New York Times*, 13 December 2006.
3. For more on this, see Mark Hitchcock, *What On Earth Is Going On?* (Sisters, Ore.: Multnomah, 2002), 55–57.

CHAPTER 10

Iraq: The New Babylon—Economic Center of World Power

1. I explore Iraq and its relationship to the end times in greater detail in my book *Seven Signs of the End Times* (Sisters, Ore.: Multnomah, 2003).
2. Barbara Slavin, "Giant U.S. Embassy Rising in Baghdad," *USA Today*, 19 April 2006.
3. Bay Fang, "An Oil Rush in (Yes) Iraq," *U.S. News & World Report*, 13 November 2006, 56.
4. Ibid.
5. Ibid.

CHAPTER 11

China Flexes Its Awesome Power

1. Richard J. Newman, "The Rise of a New Power," *U.S. News & World Report*, 20 June 2005, 40.
2. Michael Elliott, "The Chinese Century," *Time*, 22 January 2007, 32–41.
3. U.S. Department of Defense, *Quadrennial Defense Review Report*, (Washington, D.C.: February 6, 2006), 9.
4. Bibhudatta Pradhan and Anand Krishnamoorthy, "China, India to Boost Trade, Investment, Energy Ties," Bloomberg.com, 21 November 2006, http://www.bloomberg.com/apps/news?pid=20601102&sid=aFB_NIbsDUOA&refer=uk (accessed December 14, 2006).
5. Newman, "The Rise of a New Power."
6. Stephen Leeb, "A More Cautious Way to Play Energy and Chindia," *The Complete Investor* 4, no. 1 (January 2006), 2.
7. Matthew Forney, "China's Quest for Oil," *Time*, 18 October 2004.
8. U.S. Central Intelligence Agency, *The World Factbook* (Washington, D.C.: 2006). China's total manpower available for military service is estimated at 343 million (males aged 18–49), but the military manpower fit for military service (ages 18–49) is 281,240,272. This number is rising at a rate of about 13 million per year.

CHAPTER 12

Natural Disasters, Disease, and Famine Reach Everyone

1. Charles Krauthammer, "Flu Hope, or Horror?" *Washington Post*, 14 October 2005.
2. Tim Appenzeller, "Tracking the Next Killer Flu," *National Geographic* 208, no. 4 (October 2005): 2–31.

CHAPTER 13

The Last Suicidal Battle of World War III

1. Nancy Gibbs, "Apocalypse Now," *Time*, 1 July 2002, 42–48.

John F. Walvoord
The Father of Modern Biblical Prophecy

NO SINGLE INTELLECTUAL VOICE CONTRIBUTED more to the development of modern biblical prophecy than Dr. John F. Walvoord. During his six-decade-long career as an author, pastor, teacher, and educator, Dr. Walvoord articulated a comprehensive view of biblical prophecy that was based on his rock-solid belief that all the prophecies in the Bible either have been, or will be, literally fulfilled.

Dr. Walvoord began his teaching career as a professor of theology at Dallas Theological Seminary in 1936. In 1952, after the death of Dr. Lewis Sperry Chafer, the seminary's founder and first president, Dr. Walvoord became president and built it into a formidable graduate school of theology. In 1986, after serving Dallas Theological Seminary for fifty years, Dr. Walvoord became chancellor.

From the beginning of his professional career, Dr. Walvoord spoke and wrote about biblical prophecy in light of current world events. Even before the world believed there could be a Jewish return to the Holy Land or a nation of Israel, Dr. Walvoord insisted that a new Jewish state would emerge and that no one, whether it be the British, the Palestinians, or the Arab nations, could stop this inevitable fulfillment of biblical prophecy.

Before the Arab-Israeli wars of the 1960s, Dr. Walvoord maintained that Israel would win more land and power. He saw God's plan for the end times begin to unfold as the Palestinian-Israeli conflict became the focus of NATO and Western leaders. He taught that soon all the nations of the world would be embroiled in conflict leading to the events prophesied in the books of Daniel and Revelation.

Walvoord's studies led him to author, coauthor, or edit more than fifty books on Bible prophecy. One, *Armageddon, Oil and the Middle East Crisis,* became an international best seller in 1974. This work was later revised and expanded in 1990 during the Gulf War with Iraq. More than two million copies of this work are in print, and it has been translated into ten languages. This work proved the value of biblical prophecy in explaining world events.

Dr. Walvoord believed that the events of September 11, 2001, were the opening salvo to acts of sacred terror in the name of jihad that would push the world to the brink of destruction. In addition, he sensed that weapons of mass destruction would proliferate and force the West into preemptive military strikes. The need for oil would require massive military intervention to protect the oil fields of the Middle East.

Viewing current events through the lens of biblical prophecy, he believed it was evident that soon—very soon—the world would be engulfed in a terror never before imagined. In 2002, he began working on a new book to help make sense out of the confusing events that filled the headlines. From that unfinished work—and his classic *Armageddon, Oil and the Middle East Crisis*—comes *Armageddon, Oil, and Terror.*

John F. Walvoord
Bibliography

Author

The Doctrine of the Holy Spirit

The Holy Spirit

The Return of the Lord

The Thessalonian Epistles

The Rapture Question

The Millennial Kingdom

To Live Is Christ

Israel in Prophecy

The Church in Prophecy

The Revelation of Jesus Christ

The Nations in Prophecy

Jesus Christ Our Lord

Daniel: The Key to Prophetic Revelation

Philippians: Triumph in Christ

The Holy Spirit at Work Today

Matthew: Thy Kingdom Come

The Blessed Hope and the Tribulation

The Nations, Israel and the Church in Prophecy

Every Prophecy of the Bible (formerly *The Prophecy Knowledge Handbook*)

What We Believe

Major Bible Prophecies

The Final Drama (formerly *Prophecy*)

End Times

Prophecy in the New Millennium

Coauthor

The Prophetic Word in Crisis Days

Armageddon, Oil and the Middle East Crisis

Five Views on Sanctification

Four Views on Hell

Contributor

Modern Debating

Not by Bread Alone

The Sure Word of Prophecy

Winona Echoes

Light for the World's Darkness

Understanding the Times

The Word for This Century

The Coming World Church

Focus on Prophecy

Fresh Winds of the Holy Spirit

Prophetic Truth Unfolding Today

Prophecy in the Making

Prophecy in the Seventies

Jesus the King Is Coming

Founder's Week Messages

America in History and Bible Prophecy

Money for Ministries

Issues in Dispensationalism

Vital Theological Issues

Vital Prophetic Issues

Raging into Apocalypse

Foreshocks of Antichrist

Vital Christology Issues

Forewarning

The Road to Armageddon

Countdown to Armageddon

Foreshadows of Wrath and Redemption

Editor

Inspiration and Interpretation

Truth for Today: Bibliotheca Sacra Reader

Major Bible Themes (revised)

Chafer's Systematic Theology (abridged)

Coeditor

The Bib Sac Reader

Bible Knowledge Commentary (two volumes)

The Life of Christ Commentary

Mark Hitchcock
Bibliography

Author

Iran: The Coming Crisis

Could the Rapture Happen Today?

55 Answers to Questions about Life after Death

The Truth behind Left Behind (with coauthor Tommy Ice)

End Times Answers Series

   The Four Horsemen of the Apocalypse

   What Jesus Says about Earth's Final Days

   Seven Signs of the End Times

   Is the Antichrist Alive Today?

   The Coming Islamic Invasion of Israel

   Is America in Bible Prophecy?

   What On Earth Is Going On?

The Second Coming of Babylon

101 Answers to the Most Asked Questions about the End Times

The Complete Book of Bible Prophecy

After the Empire: Bible Prophecy in Light of the Fall of the Soviet Union

Contributor

Tim LaHaye Prophecy Study Bible

The Gathering Storm

The End Times Controversy

The Popular Encyclopedia of Bible Prophecy

Politics and Power in a Slave Society

J. Mills Thornton III

Politics and Power in a Slave Society
Alabama, 1800–1860

Louisiana State University Press
Baton Rouge and London

Designer: Dwight Agner
Type face: VIP Sabon
Typesetter: Graphic Composition, Inc., Athens, Georgia
Printer and binder: Kingsport Press, Inc., Kingsport, Tennessee

LIBRARY OF CONGRESS CATALOGING IN PUBLICATION DATA

Thornton, J   Mills, 1943–
  Politics and power in a slave society.

  Bibliography: p.
  Includes index.
    1. Alabama—Politics and government—To 1865. I. Title.
JK4525;1977;T48 ——   320.9'761'05   77–4296
ISBN 0–8071–0259–8

Winner of the
Jules F. Landry Award
for 1977

To the memory of my grandfather,
J. MILLS THORNTON, SR.

Contents

Illustrations

Tables

Preface

THE WORK which follows is founded upon a set of assumptions about the process of American history which, lest the reader mistake my purpose, I had better make explicit. In the first place, I believe that the history of our states is by no means entirely a function of the history of our nation. A state's history possesses its own concerns, its own actors, its own logic. It is, of course, possible to recount some aspects of national history as if the nation were a unit, just as it is possible to treat some aspects of the history of the western world as if Europe and America were a unit. At the point at which great events reach the individual, however, those events are perforce observed from the perspective of each person's past experience. And though the existence of differing local perspectives may be of no especial importance in explaining certain developments, the fact that we are a federation renders it, I think, crucial to the understanding of our politics. The voters in each state, having been exposed to local leaders, issues, and incidents, have thus known a politics not shared in anything but barest outline by voters elsewhere. The same thing might be said of the voters of a county, to be sure. Yet the nature of federalism seems to me to elevate the political life of the state to such a level of importance in the experience of a citizen that, unlike that of a county, it can readily become—must, indeed, often become—an essential factor in shaping his reactions to national questions, and to political transactions in general.

Now I also believe that all actions in history are based, necessarily, on subjective perceptions. It is possible, I suppose, for one's subjective perception of a group of circumstances to be more or less congruent with something which might be described as "objective reality." But I do think that history which seeks only to discover "what really happened" can degenerate far too easily into antiquarianism. The more important task is to recreate people's impressions of occurrences. It is probably not too much to say that history is the story of the collision of perceptions. And since American political history contains within it separate, parallel—in some respects even autonomous—sets of events in state and nation and thereby grinds different lenses through which voters must attempt to view common phenomena, it follows that state history must impinge as frequently upon national history as national history does upon state history. It follows, in fact, that state history must give form to national history, just as national history contributes to forming state history.

To put the matter another way: Abraham Lincoln was one man, and we may by diligent investigation discover his particular beliefs on a range of questions. But it is possible to maintain that when Lincoln ran for president, he became—at least as a candidate—not one man with specific views at all, but a mass of diverse mental images. Certainly the Lincoln who emerges from the pages of the Alabama press bears little resemblance to the Lincoln one encounters in the press of Alabama's balance state, Illinois. And Alabamians reacted, of course, to the Lincoln they knew. Thus national politics, which seems at first glance to be national in scope, becomes on examination quite local— quite subject, by extension, to the manipulation of characters with whom even the specialist in the period may not be acquainted.

It is undoubtedly easier to study—and vastly easier to teach— American political history as if it had taken place for the most part in Washington. Very few historians are really expert in state history, and the successful efforts to show the relationship between state and national affairs have been even fewer. The profound importance of state history in shaping national history has therefore remained largely hidden. But the phenomenon, for all that it has seldom been noticed by scholars, has been nonetheless real.

I have led the reader through this chain of observation in preparation for an attempt to defend the present work from the charge of parochialism. The reader is about to embark upon an extended account of several aspects of the early history of Alabama. It may well be that he will find out a good deal more about Alabama than he wants to know. And towards the end, after he has waded through a swamp of unfamiliar names, he may conclude with some resentment that I have attributed cosmic significance to a series of deservedly obscure proceedings. He may even, if in a waspish mood, decide that my argument reduces to the contention that the American Civil War was caused by the failure of the Alabama legislature to reelect Benjamin Fitzpatrick to the Senate in 1859. I will state that I do not in fact maintain any such position. For fear that my mere assertion fail to allay the doubts of the skeptic, however, let me offer a specific declaration of my intention in undertaking this study.

First, I have not meant to deny that the familiar sequence of escalating incidents—the Missouri Crisis, nullification, the rise of abolitionism, the Texas controversy, the Mexican War, the Wilmot Proviso, the Crisis of 1850, the Kansas-Nebraska Act, the collapse of the Whiggery and the creation of the Republican party, the Dred Scott decision, Lecompton, the John Brown raid, the Charleston convention, the election of Lincoln—is essential to the explanation of secession. Indeed, it is not only not my purpose to deny that these things were important, but it is precisely my purpose to show why they were important. To comprehend why, when a stone is thrown into a pond, there is a splash, it is necessary to understand the nature of stone, but it is equally necessary to know something about water. The present investigation is an effort to paint the portrait of a political style, a political culture. It seeks to describe, for one state, the institutional, ideological, and political context into which national events fell. I wish, if I may so phrase it, to place upon the reader the spectacles through which antebellum Alabamians peered out at their frightening world.

These remarks lead me to a second point. For anyone used to more traditional discussions of secession, the first third of this book may well seem to be a sort of extended introduction, only tangentially related to the subject. On the contrary, I regard the first third of the study as the statement of my hypothesis, and the remaining two-thirds as a test case of that hypothesis. I have not sought to explain secession directly, but rather to explain the conditions which made a decision for secession possible. In fact, I have never regarded the explanation of secession as my primary purpose, but merely as something which I had to do in order to make my case as to the nature of the state's political structure. Perhaps this point will be clearer if I offer a succinct summary of my contentions—though I do so with some hesitation, since brevity necessarily distorts the argument to some degree.

Antebellum Alabama was, I believe, a society obsessed with the idea of slavery. In the first place, the fear of an imminent loss of freedom was a part of the inheritance which Alabama's citizens had received from their Revolutionary forebears. The fear had dominated the thought of radical Whigs in eighteenth-century England and had been an essential element in the ideology of the republic's founding fathers. Modified to meet the needs of a later generation, it formed a principal item both in the allegations of the Jacksonians and in the responses of their Whig adversaries. And in Alabama this tradition was lent considerable urgency by a daily familiarity with black slavery, which served as a constant reminder of the terrible reality behind the politician's metaphor. Secondly, because servility excluded one from membership in the citizen body, an Alabamian therefore could not simply assume that his dignity as an individual was accepted; he had rather to prove his worth—his claim to possess the qualities of a free man—constantly, both to his fellows and to himself. If he wished to retain his place in society, he had to be ready at all times to fight for it. Finally, slavery guaranteed, so it was believed, that very few white men would ever have to depend directly upon other white men for their sustenance. Since Jacksonian ideology emphasized the notion that freedom is autonomy—that is, the absence of external forces manipulating one's life—the existence of slavery quite naturally came to seem an essential bulwark of freedom.

Politicians played constantly upon the fear that institutions were conspiring to limit autonomy, and thus to reduce the populace to subservience. Politics was the profession of popular representation; politicians considered it their responsibility to locate some organization or practice which would serve as a symbolic summary of the otherwise unfocused popular misgivings. Officeseekers went about their task by identifying and promising to destroy potential sources of enslavement. Government was regarded as something like a trade union of the electorate—the mechanism through which the voters, individually weak, could bring their collective strength to bear against the rich and the powerful. Throughout most of the antebellum period, therefore, Alabama's rulers strove vigorously to limit the influence of wealth—and particularly of corporate wealth—in the life of the state.

Developments within the state during the 1850s made all of these aspects of Alabama's past mighty allies of the developing southern rights crusade. The boom in cotton prices during this decade generated investment capital, permitting the construction of a rail network. Areas of the state previously isolated began to move into the market economy. The banking system, essentially abolished during the depression, was recreated. Cities grew rapidly, and a portion of the electorate, dazzled by the new prosperity, began to vote for candidates who advocated aggressive governmental programs to develop the economy and to assist the citizenry. Government at all levels became much more active; its expenditures increased enormously. A statewide public school system was created. Control of the political mechanism began slipping from the hands of poorer citizens, as the influence of great planters in the state's political life assumed significance for the first time. These events, refracted through the remaining elements of the state's traditional ideology, assumed a profoundly menacing appearance and thus intensified the fears which had been the raw material of Alabama politics from earliest days.

Just at this time, however, leadership within the Democratic party—now more than ever the state's dominant party—was passing to a second generation of politicians, less sensitive to the attitudes and apprehensions of the masses. Most of their efforts to locate symbols adequate to the creation of a political movement were clumsy and excessively conscious. Only the villains offered by the southern rights advocates among them seemed capable of striking fire with the voters. Alabamians were now gaining those contacts with the outside world which made a northern threat seem credible. And northerners were coming to demand that the South be shut out of the territories—the one hope for escape from the growing rigidity which Alabamians detected in their social order. If Republicans controlled the federal government, Alabamians concluded, a southerner would be able to go to the territories only if he were willing to abandon a truly egalitarian, democratic world for a hierarchical, elitist one, on the northern model. Moreover, Alabamians regarded Republican policies as a declaration that southerners were second-class citizens, junior partners in the American enterprise. The southern rights argument successfully defined a monster which—like the "Monster Bank" of an earlier day—was seeking to deprive the voters of the pride of freedom which was their most valued possession. And the politics of the late fifties dutifully responded to that fact.

During the fifties Alabama had been both horrified and irresistibly fascinated by the evidence, with which events of the decade were replete, of the power of organized minorities to effect their aims without the consent of the masses. The activities of corporations and urban elements within the state and of abolitionists in the North all seemed to offer proof of this capacity. Jacksonian ideology pronounced such activities an immoral use of the political process; the only moral path to a remedy for one's grievances lay through an effort to convince a majority of the justice of one's cause. But many young laissez-faire radicals took the teachings of the new age to heart. These men, who were to be the cutting edge of the Yanceyite movement, thus came to preach the liberating gospel that southerners possessed a means of sectional salvation alternative to the effort to persuade northerners of the equity of southern claims. Minorities need not wait until they became a majority; they could save themselves. Thus, while Alabamians' fears of the free-soil movement were fixed firmly in Jacksonian assumptions about the nature of the social order, the strength of the notion that secession could be an efficient defense against the menace rested on the lessons of the emerging era of industrialization and urbanization. The sectional crisis took form at the moment of conjunction between these two worlds.

I commenced this preface with an argument that the specific events of state politics, no matter how local they may seem at first glance, contributed essentially to the creation of an environment in which the acceptance of revolution was possible. I would like to conclude the preface on a somewhat different note. A majority of northerners voted for Lincoln; the Lower South states seceded within a few weeks of each other. Obviously common phenomena must have been at work in the emergency. Despite differing local perceptions of them, the specific incidents of intersectional recrimination which I recited earlier, from the Missouri controversy to the election of 1860, constitute one source of this commonality. But I would wish to point to another. I believe that the Civil War was the catastrophe of Jacksonian America, the denouement of the Jacksonian drama. Accordingly, for all that I have urged the importance of recognizing a measure of autonomy in state history, I also believe that, given a sufficient degree of generalization, the various components of the Alabama setting of the 1850s as I have described them were present in substance in each of the other southern states—and, *mutatis mutandis*, in each of the northern states as well. One of my principal aims in this volume has been to suggest the deeply important sense in which the Civil War is everywhere an outgrowth not merely of the direct sectional encounters, but also of many of the episodes and concerns of the antebellum period which did not have any explicitly sectional content. The war was the sum of the age. And thus the experience of Alabamians in these years was, at some level, the experience of all Americans.

Acknowledgments

IT IS A great pleasure for me to acknowledge the many kindnesses extended to me by friends, acquaintances, and strangers in the perhaps too many years during which this book has been in preparation. The volume presented here is based largely upon the fruits of eight years of research, off and on, at the Alabama Department of Archives and History in Montgomery—a period which, despite its length, was insufficient for me to do more than scratch the surface of the Archives' rich holdings. There is hardly a member of the Archives' research staff who has not in some way gone beyond the call of duty in my behalf. I hesitate to mention any names, since I cannot mention them all. But I must particularly thank the department's director, Mr. Milo B. Howard, Jr., who was endlessly helpful and unfailingly kind. I also wish to express especial appreciation to the late Mr. William Letford of the Civil Archives Division and to Mrs. Virginia Jones of the Manuscripts Division, the respective death and retirement of whom are blows to all students of Alabama's history.

Professors Malcolm McMillan and Allen Jones of Auburn University arranged for me to use a microfilmed copy of the Dixon H. Lewis Papers, thus saving me a trip to Texas. The Reverend and Mrs. Thomas Thrasher put me up—and put up with me—during my research at Chapel Hill and Duke. And the staffs of those two libraries were always efficient. Professor Ralph Wooster of Lamar State University provided me with the original data for Alabama which he had used in the preparation of his book *The People in Power*, thus allowing me to compare his findings with my own. I am deeply grateful to Professor Wooster for this act in the highest tradition of scholarship.

Professor Michael Holt, now of the University of Virginia, read two earlier versions of this study and offered numerous incisive, subtle and exceedingly useful comments. My argument would be far looser and the structure of the book far more confusing were it not for Professor Holt's suggestions. Professors George Wilson Pierson, Edmund Morgan, and Howard R. Lamar of Yale University encouraged me at an early stage. My former colleague Professor Michael Perman of the University of Illinois at Chicago Circle and my present colleague Professor Gavin Wright read the manuscript and made instructive observations. And Professor Eugene Genovese of the University of Rochester tendered a challenging criticism of one of my principal contentions.

I have postponed to the last the acknowledgment of by far my greatest debt, and the one which I have the most difficulty in putting into words. From Professor C. Vann Woodward of Yale University, who directed the dissertation of which this book is a revision, I received patient criticism, gentle advice and constant support. But my obligation is not limited to these contributions. I also received from Professor Woodward what I can only call a frame of mind, an understanding of what is to be gained from the study of the past. That gift is one which no thanks can repay.

I gratefully acknowledge permission to reprint lines from Robert Penn Warren's poem "Harvard '61: Battle Fatigue," from *Selected Poems: New and Old, 1923–1966*, copyright © 1966 by Robert Penn Warren and reprinted by permission of Random House, Inc.

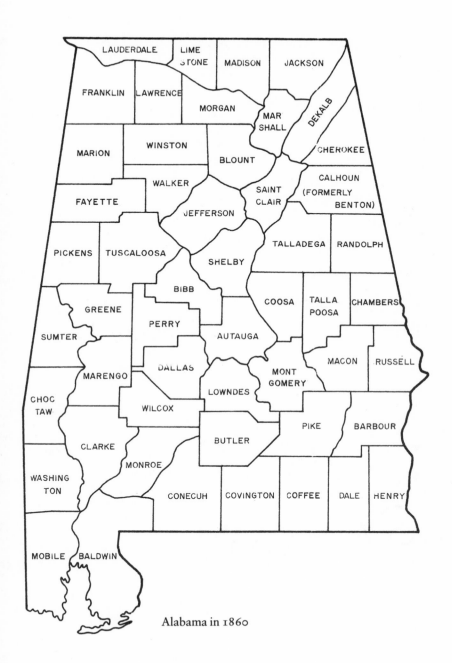

Alabama in 1860

Part One **Quirites**

Chapter I Foundations

MARK TWAIN was still an adolescent in the years during which his cousin Jeremiah Clemens served in the United States Senate from Alabama. But the young man could hardly have been ignorant of the notoriety which his distinguished relative gained during the Crisis of 1850 for delivering speeches whose vitriolic denunciations of the North and passionate proclamations of southern righteousness startled all observers. Perhaps it was at this time that Twain began to grapple with the problem which was to dominate so much of his subsequent writing: what it meant to be born a southerner. Nine years after his cousin left the Senate, Twain gave a concrete demonstration of his dilemma by volunteering for the Confederate army and then, following the briefest of service, deserting the cause. Thereafter the problem seems to have tormented him. We have from his pen a number of loving portraits of boyhood in the South, punctuated by unexpected and sharp assaults upon the region. His most moving attempt to resolve the difficulty, however, is set not in the South but in medieval England.

A Connecticut Yankee in King Arthur's Court, beneath its humor, is a tortured effort to explore the validity of the assumptions of laissez-faire America by placing them in conflict with the alien values of an earlier age. The hero is convinced of the virtues of machinery and democracy, and wishes to acquaint the sixth century with their benefits. He at first assumes that feudal civilization will crumble at his touch, but he quickly finds its foundations deeply laid. At one point he is particularly horrified to find members of the lower classes cooperating eagerly with the aristocracy to execute a group of rebels against the aristocracy's rule. The hero tells us:

This was depressing to a man with the dream of a republic in his head. It reminded me of a time thirteen centuries away, when the "poor whites" of our South who were always despised and frequently insulted by the slave-lords around them and who owed their base condition simply to the presence of slavery in their midst, were yet pusillanimously ready to side with slave-lords in all political moves for the upholding and perpetuating of slavery, and did also finally shoulder their muskets and pour out their lives in an effort to prevent the destruction of that very institution which degraded them. And there was only one redeeming feature connected with that pitiful piece of history; and that was that secretly the "poor white" did detest the slave-lord and did feel his own shame. That feeling was not brought to the surface, but the fact that it was there and could have been brought out under favoring circumstances, was something—in fact it was enough; for it showed that a man is at bottom a man, after all, even if it doesn't show on the outside. . . . Whole ages of abuse and oppression cannot crush the manhood clear out of him. Whoever thinks it a mistake, is himself mistaken.[1]

Twain was a southerner, however, and he knew that the Connecticut Yankee's tenacious faith was ill placed. Because the Yankee refused to profit from the object lessons which the sixth century so regularly presented him, because he refused to abandon his naive notions of man, he impelled the novel toward a denouement in which his dreams were rejected and his world destroyed. There have been historians who have shared the Yankee's view of the South, who have preferred his affirmations of cheering unreality to the discovery of a sadder truth. But as Twain knew—and as he was to teach his Yankee protagonist—the ideals of the antebellum South were the ideals of the southern citizenry. Students who insist upon attributing the evil of the region to a ruling class—who, in effect, absolve the populace from blame in the creation of its society—are often attempting to close their eyes to a fact which they do not wish to believe: that democracy contains no intrinsic tendency towards producing good. Democracy as a form of government is merely a mirror of men, and the insistence upon man's nobility is what brought the Connecticut Yankee to his doom.

In the present work I shall undertake to explain how the political

1. Mark Twain, *A Connecticut Yankee in King Arthur's Court* (New York: New American Library, 1963; originally published, 1889), 216, 218.

structure of antebellum Alabama permitted the adoption of secession, and why the social structure demanded the decision. The first chapter, an introduction to the larger study, will narrate briefly the events which, at the outset of the state's history, created the assumptions and the style that were to dominate the coming decades. In the succeeding two chapters I shall describe the nature of government and politics in the state during the era. And in the final three chapters I shall turn to the last ten years of antebellum life, in an effort to show how the institutions and beliefs delineated in the earlier chapters worked together with awful logic to slay the community which had produced them.

The Birth of the Style

One shorthand but nonetheless useful way of delineating the periods of Alabama's early political history is to glance at the educational background and length of service of her various congressmen. In the light of these criteria, the years during which antebellum Alabamians served in the national House of Representatives—1818 to 1861—fall readily into three periods of fourteen years each. Of the seven men elected before 1832, only two had not attended college.[2] But of the twenty men first elected between 1832 and 1846, fifteen had never attended a college. Further, the two men in the earlier period who could not claim college attendance each served but a single term. The average tenure in this period is six years six months, and discounting the two non-college men it is eight years, or four terms. In the second period the average tenure is only four years four months, and by disregarding two men with long service we obtain the more accurately descriptive figure of three years two months, or a term and a half. Clearly, the electorate in the second period chose more poorly educated representatives and turned them out of office with much greater alacrity.

For those men elected after 1846, the picture changes a bit. Of the

2. These and the following facts are from U.S. Congress, *Biographical Directory of the American Congress, 1774–1949,* comp. James L. Harrison *et al.* (Washington: Government Printing Office, 1950). I may add that one of the two non-college men, Robert E. B. Baylor, later served the cause of higher education by founding the university which bears his name.

eighteen, six were graduated from a college, an additional three attended college but did not graduate, and two others attended formal professional schools. The difference is hardly marked, however, and to balance it we find such men as seven-term Representative Williamson R. W. Cobb, who had no formal education at all; his first employment was as an itinerant clock peddler. The average time served by these men is four years three months, and if Cobb and one other perennial congressman be disregarded, the average is three years three months. We may conclude that the candidates offering themselves for office were now somewhat better educated, but that the electorate was not appreciably more satisfied with its representation than earlier. As to party balance, we note a marked Democratic predominance. Only nine Whigs were elected to Congress during the entire antebellum period, and only one of these men—Henry W. Hilliard—served more than two terms.[3]

There are factors which distinguish the third period more sharply from the second than it may appear, but we may leave them aside for the present in order to dwell upon the differences between the first period and both of its successors. One model frequently offered for antebellum political development does not seem to be confirmed by these findings. Far from encountering a rising aristocracy, we are struck by precisely the reverse—at least to the extent that the electorate's acceptance of elitism may be measured by its willingness to retain its representatives in office for long stretches and to regard academic attainments as no disqualification for preferment. We may safely assert, at any rate, that after 1832 voters were far more disposed to appraise a representative's efforts and find them wanting, and far more likely to demonstrate hostility to intellectual pretensions. A look at Alabama politics in the earliest period will help us to understand what caused this change.

Before the creation of the Alabama Territory in 1817, only two small sections of the state had been settled. The Tombigbee settlement, in present-day Washington and Clarke counties, was almost entirely isolated from contact with the outside world. Located in extreme southwest Alabama, it was surrounded on three sides by the vast wil-

---

3. In addition to the nine Whigs, two Democrats were elected as Know-Nothings in 1855.

derness of the Indian country and on the fourth by the hostile Spanish at Mobile. It was populated largely by cattle drovers. As late as 1820 it counted 643 herds of cattle over forty head each, to but 168 such herds in Madison County, the state's other frontier settlement. At the same time it reported only 1,697 taxable slaves to Madison's 5,511, and paid total taxes of $2,995.92 against Madison's $9,254.95. The latter figure, incidentally, is one-fourth of the total taxes collected by the state in the year. The Tombigbee settlement's most famous citizen was Harry Toulmin, a Scottish freethinker who fled to the region in search of a place so far from civilization that he could be safe from the Presbyterians. Toulmin, the territorial judge, represented the settlement in most of its relations with the outside world—primarily, it seems, because no one else was capable of undertaking the commissions.[4]

Madison County, in the Tennessee Valley in extreme northern Alabama, was a different case altogether. Squatters had been coming into the area since 1804, but it was not opened to purchase until the end of 1809. At the Nashville land sales of that year much of the best land was purchased by wealthy Georgians. Only about a third of the squatters were able to buy the lands which they had cleared. But many Tennessee settlers secured plots in the area. Of the original purchasers 85 percent bought small farms for homesteading.[5] The net result of the land sales, therefore, was to create a population with an overwhelming majority of small Tennessee farmers, but to place most of the best land in the hands of a wealthy and clannish band of Georgia planters. The situation was ready-made for class conflict.

The Georgians in question are a most interesting congregation. Neighbors in the Piedmont of Virginia, they immigrated to the Broad River region of Georgia about 1784, under the leadership of General George Mathews, later twice governor of that state. The settlers, who from the outset possessed a strong sense of group identity, "formed the most intimate friendly social union ever known among the same

4. Frances C. Roberts, "Background and Formative Period in the Great Bend and Madison County" (Ph.D. dissertation, University of Alabama, 1956), 411–12; Thomas McAdory Owen, *History of Alabama and Dictionary of Alabama Biography* (4 vols.; Chicago: S. J. Clarke Publishing Co., 1921), IV, 1676–77.

5. Roberts, "Madison County," 137, 200, 204–205. By 1815, some 43 percent of the three thousand squatters had purchased title to land in the county.

number of persons." The story of these remarkable people is related in the memoirs of Governor George R. Gilmer, himself one of them.[6] Since the homes of many of the Broad River people had been in the same area of Virginia, some intermarriage had already taken place, but in Georgia the intermarriage reached such heights that every member of the group was closely related to every other. They were accustomed to wielding political power and, by the time of the settlement of Alabama, had already produced a governor, three senators, and numbers of congressmen and legislators. In Alabama's early years, the cousinry dominated the state politically, economically, and socially. Though not completely homogeneous in their views, they generally shared a common social outlook which can only be described as confidently superior. In that particular sense, one might with some legitimacy characterize them as aristocrats.

The main migration into Alabama from the Broad River was not to come until 1818, and it was to be to the Black Belt, but in 1809 three of the Broad River group—Thomas Bibb, Alabama's second governor; Bibb's cousin, Leroy Pope; and Pope's son-in-law, John W. Walker—bought extensive holdings in the newly opened Tennessee Valley, and a number of their kinsmen followed them there to become even wealthier off the fertile land. Leroy Pope, who created the town of Huntsville and by a liberal application of money and influence made it the county seat, became president of the Huntsville Bank—a fact of incalculable importance for the future history of the state.[7]

It is not hard to understand the hostility aroused in the Tennesseans by the opulent Broad River settlers. The inimitable Mrs. Anne Royall described Pope's situation in 1823, somewhat more than three years after his bank's suspension of specie payment had plunged the state into crisis: "Col. Pope is amongst the wealthiest men in the state of Alabama, and lives in princely style. If any man is to be envied on account of wealth, it is he. His house is separated from Huntsville . . . and from an eminence overlooks the town. . . . On the east lies his

6. George R. Gilmer, *Sketches of Some of the First Settlers of Upper Georgia, of the Cherokees, and the Author* (Baltimore: Genealogical Publishing Co., 1965; originally published, 1855), 6. See also E. Merton Coulter, *Old Petersburg and the Broad River Valley of Georgia: Their Rise and Decline* (Athens: University of Georgia Press, 1965).

7. Roberts, "Madison County," 217,222. On the general wealth of the Broad River clans, see Gilmer, *Sketches*, 137.

beautiful plantation, on a level with the house. . . . If I admired the exterior, I was amazed at the taste and elegance displayed in every part of the interior: massy plate, cut glass, chinaware, vases, sofas and mahogany furniture of the newest style decorated the inside." [8] Naturally the small farmers were suspicious of a bank which refused redemption in specie while its president lived in such a style.

But the roots of resentment go much further back in the history of Madison. It first appeared in the open in 1810, only a year after the opening of the county. A small settlement of squatters near the future site of Huntsville had existed before the land sales of 1809. The area was generally called Hunt's Spring after the squatter who first built his cabin there. When, however, Pope laid off his town, he decided to give it a new name. Proud of his reputed relationship to Alexander Pope, he chose the name Twickenham, after the poet's home. Having already expelled Hunt from his land, Pope had now expunged the squatter's name from the landscape. The original residents were enraged. The next year Madison became entitled to three seats in the Mississippi territorial legislature, and the Georgians nominated County Attorney Louis Winston and Pope's son-in-law John W. Walker, balancing their ticket with the selection of Tennessean Peter Perkins for the third seat. But the old settlers decided to make a fight, and put forward squatter Hugh McVay and newly arrived Tennessean Gabriel Moore. McVay and Moore swept to victory over Winston and Walker, and the future tone of Madison County politics was established. The Broad River group, destined to dominate the county economically and socially, were nevertheless not to win an election for seven years, and when they finally did so, as we shall see, their triumph was fleeting. It is worth noting that both Moore and McVay were to become governors of Alabama.

The first action of the new legislators was to have the name of Twickenham changed to Huntsville. In gratitude for this blow at the privileged, the Madison County electorate consistently returned Moore and McVay to the legislature every year for the rest of the territorial period. And Moore and McVay, especially the former, con-

---

8. Anne Royall, *Sketches of History, Life and Manners in the United States* (New Haven: printed for the author, 1826), 14.

tinued vigorously to fight the battles of the masses and to oppose the Broad River forces.[9]

The creation of the Alabama Territory in 1817, however, brought rapid change to the political order. Practically all of Alabama was opened to settlement at the same time. Except for two small plots in the west and the vast territory between the Coosa River and the Georgia line, the Indians ceded the entire area of the future state in 1816. By 1817 surveys had been completed and sales begun—at Huntsville for north Alabama and at Milledgeville, Georgia, for the central and southern areas. Thereafter, the population rose phenomenally. In 1813 the population of the two Alabama settlements was 13,000. As squatters began to enter the newly ceded lands during 1816, the population rose to 25,000. By the spring of 1817 it was 33,000 and by the summer 35,000. In 1819 the number had reached 70,000 and in 1820, 127,000.[10] During this land boom period, the bulk of the Broad River community decided to follow its pioneer relatives from Georgia to the new territory. Forming a land company, the settlers selected a prominent Milledgeville friend, General John B. Scott, to handle the purchase of a tract from among the lands being offered for sale in his home town. Scott purchased a choice section on the upper Alabama River, including the future site of a part of the city of Montgomery, and in 1818 Scott's associates began to remove to the area.

The rapidly increasing population brought dreams of statehood to the newly adopted Alabamians. And because the desire for admission was so strong, the Broad River immigrants were able to transfer their political prominence to their new home. One of the most powerful men in the national government, Secretary of the Treasury William H. Crawford, was a son of the Broad River, as were both of Georgia's senators, William Wyatt Bibb and Charles Tait. The additional alliances of the Broad River were extensive. All of this influence could be mobilized in behalf of Alabama's admission, if the Broad River group desired to do so. The astute politicians within the group quickly

9. Roberts, "Madison County," 305, 307.
10. Thomas P. Abernethy, *The Formative Period in Alabama, 1815–28* (University, Ala.: University of Alabama Press, 1965; originally published, 1922), 26–27; Weymouth T. Jordan, *Ante-bellum Alabama, Town and Country* (Tallahassee: Florida State University, 1957), 22–23.

realized that they could use their power in order to strike an implicit bargain, promising the Alabamians statehood if the Alabamians in turn would bestow electoral favor upon them.

Senator Bibb, who had made himself unpopular in Georgia by voting to increase Senate salaries, resigned from Congress and accepted President Monroe's appointment as governor of the Alabama Territory. From this eminence he began the effort to have Alabama admitted to the Union as a Broad River fief. The statehood argument had telling effect even in bitterly divided Madison County. In the elections of 1817 for the first territorial assembly, Gabriel Moore and Hugh McVay were returned of course, but the county's other two seats went to the Broad River leader John W. Walker and an important ally of the group, Clement Comer Clay. Similar results appeared from throughout the state. When the legislature convened in 1818, the Broad River combination had great strength in the elective lower house, and was thus able to control the selection of the upper house as well. As soon as word of these events reached Washington, Charles Tait swung into action, had the Alabama admission bill passed by the following spring, and removed posthaste to the Alabama Territory in order to receive his reward—the new state's federal judgeship. Meanwhile, the territorial assembly, under the recently elected Broad River leadership, undertook an unfortunate experiment intended to alleviate the growing pains of Alabama's infant economy. In order to attract credit to the booming but currency-starved settlements, future Chief Justice Abner Lipscomb introduced and the legislators passed a bill repealing the Mississippi Usury Act of 1805, which had set the maximum interest on loans at eight percent. Henceforth, any interest rate specified in a contract would be legal.[11]

This action was to have dire consequences for the future hopes of the Broad River politicians but, for the present, they went from strength to strength. In the spring of 1819, they scored a sweeping triumph in the election for delegates to the state's first constitutional convention. The electorate seemed in unanimous agreement "that the most important problem facing the convention was the admission of

11. *House Journal*, 1st Sess. of 1818, pp. 22, 31–32, 41, 53, 149, 158. *Cf.* Abernethy, *Formative Period*, 137.

Alabama to the Union," [12] and that the Broad River power bloc was in the best position to effect this result. Even in Madison County, the Broad River victory was an easy one. Only Gabriel Moore among the county's eight delegates was not associated with the group. The victory was aided by the fact that many of the candidates who normally were darlings of the masses had deserted public opinion to take a stand against admission under present conditions.[13] John W. Walker was elected the convention's president, and Clement Comer Clay was appointed chairman of the committee of fifteen which drafted the constitution.

But the constitution that was produced was the most liberal of any state's at the time. White manhood suffrage was adopted. Elections were by secret ballot. No qualifications other than age, race, sex, and residence were established for any office. The voters chose state representatives for one year, governors for two years, and senators for three. Legislative apportionment was based strictly on white population in both houses. Reapportionment was made mandatory every six years. A gubernatorial veto could be overridden by a simple majority of each house. Emancipation was permitted, as was the prohibition of the importation of slaves for sale. Slaves were guaranteed jury trials when accused of crime. Lands could only be taxed in proportion to their value. All banks were required to reserve two-fifths of their stock for the state, which, if it exercised its option to buy, would appoint two-fifths of the bank's board of directors. Bank stockholders were made liable for bank debts in proportion to the amount of their stock. Four of the five members of the county governing bodies were popularly elected,[14] as were sheriffs and clerks of court. Judges were chosen by joint ballot of the legislature for life. The last provision, the single one even vaguely conservative, had been approved only after a fierce fight; it was modified by amendment within ten years.

12. Malcolm C. McMillan, *Constitutional Development in Alabama, 1798–1901: A Study in Politics, the Negro, and Sectionalism* (Chapel Hill: University of North Carolina Press, 1955), 31.

13. Roberts, "Madison County," 337, 320.

14. The constitution merely permitted this arrangement (*Alabama Constitution of 1819*, Art. V, Secs. 1, 9, 12). Its actual basis was a statute of 1821 (*Acts of Alabama*, Called Sess. of 1821, pp. 8–18; *cf. Acts of Alabama*, Sess. of 1822–23, pp. 3–5). The county judge—later styled the probate judge—served ex officio as the fifth member and chairman. His election was given to the people in 1850.

The provisions of the 1819 constitution, given the composition of the convention, might seem anomalous. In fact, however, they emphasize the existence of general attitudes which we must keep constantly in mind. The Broad River group, though it may with a degree of justice be called a branch of the "Southern aristocracy," was not at all aristocratic in the political theories it accepted. And in making such anti-elitist assumptions, the group was characteristic of a large segment—perhaps most—of the class which it represented. John W. Walker had written to Charles Tait when Tait was drafting the act authorizing the convention, "If the People ought ever to be fairly and fully represented, it is in the formation of a Constitution—which the fundamental principle of all our institutions supposes to be the act of the People themselves." [15] Such a sentiment, though expressed in this case in an effort to secure an increased membership for Walker's home county, is not at all an unusual one among Alabama's early rulers. They had gained position and power in Georgia under a professedly democratic system, and they expected to achieve success in Alabama on the same terms. In addition, it is important to note that if their political dreams failed to materialize, they would not be excessively disappointed. Their ambitions in the economic realm were equally important to them. One may even imagine that their devotion to democratic political institutions derived in part from the fact that it was in such a setting that they had converted the rather moderate means with which they had immigrated to Georgia, into the considerable wealth in which they had immigrated to Alabama. At any rate, it is certainly accurate to say that the accumulation of wealth was one of the group's primary goals.

If economics dominated some Broad River minds, it was the economy which was to bring Broad River political schemes to naught. The constitutional convention coincided with the Panic of 1819, and the effects of the depression very soon began to be felt by the farmers who were just then struggling to meet the payments on the lands which they had purchased at the government auctions. The repeal of the Usury Act, which had gone into effect at the end of February, 1818, had sent interest rates soaring and debtors were now pressed on

15. John W. Walker to Charles Tait, December 3, 1818, in Charles Tait Papers, Alabama Department of Archives and History, Montgomery.

all sides to settle their accounts. The gubernatorial election of 1819, in which William Wyatt Bibb defeated Marmaduke Williams by 1,200 votes out of 15,500 cast, was the last in which the Broad River was clearly successful. Williams, later a leading Tuscaloosa Whig, had sought to identify himself with the popular elements, but with only limited success. He was disliked in the south because he opposed Bibb's choice of Cahaba as the state capital. But the failure of the Broad River allies to hold the northern part of the state was apparent. The governor carried only two of the northern counties. And in the crucial legislative contest in populous Madison, the Broad River representatives were swept from office. Three of the new representatives installed in their places—Samuel Walker, Epps Moody, and Isaac Wellbourn—had been rejected in favor of their opponents in the election for convention delegates just a few months before. Only two of the eight representatives were even slightly associated with the Broad River forces. Gabriel Moore overwhelmed Leroy Pope in the race for the single state senate seat.[16]

In 1820 the Broad River coalition included in its number, in addition to the governor: his brother, the president of the state senate; one of the two U.S. senators, John W. Walker; the state's chief justice, Clement Comer Clay; and her federal judge, Charles Tait. But, despite this accumulation of power, the group's political ambitions were already doomed to miscarriage. In June, 1820, the Huntsville Bank suspended specie redemption. The Huntsville notes were practically the only currency in north Alabama, and the suspension hence vastly increased the antagonism of the farmers in that area to Pope and his associates. By 1823, their gubernatorial candidate Henry Chambers having been defeated for a second time by their archenemy Israel Pickens, the Broad River settlers had bequeathed the state her liberal constitution and had withdrawn into the fastnesses of their economic and social power. They continued their entrepreneurial endeavors—often with success, as we shall see. But in the state at large, the Broad River group abandoned political life forever shortly after Governor Pickens' decisive triumph.

The fact that Alabama's proto-aristocracy no longer possessed the

16. Roberts, "Madison County," 343–44.

power to transform itself into the genuine article does not end the story, however. We recall that the break which we located in our analysis of Alabama's congressmen was in 1832, not 1823. The solution to this difficulty is easily found in the character of the men who had been leading the opposition to the Broad River efforts. The farmers' battles were fought by well-educated men, often lawyers, who saw identification with the masses as a road to power and who, in addition, sincerely resented Broad River pretensions. Such a man was Gabriel Moore. We have already seen him at the age of twenty-five, leading the battle to rechristen the town of Twickenham. During succeeding years, in the Mississippi and Alabama territorial legislatures, in the 1819 constitutional convention, in the new Alabama legislature, and in the Congress, to which he was sent in 1821, he continued to fight for the people. His four terms as a congressman were devoted to efforts to secure preemption rights at land sales for squatters, to prevent their forcible removal from illegally occupied lands, and generally to liberalize provisions for land purchase. He was principally responsible for the passage of legislation along these lines in 1824 and 1826, and when a general preemption act was finally passed in 1830, though Moore was no longer in Congress, the triumph was really his. Moore's successor, Clement Comer Clay, eager to cut the ties which had bound him to the dying Broad River bloc, shrewdly took up Moore's crusade in behalf of the squatters and drove the final bill through to passage. When Moore offered for governor in 1829, no one could be found to oppose him, and the electorate elevated him unanimously.

But Moore was not a farmer. Educated at the University of North Carolina, he was regarded as one of the most successful lawyers in the state. At any rate, he was certainly quite well-to-do; in 1830 he owned 30 slaves and by 1840 he owned 79. Though his sympathies were with the lower classes, his station was not. Events after 1823 began to alienate the farmers' affections for such men as he.

The reelection of Israel Pickens as governor was not the only event which marks 1823 as a watershed. In 1823 also William B. Long, a young Kentucky attorney who had come to Alabama the year before, began the publication of the Huntsville *Democrat*. Long's frenzied excoriations of the conspiracy that, so he warned, threatened the liberties of Alabama's citizens, are ludicrous at this distance; but the conspiracy seemed a deadly serious business to the thousands of north Alabama farmers who read his published fulminations. Long called his opponents the "royal party" and he found them under every bush. Though he and his associates claimed to know exactly who their enemies were, they were capable of changing their minds as to whether a particular politician was or was not an aristocrat.[17] In any event the evil conspirators, whoever they might be, were certainly set on sucking the life blood from all sturdy sons of the soil. The Huntsville Bank was able to pay in specie, Long announced. It was merely refusing to do so. The "royal party" was seeking thus to force small farmers to sell out their holdings. Their ultimate aim might well be to establish feudalism in the Tennessee Valley.

About the time that editor Long was discovering the existence of the royal party, Governor Pickens was making the discovery which would leave him the master of Alabama politics. Coming from the quiet backwater of Saint Stephens in the old Tombigbee settlement, he had been elected in 1821 in a contest which had turned largely upon personalities, sectional rivalries and depression-born resentments against the incumbent rulers. But he had cut his political teeth in the politics of North Carolina, which state he had served in Congress for six years, and he well knew that if his career was to advance, he needed to create for himself a substantial statewide power base. Saint Stephens had afforded him no means to effect that end, but now that a bit of luck had placed him in the governor's chair, he could reveal himself to the north Alabamians as a champion of the people by locating and espousing a popular issue. He found it in a proposal for chartering a state bank. He sought to take control of the economy out of private hands and to create a public institution with a president and directors elected by the legislature. Such a bill almost necessarily drew the opposition of the state's businessmen.[18] But that opposition was grist for the mill of Long's *Democrat*, and now Long's charges were

17. *Cf.* Stanley M. Elkins and Eric McKitrick, "A Meaning for Turner's Frontier," *Political Science Quarterly*, LXIX (1954), 580. The point, of course—quite different from that which Elkins and McKitrick deduce—is that by this time there was no longer any organized effort by a coherent group to extend existing social and economic power into the political sphere; so that Long and his successor Andrew Wills could fix on any candidate as the "royalist" with about equal validity.

18. See Abernethy, *Formative Period*, 116–17.

echoed by the governor. Together they labored to convey the impression that the battle lines separated the poor but honest from the wealthy, supercilious and crooked. In 1823 Pickens was reelected and the Bank of Alabama was established. But the process of the disintegration of Alabama politics had begun. What worked for Pickens, many a neophyte politician reasoned, may work for me. Thus the key to achieving office became to convince the electorate of one's credentials as a common man.

The absurdities of the situation were demonstrated first, naturally, in Madison County. In 1825, at Long's editorial insistence, the legislature revoked the charter of the Huntsville Bank. Long thereupon offered himself and a slate of his friends for the legislature, proclaiming that the voters were being given an opportunity to show their gratitude for his achievement. The voters responded by turning out the representatives who had actually voted for the revocation, and putting Long and his friends in. Long died two weeks after the election, however, and in the following months other ambitious politicians were able to convince the voters that Long's heir apparent, former Senator William Kelly, was himself a financial manipulator of sorts. The next year, therefore, Kelly and his associates were turned out, and a third set of representatives gained office. But Kelly was not defeated yet. If he could create an issue comparable to Pickens' bank, he could yet recoup his fortunes.

He located promising material in a recent decision of the state supreme court. In 1824, the court had ruled that contracts for debt made during the period after the repeal of the Usury Act were valid only between the date of the contract and the date on which the debt first fell due, and that if the debt thereafter remained unpaid, additional interest could accrue at no more than the statutory rate, 8 percent.[19] The decision was hailed as a great blow for the people. But in 1827, with almost exactly the same personnel, the court ruled that the statute of limitations precluded the recovery of illegal interest which had been collected prior to its 1824 decision.[20] Suddenly the justices were

19. *Henry and Winston* v. *Thompson,* 1 Minor 209. The author of the principal opinion, Chief Justice Lipscomb, was also the author of the act at issue.

20. *Jones* v. *Watkins,* 1 Stewart 81. Of the justices who considered this case only John White was new.

transmuted into members of the royal party. Kelly announced a crusade to have certain of the judges impeached, and on this platform he and his allies were returned to power in Madison—the fourth change in the county's legislative delegation in as many years. The impeachment trial resulted in an acquittal, but Kelly's efforts did eventuate in a constitutional amendment limiting judicial tenure to six years.

And so, by the beginning of the decade of the thirties, the infrangible patterns of Alabama politics were established. Perhaps the last casualty of the upheaval was that first friend of the common man, Gabriel Moore. When Long had been able to present genuine evidence in support of his diatribes, Moore had listened. Thus he early called for a congressional investigation into the alleged defalcations of "royalist" John Brahan, the receiver of the Huntsville Land Office.[21] But on the whole Moore had persistently sought to chart his own course in politics, rather than rushing to pronounce each new shibboleth proposed by the *Democrat*. He had, therefore, become suspect in the very circles in which he had always been most popular. A person of Moore's wealth and education had now to be even more an adherent of democratic dogma than were the small farmers themselves, since the most innocuous deviation would be taken as proof of his already suspected duplicity.

At the end of his term as governor, Moore ran for the Senate against John McKinley, a former ally of the Broad River group who had received absolution from the *Democrat*'s editors and was now the candidate of the "popular" faction. In order to defeat McKinley, Moore accepted the support of the legislature's relatively small bloc of Nullificationists. This action made the Jackson administration suspicious of him, and the administration's coolness towards him when he reached Washington drove him towards friendship with John C. Calhoun. When, after much hesitation, Moore voted against Martin Van Buren's confirmation to the British ministry, the "champions of the people" were at last provided with a concrete action to support their allegations that the senator had deserted the true faith. They quickly launched a noisy campaign to secure his political destruction. In 1834

21. Roberts, "Madison County," 366.

the legislature formally requested him to resign. He refused, but after the expiration of his term in 1837, he was never again elected to public office. In 1843 he emigrated to Texas, and there in 1845 he died, unwept by those by whom once he had been worshipped.

What was this "royal party" which had created the structure of all future political activity? We might answer, and not without some superficial validity, that it was nothing—a figment of the demented imagination of William B. Long and of his equally vehement successor at the *Democrat*, Andrew Wills. But to give such an answer is to miss the point. The royal party was real—as real as an irrational hatred or an unnamed fear. It was the embodiment of all the insecurity of small farmers in the midst of plantations, of the poor in the midst of plenty, of a new state in the midst of old. It was an entity to whom the defiant affirmation could be made that in a democracy, numbers count. Long's bulletins from an imaginary front informing the troops that the enemy had been turned back filled his followers with fierce joy. It also diverted their energies away from any effective agitation for substantial amelioration of their hard lot. Social welfare schemes, even internal improvements projects, were wholly foreign to the government of antebellum Alabama. But the war against the phantasmal royal party gave the mass of Alabamians something perhaps more valuable. It gave them the crusade—the sense that, through cooperative political action, they could command their destiny. For better or worse, this gift was to remain Alabamians' proudest possession through the future years.

We may, then, summarize the course of early Alabama politics. An imported Georgia elite early alienated the small farmers of north Alabama, generally immigrants from Tennessee. The Broad River pioneers possessed only economic power until just after the creation of the Alabama Territory. Then, riding a popular issue—statehood—for the first time, they took power from the champions of the people, who had deserted public opinion in order to oppose admission. This development, coupled with the fact that other members of the cousinry had gained social leadership during the settlement of the Black Belt to the south, gave the Broad River group ascendancy in the state's early days. But the enactment of legislation which could be made to appear self-serving, and the intervention of an outside economic disaster, returned these men to their accustomed unpopularity and, by 1823, they were no longer a political force in the state.

Leaders in these years were drawn principally from the Tennessee Valley. There—and there alone in the territorial period—the conjunction of a small farmer majority and the makings of an aristocracy with which the majority could fight had given aspiring politicians an opportunity to prove to their constituents their devotion to the cause of the masses. South of the valley, the more homogeneous communities of both the hill counties and the Black Belt did not afford such an arena for local class conflict. This fact in great measure explains the preponderance of Tennessee Valley residents in nascent antebellum politics. But the war against the "royal party" began to undermine the influence of the shepherds who had established themselves as popular spokesmen in the clashes of early days. Politicians either vigorously espoused and reinforced the myths and prejudices of the hill-county electorate, outdoing each other in affirming the limitations of their philosophies, or else were eliminated from public office. The desperate search for issues with which to authenticate democratic credentials began with the efforts to establish a state bank and to impeach offending members of the supreme court. At first, when the politicians embraced popular prejudices, they knew better but were afraid to say so. Very soon, however, politics was dominated by men who did not, in fact, know better. The government of Alabama was then prepared to act out the antebellum drama.

The Style Acquires Substance

Alabamians were preaching the substance of the Jacksonian faith long before Jackson had become its symbol. Indeed, Jackson, because of his background in land speculation, had some difficulty in convincing Alabamians that he was a true prophet of their creed.[22] From earliest times, it is true, voices were raised in advocacy of positions that in later years the Jacksonians were to condemn as heterodox—voices that called for aid to internal improvements and the erection of tariff walls and that deprecated the notion that the preservation of the rights of the

22. *The Tuscumbian* (Tuscumbia), May 31, 1828.

states might be incompatible with an active general government.[23] Such views were to become the doctrine of Whiggery. It is, however, profoundly erroneous to suppose that these early efforts were the foundation stones of the opposition. It is equally false to maintain that the acceptance of these ideas renders the authenticity of Alabama's devotion to Jacksonian teachings suspect. Her devotion resulted from no late conversion; it represented a fundamental social commitment. Rather, the fact that such opinions should have been advanced before Jackson's accession to the chief magistracy is evidence that the policy canon of the Democrats was late in formulation and that the essence of the faith lay much deeper. The present section will define the ways in which the parties differed, with particular emphasis upon segregating mere policy differences from conflicting presuppositions.

The historic roots of the Whig party are embedded in the growth of a doctrine which both factions accepted—states' rights. The doctrines of the Jeffersonians in that regard were not current in early Alabama. In fact, perhaps the only prominent exponent of strict Jeffersonianism in the state was former Georgia Congressman Bolling Hall, who had settled in Autauga County in 1818. Hall's nephew, Dixon H. Lewis, began the process of insinuating states' rights ideals into the political oratory of Alabama by using them to attack John Quincy Adams and to exalt Andrew Jackson during Adams' tenure in the presidency. But the ideals were embraced at this period primarily because of their usefulness in furthering Jackson's campaign.[24] In 1829, Lewis was elected to Congress after a canvass turning on the issue of federal aid to internal improvements. Lewis opposed such aid even though to do so was highly unpopular at the time.[25] He was aided in achieving his victory, however, by his political sense and by his entertainment value. While his opponents confined themselves to waterborne transportation, and campaigned almost exclusively among settlers along the river banks,

23. *E.g.*, the Fourth of July address delivered by John W. Walker at Huntsville in 1811 (reprinted in Birmingham *News*, July 4, 1915); *The Tuscumbian*, December 24, 1824, January 30, 1826; Florence *Register and Public Advertiser*, August 4, 1827.

24. Abernethy, *Formative Period*, 147–51. *Cf.* Lewis' resolutions, in *Acts of Alabama*, Sess. of 1826–27, pp. 120–121, and *Acts of Alabama*, Sess. of 1827–28, pp. 169–72; and his address, in *House Journal*, Sess. of 1827–28, pp. 182 ff. See also *Acts of Alabama*, Sess. of 1825–26, p. 104, an exceedingly mild resolution which was Lewis' first tentative states' rights step.

25. The campaign may be followed in the Selma *Courier*, particularly June 18, July 2, July 9, July 16, July 23, August 20, 1829.

Lewis went out into the back country. There, with his vast corpulence, he provided speeches more amusing than a circus sideshow.[26] Thus the genuine acceptance of states' rights doctrines was still in the future.

The ideology of states' rights actually gained importance because of the continuing search by the politicians who had opposed Israel Pickens, for an issue on which to regain power. After Pickens' smashing reelection in 1823, many of the prominent leaders who had cooperated with the Broad River group began casting about for a way to dissociate themselves from that alliance. In the presidential election of 1824, the group was of course supporting its kinsman William H. Crawford. Governor Pickens endorsed John Quincy Adams and the Huntsville *Democrat* came out for Henry Clay. A great many of the north Alabama politicians formerly allied with the Broad River group—particularly such Tennessee Valley leaders as John McKinley, Clement Comer Clay, and Henry Chambers—therefore joined their fortunes with the only other alternative, Andrew Jackson. When the returns were counted, they discovered, perhaps a bit to their surprise, that their candidate had been given an overwhelming endorsement, receiving 70 percent of the vote. The Pickens forces, in uneasy alliance with such uncompromising advocates of a centralized and activist government as James Dellet, managed to deliver 18 percent of the vote to Adams, most of it from the relatively mercantile areas. And the group rounded up 12 percent for Crawford; more than half of his total came from the principal Broad River settlements, in Montgomery, Autauga, Madison, and Dallas. Henry Clay was not accorded a significant poll.

The unexpected magnitude of Jackson's triumph placed his fortunate supporters well on the road to emancipation from their past. But in south Alabama, hostility to Crawford and the group had not seemed to be of sufficient depth and intensity to warn all of the group's former allies in time that they must desert Crawford's cause. Thus, such politicians as John F. Everitt, Jack F. Ross, John Archer Elmore, Matthew Clay, James Abercrombie, George Phillips, Dixon H. Lewis,

26. On Lewis' campaigning techniques, see the unsigned obituary of Lewis by one of his contemporaries in the Dixon H. Lewis Papers, Alabama Department of Archives and History, Montgomery. Lewis weighed 350 pounds when only twenty and 430 pounds at his death.

and many of lesser stature found themselves with the albatross of aristocracy hung securely around their necks.

In an attempt to emulate the success of their north Alabama brethren, most of these south Alabama leaders scrambled into Jackson's ranks after 1824. But their migration came too late for their reputations to receive its full benefit. They actually joined the cause no later than did many of the Pickens faction. But even after Governor Pickens' untimely death in 1827, his adherents could still claim association with issues which assured them of a place in popular affections. They had created the people's bank, had forced Leroy Pope to his ruin, and even at that moment were engaged in the effort to make the state supreme court respond to the needs of debtors. The Huntsville *Democrat* thus moved easily into the role of principal Jacksonian organ and Pickens men took leading positions in the Jacksonian crusade. They saluted the men whom they found there already, including such of their old enemies as John McKinley and Clement Clay, as converts to the one true faith, effectively obscuring precisely who had joined whom.

The Crawfordite novices in the faith had no such independent issues upon which to rely. They sought eagerly to gain full acceptance from their new allies. But though Dixon Lewis was permitted to use his strict constructionist theories to assault President Adams, and though John Archer Elmore was accorded a symbolic place on Jackson's slate of electors in 1828, it was apparent that the south Alabama Crawfordites were merely tolerated, not welcomed, in the Jacksonian camp. In the popular mind they remained firmly identified as the political lackeys of the incipient elite of territorial days. As such, they were very little more popular with most voters, especially in north Alabama, than were the small group of centralizing ideologues led by James Dellet who defied public opinion to support Adams for reelection in 1828. Adams managed respectable polls in such rather commercial counties as Mobile, Tuscaloosa, and Greene, but in the state at large he received a humiliating 10 percent of the votes, to Jackson's 90 percent.

Whatever a politician's formal position in the canvass of 1828, then, the voters remained acutely aware of which leaders were generally reputed to be aristocrats and which were not. In offering a toast at a Selma banquet in 1829, one guest defiantly proclaimed, "The voters of the county of Dallas are not willing to admit that the records of the country prove that we are governed by Lords and Nobles.—If such men as Nicholas Davis, [James] Jackson of Lauderdale, [George] Phillips, [Samuel W.] Oliver, [Dixon H.] Lewis, [James] Abercrombie and others be aristocrats, we would that all our law-givers were such aristocrats." But shortly from across the board came the reply: "Harry Toulmin, Israel Pickens, Gabriel Moore, Reuben Saffold, William R. King and John Murphy—the true asserters of the enlarged rights of man in the [Constitutional] Convention of Alabama."[27]

Thus even at this date, well before the existence of formal party organizations in Alabama, and a full decade before the final definition of the issues over which the two parties were to struggle, the public seems to have had a clear sense of what characteristics would form the opposing groups of leaders. Every individual mentioned in the first toast would become a founder of the Whiggery—though Davis and Jackson would enter the party, along with James Dellet and Arthur F. Hopkins, through the tiny and despised faction of pro-Adams governmental activists, while Phillips, Oliver, Lewis, and Abercrombie would take the more usual route into the new party, through nullification. The second toast's catalog, the old heroes of the Pickens faction, was not quite so durable a list. Death had already claimed Toulmin and Pickens by this time, and excessive independence would eliminate Moore. But the political usages and general social orientation represented by these names would certainly carry forward into the emerging Jacksonian leadership. Moreover, as the toast's reference to the constitutional convention implies, while issue content in the party struggle was to be added by historical circumstance, the actual identity of the initial set of political managers had to a surprising extent been determined by the events of the earliest days of statehood.

If, however, the south Alabamians formerly associated with the Broad River settlers had not been able to locate some mechanism through which to destroy their identification with elitism, as many of their prominent early associates in north Alabama had long since succeeded in doing, then the relative continuity of factional leadership in

27. Selma *Courier*, July 9, 1829.

41744

the state might have been broken just at this time by the total triumph of that party which had been nursed in its infancy by Pickens, Long, Kelly, and Gabriel Moore, and which had recently been strengthened by the accretion of such talented manipulators as McKinley and Clay. Of course, the coalition was not entirely harmonious, as the contest between McKinley and Moore for the Senate in 1831 demonstrates. But it was sufficiently stable to portend doom for both the small group of Adams partisans and, especially, for the much larger group of south Alabama "aristocrats."

Fortunately for the ambitions of the Crawfordite remnant, the personal triumph of Dixon Lewis in the congressional elections of 1829 suggested a possible path to political redemption. In that campaign, as we have seen, Lewis had introduced into the political discourse of the state a potent pseudo-Jeffersonian brew linking strict construction and laissez-faire economics to the effort to preserve the farmer's freedom. He warned earnestly of the dangers of federal aid to internal improvements, playing repeatedly upon the popular assumption that government could easily become despotic if not restrained. He painted horrifying word portraits of a population stripped of its liberties. "It is idle to say that we must rely upon the justice and moderation of Congress as a relief from these consequences," he thundered. "When has any wise government intrusted the rights of its citizens to such deceitful securities? To quote the emphatic language of a Southern writer, 'The very definition of slavery is that political condition in which one portion of society is dependent for the enjoyment of all its rights upon the justice and moderation of another.' " [28]

Southerners knew slavery, and they sought above all else to avoid the condition. Therefore the south Alabama politicians who were searching for a tactic with which to establish their enmity towards aristocracy recognized at once the enormous power of this appeal. Young Moseley Baker, who in 1827 had become the editor of an old Broad River organ, the Montgomery *Alabama Journal*, was set to work propagating the newly rediscovered doctrines of states' rights. In 1832 Baker was detected in a scheme to defraud the Bank of Alabama, and decamped to Texas. But his successor at the *Journal*, Thomas S.

28. *Ibid.*, June 18, 1829.

Mays, carried on his work. Baker and Mays were ably supported by A. M. Robinson, first at the Tuscaloosa *Spirit of the Age* and later at the Tuscaloosa *Intelligencer*; and during the crucial years 1833 and 1834, by perhaps the most talented and effective of all the Nullifier editors, Richard T. Brumby of the Tuscaloosa *State Rights Expositor.*[29]

In connection with the developing South Carolina rationale for resistance to the tariff, the states' rights propagandists very quickly extended Lewis' oratorical conventions to the issues of free trade. One zealous member of the states' rights rank and file, a cousin of the future congressman and educator J. L. M. Curry, absorbed the line and repeated it earnestly in a letter to his uncle. The Nullification party, he said, included "every patriot who does not quail with abject and slavish fear before the Lordly Aristocrats of the North and East"; southerners had become the slaves of the tariff advocates, "and a master dislikes to let his slave go free. But we have the right and power on our side, and if we have not the firmness and valor to demand and maintain our rights, we deserve to be slaves." But, like most of his party, this writer went on to denounce Calhoun as a self-seeking politician, and to assert his continued adherence to the cause of Jackson.[30]

In truth, very few Alabamians outside the Black Belt were much exercised about the tariff. All admitted it to be sectional, partial, and unjust. But the regulation of international commerce simply seemed to a subsistence farmer in the Alabama hills, to have very little relevance to the prosaic round of his existence. Moreover, some trusted political leaders, including Governor John Murphy and Senator John McKinley, told the electorate that in the long run a tariff would force crop diversification and industrialization on the state, which would be quite a good thing. And many other politicians joined Governor John Gayle in supposing that the tariff was a mere political maneuver by Henry Clay, and would pass away with the demise of Clay's presidential aspirations.[31]

29. *Alabama Journal* (Montgomery), April 14, April 29, May 19, 1832; Huntsville *Democrat*, March 14, 1833, September 3, 1834.
30. Jabez Curry to William Curry, July 8, 1832, in J. L. M. Curry Papers, Alabama Department of Archives and History, Montgomery.
31. *Senate Journal*, Sess. of 1829–30, p. 7; John McKinley, in Tuscumbia *Telegraph and*

Even those Alabamians who did fear the tariff were not much enamored of nullification as a remedy for it. The electorate was coming slowly to embrace states' rights, but only as a political creed to be given currency by reason and argument, and consequent victory at the polls. Nullification committed the sin of challenging the perfection of the American constitutional structure, though every true citizen knew that "the wisdom of our system has secured [the rights of the states] against every emergency short of open and avowed usurpation."[32]

Nevertheless, during 1830 and 1831, warnings of threats to freedom both from the tariff and from federal aid to internal improvement did carve out for the nascent states' rights faction a secure power base in the Black Belt. The belt was the region of the state most closely tied to the national economy and was therefore the area most likely to accept the notion that policies formulated in such remote places as Washington City upon such dimly understood matters as the tax rates on imported goods, could have immediate significance for the daily lives of ordinary people. As a result, there emerged in the belt a substantial bloc of voters who believed that their continued personal independence was in danger.

In 1832 the states' rights men felt strong enough to defy the Jacksonian leadership in the state by joining in the effort to elect Philip Pendleton Barbour as vice-president instead of Martin Van Buren. Though Barbour received only 14 percent of the vote in the state at large, to Van Buren's 86 percent, the Virginian did obtain more than a quarter of the poll in eight south Alabama counties—Pickens, Greene, Marengo, Wilcox, and Lowndes in the Black Belt, and Butler and Conecuh farther south. Indeed, Barbour's slate actually carried Pickens, Wilcox, and Conecuh.[33] Moreover, in the legislative elections of the same year, the states' righters captured about a fourth of the assembly seats, virtually all of them from the belt.[34]

Patriot, June 21, 1828; John McKinley to John Murphy, May 25, 1828, in Governors' Correspondence: Murphy, Alabama Department of Archives and History, Montgomery; *Senate Journal*, Sess. of 1832–33, pp. 12–13; *Senate Journal*, Sess. of 1833–34, p. 11. Cf. George Goldthwaite to Joseph W. Lesesne, August 26, 1844, in Joseph White Lesesne Papers, Southern Historical Collection, University of North Carolina Library, Chapel Hill.

32. *Senate Journal*, Sess. of 1833–34, p. 11. Cf. *Senate Journal*, Sess. of 1831–32, pp. 46–48 and *Senate Journal*, Sess. of 1832–33, p. 14.

33. No returns survive from six of the thirty-six counties.

34. Huntsville *Democrat*, November 15, November 22, 1832.

By the time that nullification had passed its crisis in South Carolina, then, its issues had done well by the Alabama politicians who were riding them. Constant emphasis on the threat which governmental activity posed to liberty and constant reiteration of concern for the preservation of individual autonomy had emancipated the men allied with the faction from the old association with the presumptively antiindividualistic, antilibertarian values of aristocracy—at least in the Black Belt, where the populace accepted that the danger was not chimerical. Still, a fourth of the assembly seats and 14 percent of the statewide vote was not a party, by a long shot. If they had been left with the issues of the tariff and internal improvements, the states' righters would probably never have achieved broad support. They could save themselves from this fate only by linking their doctrines to some issue comprehended by a mass following. And then, in 1833, they were quite unexpectedly presented with the means for doing so—the confrontation with the Jackson administration over the removal of the Creeks.

After the Creeks had ceded their remaining lands in the state in 1832, Alabama had immediately divided the area into counties and squatters had rushed in. But federal authorities quickly began to receive allegations of widespread efforts by the settlers to defraud the Indians of the lands guaranteed to individual tribesmen under the terms of the treaty. President Jackson thereupon ordered the army to remove all white people from the cession, and to keep them out until the completion of full surveys. For the squatters this decision meant months of homelessness and privation, and they resisted. In the ensuing hostilities, a member of the newly elected Russell County Commission, Hardeman Owens, was killed by one of the federal troops. The squatters promptly indicted the soldier for murder, and Governor Gayle demanded his surrender to state officials.

Gayle went further, however, to denounce the War Department's protection of the Indians as a gratuitous affront to Alabama's sovereignty. Since the state had extended legal jurisdiction over the region, he pointed out, disputed land titles could be settled in the state courts by the ordinary process of trespass and ejectment actions. The fact that the federal government refused to trust that procedure carried with it the outrageously undemocratic implication that Alabamians could not properly administer their own affairs. In making his argument, Gayle adopted many of the oratorical conventions of states' rights theorists.[35]

The crisis itself was settled by a bit of realpolitik. President Jackson's mediator, Francis Scott Key, publicly promised to deliver the offending soldier, but in fact quietly permitted the hapless young man to desert. By that time the survey of the cession had been completed. Key therefore compelled the Indians to select their lands at once, and the army happily withdrew, leaving the Creeks to the greed of the speculators, the hatred of the settlers, and the illusory protection of the state. These devices saved face for the president, but there was actually no blinking the fact that Gayle had won. After the crisis of 1833, the Indians received no further assistance from the federal government until their final removal in 1837.

The question of land—preemption for squatters, extinction of Indian titles, reduction of federal land prices and their graduation according to the quality of the soil, or as the politicians phrased it, getting every family a farm[36] —had of course been a powerful issue from the beginning of the state's history. The villain of this piece had usually been the federal government, the agency which could, but would not, satisfy the settlers' land hunger. Many politicians—John W. Walker, Gabriel Moore, and Clement Comer Clay most prominent among them—had built their popularity by portraying themselves as congressional champions of the hard-pressed land purchasers or squatters, in

35. Gayle's involvement in the controversy is best studied through his official correspondence. See John Gayle to Jeremiah Austill, November 26, 1832, Gayle to Lewis Cass, August 20, 1833, Gayle to Robert L. Crawford, August 20, 1833, Gayle to Elijah Hitzclaw, August 20, 1833, Gayle to Edward Curry, August 20, 1833, Gayle to Thomas Woodward, August 20, 1833, Gayle to Thomas S. Martin, September 24, 1833, Gayle to Cass, October 2, 1833, Proclamation of His Excellency the Governor to the Citizens of the Counties Situated in the Creek Nation, October 7, 1833, Gayle to James Abercrombie, J. Dandridge Bibb, William D. Pickett *et al.*, January 26, 1834, all in Governors' Correspondence: Gayle. See also *Senate Journal*, Sess. of 1833–34, pp. 13–22, 77, 93; William R. de V. King to Gayle, December 6, 1833, January 4, 1834, March 18, 1834, and undated extract [internally dated to 1832], all in William R. de V. King Papers, Alabama Department of Archives and History, Montgomery. Finally, on the settlement of the controversy, see Francis Scott Key to Gayle, February 4, 1834, June 11, 1834, both in John Gayle Papers, Alabama Department of Archives and History, Montgomery. See also Huntsville *Democrat*, October 3, October 17, October 24, October 31, November 14, November 21, November 28, 1833. An earlier version of Gayle's position had been argued in federal court by Arthur P. Bagby and Henry Goldthwaite, and had been dismissed (Huntsville *Democrat*, January 5, 1832).

36. *Senate Journal*, Sess. of 1829–30, pp. 156–57.

battle with a government in which other interests were predominant and which was therefore unwilling to heed the pleas of the pioneer. Gayle's efforts, however, gave promise of opening a new route to the fulfillment of the farmers' dreams. No longer need their representatives engage in supplication before a Congress whose designs were alien to them. Now, like freemen, they could take what they wanted. The state government, it seemed—the political embodiment of the white settlers—held legitimate authority over the Indians as well. Gayle had short-circuited the mediating influences of the federal structure; he had eliminated the necessity to weigh contending interests; he had placed power directly in the hands of the people—at any rate, of the electorate of Alabama. For it was clear that the courts were sufficiently popular in their constitution that the acceptance of Gayle's case actually would place the disposition of the cession lands in the hands of the white settlers.[37]

Nullification as a weapon of South Carolina planters against the tariff had little appeal for Alabamians, and particularly little for the subsistence farmer to whom questions of foreign trade seemed as yet very far away. But a less formal brand of nullification used to increase the direct control of the subsistence farmer over his own destiny, to allow him to gain title to his own plot of earth, had great attraction indeed. It might even be made to appear as a new advance in the practice of democratic government.

In the legislative elections of August, 1833, the states' rights forces had captured their usual 25 percent or so of the seats. But after the removal crisis erupted in September, as Gayle's arguments began to take hold, a group of legislators—some of them, no doubt, motivated by personal loyalty to the governor, but others by a realization of the power of the governor's issue—moved to his support. By the time the winter's assembly session commenced, therefore, the new states' rights coalition found itself with an equal division of the members.

The breakthrough which the Creek difficulties had handed to the cause of the opposition compelled the Jacksonians to reexamine their position. In the fall, the Jacksonian leaders had denounced Gayle as a vile apostate. But during 1834 they carefully maneuvered to recapture

37. *E.g.*, George D. Shortridge to Clement Comer Clay, March 20, 1837, John A. Campbell to Clay, May 10, 1837, in Governors' Correspondence: Clay.

the allegiance of the Gayle men, finally even making overtures to Gayle himself. After all, they argued, the removal crisis was now over, and the factions in state politics could thus reform around new problems. Particularly, they sought to emphasize support for Jackson in the controversy which had been aroused by his removal of federal deposits from the Bank of the United States in the winter, and his censure by the Senate in the spring.

Though almost compelled by national events to enter this debate, the Jacksonians had great difficulty with it. In the first place, their own party was divided between those who opposed any national bank, and those who, like John McKinley, simply desired modifications in the bank's charter. In the second place, the orthodox states' rights men were not in the least backward in proclaiming their own belief that national bank charters were unconstitutional. Thus the Jacksonians were reduced to placing their adjurations upon the simple ground of personal loyalty to the president; all who did not rally to his standard in this hour of need would prove themselves Jackson's enemies.

The stage was thus set for the master stroke which would transmute the pro-Gayle coalition of the previous year into a party. The general assembly of 1834 was divided among three factions; one legislator defined them as Nullifiers, good Jackson men, and whole-hog Jackson men. It appears that the orthodox Jacksonians included perhaps 45 percent of the members, the Nullifiers about 30 percent, and the "good Jackson men"—the Gayle forces—the remaining quarter. The early weeks of the session were spent in a delicate ballet, as the Jacksonians attempted to regain, and the Nullifiers to hold, the allegiance of the third group. The Gayle men were unwilling to brand themselves as enemies of Old Hickory. They therefore voted with the Jacksonians to adopt the resolutions requesting Gabriel Moore to resign from the Senate. The Nullifiers began to worry that their newly won political strength might be melting away. They searched energetically for some expedient to hold the states' rights coalition together.

Near the end of the session, the Nullifier leaders hit upon an adroit strategem. They reworked the Jacksonians' anti-caucus oratory of 1824 into an attack on party conventions, denounced Van Buren as a power broker and political manipulator, and offered resolutions nominating an old Jacksonian, Hugh Lawson White, for president.

Then they quietly retired to the background in order not to give the movement an anti-Jackson flavor. The Gayle men subscribed at once to this nearly flawless solution. Moreover, in a monumental blunder, the Jacksonians, who were still seeking to curry the favor of the Gayle forces, agreed not to oppose the resolutions nominating White, if they were amended to deprecate any candidacy which might throw the election into the House. The resolution thus passed, and the jubilant Nullifier and Gayle leaders promptly launched their crusade, which was to dominate the coming two years, against the convention form of nomination.[38]

White was the perfect candidate for the new party, and the convention was the perfect issue. The Nullifiers lay low, and the White campaigners earnestly proclaimed that the Nullifiers were supporting White simply because they could find no candidate of their own. White was in fact, they said, the one true successor of Jackson, and the only issue was the threat to liberty posed by the existence of party conventions. A few of the White papers occasionally mentioned sectional considerations, but such matters were merely a passing concern compared to the daily hammering emphasis upon the question of whether a vote for Van Buren was not tantamount to "surrendering up our judgments and rights to the control of a few leading politicians and office-holders. . . . It is due to independence, it is due to the country, it is due to liberty itself that this odious [convention] system should be spurned from the embrace of freemen," they warned. "Let it go on a few years longer, and the elective franchise will become a mockery. . . . Yes! let our chief officers continue to be nominated and chosen in this way, and we may linger out a degrading political existence under a caucus despotism—we may wear for a while longer the forms of freemen; but our spirits will be effectually enslaved."[39] There was really never but one issue in Alabama politics: how to avoid slavery.

38. Huntsville *Democrat*, January 12, July 26, 1832, October 17, October 24, October 31, 1833, January 9, January 16, January 30, August 6, November 26, December 10, December 24, 1834, January 7, January 14, 1835.
39. Huntsville *Southern Advocate*, May 26, 1835. See also January 6, February 17, March 24, April 7, May 5, May 19, June 2, June 9, June 16, July 14, July 21, September 22, September 29, October 20, December 29, 1835, April 5, August 2, September 6, October 25, 1836.

About the spring of 1835 the White coalition gained an additional small but talented accretion, the leaders of the Adams forces of 1828. Adams' minuscule vote in that year had plunged his supporters into temporary obscurity. But with the rise of the nullification question around 1830, the strongly unionist Adams men—and a few north Alabama Crawford men—had reemerged as prominent figures in the anti-nullification coalition. Included in this number were Arthur F. Hopkins, James Dellet, Nicholas Davis, James Jackson, and John J. Ormond. They had remained adherents of the Unionist party until 1834. But though the emphasis by the Jacksonian press during that year upon the issues involved in the withdrawal of the federal deposits had had little effect upon any other political faction in the state, it had quite suddenly made aliens of this forlorn little band. In the coming year of factional maneuver, the Hopkins-Dellet group had largely held aloof.[40] In 1835, however, without fanfare they cast their lot with the anti-Van Buren effort.

The White party came up with a gubernatorial candidate against the Jacksonians' Clement Comer Clay in 1835. General Enoch Parsons had been one of the first prominent Alabamians to espouse Andrew Jackson's presidential cause.[41] His campaign, in accordance with the now-established standards of Alabama's politics, was judged by the frequency and ostentatious sincerity with which he bowed to the symbols of the democratic faith. One of Parsons' admirers described the beginning of the effort to a friend.

He came into sight of this town [Tuscaloosa] on the fourth [of July]. He had not gone very far into the main street when he found a collection assembled at the Methodist Church listening very attentively to an Oration. The General forthwith gets down, sends his man on to the tavern with the horses, and stumbles into the Church as a good old Hero should. As soon as the orator of the day had concluded, the said General starts up and gives to the sober congregation, more numerous in females than males, an address announcing himself a candidate for Governor. The matter took very well, is looked upon as the quintessence of Democratic Republickanism, and he is now styled the old Hero.[42]

40. *E.g.,* Huntsville *Democrat,* June 19, July 3, 1834.
41. Mobile *Register,* July 31, 1823.
42. Benjamin F. Porter to James Dellet, July 27, 1835, in James Dellet Papers, Alabama Department of Archives and History, Montgomery.

Clay defeated Parsons easily, with some 65 percent of the poll, the returns demonstrating the usual sectional division. But the White men retained an almost equal division of the legislature's lower house, and captured a precarious control of the Senate.[43] The Jacksonians, disturbed by the opposition's showing, were moved to summon the state's first party convention, which assembled in Tuscaloosa in December, 1835, to nominate a Van Buren electoral slate. Formal organization of the Democratic party dates from this time.[44] The action, of course, provided additional ammunition for White's propagandists.

Because of their hostility to conventions, the opposition was unable to stage a formal gathering. But later in December they did hold an open meeting at which a ticket of White electors was ratified. The electors had been carefully chosen to omit any but old Jacksonians. Included in the number, among others, were Governor Gayle, former Governor Murphy, Congressman Samuel W. Mardis, and House Speaker James W. McClung. White was damaged by the telling charge that, because his candidacy was not a national one, a vote for him was in effect a vote to decide the presidential election by intrigue in the House. Van Buren carried Alabama with 55 percent of the poll, to White's 45 percent.

Despite their loss, however, the White forces were not too discouraged. In the first place, the two-year long campaign had welded the leadership of the Nullifiers and of the Gayle faction into a firm alliance, which the Democrats initially called the "Whigs and Nullifiers," but increasingly between 1837 and 1839, simply the Whigs. In the second place, the opposition held its legislative strength, a slim majority in the Senate and a virtually even division of the House.[45] They remained confident of their issues. Through a happenstance of timing,[46] the Democrats were precluded from holding a state conven-

43. Huntsville *Democrat*, November 25, December 2, 1835; Huntsville *Southern Advocate*, December 15, December 22, 1835. About 20 percent of the representatives seem to have been Nullifier White men, and 30 percent Unionist White men.

44. The convention proceedings are printed in the Huntsville *Democrat*, December 23, 1835. The statement that the Democratic convention of December, 1838, was the state's first, offered in Allen W. Jones, "A History of the Direct Primary in Alabama, 1840–1903" (Ph.D. dissertation, University of Alabama, 1964), 13, is erroneous.

45. Huntsville *Southern Advocate*, August 30, 1836.

46. Owen, *History and Dictionary*, III, 582.

tion to nominate their gubernatorial candidate in 1837. They relied upon a legislative caucus instead, and chose a man who had only converted from the Whiggery eighteen months before, Arthur P. Bagby. The Whig candidate, Samuel W. Oliver, was as happy to crusade against a caucus as against a convention, however, and the oratory of Oliver's campaign was identical to that of White's. But Bagby beat Oliver by the customary margin, 55 percent to 45 percent, and in addition the Whigs appear to have lost control of the Senate, though they retained their strength in the House.[47]

The Panic of 1837 caused one final readjustment in the membership of the opposition, placing the nascent Whig party in the form which it was to retain through the coming decade. The leadership of the states' rights alliance, and of the small accretion of broad constructionists, was for the most part strongly commercial in its outlook. Indeed, the Black Belt Nullifiers had been drawn to the states' rights ideology initially, precisely because their involvement in the market economy made the allegation that the federal government's economic policies were a threat to freedom, seem a credible one. And the broad constructionists had generally adopted attitudes favorable to governmental activism because of their desire to obtain policies which would stimulate economic growth. In the legislature of 1840, those members who by that time called themselves Whigs, owed almost 80 percent of the total debt due from the legislators to the Bank of Alabama.[48] In addition, the opposition generally represented those counties most adversely affected by the depressed national economy, the urban and planting areas. After the panic, therefore, both the opposition politicians and a great many of their constituents began seeking some scheme of relief.[49]

47. Tuscumbia *North Alabamian*, July 21, 1837; Huntsville *Democrat*, September 5, November 11, 1837.

48. William H. Brantley, *Banking in Alabama, 1816–1860* (2 vols.; Birmingham: privately printed [Vol. I by Birmingham Printing Co., Vol. II by Oxmoor Press], 1961, 1967), II, 334–37, Appendix. The figures were $572, 596.66 of $721,909.48. It can, moreover, be noted that a very large portion of the Whig liability was owed the Mobile branch, located in the state's seaport and commercial center

49. *Cf.* James Jackson to Arthur P. Bagby, December 3, 1837, A. Q. Crawford to Thomas Tunstall, August 27, 1838, James E. Belser to Bagby, September 4, 1838, John P. Graham to Bagby, September 5, 1838, Gideon B. Frierson to Bagby, October 5, 1838, all in Governors' Correspondence:Bagby.

The solution accepted by most of the party's leaders was the chartering of a third Bank of the United States. Though the overwhelming majority of the states' rights men, converted by their pocketbooks, accepted this new position without difficulty, a small group of more consistent devotees of states' rights theories, led by Congressman Dixon H. Lewis, withdrew from the opposition coalition during the summer of 1838 in protest against what seemed to them to be a desertion of principle. By August of that year, the Whiggery was talking of running a candidate against Lewis, and at the Democratic state convention in December, the break was formalized when Lewis was unblushingly nominated to carry the Jacksonian banner in his congressional district.[50]

In part because of the defection of Lewis and his allies, but also because the bulk of the Alabama electorate was simply unconvinced of the virtues of a national bank, the Whiggery suffered a distinct defeat in the legislative election of 1838. Though party lines were still not sufficiently clear to permit a precise count, it appears that the Democrats could claim about fifty-three members in the new House, and the Whigs only some thirty-seven. And in 1839 the Whigs fell even further. By this time the party count was comparatively accurate, and produced a House containing some sixty-eight Democrats and thirty-two Whigs.[51] The opposition's decline from its equal division of the legislature in 1836 had been little short of calamitous.

In 1840, however, the Whiggery made a dramatic return to the strength it had possessed before the panic. The new House elected in that year contained fifty-one Democrats and forty-nine Whigs.[52] There were two reasons for this recovery. In the first place, at the beginning

50. Reuben Saffold to Arthur P. Bagby, May 22, 1838, Sidney C. Posey to Bagby, August 8, 1838, John Clark to Bagby, August 17, 1838, Clement Comer Clay to Bagby, January 20, 1838 [misdated; actually 1839], all in Governors' Correspondence: Bagby; Huntsville *Democrat,* December 29, 1838. *Cf.* Alexander Bowie to John C. Calhoun, April 13, 1847, in J. Franklin Jameson (ed.), *Correspondence of John C. Calhoun: Fourth Annual Report of the Historical Manuscripts Commission,* in *Annual Report of the American Historical Association for the Year 1899,* II (1899), 1109–1111.

51. Huntsville *Democrat,* December 8, December 22, 1838, September 7, 1839; Wetumpka *Argus,* March 4, 1840. In 1838 there were perhaps 42 committed Democrats, 34 Whigs, and 14 swing votes.

52. Whigs remained, however, a distinct minority of the Senate, only a third of which was chosen in any one year.

of 1839 the Whigs, recognizing their need for organization, had relented in their disapproval of party institutions so far as to hold a state convention. The party did not entirely abandon its hostility to conventions. It held a second convention at the end of 1840, and a third one in January of 1844. In addition, there was a Unionist convention composed primarily of Whigs in 1852 and a strictly Whig gathering later that year to choose electors for Winfield Scott. These five, however, were the only statewide gatherings ever held by the Whiggery. No Whig gubernatorial candidate was nominated in a convention. In 1841, James W. McClung, an anti-subtreasury Democrat who ran for governor with Whig endorsement, echoed Parsons and Oliver in making opposition to conventions a principal plank in his platform.[53] But McClung's defeat effectively ended appeals to this issue, and the Whigs themselves often resorted to district and local conventions in the coming decade. After 1839, therefore, the Whiggery may be considered to have possessed a relatively well defined party organization, at any rate equal to the structure established by the Democratic party in 1835.

Even more important in the recovery of the Whiggery was the deepening economic depression. After a conference of their presidents at Blount Springs in 1838, the state's banks had resumed specie redemption, only to be forced to a second, and even more catastrophic, suspension near the end of 1839, because of the failure of the Pennsylvania descendant of the Bank of the United States.[54] It was now clear that there would be no quick escape from the financial difficulties.

Many former Jacksonians who had initially rejected Whig proposals for rechartering the national bank began to reconsider in the light of the economic lessons which they had recently received. The wealthy Mobile industrialist and politician Adam C. Hollinger ingenuously reported an intellectual conversion about this time. He had, he said, supported Jackson "ardently, as well as his successor, under the mistaken idea that they were right in breaking down the Bank of the United States. In 1838 I began to doubt, having by chance obtained Hamilton's report, which with reading some of the writings and

53. Wetumpka *Argus*, March 17, 1841. *Cf.* March 26, June 9, 1841.
54. *Cf.* William R. Hallett to Arthur P. Bagby, November 9, 1839, in Governors' Correspondence: Bagby.

speeches of H. Clay and others, the film dropped from my eyes. I walked out of the fog [and] joined the Whigs."[55] There can be but little doubt that Hollinger's deranged affairs helped prepare him to appreciate the arguments of Alexander Hamilton and Henry Clay.

Evidently, in the years immediately after the Panic of 1837 the citizenry tended to accept the Democratic position that the commercial and speculative spirit characteristic of the Whiggery was the fundamental cause of the depression. But by 1840, after the crisis entered its second phase, a considerable number of Jacksonians joined Hollinger in changing their minds. Thus the Whigs regained their legislative strength. And when the presidential vote was counted, it was found that—though there had been an enormous increase in voter participation since 1836, from 68 percent of persons eligible, to 90 percent—yet the party division was precisely the same as in the earlier year. Van Buren received 55 percent of the total in each election, and both White and Harrison got 45 percent.

The composition and relative strength of the parties were to remain fixed for the coming decade. The narrow minority of 51 to 49 in the House of 1840 would be the Whigs' high-water mark in that body. In 1841 they settled back to forty-five seats, against the Democrats' fifty-five. They were never to control the legislature on joint ballot, though they did succeed in capturing the Senate twice, in 1849 and in 1851. They would never win a statewide office. But they could always count on some 40 to 45 percent of the vote. In that sense the magnitude of Benjamin Fitzpatrick's victory over James W. McClung in the gubernatorial election of 1841—57 percent to 43 percent—was typical of a developing pattern.

Meanwhile, the accession of the small group of states' rights ideologues such as Dixon H. Lewis and James M. Calhoun in 1838 seems to have guaranteed that the Jacksonians would maintain their rather thin but durable majority in Alabama's politics. Yet almost from the beginning the Jacksonians found that they had bought themselves trouble. The Lewis faction was difficult to control. Already by 1840 the regular leaders talked longingly of expelling the mischief makers within their ranks. The orthodoxy of the faction was called into ques-

55. Adam C. Hollinger to James Dellet, December 23, 1840, in Dellet Papers.

tion. Some old Jacksonians even threw up their hands in disgust at the party's loss of ideological consistency. As John B. Hogan sadly commented, "We have become so damnably mixed up that it is hard to know where to find myself."[56] But the Jacksonians, with the aid of their new allies, crushed the Whigs' high hopes in 1840, and thereafter condemned the Whiggery to permanent minority. The Democratic coalition was troublesome, but profitable.

The course of the opposition to a fairly equal partition of the state's electorate is a history of searching for acceptable issues with which to establish adherence to the social creed. The Whig party's roots lie in the warnings of the south Alabama Crawfordites and their allies during the late 1820s that government intervention in the economy would enslave the populace. It extended its appeal to voters who were not in the market economy in 1833, when it used its ideology in order to wrest from the grasp of federal power a farm for the hard-pressed squatter. It placed itself upon a stable footing at mid-decade by attacking the use of nominating conventions, as a menace to the continued existence of democracy. And it gained its final form after the Panic of 1837 by demanding that government at all levels come to the rescue of the stricken populace. The heart of each of these issues—including the last one, as we shall shortly see—was an appeal to the necessity for securing freedom and equality from the forces which threatened bondage. For the politician who espoused these positions, their chief value was that they served to refute the most damaging of all charges—the allegation of aristocratic sentiments. For the voter who rallied to them, their chief value was their communication of a sense that he was engaged in preserving his dignity and autonomy. Upon no other foundations could a successful political party be erected.

We have thus traced the opposition through its various metamorphoses to its formal adoption of Whig identity in 1839. But we are still a long way from answering the questions posed at the beginning of the present section—questions which go to the place of ideology in defining party membership in antebellum Alabama. It would appear at

56. John B. Hogan to Arthur P. Bagby, October 27, 1839, William R. Hallett to Bagby, February 5, 1840, in Governors' Correspondence: Bagby.

first blush that the opposition adopted and discarded ideologies with abandon, and did so with only minimal effect upon its membership. We note, however, that in the 1840s the questions at issue between the parties tended to be national in character, and that the electorate seemed deeply and genuinely divided on the merits of the debate. A closer look at the ideologies espoused by the parties in this decade will aid us in clarifying the difficulty.

The Whigs retained, as we have seen, commercial attitudes.[57] Studies of the leadership of the two parties have shown that men active in party functions were drawn generally from every economic stratum, but with perhaps a slight tendency for Whig leaders to be concentrated in the middle levels, while Democrats were a bit more evenly distributed.[58] The median slaveholding and property value for Whig legislators, as we shall see, were double those for Democratic members. The same slaveholding differentiation appears true for nullifiers as opposed to Jacksonians in 1831.[59] Of course, this finding is conditioned by the sectional nature of the parties. The Whigs and nullifiers, after all, represented wealthy counties. It would seem reasonable to suppose that their Democratic opponents in those counties were not greatly poorer than they. It is, however, significant that the wealthier counties preferred Whiggery.

The economy of the hill counties was founded upon subsistence agriculture. The planting and urban counties were, however, parts of the cash economy. Sales of merchandise in Alabama totaled something more than thirteen million dollars in 1846. Of this figure, Mobile ac-

57. On this point, *cf.* Charles Grier Sellers, Jr., "Who Were the Southern Whigs?" *American Historical Review*, LIX (1954), 335–46. I do not mean to imply that Whig leaders were uniformly, or even usually, engaged in trade, but merely that the points of view of such leaders were colored by commercial considerations, and that they tended to look kindly upon entrepreneurial speculations.

58. Thomas B. Alexander *et al.*, "Who Were the Alabama Whigs?" *Alabama Review*, XVI (1963), 5–19; Thomas B. Alexander *et al.*, "The Basis of Alabama's Ante-bellum Two-Party System," *Alabama Review*, XIX (1966), 243–76; Mary Jane Pickens, "A Critical Analysis of the Basis of Party Alignment in Autauga County, Alabama, 1836–1860" (M.A. thesis, University of Alabama, 1963); Frank M. Lowrey, "A Critical Analysis of the Relation Between Selected Factors and Party Affiliation in Montgomery County, Alabama, 1840–1860" (M.A. thesis, University of Alabama, 1964); Kit Carson Carter, Jr., "A Critical Analysis of the Basis of Party Alignment in Lowndes County, Alabama, 1836–1860" (M.A. thesis, University of Alabama, 1961).

59. A correlation of the votes recorded in *House Journal*, Sess. of 1831–32, pp. 219–23, with slaveholding statistics reveals that the median slaveholding for those taking the states' rights side was 14.5 and 13.5, respectively, while for their opponents the figure was 7 in each case

counted for about half and the twelve Black Belt counties for another quarter. The remaining thirty-seven counties, containing considerably more than 70 percent of the white population, accounted for only 25 percent of the total sales. In the same year, 43 percent of the $3,200,000 lent at interest was Black Belt capital. The Broad River center of Montgomery, with less than 3 percent of the white population, had loaned almost 11 percent of the entire figure. The Black Belt produced half of the total income of the state's lawyers and physicians, and Mobile an additional 10 percent.[60] An analysis of the debts owed the Bank of Alabama about the same time showed that a third of the total was due from citizens of Greene, Montgomery, and Mobile.[61] Such statistics could be multiplied. Clearly the whiggish counties were much more deeply involved in commercial activities than were their Democratic counterparts and had much greater familiarity with the points of view of the professional and the financier. Thus in the legislature of 1849, about two-thirds of the Democrats were farmers and a fourth lawyers, whereas only half the Whigs were farmers and a third of them were lawyers.

In the Black Belt counties, where agriculture was an extension of national and international trade, and in the hill counties, where subsistence farming was the rule, single sets of ideals came to be widely accepted in every stratum of society, and because of the reinforcement of consensus, grew into orthodoxy. Election returns from those counties, therefore, can be studied to little purpose by one who seeks to discover the foundations of party division. But in the border counties—the counties surrounding the Black Belt, which were usually closely contested between the parties—voting statistics hint at an urban basis for Whig allegiance. In Coosa County, for instance, the town of Wetumpka regularly elected a Whig mayor and was the center of the party's strength. The rest of the county, rural and small-farm, was overwhelmingly Democratic. In Jefferson, the county's one community, Elyton, was Whig; the surrounding hills were Democratic. In Tuscaloosa, the city voted Whig while a number of the rural beats

60. Based on the appendices to the *Report of the Comptroller of Public Accounts on the Subject of Taxation* (Montgomery: McCormick and Walshe, Printers, 1848), 13–21.
61. David L. Abrams, "The State Bank of Alabama, 1841–45" (M.A. thesis, Auburn University, 1965), 46.

returned Democratic polls. Urban Mobile's division is equally suggestive. The trading community which returned each fall and remained
through the season of cotton marketing but fled to New York and the
resorts with the approach of the summer tended to be Whig. The
backbone of Democratic strength was among permanent residents.
For this reason the date for holding the city elections was a matter of
bitter partisan conflict.[62]

The same distinctions apparent in the sources of electoral support
were also reflected in the themes of political oratory. A typical Whig
opinion about the troubled state bank was "that the more Banks have
to do with the merchants of the country and the less with the politicians and planters, the better. The only good Banks are those that are
purely commercial. . . . When we can see a system of banking adopted
in [our] State uniformly a faithful transcript of its commerce, we shall
then and not until then, see all the various transactions of our country
move on smoothly together."[63] Meanwhile the Democrats were told
that the Bank of the United States was strong because its supporters
were "located in Towns and commercial Cities, where unity and concentration of effort can always be had." The Democratic press asserted, "Separate these town, striped-breeches gentry from the rest,
and the concern [Alabama Whiggery] will dwindle to a mere handful."
And the party's publicists warned,

There is an incessant war waging in every commercial country between the
moneyed interests and the rights of labor. In European governments the
former have prevailed; and the people are reduced to penury and want while
their masters roll in luxurious ease. All laws in these countries favor wealth
and grind poverty. Hence the incessant wars, revolutions and massacres that
occur. . . . In the Northern and Eastern States, this system is taking deep root;
and hence in the cities of Boston, New York and Philadelphia, a frightful
proportion of the population are paupers! With us of the Southwest,
nineteen-twentieths of the freemen are agriculturists. Labor is the great controlling interest—yet even here we find men so blinded to the true interest of
the State and the people that they are ready to legislate for capital and against
labor.[64]

62. Wetumpka *Argus*, November 18, 1840, May 26, June 2, December 22, 1841; Lemuel
G. McMillion to Arthur P. Bagby, March 3, 1840, in Governors' Correspondence: Bagby; Tuscaloosa *Independent Monitor*, May 29, 1841, August 10, 1847.
63. Lewis Kennedy, in Wetumpka *Argus* , July 7, 1841.
64. *Ibid.*, September 11, 1839; Cahaba *Democrat*, quoted *ibid.*, June 10, 1840; "Raquet,"
in Montgomery *Advertiser* , December 19, 1849.

The evidence available is not, of course, conclusive. But it suggests divisions of outlook worthy of further examination. Before proceeding with our discussion of the subject, however, it would be well to indicate the great range of issues upon which the parties agreed. On the most obvious level, they accepted the presuppositions of the American social order. They agreed with John Gayle that "The general competence and increasing prosperity of our fellow citizens; our soil of almost inexhaustible fertility; our navigable streams and salubrious climate; our active and prosperous commerce; the busy scenes of industry and enterprise, which are [be]held in every direction; and our mild and equal system of laws bespeak us at once the freest and happiest people on the face of the globe." They agreed that elsewhere "the energies of man are restrained and his faculties borne down by arbitrary subjection to the will of others. But here everyone has opportunity to pursue his own interests according to his own volitions, subjected only to the restraints of equal and wholesome laws." And they joined in cheering efforts at democratic revolution in Europe and in denouncing monarchy.[65]

Moreover, they vied with each other in asserting their devotion to egalitarian and majoritarian principles. Did a Whig candidate speak haltingly and ungrammatically? It resulted from his "having been raised at the plow handles and not being by profession a debater as" was his Democratic opponent. Would congressional districting according to white population increase Democratic representation? Then the federal ratio "is tantamount to saying that the wealthy nabob with his five hundred negroes shall be estimated of the same political weight in the division of our State into Congressional Districts as three hundred and one free white men without slaves." When a Democrat announced, "We confide in the virtue and intelligence of the people," a Whig rushed to add that anyone who disagreed held principles which were "a blossom of aristocracy and [which] possess no affinity with those principles which guaranty freedom to man." The Whigs were as vigorous as the Democrats in attacking partiality to the rich.[66]

65. *Senate Journal*, Sess. of 1833–34, p. 7; *Senate Journal*, Sess. of 1829–30, p. 6: *Senate Journal*, Sess. of 1831–32, p. 46; Mobile *Register*, June 2, 1823; Montgomery *Advertiser*, January 2, January 16, 1850.
66. Montgomery *Advertiser*, July 16, August 6, 1851; Wetumpka *Argus*, June 5, June 19, 1839; *Alabama Times* (Wetumpka), quoted in Wetumpka *Argus*, March 16, 1842.

Though the parties echoed each other in such matters, they were unwilling to concede that their opponents' sentiments were genuine. When a Whig paper ventured to doubt that political institutions should always "be governed and controlled by the whim and caprice of the majority of the People—frequently by no means qualified to judge of the subject matter before it," the Democrats screamed, "Here it is, Farmers, Mechanics, laboring men," proof that the Whigs were "the aristocrats—the bankites—the soft handed and soft headed gentry." Meanwhile the Whigs, by taking the view that a legislator was absolutely bound as an agent of the people to vote in the assembly as had his county in its most recent election, maneuvered the Democrats into the admission that they believed that a representative was the sole judge of how well he reflected his constituents' opinions, and that they therefore rejected the right of the legislature to enforce popular instructions. The Whig proposal to abolish the presidential veto was to the Whig mind an effort to increase the power of the people's immediate representatives, but the Democrats thought that its aim was to "revolutionize our form of government, and erect a monarchy upon its ruins." In sum, the parties also agreed that they disagreed. It seemed to them that their differences were real and fundamental. The Whigs would have accepted the assertion of a Democratic editor that men who claim to be independent of party "are hermaphrodites in politics" and therefore "productive of no good."[67]

The sincerity of this feeling brings us back again to our effort to define the source of party difference. It was upon national issues, of course—specifically upon the virtues of the subtreasury scheme as opposed to the Bank of the United States—that the final party coalitions had formed. But as we have seen, the history of the two parties really stretches back to the earliest days of Alabama's existence.[68] Though debates on the questions which divided the parties at the federal level occupied a good deal of the state politician's time in the 1840s, an examination of the range of issues over which the parties disagreed at

67. Wetumpka *Argus*, April 1, 1840, November 10, 1841; *House Journal*, Sess. of 1840–1841, pp. 29, 85–86; Montgomery *Advertiser*, February 27, 1850.
68. Against Richard P. McCormick, *The Second American Party System: Party Formation in the Jacksonian Era* (Chapel Hill: University of North Carolina Press, 1966), 287–94, who confuses mechanisms of party governance with parties.

the state level is nevertheless a more instructive route to an understanding of party division. These issues usually seemed more immediate to the citizenry, and discussions of them were therefore more likely to arouse the deepest passions, and to reveal the most fundamental assumptions of the society.

There were, of course, areas of state policy over which the parties did not consistently differ. The table in Appendix I reveals that the primary subjects which did produce profound disagreements were proposals which tended to pit the values of an organized and style-conscious urbanism against the more traditional values of an individualistic and isolated rural world—proposals which often, though by no means exclusively, involved governmental activity to develop the economy. In order to elucidate the nature of these differences, we may glance at three areas of particularly heated controversy: banking policy, attitudes towards corporations and in particular towards aid to internal improvement, and accusations by the Democrats of class bias on the part of the Whigs.

Many of the Whig leaders, especially Arthur F. Hopkins and James Jackson, had opposed the Bank of Alabama at its inception.[69] They argued that such was the nature of man that unless the private interests of the directors and management were at stake in the success of the bank, its affairs would not receive the careful supervision necessary. They therefore urged the sale of stock in the bank to the public to the amount of three-fifths of its capitalization. The Pickens party feared that the Broad River group could thus gain control of the institution. In addition, at this early period their faith in human nature was as yet boundless; they hailed the bank's profits as a refutation of their opponents' calumnies against a public-spirited citizenry.[70] In fact, the bank's early success was a function of the booming economy. Nevertheless, that success, coupled with the fact that the bank had come to symbolize popular control of the marketplace, made criticism of the institution during coming years akin to political heresy.

By the middle 1830s a few voices within the Democratic party were beginning to be raised in censure of the conduct of the bank. But

69. Brantley, *Banking in Alabama*, I, 137, 224–25.
70. E.g., *Senate Journal*, Sess. of 1830–31, pp. 10–12.

the censure was founded upon assumptions very different from those which Pickens' opponents had earlier held. While the Broad River allies had feared that the bank was not sufficiently tied to the commercial community and did not take sufficient account of self-interest as a proper economic motive, the Democratic dissidents led by John B. Hogan thought that the bank's directorate was not really dedicated to the communal good, but used its power to enrich a limited group. Hogan told the legislature that the sin chiefly to be suspected of any bank, the matter most carefully to be investigated, was "if a fair and equal partition of the benefits of that institution has been made among the applicants at large; and if some individuals have not been favored to the exclusion of others equally entitled to a discount." [71]

Such debate came too late to reform the bank. Few politicians other than Hogan were able to summon sufficient courage to attack the bank openly until the legislative session of 1836. [72] By that time the crash was only four months away. But between the initial suspension of specie payment in 1837 and the final decision to abolish the bank in 1842, criticism such as that in which Hogan had indulged as early as 1834 became a commonplace. Although the Democrats continued to have a pro-bank faction—Nathaniel Terry, Bolling Hall, and the Tuscaloosa *Flag*, for instance—the debate became more and more a party division. The Democrats at first claimed that there was nothing intrinsically wrong with the bank; the fault lay in its managers, who had engaged in political corruption and favoritism, aided by a defective method of choosing directors. The Whigs felt that the directors had generally done as well as they could have under the circumstances. Rather, the fault of the system was in its subservience to agriculturists, the dominant interest in the political sphere as in the society. The bank needed experienced financiers as managers and a loan policy designed to facilitate commerce rather than to aid planting. They continued to advocate the sale of three-fifths of the bank's stock to the public, an action which would largely eliminate the institution's character as a public servant and would connect it closely with the state's financial powers.

71. John B. Hogan to Arthur P. Bagby, January 2, 1840, in Governors' Correspondence: Bagby; Brantley, *Banking in Alabama*, I, 295–98, 415.
72. Brantley, *Banking in Alabama*, I, 332–33.

By the early 1840s, each group had modified its position to some extent. The Whigs had abandoned their plan to sell shares to the public, for they now felt that the bank was in such a poor business position that no one would invest in the stock. They instead advocated outright abolition of the state institution and conversion to a system of private chartered banks. The Democratic leadership still clung to the notion that salutary modifications could convert the bank into the public servant which Pickens had contemplated. But many hill-county Democrats were now convinced that no bank in any form could ever be friendly to the popular welfare. The very congregation of capital was intrinsically corrupting, and whoever sought to manage such an institution was corrupted by it.

In the session of 1842 there were enough Democrats of this mind to effect, together with the Whigs, the final dissolution of the bank. There were not, on the other hand, enough Whigs to create a private banking system in its place. For the remainder of the decade the state had only one bank—the Bank of Mobile, which had been chartered in 1818. The debate continued, however, and the contraction of note circulation which followed the abolition of the banking system did the loudest talking. By 1849 most Democrats were convinced of the wisdom of the Whig proposals. The legislative election of that year resulted in the triumph of private bank advocates, led by Governor Henry Collier, who without crediting the Whigs, adopted and endorsed their policies completely in his first message to the legislature. During the 1850s the statewide system of private banks of which the Whigs had dreamed was created.[73]

The Jacksonians' changing attitude toward the bank is an index to the fundamental disillusionment that overtook them in the 1830s. In the preceding decade, even before the rise of Jackson, the outlook of the Pickens-Kelly adherents had been colored by deep and extraordinary trust in the capacity and the goodness of the Alabama farmer. The bank which they constructed presupposed these qualities in the

73. Among the more important sources for the banking debate are *Senate Journal*, Sess. of 1835–36, pp. 7–8; *Senate Journal*, Sess. of 1839–40, pp. 6–20; *Senate Journal*, Sess. of 1841–42, pp. 13–15; *Senate Journal*, Sess. of 1849–50, pp. 315–16, 348–53; *House Journal*, Sess. of 1839–40, pp. 154–60; *House Journal*, Sess. of 1849–50, pp. 25–26, 200–217; Wetumpka *Argus*, July 7, October 6, November 10, December 15, 1841; Tuscaloosa *Flag*, quoted in Wetumpka *Argus*, September 8, 1841; Selma *Free Press*, November 21, 1839.

legislators, the borrowers, and the directors. A quietly growing suspicion of all three groups marked the early 1830s, so that when the Panic of 1837 plunged the bank into suspension, the bitter Jacksonians were prepared to believe that the disaster was a product not of the economy but of evil men. The institutions which appeared to have perverted fellow citizens in whom the Jacksonians had formerly placed faith took on therefore peculiarly moral qualities. Democrats enthusiastically espoused the reductionist anti-institutionalism which constituted in their minds the chief virtue of Van Buren's subtreasury scheme. From that point, it was an easy jump to the extreme notions of Senator Mace T. P. Brindley—that God, through the Bible, had forbidden banking; that "banking and paper money is in conflict with justice, equity, morality and religion," that there is "nothing evil that it does not aid—nothing good that it is not adverse to." [74]

In this light the victory of William Henry Harrison in 1840 marked the final demise of a noble vision. At first the Democrats were moved to righteous anger by the Whigs' appropriation of the symbols of democracy during the campaign. By the use of "banners of Cider Barrels, log cabins, coonskins, gourds and a hundred other such fooliries," the Whigs were "practicing the most corrupt and unprincipled acts that ever men did, by misleading the ignorant portion of the people." [75] After all, they assured themselves, the basic difference between the parties was that the Democrats had confidence in, but the Whigs distrusted, "the integrity and capacity of the People for self-government." [76] But at the conclusion of the election, an old Jacksonian sadly wrote a more recent convert, "We have recently seen how easily [the people] can be led by clamor and denunciation"; and a few years later he commented bitterly, "Man is I believe a selfish animal by nature and is rarely governed by motives unconnected with self." [77] This transformation in attitude was a product of many events, but not least, of the circumstances surrounding the failure of the bank. Thus, while the Whigs were migrating from strict to broad construction, the

74. *Senate Journal*, Sess. of 1849–50, pp. 315–16, 348–53.
75. Samuel Forwood to William S. Forwood, October 5, 1840, in William S. Forwood Papers, Southern Historical Collection, University of North Carolina Library, Chapel Hill.
76. Wetumpka *Argus*, March 11, 1840.
77. William R. de V. King to Arthur P. Bagby, February 14, 1841, King to Catherine Ellis, June 6, 1847, both in King Papers.

Jacksonians were abandoning their optimistic assessment of the common man for the notion that power and wealth would transmute his good qualities into sinister ones. The Jacksonians had always accepted the existence of malefactors, of course. But the notion that institutions could—indeed, almost inevitably would—corrupt mere men, and the notion that the masses could be brought by demagogy to endorse such corruption at the polls, were ideas which had never before played a significant role in their thought. Therefore, the Jacksonians were on their guard against their countrymen. In league, those countrymen could well threaten the continued existence of equal rights—in fact, of freedom itself.

One of the first products of this new attitude was the Democratic position on relief for the bank's debtors. Earlier, debtors had seemed an unfortunate class to whom the charity of the state should be extended.[78] But now they were pictured as a group who had plotted to rifle the bank of its resources. A Wetumpka meeting concluded angrily that there was "no excuse for an attempt to shift the debt from the shoulders of the adventurers and speculators who have been rioting in their borrowed wealth, to the yeomanry of the country, who must bear the hand of the Tax gatherer when he calls upon them to make up for the defalcations of this class of debtors." It was regularly pointed out that the debtors were only a small proportion of the electorate—400 men out of 1,800 in Montgomery County, where the number of debtors was high.[79] The hard-pressed borrower was now a member of an elite, and a threat to democracy. Benjamin Fitzpatrick thus was swept into the governorship in 1841 over James W. McClung upon the assurance, "I have never borrowed a dollar from a bank, neither was I ever president or director of one. I am a tiller of the earth and look to that as the only source of prosperity and wealth."[80]

But the election in which indebtedness to the bank played its most important role was that of 1845. Nathaniel Terry, himself heavily in debt,[81] achieved the regular Democratic nomination by manipulation

78. Selma *Courier*, January 3, 1828.
79. Wetumpka *Argus*, November 13, November 20, November 27, 1841.
80. William W. Duncan, "Life of Benjamin Fitzpatrick" (M.A. thesis, University of Alabama, 1930), 43. *Cf*. Abrams, "State Bank," 17.
81. Terry owed $46,000 in 1840 (Brantley, *Banking in Alabama*, II, 336, Appendix), but had reduced his debt to $33,300 by 1843 (Abrams, "State Bank," 12).

of the convention machinery,[82] and launched a campaign based upon a program of debtor relief. He called for repeal of the newly adopted Debt Collection Act of 1845, saying that this attempt to force collection on a people unable to pay would end in compelling repudiation of the state's outstanding bonds. Terry's nomination brought Joshua L. Martin, an anti-debtor Democrat, into the field as an independent, advocating strict enforcement of the Debt Collection Act's tough provisions. The Whig candidate, Nicholas Davis, then withdrew, and Martin won with 55 percent of the vote to Terry's 45 percent.

The Whigs tended to sympathize with Terry's point of view. They did not accept the new Jacksonian suspicion of the debtor class. Rather, the debtors appeared to them as victims of economic circumstances. But Terry was a fiercely partisan Democrat, the author of the General Ticket Law; and support for Martin gave promise of permanently splitting the Democratic party. The Whigs were therefore better united than were the Democrats. Martin's victory was the product of a combination of Whig partisanship and Jacksonian apprehensions. Terry was left with Whig debtors and those Democrats who, like himself, had gotten involved with the bank when it was a proof of popular sentiments to do so, and were still to some extent hypnotized by the Pickens dream of a capitalist institution made subservient to the people. Terry's defeat was the death of such optimistic notions; it was the triumph of the new age, to be ruled by vague and uneasy fear.[83]

If the political dominance of undefined anxiety was a relatively late phenomenon, coincident with the failure of the state bank, class hatred and fear of corporate wealth was a continuing theme in Alabama history. Such hatred could coexist both with the earlier Jacksonian faith in the masses and with the later disillusionment. In the former view, capitalists were the enemies of the common man; in the latter, they were his manipulators. In either case, they were evil. It was in their attitudes toward corporations, and specifically towards state aid to corporations, that the parties were most sharply divided. In the 1820s

82. Jones, "Direct Primary," 21–24.
83. Abrams, "State Bank," 53, 61–63; Greensboro *Alabama Beacon*, August 16, August 23, August 30, 1845. Of the twenty-eight counties carried by Martin, Polk had carried fourteen the year before and Clay also had carried fourteen. Of Terry's twenty-one counties, Polk had taken sixteen and Clay five.

there had been little opposition to internal improvements undertaken at state expense. Such publicly owned facilities were in keeping with the conception underlying the Bank of Alabama. Indeed, the populace frowned upon attempts by private enterprise to compete with public efforts.[84] The growing strength of the Nullifiers put an end to requests for federal assistance in financing these ventures, but hostility to the state's undertaking them when it had the money to do so increased much more slowly. The state's Board of Internal Improvements was abolished at the beginning of 1832, but as late as 1836 Clement Comer Clay proposed an ambitious program including both canals and railroads. Both Governors Bagby and Fitzpatrick, moreover, claimed that they would not be averse to such endeavors if there were no depression, and Bagby even suggested a plan to pay for them.[85] But by the late 1840s the Jacksonians no longer looked favorably even on communal projects.

State aid to privately financed improvements, particularly railroads, had a different history, however. From the beginning Whigs favored it and Democrats did not. Democrats proclaimed their determination to "defend honest labor against the grasping avarice and grinding oppression of chartered monopolies and associated wealth."[86] Whigs concurred in the opinion that such aid would help end the depression, and felt in addition that facilitating commerce would increase the state's wealth.

Democrats did not doubt that railroads would improve communication and strengthen the economy. But they feared the power which corporate wealth would thus gain in the life of the state. They believed "that money governs despite laws and constitutions" and that "the money power in every country is at war with every interest." The notion that a railroad could really be a blessing to the community seemed

84. See, *e.g.*, the Memorial of the Tuscumbia, Courtland and Decatur Railroad to the Legislature of Alabama, in Governors' Correspondence: Bagby

85. *Senate Journal*, Sess. of 1832–33, p. 11; *Acts of Alabama*, Sess. of 1829–30, pp. 7–10; *Acts of Alabama*, Sess. of 1831–32, p. 23; *Senate Journal*, Sess. of 1836–37, pp. 18–19; *Senate Journal*, Sess. of 1839–40, pp. 9–10; *Senate Journal*, Sess. of 1840–41, p. 14; *Senate Journal* , Sess. of 1841–42, p. 94. See the folder marked "Board of Internal Improvements," in Governors' Correspondence: Samuel Moore, for a sample of that board's activities.

86. Montgomery *Advertiser*, October 31, 1849. By that date, however, it was possible, at least in south Alabama, to add that one looked favorably on enterprise "that does not seek to foster itself at the expense of other paramount interests."

ludicrous to them, therefore, and they ridiculed the earnest promises of economic greatness in which the railroad advocates indulged. "A corporation, that is a co-partnership without soul or body, is formed and presents itself before the Legislature, and after expressing the greatest compassion for the ignorance and want of sense generally of the people of Alabama in attending to their affairs, kindly proposes to extend a helping hand to them to *develope* their resources, and upon the simple condition that said benighted people should first *develope* two and a half millions of dollars of their money for the special benefit of said intangible corporation." No, they concluded, "if we have not the internal improvements that older States can boast of, let us be able to glory in the fact that Alabama . . . knows no creditor, and has a population neither seeking nor needing the patronage of State credit."[87]

These thoughts had great appeal for the small farmer, who agreed with the characterization of aid to improvements as a "fascinating and captivating doctrine of seeking your own good at the expense of other men's toil and sweat."[88] Therefore, from the time governmental assistance to corporations was first seriously sought during the Panic of 1837[89] until the middle of the 1850s, the Democrats were able to defeat all such schemes. But in the final decade of the antebellum period the tide began to set in favor of aid, and in 1859 a general program of assistance was enacted. Thus, in the realm of internal improvements as with banking, the doctrines of Whiggery triumphed as the Whig party died.

The belief that aid to internal improvements and chartered banks were legal ruses whereby the wealthy were permitted to become parasites upon the suffering masses led naturally to the adoption by the Democrats of the oratory of class conflict. They painted fanciful portraits of Whig politicians "with kid gloves, french pumps and cambric handkerchiefs . . . receiving with a complacent bow the lordly aristo-

87. *Ibid.*, December 19, 1849, January 20, 1852.
88. Felix G. Norman to George S. Houston, May 15, 1846, November 10, 1846, both in George S. Houston Papers, Duke University Library, Durham.
89. *E.g.*, George W. Owen to Clement Comer Clay, December 16, 1836, and Resolutions and Address of the Internal Improvements Convention Held in Montgomery, Alabama, March 9 and April 1 (respectively), 1837, all in Governors' Correspondence: Clay.

crats, and turning the door on every log cabin boy who dares to present himself for admission!"

The ruffle-shirted counter hopper, rolling in the wealth acquired by driving shrewd bargains with the plain and unassuming farmer, has the high privilege of sauntering through those magnificent halls and of drinking champaigne [*sic*] and other costly wines provided for their delicate palates; while the honest but poor inmate of the log cabin must not enter for fear, it may be, of soiling the polished floor! and of offending the gaze of those princely exclusives!

The Democrats, as in this passage, often sought to identify the Whigs with mercantile elements—"counter hoppers"—and themselves with the farmers. But in the Democratic nightmare, Whiggery was allied with all types of wealth. They assured their followers that "amidst their [Whig] ravings we catch glimpses of their true thoughts and their true motto—'the supremacy of the Rich over the Poor'—the friend of the Wealthy Planter—the Legislative foe of the hard-handed but poor tiller of the soil!" And they warned that the "ignorance, poverty, filthiness, vulgarity and indecency" of the small farmer "have been standing themes of their [Whigs'] reproach and ridicule for years." [90]

These allegations were repeated so vehemently that they gained credence. The Whigs did not, of course, hold such elitist views. Sometimes their opinions were absolutely indistinguishable from those of the Democrats, as when the Whig Tuscaloosa *Monitor* denounced the tariff as calculated to "raise up aristocratic fortunes to the manufacturers of the north." [91] The trouble was that the doctrines of Whiggery were oriented towards business, and as long as the populace regarded business as its enemy, the Democrats could seize upon the most unlikely, even completely inconsequential, Whig proposals and make them appear to have a sinister turn. Thus, granting President Harrison's widow the franking privilege and $25,000 led to the announcement, "A system of *pensioning* the aristocratic families of this country has been commenced." In surveying the provisions of a new tariff, the Democratic Tuscaloosa *Flag* announced itself outraged at the Whigs

90. Wetumpka *Argus*, February 24, 1841, February 10, 1841 (both presumably from the pen of William L. Yancey); Montgomery *Advertiser*, November 11, 1851.

91. Tuscaloosa *Monitor*, quoted in Wetumpka *Argus*, November 3, 1841. Cf. the speech of Hardin Perkins in Wetumpka *Argus*, December 1, 1841.

for "exempting from tax physic poison, gewgaws, gold and silver epaulettes, statuary, engravings and railroad corporation iron." The implications in this catalog are so obvious, and so patently absurd, as to be laughable; but there was doubtless a portion of Alabama's electorate which was not amused. We are told that a proposal to create the rank of lieutenant general, and another to tax coffee and tea, were "dangerous" issues with the voters.[92]

In 1841 Congressman David Hubbard put into writing his personal formulation of the essence of the Democratic creed: if "you feel sufficiently confident in your own exertions that you don't need any system of *Government Charity* to enable you to make a support for yourself and family," and if "you have too strong a sense of meum and tuum (mine and thine), to desire that Government shall step in between us and take that which belongs to me and was intended for the support of mine, and give it to *thee* for the support of *thine*—If this is your feeling, you are in heart a Democrat, and we are 'brothers in the faith.'" And a Democratic paper phrased the concept: "The laboring class of the people depend for their prosperity and happiness upon the principle of equal rights; legislation should leave them to the free exercise of their skill and industry under the General Law which gives to no class rights or privileges not equally enjoyed by all."[93]

We come thus to the core of the ideological differences between the parties. We encounter the fundamental divergence at the nexus which links power and freedom. Alabama farmers seem always to have been fearful for their freedom. The fewer contacts they had with the world, the better they liked it. They sought individual autonomy. They resented the necessity of dealing in bank-made paper; they resented the necessity of buying their land from the government; they resented the necessity of paying taxes and otherwise encountering the state; they resented the necessity of selling their crops and obtaining supplies from afar. Whenever power impinged upon their lives, they reacted with

92. Wetumpka *Argus*, October 6, 1841; Tuscaloosa *Flag*, quoted in the *Argus*, September 8, 1841; M. C. Gallaway to George S. Houston, January 26, 1847, in Houston Papers. *Cf.* Gallaway to Houston, December 22, 1846, in Houston Papers; Wetumpka *Argus*, September 15, 1841; Robert T. Scott to Clement Claiborne Clay, July 7, 1858, in Clay Papers, Duke University Library, Durham.

93. David Hubbard to George S. Houston, February 24, 1841, in Houston Papers; Wetumpka *Argus*, March 11, 1840.

suspicion and perturbation. It was this feeling which gave invulnerability to the various symbolic issues—preemption for squatters and Indian removal, the Huntsville Bank and the Bank of Alabama, aid to railroads and, at the end, southern rights—which shaped and governed antebellum politics.

The fears, however, were given political form by history. In the early years, the corruption of power was something that happened to the opposition; one's own allies were impervious to its blandishments.[94] The day was still far off when a politician could gain popularity by opposing a project intended for the especial benefit of his own district.[95] It is not surprising that the first group to espouse a political ideology as a direct result of its feeling threatened by power was the group most thoroughly involved in the national economy. The tariff was not an immediate menace to the interests of any group except the planters and their ancillaries, the factors. It was difficult, therefore, for the anti-tariff forces to communicate their alarm to other social groups. The federal government was as yet so far removed from the subsistence farmer and from the small market farmer that they did not perceive it as a force in the determination of their welfare.[96] Most Alabamians had contact with the general government only in the process of acquiring land.

It was a Jacksonian governor, John Gayle, who made the doctrines of state sovereignty relevant to the small farmer. Gayle backed into the Whig party during the latter 1830s, but at the beginning of his governorship he had no connection with the opposition. It was ironic, therefore, that his actions had the effect of popularizing states' rights ideas. He strengthened the Nullifiers' case in opposition to the Democracy, but by the time he himself was willing openly to declare himself a Whig, in 1840, his former allies the Jacksonians had become the principal exponents of strict construction. He thus became a victim of the historical movement which he helped to set into motion.

Meanwhile, the growing Jacksonian disillusion with the ability of men to control impersonal forces caused them to lend more and more

94. *E.g.*, Tuscumbia *Telegraph*, November 7, 1827.
95. As was the case with George S. Houston's opposition to the repair of the Muscle Shoals Canal; see Felix G. Norman to Houston, May 15, 1846, in Houston Papers.
96. Selma *Courier*, September 18, September 25, October 9, 1828; "A Southern," in the *Courier*, July 16, 1829.

credence to the fear of power upon which the strength of the states' rights group was founded. The bulk of the Nullifiers, however—as opposed to the handful of Jeffersonian ideologues who were the intellectual godfathers of strict construction in Alabama—had practiced selective states' rights. They had feared power when it was directed against them, but they had viewed it as useful if friendly to their interests. The bitter Jacksonians were far more absolute. They themselves had been in control of the government at the time the events which now appeared threats had materialized. Their fears could not therefore be directed against men or parties; instead, they inveighed against the formless threat of power itself. And thus the parties of the 1840s were formed.

It is important to note that the Whigs did not abandon their early fear that the government could become a despotism. It was just that the Jacksonians moved beyond the Whigs to the position that an active government would necessarily become a despotism—as would any power center, such as a corporation, a bank, or any other collective force which impinged upon individual autonomy. Party debates were thus in essence a conflict between the Whigs' maintenance that the power of collective action could be harnessed to benefit society, and the Democrats' maintenance that no hand was strong enough for the reins. The only collective actions acceptable to the Democratic party were defensive ones—using the government to rescue the populace from the machinations of the powerful. The Democracy itself, Democrats believed, was not an institution at all, but only an alliance formed to nudge the government into such defensive efforts. Whigs sought office by pointing to physical improvements erected at their instance to the advantage of the community. Democrats sought office by pointing to the number of institutions which they had aided in destroying or dismantling.

In this light we may solve the puzzle with which we began the present section. If one looks at the events of party formation synchronically, one does not see consistent ideological commitments. The states' rights views of the opposition in the 1830s appear in conflict with the broad construction and governmental activism which it advocated in the 1840s. The Jacksonians' construction of financial institutions and their oratory of faith in the common man appear inconsistent with their later position that any governmental aid to institutions would be subversive of the individual's freedom and autonomy, and that the masses were always subject to domination and cozenage by power centers. When one views ideology diachronically, however, with an awareness of the centrality of attitudes towards power, themes emerge. From earliest days, the Democrats believed that the substance of freedom was lack of economic dependence upon other men. The absence of economic dependence took on moral overtones for them; it was necessary to the affirmation of manhood, to thinking uninfluenced by others, to the self-reliant behavior of the free man—the ideals of the social faith. The Whigs were equally dedicated to these ideals of conduct, but to them, the only effective mechanism for the achievement of the ideals was the amassing of a "competence," of sufficient wealth for one's ordinary needs. Therefore, the road to freedom was the road to prosperity and economic development. The Democrats sought to destroy private banks, to erect user-owned institutions, and later to cripple or destroy corporations. The Whigs cast about for ways to increase the money in circulation and to facilitate commercial intercourse, and they fought legislation which appeared likely to diminish the prosperity of the state. At first, they put the tariff into this category, though later many of them relented, on being convinced that protection would in fact enhance Alabama's commercial position. When they were fighting the tariff, however, they warned that it would lead to slavery, precisely because increasing wealth was to their minds the path to freedom.

The goal of antebellum society, in sum, was individual liberty. The Democrats sought this goal by decreasing interaction; the Whigs by extending affluence. But each party accepted the fundamental notion that liberty was economically defined. Indeed, we observe that Democratic dogma had its greatest strength in the depressed 1820s and 1840s, while Whig ideas gained their most general acceptance in the periods of prosperity, the middle 1830s and the 1850s. At base the entire society joined in sanctioning certain concepts: that freedom was the greatest of all possessions; that it was maintained through economic action; that power could be destructive of it; and that the function of the state was to preserve it.

It is of the greatest importance to note, in conclusion, that the final issue of the antebellum period, southern rights, also derived from these concepts, and specifically from their Democratic descendants. The exclusion of slavery from the territories was a declaration "that a free citizen of Massachusetts was a better man and entitled to more privileges than a free citizen of Alabama." To the voters it presented the question, "Will you submit to be bridled and saddled and rode under whip and spur" or affirm, alternatively, "the great doctrine of *Equality*: Opposition to ascendancy in any form, either of classes, by way of monopolies, or of sections, by means of robbery."[97] The northern political hegemony was manipulating its power to abridge the freedom of southerners, to bar them from settling on the new lands, to mark them as second-class citizens. Despotism threatened; the state had limited the autonomy of the citizenry. This rationale had deep roots in Alabama oratory—and in Alabama fears. We shall explore the southern rights movement in detail in succeeding chapters. It will become clear that the threats which sustained Jacksonian dominance at the polls were also at issue in the sectional crisis. For the present, however, let us turn to an examination of the specific institutional mechanisms through which the society undertook the activity which it most dreaded: the use of power.

97. "Burleigh," in Montgomery *Advertiser*, June 25, 1851.

Chapter II The Legislature

GOVERNOR Arthur P. Bagby was moved almost to rhapsody by the assembling of the Alabama legislature in 1841. "Nothing," he told the members, "is better calculated to illustrate the excellence and beauty of our representative system than the recurrence of the seasons and of events, by which the chosen representatives of a free people annually assemble at the capitol of the State for the purpose of making suitable returns for the confidence reposed in them by the enactment of wise and salutary laws, and throwing additional safeguards around the essential rights of life, liberty and property." [1] That the convention of a legislative body should inspire a sober observer to thoughts of beauty, may seem puzzling—and perhaps a trifle ludicrous—today. But a sensitive visitor to the era cannot fail to discern that antebellum Alabamians quite frequently felt for their legislature a regard, and attributed to its efforts an importance, which would be out of place in the modern world.

On the most obvious level, the importance attributed to the body may be easily explained. The legislature was very nearly the whole state government, and a major force in local government as well. It elected every state official other than the governor: the secretary of state, the treasurer, and the comptroller of public accounts; circuit, equity, and appellate judges; [2] the attorney general and the circuit solicitors. And its discretion reached deep into local communities. Until 1850 it chose the county judge, who was the fifth member of, and presided over, the county governing body. It elected at one period in

1. *Senate Journal*, Sess. of 1841–42, p. 10
2. After 1850, however, the election of circuit and county judges was given to the people.

the state's history, the presidents and the boards of directors of each of the five state banks, and two-fifths of the directors of the two private banks. It chose the commissioners who supervised such works of internal improvement as the state undertook, and who disposed of the state's public lands. It elected the trustees of the University of Alabama and, after the office was created in 1854, the state superintendent of education. It even appointed the physicians who sat on various municipal boards of public health.

In addition to these and a number of other direct selections of personnel, the legislature regulated by statute a thousand areas of life. It ordained the structure of city and town governments. It established maximum rates for county taxation, and of course formulated the state's own tax policy. It chartered corporations, banks, schools and churches, and imposed on them such limitations and requirements as it desired. It defined as socially disruptive such conduct as met with its disapproval, and prescribed such punishment for the conduct as it saw fit. In short, the government was as active as the legislature ordered, in such fields as the legislature ordered.

The evident political importance of the assembly, however, is a mere hint at its real significance as a social force. Its actions gave concrete expression to the ideals of the populace, and specific legal and institutional form to the generalized precepts of the social philosophy. No governmental institution more clearly reflects the soul of antebellum Alabama. When, therefore, we have formed an appreciation of the nature of the institution—its strengths and weaknesses, its members, its functions—we will have taken a long step towards understanding the condition of that soul.

Personnel

The legal qualifications for membership in the legislature give but little intimation of the sort of men who sat there. Any person could be chosen who was a white male citizen, two years a resident of Alabama and one year of the district for which he stood, and who was at least twenty-one in the case of representatives or twenty-seven in the case of senators. Anyone who held a governmental office of profit, or who, having once been a receiver of public funds, was in arrears in paying over the funds he had held was, however, ineligible.[3] The prohibition against membership by holders of other offices ordinarily went unenforced, but in 1839 the House expelled five members and the Senate three for violation of the section. Doubtless the prohibition would not have been enforced in 1839 had not Jeremiah Clemens, angered when another member of the House questioned his right to a seat, insisted on the investigation of each legislator for compliance with the constitutional rule. Even so, the Senate waited until the final day of the session to expel its three offending members. And the people of Jackson County, incensed at the expulsion of their representative, promptly elected him to the vacancy, forcing the House to expel him a second time.[4] As this episode demonstrates, the voters of Alabama could really send almost any member of the electorate to the assembly, whatever may have been the legal requirements.

Assembling economic data on Alabama's legislators is not an easy task. Before 1850 the census did not attempt to gather such information. Fortunately for our purposes, however, one important species of property also constituted a portion of the population—the slaves. To the extent that slaveholding is an index to economic status—and in antebellum Alabama it most often was—we may also determine the position of legislators in 1830 and 1840.[5] In order to minimize temporal distortions in the data, we shall examine only the legislature elected in the year in which the census was taken, and the legislatures in the years immediately before and after that year. For the three assemblies surrounding 1830, the median slaveholding is nine. For the assemblies prepared from the census of 1840, the median figure is 9 and one half.

In the legislatures of 1830, there were twelve non-slaveholders and ten holders of more than fifty slaves. One-fourth of the legislators owned four or fewer slaves; three-fourths owned twenty or fewer.

3. *Alabama Constitution of 1819*, Art. III, Secs. 4, 12, 26, 27.
4. *Senate Journal*, Sess. of 1839–40, p. 330; *House Journal*, Sess. of 1839–40, pp. 97–100, 105, 110, 233; Virgil L. Bedsole, "The Life of Jeremiah Clemens" (M.A. thesis, University of Alabama, 1934), 7–8.
5. Unsettled conditions in the early statehood period led to a failure to take the census of 1820 in most of Alabama's counties, and to the loss of the manuscript returns for many of the remainder. Only eight counties have extant returns.

These figures are particularly instructive because, as we shall presently see, farmers—the occupational group most likely to own slaves—dominated the legislature. There was only minor variation among the three legislatures in question. Dividing the legislators by houses produced a slight differential. The median slaveholding for senators is twelve; for representatives, eight.

One should also bear in mind that the figures given here may actually overstate the slaveholding of the legislators. Of the 174 men who sat in the three legislatures in question, I located only 149 in the census returns. On the assumption that the census taker would have been quite unlikely to have overlooked a vast plantation in the course of his circuit of the county, it is probably reasonable to expect that the 25 missing members lived in more humble circumstances.

Investigation of the three legislatures surrounding 1840 produced similar results. One significant variation was the increase in the number of non-slaveholders, from 12 in the group of 1830 to 27 in the group from 1840—an increase from just over 8 percent of the total to nearly 12 percent. The 1840 figures also show a rise in the number of men holding more than fifty slaves from a bit less than 7 percent of the total to 10 percent. As in 1830, a separation of the legislators by houses produces a higher median figure for senators. For the 39 senators for whom we have data, the median slaveholding is nineteen. The median for the 110 representatives found is eight.

A new variable present in the 1840 legislatures is party affiliation. I was able to discover slaveholding figures for 212 legislators for whom I also determined a party affiliation—83 Whigs and 129 Democrats. The median holding for the Democrats was seven; for the Whigs, double that, 14 and one half.[6] This differential is of course partially attributable to the fact that those counties in which the Whigs were strong enough to elect their legislative candidates were also generally the counties in which both the number of slaveholdings and the average number of slaves held were significantly above the usual figures for the state as a whole. It is probable that the defeated Democrats in those counties were also well-to-do. The differential may be considered,

6. For a graphic representation of these various findings, see J. Mills Thornton III, "Politics and Power in a Slave Society: Alabama, 1806–1860" (Ph.D. dissertation, Yale University, 1974), 573–82.

therefore, a commentary more upon the sectionalism of Alabama politics than upon the economic status of the Whig party's membership.

I must offer once again the caveat that, since I was able to locate
only 219 of the 267 men who sat in the legislatures in question, it is
possible that the median figures given here somewhat overstate the
actual ones. I may also note that, if as seems probable, both the
number and size of slaveholdings increased in the decade from 1830 to
1840, then the fact that the median legislative holding remained constant at nine is the more remarkable and may represent a relative decline in the economic status of the legislator with a median holding.[7]

Estimating social status on the basis of slaveholdings is a tricky
business at best. We may easily imagine a thousand reasons why the
status apparently indicated by a holding is not an accurate classification for some particular individual. But if we make no such effort, our
economic data must remain of mere antiquarian interest. As a rough
guide to the status indicated by the various figures developed in this
study, we may adopt the typology offered by Ulrich B. Phillips.[8] He
calls twenty slaves "roughly a minimum for the plantation method" of
agriculture. He ranks holders of from five to nineteen slaves "as a middle class of large farmers and comfortable townsmen." Holders of
fewer than five slaves, including the vast numbers of non-slaveholders,
are left presumably to be classified as a lower-middle and lower grouping. If we add to this typology a final boundary line not suggested by
Phillips, letting fifty slaves mark the division between small planter and
large planter, then we may summarize, without however any pretensions to refinement, the class composition of the legislatures for which
we have data.

As the state emerged from its first decade, about a quarter of its

7. Whether or not the number and size of slaveholdings actually did increase in the decade
remains an open question. Though such figures could be developed, albeit with some difficulty,
from the manuscripts of 1830 and 1840 (and for that matter, from all the previous censuses), it
was not done at the time nor, as far as I know, has it been done since. In 1850 these figures were
gathered for each of the southern states, but for some unaccountable reason were not broken
down by county, making them less than fully useful. Only in 1860 was a complete county-by-
county inventory made, and even then it was almost left out of the published returns. Omitted
from the volume on population, it was added as an afterthought to the volume on agriculture
(*Census of 1860*, II: Agriculture, clxxii, 223–48). The collation of similar statistics from earlier
censuses would be a project well worth the time of a person so inclined.

8. Ulrich B. Phillips, *Life and Labor in the Old South* (Boston: Little, Brown and Co.,
1963; originally published, 1929), 339.

legislators were planters and about a quarter members of the lower-middle and lower classes. Half of the members belonged to the "middle class of large farmers and comfortable townsmen." Large planters constituted less than 7 percent of the total. After a decade of unexampled prosperity culminating in a disastrous panic and the beginning of a crushing depression, we find that the power of the large farmer middle class has been eroded from above and below. Members of the lower-middle and lower classes increased their percentage from a quarter to a third, as did the planting group, so that in 1840 the three social divisions each had an approximately equal percentage of members in the legislature. Large planters increased their representation somewhat, from about 7 percent to 10 percent, and small planters rose from 18 percent of the 1830 group to more than 22 percent in that of 1840. As in the legislatures as a whole, both the small planters and the lower-middle and lower grouping bettered their positions in the Senate at the expense of the middle class.

The final decade of the antebellum period witnessed further significant changes in the class composition of the legislature. I shall, however, reserve the discussion of the later assemblies to another chapter.[9]

For the present, let us turn to a second important element in our developing portrait of Alabama's legislators: information on their occupations. At all times farmers dominated the assembly. Law was the only other vocation which consistently had substantial representation. In the Legislature of 1828, some 72 percent of the members were agriculturists and 16 percent lawyers. The remainder pursued a variety of occupations.[10] In 1840, 70 percent of the House called themselves farmers, as against 12 percent identified as lawyers, and the remainder scattered.[11] In 1849, among those legislators found in the census, 59 percent were farmers and 26 percent lawyers. There was a small variance in the composition of the two houses.[12]

9. See pp. 297–99 herein.
10. Tuscaloosa *Chronicle*, quoted in Selma *Courier*, December 18, 1828.
11. Wetumpka *Argus*, January 20, 1841.
12. The House was composed of 63 percent farmers and 25.5 percent lawyers, whereas the Senate contained 48 percent farmers and 30 percent lawyers. *Cf.* Ralph A. Wooster, *The People in Power: Courthouse and Statehouse in the Lower South, 1850–1860* (Knoxville: University of Tennessee Press, 1969), 123.

The census of 1840 provides us with a unique opportunity to determine the full extent of involvement with agriculture by men for whom farming was not their primary occupation; for that census undertook to list after the name of the head of the household the number of members of the household engaged in each of the important occupational classifications. Thus, even if the legislator himself is, for instance, a physician, the fact that other members of his family are working his farm is readily apparent. Of the 194 legislators whose occupations I located in the 1840 census, more than 84 percent had some direct connection with agriculture. About 68 percent of the legislators were entirely dependent on farming. Some 20 percent of the members found had an immediate interest in the learned professions. Almost 9 percent of them were involved in manufacture and trade, and a bit less than 6 percent in commerce. Thus, while a third of the men had some non-agricultural income, half of that third also were engaged in agriculture. Among Democrats, 88 percent were connected with agriculture, and about 19 percent with the learned professions. Among Whigs, 78 percent had some connection with agriculture, and 22 percent with the learned professions.

To complete our collective biography of the legislators, we may note briefly two other areas of classification: birthplace and age. Alabama's legislators were almost all southerners, usually Georgians or South Carolinians by nativity. North Carolinians were a significant group early in the antebellum period, but lost ground as time passed. And of course when the state had reached a sufficient age to admit of it, native Alabamians became an important element.[13] We cannot determine age from the census returns before 1850. In the assemblies of 1849 and 1859, most legislators—a bit less than 69 percent in each case—were in their thirties or forties. In the earlier session, senators tended towards somewhat greater age than did representatives; but in the later assembly, no such distinction was apparent.[14]

These various statistics naturally lead us to ask to what extent Alabama's legislators were representative of the society as a whole. But the question is not an easy one to answer. Some things may be said immediately. In 1845 there were 642 practicing attorneys in Alabama,

13. Wetumpka *Argus*, March 4, 1840, January 20, 1841; Wooster, *People in Power*, 121.
14. Wooster, *People in Power*, 121.

and 75,341 adult white males,[15] so that practicing attorneys were somewhat more than eight-tenths of 1 percent of the electorate. That lawyers were 12 percent of the House in 1840 is gross over-representation, even when allowance is made for the perhaps considerable number of attorneys who did not practice. Similarly in 1850, the first year for which the statistic is available, slaveholders constituted just over 31 percent of the electorate. But non-slaveholders were 12 percent of the legislators of 1840 and perhaps a fourth of the assembly in 1849. These men, then, sat for at least two-thirds of the voters. Such comparisons could be multiplied. If one expects the democratic process to generate proportional representation of interest groups, or even closely to approximate such a situation, then the Alabama legislature was an unrepresentative body.

Surely, however, such a notion is too naïve to receive credence. The democratic process was intended to produce responsive representatives, not scale models of the social hierarchy. We may dismiss out of hand, therefore, the argument that merely because certain segments of the society had a voice in the legislature larger than their share of the electorate, the assembly was therefore unrepresentative. In numerical terms it was, of course; but in functional terms it may well not have been.

Nevertheless, there may possibly be percentages of malrepresentation which are sufficient to classify a legislative body as presumptively unrepresentative, pending examination of its behavior. We may consider whether any of Alabama's legislatures must be included in that group. The legislature was at all times wealthier on the average than was the population as a whole. The median slaveholding among the legislators found in the 1830 and 1840 censuses was, in each case, nine, but for the whole electorate it was zero. Similarly, as we shall see in due course, the median real estate value in the assembly of 1859 was more than $9,000, but the mean for the electorate at the time was about $2,100; and the personal property holding figure was more than $25,000 among the assemblymen, but about $5,000 among the populace.

The differentials in these comparisons should not surprise us, how-

15. Tuscaloosa *Monitor,* quoted in Tuscumbia *North Alabamian,* November 14, 1845; Tuscumbia *North Alabamian,* January 3, 1845.

ever. In considering them, we must keep in mind that the nature of involvement in politics at the elective level—the campaigning and electioneering, the development of a "district-wide name"—may often make at least moderate means an almost essential adjunct to the effort. A property value for officeholders of five times that for the average of the electorate is, in fact, probably not extraordinary.

Other points deserve greater emphasis. At no time did large planters control—or even come close to controlling—the legislature, numerically. Throughout much of the antebellum period they were a very small part of the legislature, and even in the final decade of these years, when they did increase their role, they represented no more than a quarter of the seats. At all times in the antebellum period, poorer elements in the state had a significant voice in shaping its legislation. In fact, the extent of their power—a fourth to a third of the legislature—would be a rarity in assemblies of our own time, and can perhaps be regarded as rather an achievement for such bodies in the nineteenth century.[16] A half to three-fourths of the legislators were clearly outside the planter class. Small planters and large planters often had differing interests, and one may well question the validity of regarding them as a unitary economic bloc. But even if they may properly be treated as a single classification, their number to the very end of the antebellum period, as we shall see, was at least balanced by that of non-planters. Moreover, the number of large planters who attained office remained small. In 1860, there were 1,654 owners of more than fifty slaves in Alabama.[17] Of this number, only 164—less than 10 percent—had ever been elected to the legislature. And con-

16. No comparable study of northern legislatures in the antebellum period has yet been made. Indeed, except for the censuses of 1850 and 1860, no data would be available, since slaveholding figures would not exist. As to the southern states, Ralph A. Wooster's *The People in Power*, cited above, indicates that Alabama did not differ significantly from her sisters, with the possible exception of South Carolina, whose legislators showed a somewhat greater tendency to wealth. For the present day, a number of studies have pointed to the American practice of choosing lawmakers from the higher socioeconomic strata. See Donald R. Matthews, *The Social Background of Political Decision-Makers* (Garden City, N.Y.:Doubleday, 1954) and the same author's "United States Senators—A Collective Portrait," in Samuel C. Patterson (ed.), *American Legislative Behavior, a Reader* (Princeton: Van Nostrand, 1968), 130–44. None of the modern studies can be so explicit as the present one in stating economic position, however, because such statistics are scarcely ever put in the public domain.

17. A convenient listing is Joseph K. Menn, "The Large Slaveholders of the Deep South, 1860" (Ph.D. dissertation, University of Texas, 1964), 220–34, 262–541.

siderably more than half of that group—90 of them—came from just the thirteen counties of the Black Belt. Our statistics do not appear on their face, then, to relegate Alabama's legislature to unrepresentative status. Quite to the contrary, they seem to point to an assembly representative perhaps to a surprising degree.

In the final analysis, however, the question of the extent to which the legislature was a functionally representative body can be answered only by an examination of its actions, and that must await the final section of this chapter. For the present, let us turn away from our statistical portrait of the legislators to literary sources, in an attempt to depict legislative personnel with more depth and color than numbers can offer.

By traditional standards, Alabama's legislators were men of modest talents at best. In the formative years, indeed, men who were experienced in affairs of state were often shocked at what they regarded as incompetence. John M. Taylor, the Virginia-bred lawyer who had played an important role in the constitutional convention of 1819 wrote of the first legislature:

Many men who possess an uncommon portion of the milk of human kindness anticipated an improvement in the measures which would be pursued by our Solons after they had been long enough together to become acquainted with each other and with parliamentary rules and usages. Never was calculation farther from being correct. As they know each other better, finding but little mental disparity among them, many who were previously doubtful whether they were *compos mentis* or not, are now clearly convinced that they are really wise men, and that their names will be handed down to posterity for their admiration and reverence; when there is only one circumstance which will prevent the whole body from becoming a bye-word more forcibly to express folly, and I much fear something like corruption; I mean the probability that in a year or two all their laws will be repealed, and in one or two more, forgotten.

Nor were such sentiments confined to the Broad River group and their associates, for even Israel Pickens was moved to scorn for these "appropriate productions of an *infant* state." [18]

18. John M. Taylor to John W. Walker, December 8, 1819, Israel Pickens to Walker, January 27, 1820, both in John W. Walker Papers, Alabama Department of Archives and History, Montgomery. For more in the same vein, see John McKinley to Walker, December 20, 1819 and Taylor to Walker, January 20, 1820.

Taylor was wrong, however, in imagining rapid obscurity for the proceedings of the first legislature. Rather, they were typical of those which were to follow. By 1826, a Tuscaloosa paper was openly lamenting, "It too often happens that men of the lowest grade of intellect are found in our Halls of Legislation." [19] But the legislators perhaps possessed a kind of competence which, because it was alien to the men who viewed the assembly with such distaste, was often overlooked. Clement Claiborne Clay, a splenetic young man who did not easily bestow praise, wrote his mother on first entering the legislature that it contained "a great amount of natural talent and statesman-like ability." [20] It was "natural talent" rather than cultivated expertise that marked the assemblymen, if anything did.

An episode in the session of 1834 casts light on the legislative turn of mind. In 1828 the legislature artificially expanded the size of the counties bordering the Creek Indian territory in order to establish Alabama's sovereignty in the area. These acts were a mere maneuver in the dispute with the federal government over Indian removal. James Abercrombie, the senator from Montgomery, moved in 1833 to that part of the Creek territory ostensibly included within Montgomery, and argued that he had not thereby forfeited his seat. But the Senate expelled him, in a struggle pitting the forces of legalism against the ordinary practical legislator. The minority pointed out that the law was on the books and that if the legislature refused to follow statutory dictates, it would in effect be declaring its own act void. But the majority replied that, whatever might appear from the face of the act, when it was passed it was intended only to regulate Indians. They refused to be bound by the literal meaning of their laws, but enforced instead a common sense intent. [21]

The legislators debated without flair, [22] managed their affairs with-

19. *Alabama Sentinel* (Tuscaloosa), June 17, 1826. On the third legislature, *cf.* "Censor," in *Alabama Republican* (Huntsville), December 28, 1821.

20. Clement Claiborne Clay to Susanna Withers Clay, December 23, 1842, in Clay Papers, Duke University Library, Durham. *Cf.* Samuel Forwood to William S. Forwood, December 11, 1839, in William S. Forwood Papers, Southern Historical Collection, University of North Carolina Library, Chapel Hill.

21. *Senate Journal*, Sess. of 1834–35, pp. 20–23, 66–68, 75, 172–80, 183–84. This encounter contributed importantly to the developing consciousness of party difference (Huntsville *Democrat*, December 10, 1834).

22. E.g., *Senate Journal*, Sess. of 1830–31, pp. 120–23.

out excessive resort to parliamentary procedure, but brought to bear on their duties the intelligence of men schooled by observation and events. Often they failed to understand the long-term best interests of the state. Usually they found themselves, when attention turned to complicated national affairs, at the mercy of those men who, because of superior academic attainments, affected to understand such things. But they knew very well what would please their constituents and what would not.

The most important day in the legislator's year was the day each August when he was summoned before the sovereignty of Alabama to have his actions approved or disapproved. Voting was by ballot, but a number was placed on each ballot corresponding to a number by the voter's name on a master list, so that it was possible later to determine how each man had used his franchise. It was regarded as insulting to challenge another man's right to vote, and the action was seldom taken. In one contested election it was revealed on examination that ten minors, eleven nonresidents and a felon had voted, and one man had voted twice.[23] But despite these aberrations, elections were on the whole fair tests of popular strength.

They were preceded by the most intense campaigning. In 1847, Tuscaloosa produced eight candidates, five of them Democrats, for her three legislative seats. "Poor devils!" wrote an observer, "What a time they have of it—riding ten or twelve miles in the hot sun and speaking every day. They have been at it for a month, and continue until election day,"[24] a two-month long canvass. In addition to the formal speeches, "electioneering"—swapping stories with the voters and treating them to free drinks—was usually expected. On at least one occasion, however, the practice was suppressed on the ground that it was an encouragement to intemperance.[25]

Parties were important determinants of voting behavior, but they were not quite so well disciplined in legislative as in gubernatorial or presidential elections. Sometimes local jealousies or personal interests

23. *Senate Journal*, Sess. of 1829–30, pp. 55–56. An act of 1842 attempted to deal with this problem (Wetumpka *Argus*, January 19, 1842), but evidently with only limited success.

24. Rufus H. Clements to Jefferson Franklin Jackson, July 21, 1847, in J. F. Jackson Papers, Alabama Department of Archives and History, Montgomery.

25. Selma *Courier*, August 14, 1828, May 21, May 28, July 30, 1829.

were more important than party drill.[26] The Democrats were so much the majority party in so many counties that they were plagued by an excess of ambitious candidates. Often the party's inability to persuade its aspirants to limit their number to the number of places open led to a Whig's being able to sneak into a seat normally Democratic.[27]

Before the rise of formal parties in the late thirties, and to a considerable extent even thereafter, intracounty sectionalism was a powerful voting determinant. Especially was sectionalism a force in such counties as Franklin, St. Clair, Dallas, and Greene, where important physical obstructions—mountains in the case of the first two, rivers in the case of the others—hindered communication. Hostility to urban centers could also be generated by attacks on capitalists, who did not "accumulate [their] wealth by the ordinary process of mental and physical labor."[28]

The third great voting determinant, and socially perhaps the most significant one, was the sentiments of the candidates, as revealed in their oratory. Politicians sought constantly to "ride a hobby," as they said: to locate and exploit a popular issue. The issue might be one of local interests: Governor Henry W. Collier launched his political career with a pledge to have a capitol building erected in Tuscaloosa.[29] It might be personal: Griffin Lamkin gained a seat by emphasizing his service as commandant of the Madison County militia.[30] But usually, following in the footsteps of Kelly, Long, and Pickens, the candidates based their campaigns on attacks upon some concentration or use of power—the national bank or the state bank, the federal government, the state government, taxation, the courts, the schools, party conventions, corporations.[31] Wherever power existed, it could be made to

26. Particularly in faction-ridden Mobile: John B. Hogan to Arthur P. Bagby, January 2, 1840, in Governors' Correspondence: Bagby, Alabama Department of Archives and History, Montgomery; Hogan to Hugh McVay, August 27, 1837, in Governors' Correspondence: McVay.

27. *E.g.*, Sidney C. Posey to Arthur P. Bagby, August 8, 1838, in Governors' Correspondence: Bagby.

28. *Franklin Enquirer* (Tuscumbia), May 5, 1824; John C. Pickens to Samuel Pickens, June 28, 1827 and the beat returns for the general elections of 1831 in Greene County, both in Pickens Papers, Alabama Department of Archives and History, Montgomery; Selma *Courier*, June 26, July 17, July 24, 1828; Wetumpka *Argus*, September 11, 1839.

29. *Alabama Sentinel* (Tuscaloosa), June 3, 1826.

30. *Alabama Republican* (Huntsville), July 15, 1819.

31. William Winter Payne to Arthur P. Bagby, July 23, 1838, in Governors' Corre-

appear evil; wherever power was used, it could be denounced as oppressive.

The electorate listened carefully to such pronouncements—indeed, too carefully, in the opinion of some early observers.[32] The practice, which was a common one, of groups of voters demanding through the press printed statements of the legislative candidates' positions on public issues, drew the ire of a Selma correspondent. "The only honest and fair mode of election," he concluded, "I deem to be this—to vote for men in whose honesty, integrity and talents we can confide, requiring no further pledge than their own character and their oath of office. He who gives more does not go into office independently. . . . A man who will very readily pledge himself, I would not very readily believe." The mode of election proposed by this correspondent was the one common in the Jeffersonian world, and the correspondent's letter clearly reflects Jeffersonian presuppositions. But Selma, and Alabama as a whole, had moved into the new Jacksonian age. The voters no longer confided in the character and integrity of their representative; he was their dependent. And so a letter in reply denounced the "anti-republican character" of the earlier letter. "This writer, I suppose, would have us take all this [the qualifications of an office seeker] for granted upon the say-so of the friends and partizans of the candidates" or give credence "to the things that the candidates themselves may whisper secretly in their ears. But no! the people of this county will never consent to rely upon this information. . . . They wish things told to them in such a way that there can be no mistake, no prevarications, no misrepresentations." The candidates must state "fully and explicitly their views."[33] The spirit of deference, if it had ever existed in Alabama, was dead; for the rest of the antebellum period elections would belong to the electorate.

Though the notion that "every man is born a legislator"[34] was

---

spondence: Bagby; Wetumpka *Argus*, July 7, December 22, 1841; William W. Parham, in *The Tuscumbian* (Tuscumbia), July 18, 1825; Thomas Livingston Bayne to Jefferson Franklin Jackson, July 20, 1849, in Jackson Papers; *Senate Journal*, Sess. of 1841–42, p. 93; *Senate Journal*, Sess. of 1859–60, pp. 16–17; Hugh Lawson White Clay to Clement Comer Clay, July 5, 1845, in Clay Papers; Felix G. Norman to George S. Houston, January 23, 1848, in George S. Houston Papers, Duke University Library, Durham.

32. E.g., *The Tuscumbian*, June 20, 1825.
33. Selma *Courier*, July 17, July 31, 1828.
34. *The Tuscumbian*, June 27, 1825.

widely, if tacitly, held, the voters nevertheless often chose as their representative one of the leading men of their community. In the early years, when the militia was a powerful force in local government, legislators were often drawn from its officer corps.[35] But militia officers were themselves, of course, elected officials, chosen from the lower ranks. Activity in county politics could also make a man's name familiar to his neighbors. Indeed, as we have seen, a number of legislators in 1839 were actually holding local office at the same time at which they were serving in the legislature. Lawyers, who met a great many people in the course of riding their circuits, had some advantage in becoming well known. Wealth, too, could give one a reputation in the neighborhood. Jacinth Jackson, who sat as the member for Pike in 1829 and 1830, was known for his ownership of a two-story frame house. But he was almost illiterate, and, made to feel his lack of learning while serving in the House, he enrolled in the same "old field school" which his children were attending and studied his lessons along with them. Later he became a large planter, but he remained unfamiliar with the constraints of grammar and spent years trying to prevent his brilliant son from attending college.[36]

The point to be emphasized is that a man's position in the local community is not an index to his position on a large stage. Even though Jacinth Jackson was a man of some substance in Pike County, when he entered the legislature he encountered men of far greater economic and intellectual stature than he. If he were sufficiently rooted in the outlook and prejudices of the community from which he came, he would react to these men as would the other citizens of Pike; he would, in other words, represent his constituency. It is usually, therefore, from the composition of the statewide electorate and from the composition of the legislature itself rather than from the composition

35. John Watkins to Thomas Bibb, September 4, 1820, Governors' Correspondence: Thomas Bibb.

36. W. Wallace Screws to Jefferson Franklin Jackson, July 3, 1858, Frederick J. Kingsbury to Eleanor M. Jackson, August 12, 1903, Jacinth Jackson to Jefferson Franklin Jackson, January 17, 1852, Jefferson Franklin Jackson to W. L. Cowan, April 6, 1839, Jefferson Franklin Jackson to A.K. Merrill, July 13, 1840, all in Jackson Papers. Menn, "Large Slaveholders," 507, records Jacinth's holdings as 55 slaves, $15,800 in real estate, and $66,675 in personal property at the end of the antebellum period, by which time he had moved to Sumter County. Jefferson, his son, later earned degrees from both Yale and Harvard, and was elected to Phi Beta Kappa at the former institution.

of the local population that the class position of legislators must be determined.[37]

Once the electorate had chosen its representatives, it kept tight rein on them through the power of instruction. Almost from the beginning, legislators acknowledged an absolute duty to follow instructions. Indeed, thinking for oneself was very nearly a sin. A newspaper correspondent wrote, "Who would willingly come into office intending to act from conclusions of their own, formed in reason, justice or passion, in opposition to the will of their constituents? If no man would (and it is evident no honest man [would]), none should hesitate to express the sound convictions of their minds in the most public and unreserved manner." And he added happily, "The people's will is the law—'they can do no wrong' in this country; and where is the man that dares brave their decrees?" The notion that the opinions of the representative, even when "formed in reason," are utterly irrelevant to the legislative process, is a startling one, but it was so widely held that the next week a correspondent derided these views as being too obvious to require saying: "Who did not know this?" he asked.[38] Candidates requested as part of their campaign oratory, to be instructed. And when presented with difficult issues during the course of the session, assemblymen wrote home begging orders. Of course, they often suggested in what way they would wish to be instructed. But when the proper instructions were not forthcoming, they did not hesitate to vote against their sense of what was in the public interest in order to fulfill what they took to be their constituents' desires.[39]

37. Jacinth Jackson owned ten slaves in 1830. The failure to realize the distinction between local and legislative status renders defective the work of Richard E. Beringer, "A Profile of the Members of the Confederate Congress," *Journal of Southern History*, XXXIII (1967), 518–41, esp. 532, 536. Beringer undertakes to compare the property holdings of the congressmen to the mean for the counties in which they resided. Because he finds a substantial number of congressmen whose holdings were six times or more greater than the average for their immediate neighbors, he concludes that the congress was unrepresentative. But the comparison is not, in fact, very instructive. Officeholders must be judged by the stage on which they act—in the case of congressmen, the whole nation. The fact that a holder of ten slaves may be well-to-do by the standards of some small-farm county does not mean that he will feel himself any the less poor when he encounters a Louisiana sugar baron. Actually, though Beringer fails to appreciate the implications of his figures, they appear to prove that the Confederate Congress was, in relative terms, quite representative indeed.

38. Selma *Courier*, July 10, July 17, 1828.

39. *The Tuscumbian*, July 18, 1825; Hugh Lawson White Clay to Susanna Withers Clay, December 15, 1845, Clement Claiborne Clay to Clement Comer Clay, December 22, 1845, De-

Such action was perfectly acceptable. During the congressional canvass of 1851, the Whigs pointed out that the Democratic nominee, John Cochran of Barbour, had years before, when representing Benton County in the legislature, voted for the White Basis Bill, detested by the Whigs. But, responded the Democrats, Cochran had had no choice in the matter, for at that time he resided in Benton, and even the Whigs "will recognize the right that the people of a county should have their views carried out by their representative and that Colonel Cochran was bound to vote as they desired." He had only followed the "known wishes and instructions of the people" of his county.[40] There were even efforts to have the legislature enforce the right of instruction against its members,[41] but they were rejected, and the imposition of sanctions left to the voters.

The voters used their powers with great freedom, and rates of reelection to the Alabama legislature, from the very beginning, appear to have been quite low. It would, of course, be quite difficult to discover how many legislators actually sought reelection and were defeated. But we can determine the turnover rate in the period. During the antebellum era there were 3,220 legislative places to be filled, and they were occupied by 1,622 different men. This ratio informs us both that the average legislator could expect just two terms, and that in any given session, half of the members were likely to be new men. Only 186 assemblymen—a bit more than 11 percent of the antebellum total—managed to serve four or more terms.

The men who sat in the legislature were little concerned with the preservation of parliamentary decorum. From the state's earliest days, sessions were boisterous and even violent. Sometimes the disorders were mere breaches of etiquette. More often they were acrimonious personal disputes which disrupted assembly sessions, and which usually required a committee investigation, though occasionally they could be settled by less formal intervention. But at least as frequently,

---

cember 24, 1845, and January 9, 1846, all in Clay Papers. *Cf.* George S. Walden to Bolling Hall, September 6, 1853, in Bolling Hall Papers, Alabama Department of Archives and History, Montgomery.

40. Montgomery *Advertiser*, August 6, 1851. The White Basis bill had inaugurated the practice of apportioning congressional districts solely on the basis of white population, thereby reducing the power of the whiggish plantation counties.

41. *House Journal*, Sess. of 1840–41, pp. 29–30, 85–86.

sessions were marked by childish displays of misconduct. In 1849, during a debate on an appropriation for the University of Alabama, the members got into a spitball fight. In 1852 another spitball fight led to a violent argument. On the same day opponents of the bill under consideration, to charter a railroad, drowned out with sustained coughing the clerk's efforts to read it. And in 1846, when future governor and Confederate attorney general Thomas Hill Watts called future supreme court justice Thomas J. Judge ignorant, actual fisticuffs ensued. Examples of this sort could be multiplied. The formality and restraint of legislative proceedings evidently seemed silly to the legislators, and their behavior demonstrated their contempt for such concepts.[42]

There were always rumors current of corruption among the legislators. Occasionally they were true. Moseley Baker, one of the state's most important Nullificationists, swindled the Bank of Alabama out of $21,800. He decamped to Texas, where he became a leading citizen and eventually repaid the stolen funds. Erasmus Walker, a representative from Dallas who acted as an agent to handle applications from distant counties for loans at the state bank, was caught pocketing funds sent him to be paid to the bank. Dixon Hall, Benjamin Davis, and John A. Whetstone, all prominent politicians in Autauga, were implicated in an attempt to defraud the bank of $15,500, and Whetstone was forced to withdraw his candidacy for the assembly as a result of the affair.[43] But such instances of overt dishonesty were rare. Somewhat more common was influence peddling. Senator James F. Roberts' heavy indebtedness to the Mobile branch of the state bank evidently made him a willing tool in an effort to discredit the few who sought to make public the dubious business practices of that extraordinarily mismanaged institution. And the banks were certainly not

42. Israel Pickens to William B. Lenoir, November 19, 1821, in Pickens Papers; *Alabama Republican* (Huntsville), November 23, 1821; *Senate Journal*, Sess. of 1830–31, pp. 120–23, 137, 151–52, 185–86; *House Journal*, Sess. of 1839–40, pp. 286–96; Montgomery *Advertiser*, January 23, 1850, February 10, February 17, 1852; Clement Claiborne Clay to Clement Comer Clay, January 18, 1843, January 21, 1846, both in Clay Papers. *Cf.* Wetumpka *Argus*, January 12, 1842. Watts and Judge later became law partners.

43. *Senate Journal*, Sess. of 1833–34, pp. 128, 148; Wetumpka *Argus*, June 23, 1841 (these charges, however, were never proven). On bank frauds generally, *cf. House Journal*, Sess. of 1841–42, pp. 354–55.

above attempting to buy a member when they thought him on the market.[44]

However, even if we make the most generous allowances for the substance behind the rumors, still the number and frequency of these reports strains credulity. Any event out of the ordinary was likely to produce tales of dishonesty. Land, for instance, had been very much overpriced at the sales of the territorial period. But the populace had not realized the extent of the overvaluation until commissioners were appointed to classify the 400,000 acres given the state by the United States to finance the building of the Muscle Shoals Canal. When their report showed the lands to be worth much less than had been expected, the Huntsville *Democrat* promptly stated that the classification had been a "tissue of iniquity" and a "second edition of the Yazoo fraud, engineered by the Alabama Legislature." When *Democrat* editor Thomas J. Sumner was ordered to present his evidence to the assembly, it became clear that his unhesitating assertion had been nothing more than the suspicion of his fevered imagination. He had merely assumed that corruption must exist in such a situation.[45]

One reason for the readiness of Alabamians to charge dishonesty is that they defined the term so that it included acts normal to the legislative process. Clement Claiborne Clay wrote to his father, "The Removal question [the bill to move the capital from Tuscaloosa to Montgomery] is playing havoc with men's virtue. High bids are offered for removal votes, as I know by *intimations as broad as dared be made to me.* And it is thought Winston (!!) and possibly other senators are in the market." It would certainly appear that we have here discovered a case of corruption, involving no less than that Cato figure John A. Winston. But Clay adds, "He [Winston] will vote for removal for a seat in the *U.S. Senate*, and if his vote is needed, his price may be paid!" On another occasion, we find an observer writing of the election of five men to the supreme court, "More corrupt proceedings I never witnessed than were carried on in our Assembly. The most open

---

44. *Senate Journal*, Sess. of 1835–36, p. 165; Samuel F. Rice, in Wetumpka *Argus*, December 29, 1841; *House Journal*, Sess. of 1841–42, pp. 191–95. For Roberts' debt, see William H. Brantley, *Banking in Alabama, 1816–1860* (2 vols.; Birmingham: privately printed [Vol. I by Birmingham Printing Co., Vol. II by Oxmoor Press], 1961, 1967), I, Appendix.

45. *House Journal*, Sess. of 1829–30, pp. 93–94; *Senate Journal*, Sess. of 1829–30, pp. 129–32.

and barefaced swapping of votes." The negotiation and compromise almost necessarily incident to the enactment of legislation, then, appeared *per se* corrupt in the eyes of many antebellum Alabamians. One group of legislators found reprehensible the inclusion, in a bill to aid internal improvements, of a large group of projects not one of which alone could have commanded a majority, but which together added a sufficient number of votes to achieve passage.[46]

The problem, however, is more than a mere matter of definition. When the inclusion of a number of local projects in a bill in order to create a majority is a questionable practice; when the swapping of votes is corruption; when dishonesty is assumed without evidence, we must have, in fact, suggestions of deep doubts about the social role of the legislature. In the society which we are exploring, power is by its nature sinister, for power always limits freedom. All centers of power are, therefore, suspect, and anyone who exercises authority labors under the presumption of corruption. Alabama's legislators were, by and large, simple men. Their abilities were not great enough to enable them to grapple successfully with the problems with which the state was faced. And every failure, given the presumption of guilt, was taken by the masses as further evidence of corruption. And every such conviction reinforced the social bias against the use of power.

In the crisis of 1837, as the state was swept up in the vortex of financial panic, men who knew the legislators well hesitated long before summoning them into session. Mobile Democratic boss Thaddeus Sanford wrote Governor Clay, "We are in a condition of pecuniary distress that surpasses anything of the kind that I ever contemplated. . . . House after house of large means, and of resources hitherto considered unbounded has been prostrated and scarcely anything is left but one general scene of devastation and ruin." Still he had resisted the pressure to urge a special session because "I have feared the action of the legislature on such delicate and important subjects in a season of universal panic, especially when I recollect the materials of which it [the legislature] is composed." Judge William D. Pickett wrote, "I am of the opinion that there will be more danger and injury

46. Clement Claiborne Clay to Clement Comer Clay, January 9, 1846, in Clay Papers; John M. Taylor to John W. Walker, January 20, 1820, in Walker Papers; *Senate Journal*, Sess. of 1859–60, pp. 341–42.

likely to occur from the sudden assemblage of the Legislature than good. I should fear that any remedies that a heated and interested Legislature could devise would work ultimate harm to the body politic. That detriment will likely operate upon the class called creditors." And Sidney C. Posey said, "Under the existing alarm and pressure . . . I have no doubt the Legislature would be hurried into some measure of supposed relief which would be highly impolitic and ultimately injurious to the State." [47]

These forebodings were completely justified. The acts of the special session of 1837—requiring the banks to increase their already bloated note circulation by $5 million and to suspend the collection of $5 million of their debts—were disastrous in their consequences. But it is important to note that the men who predicted this legislative calamity attributed it to its proper cause: the limited talents of the assembly members and their eagerness to aid the citizenry. The central political event of the early 1840s was to be the oratorical transmutation of this bumbling effort to help into a malevolent exercise in self-interest. Where power was concerned, failure was corruption. Thus the men who sat in Alabama's legislature, on many occasions when they did their best to serve, reaped for their efforts harvests of scorn, usually deserved, for their ineptitude, and suspicion, usually groundless, of their honesty.

And yet we opened the present discussion with a most forceful statement by Governor Bagby of a quite different attitude. When the legislature attempted a positive exercise of power, and the effort failed, the legislators became subject to their constituents' hostility to power. But ordinarily the legislators knew better than to attempt positive action. They knew that the majority of Alabama's voters had given the assembly not a positive but a negative commission—the passage of laws to restrict, regulate or destroy concentrations of power in the private sector. When the legislature confined itself to activity of that kind, it was not a threat to the citizenry but their collective voice, their sword in the struggle for freedom. The Jacksonian generation differed from its Jeffersonian predecessor precisely in realizing that, though

47. Thaddeus Sanford to Clement Comer Clay, April 22, 1837, William D. Pickett to Clay, May 1, 1837, Sidney C. Posey to Clay, May 9, 1837, all in Governors' Correspondence: Clay. *Cf.* William Fleming to Clay, May 15, 1837, in Governors' Correspondence: Clay.

government could easily become oppressive, it could also, if carefully controlled, be a potent weapon against certain forms of oppression in the economy and the social structure. It was such considerations which seemed to Governor Bagby to clothe the annual meeting of the assembly in garments of beauty; the assemblymen had come together in order to throw "additional safeguards around the essential rights" of the populace. We shall turn to that aspect of the legislature's functions—the aspect which rendered the body respected, and even perhaps beloved—after we have explored the formal mechanisms of the legislative process.

The Institution

The Alabama legislature met annually until 1845, but biennially thereafter. It convened in November[48] and met for about two months when sessions were annual. Biennial meetings lengthened the sessions to about three months.

At the urging of Governor Bibb, the territorial assembly made itself one of the best paid legislatures in the United States, at five dollars a day while in session. But the angry cries of the people were not long in being heard. One candidate for office charged that the members were "living at their ease" on their "extravagant salaries," which were "drawing money from those that have not got it to spare, and giving it to them that do not earn it." The salaries, he argued, were obviously too large because they exceeded even what the farmer would "give the laborer per year that is undergoing all the inclemency of the weather." Here were precisely the sorts of arguments best calculated to scare Alabama lawmakers out of their wits. The charge that they were earning more than would a farm laborer was too much for them, and they scurried to reduce their pay to four dollars per diem.[49] Legislative

48. In 1819 the assembly convened in October, and from 1842 to 1847 it convened in early December, but for the rest of the antebellum period it began its sessions in November.
49. *Alabama Republican* (Huntsville), June 1, 1821 (only Mississippi and Georgia paid as much as $5); Job Key, in *Alabama Republican*, July 13, 1821; *Acts of Alabama*, Called Sess. of 1821, p. 23; *cf. House Journal*, Sess. of 1842–43, pp. 471–72. The legislators also received $4 for each twenty miles traveled in a single round trip to the capital. The speaker of the House and the president of the Senate received $6 per diem and the clerk of the House and secretary of the Senate $7 per diem.

compensation remained at four dollars throughout the antebellum years.

This episode is another example of the fatal subservience of the Alabama political system to the demagogic appeal. The electorate was at all times deeply fearful that the government would accumulate power and wealth at the expense of the citizenry. Any action which could be interpreted as a symptom of the beginning of this process was, therefore, subject to the uses of the aspirant for office. Governor Bibb's motives in suggesting adequate compensation to the legislators had been the best: to enable the poor to enter public life.[50] But, as the legislators instinctively realized, it was the attack of the demagogue which would strike home with the electorate, not the arguments of Bibb. Indeed, even after the reduction of the lawmakers' salaries to a low level, charges of legislative extravagance continued to be a staple of political harangues for the rest of the antebellum period.[51]

Unlike many southern states, Alabama never had to fight the battle to democratize the basis for apportioning legislative seats; it was always white population. Nevertheless, this guideline left much room for maneuver, and in many a session of the legislature apportionment was, as a contemporary said of the fight in 1851, a "vexed question."[52] Considering the political sensitivity of the operation, the legislature came reasonably close to fulfilling its constitutional mandate. It produced some sort of reapportionment after each state census, which was taken every six years.[53] And the apportionments enacted reflected reasonably well the distribution of the population. Under the plan of 1839, for instance, a minimum of 42.6 percent of the white population could elect a majority of the House and 41.2 percent a majority of the Senate. Under the plan of 1851 the respective percentages were 43 percent and 45.3 percent.

Given the constitutional limitations of at least one representative and no more than one senator to a county, these figures are not exces-

50. *Journal of the Legislative Council*, 1st Sess. of 1818, pp. 7–8.
51. E.g., Tuscaloosa *Flag*, quoted in Wetumpka *Argus*, January 20, 1841.
52. Montgomery *Advertiser*, January 27, 1852.
53. In 1850 the constitution was amended to require a state census in 1855 and every tenth year thereafter, and to extend the intervals between apportionments accordingly. The legislature reapportioned itself eight times in the antebellum period—every three years from 1819 to 1827 and every six years from 1827 to 1856.

sively askew. As we would expect, however, legislators sought whenever possible to gain partisan advantage through the apportionments. The legislature of 1839 was controlled by the Democrats. Of the eight counties which in the apportionment of that year were grossly and volitively over-represented, three were Democratic counties and an additional four were closely contested between the factions. The Democrats presumably hoped to win the allegiance of these counties by reward. Similarly, the Whiggery having gained unusual strength in the legislature of 1851, half of the twelve grossly and volitively over-represented counties in that year were in the Black Belt.[54]

The citizenry placed heavy pressure upon the lawmakers to finish their work expeditiously and adjourn. Like attacks upon legislative compensation, charges of sloth could easily be transmuted into the allegation that the legislature was unmindful of a populace groaning under the weight of the exactions necessary to finance a session. Therefore the members generally met for three hours in the morning, three in the afternoon, and an additional two in the evening, six days a week, while in session. Nor did they take holidays, even for Christmas. There can be no surer indication of the great changes which overtook Alabama in the final decade of the antebellum period than the decision of the legislature in 1849 to permit a Christmas recess. But even at the very end of the antebellum years, Christmas vacations still brought horrified protests.[55]

The opposition to lengthy sessions led directly to the adoption of biennial meetings. This method of limiting the government's power to

54. I speak here only of the House of Representatives. By the phrase "grossly and volitively over-represented" I mean counties which were allotted more than the constitutional minimum of one representative and which thereby were given a white population per representative at least 400 below the median ratio for the whole House (3,138 to 1 in 1839 and 4,200 to 1 in 1851). The counties which fall into this category in 1839 are Lawrence, Tuscaloosa, Blount, Jefferson, Shelby, Greene, Marengo, and Monroe; and in 1851 are Franklin, Blount, Bibb, Shelby, Dallas, Lowndes, Macon, Marengo, Sumter, Wilcox, Butler, and Henry. It is to be noted that four of these latter counties (Bibb, Shelby, Butler, and Henry) had been carried by the Southern Rights ticket. The fact that they were rewarded by a Unionist legislature probably indicates the proficiency with which the Southern Rights Democrats in the House contrived an alliance with the Union Democrats during the course of the session.

55. *House Journal*, Sess. of 1849–50, pp. 249–50; *House Journal*, Sess. of 1859–60, pp. 205, 459. The custom of meeting on Christmas Day sometimes brought trouble, however. At one such meeting in 1841, two representatives doused a third with a bowl of eggnog on the floor of the House (Wetumpka *Argus*, January 19, 1842). Failure to schedule evening sessions could also bring outcries: *House Journal*, Sess. of 1841–42, pp. 128, 147.

act, and of curtailing its expenditures, had great support from the earliest days of statehood. By 1846 pressure for the reform had become so strong that it swept the state—receiving the approval of 91.5 percent of the voters expressing an opinion, and even carrying with it through the legislature a highly controversial rider removing the state capital from Tuscaloosa to Montgomery. Despite this prodigious endorsement, the scheme had not been in operation five years before the state's Democratic organ pronounced it a failure. And the constitutional convention of 1861 abandoned it for a return to annual meetings.[56]

This episode is typical of how reform could find great popular favor merely by the constant repetition of the assurance that its consequence would be the limitation of governmental power. Early in the debate, leaders pointed out that biennial meetings would result in longer sessions, with no net gain to the treasury.[57] But as time passed, opposition to the amendment came more and more to be equated with opposition to its goal, until eventually there was no dissent to be heard. The natural result of the oratorical methods of the period, when they were used persistently and skillfully, was just such a process of gradually gathering unanimity.

The legislature in Alabama was essentially an autonomous institution. The governorship was little more than a salaried honor. The governor's most important act each year was the preparation of his annual message to the opening meeting of the legislature. With the recommendations in his message, he exercised such impact as he had upon the legislative process. Each house referred the various gubernatorial suggestions to appropriate committees for study. Moreover, his arguments could sway public opinion. The message was reprinted verbatim in every important newspaper in the state, and was the subject of close scrutiny and extensive comment, both public and private. But after the delivery of the message, the governor usually faded into the shadows for another twelve months. He possessed only a suspensive veto; a

56. *The Tuscumbian*, December 31, 1824; Selma *Courier*, August 14, 1828; *House Journal*, Sess. of 1830–31, p. 99; Malcolm C. McMillan, *Constitutional Development in Alabama, 1798–1901: A Study in Politics, the Negro, and Sectionalism* (Chapel Hill: University of North Carolina Press, 1955), 51–63; Montgomery *Advertiser*, February 27, 1850. Each session, under the terms of the constitution of 1861, was limited to thirty days, however. The constitution of 1865 again ordered biennial sessions.

57. *House Journal*, Sess. of 1829–30, pp. 191–93.

simple majority in each house could override it. Governors in any case very seldom used their veto. When they did so, they usually held themselves motivated by constitutional considerations rather than by mere questions of policy. At the very least, they alleged a severe defect in the law which had not come to the legislature's attention.[58] The governor's power to make temporary appointments to vacant offices when the legislature was not in session did give him a bit of patronage to distribute—particularly after the adoption of biennial meetings.[59] But for the most part the substance of state government remained in the hands of the assembly.

There were few formal ties between the governor and his party in the legislature. It was apparently felt that the bond of common membership in the Democratic party should be a sufficient link. The choice of the speaker of the House and the president of the Senate, for instance, was strictly the responsibility of the majority caucus in the respective houses. Though the campaigns for these places were aggressive, the governor did not ordinarily express a preference among the contenders.[60] Indeed, it was rare even for him to designate floor leaders to press his legislative proposals. Rather he depended upon party regularity to effect his aims. Possibly the failure of the state's governors to attempt to gain a more active role in legislative affairs is an aspect of the society's fear that strong leadership foreshadowed despotism. After the disintegration of parties in the late 1850s, presiding officers were chosen, as they had been in the 1820s, by open vote of the whole house; and the elections were often bitter, multiballot affairs.[61]

The legislative offices were worth the struggle. The speaker had absolute power to appoint all committees in the House. Senate committees were continuing bodies, but the president assigned new mem-

---

58. E.g., *House Journal*, Sess. of 1840–41, p. 333; *House Journal*, Sess. of 1849–50, pp. 286–87, 333–34; *Senate Journal*, Sess. of 1835–36, pp. 161–62; *Senate Journal*, Sess. of 1859–60, pp. 371–72, 387. It was this tradition which made John A. Winston's course so remarkable.

59. E.g., *Senate Journal*, Sess. of 1849–50, pp. 53–55. The governor could also pardon criminals and summon special sessions of the legislature. But public disapproval of the expense involved militated against the use of the latter power. Only four special sessions were held in the entire antebellum period.

60. A typical race for speaker was Bolling Hall's in 1853: see George S. Walden to Bolling Hall, September 6, 1853, John Hardy to Hall, October 13, 1853, Benjamin Fitzpatrick to Hall, October 5, 1853, all in Hall Papers.

61. *House Journal*, Sess. of 1859–60, pp. 4 ff.

bers to the various vacancies on them. And both officers by their rulings greatly influenced the course of debate—though, since they were often ignorant of the niceties of parliamentary procedure,[62] appeals from their decisions were frequent and occasionally successful.

Perhaps the assembly's most significant organizational deficiency was its inability to exercise sufficient superintendence over the state's two financial officers, the treasurer and the comptroller of public accounts. Legislators had neither the time nor the inclination to undertake more than a cursory audit of the state's books. In 1849, some $21,500 in gold and silver was discovered stuffed in a flour barrel in the basement of the old Bank of Alabama in Tuscaloosa. It had been stored there by the treasurer, and faulty bookkeeping apparently had allowed it to be forgotten. More seriously, Treasurer Samuel G. Frierson stole more than $14,500 from the state in the early 1840s. And Comptroller Jefferson C. Van Dyke took more than $20,000.[63] Such incidents were virtually unavoidable as long as most real authority in the state was committed to a temporary body with a highly unstable membership.

One of the most common criticisms of the legislature was the amount of legislation it produced applying only to one county, locality, or person. In 1851, for instance, precisely 42 of the 452 bills enacted were general laws. The result of this situation was constant agitation for the legislature to delegate more of its responsibilities to the county commissions and to the courts; and for the enactment of such self-operating laws as general incorporation statutes.[64] But the legislature strongly resisted such suggestions, primarily because its power over local affairs made the individual legislator extremely influential in his own community and could, if he drew his bills well, advance greatly his standing with his constituency, and thus his personal career. Lawmakers tended, therefore, to pay particular attention

62. *E.g.*, Felix G. Norman to George S. Houston, February 10, 1848, in Houston Papers; *House Journal*, Sess. of 1849–50, pp. 485–90.

63. Montgomery *Advertiser*, November 28, 1849, November 4, 1851; *Senate Journal*, Sess. of 1849–50, pp. 97–98; *House Journal*, Sess. of 1849–50, pp. 113–14. On another occasion (*House Journal*, Sess. of 1849–50, pp. 479–81), more than one million dollars in unissued state bonds was found in the capitol. On Van Dyke, *cf. Senate Journal*, Sess. of 1833–34, p. 128.

64. Montgomery *Advertiser*, January 30, 1850, February 24, 1852; *House Journal*, Sess. of 1849–50, p. 222. *Cf.* Henry Hitchcock to John W. Walker, January 2, 1821, in Walker Papers; Wetumpka *Argus*, January 20, 1841.

to local opinions and needs. This arrangement contained, of course, both salutary and destructive implications; it encouraged both active representation and pandering to provincialism and prejudice.

One member who was far from innocent of the charge himself commented that the thing principally wrong with the legislature was the propensity of its members to make speeches, so "that it is quite difficult to despatch the simplest proposition under hours of debate." As the term was used in the assembly, "debate" meant not so much an interchange of comments as a series of long, carefully prepared speeches, delivered without notes. The session usually began each year with a debate on national affairs, and ambitious young men hopeful of advancement to Congress used this opportunity to display to the party elders their oratorical powers and ideological fervor. But speeches upon local issues were at least as important. It was customary for members to have their speeches printed and distributed among their constituents as proof of their zeal in guarding the citizenry from threatened legislative harm. An impressive effort in debate could do much to advance a career. Towards the end of a session, however, legislators grew tired of excessive speechmaking, and often voted cloture. It took only a simple majority to order the previous question, and the device was frequently used, often against the minority Whigs.[65]

Votes in the legislature—both for measures and for men—were frequently affected by legislative horsetrading. Though the practice of building a majority for one measure by agreements to support other pending proposals was regularly condemned, it was common. Moreover, the use of such tactics was even more prevalent in the votes for the numerous officials chosen by legislative election. The various candidates visited the capitol to bargain for the places they sought. Votes were swapped and influence brought to bear. Multi-ballot elections often produced compromise candidates, whose qualifications might well resemble those of one gentleman for whom it was claimed that he was "bland and courteous in his manners." It is easy to believe

65. Clement Claiborne Clay to Clement Comer Clay, January 21, 1846, Clement Claiborne Clay to Susanna Withers Clay, December 23, 1842, Clement Claiborne Clay to Jones Withers Clay, January 8, 1845, Clement Claiborne Clay to Clement Comer Clay, January 30, 1843, all in Clay Papers; Wetumpka *Argus*, December 30, 1840, November 17, 1841; Montgomery *Advertiser*, December 12, 1849. On at least one occasion the Whigs sought to make the invocation of cloture more difficult, but failed (Wetumpka *Argus*, November 10, 1841).

that in votes involving men, political negotiation and influence were more often than not the factors determinative of the outcome. Probably, however, such elements were less important in the passage of statutes. Alabama legislators were always aware that their constituents would scrutinize the provisions of new laws, in search of the beginnings of tyranny.[66]

Groups, Blocs, and Parties

"Sent up by the people to sit in the temple which they have dedicated to civil liberty, we should be as free from the passions of discord and party animosity as when convened to worship in the temples of our religion."[67] So spoke Governor John Gayle to the legislature of 1832. But neither that nor any other session was free from the passions of party; various issues produced various blocs, but the existence of blocs was always an essential element in the legislative process.

Economic groupings, though probably the most significant of the legislature's voting combinations, coalesced only occasionally, in response to specific proposals. Table 2 in the Appendix lists roll call votes which give evidence of having produced divisions along economic lines. Two generalizations appear supportable. The first is that, as we would have expected, the issues in question most frequently involve the use of power by the state or the creation of power centers in the private sector. The poorer elements in the assembly tend to favor reducing taxes and adopting such proposals as biennial sessions of the legislature. They tend to oppose aid to internal improvements or the chartering of banks or railroads. In addition, it is clearly the wealthier elements who favor such undertakings of state paternalism as public aid to education or mental health. Moreover, the poorer legislators usually oppose women's rights bills and, with some

66. Huntsville *Democrat*, January 30, 1834; Montgomery *Advertiser*, February 27, 1850; Wetumpka *Argus*, December 30, 1840; John B. Hogan to Arthur P. Bagby, November 22, 1838, in Governors' Correspondence: Bagby; Hugh Lawson White Clay to Clement Comer Clay, December 9, 1845, in Clay Papers; Clement Comer Clay to Dixon H. Lewis, October 20, 1845, in Dixon H. Lewis Papers, University of Texas Library, Austin; Leroy Pope Walker to Bolling Hall, November 1, 1851, Jonathan Haralson to Hall, August 26, 1853, John Gill Shorter to Hall, August 16, 1853, in Hall Papers; *House Journal*, Sess. of 1831–32, pp. 119–20; John F. Moseley to Clement Comer Clay, February 12, 1837, in Governors' Correspondence: Clay.

67. *Senate Journal*, Sess. of 1832–33, p.6.

variation, favor the prohibition of liquor sales. Doubtless the spirit of progressivism which characterizes the attitudes of the wealthy on a number of issues reflects their usually better education. But the position of the poorer groups on each issue except temperance is in fact opposition to the concentration of power in institutions. Their approval of state enforcement of morality is, most probably, an expression of hostility on their part to what they took to be a rather dissolute life style among the planters. And upon this question they demonstrate some inconsistency.

The second point which emerges from these roll call analyses is that class divisions within the legislature became rather more frequent as the years passed. The situation reflects the changing locus of class power in the state's politics. About 1830 the ideals of the poorer classes were so fully dominant that such wealthy persons as had achieved office felt it necessary to outdo their poorer colleagues in subservience to these ideals. Very few votes show any class division at all, because for all practical purposes no proposals were made which challenged the popular hegemony. Such roll calls as reveal economic divisions are upon absurdly egalitarian or demagogic proposals: forbidding judges to charge juries unless requested by the jury to do so, for instance, or refusal to complete the construction of the capitol. In these cases the wealthier legislators adopted an ostentatiously popular position, and left the bills to be defeated by poorer members, who could, by virtue of their economic status, afford to bring common sense to bear on the question. For that reason the earlier votes, when there is any division at all, usually have the larger slaveholders supporting the more extreme efforts to limit infringements upon individual autonomy. Nevertheless, it is clear that larger slaveholders were more likely to align themselves against the administration of President Jackson.

By about 1840 the roll calls show wealthier members beginning to favor the use of power. Though there were still many individual exceptions among the legislators, the existence of a national party committed to governmental activity in the economic sphere had encouraged the open expression of such views. But members who held to the notion that power must be restricted were as yet a clear majority on most questions—so much so that proposals seeking to challenge the regency of this idea were still seldom brought forward. Much legislative business therefore did not provoke division along economic lines.

Analyzing the data by party seems to reveal that, whereas the Democrats' factionalism may well have been based upon economic status, the Whiggery's internal division was more often along urban-rural lines. Particularly by 1850, but also to some extent a decade earlier, a range of issues involving taxes and ventures of state paternalism tends to produce an agrarian alliance of wealthy Whig planters and poor Democratic farmers on one side and, on the other, a bipartisan grouping, united in defense of a nascent urban progressivism, of relatively well-to-do Democrats and of Whigs whose investments were not concentrated so heavily in land.

By the end of the antebellum period, a great many of the roll calls reveal class conflict. In these years the elements formerly dominant in the political structure were fighting for survival—and often losing to the newly powerful coalition of wealthy activists. Aid to internal improvements, the chartering of corporate privilege, public efforts in the fields of education and health—all were driven through the final assemblies over the opposition of poorer or more rural legislators. Cleavages along the faultlines of class had become a fact of life in the legislature.

An examination of the committee system in the assembly further emphasizes these observations. Committees were an important element in the legislative process. Bills were usually assigned for study to an appropriate standing committee, though they need not be. It was not the practice of committees to bury bills; proposals were ordinarily all reported, either as expedient or inexpedient. If a bill was reported as inexpedient, its sponsor then asked the whole house to refuse to concur in the committee report. Therefore the legislature had as a matter of course the right to review controversial committee decisions. The extent of a committee's influence was, as a result, dependent upon the extent of the confidence which the legislators placed in the judgment of the committee members. If a committee was known for careful and sober study of the proposals which passed before it, the house was usually inclined to affirm the committee's rulings.

Committee chairmen depended for their power, as did their committees, upon their respective reputations for knowledge and judgment. When a bill had been given a favorable report by a committee, the chairman, rather than the bill's author, ordinarily managed the bill on the floor. Thus chairmen were among the most prominent members in debate, and a chairmanship might well further a politician's career. But the influence of a chairman upon the legislative process could not be greatly disproportionate to his talent.

In the light of this account, it should be clear that committees were not quite so important in the antebellum legislature as they often are in bodies of like character. But they were indeed important, and a study of their membership can tell us much about the location of economic power in the legislature. An effort to summarize the economic composition of the committees in various assemblies produces an interesting pattern.[68] The committees were appointed by the presiding officers of each house, and those officers seem to have paid close attention to the economic status of the legislators in making their assignments. Before the final decade of the antebellum period, it appears to have been the custom to form the unimportant committees—the committee on the state capitol, for instance, or on county boundaries—almost entirely from either the poorest or the wealthiest legislators, while reserving the important committees predominantly for members of the middle class. Such discrimination was not crudely done, of course, and members from all economic strata turn up on all the various committees over a period of years, but median figures for the committees suggest strongly that the legislative leadership did indulge in the practice of placing unusually rich or poor members in a sort of economic quarantine.

Among the committees of first rank, only Ways and Means, the tax committee, shows any real tendency to domination by the planter members. This tendency, however, is not especially significant. Though Ways and Means drafted each revenue act, the bill then went before a committee of the whole in each house where it could be extensively amended to reflect the views of the general membership. In fact, no bill received such close scrutiny and thorough revision. The actual influence of the Ways and Means Committee upon the revenue act was, therefore, small. Our discussion of the state's tax structure in the

68. For a table including such data, see Thornton, "Politics and Power," 595–600.

next section of the present chapter will show that the tax burden fell with unusual weight on the wealthy. It was hence most probably to prevent disaffection among the most heavily taxed elements of the population that the legislative leadership allowed them their apparent influence in the process of enacting the taxes.

In the final years of the antebellum period, the practice of relegating poor legislators to the most unimportant committees continued. But now they were no longer joined there by the rich. Rather the wealthy legislators began to receive commanding positions on the committees with real responsibility. The beliefs of these new rulers is shown clearly in the number of men who called themselves members of the "Opposition" who received choice committee assignments. Only fifteen of the one hundred representatives in 1859 fell into this category, but they held four of the nine seats on the Judiciary and Internal Improvements committees, respectively, and three of the nine on the Committee on Corporations. In contrast, many unimportant committees were wholly Democratic. Clearly by 1859 the center of economic power in the legislature had shifted to a wealthy group oriented towards whiggish goals. But this development is quite a late one, and beyond the scope of the present chapter.

Committee chairmen were no wealthier as a group than was the whole legislature. In fact, the median levels among chairmen so closely coincide with those for all legislators in each session examined that the coincidence may give evidence of design. In 1849 and in 1859, however, the group of chairmen contained a significantly higher proportion of lawyers than did the assembly as a whole, particularly so in the former year.

In addition to economic groupings, legislative voting at various times gave evidence of other nonparty blocs. In the early years legislators sought to fasten on Alabama laws patterned on those of their native states, thus producing immigrant alliances. Far more important was sectional jealousy within the state. Such rivalries played an important part in achieving the consistent defeat of internal improvement projects. Indeed, when an aid bill for internal improvements finally did pass, it was only by including projects from all sections. The chartering of banks and the location of the capital also became enmeshed in sectionalism. And a violation of the custom of allotting one U.S. senator to north and one to south Alabama could even make a devoted party organ desert the partisan for the sectional banners.[69] But just as sectionalism had deeper roots than mere differing residence, so all of these controversies contained elements of far more profound cleavages in the society, and it is difficult to determine the extent to which simple sectionalism is at work in the votes. Hostility to banks and internal improvements was symptomatic of economic divisions, and the removal of the capital was intimately bound up with the question of internal improvements, as the letters of Clement Claiborne Clay make clear. Moreover, even the sectional disputes over the state's U.S. Senate seats were often at base ideological. For instance, the appointment of William R. King to replace Arthur P. Bagby in 1848 produced little opposition in north Alabama, even though it gave south Alabama both senators. King's residence was wrong, but his politics were right. It was only when Benjamin Fitzpatrick was named to succeed Dixon H. Lewis later in the same year that the sectional storm which eventuated in the election of Jeremiah Clemens arose. Fitzpatrick was a south Alabamian in beliefs as well as in domicile.[70] Sectional blocs in the legislature, therefore, are usually adumbrations of other divisions.

Within the parties, powerful or rising politicians gathered about themselves lesser figures who hoped to advance their own fortunes by the association. Thus a number of votes for a proposal or a candidate could often be had by gaining the approval of a single man. Sometimes the man was a county boss who could dictate the course of his county's members. A politician might link others to himself by performing personal services, such as arranging a bank loan, or simply by making himself agreeable and thus cultivating friendships. Once such a group was created, the man who controlled it could become quite influential, and his support was eagerly solicited. Alternatively, a powerful figure might undertake a concerted campaign to have his friends and as-

69. Thomas Casey, in Selma *Courier*, February 14, 1828; *Senate Journal*, Sess. of 1835–36, p. 9; *Senate Journal*, Sess. of 1859–60, pp. 341–42; *House Journal*, Sess. of 1859–60, pp. 403–409; Montgomery *Advertiser*, January 16, 1850; Clement Claiborne Clay to Clement Comer Clay, December 22, 1845, in Clay Papers; *Jackson County Democrat*, quoted in Montgomery *Advertiser*, March 13, 1850.

70. See pages 136, 182–83 herein. *Cf.* James E. Saunders to George S. Houston, July 19, 1848, Clement Comer Clay to Houston, undated postscript to a letter the body of which is missing [dated internally to mid-December, 1848], both in Houston Papers.

sociates elected to the assembly in order to effect some legislative goal.[71]

The final factor determinative of nonparty blocs is also the most elusive—ideology. At some periods, on some issues, ideological groupings appeared to develop some degree of organization and continuity.[72] But ordinarily such groups were merely individual legislators whose views on a question of public policy happened to coincide. The degree to which ideology was derivative from other factors—nativity, occupation, residence, wealth—is a question of philosophy rather than of fact.

In the long run, only the formal parties preserved any coherence as legislative voting blocs, and they did so only because of the unremitting efforts of party leaders. The Whigs came within a single seat of capturing the House in 1840, and actually controlled the Senate by one vote in both 1849 and 1851, but in every other session the legislature was consistently, and often substantially, Democratic. Instilling party discipline was, however, no easy task. No situation would make the party leadership happier than that described by a lobbyist in 1852: "Party lines and the subdivisions are so accurately defined, and spring up so immediately on every bill, resolution and in fact every word that the true purposes of Legislation are much retarded, or lost sight of." [73] But the situation in 1852 was not at all a natural one. It was carefully manufactured.

The parties were divided primarily over national economic questions, and over those state policies which were logical extensions of such national questions. In sessions during which national affairs were not brought up, or when the two state parties were in agreement on their attitudes toward the great national question of the moment, par-

71. John Gaddis Winston to Dixon H. Lewis, January 4, 1848, Clement Comer Clay to Lewis, October 20, 1845, both in Dixon H. Lewis Papers, University of Texas Library; John Hardy to Bolling Hall, January 28, 1853, John Gill Shorter to Hall, August 26, 1853, both in Hall Papers; undated, unsigned obituary of Dixon H. Lewis by one of Lewis' contemporaries (MS in Dixon H. Lewis Papers, Alabama Department of Archives and History, Montgomery); John L. Hays to Clement Claiborne Clay, June 1, 1857, in Clay Papers.
72. John S. Kennedy to George S. Houston, February 29, 1848, in Houston Papers.
73. Tuscaloosa *Flag,* quoted in Wetumpka *Argus,* August 25, 1841 (the figures in Wetumpka *Argus,* August 26, 1840, are apparently erroneous); Montgomery *Advertiser,* November 18, 1851; A. Lopez to John Bragg, January 24, 1852, in John Bragg Papers, Southern Historical Collection, University of North Carolina Library, Chapel Hill.

tisan hostility in the legislature might threaten for the moment to abate. To prevent this situation, Democratic votaries usually had introduced at the outset of each session a set of resolutions taking a strongly partisan position on national affairs. The resultant debate served to arouse party consciousness. New members were carefully impressed with the necessity of maintaining party regularity if they desired to rise in politics. Party elders actively sought legislative leaders who were adept at the maneuvers necessary in order to preserve discipline among the troops.[74]

The parties did not elect formal leaders other than the speaker of the House and the president of the Senate. There were always, however, drillmasters: legislators more partisan than their colleagues, and as a result more active in party affairs. Those legislators who professed membership in a party but who were not actively partisan might not regard their more partisan colleagues as their leaders. But the most partisan members became de facto a party leadership, for it was through their manipulation of measures and emotions that the restraints of party were imposed. Their lack of titles is unimportant; anyone who studies the assembly comes quickly to realize their power.

When the Democratic majority was large, restrained measures proved at least reasonably effective in attaining the leadership's goals. But when the Whigs succeeded in narrowing the gap, the Democratic drillmasters found it necessary to pursue a course even more offensively partisan than customary. Only thus could they arouse sufficient interparty bitterness to enforce party-line voting. It was frankly with this end in view, for instance, that the leaders hit upon the stratagem in 1840 of abolishing all congressional districts in favor of general ticket voting; it appeared to them to be "the best means for drawing the party lines as soon as possible" after the legislature convened. Accordingly the general ticket was driven through the legislature amidst scenes of unparalleled bitterness and turmoil, accompanied by Democratic protestations of devotion to orderly debate and majority rule.[75]

74. *House Journal*, Sess. of 1839–40, p. 375; Montgomery *Advertiser*, November 28, 1849, February 27, 1850; Wetumpka *Argus*, November 17, 1841; Leroy Pope Walker to Clement Claiborne Clay, November 20, 1858, in Clay Papers; Clement Comer Clay to Arthur P. Bagby, January 20, 1838 [misdated; actually 1839], in Governors' Correspondence: Bagby.
75. Nathaniel Terry to Arthur P. Bagby, September 19, 1840, in Governors' Corre-

The reason for these Byzantine efforts to create party strife is straightforward: patronage. The national parties offered differing programs, of course, and the state parties frequently endorsed alternative proposals in state affairs as well, particularly upon economic questions; but the leaders of the Democratic party always acted as if their primary function was to gain as many offices as possible for the party faithful. Their task was made difficult by the fact that the legislator not directly involved in party affairs was less concerned about party in making his choice among candidates than about men. Throughout the antebellum period the Whigs were thus able to win some offices at the hands of the assembly. Whigs preached constantly the injustice of "proscription"—by which they meant their own exclusion from office. The Democrats listened and responded not so much out of a sense of fair play as because the charge of proscription was effective with the electorate. It aroused fears, always lurking just in the background, that a party to whom absolute power was committed would become despotic. Democratic legislators who sensed that this issue could spell doom for their party's hegemony were thus placed in the position of allowing Whigs to achieve office in order to disprove a principal charge of Whig oratory. Whigs were occasionally elected to county judgeships in Whig counties. They controlled the branch state banks at Montgomery and Mobile, and had great power in the bank at Tuscaloosa. And within the legislature, too, they were given place beyond their numbers.

The Whigs were always allowed substantial, though minority, representation on the most important committees. The extraordinary thing is that they were also allowed a number of committee chairmanships—ordinarily one-third, though in the Senate of 1849, which the Whigs narrowly controlled, they took a half of the positions.[76] Even more startling is that the Whigs actually were given control of some committees. These concessions were a calculated reply to the allegations of proscription.

---

spondence: Bagby; *House Journal*, Sess. of 1840–41, pp. 290–96, 313–14; Wetumpka *Argus*, January 6, January 13, 1841.

76. In 1840 the Whigs had only one-fourth of the Senate chairmanships, but one of these chairmen was given a most important committee, the judiciary. For a table of the party composition of committees at selected sessions, see Thornton, "Politics and Power," 597–600.

While blunting the thrust of the Whig oratorical effort, the Democratic leadership allotted control of committees in a cleverly partisan manner. First of all, the Whigs were given one or two unimportant committees: the committee which considered petitions for divorce was a favorite, since its decisions almost invariably made someone angry. In addition, however, Whigs were usually given control of two important units—internal improvements and education. The strategy in this practice is clear. The Whigs were pledged as a party to the advocacy of these two unpopular causes. The electorate's hostility to any governmental activity in these areas was evident, and the Whigs might have been inclined to allow the subjects to rest until such time as they had succeeded in gaining a majority upon some other issue. But by placing Whigs in control of the relevant committees, the Democrats virtually forced the Whigs to keep bringing out bills, which the Democrats could then defeat on the floor. Control of these committees was thus a short-term concession which in the long run reinforced Whig identification with measures which the society rejected.

The Democratic leaders were willing to give some positions to Whigs as elements of strategy. But the members of the Democracy in the legislature who were less involved in party affairs were often willing to give away a good deal more. It was this attitude that the drillmasters had constantly to curb. The danger was that friendship across party barriers might carry over into the numerous elections which the legislature made. Denouncing "temporizing politicians," the partisan leaders proclaimed that they would "show no quarter"; they were even willing to stoop to patently unconstitutional means to preserve Democratic control of patronage. They realized that it was a powerful tool in perpetuating their statewide majority. Indeed, when interparty coalitions were attempted, patronage was usually the rock upon which they foundered.[77]

Party governance in the legislature was provided by the caucus. Caucuses antedated parties. They grew out of the informal consultations of legislative allies by which gubernatorial candidates were

77. Nathaniel Terry to Arthur P. Bagby, September 19, 1840, Philip Phillips to Bagby, undated [August, 1840], both in Governors' Correspondence: Bagby; Montgomery *Advertiser*, August 13, 1851.

nominated in the early years.[78] Rules in the caucus were not fixed; usually, but not always, a two-thirds vote was necessary for nomination. Voting was by secret ballot.[79] Members ordinarily accepted the caucus decision, but occasionally the fight would be carried to the legislature. In such cases, as in the election of Jeremiah Clemens to the United States Senate, one of the contestants might attempt to effect a deal with the minority party. It was precisely this possibility, of course, that the caucus was intended to forestall. The caucus is a difficult institution to study, as its deliberations were seldom discussed. It appears, however, that, towards the end of the antebellum period, the parties increasingly became alliances of personal blocs to which lesser politicians had attached themselves. In this situation the caucus, because of its secret voting, remained one of the most independent of the institutions of party governance. Party leaders tried to work their will within the caucuses, and it seemed to at least one veteran politician that their influence in these gatherings was increasing, but the leaders themselves knew that their control was far from ironclad. They even sought the abandonment of the secret ballot in an attempt more fully to dictate the legislature's choices.[80] But the effort failed. Doubtless the power of the leaders—the "wireworkers," as contemporaries called them—was great, but the caucus remained primarily a legislative institution.

The precise nature of party influence in the legislative process is difficult to determine. In sum, however, it does appear that despite the substantial differences between the parties in both policies and social philosophy, partisanship in the assembly was perhaps as much manufactured as real. Parties as coherent groups were, on the whole, more effective as electoral than as legislative organs. Nevertheless, largely because the constitution of 1819 committed the election of so many

78. Henry Hitchcock to John W. Walker, January 2, 1821, in Walker Papers; *Alabama Republican* (Huntsville), January 19, February 2, February 9, February 16, March 9, 1821.

79. Clement Claiborne Clay to Clement Comer Clay, postscript to a letter from Virginia Tunstall Clay to Susanna Withers Clay, December, 1844, John D. Phelan to Clement Claiborne Clay, April 22, 1857, both in Clay Papers.

80. Joshua L. Martin to Bolling Hall, September 18, 1853, in Hall Papers; John D. Phelan to Clement Claiborne Clay, April 22, 1857, John Gorman Barr to Clay, May 2, 1857, J. M. Hudgins to Clay, May 11, 1857, Theophilus L. Toulmin to Clay, May 30, 1857, all in Clay Papers.

important officers to the legislature, the Democratic drillmasters were usually able to keep the pilot light of partisan passion burning.

Measures

"Too much legislation kills": the sentiment was widely shared. And yet it was admitted that "the first great object of every government should be to afford the citizens protection . . . from the encroachments of the strong and the machinations of the wicked." [81] With these two assertions the boundaries of legislative action were defined. It was the function of the assembly to protect popular liberty; to interpose itself between the citizenry and concentrations of power not subject to popular control. If it did less, liberty was endangered. But if it did more—if it sought to make the government into a rival for power—then fears were equally justified. The dilemma of legislation was always, therefore, how much action was too much.

One candidate for an early legislature informed the voters, "In the first place, I am opposed to oppression, and think government should avoid it as much as possible." This extraordinary statement immediately informs us that the word "oppression" as used here has a meaning different from the common understanding of it today. What we mean by oppression, government can always avoid. But in antebellum Alabama, oppression meant the use of power, and that is sometimes unavoidable. The same writer later makes his ideal clear. He tells us that we must emulate the customs of the founding fathers "so far as not to press on each other." [82] The goal of legislation, then, should be to isolate the citizens one from another; to guarantee—indeed, to enforce—individual autonomy.

The legislative fear of seeming to be too powerful could lead the lawmakers to ludicrous extremes. State Architect William Nichols was investigated, hounded, criticized and finally forced to resign, evidently because he designed a state capitol too grandiose for the legislators. They refused to complete the building. And the president's home at the University of Alabama was even worse—a "palace," a "stupendous

81. Wetumpka *Argus*, January 1, 1840 (*cf.* Montgomery *Advertiser*, February 24, 1852); *Senate Journal*, Sess. of 1831–32, p. 46.
82. *Alabama Republican* (Huntsville), July 13, 1821.

model of architectural display"; it was "altogether too large for the President. He could never occupy half its rooms."[83] Such issues were not trivial to the legislators, or to their constituents; lavish buildings could represent the first steps down the road to despotism. Some legislators even founded their careers on such nightmares. "Voting against appropriations," wrote one senator of his colleagues, "is the safe and popular side, and then why need they think. It is said of one who was a member twenty or thirty years that in all that time he voted on every appropriation and tax bill and *always in the negative*. Had he lived a thousand years he would have been a member all the time."[84] Even the notion of licensing physicians and lawyers was deeply resented as unwarranted, "oppressive" governmental action. There were constant—and sometimes successful—efforts to have persons declared doctors or lawyers by legislative fiat, despite their lack of qualifications.[85]

There were, of course, many more mundane examples of this attitude at work. The state regularly hired fewer persons than were necessary to carry on its business. And it habitually underpaid such officers as it had.[86] These complaints were particularly true in the court system. But the practices extended into all areas of the government, and sometimes led to financial loss. During the late 1820s, when the state was still undertaking internal improvements projects, it appropriated a total of more than $136,000 to this end. Almost every penny, however, was wasted because the legislature refused to hire engineers to plan the works. In some cases, the "improvements" created new obstacles to navigation which had later to be removed.[87]

83. *Senate Journal*, Sess. of 1829–30, pp. 7, 93; *House Journal*, Sess. of 1829–30, pp. 137, 209–10; *House Journal*, Sess. of 1830–31, p. 249; *Senate Journal*, Sess. of 1831–32, p. 15; *Senate Journal*, Sess. of 1830–31, pp. 13, 117; *House Journal*, Sess. of 1841–42, pp. 201–202; Wetumpka *Argus*, December 15, December 22, 1841. Ostensibly Nichols was investigated for corruption in the letting of contracts. But even after he was exonerated, legislators remained hostile to his efforts. The bill abolishing the Board of Internal Improvements was explicitly intended to eliminate Nichols' job.
84. Jefferson Buford to Jefferson Franklin Jackson, June 12, 1849, in Jackson Papers.
85. *House Journal*, Sess. of 1849–50, p. 260; *House Journal*, Sess. of 1859–60, pp. 494–95; Montgomery *Advertiser*, January 30, 1850.
86. Alexander Bowie to Arthur P. Bagby, October 25, 1840, Anderson Crenshaw to Bagby, September 15, 1840, both in Governors' Correspondence: Bagby; *House Journal*, Sess. of 1849–50, pp. 36–37; *Senate Journal*, Sess. of 1836–37, pp. 19–20.
87. *House Journal*, Sess. of 1849–50, p. 222; *cf.* Thomas Fearn to John Murphy, July 27, 1828, in Governors' Correspondence: Murphy.

It is abundantly clear that the state government was philosophically committed to inaction, to restraining its power within carefully constricted bounds so as to pose no threat to individual liberty. The other half of the legislature's duty, however—the necessity to defend the citizenry from the encroachments of private power concentrations—is less often documented. The legislature acted on a broad front to diminish the power of wealth. We shall glance at only three of the areas of activity: tax policy, aid to railroads, and the regulation of banking.

In his first inaugural address, Governor Benjamin Fitzpatrick succinctly stated the antebellum attitude toward taxes: "The essence of modern oppression is taxation. The measure of popular liberty may be found in the amount of money which is taken from the people to support the government; when the amount is increased beyond the requirement of a rigid economy, the government becomes profligate and oppressive."[88] Holding these views, legislators naturally examined revenue measures with the most careful scrutiny. Only in the final decade of the antebellum period did the total state tax become really substantial. Tax policy could not, therefore, be so effective a tool in shaping society as it might otherwise have been. Nevertheless, the revenue acts from the very beginning show clearly the objects of legislative hostility, the groups whom the legislators sought to restrain.

The graphs on the following pages illustrate the relative weights of the various sources of the tax dollar in a number of fiscal years. The principal source of revenue for almost all of the antebellum period was the tax on slaves. The Mississippi Territory had taxed slaves at one dollar a head. In 1819, with the government in the hands of the wealthy Broad River group, the slave tax was repealed. When, however, a substantial deficit in the state budget was produced, the tax was hastily reinstituted and remained a permanent fixture of subsequent acts.[89] Though its amount varied, for most of the antebellum period the tax on slaves was a sort of poll tax, but with increasingly subtle distinctions based on the ages of the slaves. An attempt to base the tax

88. *House Journal*, Sess. of 1841–42, p. 93.
89. *Alabama Republican* (Huntsville), December 8, 1820. The summary of the development of tax policy contained in Albert B. Moore, *History of Alabama* (Rev. ed.; University, Ala.: University Supply Store, 1934), 236, is erroneous.

at least partially on the market value of the slaves was tried briefly in the late 1840s.

The only other important source of income was the tax on land. One of the most heated struggles of the antebellum period resulted from efforts to alter the basis for assessing the real estate tax from the "classification" to the "*ad valorem*" method. Under the former system, all land was placed in one of four categories according to quality, and a rough assessment of value per acre thus formed. The latter method required the determination of the market value of each piece of land. In each case, the tax was taken as a percentage of the valuation. The *ad valorem* tax more accurately reflected the wealth of the landowner, but required a much larger staff of officials to administer it. A sort of partial *ad valorem* assessment was adopted in 1842, but full conversion to *ad valorem* taxation was finally effected only in 1848, after an enormous clerical effort and a great deal of public resentment at the expansion of the bureaucracy.[90] Under both systems, however, the owners of the best lands paid the highest taxes.

These two taxes—on land and on slaves—together produced about 70 percent of Alabama's revenue. The remaining 30 percent was derived largely from taxes on luxuries and on capital. The former group of taxes was aimed directly at the state's wealthiest citizens; it included taxes on such items as pleasure carriages and race horses, gold watches and private libraries, and household furniture of more than two hundred dollars in value. Indeed, practically every external mark of the planter's life-style was taxed.

Taxes on capital are even more interesting. From the outset the state taxed money loaned at interest and stock held in banks. But as the antebellum period advanced, more and more such taxes were enacted. In 1846 there were taxes on all capital over five hundred dollars invested in manufacturing,[91] on money loaned at interest, on the purchase of bills of exchange, drafts and certificates of deposit, on the income of transportation and insurance companies, and on savings

90. *House Journal*, Sess. of 1849–50, pp. 18–19; C. C. Gewin to George S. Houston, May 22, 1848, in Houston Papers. The *ad valorem* method had been used early in the 1820s, but had been abandoned late in that decade in favor of the easily administered classification system.

91. This tax was payable whether or not the corporation in question was making money: *House Journal*, Sess. of 1849–50, pp. 289–91.

Politics and Power in a Slave Society

1847

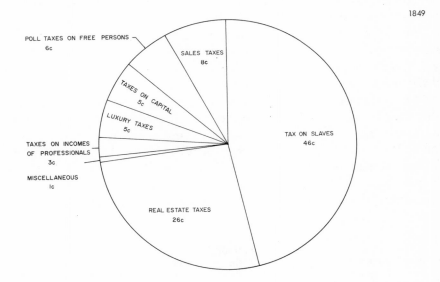

1849

Sources of the State Tax Dollar in Various Fiscal Years

1855

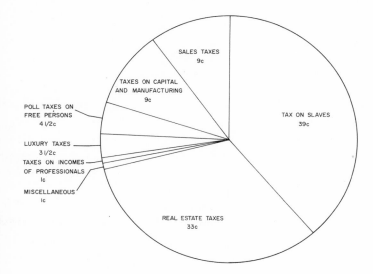

SALES TAXES
9c

TAXES ON CAPITAL
AND MANUFACTURING
9c

POLL TAXES ON
FREE PERSONS
4 1/2c

LUXURY TAXES
3 1/2c

TAXES ON INCOMES
OF PROFESSIONALS
1c

MISCELLANEOUS
1c

TAX ON SLAVES
39c

REAL ESTATE TAXES
33c

1860

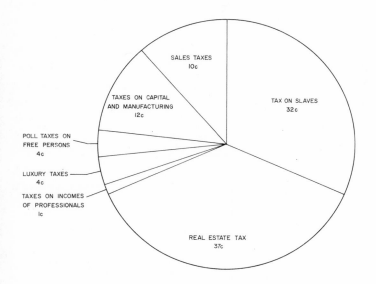

SALES TAXES
10c

TAXES ON CAPITAL
AND MANUFACTURING
12c

POLL TAXES ON
FREE PERSONS
4c

LUXURY TAXES
4c

TAXES ON INCOMES
OF PROFESSIONALS
1c

TAX ON SLAVES
32c

REAL ESTATE TAX
37c

held in cash. The 1850s saw a further increase in these taxes, both in number and in amount. Taxes on capital rose from a bit more than 6 percent of the state's revenue in 1846 to 11 percent in 1860. These levies were enacted to prevent capital not reinvested in agriculture from thus escaping taxation, but they became a particular source of complaint because they sometimes taxed nonagricultural investments at a higher rate than were land and slaves.[92] The taxes on the gross personal incomes of lawyers, doctors, public officials, and the officers of corporations, on commissions charged by factors and commission merchants, and on fees for the storage of cotton reflected the same desire to see that non-farm income did not escape governmental exactions.

From the beginning of the antebellum period a sales tax was levied which may possibly have been passed on to the consumer. By the end of the period this tax was some 8 or 9 percent of the state's revenue. Other than this tax, the only source of revenue which was assessed against voters regardless of their condition was the poll tax, a nominal sum which was levied on all white males between 21 and 45. It represented only 3 or 4 percent of the state's tax income.[93]

It is important to note the stability of Alabama's tax structure. Throughout the antebellum years, the same general objects were taxed and, though rates rose slowly, the various categories continued to bear roughly the same proportions of the total tax load.[94] We may therefore make a general, if crude, estimate of tax incidence in the antebellum period. It would appear that the wealthiest third of the citizenry paid at least two-thirds of the state's taxes. The entire tax structure was directed at wealth. Though there was a whole class of taxes—the income and capital levies—directed at wealth derived from nonagricultural sources, the tax burden was borne fundamentally by planters. They paid taxes on their slaves and taxes on their plantations, and additional taxes on the luxuries which made their positions worth

92. *Ibid.,* 330–31.
93. License fees, chiefly on taverns and traveling salesmen, were also fairly important for most of the antebellum period.
94. Compare, for instance, the provisions of the Revenue Act of 1820 (*Acts of Alabama,* Sess. of 1820–21, pp. 10–13) with those of the Revenue Act of 1850 (*Acts of Alabama,* Sess. of 1849–50, pp. 3–36). One must bear in mind, of course, that the state levied no taxes other than license fees from 1836 to 1842.

seeking. Indeed, since large planters usually were the only persons in the society with excess capital sufficient to engage in speculation, they paid much of the capital taxes, too. And if, instead of reinvesting in agriculture or investing in some other enterprise, they sought to save their profits, they were subject to the "idle money" tax.

Taxation was oppression, as Governor Fitzpatrick had said. It was necessary, of course, that a portion of the community be oppressed in this way. But in laying imposts, the legislators could be counted on to know which of the voters had elected them.

If tax policy showed legislative awareness of the true source of political power, efforts to aid internal improvements revealed something equally as significant—a profound hostility to corporations. In the early years the legislature hesitated even to charter such companies, much less to offer them governmental assistance. The charters were regularly restricted and sometimes rejected. The state's first railroad, a short line to circumvent the Muscle Shoals, was chartered only after a prolonged legislative battle. And even after this breakthrough, the governor was constrained to continue frequent exhortations to the legislators not to dismiss railroad charter bills out of hand.[95]

At least by the end of the 1830s, however, opposition to the very existence of railroads had declined. The struggle now centered around state intervention in aid of such efforts. The career of one such company will illustrate the nature of the conflict. The West Point Railroad was financed by Broad River capital, and doubtless that fact intensified legislative opposition to it. It was intended to run from Montgomery to West Point, Georgia, there to link with a road from West Point to Atlanta. The company received its initial charter in 1832, but failed to organize and was rechartered in 1834. This charter, under which the company operated until it was sold in a consolidation in 1870, contained a provision common to corporate charters granted in Alabama in the early years: no stockholder, no matter what his investment, was permitted to vote more than 100 shares of stock.[96] Such

---

95. *Senate Journal*, Sess. of 1833–34, pp. 127, 170, 172; *Senate Journal*, Sess. of 1831–32, pp. 73, 85–87, 103–104, 110 and *passim*; *House Journal*, Sess. of 1831–32, pp. 143–45, 162, 165; *Senate Journal*, Sess. of 1834–35, pp. 7–12; *Senate Journal*, Sess. of 1835–36, p. 9.

96. *Acts of Alabama*, Sess. of 1834–35, pp. 118–24. For the postbellum history of the company, see Richard E. Prince, *Steam Locomotives and History: Georgia Railroad and West Point Route* (Green River, Wyoming: Richard E. Prince, 1962), 55–65.

provisions represented an effort by the legislature to increase the participation of small stockholders in the management of companies.

Risk capital was scarce in Alabama, and the company had much difficulty with investors who failed to complete pledged payments on their stock. Indeed, in the Panic of 1837 the company had to declare 65 percent of its stock forfeited, and only frenzied efforts kept the enterprise alive. Yet, at a personal loss of some $200,000, two of the Broad River capitalists, John B. Scott and Abner McGehee, undertook to build the road with their own slaves. By 1840, in the midst of the most daunting circumstances, 88 miles of the road's 116-mile route had been graded, and in May, the first twelve miles were opened to traffic.[97] At this point financial difficulties forced the company to turn to the legislature for aid.

The company asked not for cash but for the state's endorsement of $900,000 in corporate bonds which the railroad proposed to issue. In exchange, the railroad offered mortgages on $2,400,000 of property, including mortgages on the real estate of each stockholder to the value of his stock. Despite the substantial progress which had been made in building the road and the ample security which was tendered, the legislature rejected the company's pleas. The road was sold under foreclosure.

The reorganized corporation, more firmly than ever under Broad River control, was presented with a new opportunity for gaining the state's assistance by the federal government. In 1841 Congress granted Alabama some $234,000 on condition that Alabama would use the money to build improvements from the Tennessee River to Mobile and from West Point across the state towards Mississippi. There was much grumbling in the legislature about the attachment of these conditions but they were eventually accepted. Yet the legislature adamantly refused to give the West Point Railroad any portion of the funds. Years of coaxing and persuasion finally induced the legislature, in 1844, to loan the West Point $117,000—money which the road reasonably felt was due it outright under the terms of the congressional donation—on pledge of adequate security to repay the sum with interest within ten

97. Mildred Beale, "A Biography of Charles Teed Pollard" (M.A. thesis, University of Alabama, 1928), 23–26; Wetumpka *Argus*, June 10, 1840 (an account of the first train's run by William L. Yancey, who was along for the ride).

years. But the governor then rejected all security which the company could offer. Only when, in desperation, five of the Broad River group gave the state first mortgages on their own property did the governor finally release the principal.[98]

The state loan was a tiny sum compared to the $1,500,000 spent in constructing the railroad, but it was enough to enable the company to weather the crisis of its reorganization. In 1851, largely as a result of the loan, the railroad reached West Point, fifteen years after construction had commenced. In 1854 the connection with Atlanta was opened.

The legislature's refusal to pay over to the West Point funds due it—funds not even derived from state taxation, but accruing from a federal grant[99] —without years of persuasion and the satisfaction of unusual demands for security, and then only as an interest-bearing loan, is a case only a trifle more extreme than most. It is certainly not out of character with the assembly's pattern of behavior. Time and again, when a small loan or expenditure could have added millions of dollars to the commerce of the state by facilitating trade, the legislature refused to act. A loan from the Bank of Alabama at Decatur to aid in the construction of the Tuscumbia Railroad aroused a storm of protest.[100] Even as late as the 1850s, obtaining a loan to aid a railroad involved years of supplication before an assembly obsessed with the goal of liquidating the state debt.[101]

Nor were the legislators' hearts hardened only towards railroads. The federal government donated 400,000 acres of public lands to Alabama, the proceeds from the sale of which were to be used to construct a canal around the Muscle Shoals. In 1831 the canal was com-

---

98. Beale, "Pollard," pp. 27, 35; *Senate Journal*, Sess. of 1841–42, p. 26; Wetumpka *Argus*, December 22, December 29, 1841.

99. The grant represented 2 percent of the proceeds of federal land sales in Alabama. The money had been set aside by the act of admission in 1819 for use, under the direction of Congress, to build roads into the new state. But Congress, never having appropriated it to this purpose, decided simply to turn it over to the state with the stipulations recited in the text. Of course a portion of the money was "due" the West Point only by implication.

100. *Senate Journal*, Sess. of 1839–40, pp. 231–42, 308–321. Hostility to this loan was exacerbated by the bank's interlocking directorate with the railroad. *Cf.* Wetumpka *Argus*, January 1, 1840.

101. Clement Claiborne Clay to Clement Comer Clay, December 27, 1849, Virginia Tunstall Clay to Susanna Withers Clay, January 1, 1850, Clement Claiborne Clay to Clement Comer Clay, November 23, 1855, all in Clay Papers.

pleted at a cost of some $645,000. Some years later the canal was damaged by a freshet. Just $2,000 would have sufficed for repairs, but it would have required the expenditure of $2,000 from state funds rather than from a federal grant. The legislature refused; the canal benefited Tennesseeans more than Alabamians, legislators announced. Exhortation and cajolery came to naught. By 1847 the estimated cost of repairs, as a result of the canal's neglect, had risen to $50,000. It was never fixed. A $645,000 investment and many times more in the value of the commerce which would have been generated were sacrificed.[102]

The Muscle Shoals Canal was a direct effort by the state to further transportation, but it is very nearly unique in the history of Alabama. After 1832, the legislature never again initiated an internal improvements project, and regularly rejected pleas to aid private ventures in the field. A contributory factor in maintaining this attitude was the state's fiscal condition after the failure of the state bank. But the fundamental reason was expressed by a veteran Democratic legislator when a bill to charter a railroad was under consideration in 1848. He distrusted corporate charters, he said. "They always open the door for honest industry to be swindled by privileged monopoly, and as such are cursed fungous excresions [sic] upon the country." Corporations were "an invention of monarchs" which had "become the instrument through which a moneyed aristocracy proposed to govern a confiding people."[103]

A future president of the state senate, Benjamin C. Yancey, stated the position a bit more fully:

Inequality in wealth will ever exist while there is a difference in the virtue, intelligence and industry of the people. But the policy of all political systems established for the happiness of the mass, and especially of our Republican

102. Report of James Irvine *et al.*, Commissioners of the Muscle Shoals Canal, to the Governor [January, 1838], in Governors' Correspondence: Bagby; John R. Henry to George S. Houston, December 25, 1847, in Houston Papers.

103. *Senate Journal*, Sess. of 1832–33, p. 11; *Senate Journal*, Sess. of 1835–36, p. 6; *House Journal*, Sess. of 1840–41, pp. 299–304; George W. Owen to Clement Comer Clay, December 16, 1836, in Governors' Correspondence: Clay; Ezekiel Pickens to Arthur P. Bagby, September 10, 1838, in Governors' Correspondence: Bagby; Felix G. Norman to George S. Houston, January 23, 1848, in Houston Papers; John W. Bridges to Bolling Hall, October 5, 1853, in Hall Papers; Cahawba *Southern Democrat*, December 16, 1837; Wetumpka *Argus*, July 15, 1840, December 15, 1841; Montgomery *Advertiser*, January 27, 1852.

Government, is to diminish these inequalities by guarding against the undue aggregation of capital in the hands of a privileged and speculating few and protecting the people in the enjoyment of the fruits of their labor. All monied [*sic*] corporations are opposed to this policy. Their special privileges and selfish combinations impede the natural tendency of capital to an equal distribution among the people; they are exempted from liabilities to which the unincorporated people are subject, and enjoy privileges not enjoyed by the people in business. . . .

Incorporated companies create no wealth; they fatten upon the labor and industry of the poor man who lives by the sweat of his brow.—Let these combinations then of wealth against labor, of the rich against the poor be regarded as engines of popular oppression.[104]

Such sentiments were widely held; their roots did not stop in the topsoil of Jacksonian oratory but ran deep, searching out the well-springs of agrarian fears. Politicians not only voiced them but, at least until the 1850s, acted on them. The changes in policy during the final decade of the antebellum years are the subject of another chapter.[105] It is important, however, to note that many Jacksonian legislators held tenaciously to an attitude of hostility towards capital, even after the position was no longer politically dominant. As late as 1860, when a general program of state aid to railroads was finally undertaken, the minority in the assembly warned that the passage of the bill was "about to be effected by a combination of certain railroad interests: a combination not only powerful to-day, but if not checked, fearful in its threatenings to the future legislation of the State." And, they said, the "tendency of such legislation is demoralizing, and its ultimate effect will be to deliver over the government of the State to the control of a combination of corporations."[106]

The most severe test for this attitude was surely the legislature's relationship with the Bank of Alabama. One may only with the greatest difficulty conceive of an institution more likely by its constitution to lead the legislators away from their stern opposition to concentrations of capital. A close examination reveals, however, that the assembly emerged from the episode with its principles but slightly sullied.

104. Wetumpka *Argus*, August 21, 1839.
105. See Chapter V, herein.
106. *House Journal*, Sess. of 1859–60, pp. 391–92; *Senate Journal*, Sess. of 1859–60, pp. 341–42.

The presidents and directors of the Bank of Alabama and of its four independent branches were elected by joint ballot of the legislature.[107] Before the creation of the four branch banks, legislators were charged with the selection from among the paper offered to the bank for discount, the names of the men from their counties most likely to be good risks. Even thereafter, the presence of a legislator's name on a note as endorser carried great weight with the bank directors who sought reelection at the legislature's hands. The electioneering which surrounded the balloting for directors could decide the fate of important unrelated measures. The banks used personal favors and entertainment to prevent legislative investigations. A legislator who asked a personal loan was seldom refused. Indeed, such loans might be used to influence legislative actions. Moreover, the dependence of the banks on the legislature provided some assemblymen with irresistible temptation to corruption.[108]

These structural defects in the organization of the banks went unchallenged primarily because of the bank's history. As we have seen, the public ownership of the bank was contrasted in the public mind with Pope's evil Huntsville institution. The notion of having a bank entirely subservient to political institutions, and hence to the popular will, was the idea with which Pickens had destroyed the Broad River's early hegemony. In the following years, for a politician to announce himself as opposed to the constitution of the Bank of Alabama was to declare for the rule of a financial aristocracy. The bank had become a symbol of open government, popularly controlled, and as such was beyond criticism. Gayle's hesitant but thoughtful critique of the institution in 1835 did as much as anything else to drive him into the ranks of the nascent opposition. He had typed himself—by this and other actions—and his disclaimers were not heard.[109]

107. The Bank of Alabama, located at Tuscaloosa, was created in 1823. Branches at Decatur, Montgomery, and Mobile were added in 1832 and another, at Huntsville, in 1835. The branches were independent of the mother bank.

108. Brantley, *Banking in Alabama*, I, 264; *Senate Journal*, Sess. of 1835–36, p. 8; *Senate Journal*, Sess. of 1839–40, p. 18; *House Journal*, Sess. of 1841–42, pp. 191–95; John B. Hogan to Arthur P. Bagby, January 2, 1840, in Governors' Correspondence: Bagby; Wetumpka *Argus*, December 29, 1841. See pp. 76–77 herein.

109. *Senate Journal*, Sess. of 1835–36, pp. 7–8. Despite his support for White in 1836, Gayle did not finally declare himself a Whig until 1840; see John B. Hogan to Arthur P. Bagby, October 27, 1839, in Governors' Correspondence: Bagby.

The bank's relationship with the legislature thus was extremely unhealthy. The directors were dependent on the legislators for place, but the bank's structure was immune from legislative question. But to stop with this observation is to miss an important aspect of the connection. Given the fact that the relation was inherently defective, the legislators in fact behaved with great propriety. The situation could have generated the most extraordinary corruption. It did not.

In the first place, legislators did not, by and large, use their position to gain large bank credits. In the Senate of 1836, the year before the crash, 20 percent of the members held no loans from the banks, and 80 percent owed less than $5,000. Only three senators owed more than $10,000, and James F. Roberts of Mobile alone had a really substantial debt—$75,000. Of the 133 legislators in 1840, a third were unindebted, and considerably more than half owed less than $1,000. Only something over 18 percent of the legislators owed more than $5,000.[110] In both cases, these figures include debts for which the legislators were not directly liable, but were merely sureties. Of course there were legislators who allowed themselves to become deeply indebted, and then to be made apologists for the bank: James F. Roberts was one such, Nathaniel Terry another. But these men were exceptions. Lawmakers usually avoided becoming financially subservient to the institution which they governed.

In the second place, the loans made by the banks, even if, as seems difficult to believe, they were often a result of political interference, were usually sound. Contemporary observers, and historians since, appear mesmerized by the growing amounts of bad debts in the early 1840s. At each session of the legislature, the total grew larger. The inference is often drawn that the banks had made many poor loans. On the contrary, the figures actually reflect the financial extremities into which the depression cast even some of the community's most substantial citizens.[111] Commentators too infrequently glance at the

110. Brantley, *Banking in Alabama*, I, 408, II, 334–37, Appendices.
111. Cf. *Senate Journal*, Sess. of 1839–40, p. 12; *Senate Journal*, Sess. of 1849–50, p. 204; David L. Abrams, "The State Bank of Alabama, 1841–45" (M.A. thesis, Auburn University, 1965), 43–45, 60. Henry Hitchcock, for instance, was one of the state's most important entrepreneurs. At the beginning of 1837 he was worth more than a million dollars. By the end of April he had lost his entire holdings: Henry Hitchcock to his wife, April 13, April 30, 1837, in Henry Hitchcock Papers, University of Alabama Library, Tuscaloosa.

efforts of Francis Strother Lyon, the commissioner who supervised the liquidation of the banks. His reports, however, tend to confirm the ultimate security of the loans. It was, after all, Lyon's success in recovering so many "bad" and "doubtful" debts as prosperity returned, coupled with his use of the school fund for bank rather than school purposes, which made his liquidation program possible, and which gave Lyon his reputation as a financial wizard in the minds of politicians who had prematurely written these loans off.[112] Lyon's achievement is a tribute to his talents in the management of financial affairs, but it is also to some extent a confirmation of the judgment of the bank directors of the 1830s. We must remember that the bank failure was the central issue in the politics of the 1840s, and that hence many of the charges commonly hurled prove on investigation to have been little more than fevered imaginings or demagogic oratory.

We need not, of course, dismiss the preliminary findings of the joint committee appointed by the legislature in 1841 to investigate the bank in order to take this position. There is no doubt that corrupt dealings surrounded the banks, particularly in their last years, and that men of wealth and power were involved. But the banks' business would appear to have been too diverse and conducted on too large a scale to have been infected fundamentally by such avaricious maneuvers.[113]

There is a final aspect to the legislature's relationship with the bank which is quite instructive. While the legislators only rarely sought to employ the institution to their own advantage, they had a marked and highly detrimental effect on it as a result of another source of behavior—immense economic ignorance. John B. Norris, an experienced financier and one of the later presidents of the Mobile branch, cried in utter frustration,

I am not astonished at the course things are taking in the Legislature, and unless they do much better than I expect, they will certainly destroy all the Banks. . . . There is no financial ability in any country, with all the original capital of the State Banks in specie, that could sustain the credit of our State

112. *House Journal*, Sess. of 1849–50, p. 216; Montgomery *Advertiser*, December 5, 1849.

113. *House Journal*, Sess. of 1841–42, pp. 354–55. A thorough and scholarly study of the Bank of Alabama still awaits doing, though the materials are available. The books of the five banks and the complete correspondence of the Mobile branch remain in the Alabama Department of Archives and History, essentially unexamined by students of the subject.

Institutions under such improvident Legislation. To persons who are acquainted with the situation of the Banks, the various propositions relative to the Banks [in the legislature] are perfectly astounding. Does any member of the Legislature suppose that any man having the necessary qualifications to manage the Banks can be induced to continue from year to year to labour for the benefit of the Banks and receive his compensation in abuse without measure?

And William R. Hallett, who headed the private Bank of Mobile, commented, "I am disgusted with the proceedings of our Legislature. It looks to me as though the members were determined to break down every Bank in the State. If the Legislature aims at correcting abuses, their proceedings go to show that they do not know what they are doing." [114]

The personal abuse of which Norris spoke was a product of the post-suspension era, when politicians began accusing the bank personnel of general dishonesty and malevolence. But the "perfectly astounding" legislation had a long tradition. In 1828, for instance, the assembly directed the bank to borrow a large sum of money in New York in order to loan it out to hard-pressed debtors of private institutions, thus allowing the debtors to meet their previously contracted payments. When Governor Gayle was attempting to sell the bonds the proceeds of which were to form the capital of the new Huntsville branch, he confessed bitterly that the legislature's plan for issuance of the bonds was "the very worst that could have been adopted." He was "almost tempted," he said, to ignore the legislature's instructions. The assembly regularly mismanaged bond issues, putting the state to much extra expense, and sometimes making the securities simply unsalable. The statute books are, in fact, littered with fiscal blunders and absurdities. Not the least of these follies is the extraordinary decision in 1836 to abolish all state taxes and to finance government from the income of the banks. [115]

114. John B. Norris to Arthur P. Bagby, January 14, 1840, William R. Hallett to Bagby, January 10, 1840, both in Governors' Correspondence: Bagby; see also Hallett to Bagby, January 18, 1840, Norris to Bagby, January 18, 1840, John Martin to Bagby, January 30, 1840.
115. Selma *Courier*, January 3, January 31, 1828; John Gayle to Bartley [letter addressed to Benjamin] M. Lowe, March 20, 1835, in Governors' Correspondence: Gayle; William R. Hallett to Arthur P. Bagby, December 24, 1838, in Governors' Correspondence: Bagby; *Senate Journal*, Sess. of 1841–42, p. 13. Something of a highpoint of economic ignorance, I think, is reached by Governor Bagby in *Senate Journal*, Sess. of 1839–40, pp. 10–11.

There is, however, one fundamental attitude unifying all of the legislature's actions toward the banks, and explaining many of the more bizarre decisions of the bank directors themselves. Henry W. Collier, the most knowledgeable of the state's antebellum governors in financial affairs, stated the situation precisely: "The banks were regarded as the property of the people not only collectively but individually."[116] The legislature and likeminded directors believed that the institutions' primary goal was service to the citizenry—the banks' owner-customers—and that the private profit of the banks must be sacrificed to the welfare of the populace. The directors tried ordinarily to select the best loans from among the paper offered them for discount, but the thought of simply refusing loans—of curtailing accommodations in order to regulate note circulation in the interest of the bank—was foreign to them. The bank had not been erected for that purpose.

The story of the legislature's relationship with the state bank is not, then, a history of self-interest and avarice so much as it is the chronicle of a group of pathetically naïve men seeking eagerly to further the general welfare through the use of institutions which they had not the skill to manipulate. No episode in antebellum history would appear at first glance to give stronger evidence of sordid cupidity and lack of concern for the populace on the part of the legislators. No episode gives on closer examination more convincing proof of legislative dedication to making capital and its derivative institutions subserve the aspirations of the whole society. With the Bank of Alabama, the state's lawmakers went beyond efforts to limit the power of corporate wealth to an attempt to design an institution which would eliminate private profit altogether from the operations of the credit and currency mechanisms.

Legislators talked a good deal about democracy: gubernatorial nomination of bank directors was "undemocratic"; the white basis for congressional districting was "democratic."[117] The student notes,

116. *House Journal*, Sess. of 1849–50, p. 203.
117. *Senate Journal*, Sess. of 1841–42, p. 14; *Senate Journal*, Sess. of 1835–36, p. 8; Wetumpka *Argus*, November 24, 1841; Montgomery *Advertiser*, August 6, 1851. The general ticket system was also called democratic: *Senate Journal*, Sess. of 1840–41, p. 18.

however, that legislators were very slow to diminish their own powers. They did not finally turn selection of the judiciary over to the people until 1850, for instance. Democracy was a concept towards which all politicians did regular obeisance; it was a word which possessed great force, and if fastened securely onto a man or a program, could dictate popular support. But "democratic" is doubtless not the word with which to characterize the Alabama legislature. The membership of that body did not by any means constitute a microcosm of the wealth distribution within the society, though within broad limits it was probably reasonably representative. Power within the assembly was disproportionately in the hands of certain economic groups, and particularly, of certain partisans who by virtue of their devotion to the preservation of party drill created for themselves leadership roles. Most legislators remained passive, content with the power which their positions gave them in their local communities. They usually allowed themselves to be guided by the caucus and by the divisive or symbolic issue. These traits may not have been unusual in nineteenth-century state legislatures, but they certainly do not describe a genuinely democratic representative body.

And yet, one cannot visit Alabama's antebellum capitol without sensing that a remarkable spirit pervades its chambers. It is as if that propaganda which for decades—stretching back long before the Revolution—had extolled the virtues of the simple farmer in his humble cot, had here at last fallen on fertile ground. The assembly, to the extent of its limited knowledge and information, and its constricted conception of its authority, sought actively to be his champion.

It is important to note that the essence of legislative apprehension was not merely wealth, but the concentration of wealth. As a result, legislators differentiated to some extent between wealthy planters who reinvested their profits in agriculture and those who diversified their holdings by investing in commerce or industry. The planter who remained on his farm—who kept to himself and knew his place—was regarded as simply an agriculturist whose operation was on a larger scale. After all, he worried about the same weather conditions and followed with the same avidity the growth of the various crops. Farmers might resent such a man; they insisted, through their repre-

sentatives, that he carry an uncommonly large share of the tax burden.
But they saw no reason to fear him. His occupation was too much like
their own.

The wealthy could easily transmute themselves into enemies of
popular liberty, however, by cooperating together. When planters
sought to further their interests—their "selfish ends"— "by congregat-
ing their fortunes," as Benjamin C. Yancey had phrased it, resentment
towards them turned at once to alarm. A corporation was an institution which enabled a planter or other well-to-do investor to emerge
from the isolation of his individual fortune into a legal alliance
through which he and his fellows could control the destiny of other
men. Such unions of capital were the objects of particular governmental hostility.

At the very least, then, the Alabama legislature emerges as having
more fully typified the society which elected it than is often thought.
Legislators listened to the voice of the masses, exerted themselves to
placate popular fears, and pandered to social prejudice. We may grant
that they seldom exhibited leadership or foresight; indeed, they
explicitly rejected such qualities in favor of popular instruction and
faithful agency. Surely, however, it is cruel to ignore the substance of
their proudest claim: that they sought with a will to protect the
citizenry from such phantasms as the citizenry from time to time perceived.[118]

118. Wetumpka *Argus*, August 21, 1839.

Chapter III The Parties

HOWEVER responsive the legislature may have been to the needs of the society, one could argue with much apparent cogency that the structure of the parties placed the substance of power in the hands of a political elite. Although conventions greatly limited the ability of the electorate to choose its officials, the membership of the conventions was not especially representative, and the procedure of the conventions—particularly at the county level—delivered effective control of the meetings to a small group of managers. In fact, it might be said that a political party at this period was not much more than a confederation of political managers.

But such an argument, even though its premises may be individually correct, would actually rest upon a profoundly erroneous understanding of the nature of the party structure itself. A closer examination of the parties will reveal them not as elitist institutions, but as subtle agents of the social faith. Reaching deep into the citizenry, the parties were perhaps the most comprehensive and assiduous reflectors of Alabamians' desires. In the present chapter, we shall attempt to define the true sources of power within the parties, to explain the interaction between the parties and the society at large, and thus finally to gain additional insight into the nature of the society's unspoken assumptions. Our discussion, focusing first on the state and then on the local level, will in each case begin with a brief description of the formal party mechanisms and will then turn to the real, though unofficial, machinery of party governance.

Organization at the State Level

From the state's earliest days, legislative leaders of the two opposing factions had held consultations to choose gubernatorial candidates,[1] and from earliest days they had met excoriation for doing so. The legislature was charged, "in the omnipotence of its pretensions," of attempting "to prescribe to the people who shall be their Governor and their Representatives in Congress."[2] The factional caucuses at this early stage were extremely informal affairs. During the course of the legislative session, lasting six weeks or more, the leaders discussed the available men, and eventually agreed upon a mutually acceptable figure.

One early device, adopted in connection with the selection of presidential electoral slates in 1824 and 1828 to avoid arousing the popular fear of clique rule, was to announce a general meeting of all the adherents of a faction who happened to be in the capital city on the day selected. As a student of antebellum Alabama might expect, a "meeting composed promiscuously of members of the Legislature and other citizens" could be called "wholly unexceptionable," while an effort "to exclude all but members of the Legislature from the right to participate in the nomination of candidates" was regarded "as a gross usurpation of power, and as an attempt to establish an aristocracy."[3]

The state's first real convention, with delegates formally selected by county meetings, was the Democratic gathering of 1835 which selected the Van Buren electoral ticket for the following year's presidential canvass. Thereafter the Democrats held a statewide convention in the winter of every fourth year to choose presidential electors and national convention delegates, and in the spring of every second year to nominate a gubernatorial candidate.[4] In sharp contrast, the

---

1. See Henry Hitchcock to John W. Walker, January 2, 1821, in John W. Walker Papers, Alabama Department of Archives and History, Montgomery, for an account of one such decision.
2. *Alabama Republican* (Huntsville), January 19, 1821. *Cf.* February 2, February 9, February 16, March 9, 1821.
3. *House Journal*, Sess. of 1831–32, pp. 233–34. *Cf.* 171, 176, 178.
4. No convention was held, however, on five occasions: in 1837 Governor Clay's sudden resignation forced the party to resort to a legislative caucus; in the spring of 1839, in 1843, and in 1855 the incumbent governor had no opposition for renomination; in 1851 the party was so deeply divided over the Compromise of 1850 that no meeting was possible.

Whiggery, as we have seen, held only four conventions, the first one in 1839.[5]

Although, except in the case of Nathaniel Terry in 1845, the Democratic conventions virtually chose the governor—in addition to making numerous other important decisions—it was nevertheless difficult to get the electorate to take an interest in the affairs. The unpopular nomination of Terry led many to pay greater attention to the conventions, but it was still not uncommon for a few of the sparsely settled Wiregrass counties to send no delegates, and for other counties—particularly the more remote hill counties—to be represented only by their legislators, or even by someone who happened to be among the spectators and was invited to take a seat.[6] Indeed, such was the level of absenteeism that getting a candidate's supporters to show up may well have been his campaign manager's major problem.[7] The fact that so few men were willing to travel to the capital for the meeting explains the timing of conventions. Winter conventions coincided

5. The conventions of 1839, 1844, and 1852 were held to choose presidential electors and, in the case of the first two, national convention delegates. The convention of 1840 was intended to nominate congressional candidates, though in the end it declined to do so because of the pending General Ticket bill. There was also a Unionist state convention in 1852, three Know-Nothing state conventions in 1855 and 1856, and a Constitutional Unionist convention in 1860.

6. These and other generalizations about party conventions are based upon convention journals. I was unable to locate the journal of the Whig convention of 1844. The journal of the Whig convention of 1839 is in pamphlet form in the University of Alabama Library, Tuscaloosa, and that for 1840 in the Tuscumbia *North Alabamian*, January 9, 1841. The journal of the Unionist convention of 1853 is in the *Alabama Journal* (Montgomery), January 22, 1852, and that of the Whig convention of that year also in the *Alabama Journal*, September 3, 1852. The journal of the American party convention of 1856 is in the *Sumter County Whig* (Livingston), February 20, 1856. The Know-Nothings also held two conventions in 1855; both were secret sessions, but a list of probable delegates to the first of them, excluding Mobilians, is in the Montgomery *Advertiser*, January 17, 1855. The Constitutional Unionist convention journal is in the *Pickens Republican* (Carrollton), July 12, 1860. Democratic convention journals may be seen in the following sources: Huntsville *Democrat*, December 23, 1835; Wetumpka *Argus*, January 29, 1840 and January 13, 1841; Huntsville *Democrat*, December 14, 1843 and May 21, 1845; Eufaula *Democrat*, May 19, 1847; Huntsville *Democrat*, March 8, 1848 and June 20, 1849; Montgomery *Advertiser*, January 27, 1852, May 11, 1853, January 11, 1856, June 3, June 10, 1857, and May 18, 1859. The proceedings of the convention of January, 1860, are in the bound volumes of pamphlets in the J. L. M. Curry Collection in the Alabama Department of Archives and History, Montgomery, Vol. XXVII, No. 36; and of the June meetings in the Montgomery *Advertiser*, June 13, 1860 (Yanceyite) and Montgomery *Confederation*, June 8, 1860 (Douglasite).

7. Percy Walker to Joseph W. Lesesne, December 10, 1843, in Joseph W. Lesesne Papers, Southern Historical Collection, University of North Carolina Library, Chapel Hill; John Hardy to Bolling Hall, April 23, 1853, in Bolling Hall Papers, Alabama Department of Archives and History, Montgomery.

with the legislative sessions so that legislators could be used as delegates. And both winter and spring conventions were scheduled to coincide with the two annual terms of the state supreme court, so that lawyers who had cases to argue before the court could be appointed delegates.

This arrangement, though really a practical necessity, had the effect of giving to lawyers a much stronger voice in party affairs than they had in the governmental apparatus. Page 121 contains a table stating the percentages of attorneys and of legislators who served as delegates to the various conventions.[8] Full data are not available for the Whiggery, but it appears that lawyers may have had an even larger role in that party than in the Democracy. Only in the final decade of the antebellum period did Democrats equal the level of lawyer participation achieved by the Whigs in 1839. At the same time, in no winter convention did the Democrats even approach the low level of legislative participation which the first Whig convention showed.

The state's bar was of course most numerous in the Black Belt, which was also the area most involved with the market economy. We may not be surprised, therefore, that attorneys—agents of the world of contract and commerce—should be so strong in the Whiggery. But it appears that even the Democracy in the market regions was disposed to give substantial power to lawyers. A uniformly high percentage of the attorneys who served as Democratic delegates was sent by the Black Belt and Mobile. The hill-county Democracy, on the other hand, appears to have drawn its party leaders, as it did its ideology, primarily from the ranks of farmers.

It should also be noted that the power of the bar within the Democratic party increased steadily during the antebellum period. More and more ambitious Black Belt attorneys seem to have deserted the Whigs for the party which controlled statewide office and monopolized state patronage. And at the end of the 1850s lawyers at last began to be

8. The percentage of lawyers was determined by comparing the lists of delegates either to the roll of the bar for 1845 in William Garrett, *Reminiscences of Public Men in Alabama for Thirty Years* (Atlanta: Plantation Publishing Company's Press, 1872), 780–791, or to the roll of the bar to be found in Governors' Correspondence: A. B. Moore (dated internally to about 1855). The conventions of 1848, 1849, and 1852 were checked in both lists. When a convention did not meet during a legislative session, members of both the immediately preceding and the immediately following session were counted as being legislators.

Analysis of Delegates to State Political Conventions*

	Year	Time of year	% of legislator-delegates	% of lawyer delegates	Total % legislators or lawyers
WHIGS	1839	Winter	19.0	32.0	47.0
(Unionist)	1852	Winter	38.4	27.0	50.4
	1852	Summer	6.3	17.2	23.4
(American)	1856	Winter	37.1	24.8	54.3
(Constitutional					
Union)	1860	Summer	2.9	11.2	13.7
DEMOCRATS	1835	Winter	22.5	10.0	29.6
	1839	Winter	50.0	16.0	62.0
	1840	Winter	42.0	20.0	56.0
	1844	Winter	45.0	25.7	62.0
	1845	Spring	15.0	27.7	40.4
	1848	Winter	35.0	27.7	54.2
	1849	Spring	2.0	28.0	28.5
	1852	Winter	32.9	33.5	58.7
	1853	Spring	8.7	21.0	26.0
	1856	Winter	24.0	28.0	46.4
	1857	Spring	11.0	31.5	40.0
	1860	Winter	25.0	33.0	51.4

* See notes 6 and 8 to this chapter.

Residence of Lawyer-Delegates to Democratic State Conventions

Year	% of Lawyer-Delegates from Black Belt	% of Lawyer-Delegates from Black Belt and Mobile
1835	28.6	42.9
1839	33.3	38.9
1840	35.7	35.7
1844	34.5	37.9
1845	38.5	46.0
1848	44.2	51.9
1849	59.2	64.8
1852	50.0	60.7
1853	58.6	69.0
1856	45.0	47.5
1859	39.2	47.3
1860	39.8	43.1

accorded some degree of leadership even in the hill counties. These changes within the Democracy go hand in hand with the decline of the party's devotion to the doctrines of agrarian radicalism.

It is nevertheless essential to emphasize that at all times a great number of delegates—some 40 percent or more in winter conventions and up to three-quarters in spring conventions—were neither legislators nor lawyers. They had, we must presume, been stirred to journey to Tuscaloosa or Montgomery specifically in order to attend to the affairs of their party. These men were the devoted county workers, the committed partisans, who formed the most energetic element in the party's efforts to organize and influence the electorate.

This group of ardent laborers in the party vineyard was even more in evidence at the district conventions to nominate congressional candidates.[9] Legislators almost never went as delegates to such meetings, and lawyers were few in number—seldom more than three or four of the members. The gatherings were small, with most of the delegates coming from the county which was the convention's host. Men who came all the way from the neighboring counties to attend district conventions were ordinarily either zealously dedicated to the party or were political associates or clients of a candidate for the nomination. The delegates from the other counties in the district had a disproportionate voice in the conventions because, so far as I have been able to discover, congressional district conventions uniformly followed the practice of allotting to each county's delegation, no matter what its size, the same number of votes as the county had in the legislature.

The basis for apportioning votes at state conventions was a matter of heated controversy among the Democrats. If each county were allowed as many votes as it had members of the legislature, the areas in which the Whigs were strong would be given excessive power. South Alabamians noted, however, that the prospect of exercising such power might attract additional support for the Democrats in the Black Belt. North Alabamians were unconvinced, and favored instead giving each county one vote for every two hundred or three hundred votes

9. Journals of representative congressional district conventions are in the Tuscumbia *North Alabamian*, February 20, 1841; Pickensville *Register*, June 3, 1843; Tuscaloosa *Independent Monitor*, April 20, 1847; Montgomery *Advertiser*, May 14, June 18, 1851; Wetumpka *Spectator*, June 4, 1857.

cast by it for the Democratic presidential nominee in the preceding election. In the first four antebellum conventions the legislative representation basis was used, but in all succeeding gatherings the presidential poll basis was adopted. South Alabamians continued to fight the method vigorously, however, and their losing record is an index of north Alabama's power rather than of resignation on the part of the southern counties.

The last great victory by north Alabama in this long-running feud was in the convention of 1853. As a result of the decline of the Whiggery, the vote for Franklin Pierce had been substantial in 1852 even in the Black Belt. But the north Alabamians forced the use of the 1848 return for Cass as the base upon which vote allotments were figured. Alabama's overwhelming endorsement of James Buchanan in 1856, however, left the north Alabamians no longer able to hold the line. On the basis of the Buchanan poll, south Alabama was able, in the final three antebellum conventions, to regain the sizable vote it had lost in 1845.

The key to many a convention was the selection of its temporary chairman, since the rules gave to the chair the power to name the members of all committees. It was the procedure of the convention for the temporary chairman to appoint a committee to select the convention's permanent officers—a slate which was always accepted unanimously. The permanent chairman thereupon appointed a resolutions committee and such other committees as were necessary, including sometimes committees to nominate candidates. Thus the faction which organized the convention had taken a long step towards controlling it. The temporary chairman, it appears, was simply the choice of the man who was able to get to the podium first. The south Alabama element gained control of the Democratic convention of 1848 by the following farcical expedient, as described by a delegate:

By a trick at the outset we [the north Alabama politicians] lost the inside track. The arrangement amongst our friends . . . was to make [Nathaniel] Terry chairman, which would have secured the nomination of electors and delegates of the "purest water." William B. Martin was to make the preliminary motion for filling the chair and did so, but Col. [John]Erwin, holding his watch in his hand, announced that the hour of 7 had not arrived—and when the minute hand reached the zenith, he pompously moved that the Speaker of the House [Leroy Pope Walker] should take the chair. In that way we lost the first trick and they gained the Presidency by constituting the committee to recommend the officers to their liking.[10]

These doings seem ludicrous until we recall that the convention of 1848 was the body which adopted the Alabama Platform, and that therefore this bit of childish chicanery led America another step down a path the end of which was the death of 600,000 of her sons. Upon such institutions, with such imperfections, was the government of the antebellum Union dependent. It is not ludicrous; it is grotesque.

The procedure of a convention was so flexible, however, that any group with skilled floor managers and strong backing could overcome even so great a setback as the loss of the chair. In 1848 the north Alabama group still managed to secure a number of the nominations for men acceptable to it. It was not, therefore, that conventions were impervious to the will of a majority of the delegates. It was just that in order to effect that will, the majority had either to be in control of the chair and of the various committees, or it had to have clever managers who knew when and how to wrest power from the convention's officials. The convention as an institution did not go out of its way to consult its delegates; it was subservient instead to the desires of its officers. The delegates could make themselves heard, but they would have to shout. And even so, if they shouted at the wrong time or over the wrong issues, they might find their cries drowned out.

In the nomination of candidates, compromise and quiet negotiation predominated over floor fights. Conventions were conceived as a way to unify the party, and there was as a result great pressure on an aspirant to yield his ambitions when they threatened to become divisive.[11] Candidates therefore took private polls of the delegates and when they concluded that they did not have a majority, they often withdrew their names before or shortly after the balloting began. Bitter multiballot contests were not rare, especially in struggles for the gubernatorial nomination, and they seem to have become increasingly acrimonious affairs later in the antebellum period, when Democratic convention endorsement had clearly become tantamount to election.

10. James E. Saunders to George S. Houston, February 26, 1848, in George S. Houston Papers, Duke University Library, Durham.
11. I have encountered no more instructive look inside an Alabama convention than Charles P. Robinson to John Bragg, January 21, 1852, in John Bragg Papers, Southern Historical Collection, University of North Carolina Library, Chapel Hill.

Even as late as 1857, however, the old spirit of self-sacrifice for the good of the party still was to be found.[12]

The growth of multiballot engagements was encouraged by the adoption in Democratic conventions after 1845 of the two-thirds rule for gubernatorial nominations. The requirement was a response to Nathaniel Terry's successful manipulation of the convention machinery and was intended to make such factional choices impossible. It increased the likelihood that no strong or controversial figure could obtain nomination and gave hope to politicians whose claims to be chosen were increased when the party sought a compromise candidate.[13] But the majority rule was retained on all questions except the selection of a gubernatorial nominee, so that the two-thirds majority is not a full explanation of the propensity of the parties to choose moderate candidates.

The necessity to build a majority at the polls was an even more influential factor. Men who were regarded as extreme partisans or as having extreme views on sensitive issues could not ordinarily be nominated.[14] Thus the structure of the two-party system itself contributed importantly to the choice, in those areas of the state in which the parties were evenly matched, of candidates who were not strongly identified with attitudes which would alienate definable factions or blocs of votes. Still, it must be noted that the nature of a "moderate" position changed with time and locality: at one period it might be a southern rights advocate; at another, a Union Democrat; an opponent of all banks or an advocate of mild banking reform measures; and so across the whole range of political positions in Alabama history. Political leaders shaped their nomination to the exigencies of the situation, and an ambitious candidate could modify those exigencies by recognizing and exploiting some popular issue. The general rule, therefore, that conventions tended to settle on nominees who would offend the least number of factions, is subject to a caveat: the unceasing effort by every

12. John E. Moore to Matthew P. Blue, June 12, 1857, in M. P. Blue Papers, Alabama Department of Archives and History, Montgomery.

13. *E.g.*, Felix G. Norman to George S. Houston, February 14, 1847, in Houston Papers; Eufaula *Democrat*, January 13, 1847.

14. *E.g.*, William R. Hallett to Arthur P. Bagby, November 9, 1839, in Governors' Correspondence: Bagby, Alabama Department of Archives and History, Montgomery; John Hardy to Bolling Hall, May 13, 1853, in Hall Papers. *Cf.* Garrett, *Reminiscences*, 92.

politician to make certain that his own position on each public question was the popular one produced constant alterations in the formulation of the partisan creed. And whenever a strong leader was able to forge his own majority upon an issue, party institutions were always sufficiently responsive to public opinion to insure him of receiving the rewards at their disposal.

Thus there existed a certain tension between the needs of the party and the needs of the political aspirant. In the final analysis, the politician's fate was in his own hands. There were, it appears, two basic strategies which could give him power. He might choose to play the game defensively, adopting the orthodox view upon supposedly settled questions and watching constantly for the emergence of new issues, ever nervously poised to jump to the more popular side. If he adopted this pattern for his career, he became in the language of the time a "trimmer"—one who trimmed his sails to each new political breeze. Such a course might take him far; it carried William R. King to the vice-presidency of the United States and John McKinley to a seat on the Supreme Court. But for the maladroit, this tactic could lead to disaster. Nathaniel Terry's devotion to the Bank of Alabama had seemed the quintessential mark of the democratic statesman when he had formed the attachment, but he had allowed himself to become so deeply involved with the institution that he was unable to detect the shifting of the center of Alabama politics upon the question during the early 1840s. In 1845, therefore, he found himself unexpectedly delivered up as a sacrifice to the gods of the social faith.

Alternatively, the politician might decide to pursue an offensive strategy, gambling that he could create a new symbolic issue. The odds were not encouraging. After initial success, most of the politicians who took this path—for instance, Kelly with the big-interest cases, Gayle with Indian removal, Gabriel Moore with squatter preemption, Martin with liquidation of the state bank, Winston with railroad aid, to some degree Fitzpatrick with southern rights—were destroyed by the changes which their issues wrought in the structure of politics. But there were always ambitious men who were willing to try.

Though probably virtually all politicians indulged dreams of riding a hobby to unchallengeable eminence, perhaps a majority of the state's politicians in practice remained trimmers. And despite the fact that these men actually kept their popularity, and thus their offices, by their own careful attention to the public mood, yet because they lived upon issues which were not of their own creation; because their following was, at least in good part, gathered by the sensitivity with which they judged whether or not a new issue was a successful incarnation of the general partisan ideology; because they were, in a sense, parasites on the more aggressive politicians, they therefore were peculiarly susceptible to the misapprehension that whatever place they had achieved, they owed to the party. For them, the convention came to seem the mechanism which had bestowed their power. Primarily for this reason, also—because they tended to view themselves as sons of a party to which they owed filial duty and to whose paternal wrath they were subject, rather than because they were especially deeply inspired by the party's gospel—these politicians were often willing to stand aside in order not to divide the common effort.

For the other group of dominant figures, the convention was the barometer of the popular acceptance of their issue. While they had access to the fears of the electorate, they could expect the party's nomination. But when their hour was past, the convention was among the first institutions to turn upon them. Party workers secretly resented politicians whose popularity was great enough to make them relatively independent of party machinery.[15] And there were always many suitable rivals awaiting the fall, whose success would not compel all other politicians to redraft their credentials as champions of the masses.

Whichever route the politician chose to political influence, the convention ordinarily had but one index in weighing his qualifications—the extent of his popularity. In a county in which one party was dominant, other elements might be considered. But when the opposition brought out a vigorous candidate, the party sought not talents but strength. Strength might mean a clear personal identification with an issue, but at least as often it implied simply an ability to rehearse the current articles of the faith convincingly, usually coupled with an engaging character and an ability to tell a good story.[16] The convention

15. *E.g.*, Leonidas Howard to Bolling Hall, June 2, 1849, in Hall Papers.
16. William R. Hallett to Arthur P. Bagby, November 9, 1839, Hallett to Bagby, November 27, 1838, both in Governors' Correspondence: Bagby. Note that in the letter cited in note 11 above, popularity was, at least ostensibly, the sole reason for the hostility to the choice of Tristram B. Bethea.

was first and foremost a party organ; compromise was its fuel and victory its goal.

Next to the convention, the most important element in the party structure was the legislative caucus. We have already encountered this institution in our discussion of the assembly. Like the convention, it met only when rival aspirants from the same party threatened to disrupt party harmony and allow an opposition victory. The Democratic caucus voted by secret ballot and for important offices sometimes required a two-thirds majority for nomination. The decisions of the caucus, like those of the convention, were enforced only by the feeling which most politicians had of deference to party authority, by the pressure of disapproval from fellow party members, and by pleas and threats from the party newspapers. Bolters received frequent reminders from the party leadership that "parties or associations of men can never succeed without occasionally making sacrifices of feeling and this they ought to do cheerfully to promote principles." [17]

The third great element in party governance is perhaps the most infrequently noticed—the party press. As we shall see, the editor of the local party paper was an essential member of the county leadership. Similarly, the editors of the great urban organs were at the very heart of power at the state level, wielding influence at least equal to that of the office holders. Among the party papers, the press at the capital was the acknowledged leader. One Democrat lamented "that the press generally are so tender footed in regard to rebuking the insolence of the central organ at Montgomery [the *Advertiser*]. If the Democratic party were slaves and the editor [M. P. Blue] their legally constituted owner, he could not speak in tones of more mandatory authority." [18] The organ could lose some of its influence if it allowed itself to get badly out of step with the party. But ordinarily the editorial opinions of the capital papers were taken as ex cathedra pronouncements. Their

17. James W. McClung to Rush Elmore, July 18, 1847, in Dixon H. Lewis Papers, University of Texas Library, Austin; Montgomery *Advertiser*, December 5, 1849, February 27, 1850; James G. Lyon to Arthur P. Bagby, September 15, 1839, in Governors' Correspondence: Bagby. The only formal record of the deliberations of a caucus of which I am aware is the Know-Nothing campaign tract, [Johnson J. Hooper,] *Proceedings of the Democratic and Anti-Know Nothing Party in Caucus; or the Guillotine at Work at the Capital During the Session of 1855–56, By an Eye Witness* (Montgomery: Barrett and Wimbish, Book and Job Printers, 1855).

18. J. D. Williams to Clement Claiborne Clay, June 11, 1857, in Clay Papers, Duke University Library, Durham.

circulation extended throughout the state. The gatherings which drafted the calls of conventions often met in their offices, and their columns were used like whips to enforce party discipline. Politicians often were forced to approach an editor as suppliants, begging for his endorsement. The important papers suggested candidates for office, and conventions sometimes did little more than ratify these suggestions.[19]

An editor had to be a devoted partisan since, particularly in rural areas, he seldom made much money. His subscribers took his paper in order to discover the party line on public events, and if his politics failed to remain pure, he lost his following.[20] His function therefore was constantly to apply party principles to developing circumstance in such a way as to accord with the prejudices of the community. Only thus did his arguments become convincing. Indeed, the ability to bring principles to the support of prejudices was the essence of the editorial talent, and the most efficacious aid which the editor could offer his party.

The editor's vociferous partisanship was the characteristic which presented the most important obstacle to his using his power within the party in order to attain office. The course which his position dictated towards the opposition alienated many voters who might normally have been his friends.[21] The other party would not vote for him, and his own, though willing to hail him as a leader, was unwilling to nominate him for fear that even a small defection from his ranks would deliver the day to his opponent. A few editors gained important office. But on the whole the editorial corps was confined to aiding in the nomination and election of other men.

The fact that editors could gain party but not governmental power points to an important aspect of party structure. Whereas the achievement of elective office required a broad base of popularity, ac-

19. Montgomery *Advertiser*, June 4, 1851, February 3, February 10, 1852; Mobile *Register*, quoted in Montgomery *Advertiser*, May 28, 1851; B. F. Pope to Clement Claiborne Clay, June 23, 1847, in Clay Papers; Rufus Blue to Matthew P. Blue, October 12, 1853, William F. Samford to Blue, February 11, 1857, both in M. P. Blue Papers.

20. Wetumpka *Argus*, December 29, 1841; *The Tuscumbian* (Tuscumbia), November 22, 1826; *Alabama Sentinel* (Tuscaloosa), June 10, 1826; "Many Democrats," in Montgomery *Advertiser*, November 4, 1851.

21. Rufus Blue to Matthew P. Blue, April 16, 1858, in Blue Papers.

cession to place within the parties turned on devotion to and labor in behalf of the party. Persons chosen to such positions therefore tended to be aggressively, even blindly, partisan. Jesse Beene, for instance, was president of the Democratic convention in 1839. He was probably even more partisan than most such officials. On assuming the chair, he told the delegates that every Whig was "untiring in his exertions to pull down the fabric of liberty based upon the Constitution and prostrate the rights of the people, for the purpose of advancing upon the ruins thereof, Aristocratic power." Beene was thereupon chosen a delegate to the Democratic national convention.[22]

It is no wonder that the Whigs were furious at Beene's address. It is no wonder that he was known to Democratic leaders as an unpopular man.[23] The wonder is that he could have been chosen to any position at all. But genuine commitment to a party appears to have induced a state of mind almost akin to insanity. When the Whigs brought out no gubernatorial candidate, the Democrats feared a secret nominee. When the Whigs, unable to agree among themselves, brought out four candidates for a single legislative seat, the Democrats thought it a plot to draw more Democrats in the race and thus to fragment the vote. The most vigorously advanced opinions of the opposition were held to be cynical positions assumed solely in order to achieve office.[24] Since the partisans were capable of accepting such notions as these, Beene's phantom must have seemed to them a threat of some substance. But his accusations were never likely to generate any substantial following because they were directed against a large portion of the citizenry. They were no more absurd, intrinsically, than were many of the charges hurled at banks and corporations, but the electorate's involvement with those institutions was not at all comparable to its experience with the party system. Many voters might never have met a bank president. But the parties were broadly based in the society. A charge that the Whiggery had been responsible for a slave revolt in

22. Wetumpka *Argus*, January 29, 1840.
23. *Ibid.*, April 15, 1840; William R. Hallett to Arthur P. Bagby, December 10, 1838, in Governors' Correspondence: Bagby.
24. Wetumpka *Argus*, July 24, 1839, May 26, 1841; Huntsville *Democrat*, May 8, 1844; Montgomery *Advertiser*, March 27, 1850.

Louisiana,[25] therefore, could only appear to the masses as questionable.

The fact that these charges were regularly made is, however, a matter of significance. They must have had the ring of truth at least to those who made them. It was men of the sort who hurled these accusations who were galvanized by the name of party, who were inspired to labor long hours to insure success at the polls, who would travel many arduous miles in order to attend a party convention. And it was they who were ordinarily elected to party offices, particularly to membership on the party executive committees. When the Mobile Whig committee published a bitter attack on the Democrats, an old politician hastened to assure the governor that, although it bore the signatures of all six committeemen, "It is signed by men but little known and of no influence in our community. The one who heads the committee [H. B. Gwathmey] would not have been known but for his untiring zeal" in the service of his party. His opinions received no credence except among his fellow "violent partizans."[26] In all these respects the Mobile committee and its chairman were typical.

The contemptuous tone of this description is also noteworthy. Though the partisans received party office, the politicians trusted them with little authority. The executive committees were in theory responsible for issuing the call for a convention, but in fact the call was usually drafted by a group of political leaders. The one element among the partisans which did have access to the inner circles of party power was the newspaper editors. Other than the voice of the editors, however, the sound at the seat of power was usually the sound of political pragmatism. The partisans supplied the parties with manpower and dedication in campaigns, and a significant portion of the delegates to the party conventions. The editors supplied ideology, aided in keeping the party organization in repair and galvanizing the party workers, and by their oratory and example worked to control selfish fac-

---

25. Wetumpka *Argus*, September 30, 1840.
26. Abner S. Lipscomb to Arthur P. Bagby, September 14, 1838, in Governors' Correspondence: Bagby. William L. Barney, *The Secessionist Impulse: Alabama and Mississippi in 1860* (Princeton: Princeton University Press, 1974), goes badly astray in failing to understand the actual character and functions of the party executive committees, both state and county.

tionalism. But the real leadership in the parties came, as we shall presently see, from a third source—the professional politicians.

From the beginning there were factions within the parties, ideological, sectional, and personal. Since the parties each had rather clear ideological positions, the one important intraparty divergence of an ideological sort was the disagreement among the Democrats over southern rights. The fascinating story of how the conflict between the mass of the party and the small group of southern rights advocates within it winds through the party's history is deserving of much more extended treatment than the limits of the present study allow. Suffice it to say that, until the final decade of the antebellum period, the men who had followed Dixon Lewis out of the Whig party in the summer of 1838, in protest against Whiggery's endorsement of rechartering the national bank, made few converts to their extreme strict constructionist outlook within the Democracy, and thus remained a small minority whose numbers were, however, relatively stable. At the county level they could claim significant concentrations only within the parties of some of the Black Belt counties, where there were few Democrats anyway, and in Mobile. Often the Jacksonians became angry at them, and occasionally even were ready to declare that "they care nothing for us and our cause and are as much sold to John C. Calhoun as ever a sorcerer was to the devil. . . . I sincerely think the impending battle will be more successfully fought if our ranks were purged of all pretended democrats. For policy's sake we have forborn long enough. The true policy now is 'He that is not for us, is against us,' and must 'bundle and go.' The appeal must be made [only] to the yeomanry of the country."[27] But the sad fact was that such bluster dashed itself against the political reality that, if the numbers of the southern rights group were stable, so were the numbers of the Jacksonians and of the Whigs; and the Democratic majority over the Whigs was only some five thousand votes. The Democrats thought that they needed their southern rights allies in order to remain in power and the southern rights forces knew that they needed membership in a party in order to have access to office. And so, each time the southern rights

27. James E. Saunders to George S. Houston, December 3, 1847, in Houston Papers. See also Thaddeus Sanford to John Bragg, March 13, 1852, in Bragg Papers.

men returned to the party fold, the Jacksonians joined in the lame conclusion, "Well, if they will stick at last, I am content." [28] Such was the course of this dispute from its inception in 1838 until the last five years of the antebellum era.

The conflict between north Alabama and south Alabama is a much more important and pervasive phenomenon. Each party sought to overcome its narrowly sectional base by playing to the voters in the other section. Thus, ironically, residents of the Tennessee Valley, where there were rather few Whigs, were an important leadership group in the Whig party and south Alabamians, who seldom could carry their counties for the Democrats, had great strength in Democratic councils. But the place within Whiggery of such men as Arthur F. Hopkins, James Jackson, Nicholas Davis and his two sons Nicholas, Jr., and Ripley, Jesse W. Garth, William B. Figures, and other north Alabamians is not as portentous for the future as the corresponding situation among the Democrats. Alabama's Whigs had been so long a minority that their differences were submerged in their desire for victory. Within the Democracy, however, fissures had begun to emerge. Indeed, one Democratic editor confessed that he feared that the party could be reunited only by being defeated. [29] The divisions were serious primarily because they became rather subtly involved with attitudes towards abolitionism.

The Democrats had always made more of the abolitionist threat than had the Whigs. The Whigs were hostile to abolitionism, of course, but they already held the allegiance of the state's great slaveowning regions. The Democats, on the other hand, had to shake the planter's faith in Whiggery if they were to make inroads into the Black Belt. Particularly during the campaign of 1840, they began emphasizing their belief that broad construction played into abolitionist hands. The conviction was doubtless genuine and deeply held, but in the course of making it a part of political oratory, the Democrats so simplified the reasoning involved that they soon were arguing that the American System was a plot conceived specifically in order to free the slaves. Such notions were emphasized on the state level particularly

28. Thaddeus Sanford to John Bragg, June –, 1852, in Bragg Papers.
29. M. C. Gallaway to George S. Houston, June 7, 1845, in Houston Papers.

when it was necessary to attempt to win the acquiescence of the planting regions to some proposal—the general ticket, for instance.[30]

The involvement of Whiggery with abolitionism was a truth accepted by Democrats regardless of region. But a variety of circumstances led south Alabamians to talk about the issue more often. Their section, as we have seen, was much more deeply involved with the national economy, and therefore the federal government seemed a more immediate power to its citizens. A threat to slavery from such a quarter became, as a result, a bit more believable. The few strict constructionist Calhounites in the party were concentrated in a number of the southern counties, and their presence compelled the party leaders there to emphasize this aspect of party ideology to mollify an always restless group of supporters. And there was always the hope, belied by voting statistics but tenaciously held, that the argument could drive a wedge between the Whig merchants and lawyers and their planter allies.

The constant repetition of this theme in the south, however, created subtle divisions within the party leadership. Southern politicians grew to think of the matter as a principal element in the Democratic creed, whereas in north Alabama it still seemed secondary to financial and other issues. This difference was one of emphasis, but given the sectional rivalry for influence within the party, it came to be considered a rather important disagreement. North Alabama Democrats feared that the nomination of a south Alabamian would not sufficiently excite their constituents because he would be accentuating questions with which north Alabama voters were not deeply concerned, and south Alabamians opposed the nomination of northerners for the same reason. Local success at the polls was thus at the heart of the sectional factionalism.

The north Alabama Democratic politicians of course represented the greater number of Democratic voters, but a number of factors re-

30. Wetumpka *Argus,* January 29, February 26, September 23, December 16, 1840, July 21, 1841; David Hubbard to George S. Houston, February 24, 1841, in Houston Papers; William R. de V. King to Arthur P. Bagby, February 14, 1841, in William R. de V. King Papers, Alabama Department of Archives and History, Montgomery; William R. Hallett to Arthur P. Bagby, November 19, 1838, September 5, 1840, in Governors' Correspondence: Bagby; "One of the People," in Montgomery *Advertiser,* June 25, July 23, 1851; *Senate Journal,* Sess. of 1840–41, p. 18.

duced their influence within the party merely to parity with that of their south Alabama competitors. Nomination of candidates from areas in which the party was not strong was a way of diminishing the party's sectional identification, and also gave promise of gaining for the party a number of voters who ordinarily would have voted for the opposition but who were attracted to the individual candidate because of personal friendship. Hill-county residents, in ordinary circumstances, were certain for the Democracy, and Black Belters for the Whiggery, so that a Democrat from the hills or a Whig from the Black Belt could offer no dowry of unexpected ballots. Moreover the partisans who constituted a significant portion of the convention delegates were much moved by the argument that, while north Alabama Democrats could expect office from their constituency, south Alabamians labored long for the party with no hope of reward at the local level. South Alabama politicians played on this feeling by referring to themselves as "few and faint, but fearless," and by saying, in the words of one of the few Black Belt Democratic legislators, "It is true that the Democratic party in this State are under many obligations to our Northern friends, but we are indebted perhaps to the masses in that quarter for their firm consistency as much as we are to their public men; for they have not encountered the difficulties and suffered political emolation [sic] as the publick men in the South have done. With them victory has been achieved without a struggle and they bring no scars from the battlefield." Finally, north Alabama was so firmly Democratic in its sympathies that the region became overstocked with ambitious politicians of that party. "The fact is," said an observer, "they are in each other's way and it is impossible to get their social influences to unite"; or as another remarked, "There is so much jealousy amongst the public men in that section of the state that they will betray a common cause before they will sustain a rival." South Alabamians' minority status encouraged an unwillingness among them to indulge personal rivalries. All of these factors gave south Alabama Democrats a strength within the party far beyond their numbers.[31]

31. P. H. Earle, George W. Gayle, T. E. B. Pegues *et al.* to Arthur P. Bagby, October 14, 1840, in Governors' Correspondence: Bagby; John W. Bridges to Dixon H. Lewis, November 6 [?], 1844, in Lewis Papers, University of Texas Library; James E. Saunders to George S. Houston, July 19, 1848, in Houston Papers.

The Whigs regularly nominated north Alabamians to statewide office, but elected only south Alabamians, since only in those districts could they command a majority. But the Democrats were forced to make sectional compromises in their tickets. One of the United States Senate seats was north Alabama's and one the south's. For only two of the forty-one years of antebellum statehood was this rule violated.[32] Between 1830 and 1860 the Democrats ran ten men for governor, five from each section. From the selection of Benjamin Fitzpatrick in 1840—the first time that a candidate for governor was chosen by convention—to the end of the antebellum period there were six Democratic gubernatorial nominees, three from each section. The residence of the nominee was carefully weighed in connection with political events. When the party sought to defeat the north Alabama maverick Joshua L. Martin in 1847, it turned to Reuben Chapman, a Tennessee Valley congressman whose primary economic interest was a large plantation in the Black Belt county of Sumter.[33] The campaign of a north Alabamian for senator might often be linked with that of a south Alabamian for governor.[34] Though immediate circumstances governed which candidate's sectional credentials were most advantageous in any one year, over a long enough period each section received fair consideration. Such was the case, however, only because Democratic politicians were always ready to insist on full representation for their own region.

32. From February 17 to November 27, 1826, Israel Pickens and William R. de V. King sat together in the Senate; and from July 1, 1848, to November 30, 1849, two south Alabamians again were senators, at first (July 1 to November 25, 1848) King and Dixon H. Lewis and thereafter King and Benjamin Fitzpatrick. In both 1826 and 1848 the brief conjunctions resulted from gubernatorial appointments to complete unexpired terms. A principal factor in the destruction of Governor Reuben Chapman's career was his appointment of two south Alabamians in 1848. For a bit more than six years (November 24, 1841, to July 1, 1848) Arthur P. Bagby, originally a resident of Monroe County and later of Montgomery, sat in the Senate with south Alabamians, at first King and then Lewis. But during this time Bagby claimed Tuscaloosa as his residence and was regarded as the north Alabama senator: Clement Comer Clay to George S. Houston, July 29, 1848, in Houston Papers. On this point, however, see the letter and speech of Jeremiah Clemens, in Huntsville *Democrat*, February 5, 1842, and the editorial comments, February 12, 1842.

33. Clement Comer Clay to George S. Houston, undated postscript to a letter the body of which is missing [dated internally to mid-December, 1848], in Houston Papers. In 1860 Chapman held 106 slaves on his Sumter plantation: Joseph K. Menn, "The Large Slaveholders of the Deep South, 1860" (Ph.D. dissertation, University of Texas, 1964), 505.

34. John Cochran to Clement Claiborne Clay, May 9, 1857, in Clay Papers; John W. Bridges to Dixon H. Lewis, November 6 [?], 1844, in Lewis Papers, University of Texas Library; Wetumpka *Argus*, December 2, December 9, 1840.

Before leaving the subject of factions based on area of residence, we must emphasize the distinction between the south Alabama faction and the Calhounites. The tendency to identify these two groups[35] has derived, perhaps, from a larger misconception of the nature of the party structure in Jacksonian America. The fascination with the Jacksonians' hostility to capital has obscured the sectional elements in the Jacksonian alliance.[36] The Jacksonians were hostile to capital, of course, and in no region more so than in the South. But southerners were at all times frightened by the prospect of slavery's involvement in federal politics. The Jacksonians, north and south, were perforce committed to the maintenance of an intersectional party organization. Northern Jacksonians were as concerned as were southerners, therefore, to suppress the agitation of the slavery question. The Democratic politicians and press throughout the country agreed upon a policy of noninterference. South Alabama politicians thus were not in disagreement with their party nationally in their concern for southern rights. Their anxiety about the issue put them occasionally a few steps in advance of the mass of the Democracy in their views upon related questions, but the mass always soon caught up. Their devotion to the Jacksonian creed did not stop short at the mention of slavery; on the contrary, the existence of slavery was one of the elements which insured that their zeal in the faith would not flag. The Democratic party, whatever else it was, was everywhere the party which opposed allowing the sensitive relations of master and slave to become a subject of political debate. The southern Jacksonians were convinced that as long as the party existed, and as long as their efforts prevented it from deserting its strict constructionist principles as had the earlier Jeffersonian coalition, they had only to defeat the Whigs to rest easy on the score of slavery.

35. *E.g.*, Albert B. Moore, *History of Alabama* (Rev. ed.; University, Ala.: University Supply Store, 1934), 159–61 and 162–207, 238–68, *passim*.

36. *E.g.*, Arthur M. Schlesinger, Jr., *The Age of Jackson* (Boston: Little, Brown and Co., 1945). Richard H. Brown's useful article "The Missouri Crisis, Slavery, and the Politics of Jacksonianism," *South Atlantic Quarterly*, LXV (1966), 55–72, has begun the effort to restore the South to its rightful place at the heart of the Jacksonian movement. It must always be borne in mind, however, that while northerners agreed with southerners in suppressing the agitation of slavery, southerners were at least as devoted as northerners to the limitation of the power of capital, a point which Brown misses. Jacksonianism was a genuine intersectional alliance on every level.

It was precisely upon this point that the south Alabama Democratic politicians differed with the small band of admirers of John C. Calhoun who gathered around Dixon H. Lewis. Only Lewis of the group achieved high office; their views were simply too extreme to receive favor from delegates or voters. Sometimes their intelligence gained them places in the judiciary, as it did with John A. Campbell, Joseph White Lesesne, and Henry and George Goldthwaite. William L. Yancey was sent to Congress before his affiliation with this group, and Percy Walker gained a single congressional term as a Know-Nothing in 1855. But more typically these men engaged in the private practice of law as, for much of their lives, did Thomas Williams, Thomas S. Mays, and Robert G. Scott, and exercised such influence as they had through personal friendship. They were convinced that the welfare of the South could not be trusted to the vagaries of national politics. The interest of the Democratic party in suppressing all discussion of slavery seemed to them a very weak reed upon which to lean. Rather, they dreamed of a South freed from the intersectional ties of party, aware of its regional interests, demanding formal guarantees for its institutions. As Senator Calhoun himself told Chancellor Lesesne, "There is not the slightest chance" of reforming the government through the existing parties.

The leaders on both sides are thoroughly rotten—incorrigibly so—mere spoilsmen and hollow hearted hypocrits [sic], without a particle of regard for principles and perfectly indifferent to country. I am disposed to believe that the only chance for reformation is to break up the present party organization; that, that can only be done by breaking up party machinery, and especially the [national] convention; and that, that can only be done by running as the people's candidate one of wide spread popularity. . . . I also am inclined to believe that it is the only way in which the South can be united, and thereby avert the calamity impending over it.[37]

Holding such principles, the Calhounites could hardly be ardent Democrats. From the moment they joined the Democracy, they were uncertain allies, deserting the party in local races and in national ones.[38] But support for Whig candidates was ordinarily out of the question for them because of ideological considerations, and their

37. John C. Calhoun to Joseph W. Lesesne, July 19, 1847, in Lesesne Papers.
38. *E.g.*, John B. Hogan to Arthur P. Bagby, January 2, January 10, 1840, in Governors' Correspondence: Bagby.

numbers precluded an independent effort; so the Calhounites were condemned to wasting their talents on attempts to convince devoted Democrats that the Democratic party did not afford southern rights sufficient protection. At the very end of the antebellum period, this debate became the central issue of Alabama politics, but for most of the era the Calhounites' position seemed patently contradicted by events. In sum, then, the south Alabama Democrats, even though they tended to emphasize southern rights more heavily than did their north Alabama brethren, were Jacksonians to the core, and confident that their party was the South's shield and buckler. The followers of Calhoun were a vexatious but small minority who had little influence within the party. The primary effect of their existence was to cause south Alabama politicians to discuss southern rights questions somewhat more often than they otherwise would have.

The third sort of factionalism within the party—that derived from the rivalries of aspiring politicians—is the most important. As we have seen in our study of the legislature, lesser politicians in antebellum Alabama tended to attach themselves to greater ones, producing within the parties an almost feudal hierarchy of personal blocs. Of course the influence of such blocs may be overstated. The ideological lines which divided the parties in Alabama were drawn with sufficient clarity that no politics based merely on personal rivalry could develop. Editorial exhortations to party unity were frequent and eloquent, and party leaders accepted their arguments. John J. Seibels denounced the existence of cliques within the party: "We detest all such bodies or associations and shall be after them, as the saying goes, 'with a sharp stick.'" On the one hand, Seibels at the very moment he penned these words was the chief propagandist for the powerful "Montgomery Regency," headed by Benjamin Fitzpatrick. Seibels' words thus appear hypocritical. On the other hand, Governor Fitzpatrick himself proudly proclaimed, "I have always been a caucus and a party man." [39]

Both of these men were as loyal to the party as they claimed. They merely practiced a sort of self-deception common among Alabama

39. Montgomery *Advertiser*, January 2, January 30, July 31, 1850, April 2, December 2, 1851; Wetumpka *Argus*, March 31, 1841; W. D. S. Cook to George S. Houston, December 25, 1848, J. McDonald to Houston, January 17, 1849, John S. Kennedy to Houston, April 22, 1848, all in Houston Papers; Benjamin Fitzpatrick to Bolling Hall, October 5, 1853, in Hall Papers.

politicians. The cliques to which they belonged did not seem to them institutions, but rather merely aggregations of friends formed to share patronage. They did not fully appreciate the role which such blocs played in party governance. Of course, they knew that enmity to a bloc was an offense which had to be punished, the punishment being the withholding of the patronage for which the offender had looked to the bloc. But in their own minds they were enforcing party rather than bloc discipline. The blocs had become so interwoven into the fabric of the party that an individual's display of independence appeared to most politicians as a revolt against the entire partisan institutional structure. Note, for instance, the particular phraseology in one letter advising a patronage boss of a recent act of impertinent self-reliance in the ranks. "The Fitzpatrick party I presume are acquainted with his [A. B. Clitherall's] proclivities" and they "ought to teach him a lesson that will *cool* his aspirations and satisfy him beyond a reasonable doubt that *He* is not the Democratic Party of Alabama." [40]

This strange self-deception derived, we may surmise, from the fact that cliques were, in the political ideology of the state, evil and oppressive mechanisms. Since one does not usually suppose that a group to which one belongs is evil and oppressive, it followed that the group was not a clique, at least as the term was generally understood. This denial of the power of the personal blocs kept them in fact subservient to the party. Because almost everyone accepted the necessity for party unity, the party was thus able to maintain a semblance of coherence. Quietly but inexorably, however, more and more power within the parties—particularly within the Democracy—came to be exercised by the leaders of blocs.

Patronage was the reason for the existence of such cliques, and the glue which held them together. Loyalty to the party was an important element in gaining office, of course. As early as 1837, and regularly thereafter, work in the party cause was mentioned as a qualification. But within that framework, office was allotted by the appointing authority fundamentally upon considerations of friendship. If one did not know intimately the person who was to make the appointment, one gathered recommendations from politicians who did. Con-

40. J. N. Carpenter to Bolling Hall, October 1, 1853, in Hall Papers.

gressmen were flooded with such letters. While federal patronage came directly from the congressmen of the appropriate party, state patronage required a more highly articulated network of relationships, since state posts were ordinarily filled by legislative election. It was out of this welter that the personal blocs grew up. The applicant desired the office. The appointing authority wished to be certain that the choice would carefully tend the interests of his benefactor. The person who had recommended the applicant desired to please both appointer and appointee, in order to use their friendship to further his own career. Since there were many offices available and many persons, especially at the state level, involved in filling them, quite extensive connections were formed quite rapidly, and any one politician owed fealty to a number of such blocs.[41]

In a political race, these debts were called in. When an officeholder was indebted to more than one of the contestants, he usually aided the one he thought would be of greatest use to him in the future. Thus the more powerful dispenser of patronage became more powerful still, and went from office to office with a lengthening chain of adherents favorable to his advancement. Intraparty struggles usually took place in the half-light of backstage maneuver.[42] Therefore, binding to oneself sufficient party workers and legislators to control conventions and caucuses was as essential to the art of politics as was oratorical power and skill in the manipulation of symbolic issues. But it must be borne in mind that, however strong a personal bloc might appear, it could unravel overnight if its adherents began to doubt the ability of its leader to deliver future rewards. Thus these blocs were ultimately sub-

41. John Clark to Arthur P. Bagby, November 13, 1837, in Governors' Correspondence: Bagby. See the various letters in the Jefferson Franklin Jackson Papers, Alabama Department of Archives and History, Montgomery, recommending Jackson for U.S. Attorney in 1849; also Leroy Pope Walker to Bolling Hall, November 1, 1851, John Gill Shorter to Hall, August 26, 1853, both in Hall Papers. The John Bragg Papers are filled with correspondence of this sort; particularly interesting is Thomas McGraw to Bragg, February 26, 1853. Other letters which illuminate the operation of the patronage system include Theophilus L. Toulmin to Arthur P. Bagby, May 6, 1838, in Governors' Correspondence: Bagby; Williamson R. W. Cobb to Clement Claiborne Clay, June 12, 1857, in Clay Papers; James E. Saunders to George S. Houston, March 6, 1846, Samuel J. Leggett to Houston, January 7, 1848, in Houston Papers; W. Medill to Samuel Pickens, September 6, 1845, in Pickens Papers, Alabama Department of Archives and History, Montgomery.

42. E.g., John Hardy to Bolling Hall, January 13, January 28, April 23, 1853, in Hall Papers.

ject to the discipline of the popular will. If a politician ran afoul of some emerging sentiment and began to lose public favor, his empire would come crashing down.

Personal blocs existed to dispense patronage but, even though their members were not fully aware of the implications of the blocs' power, nevertheless the very existence of blocs came to have an important influence upon the development of the political process. When a bloc leader became closely identified with some position or proposal, it was in the interests of his friends to sustain him ideologically in order to prevent his losing popularity, and thus office. As a result, patronage alliances came to have doctrinal correlatives. They were mechanisms whereby the political ideas of party leaders were extended deep into local communities, to the beat level and to the postal district. They informed and aroused the populace about pending bills. They disseminated particular views of unfolding events. They allowed politicians, in short, to lead men and to shape events more effectively than ever. Issues which had seemed far away and of no relevance to the voter became immediate and important to him. The electorate thus became more and more involved with political affairs, more and more fearful that erroneous decisions at the polls could threaten the continued existence of freedom, more and more convinced that the affairs debated at Tuscaloosa and Montgomery, and even at Washington City, were matters of terrible, of incomparable moment.

The power supplied him by the personal bloc was the primary source of the professional politician's influence within the party structure. He probably did not himself appreciate the extent to which he manipulated popular notions. He felt himself subservient to the voters' will, as indeed he was. But that will was formed from an interaction between the electorate's rather inchoate fears and the politician's efforts to direct those fears towards some specific man or proposal on the current scene—to name the nameless terrors of the night.[43] Because he thus gave shape to the general ideological principles upon which the parties were founded, the politician earned the applause and

43. Of course these remarks are more fully applicable to Democrats than to Whigs. The Whig politician sought to give specific form to the nameless hopes and vague aspirations of the populace more often than to its fears. Throughout this section, I have felt justified in placing the greater stress upon the practices within the Democracy, because that party was so much the more influential one in the political history of the state.

devotion of the editors and partisans. Because he had that applause, he could gain power. Because he had power, he could give office to his followers, particularly to other politicians. Because he thus built a personal bloc, he could disseminate his ideas ever more widely. And thus he rose to eminence. And, as long as he made no false step which damaged his rapport with the people's will, he entered each convention as a hero in the partisan wars, a man whose views were honored by many delegates.

It was by such methods as these that control of the parties at the statewide level fell into the hands of a relatively restricted number of professional political leaders. The course of the parties and the spoils of power were matters determined by negotiation, compromise, and occasional conflict among these leaders. The convention and the caucus were the institutions within which the conflict was fought out. The party, through its editors and its ideology, and the acceptance of the need for unity in the service of the ideology, was the institution which compelled the more or less graceful surrender of the leader whose adherents proved the less numerous. One final element in the party structure has yet to be explored, however. We must consider the question of how, at the end of the partisan power chain which led from the party leaders down through their adherents to the county and beat levels, the parties organized the electorate in support of their notions. Let us turn next to that question.

County and Beat Organization

There were three alternative ways in which candidature was established at the county level in Alabama, and they reveal once again the difficulty of reconciling the necessity to develop party machinery with the society's fear of organized power. The most frequently mentioned method of nomination is the county convention. It was used by both parties in closely contested counties because it effectively brought together the various county leaders and factions, and galvanized and focused the efforts of party workers. As we have seen, however, the populace was always suspicious of conventions, as of other institutions, because of their purported potential for oppression. In counties in which one party held a large majority, the practical justification for conventions lost its force, and the electorate therefore would not often tolerate their use. In Democratic counties there was usually no nominating mechanism at all. Candidates merely announced their availability in the press, and the electorate was permitted to choose its favorite from the field on the day of the general election. This practice occasionally permitted a Whig to sneak into office because of the fragmentation of the Democratic vote.[44] When that prospect appeared particularly threatening, a Democratic county convention might be hastily summoned, but since these counties had no tradition of county conventions, the candidates often regarded them as usurping authority rightfully belonging to the people, and refused to abide by their decision.

After 1845 some of the solidly Whig counties used a device which eliminated the danger that a member of the opposition might gain election because of the division of the majority—the direct primary. Under this system, only Whigs were permitted as candidates. In at least one primary county, Macon, and probably in most of them, Democrats were permitted to vote in the Whig election, since all of the contestants were Whigs. In such cases, the general election became a formality. The participation of Democratic voters most likely had the effect of strengthening the hand of southern rights as against unionist Whigs. It appears that the primary was most widely used in the eastern Black Belt.

The Democrats reacted with horror to this Whig innovation. Tennent Lomax wrote in 1849, "Under the burning sun of party spirit, many noxious weeds have sprung up and infected the pure atmosphere of this happy land—but this system of beat elections is the worst. It [will] . . . kill every flower of virtuous principle which blooms in our borders. . . . It is a horrid tyranny in disguise. . . . This miserable system of beat elections for candidates of a party erects party into a grinding tyranny which crushes every man who has the boldness to oppose party, or even to differ from party, no matter what wickedness party may commit." This outburst, apparently so irrational, in fact is another aspect of the social faith. Primaries, in Lomax' view, could

44. Montgomery *Advertiser*, quoted in Wetumpka *Argus*, September 1, 1841; Sidney C. Posey to Arthur P. Bagby, August 8, 1838, in Governors' Correspondence: Bagby.

strengthen parties by broadening their base of support, and thus might create permanent, resilient concentrations of power. The consequence of this process would be a party mighty enough to dragoon support from its followers—a "grinding tyranny." Just as the Whigs had resisted the convention, therefore, the Democrats refused to adopt the primary system. They echoed earlier Whig oratory in maintaining, in the words of a Benton County gathering, that "political caucuses and conventions should only be resorted to when absolutely necessary to prevent the defeat of our principles," and whenever practicable, moreover, they moved to dismantle such machinery.[45] Here again, as in so many other situations, the society tended to see institutions as engines which gathered momentum of their own and were always liable to crush under their weight the puny mortals who sought to guide them. Each party claimed in theory that it was merely a temporary expedient, formed to save the American experiment from the vicious designs of ravening despots. And to a rather startling extent, each party stood prepared to act as if the fiction were true.

Ironically, the fear that the primary would strengthen the power of party was misplaced. The party structure in the primary counties was almost as weak as in the free-for-all hill counties. Only in the competitive counties where conventions were used were lines of party authority clearly recognizable. When the entire electorate chose the party nominees, power was so widely diffused that leadership within the party apparatus seldom had the means to develop any strength. As at the state level, however, real leadership was exercised through informal structures outside the official apparatus. We shall explore this point fully later in this section.

It is worth emphasizing the extent to which the choice of legislators and local officials was directly in the hands of the people, at any rate in institutional terms. County conventions, as we shall see, were subject to considerable manipulation, but probably a majority of the counties did not use them in the nomination of officials. A large percentage of the men who sat in the legislature, therefore, owed their place to the electorate far more than to the party. It is for this reason,

45. Allen W. Jones, "A History of the Direct Primary in Alabama, 1840–1903" (Ph.D. dissertation, University of Alabama, 1964), 1–52, esp. 30, 46, 51–52.

at base, that the legislative devotees of party had so much difficulty enforcing party discipline on their ostensible allies in the assembly.[46] It was necessary to define the differences between the parties for the benefit of many legislators and thus to give immediacy to their feelings of membership in their respective political organizations. Hence, partisan resolutions were introduced and interparty bitterness deliberately exacerbated at the outset of each session. The party had to instill in its more democratically chosen representatives the knowledge that the opposition was the enemy.

Even the counties which did not nominate officials by convention, however, used conventions to fill party posts such as delegates to the state convention. A brief discussion of the structure of the county convention, therefore, would not be amiss. It was the custom simply to put a notice in the local party press stating the time and place at which the meeting was to be held, and to count anyone who showed up as a delegate. This mass meeting form of nomination continued to exist throughout the antebellum period; the rather more formal sort of convention, to which delegates were elected at beat meetings, did not come into general use in these years. Thus any reputable citizen of the proper party affiliation could participate in local party affairs if he desired to do so. But these county conventions were in some respects cut-and-dried affairs.

The county convention opened, as did the state gathering, with some delegate's being "called to the chair." The chairman, ordinarily by prearrangement, then called on a prominent citizen to "explain the objects of the meeting." That gentleman concluded his address by introducing a set of resolutions. The resolutions had been drafted in advance. Ordinarily they were written in the offices of the local party newspaper, at a meeting attended by a few representatives of the various county factions, and they usually embodied some acceptable procedural compromise.[47] They had three purposes: to pronounce upon the issues of the day, to dictate by what method the convention would proceed to nominate candidates for the various posts open, and to

46. See pp. 93–94 herein.
47. J. Withers Clay to Clement Claiborne Clay, December 16, 1844, in Clay Papers, is an account of one such meeting.

recommend means to strengthen the county party organization for the coming contest.

The last-named was the simplest task. A county executive committee—called alternatively a "committee of correspondence" or a "vigilance committee"—was named, either in the resolution itself or by the chairman. It was ordinarily composed of the partisans who, as we have seen, staffed the formal but largely powerless party administrative bodies. By thus giving these men nominal position, the party leaders insured their untiring aid during the campaign without according them the substance of power. Sometimes a politician or two was added to the committee for ballast.

There were at least three different methods of nomination. The nominees had sometimes been agreed upon among the party leaders in advance. Their names were then merely listed in the initial set of resolutions. Alternatively, the resolutions might empower the chairman to name the nominees.[48] This course probably implied that general guidelines for choosing the several candidates had been accepted by the various factions, but that the specific identity of the nominees had not been settled. But the most frequent method of nomination was the appointment of a nominating committee, which withdrew and returned some time later with the slate. The names were then accepted by acclamation. In none of these procedures did the delegates have any real voice. The nominating committee consisted of a few—three to seven, usually—prominent men. In the Coosa County Democratic convention of 1841, for instance, it was composed of the editor of the local party paper, the county's representative in the legislature, and the party's grand old man in that county, a former senator.[49] Opening the floor to nominations was a practice almost never used. The choice of a candidate was a delicate art, requiring shrewd and candid consideration of various factors which, if discussed openly on the convention floor, might be offensive or painful to some of the aspirants and their

48. *E.g.*, Wetumpka *Argus*, December 16, 1840; Montgomery *Advertiser*, June 4, December 2, 1851.

49. Respectively, William L. Yancey, A. B. Dawson (who was actually the immediate past state representative; the current representative, W. W. Morris, was absent at the legislative session), and Howell Rose: Wetumpka *Argus*, November 25, 1840. *Cf.* William R. Hallett to Arthur P. Bagby, November 9, 1839, in Governors' Correspondence: Bagby.

friends, and in any case was hardly likely to aid in conciliating all factions in the county. Professional politicians kept such important decisions in their own hands. In that sense the convention was more a ratification meeting than a party organ.

The practice of having the convention pronounce upon current issues transformed it into an important gathering, however. In this phase of the convention's work the delegates did participate. It was the custom to consider all the questions, both national and state, which were of general concern at the time.[50] On many issues, of course, the delegates were all like-minded. But when there were divisions, each side brought out its arguments, debate was joined, and the delegates then voted. If a gubernatorial contest was pending, the various contenders were praised in turn by their friends, and the convention proceeded to nominate a candidate to the consideration of the state convention, to instruct its state delegates, or to take some other action to indicate its choice. If the delegates were deeply divided, they might adopt a resolution listing various acceptable figures. They debated national affairs, and similarly announced their conclusions by resolution. It was at such gatherings as these that legislators were given instruction on pending questions.[51]

These activities were followed with the most intense interest in political circles. They were the antebellum order's form of the modern public opinion poll. Politicians determined the electoral mood on the basis of county convention votes, and adjusted their actions accordingly. If the debaters on each side of the question had been able, the public decision as expressed in a convention resolution could have profound impact on governmental attitudes. The delegates were not to be trusted to choose the nominees, but they were taken to be fairly representative of the electorate, which would have the final decision at the polls, and their choice between conflicting arguments presented to them was taken to presage the voters' choice. County conventions therefore had enormous influence in political life, but not at all in such ways as one would ordinarily suppose. They were influential not in

50. See, for example, the county convention resolutions in the Wetumpka *Argus*, July 14, September 15, November 3, November 10, 1841.

51. *Ibid.*, December 2, 1840; J. Withers Clay to Clement Claiborne Clay, April 11, 1845, in Clay Papers; Edward A. O'Neal to George S. Houston, February 6, 1848, in Houston Papers.

determining the identity of personnel but in governing the substance of policy.

The persons nominated were, in those counties which used conventions for the purpose, chosen by an exceedingly undemocratic procedure. Of course they need not therefore be unpopular. Indeed, the degree of their popularity was the single most important factor in their choice; a candidate was of little use to anyone if he could not win at the polls. It remains nevertheless true that the legislature presented the anomalous picture of a body composed partially of men chosen directly by the electorate and partially of men picked initially by a tiny clique of leaders and only, as it were, ratified by the populace. A glance at the one function performed everywhere by convention, the selection of delegates to the state convention, casts the situation into a rather different light, however. We see reflected in the county delegations the number of considerations which the men who picked the candidates for office had to balance. It was the custom to pick very large delegations: nine men were to split Coosa's one vote at the Democratic convention of 1840; twelve were chosen from Tallapoosa, fifteen from Bibb, and twenty-three from Autauga, though Tallapoosa had only one vote, Bibb two, and Autauga three. In 1851 Benton County Democrats named sixty-six delegates to cast the county's four votes![52]

The insistence of the counties upon selecting large delegations doubtless stemmed to an extent from the absenteeism; they hoped by naming many to have at least some representation. But an equally important reason was the necessity to placate the numerous factions into which every county party was split. There were familial divisions and friendship blocs. In addition, there was often intense intracounty sectionalism. And there were always many local issue groups.[53] All of these diverse elements went into the politicians' calculation as they weighed the choice of possible candidates.

In a convention delegation, all groups could have a share. But in a nomination for a governmental position, one man had to be found

52. Montgomery *Advertiser*, December 16, 1851; Wetumpka *Argus*, in 1840, *passim*.

53. M. C. Gallaway to George S. Houston, November 19, 1846, O. H. Bynum to Houston, January 22, 1847, Gallaway to Houston, February 18, 1847, June 23, 1846, all in Houston Papers; James Jackson to Bolling Hall, Sr., July 11, 1822, H. Sample to Bolling Hall, June 28, 1853, both in Hall Papers; Montgomery *Advertiser*, quoted in Wetumpka *Argus*, September 1, 1841.

who would please all, at the least most, of them. Obviously, any such man had to remain in close accord with popular sentiments and sympathies. In that sense, nominations, even in the convention counties, remained ultimately subject to the will of the electorate. And political managers could never consider the populace a docile mass, because parties were not capable of dictating the course of their members in the way that the anti-institutionalist Democrats feared. There were always alternative power centers in the society which could separate voters from the party standard, and the adherence of those alternative power centers to the party in any one election could be effected only by involving their loyalties in the canvass. In the convention counties—those in which two-party competition was keen—the populace was in fact politically volatile, and desertion of voters to the opposition was an ever-present danger. Hence candidates in the convention counties were no less solicitous of the people's views than were candidates in the one-party counties, in which the choice of officials was made directly by the people.

Whatever the qualifications we may cast around our portrait of the county convention, however, we must acknowledge that embedded inescapably in the very structure of the institution is the assumption that the party was not a union of voters but a union of politicians formed to influence voters. Party leaders saw it as a mechanism through which correct doctrine could be conveniently communicated to the masses and the masses thus energized into action. In this view the antebellum party was rather like the medieval church. It existed to redeem, not to enshrine, the laity; but if the laity ceased to heed the teachings of the church, the church would thus lose its secular substance, and therein lay the power of the laity to guide the application of the dogma.

Elections at the county level were no less fiercely partisan simply because they were in a geographically constricted sphere. When a school master differed in politics from the Sixteenth Section trustees, he could expect to be dismissed. Party hatred surfaced even over the appointment of notaries public. Party leaders paid to have voters brought in from neighboring states; election day produced knife fights; ballot boxes were stuffed; naturalized citizens, overwhelmingly Democratic, were intimidated from voting by Whigs. On one occasion, two enterprising Whigs even traveled through rural Jackson County spreading the wrong election date, and thus reducing the Democratic turnout. It is impossible to ascertain the number of close local elections whose outcome was determined by such corruption, but its existence is evidence at least of the fact that the parties fought without quarter.[54]

If the partisans were numerous, devout and active, however, real power at the county as at the state level rested with the calmer and more calculating professional politician. No single element was more important in achieving electoral success than wise and agile leadership. Indeed, the Whigs held their own with the more numerous Democrats in a number of counties only because, as the Democrats candidly admitted, Whig leaders were generally the more talented.[55] The men who became successful party leaders were often officeholders. They were concerned primarily to bring the party victory at the polls, and were alert to modify party positions to insure the broadest electoral support possible. Their greatest problem was usually bringing unity to the party by compromising factional differences. The men who arranged the compromises were the real powers in the county parties. One may call them "bosses," but the term probably carries erroneous connotations. They were less bosses than conciliators, men who kept the party together and its program in accord with the current popular mood.

The success of efforts at factional conciliation varied widely from county to county. On page 152 is a map of the state on which is represented the extent of legislative repetition in the antebellum period—that is, the ratio of the number of men elected to the legislature to the number of seats available to be filled.[56] Strange yet undeniable patterns emerge. The Tennessee Valley forms a recognizable

54. Lemuel G. McMillion to Arthur P. Bagby, March 3, 1840, John A. Campbell to Bagby, February 20, 1840, Thaddeus Sanford to Bagby, August 3, 1840, all in Governors' Correspondence: Bagby; William H. Gasque to John Bragg, December 10, 1851, in Bragg Papers; Hugh Lawson White Clay to Clement Comer Clay, May 26, 1841, in Clay Papers; Montgomery *Advertiser*, August 27, 1851.

55. Sidney C. Posey to Arthur P. Bagby, August 8, 1838, John J. Roach to Bagby, July 29, 1840, Clement Comer Clay to Bagby, January 20, 1838, all in Governors' Correspondence: Bagby.

56. I have excluded from the map the counties of Choctaw and Winston because they were created so late in the period (the former in 1848 and the latter in 1850) that they were represented in too few legislatures to establish any meaningful pattern. For a table of the various county percentages, see J. Mills Thornton III, "Politics and Power in a Slave Society: Alabama, 1806–1860" (Ph.D. dissertation, Yale University, 1974), 570–71.

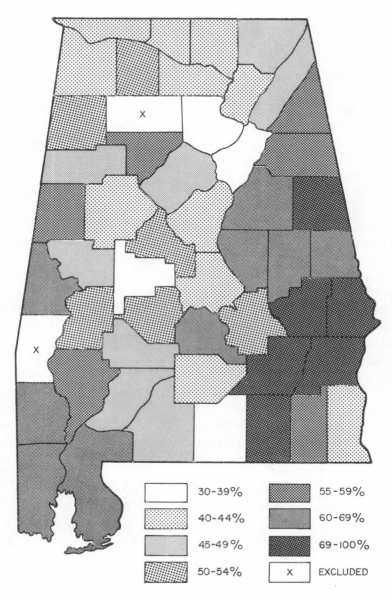

Map of Legislative Repetition

group, with its two Appalachian counties on the east separated from the rest. But the southwestern counties are grouped, as are the south-eastern ones. Three of the central Black Belt counties form a unit, and down the center of the state, Tuscaloosa, Shelby, and Autauga fall together. The east central hill counties are another bloc. Benton and Cherokee are a unit, as are Blount and Saint Clair. The observer will detect a number of other conjunctions. Traditional geographical groups fail to hold. The Wiregrass has no unity. Covington ranks as the most politically stable county in the state. But the ratio in Covington's volatile neighbor Coffee County is 76.9 percent; it changed its representatives almost whenever it had the chance. And Dale and Henry each have their own categories. The Black Belt is similarly fragmented, and the hill counties produce no pattern. The point is that the organizing principle which governs the index of political stability is neither geographical nor economic, is based neither on class nor on crop nor on wealth. It is institutional.

Communities develop political styles; that is the legacy which history leaves to political science. Styles can be altered suddenly, of course, in the crucible of war, revolution, or constitutional reform. But ordinarily they grow quietly, and the citizenry is often unaware that a style exists. Political goals have always been pursued in this fashion, the people say; it cannot be otherwise. Thus, for all its quiet growth, the grip of the style is iron when it reaches maturity. The process of development is hard to chart. Unlike constitutional development, it leaves behind not formal structures but ways of looking at the political process. Its growth is mostly by unconscious absorption of example from predecessors in one's own community and in immediately neighboring ones. But because it is of the nature of a political style that the populace does not notice subtle distinctions among communities, but assumes the general existence of its own experience and the applicability of its own notions to units with an identity of external, formal political institutions; therefore such examples do not gain great currency. They seem trivial, not worth repeating, and make progress only as apprentice politicians note the handling of a certain situation by a fellow, and silently mark the lesson down for future use. In this way some counties developed intransigent factional leaders and even situations in which politicians feared to league and contests remained at the level of every man for himself. Other counties developed traditions of compromise, leaders adept at conciliation, factions which consciously subordinated themselves to the party. And still other counties developed single-faction or machine control; it was simply the way one sought office that one sought the endorsement of some particular circle, and the power of the circle thus grew. No one thought to remark upon these differing styles; things were the way they were. For this reason the index of political stability tends to group in small geographical pockets. Such is the force of tradition and example.

The most stable counties were usually those in which power was firmly in the control of a limited group of leaders. Perry County was particularly stable. There government was committed to a very few men, associates and friends of the King family. Perry is perhaps the only county in Alabama, in addition, in which the political leadership was deeply involved with the community's wealth. The King brothers were extensive planters and railroad builders, and their allies were similarly well-to-do.[57] At the other extreme are the Creek Cession counties—the counties opened to settlement during the Gayle administration—all of which had extremely volatile political climates. The ratios of these counties range from 66 percent in Talladega to a phenomenal 83.3 percent in Randolph, the state's most unstable county. In Randolph political alliances were temporary affairs, and politicians found it almost impossible to achieve reelection. Almost the only men who had any success at office holding in the county were the Heflin family, who seem to have been aided by an extensive family connection all residing in the locality. In those Creek Cession counties lying in the Black Belt, the use of the primary for nomination may have been a factor in the rapid turnover.

Between Perry and the Creek Cession counties could be found every degree of organization in political life. In the Tennessee Valley, the same men were regularly returned to the legislature; in the southwest, they rather seldom were. Behind each county ratio stands a county style. Most often that style turns on the extent to which leaders were willing to curb their ambitions in the interests of the party. And

57. An interesting biographical account of one of the Kings, Elisha, is in Weymouth T. Jordan, *Ante-bellum Alabama, Town and Country* (Tallahassee: Florida State University, 1957), 41–61; see also *ibid*, 22–40.

with that statement we sum up the essence of partisan politics at the county level. The party was the institution within which discipline was imposed on county politics, but the amount and form of that discipline were fixed by the intangible conventions of conduct which governed the behavior of politicians one towards another.

The structure of county parties was, then, basically similar to that at the state level—conventions more responsive to manipulation than to the will of the delegates, institutions of party governance staffed by dedicated partisans and kept almost powerless, real control resting in the hands of professional politicians, and actual decision making a matter of negotiation or conflict among those politicians, with the electorate the final judges of success. We turn next to the beat, the smallest unit of civil government, to examine how the party acted at that level at which it finally reached the voters.

The beat meeting was, for all practical purposes, identical in constitution to county conventions. All who desired to attend were welcome, making it possible for the opposition, when of a mind to do so, to attempt to pack the meetings.[58] As with county conventions, resolutions drafted in advance were offered by prearrangement and, though they could be amended from the floor, were ordinarily adopted unanimously. The meeting had a lineage stretching back before the formal organization of parties, and this mode of expressing public opinion continued to be used for a great variety of purposes—to protest taxes, to investigate alleged bank frauds, to denounce pending legislation, as well as generally to announce the views of the populace upon public events.[59]

If the similarity of the beat meeting to such bodies at the county and state levels makes one think that the structure of power will also be similar, however, the beat holds a surprise. Professional politicians took a hand at organizing the meetings, of course, but at the beat level the partisans, whom we have become accustomed to finding shunted onto powerless committees, at last come into their own. To understand the nature of beat politics, we must understand the concept of

58. *E.g.,* Thaddeus Sanford to John Bragg, June – , 1852, in Bragg Papers; *Montgomery Advertiser,* October 9, 1850.

59. C. C. Gewin to George S. Houston, May 22, 1848, Felix G. Norman to Houston, November 10, 1846, both in Houston Papers; Wetumpka *Argus,* June 23, June 30, July 14, July 21, July 28, August 4, 1841.

the "two-step flow of communications" as used in political science.[60] Investigations of voter behavior in modern presidential contests revealed that the most important voting determinant was neither the speeches of the candidates nor the interpretations of the mass media, but casual contacts and conversations with friends and acquaintances. Some people in the community were deeply concerned about the election and followed it closely. They digested the conflict as it was presented in the press and, by word and attitude, conveyed their conclusions to others. These people were not so much real party workers as ordinary citizens, of every sort of background, who found themselves caught up in the passing events and communicated a sense of involvement to acquaintances. Thus were sympathies of the otherwise apathetic given direction.

So it was in antebellum Alabama. When the politicians summoned a beat meeting, the committed came; they simply cared enough to make the effort. A few of the most active and influential of these people were incorporated into the formal party apparatus, placed upon the county executive committee or sent as delegates to the party conventions. Most received no formal post. They believed, however, and in countless personal contacts they passed on that belief, to the agnostic and even to the heathen.

Line Creek was a community of farmers whose holdings generally were of only moderate size. It was located in southeastern Montgomery County, on the border with Macon.[61] Through the years it had regularly returned a Whig majority. Suddenly, during the Crisis of 1850, twelve Whigs from the area, describing themselves as "no office-seekers—but simply cotton-producers and slave-owners," dispatched a letter to their state organ, the *Alabama Journal*, denouncing it for being "rather non-committal—silent on the subject of Southern wrongs," while "fifteen sovereign States of this Confederacy are dis-

60. The theory of the two-step flow was first advanced in Paul Lazarsfeld, Bernard Berelson, and Hazel Gaudet, *The People's Choice: How the Voter Makes Up His Mind in a Presidential Campaign* (New York: Columbia University Press, 1944), 150–58. For the later development of the idea, see the Preface to the 3rd edition (1968), vi–viii, and the various studies there cited.

61. Warren Irving Smith, "Structure of Landholdings and Slaveownership in Ante-bellum Montgomery County, Alabama" (Ph.D. dissertation, University of Alabama, 1952), 120, 126; Frank M. Lowrey, "A Critical Analysis of the Relation Between Selected Factors and Party Affiliation in Montgomery County, Alabama, 1840–1860" (M.A. thesis, University of Alabama, 1964), 8, 11, 15.

franchised. . . . The agricultural and producing States of this Union are to be plundered in order to erect a stupendous system of largesses to enrich the already overgrown and pampered monopolists of the North." They therefore canceled their *Journal* subscriptions. A few weeks later a southern rights meeting attended by 1,500 persons was held in the beat and it proceeded to adopt militant resolutions. In the presidential election of 1852 the beat gave 74 percent of its vote to the quixotic effort of the southern rights forces to elect George M. Troup—the only beat in the county carried by the Troup campaign. Franklin Pierce received 26 percent of the vote, but not a single ballot was cast for Winfield Scott, who won the county, taking eight of its twelve beats. Clearly, something curious had happened to the Line Creek Whiggery.[62]

Investigation reveals the probable cause. There resided in the beat a country doctor, James W. Pierce. Doctor Pierce was a Whig, and in the course of his rounds he doubtless had occasion to discuss politics on a casual basis with his patients and their families. In 1850 he became convinced that the South stood in mortal danger from northern aggressions. His name headed the list of twelve Whigs who repudiated the *Journal.* He introduced the radical resolutions adopted by the beat meeting. He even went as a delegate to the statewide southern rights convention at the beginning of 1851 and was appointed to the powerful resolutions committee. There were only about one hundred voters in the Line Creek beat[63] so that Doctor Pierce's conversion of eleven other residents to his views created a large bloc of committed partisans among the beat's Whigs. Their own dedication brought over others, unsure or apathetic in the face of the national debate. After all, they probably reasoned, if this physician, a man who offered my family aid and sympathy in times of illness, is convinced that we are in danger, and if a group of my friends engaged in the same occupation as I am agree with him, the danger may well have substance. Thus, by 1852 there was not a single Whig in Line Creek prepared to support his party's national nominee. The conversion was complete; Line Creek

62. Lowrey, "Montgomery County," 1–28; Montgomery *Advertiser*, August 27, September 11, October 2, 1850, February 9, 1851.
63. In fact the beat cast exactly 100 votes in the 1840, 1852, 1856, and 1860 presidential contests. Between 1852 and 1856 the name of the beat was changed to Greenwood. Lowrey, "Montgomery County," 9, 16, 21, 25.

remained a solidly southern rights precinct for the remainder of the decade.

This sort of personal interaction is exactly the sort of political persuasion which political scientists have discovered among the electorate of our own day. Moreover, it explains data which have been developed by other historians. Thomas B. Alexander and his student Peggy J. Duckworth, in their analysis of Black Belt Whigs in the secession crisis,[64] discovered in every county which they studied certain beats whose behavior was as anomalous as that of Line Creek in 1850, and they suggested that the behavior of beat leaders was the principal explanatory factor. It should be emphasized, however, that such leaders were drawn from many social and occupational groups.[65] The beat might be responsive to a prominent man; such, evidently, was the relationship between the electorate of Chestnut Creek beat in Autauga County and its most famous citizen, Bolling Hall, Jr. But leaders were far more often drawn from the more humble stations; a leader was merely a man whose judgment his neighbors trusted.

The existence of the beat leadership system also explains the findings of two other students of Professor Alexander. Hoping, presumably, to find geographical correlatives of partisan behavior at the precinct level, they mapped voting returns in the neighboring and geographically quite similar counties of Lowndes and Montgomery.[66] The beats demonstrated great consistency in their respective party allegiances through time. But in Lowndes the Whig beats were, on the whole, in the southern hilly area of the county, and the Democratic beats to the north, in the Black Belt; while in Montgomery the situation was reversed, the Whiggery being stronger in the Black Belt and the Democracy in the southern hills. The point actually demonstrated

64. Thomas B. Alexander and Peggy J. Duckworth, "Alabama Black Belt Whigs During Secession: A New Viewpoint," *Alabama Review*, XVII (1964), 181–97.

65. That is the real point—though it is never very clearly made—of the various Alexander articles cited in note 58 of Chapter I, herein. The men for whom Alexander and his students gathered data were persons whose names appeared as delegates to county conventions or as participants in beat meetings or rallies. Thus the real significance of their findings is not so much that there were no important divergences between the parties as that both parties' leadership was well distributed through the various economic strata.

66. Lowrey, "Montgomery County," 8–9, 11–12, 15–16, 20–21, 24–25; Kit Carson Carter, Jr., "A Critical Analysis of the Basis of Party Alignment in Lowndes County, Alabama, 1836–1860" (M.A. thesis, University of Alabama, 1961), 7–8, 10–11, 14–15, 18–19.

by these findings is that the critical variable in determining a beat's political loyalty was not its location, and consequent economic structure, but the continuity and effectiveness of the political leadership exerted within it. Over the years the residents of the beats adopted one or the other party and stayed with it, largely because of the activities of the beat partisans, who zealously reinforced the ideological inertia of the mass of voters by countering any arguments which might have had the strength, unanswered, to have weaned away a number of adherents. Most beats, therefore, developed a partisan identity. A county often had only one or two swing beats; they determined the outcome of the election in closely contested areas.[67] Such divided beats were not without their partisans, of course, and in countless fierce engagements the partisans demonstrated beyond cavil the political utility of ideological devotion. But ordinarily the partisans had only to see to the preservation of the status quo in a beat which regularly accepted the reassurances of the men in whom it placed its faith that, whatever the opposition might aver, this year as last, all truth lay on the customary side. Beats very rarely deviated from their usual voting patterns. That was perhaps the most signal product of the fervor of the beat leaders, who never for long allowed a doubt to go unallayed.

A knowledgeable politician wrote to an officeholder seeking reelection: "Would it not be well for you to procure from some friend in the [various] counties the names of six or a dozen of the leading men in each? I do not mean of those who are known *out* of their counties as *prominent* men, but of those who at the different precincts are the *working* men at elections, and who control their little coteries of county politicians."[68] The leaders at the precinct level, then, were not the "*prominent* men" well known for their involvement in politics, but the "*working* men"—the partisans, the men convinced of the necessity of victory for the cause if disaster were to be avoided, and successful at communicating their own sense of urgency and dedication to their acquaintances. Their commitment to the faith usually precluded any facility at compromise, and they thus never rose in the party or in the government. But they were not without power. A single beat could be crucial in the decision of an election and the men who were influential

67. *E.g.*, S. G. Forbes to John Bragg, February 24, 1853, in Bragg Papers.
68. Gabriel B. DuVal to Clement Claiborne Clay, May 14, 1857, in Clay Papers.

within it might be pursued and courted by aspirants for county office. Hence many professional politicians at the local level or in the legislature owed their seats to the partisans, and were eager to please them. Statewide office was of course further removed from such influence, but even there the beat leader received respectful attention.

It was because power in the last analysis rested so heavily on these beat partisans that Alabama politics was marked to such an extent by ideological conflict, by the tendency to transmute every issue into a matter dispositive of the very existence of the Republic. It was necessary to arouse and hold the allegiance of the local leaders if the party hoped to achieve electoral success. Politicians therefore were forced to hide the strife for office under a veil of eschatological oratory. As long as they were able to do so, their popularity would reach to the beats and the branch heads. The men who cared about such things would continue to admire the state's political leadership, and would continue to say so both to the electorate who sought their guidance and to the local politicians who owed them gratitude. At the state and county levels, in short, the parties were leagues of aspirants to office, but the view from the beat transformed them into alliances of evangels, met to warn the populace against the machinations of avarice and evil.

Epilogue—Who Governed?

In the last three chapters we have encountered antebellum politics, in both its institutional and its ideological masks, at every level of its operation. It might be well before examining its death throes to summarize briefly the characteristics of its earlier virility. Alabamians were a diverse and complicated people; the foci of power in the state were appropriately manifold.

The state government was, for all practical purposes, the state legislature. Its membership was drawn from every stratum of the electorate, but until the final decade it was dominated by middle-class farmers. The very rich and the very poor were shunted into less important committees. The tax structure was distinctly weighted against wealth. The government sought actively to limit the might of corporate capital. Political leaders took this course in response to popular fears that aggregations of power were inherently threats to the autonomy of the individual citizen.

The most important group in the legislature was the group in the majority party which successfully forced partisan bitterness on the assembly's deliberations in order to insure Democratic unity in the distribution of patronage. These men viewed the party as an alliance formed primarily to gain office. They manipulated ideology to control members whose sense of loyalty to the party was less strong, who thought of the party as merely a league of citizens with similar views on public issues. Members whose commitment to the party as an organization was weak often came from counties in which the one or the other party was so fully dominant that interparty contests at the local level were rare.

Those politicians strongly devoted to the party as the mechanism whereby office was distributed were the leaders who controlled the internal party organizations, particularly among the Democrats. Patronage was to them the principal goal of partisan activity. Within the parties they formed personal alliances to influence the nominating process, and such alliances developed into articulated relationships through which the ideological positions of leaders at the higher levels were communicated to the beat. At the beat, however, the message was entrusted to the one group which was more than ordinarily convinced of its veracity, the beat partisans. These men, the foundation of party strength, galvanized the electorate into action by transmitting to the ordinary voter a sense that the issues under debate possessed apocalyptic significance. At this level the electorate held ideals rather than policy views. Primary among the ideals of antebellum Alabama was freedom, the preservation of the autonomy of the individual in the face of institutional attempts to abridge or manipulate it. The conviction of the beat partisan coupled with the verbal skills of the politician and the newspaper editor to give form and direction to these ideals. The fundamental business of Alabama politics, therefore, was the manipulation of the popular dread of manipulation.

All leadership, as Tolstoy would have it, is a kind of flight. In that sense, leadership in antebellum Alabama was an utter rout. Yet if Alabama politicians were subservient to general social ideals, they exercised leadership—at any rate, the leadership of the panderer—in transforming ideals into governmental policies. This leadership was discreet, cumulative, and on the whole predictable. It was based on the fundamental axiom of antebellum political life: give the public what it wants. But as the eunuch shapes the desires of the emperor, as the motion picture mogul gives direction to the tastes of the masses, to that extent, at least, politicians led the people of Alabama. Government, in short, was a mutual enterprise, and its institutions were designed to facilitate the cooperative effort. Each of the various elements in the society played a role. In fact, each played many roles. In seeking to describe the workings of this process, I have doubtless overly schematized it. Beat partisans were not devoid of guile in engineering the victory of their party. Politicians were often—indeed, usually—convinced of the truth of the positions which they took. But there remained subtle differences between the motivations of the two groups, and emphasis upon those differences has explanatory value.

Who governed antebellum Alabama, then? The answer is that Alabamians governed themselves. Wisdom was not always theirs, of course, nor virtue nor even benevolence. Men are condemned to mortality, and their mistakes in masses are quite as real as their mistakes as individuals. But whatever the society may have been, it was the creature of all its members. In the final decade, as antebellum Alabama moved with gathering momentum towards self-destruction, its citizens universally knew what later students have not always perceived: that they were all in it together.

Part Two **Commilitones**

Chapter IV The Bounds of Crisis

The Crisis of 1850

It has been the fashion among some students of the Crisis of 1850 to pretend that a listener, if sufficiently attentive, can hear the thunder of the guns of Gettysburg in the debate over the Georgia Platform.[1] The sounds which reach the present writer's ears, however, only emphasize that the decade which intervened between 1850 and 1860 was marked by the creation of very new social conditions, in Alabama as elsewhere. The electorate accepted in 1860 what it had rejected in 1850, not merely because affairs had taken a more serious turn at Washington but also because the voters were residents of a new world, which made new demands of them and to which they were compelled to offer new responses. The events of 1850 represent the natural consequence of the political order which we have described; by 1860, that order had been genetically altered and the secession which it produced was a sort of mutant—short-lived and ugly, but undeniably a legitimate offspring. If we are to understand how this tragic child came to be conceived, we must first examine the events which a decade earlier had led to a stillbirth.

Southern rights issues were quite late in becoming an important component of the oratory of political conflict in Alabama. During the

---

1. Professor Avery O. Craven, though of course noted as a champion of the belief that the sectional conflict was repressible, joins his irrepressible opponents in disseminating this notion: e.g., *The Growth of Southern Nationalism, 1848–61* (Baton Rouge: Louisiana State University Press, 1953), 36–141, Vol. VI of Wendell Holmes Stephenson and E. Merton Coulter (eds), *A History of the South* (10 vols.; Baton Rouge: Louisiana State University Press, 1948—).

state's first decade the citizenry was preoccupied with other questions. In the midst of the Missouri Crisis, a Huntsville newspaper had condemned congressmen for spending so much time debating the matter, since "the question to be settled is of infinitely less importance to the nation than the time consumed in their discussion" of it.[2] The Nullifiers had warned of the dangers of broad construction to the liberties of southerners, but had seldom indulged in allegations that the state's Jacksonians were consciously inimical to the region's rights. Instead, Nullifiers ordinarily claimed to be cautioning the electorate against errors into which it had been led simply by fuzzy thinking. In 1832 they had questioned the depth of Van Buren's sympathy for southern interests, of course, but they had not impugned the fidelity to their section of his Alabama supporters.

In the presidential campaigns of 1836 and 1840 references to southern rights are to be found. The supporters of White called on voters to rally to his cause on the ground that, as a southerner, he was presumably sounder on such matters than was the New Yorker Van Buren. And the Democrats in 1840 stridently proclaimed the greater reliability of the strict constructionist Van Buren than of the allegedly broad constructionist Harrison. But in each case such arguments were clearly supplementary to the main questions of the canvass—in 1836, whether Van Buren's penchant for political manipulation and his willingness to accept a convention nomination rendered him no true priest of the Jacksonian faith; and in 1840, whether the subtreasury or a new Bank of the United States was the better remedy for the depression. Moreover, in the quadrennial intervals which separated the presidential campaigns, southern rights largely dropped from political discourse. The banking issue, both in its national and in its state form, dominated the partisan debate.

In the presidential campaign of 1844, for the first time the principal question dividing the parties became whether the opposition might not be lying when it claimed to desire the South's best interests—in this case, in the shape of Texas. Texas as a political issue burst upon the state virtually without warning when President Tyler proposed to add the area to the United States. Alabamians had followed the Texans'

2. *Alabama Republican* (Huntsville), March 16, 1821.

struggle for independence sympathetically, and had contributed both soldiers and settlers to the infant republic. They were certainly pleased by Tyler's recommendation. But there had been no significant agitation for annexation, nor any sense that Texas' fate was connected with the security of the South within the Union. The antagonism to Tyler's efforts both surprised and irritated the state's voters. It seemed distinctly un-American, for it implied that the nation was not a whole, that the expansion of the South and the expansion of the nation were not the same thing. And its treatment of the South as a section conjured the frightening specter of northerners' uniting to condemn the South to minority—a status equivalent, in the view of the Jacksonian generation, to inequality. Each of the parties in Alabama therefore scrambled to proclaim itself the vanguard of the annexation movement.

In the spring of 1844, when it was assumed that the opposing presidential candidates would be Clay and Van Buren, the Whigs launched a noisy effort to prove that Clay, as a southerner, was more likely to press Texas' admission unrelentingly. When both men subsequently announced themselves opposed to annexation, each party sought to claim that its champion was nevertheless the sounder one— the Whigs because Clay was a southerner, the Democrats because Van Buren opposed annexation only as a violation of American treaty obligations to Mexico whereas Clay questioned its constitutionality. Only when the Democrats nominated Polk did the issue suddenly become clearly drawn. Thus, ironically, the harvest of Democratic victory in 1844 had been sown by both parties, with warnings similar to those of a Democratic paper, that northerners were "not content with denouncing the South and Southern institutions, and spurning us as an unclean thing, loathsome and degraded."

But they must now endeavor to weaken our political influence in the national government—aye, destroy it altogether—by cutting off this last hope for maintaining political equality . . . If Texas then is lost, we are undone—the Whigs of the North will be our masters and we will be their slaves, if we will patiently submit . . . if in the action of the national government, southern are to be postponed to northern interests and to be regarded as altogether subordinate in their nature—if the Southern States are to become vassals of the North, instead of being equal and independent members of the confederacy, we will cry loudly for disunion. Nothing, however, short of the principle of self-preservation would drive us to a measure so hateful in its character, so baneful in its consequences. It will be a matter of ultimate necessity, to which God grant that we may never be reduced![3]

In later years, Alabamians would become increasingly pessimistic about the possibility of their being accorded true equality. But at this early period, talk of disunion was still aggressively unionist in its premises. Resting as it did squarely upon the un-American character of discriminating against a portion of the polity, it demanded what it subsequently was to deny that the political system could possibly produce—full southern participation in the American adventure. The Whiggery, now stuck with an anti-Texas candidate, made the best of a bad situation by replying from the same nationalist presumptions. Its orators, who had themselves used virtually identical language in the spring, began charging in the late summer that threats of secession were unpatriotic, and that all voters who desired to preserve the Union should support Clay. The Democrats replied that the northern Whiggery was on the verge of becoming an openly abolitionist, and thus disunionist party, while the Democracy sought a genuine union. Polk received 59 percent of the state's vote, to Clay's 41 percent.[4]

Polk's election and the admission of Texas which followed eliminated southern rights from the partisan dialogue for another four years. The state's attention turned back to the events surrounding the Debt Collection Act of 1845, Terry's manipulated nomination and Martin's revolt, and later to the nation's bloody encounters in the halls of Montezuma. Still, the canvass of 1844 left an inheritance. In the first place it gave the parties their initial taste of a campaign based on the territorial question. Secondly, rather more as a result of the intervention of adventitious circumstances than not, it made the Democratic party appear somewhat more radical on southern rights than its rival. But it is important to note that—particularly in view of its Nullificationist past—the Whiggery could certainly claim no clear identification with unionism. That association was encouraged perhaps by the events of 1844, but the Whigs would not aggressively embrace unionism until the Crisis of 1850. And, as we shall discover, in the late

3. Huntsville *Democrat*, May 15, 1844; *Cf.* April 3, April 23, May 1, May 8, June 12, June 19, July 3, 1844.
4. *Ibid.*, July 17, September 11, September 25, 1844, February 5, August 6, 1845.

fifties the opposition again sought to dissociate itself from the position.[5] Probably the most portentous result of the canvass for the future, however, was the election of Dixon H. Lewis to the United States Senate.

As we have seen, Lewis had joined the Democrats in 1838 in protest against the Whigs' acceptance of the policy of rechartering the Bank of the United States.[6] In the spring of 1844, Senator King had resigned his seat in order to become minister to France, and Governor Fitzpatrick, Lewis' brother-in-law, had appointed Lewis to serve the seven months until the next legislative session. Lewis' close association with the Nullifiers a decade earlier rendered his orthodoxy suspect in the eyes of many Jacksonians. But the Democrats' embrace of the Texas crusade just at this time suddenly transfigured Lewis. His role as a champion of the cause of Polk and Texas was, as it happened, entirely consistent with the ideas which he had long preached. By the time the legislature assembled in December, therefore, even the most uncompromising Jacksonians had come to look upon him as a spokesman for the principles of the newly elected administration.[7] He was chosen easily to fill the remaining four years in King's term. At the end of 1847, though, when Lewis came up for election to a full term, things had greatly changed. Lewis, like his friend John C. Calhoun, was distinctly unenthusiastic about the Mexican War, and thus had earned the Polk Administration's enmity. And William R. King, back from France, wanted to return to his familiar post in Washington. The stage was set for perhaps the most important senatorial election of the antebellum period.

Because of the significance which southern rights questions were later to assume in politics, there is a tendency to believe that positions on such issues must have been well defined from an early date, and thus to trace supposedly consistent Unionist and Southern Rights factions far back into the history of the Democratic party. King and Lewis are sometimes pictured as the candidates of these factions. Lewis was, of course, a member of the small band of uncompromising Calhounites. But as we have seen, it is profoundly misleading to identify this

5. See pp. 360–64 herein.
6. See pp. 35–36 herein.
7. *E.g.*, Huntsville *Democrat*, December 4, 1844.

group with the south Alabama Democrats who, for the most part, took up Lewis' cause. The reaction of Alabama politicians to the Crisis of 1850 was importantly determined by the outcome of the King-Lewis contest, but more because of the personal rivalries and sectional jealousies which it engendered than because of the presumed ideological content of the election. The circumstances of Lewis' victory compelled him to seek the adoption of the Alabama Platform as a stratagem to repair his damaged position within the party. The failure of the platform encouraged the Whigs to portray Taylor as a nonpartisan southern candidate. The strength of Taylor's showing led the parties to assume equally aggressive stances on southern rights. And the efforts of each party to gain for itself identification as the only true advocate of southern rights is the essence of the politics of 1850. In order to demonstrate the validity of these contentions, we must turn to a detailed analysis of partisan maneuver in the period between 1848 and 1852.

The friction between north Alabama and south Alabama Democrats was greatly exacerbated by the collision between King and Lewis. Indeed, we are told that the hatreds thus wakened were still being felt within the party as late as 1855.[8] The sectional factions came to use bitterly descriptive labels for each other. "Hunkers," the south Alabamians called their north Alabama brethren, identifying them with the Democrats' loyalist faction in New York, and by implication reminding the public that they in the southern counties were not blindly devoted to party but realized that some issues were of such importance that they transcended the necessity for partisan success. The north Alabamians responded with the derisive appellation "the Chivalry" for their south Alabama allies; they sought to picture the southerners as an elitist group, without any mass following in their own whiggish counties, and verging in their ideas towards Alabama's *tertium quid,* the Calhounites who were the Democrats' reluctant friends in the Black Belt. The polarization was, we must again emphasize, inaccurate. The Hunkers never doubted that slavery was an essential element in south-

8. Montgomery *Advertiser,* November 21, 1855.

ern civilization which must be defended from all attack; they were simply not so quick to conclude that an attack had been launched. And the Chivalry did not endorse Calhoun's third-party notions; they were good Jacksonians who accepted Calhounite support as reluctantly as it was given and who desired party victory whenever it could be had without endangering slavery.[9] But the King-Lewis encounter did make the relatively narrow areas of disagreement between the two factions seem more significant than they had in the past. Lewis had much closer personal relations with Calhoun and his followers than did the mass of Lewis' supporters in the election, and King evidently had the quiet backing of the national administration.[10] Moreover, Lewis' candidacy brought into open alliance a group of Montgomery Calhounites led by Lewis' brother-in-law John Archer Elmore, and some of the most prominent leaders of the Chivalry led by another of Lewis' brothers-in-law, former governor Fitzpatrick. This alliance was dictated to a considerable extent by family ties, but King's forces emphasized its existence, and dubbed it the "Montgomery Regency," or alternatively the "Brass Band."[11] During the Crisis of 1850, Elmore and his friends went their own way, but the name "Montgomery Regency" continued to be applied to Fitzpatrick's clique for most of the coming decade.

Despite these seeming evidences of ideological conflict, the senatorial contest did not turn to any great extent on such questions. Lewis' relationship with Calhoun—as distinguished from Lewis' own devotion to strict construction—stretched back less than a decade, and was terminated as a result of the events of this election.[12] Lewis' victory is most importantly attributable to his vigorous appeal to party loyalty; he argued tellingly that it was destructive of the party to turn out an

9. See pp. 132–39 herein.
10. Dixon H. Lewis to Joseph W. Lesesne, April 6, 1846, in Joseph W. Lesesne Papers, Southern Historical Collection, University of North Carolina Library, Chapel Hill; J. W. Beckett to Lewis, November 25, 1847, Alexander Wells to Lewis, December 21, 1847, Thomas S. Mays to Lewis, August 11, 1848, all in Dixon H. Lewis Papers, University of Texas Library, Austin. *Cf.* John McCormick to Lewis, October 19, 1847.
11. James E. Saunders to George S. Houston, December 26, 1848, R. C. Brickell to Houston, January 16, 1849, both in George S. Houston Papers, Duke University Library, Durham. *Cf.* John S. Kennedy to Houston, February 29, 1848; and Eufaula *Democrat*, December 22, 1847.
12. John C. Calhoun to Dixon H. Lewis [internally dated to the period 1837–41], in Lewis Papers, University of Texas Library; Calhoun to Joseph W. Lesesne, February 11, 1848, in Lesesne Papers.

officeholder in favor of a challenger. Party discipline demanded that internal revolts be suppressed.[13] Still, before the balloting could achieve a choice, the north Alabamians forced Lewis to swear in writing that he would support every Polk administration measure, particularly those dealing with the war, and to announce publicly that he would take no part in the choice of the Democrats' presidential candidate in 1848.[14]

The encounter was, then, deeply divisive, not so much because of the ideological differences between the sectional factions but rather because the Chivalry resented what seemed to them cavalier disregard for the demands of the party alliance. The south Alabama Democrats were nettled by any hint that they were the party's stepchildren. The animosities thus aroused carried into the presidential campaign of the following year, and the election of 1848 in turn determined the form of Alabama's response to the Crisis of 1850.

The Chivalry strongly supported Justice Levi Woodbury for the Democratic nomination, both because they believed his views on slavery most favorable to the South and because Woodbury's son was a friend and former neighbor of Senator Lewis. Lewis evidently approved of his associates' course.[15] Probably chiefly as a way to vindicate the legitimacy of their membership in the Democracy, to demonstrate that they were not members of a fringe group as the Hunkers implied, the Chivalry sought to bind all of Alabama's national convention delegates to Woodbury by the use of a subterfuge. In a series of resolutions which have become known as the Alabama Platform, they succeeded in having the state convention instruct the delegation to vote for no candidate who would not forthrightly declare himself in favor

---

13. Dixon H. Lewis to Tandy W. Walker, September 23, 1847, John Gaddis Winston to Lewis, January 4, 1848, in Lewis Papers, University of Texas Library; John S. Kennedy to George S. Houston, February 29, 1848, in Houston Papers; Huntsville *Democrat*, October 20, 1847.

14. Dixon H. Lewis to William L. Yancey, June 29, 1848, in Dixon H. Lewis Papers, Alabama Department of Archives and History, Montgomery; James E. Saunders to George S. Houston, January 25, 1848, Felix G. Norman to Houston, January 7, January 23, February 10, 1848, all in Houston Papers.

15. Ralph B. Draughon, Jr., whose careful investigation of the origins of the Alabama Platform is most instructive ("William Lowndes Yancey: From Unionist to Secessionist, 1814–1852" [Ph.D. dissertation, University of North Carolina, 1968], 177–200), feels that Lewis played an active if discreet role in directing Woodbury's campaign in Alabama. At any rate, the senator certainly offered moral support to the movement. Woodbury's son Charles had resided in Lewis' home county of Lowndes until 1845.

of congressional protection of slavery in each territory until the moment, at the time of the assembling of the territory's constitutional convention immediately before admission, when the territory decided whether it was to be slave or free. The Chivalry believed that Woodbury would do so, but were certain that no other prominent candidate would. Woodbury, too, however, refused any such statement, and the plan collapsed. Most of Alabama's delegates accepted the nomination of Cass.[16]

The Alabama Platform came, at least for the most part, from the pen of William Lowndes Yancey, a Montgomery attorney who at this time occupied a rather equivocal position between the small Calhounite group in his city and the Montgomery Regency clique.[17] In obedience to the spirit of his resolutions, he walked out of the Baltimore convention. The rejection of the platform, he said, demonstrated that northern Democrats, who claimed to be strict constructionists, were in fact willing to compromise true constitutional principles in order to win elections. Men who would compromise on the Constitution were, he added, unsafe allies for the South; her only recourse was the formation of a wholly southern third party.[18] He returned to Alabama and began attempting to create such an organization in his home state. This effort threw him into the arms of the orthodox followers of Calhoun. In order to understand their course in 1848, we must briefly retrace our steps.

Though Senator Lewis had given pledges of loyalty to the Democratic party, the extreme southern rights men who had rallied to his

16. The essential documents on this episode are: William L. Yancey to Dixon H. Lewis, February 15, 1848, Leroy Pope Walker to Lewis, February 28, 1848, Rush Elmore to Lewis, March 2, 1848, J. L. M. Curry to Lewis, March 30, 1848, all in Lewis Papers, University of Texas Library; Lewis to Yancey, June 29, 1848, in Lewis Papers, Alabama Department of Archives and History; James E. Saunders to George S. Houston, January 25, 1848, John Bragg to Houston, February 22, 1848, Saunders to Houston, February 26, 1848, Reuben Chapman to Houston, March 29, 1848, A. C. Matthews to Houston, April 3, 1848, Saunders to Houston, April 3, 1848, Felix G. Norman to Houston, April 13, 1848, Chapman to Houston, April 13, 1848, Matthews to Houston, June 6, 1848, Saunders to Houston, June 7, July 1, July 19, 1848, all in Houston Papers; Huntsville *Democrat*, May 17, 1848; Tuscumbia *North Alabamian*, June 30, 1848; *Journal of the Convention of the Democratic Party of Alabama, Begun in the City of Montgomery, February 14, 1848*, pamphlet in Alabama Department of Archives and History, Montgomery.

17. Professor Draughon believes ("Yancey," 187) that the positive protection plank in the platform was written by John Archibald Campbell.

18. This is the substance of Yancey's highly controversial "Charleston Speech," the text of which is in the Tuscumbia *North Alabamian*, June 30, 1848.

support because of his friendship with Calhoun had made no such promises. Indeed, neither before nor after their involvement in the King-Lewis encounter did they abate their efforts to find a presidential candidate sufficiently popular to win without a party nomination. At the suggestion of Calhoun himself, their hopes in the late summer and early fall of 1847 came to center on the victorious General Taylor.[19] This circumstance caused visions of an electoral triumph to appear to the startled Whig leaders. They had never carried the state, but if any portion of the Democrats were weaned away, they would have a chance of doing so. They therefore eagerly played to the Calhounites' dream of a mass movement created outside the party apparatus by the sheer force of character and popularity of some folk hero.

In November, 1847, the Whigs arranged a "nonpartisan" mass meeting of Taylor's supporters in the Montgomery area to invite the formation of a similarly "nonpartisan" Taylor electoral ticket. In February, thirty-five of the forty-four Whigs in the legislature issued a statement calling on the state's Whiggery to abstain from participation in the national Whig convention, but instead to support the nonpartisan Taylor movement. And in March a state mass meeting named an appropriately bipartisan electoral ticket, pledged to Taylor regardless of the outcome of the Whig convention.[20] At each of these meetings the Whigs issued statements studded with phrases conjuring up the Calhounites' own personal myth: the stern Roman virtue of some unbending Old Republican lifting America above the corruption of parties and the competition for spoils to the golden past when Calhoun had received the admiration of a nation rather than of one section only. Taylor, the Whigs trumpeted, was that messiah.

A few Democrats, most notably former congressman James E. Bel-

19. John C. Calhoun to Joseph W. Lesesne, July 19, 1847, in Lesesne Papers; John A. Campbell to John C. Calhoun, December 20, 1847, in J. Franklin Jameson (ed.), *Correspondence of John C. Calhoun: Fourth Annual Report of the Historical Manuscripts Commission*, in *Annual Report of the American Historical Association for the Year 1899*, II(1899), 1152–55. *Cf.* Daniel Chandler to Jefferson Franklin Jackson, February 7, 1849, in J. F. Jackson Papers, Alabama Department of Archives and History, Montgomery.

20. A minority of the Whig leadership, more zealous in its devotion to the party, got up a series of sparsely attended conventions in the congressional districts, which sent an Alabama delegation to the national gathering. There the state's delegates divided eight for Taylor and one for Clay. See Tuscumbia *North Alabamian*, December 10, 1847, January 21, March 10, April 28, May 26, 1848; Huntsville *Democrat*, June 28, 1848.

ser of Montgomery and Samuel F. Rice, a young Talladega attorney who was to become an important scalawag during Reconstruction, rallied to Taylor's cause at once; but most orthodox followers of Calhoun vacillated. Alabama Whigs claimed that Taylor's was a nonpartisan campaign, but he himself seemed to be edging towards a formal Whig candidacy. The state Whiggery replied that Taylor was already the people's candidate, in the race by virtue of nominations made at county and state nonpartisan conventions. Now, if he received the Whig nomination, the effect was not, so they said, to bring him forward as the Whig candidate; rather, such a nomination represented merely an endorsement by the Whiggery of his nonpartisan crusade—a recognition by the Whigs that they must bow to the inevitable.[21] The explanation seemed contrived; the Calhounites waited and watched.

Thus the Calhounites were available in the early summer of 1848 when Yancey began seeking the formation of an all-southern party. It was not what they really wished, of course; their crusade was to have been national, a sort of mass realization that the South's grievances were just. Still, a southern party was better than an active campaign for the candidate of one of the old parties. It was essential that some effort be made; John A. Calhoun, a Eufaula lawyer who was the senator's nephew, explained the urgency of the case. "All the old issues," he said—the tariff, internal improvements—"are almost obsolete." The South's "present evils have been brought on us chiefly by the idea of the Northern Democracy that we will compromise." We must "disabuse their minds of this idea" by "disregarding all other questions until we have settled the Slavery question." Of course such a determination would lead to Democratic defeat, but "we are not answerable for results, but alone for the proper discharge of our duty. . . . It is the meek and timid who are fit to be made slaves of, not the bold and brave. It is true that we have a divided rank among us. But *we* have the right, and though we may now be defeated by our divisions, yet ultimately our weaker brethren must fall in with us, and we must succeed."[22] The death of the old issues, in other words, opened the door

21. Resolution 3, Resolutions adopted by the Taylor mass meeting at Montgomery, January 8, 1848, in Tuscumbia *North Alabamian*, January 21, 1848.
22. John A. Calhoun to Joseph W. Lesesne, July 10, 1848, in Lesesne Papers.

for a new organizing principle to replace the former economic one. If the slavery question were offered as that principle, though the cry might at first divide the troops, the sheer force of the righteousness of the cause would soon create a majority. The Calhounites possessed an almost Wagnerian faith in the power of "the right," and in the strength of personality it engendered in its adherents. Positive action in this particular election was essential if slavery was to become the new organizing issue. And so Yancey's pleas fell on listening ears.

By late June, the third-party movement was very near a formal debut. "Taylor's position in the late Whig convention has thrown into our arms all those Democrats who were for him heretofore," Yancey joyfully reported to Calhoun on June 21. Belser would resign from the Taylor electoral ticket, he said; Campbell in Mobile and Elmore in Montgomery were leading a number of prominent southern rights spokesmen to the cause. They had even set the date for a state convention—July 12—and were planning to bring out a ticket of Littleton Tazewell and Jefferson Davis.[23] But just at this moment, with optimism running high, the fatal blow fell.

In early July Yancey received from Dixon H. Lewis a lengthy letter which ended the third-party campaign in 1848 and laid the foundation for the bitter struggle of 1851 within the Southern Rights movement. Lewis refused all aid to Yancey's effort. He attributed it all to Yancey's pride, wounded in the Baltimore debacle. Lewis announced that, since he held office at the hands of the Democratic party, he could not refuse to support its nominee, not because his own views coincided with those of Cass, for they did not, but solely because Cass was a Democrat, nominated with southern votes. Moreover, Lewis added, Yancey could effect his views more easily from within the Democracy. "You have given me the names of several of the most respectable men in the State [as supporters of the third party]. I know none more so. They are now all Democrats (anti-Hunkers) and with half the activity and zeal required to start a new Party, they might, to any desirable extent—in spite of [George W.] Gayle, [William R.] King, etc.—control the party to which they now belong. Cut off these gentlemen, however, into a

23. William L. Yancey to John C. Calhoun, June 21, 1848, in Jameson (ed.), *Correspondence of Calhoun*, II, 1177. (The name "Mayo" in the text is presumably a misreading for "Mays" and refers to Thomas S. Mays.)

separate party—and how powerless! With all due respect to them and to you, I doubt if they could carry a single County in the State." [24] The letter left the third-party advocates stunned. Lewis did not understand the new situation. He still imagined that Senator King and King's relative and campaign manager George Gayle were the great enemies. He still believed that winning was the chief end of political activity. In short, he was a victim of that most debilitating of diseases, the spirit of party.

Without Lewis' support, the third-party movement could not continue. Most of its potential recruits would refuse to join if by doing so they damaged Lewis' position. And so the July 12 convention was never called. Belser remained a Taylor elector. Most of the southern rights men drifted listlessly through the fall campaign. Yancey denounced Cass as an advocate of popular sovereignty in the territories, but did not endorse Taylor. Most of the Calhounites took no public position, though many probably voted for Taylor. Two weeks before the election, Senator Lewis died. But his quiet murder of the third-party movement in July had repercussions long after he was buried. Southern rights men already distrusted parties. But after Lewis they began to distrust politicians. Few would ever again, without misgivings, commit their cause into the hands of a political leader.

The next step in the unfolding of the Crisis of 1850, however, has its roots in the reaction of the regular Democrats, as opposed to the southern rights men, to the election of 1848. At the end of 1847, when the threat of a southern rights defection from the party had seemed real, the Democrats had been fearful. In response to the mass Taylor rally of January 8, 1848, the Democrats organized a meeting of their own at the end of the month at which they had some of their young southern rights firebrands who were still loyal—Yancey, Adam C. Felder, Henry Churchill Semple, Rush Elmore—denounce the Taylor movement, on the perfectly correct ground that no one in fact knew what Taylor believed, that the enthusiasm for him was founded solely upon the circumstance of his being a large slaveholder. A Whig legislator confessed that this meeting had arrested the threat to the Demo-

---

24. Dixon H. Lewis to William L. Yancey, June 29, 1848, in Lewis Papers, Alabama Department of Archives and History, Montgomery. See also Yancey to Lewis, July 6, 1848, in George Petrie Papers, Auburn University Library, Auburn.

crats, and that party lines were now firm. And A. B. Moore was able to report from the western Black Belt that the Taylor fever there was subsiding. The Democrats' professional managers, who about Christmas time had been worried, were now confident. From Mobile, Montgomery, and the Tennessee Valley came assurance that any sound Democrat would carry the state.[25]

By the summer, trained Democratic observers were even committing themselves to figures. A Florence editor put Cass's majority at seven thousand. A hill county legislator ventured eight thousand. Wily former governor and senator Clement Comer Clay actually expected a margin of ten thousand. Nor were south Alabamians less optimistic. Former congressman James Lafayette Cottrell, living in Lowndes in the heart of the supposed defection, pronounced the state absolutely safe for Cass, and said that he found Taylor quite unpopular because of his refusal to clarify his position. A Wilcox County resident expected Cass to win by a very large majority, and even looked for Whig desertions to the Democracy. A powerful Mobilian gave similar assurances. And by August, one of Cass's most bitter opponents, the Calhounite leader Thomas S. Mays, reluctantly conceded Cass the edge.[26]

There was thus an enormous gap between the Democratic leaders' considered expectations and the extraordinary reality when the returns were received: 31,173 for Cass and 30,482 for Taylor, a majority of 691 votes, so thin that a recount might actually see it disappear. What

25. Eufaula *Democrat*, January 26, 1848; Huntsville *Democrat*, August 30, September 6, 1848; Thomas M. Peters to George S. Houston, January 27, 1848, James E. Saunders to Houston, January 25, 1848, Felix G. Norman to Houston, January 15, 1848, Edward A. O'Neal to Houston, February 6, 1848, all in Houston Papers; A. B. Moore to Dixon H. Lewis, January 28, 1848, in Lewis Papers, University of Texas Library. Rush Elmore was appointed by Pierce as a federal judge in the Kansas Territory. Both Felder and Semple were cooperationists in 1860, and became prominent scalawags during Reconstruction. It is worth noting that, whereas almost no members of the old Chivalry became Republicans, a not inconsiderable number of the extreme southern rights men of 1850 did so.

26. M. C. Gallaway to George S. Houston, June 25, July 23, 1848, Oakley H. Bynum to Houston, July 12, 1848, Clement Comer Clay to Houston, July 19, 1848, James Lafayette Cottrell to Houston, May 13, 1848, James E. Saunders to Houston, June 7, July 1, 1848, all in Houston Papers; J. F. Dortch to Dixon H. Lewis, July 23, 1848, Thomas S. Mays to Lewis, August 11, 1848, both in Lewis Papers, University of Texas Library. To the same effect are: Felix G. Norman to George S. Houston, July 27, 1848, James A. Cody to Houston, April 30, 1848, A. C. Matthews to Houston, June 6, 1848, Clement Comer Clay to Houston, August 3, 1848, all in Houston Papers.

had happened? A part of the answer lies in abstention. The poll in 1848 was more than 1,700 votes less than that of 1844 and almost 900 less than in 1840, despite nearly a decade of population growth. In mid-summer the postmaster at Tuscumbia, though confessing that he did not know of a single Democrat who would vote for Taylor, still had complained of a "great apathy among our politicians" and "a kind of unfixedness among the people." The most persuasive explanation for this "unfixedness" was offered by a Democratic precinct worker in a hill county beat with the colorful name of Buzzard's Roost. In February he had reported his beat safe. In December he admitted, "How wofully [*sic*] we were mistaken in the result of the presidential election. . . . I counted 23 Democrats that did not come to the election [in the precinct] and only three Whigs, and I then give [*sic*] it up. Not a single Democrat that voted here voted for Taylor, but they don [*sic*] the mischief by not voting at all. I believe Alabama is as democratic as she ever was, but there was [*sic*] so many misrepresentations of Cass, being a northern man and would turn out like Van Buren, was what done the business [*sic*]." [27]

North Alabama farmers were loyal party men, but the doubts of some Democratic leaders, though not sufficient to make the masses Whigs, were sufficient to make them fear that they were being "slickered." Throughout antebellum history, one of the principal sources of the yeomanry's resentment against the outside world was the possibility of being "slickered." And so when the off chance that Cass might be a crypto-abolitionist was pointed out, they were willing to stay at home. Of course, the central question in the situation is why these small farmers should have so feared emancipation, but we must postpone our consideration of that problem for a bit.

Abstention, then, was the chief difficulty in north Alabama. But coupled with it was what appears to have been a not inconsiderable desertion of Black Belt Democrats to Taylor's cause. In solidly Whig Montgomery County, for instance, Clay had led Polk by 180 votes in 1844 and Scott led Pierce by 144 votes in 1852, but in 1848 Taylor beat Cass by 469 votes.[28] The Democratic leaders who had made

27. J. J. Bell to George S. Houston, July 18, 1848, William Dickson to Houston, February 18, December 17, 1848, all in Houston Papers.
28. The figure for 1852 does not include 98 votes cast for Troup.

north Alabamians doubt were, of course, for the most part south Alabamians, and there the slavery question was even more potent. In both sections, therefore, the foundation of Taylor's unexpected strength was the slavery question, and the point was not lost on politicians in either party.

A subsidiary point, however, does seem to have been lost, at least for a time, in the shock of Taylor's showing. Taylor had not been offered as a candidate who would defend the South from northern aggressions but as a candidate who would end the aggressions. The Whig rhetorical line had been that Taylor's universal popularity would unite Americans again, would end intersectional bickering; because he was identified with no section or faction, having held aloof from politics previously, he could "afford us that unity and confidence which will make us harmonious at home and respected abroad" and could allow himself to be guided solely "by the lights of the Constitution and the highest example of the republican Presidents who aided in forming it." [29] Such statements were directed at a wider audience than merely the Calhounites. They resonated with perhaps the most fundamental of all chords in Alabama, the longing to be left alone. The vote for Taylor, therefore, to the extent that it was a response to the oratorical appeals in Taylor's behalf, was not a call for an active defense of slavery, but was a request to be left in peace with slavery. The frantic Democratic politicians did not see the distinction until it was too late for them—until, in fact, the spring of 1851. The Whigs had gotten the point somewhat earlier, but even they had at first been somewhat confused about the nature of the issue they were riding. And so the parties' discussions of national questions, particularly during 1849 and 1850, became almost entirely a southern rights shouting match.

The Whigs captured control of the state Senate in the legislative elections of August, 1849—the first time the party had ever controlled either house of the assembly. This canvass turned not on national issues but on the question of creating a system of private banks in the state to supply the void of banking facilities and the deficiency of currency which had existed during the preceding decade. Whig support of the proposal gave them most of their victories. Still, it appeared to

29. Tuscumbia *North Alabamian,* December 10, 1847.

dazzled Whig leaders as if Democratic blunders had presented them with both a national and a state issue on which to build a majority. They did not propose to allow either question to rest.

In both Alabama and Washington, members of the state's Whiggery adopted an increasingly aggressive tone on the pending California question and related matters. Alabama's most prominent Whig congressman, Henry W. Hilliard, told the House towards the close of the year:

A brave, generous, high-spirited people, who comprehend their rights and who know how important it is for free States to resist the first encroachment of tyranny, in whatever shape it may come, will under the pressure of a great necessity, break off an alliance which employs the machinery of a common government against them, without pausing to cast up its value. . . . It is of no avail that you point to a future of convulsion and blood which lies beyond the hour of our separation. Anything is to be preferred to an ignominious submission to tyranny—tyranny which revels in the mere wantonness of its strength. Men resign life rather than submit to that which robs life of its value.

And he added a final warning to his northern colleagues. "If you will not regard the remonstrances of a people now thoroughly roused by the unjust measures with which they are threatened, my mind is made up to stand with the people of that oppressed section of the Union in resistance to your measures and your power." [30] These sentiments would have been radical in the mouth of any representative, but in the mouth of Henry Hilliard—a careful conservative who was Alabama's closest analogue to Daniel Webster—they were simply extraordinary.

The Democratic party, meanwhile, was faced with the beginning of a rout, and its leaders were in despair. The party's state organ, the Montgomery *Advertiser*, warned, "The whig party of Alabama has been for years on the advance, while ours has been retrograding. So long have the democrats been in power in this State, that they have not perceived the fearful inroads of the opposite side." [31] But those inroads were now coming home to them. They had been forced to dump their incumbent governor, Reuben Chapman, after only a single term—the

30. *Congressional Globe*, Appendix, 31st Cong., 1st Sess., Vol. XIX, Pt. 3 (originally Vol. XXII, Pt. 1), 33–34 (speech of December 12, 1849). Hilliard reiterated these opinions in equally strong terms on February 14, 1850: *Congressional Globe*, 31st Cong., 1st Sess., Vol. XIX, Pt. 1 (originally Vol. XXI, Pt. 1), 358–61. *Cf. Alabama State Gazette*(Montgomery), July 21, 1849.
   31. Montgomery *Advertiser*, October 24 [?], 1849.

only time in antebellum history that an incumbent Democrat was denied a second nomination. They had replaced Chapman at the head of their ticket with Henry W. Collier, whose views on the bank question were, without qualification, Whig; by doing so they had been able to retain control of the legislature, but only barely.[32] And now they found themselves faced with the politically dangerous prospect of being "outniggered" by the opposition on national issues. The final blow came in the form of the election of Jeremiah Clemens to succeed Dixon Lewis in the U.S. Senate.

The warning from the *Advertiser* quoted in the preceding paragraph had been issued in connection with a plea to all Democratic legislators to caucus and present single candidates for the Senate seats, both of which were to be filled at the 1849 session of the assembly. With its greatly diminished legislative majority, the Democracy could not afford any defectors. A caucus was accordingly held, and Benjamin Fitzpatrick was chosen to fill Lewis' place. Fitzpatrick, the head of the Montgomery Regency, had been given the interim appointment after Lewis' death, and the choice had received the most impassioned and vitriolic denunciations in north Alabama. Indeed, it had been one of the principal causes for Governor Chapman's political downfall.[33] In the light of the past controversy, some twenty north Alabama Democrats refused to accept the caucus decision, and nominated Clemens, a young Huntsville attorney.

Fitzpatrick was nevertheless only two votes from victory when the

32. Chapman's and Collier's differing views on banks may be found in *House Journal*, Sess. of 1849–1850, pp. 25–26, 200–217. Of course Joshua L. Martin had been limited to one term, but he was not a regular party candidate.

33. On the appointment of King to succeed Bagby, see Dixon H. Lewis to Reuben Chapman, June 16, 1848, in Lewis Papers, University of Texas Library; Reuben Chapman to George S. Houston, June 23, 1848, M. C. Gallaway to Houston, June 25, 1848, James E. Saunders to Houston, July 1, 1848, Robert C. Brickell to Houston, July 4, 1848, Oakley H. Bynum to Houston, July 12, 1848, Saunders to Houston, July 19, 1848, Gallaway to Houston, July 23, 1848, Felix G. Norman to Houston, July 27, 1848, Clement Comer Clay to Houston, July 29, August 3, 1848, Chapman to Houston, August 6, 1848, A. C. Matthews to Houston, August 7, 1848, Gallaway to Houston, September 4, 1848, all in Houston Papers. On the appointment of Fitzpatrick to suceed Lewis, see M. C. Gallaway to George S. Houston, November 2, 1848, Clement Comer Clay to Houston, undated postscript to a letter the body of which is missing [internally dated to mid-December, 1848], Joseph A. S. Acklen to Houston, November 28, December 10, 1848, Daniel Coggin to Houston, December 24, 1848, James E. Saunders to Houston, December 26, 1848, David P. Lewis to Houston, January 8, 1849, Robert C. Brickell to Houston, January 16, 1849, all in Houston Papers.

assembly adjourned for the evening after three ballots. That night the Whigs caucused. What happened at the caucus became obscured in recrimination in later years. It appears, however, that Clemens authorized L. Ripley Davis, a Tennessee Valley Whig legislator, to assure the caucus that he was favorably disposed towards Taylor because Taylor was a southerner. The caucus demanded something in writing and Clemens agreed to write a letter to a friend, Thomas Wilson, stating that he intended to offer no factious opposition to the Taylor administration, and would stand with Taylor against free-soilism. Clemens' managers in the caucus may have added even stronger assurances without his knowledge. Later, after Taylor had revealed his surprisingly nationalist position on the sectional issues, the Wilson letter became useless to the Whigs, but the southern rights forces, angered by Clemens' support for the Compromise of 1850, eventually picked up the charge of a deal in distinctly slanderous terms and made it a major issue against the senator.[34]

Whatever in fact transpired at the caucus, the next morning the Whigs withdrew their candidate, and fifty Whigs joined with seventeen north Alabama Democrats to send Clemens to the Senate. The Montgomery *Advertiser* moaned that "in the defeat of one of these [caucus] nominees, the Democratic party itself has been overthrown . . . and we trust that we may be false prophets when we predict that it is a blow from which our party will, if ever, take years to recover. We have been torn loose from our moorings; we have neither rudder, chart nor compass; the old and time-honored landmarks of our party have been bleared over and blotted out, and our glorious old ship lies at the mercy of a coalition."[35] It was clear to the Democratic leadership by the end of 1849, therefore, that their plight was desperate and called for immediate action.

The course which they thereafter pursued was clever. Throughout the deepening sectional crisis, the Democracy had sought to outdo the

34. Vergil L. Bedsole, "The Life of Jeremiah Clemens" (M.A. thesis, University of Alabama, 1934), 22–29, contains a convenient summary of the conflicting evidence on the episode. *Cf.* Montgomery *Advertiser*, October 21, 1851, March 2, March 23, March 30, 1852, and Huntsville *Democrat*, quoted in Montgomery *Advertiser*, October 28, 1851.

35. Montgomery *Advertiser*, December 5, 1849. Fitzpatrick had also received strong opposition from a north Alabamian, L. Pope Walker, within the caucus: Montgomery *Advertiser*, September 14, 1853.

Whiggery in condemning northern aggressions. Indeed, this competition had to some extent contributed to exacerbating the crisis itself, by driving the state's spokesmen to extreme and intransigent oratory. But at the beginning of the legislative session of 1849, the Democrats ceased including partisan digs in their pronouncements and instead began calling loudly for all southerners, regardless of party affiliation, to unite against the common foe. The plea was hardly an unusual one, of course; many southern leaders had made it in the preceding months. But it gave promise of being particularly useful to the Alabama Democracy. First of all, it pleased the Calhounites, who were still flirting with the Whigs; for a central tenet of the Calhounite faith was a condemnation of parties. But more importantly, it placed the Whigs in the position of having to live up to their professions; for during the 1848 campaign, needing Democratic votes, the Whigs had frequently called on southerners to rally to Taylor's cause without regard to party, in order to suppress sectional agitation. Yet, if Whiggery did unite with its opposition on the question, it would abandon the issue through which it hoped to carve out an electoral majority.

The winter of 1849–1850, therefore, is marked by repeated calls for unity and by quiet but pervasive partisan maneuver. There was doubtless less overt partisanship during this session of the assembly than at any other session during the existence of the two parties. Indeed, the lack of party conflict was a matter of widespread comment. The only true party debate after the election of Clemens occurred towards the end of January over a patronage question. And some Democrats even sought to suppress that debate on grounds of the necessity for southern unity.[36] There was, however, never any real possibility of the formation of a grand coalition. Party leaders on each side were proceeding with utmost caution in order to retrieve from the session the maximum factional advantage.

The issue around which the parties did their careful dance was the proposed Nashville convention. Early in the session, the state's congressmen had sent from Washington a letter informing the legislature that northern fanaticism had thus far prevented the selection of a Speaker of the House. In response, a state House committee prepared to re-

36. *Ibid.*, January 23, February 27, 1850; *Senate Journal*, Sess. of 1849–1850, p. 491.

port resolutions endorsing the Nashville meeting and providing for the election of the delegates to it. Before the committee could report, however, the Whigs obtained the House's adjournment and thereafter prevented the body from reassembling, for lack of a quorum, until the national House had time to effect the choice of a presiding officer. Then the resolutions were returned to committee for redrafting in light of changed circumstances. A new effort to get House endorsement for Nashville was gutted by a committee headed by the powerful Montgomery Whig Thomas Hill Watts, who quietly inserted a provision that the state's participation in the Nashville convention would become operative only if Congress enacted the Wilmot Proviso. These resolutions were sent on to the Senate, where a strengthened set by John A. Winston was substituted. The Winston resolutions were returned to the House when less than a week remained in the session, however, and twenty-three Whigs joined fourteen Democrats in sending them to burial in a committee, in order to act on a mass of important pending legislation.[37] Thus no single set of resolutions was passed by both houses.

Perhaps the source of all this complicated maneuvering was the Whig fear of popular election of the Nashville delegates. A nonpartisan canvass for office, with both parties espousing the same principles, would completely eliminate the possibility of Whiggery's building a majority with the issue. And if the election resulted in the choice of a substantial number of Democratic delegates, the Democrats might even succeed in stealing the issue altogether. The Whigs were able, instead, to force the choice of Nashville representatives by a method which contained no such threat. Near the end of the session, when it had become evident that the legislature would not order a popular election, all of the members of the assembly were summoned to an informal meeting. There a bipartisan slate of delegates with no official standing was chosen, two Whigs and two Democrats from each congressional district, and four Whigs and four Democrats at large. Shortly thereafter the assembly adjourned, with the partisan status quo on the sectional question still intact.

At the end of February, however, for the first time since the preced-

37. Montgomery *Advertiser*, February 20, 1850.

ing November, the press of both parties suddenly blossomed with partisan attacks once more. The Compromise had made its appearance, and the parties had commenced to adjust their positions accordingly. The Whigs who had been appointed Nashville delegates began to have second thoughts. In the event, half of the Whigs did not attend, and of the nine who did, six voted against Robert Barnwell Rhett's address. On the other hand, thirteen Democrats were present, only two of whom opposed the address.

It is essential to note, however, that the Compromise of 1850 was probably not so much the cause as it was the trigger of this reorientation. Political leaders were certain to regard as weak any position which necessitated a considerable exertion merely to maintain the status quo. Strong positions pay dividends. Throughout the winter, therefore, the Whiggery was actually seeking a way to differentiate itself from its opposition, leaving that opposition on the unpopular side. The Compromise provided an opening for the graceful execution of just such a maneuver. As the Whigs were well aware, the popular issue in 1848 had been the prospect of achieving sectional peace, of ending the irritation of the slavery wound. But the intervening party shouting match had so escalated oratory that the politicians now seemed to be saying that peace could be achieved only through war, at the very least a war of words. This proposition was a form of double-think for which the masses were not yet prepared. The Whigs, knowing how they had won in 1848, quickly sensed the difficulty. The Compromise thus fell like manna from Washington. It would be a final adjustment of all outstanding issues; after its passage, there would be no need for further debate or agitation, and at least a substantial portion of the credit would belong to Mr. Clay and his Whigs.

Not all of the Whig leaders accepted this reasoning. The party's state organ, the *Alabama Journal*, did not finally acquiesce in the Compromise until September, when word reached Montgomery that the last of the Compromise bills had been passed. But throughout the spring and summer, while Whig politicians busily explained and rationalized their earlier statements, the movement of the party press proceeded inexorably. In August only two Whig papers remained opposed to the Compromise and only four Democratic papers remained favorable to it; in the fall there was one defection from each group, leaving the Marion *Commonwealth* as the only southern rights Whig paper, and the Democratic presses in the three Tennessee Valley cities of Florence, Athens, and Guntersville alone in their unionism.[38] And the Whig promise of a restoration of national amity had the same galvanic effect which it had had two years before. Whig politicians once again found themselves riding the crest of a wave.

The point, of course, is not that the passage of the Compromise was unimportant. If it had been defeated, the Whigs would have come scrambling back to their earlier southern rights position. The point is rather that the startling effect which the Compromise had on Alabama politics resulted from the fact that it allowed the Whigs both to assume a position consistent—at any rate, acceptably consistent—with the line they had recently been pushing and at the same time to assume a position clearly differentiating them from their opponents. Whigs could not have announced suddenly that the threat of northern aggression was not real; but they could and did proclaim that the threat, though real, was about to be arrested. In this sense, the Compromise represented total southern victory. It is a curious sense to be sure, for the Democratic press was certainly correct in asserting that the 1850 measures represented not a compromise, but an abandonment by the South of certain of her rights in hopes of being left with the remainder—what was to be known in another century as appeasement.[39] But for the Whigs, the actual provisions of the Compromise were unimportant; the victory lay in its passage—that is, in the prospect of ending sectional bickering, of being left in peace.

When the Whigs assumed their "southern rights with peace" ground, they left the Democrats in possession of the "southern rights and resistance" position. The Democrats soon began to find the height a difficult one to hold. In the first place, the three Tennessee Valley Democratic papers which supported the Compromise proved to be the tip of an iceberg. It became apparent that, despite the best efforts of the party leadership, a massive defection was underway in north Alabama. Even the most vigorous Democratic unionist was prepared

38. *Ibid.*, August 21, October 16, December 4, 1850, January 1, 1851. And by the spring the Florence *Gazette* was the sole Democratic pro-Compromise paper (see Montgomery *Advertiser*, March 5, 1851).
39. *Ibid.*, May 29, 1850.

for resistance if it were necessary,[40] but in those circles it no longer appeared necessary. By the thousands, north Alabama Democrats trooped into the Whig ranks during the fall, dragging their politicians behind them. In the second place, the Whigs received their new allies carefully, placed them in positions of responsibility and, when the time came to choose legislative tickets, made the selections on an apparently nonpartisan basis. Thus, by the time of the second Nashville convention in November, it was evident to loyal Democratic leaders that the disaster which they had barely avoided the year before, threatened again.

In contrast to the twenty-two delegates who had come to Nashville six months earlier, only eight Alabamians attended the sequel. The Democratic party was reconsidering its stand. Strains had been manifest ever since the Whig recantation in February. During the spring, the Democrats had been forced regularly to reiterate that the first Nashville meeting was not secessionist but merely consultative, intended to gather public opinion.[41] But the desertions following the passage of the Compromise forced even more strenuous efforts. By the winter, the leadership had abandoned its effort to unite all southerners on sectional grounds, had frankly embraced the old party standard, and was proclaiming that Unionism was merely a Whig plot to get into power and enact the American System. Most of the Democratic press had gone too far in its advocacy of southern rights simply to desert the cause. They were able to adjust to realities, however, by calling for a variety of mild remedies, such as commercial nonintercourse. The party's state organ admitted that it had been secessionist only a few months before, but simply stated that secession could not be achieved, and that therefore it sought cooperation with all who advocated any form of resistance, however weak.[42]

40. M.C. Gallaway to George S. Houston, December 31, 1848, David P. Lewis to Houston, January 8, 1849, W. T. Minor to Houston, January 12, 1849, Robert C. Brickell to Houston, January 16, 1849, all in Houston Papers.

41. See the county convention resolutions in the Montgomery *Advertiser*, April 17, April 24, May 1, May 15, May 29, 1850.

42. *Ibid.*, October 30, December 4, December 25, 1850, January 22, January 29, February 5, February 12, March 26, April 30, 1851. *Cf.* William R. de V. King to Bolling Hall, November 19, 1850, A. B. Moore to Hall, November 15, 1850, Walter H. Crenshaw to Hall, January 11, 1851, all in Bolling Hall Papers, Alabama Department of Archives and History, Montgomery; King to Thomas D. King, November 21, 1850, William R. de V. King Papers, Alabama Department of Archives and History, Montgomery.

By the time the legislative contest got underway in the spring, then, the form of the encounter was already clear. The Unionists insisted that the Southern Rights[43] forces were at heart secessionists, so that all who opposed secession were Unionists. The Southern Rights party said that the Unionists were unwilling to resist northern aggressions in any way, so that all who did not simply glory in the terms of the Compromise were Southern Rights men. And as to the former party issues, the Unionists insisted that the sectional crisis forced their renunciation, at least temporarily, while the Southern Rights group reiterated that Unionism was a front for Whiggery. Thus each party sought actively to gather into its fold as many as possible of the moderates, and particularly of the north Alabama Democrats, whose attachment to the Unionists was assumed to be uneasy. The Southern Rights forces lost the first battle; the election was an overwhelming Unionist triumph. But in the end the Southern Rights Democrats won the war, for when the new legislature convened, most of the Unionist Democrats were maneuvered into breaking with their Whig allies and reuniting with their Southern Rights enemies upon the old Democratic platform.

Meanwhile, however, in the spring the genuine southern rights advocates broke with the Southern Rights party because the Democratic politicians who were the party's leaders had adopted a policy of only moderate resistance. The genuine southern rights men refused to cease recommending that the South at least prepare for eventual secession. They held a state convention in Montgomery in February and repudiated the newly softened Democratic position. The Democratic leadership had sought to keep lines open to its southern rights element even into the new year.[44] Former governor Arthur P. Bagby actually went as a delegate to the state southern rights convention, and there got himself appointed chairman of the resolutions committee. He reported a platform which—as was the ordinary practice of Democratic politicians—took quite strong ground in its preamble, but in the resolutions demanded no real action; in this case, the resolutions merely

43. I have been rather at a loss to fix upon a terminology which would distinguish the Southern Rights Party—the Democracy without its north Alabama wing—from authentic advocates of the theories of southern rights. I have, rather arbitrarily, capitalized the political faction to distinguish it from the faith.

44. Montgomery *Advertiser*, January 1, January 8, 1851.

called for adopting whatever remedy was suggested by the proposed southern congress, which the Nashville convention had called to meet in Montgomery.

True southern rights men had been fooled too often by the politicians' device of coupling strong preambles and weak resolutions, however. On this occasion, they outmaneuvered the professional manipulators. George W. Gayle, the state's most extreme southern rights advocate, offered a substitute calling for secession, either together with other states, or alone if necessary. This sentiment was so radical that Yancey's substitute, offered next, looked like a compromise, and was adopted overwhelmingly by the delegates. It announced that secession was now a mere question of time, and called on Alabama to begin preparations for it, promising to "exert all the agencies in our power—political, industrial, commercial, social and educational—to prepare the State for that crisis which federal policy, perverted and distorted by the anti-slavery spirit, has forced us to contemplate."[45]

In terms of concrete action, Yancey's platform implied exactly the sorts of policies that the Democrats were now advocating—commercial nonintercourse with the North, direct trade with Europe, and the development of southern industry. But the Democratic leadership, having belatedly recognized the profound desire of the electorate for sectional peace, was offering these proposals as remedies which would be sufficient to rebuke the North into silence. Yancey rather envisioned them as steps preparatory to war. He held out to the voters the prospect of protracted struggle and turmoil.

The Democratic party could not afford to have its program—a path to an end to agitation alternative to endorsement of the Compromise—identified with continued crisis. Still, an effort was made to hold the allegiance of the southern rights men. The *Advertiser* suggested that Yancey's resolutions were not intended as a platform for the southern rights movement in Alabama but as an expression of the delegates' opinions. Other views, it said, were welcome in the crusade. But the leading delegates at the convention replied with a public statement affirming that the resolutions were indeed a platform,

45. *Ibid.*, February 19, February 26, 1851.

and that all who differed were no true advocates of the faith.[46] An open break followed soon thereafter.

At first, some orthodox Democrats were pleased to see the southern rights zealots embrace so suicidal a position. Senator King laughed that "Yancey, George Gayle and company will be reduced to the necessity of seceding alone," since the Montgomery Platform had alienated so many "who, not understanding the object they had in view, had been acting with them." Their extreme statement had, he said, "subjected them to ridicule."[47] But such badinage was quickly silenced as the internal struggle grew more and more heated. Throughout the spring, the Democrats were forced to devote much of their attention to the tiny dissident group rather than to the Unionist opposition, both because it was essential for the Democracy to distinguish its position from that of the extremists and because a southern rights attack on politicians who were regarded on the national scene as southern rights advocates was especially galling. By late April, the controversy had become so intense that Yancey purchased part ownership of a small Montgomery weekly, the *Atlas*, and lent his pen towards making it the organ of the fire-eaters, with vitriolic assaults on Democratic officeholders and on the regular party press. Evidently the squabble was exacerbated by mutual suspicions created during the 1848 presidential campaign.[48]

The difficulty was papered over in June. The second state southern rights convention, meeting in Montgomery in mid-month with Yancey as chairman of its resolutions committee, adopted a conciliatory platform which recommended war only if another state seceded and the federal government then tried to coerce her. The Democrats were willing to accept this formulation. Yancey having declined to run for Congress, John Cochran, a Eufaula lawyer with ties to Hunker, Chivalry, and fire-eater factions, was chosen as a compromise candidate. The fire-eaters abandoned efforts to bring out a gubernatorial candidate

46. *Ibid.*; Montgomery *Atlas*, May 21, 1851.
47. William R. de V. King to William T. King, March 27, 1851, in William R. de V. King Papers.
48. Unfortunately, only two issues of the *Atlas* appear to have survived, but the controversy may be studied from the other side through the Montgomery *Advertiser*, March 19, May 7, May 14, May 21, May 28, June 4, June 11, June 18, June 25, 1851; *cf.* also December 12, December 19, 1849, August 27, November 4, 1851, and Montgomery *Atlas*, May 21, 1851.

against the incumbent moderate Democrat Henry Collier. The question had been hotly contested at the June convention. George Gayle had proposed a nomination, but Yancey had persuaded the delegates to reject the motion, 22–37. He had done so, however, mostly by debating the question until the early morning hours, by which time thirty-two delegates had absented themselves. Yancey's resolutions, his withdrawal from the congressional race, and his suppression of the nomination movement all predisposed the regular Democrats to compromise with him. In the two counties most deeply divided by the quarrel, Dallas and Montgomery, fusion tickets were effected in the local legislative races. Thus by July, a month before the election, the Southern Rights forces could claim with at least a semblance of truth to be acting in concert.[49]

The election did not turn in all cases on the sectional issue. In Dallas the Unionists offered a ticket of two Whigs and a Democrat and the Southern Rights party a ticket of two Democrats and a Whig. The traditional party affiliation of the county proved too strong for the new issue; the voters elected the two Whigs from the Unionist list and the one Whig from among the Southern Rights candidates. In Mobile, state aid to internal improvements was an issue in the balloting. In Sumter, where the right of a state to secede was hotly debated, the electorate gave no very clear decision; it selected two Unionists and two Southern Rights men. In Barbour, fraud and foul play were widespread. In Choctaw, the Unionist legislative candidate was murdered by a southern rights man a week after the election. In Dale there was a tie, and the sheriff decided the race with a casting vote.[50] But the overall pattern in the election was clear. Half of the eighteen counties which the Southern Rights legislative candidates carried were the non–Black Belt counties of the first and the third congressional districts. These two were the only districts in which the Southern Rights congressional candidate won. Probably, then, a large proportion of the

49. Montgomery *Advertiser*, May 14, May 28, June 4, June 11, June 18, June 25, August 6, 1851, and William L. Yancey to George W. Gayle *et al.*, a committee, May 10, 1851, draft in William L. Yancey Papers, Alabama Department of Archives and History, Montgomery, printed in Montgomery *Atlas*, May 21, 1851. On Cochran, see John A. Calhoun to Joseph W. Lesesne, February 19, 1848, in Lesesne Papers; Gappa T. Yelverton to Bolling Hall, October 18, 1853, in Hall Papers; *Alabama Journal* (Montgomery), July 19, 1851.

50. Montgomery *Advertiser*, August 13, August 20, August 27, September 23, 1851.

Southern Rights legislators obtained office only by riding the coattails either of John Bragg or of Sampson Harris.

Moreover, this fact serves as a preface to an even more startling observation. Bragg had been elected to Congress only because he was the more moderate of the two candidates in the race. The Unionists had nominated Charles C. Langdon, the editor of the Whig Mobile *Advertiser* and the mayor of Mobile. Langdon, a native of Connecticut, was by far the most enthusiastic proponent of the virtues of the Compromise among the state's prominent public men. Indeed, he had embraced it so joyfully, and had repeated so often that the Southern Rights Democrats were as bad as the abolitionists, that during 1850 he became a lightning rod for violent controversy. A southern rights Whig, Hilary Foster, published a series of five pamphlets attacking Langdon, to which Langdon replied in eighteen pamphlets. In June, Langdon fought a duel with the temperate assistant editor of the Mobile *Register*. The Democrats did not hesitate to call Langdon's "the feeble voice of the traitor in [our] midst."

In sharp contrast to Langdon's well-established image as an extremist, Bragg took middle-road ground. He occupied the relatively nonpolitical position of circuit judge. He was suggested for the nomination by the Mobile *Register*, whose restrained comments on the Compromise had actually come close to an endorsement of it. At the district convention his opponents withdrew in his favor without the necessity of a contest. In the campaign, he denied that the Compromise would justify secession, and went further to deny that secession was a constitutional right, though he did admit that it was a necessary attribute of sovereignty. Moreover he refused to state what he thought Alabama should do in the event that South Carolina seceded. In short, Bragg's position closely approximated that taken by most of the Unionist candidates elsewhere in Alabama. He was endorsed by Senator King. Some Black Belt southern rights men called him a secret Unionist.

Because of the particular set of circumstances, the Democracy was successful in the first district in doing what it could not do elsewhere; it convinced the voters that southern rights meant moderate resistance and Unionism meant base submission. Thus, in a sense that passes beyond doublethink to a kind of truth, the victory of the Southern

Rights candidate in the first district was a victory for Unionism. It represented a repudiation of extremism in favor of what Unionism ordinarily made a point of offering—peace with honor.[51]

The only other Southern Rights Democrat who won was the incumbent in the third district, Sampson W. Harris. Harris' case was somewhat less spectacular than Bragg's, but he too was aided by an unusual turn of events. Harris had been perhaps the most radical and uncompromising Southern Rights advocate among Alabama's congressmen in the debates of the previous session. In their effort to make it clear to the voters why no politician could ever be a real southern rights man, therefore, the fire-eaters singled out Harris and launched against him a campaign approaching a blood vendetta. The two fire-eater presses, the Cahaba *Gazette* and the Montgomery *Atlas*, attacked him unremittingly. When Harris was goaded into publishing a lengthy exposition of his views, the radicals fell upon it; Yancey's *Atlas* proclaimed, "We recognize no more dangerous enemy to the true interest of Alabama than such counsellors as the Hon. S. W. Harris." The Cahaba *Gazette* stated that true southern rights men would vote for the Lowndes County radical Cornelius Robinson. And the state's most extreme secessionist, George Gayle, publicly endorsed Harris' Unionist opponent William S. Mudd, a former Jefferson County legislator who was later prominent in the founding of Birmingham. Gayle reasoned that since Mudd endorsed the Georgia Platform, which pledged to secede at once if northern aggressions continued, whereas Harris opposed separate state secession under ordinary circumstances as impolitic, it therefore followed that Mudd was more likely eventually to endorse Alabama's secession than was Harris. The position was doubtless idiosyncratic, but the regular Democratic press seized it as proof that Union Democrats would be safer with Harris than with Mudd. It appears that these developments had the general effect of giving Harris a more moderate image than he deserved, and that fact, added to hill-county Democratic loathing of Mudd's orthodox Whiggery, gave Harris a rather narrow majority.[52]

51. *Ibid.*, January 30, March 13, April 24, June 5, July 10, 1850; May 28, June 4, July 9, July 23, August 6, September 10, 1851.
52. *Ibid.*, May 7, May 14, May 28, June 11, July 30, 1851; Montgomery *Atlas*, May 21, 1851.

As we have already stated, nine of the eighteen counties which the Southern Rights legislative tickets managed to carry were in either Harris' or Bragg's district, and coattail riding evidently was a factor in these victories. Since the vote for both Harris and Bragg was in large measure a repudiation of extremism, as was the vote for the Unionists everywhere else, it follows that even the Southern Rights successes did not represent the triumph of southern rights principles, but rather an affirmation of the overwhelming importance of the factors which built the Unionist landslide. As huge as that landslide appears at first glance, more careful analysis reveals that it was even larger than it looks; in every section, among every class, the acceptance of the Unionist approach to the problems of the South was of a sort that drew near the limit of unanimity. And Southern Rights candidates survived, when they did, only when accident or effort clothed them in Unionist garments.

The Unionist victory was so decisive that its sequel, the almost immediate dissolution of the Unionist party, must startle the observer. In fact, however, that event may be easily explained. The Unionists had not merely won; they had swept the field. Their doctrine now stood unquestioned, at least among politicians. As early as the end of September, the state Democratic organ advised the termination of all southern rights agitation on the part of its political brood; there was no need to agitate the question in any case, it said, for abolitionists would drive the South out of the Union eventually, no matter what southern politicians did. Having adopted that position, the paper could immediately begin to upbraid any Unionist press which so much as mentioned the lately concluded debate. During the canvass, the Unionists had over and over called for an end to any further discussion of sectional issues. In the face of silence from the Democrats, therefore, the Whigs' own oratory now dictated their quiescence. Their position was impossible. If they did not continue focusing attention on the one issue which they had in common with their north Alabama Democratic allies there would cease to be any issue before the public upon which to hold the party together. But if the Whigs followed the logic of this observation to continued discussion, they would run afoul of that deep public desire for an end to polemic which had earlier propelled them to victory, would allow the Southern Rights Democrats to appear the more peace-loving party, and would subject themselves to the charge of inconsistency and of cynical irritation of an extremely sensitive wound. The Unionists were, of course, intimately familiar with the efficacy of such allegations. The dilemma was insoluble, but the Whig press was quickly plunged into internal bickering in the attempt to solve it.

While the Whiggery was thus occupied, Southern Rights Democrats used the prospect of patronage to wean away the north Alabama element in Unionism. Overjoyed at the prospect of controlling a legislature for the first time in the state's history, Whigs swamped the assembly with applications for the many offices which the legislators filled at each session. The Whig legislators made an effort to keep their north Alabama allies in mind. They voted for a Tennessee Valley Democrat for speaker, only to discover that he was a secret sympathizer with the effort to reorganize the Democratic party. The Southern Rights forces had maneuvered the Whigs into accepting him by putting up as a red herring a popular legislator widely suspected of collaboration with the Southern Rights men, thus causing the Whigs to desert their favorite candidate for the third man in the race, whom they took to be a Democratic Unionist. In the next election, for clerk of the House, Whigs discovered that north Alabama Democrats would vote for a Southern Rights man in preference to an orthodox Whig if there were only two contestants in the field. The Whigs were now placed on their guard, and the Southern Rights faction thereafter sought occasions for intensifying the mutual suspicions in the Unionist camp.

Meanwhile the Whiggery had taken complete control of the Senate. As a safety device in constructing their fusion tickets the previous summer, Whigs had ordinarily placed a genuine Whig in the Senate slot, on the assumption that if the uneasy Unionist alliance broke up in the House, they would still control one house outright, and could stave off disaster. The precaution may have been father to the fact, by alienating north Alabama politicians; but in any case when the Senate convened it chose a Whig president and secretary. The Senate president followed the usual practice of giving each group some committee chairmen; more than a third of his appointees were Southern Rights

Democrats. But the House speaker named only four Whig chairmen, one of whom was a southern rights Whig.

At the conclusion of these transactions, each group charged the others with duplicity. The Whigs sought to save the Union party by introducing resolutions approving of the Compromise and by attempting to obtain reelection for Senator Clemens. Such maneuvers were, as we have seen, time-honored devices for delineating party lines at the commencement of a session. But in this case both efforts failed in the House, now bitterly divided by patronage contests. In the vote refusing to bring on the Senate election, only sixteen of the thirty-one Union Democrats stood with the Whigs, though every Whig in the body voted affirmatively. This vote, recorded in the first week of the session, reveals the fatal effect which the patronage contests in the weeks leading up to the opening gavel had had on the Unionist alliance.

The moderate Democratic leadership had worked hard in late October and early November to effect this result. Senator King had come to Montgomery and together with John A. Winston and John J. Seibels had struggled tirelessly to achieve reorganization. They had used no magic weapons; the aging glue of patronage and spoils, coupled with hill-county resentment of Whig superiority in the Unionist effort, had been enough. Official reorganization took place at a Democratic convention in January, by which time the number of Democrats still cooperating with the Whigs in the legislature had been reduced to a dozen, only five of whom were residents of normally Democratic counties. But the real work had been done in the last two weeks of October and the first two weeks of November, accompanied by a vociferous attack on the circumstances of the Unionist champion Clemens' election in 1849 and by such potent appeals as the following.

Seibels' Montgomery *Advertiser* proclaimed that the sturdy north Alabama Democrat's "ignorance, poverty, filthiness, vulgarity and indecency have been standing themes of their [Whigs'] reproach and ridicule for years" but that "being now tired of their repeated drubbings, they [the Whiggery] propose to descend from their stilts and kindly take charge of the 'barefoot' democracy, as they have been in the habit of styling the gallant democracy of North Alabama, and direct their movements for the future." Senator King warned pointedly that the distinctions between Unionists and Southern Rights men "should no longer exist, and he who would attempt to keep them alive will prove himself to be more of a whig than a democrat." No politically ambitious legislator could have missed the implication of this assertion. Philip Phillips, the leader of the internal improvements advocates in the legislature, joined the cry that Unionism was a Whig plot. It was, he cautioned, "an illusion worked up by wise men to please the fancy of weak brethren," thus appealing to north Alabama fears of cunning manipulators. The Mobile *Register* believed that only the destruction of Unionism could restore "the good old rule of a strict construction of the Constitution" and prevent the government "from becoming one broad and unrestricted empire—a despotism with the head at Washington." And future governor Winston ranted that no Democrat desired the friendship or aid of any Whig.

North Alabamians were easily convinced. They had always been loyal party men, convinced of the Democracy's dogma. It rarely occurred to them to question the sincerity of traditional appeals, for the appeals seemed to them so intrinsically persuasive. It appeared entirely reasonable, therefore, that the south Alabamians would believe the words they uttered—as in fact, within the limits of human hopes and fears, the south Alabamians did. The state's only prominent Union Democratic paper thus greeted the overtures of its former party associates with frank elation. "It affords us unspeakable pleasure to announce that there is a probability for future harmony and union in the democratic party. . . . We have regretted, deeply regretted that necessity forced us to differ with many of our Democratic friends in regard to the compromise." However, "we sacrificed no principle of democracy—for while battling for the compromise we still cherished the same firm, fixed and undying devotion which we have always manifested for the democratic cause. But now that the struggle has passed—the Union saved . . . [and] there is no longer an organized resistance to the compromise, we hold ourselves in readiness to fall back on old issues, and to organize the party preparatory to the presidential election." It added that "secession and disunion [are] buried in the tomb of obsolete ideas." [53]

53. Montgomery *Advertiser*, November 4, November 11, November 25, December 2, 1851.The process of reorganization is best studied through the Montgomery papers. In addition

For months after the doom of Unionism was fixed, the Whigs continued to fight among themselves about efforts to save it. The dominant element in the state party initially desired to do so, and in January joined with the Democrats who remained loyal to the cause to hold a Unionist convention. They named delegates to a proposed national convention and an electoral ticket for its nominees, rejecting attendance at the national Whig meeting. No national Unionist convention materialized, however. The only practical result of the Whig maneuver, therefore, was to deny to the Alabama Whiggery again in 1852, as in 1848, an official representation at the general gathering of the party. An irregular delegation was chosen by partisans of Millard Fillmore at a number of local meetings in May, and it cast the state's vote for the president. There was little enthusiasm for the nomination of Scott in any section of the party. During the summer, however, the eager acceptance of Pierce's candidacy by all factions within the Democracy made any further thought of preserving Unionism clearly absurd. In September, therefore, the Whigs held a state convention, nominated a slate of Scott electors, and rather glumly plunged into their last presidential campaign as a party.[54]

Thus did Alabama steer, as the Unionist orators were fond of saying, between the Scylla of disunion and the Charybdis of dishonor. Charybdis need not detain us, but Scylla deserves a few remarks. It was a perfectly rational observer who, in 1852, pronounced disunion "buried in the tomb of obsolete ideas." He had, however, embalmed the notion a trifle prematurely. If we are to understand the victory of secession in 1861, it will be useful to recapitulate the reasons for its overwhelming defeat a decade earlier.

It would be easy to say that the state had been saved by the spirit of

---

to the dates cited, see September 3, September 10, September 30, October 7, October 14, October 21, October 28, November 18, December 9, December 16, December 23, December 30, 1851, January 6, January 27, February 3, February 10, February 17, February 24, March 2, May 4, September 15, December 22, 1852, January 26, February 16, 1853; *Alabama Journal* (Montgomery), January 22, 1852. See also William R. de V. King to Thomas D. King, December 5, 1851, in William R. de V. King Papers; Thomas E. Johns to John Bragg, December 10, 1851, Herndon L. Henderson to Bragg, January 15, 1852, Charles P. Robinson to Bragg, January 21, 1852, all in John Bragg Papers, Southern Historical Collection, University of North Carolina Library, Chapel Hill.

54. *Alabama Journal* (Montgomery), January 22, September 3, 1852; Montgomery *Advertiser*, March 2, March 16, April 13, April 20, April 27, May 11, May 19, May 26, July 14, July 21, September 8, 1852.

party, but the contention would not be precisely correct. To be sure, the association of the Compromise with the names of Clay and, later, of Fillmore drew the Whigs ineluctably to its support. To be sure, without the collaboration of the Black Belt which the Whiggery delivered the Unionist Democrats would have been unable to defeat the Southern Rights movement alone. To be sure, the primary difference between 1851 and 1861 was that in the former year the Black Belt voted with the north Alabama Democrats, whereas in the latter year it voted with the south Alabama Democrats. To be sure, the Black Belt was able to make this transference only because the Whig party was no longer in a position to hold the electorate of the area in line. But however obvious, however cogent these observations may be, they are only part, and by no means the most important part, of the story. They assume as fixed too many factors which were really variables. The spirit of party certainly shaped the course of the Crisis of 1850, but the outcome of the Crisis is far more directly attributable to the spirit of politics, to the ordinary operation of the political structure.

The Crisis had its roots planted firmly in the search for new political issues with which to create electoral majorities. It escalated when politicians scurried to outdo each other in getting on the right side of the new organizing principle. The effort to outdo others transformed southern rights oratory from the desperate demands to be left alone, current in 1848, to the bellicose threats to work out southern salvation with diligence, which abounded in 1849. But political oratory was constantly being test marketed; politicians were intensely sensitive to popular acceptance. They pushed each issue, step by step, towards extreme formulations, constantly seeking to discover the boundaries beyond which the people would begin to reject the cause; for it was just short of the boundary that the politician found that magic height upon which he was transfigured into the champion of a social crusade. He had, in the phrase of the time, "mounted a hobby." To do so was every politician's dream. The search for the proper hobby was not, of course, wholly cynical; the politician normally was directed to some extent by his own emotions. But there was often more of what we would call cynicism in the process than the present century could justify.

The Jacksonians did not consider the conscious effort to locate, or even to create, hobbies as quite so immoral an enterprise as we might, because they conceived the role of the politician in society in a way no longer current. Politics was the profession of popular representation. The commitment to the right of instruction is no mere theoretical oddity; it is a profoundly enlightening insight into the vision of an age. The politician's function was not to guide, but to represent. Thus, in very nearly the same way that a merchant must seek to know and to satisfy the needs of his customers, it was the politician's positive social duty to discover and give voice to the will of his constituency. In a sense his place in the scheme of things is now occupied by the advertising man, for it was his job to give concrete form to previously amorphous desires or fears.

The advertising man is limited by his ability to create a market for his product. As an invisible hand guides transactions in the marketplace, so invisible barriers confined nineteenth-century politics. The power of public opinion, and its immaturity, may well have been greater at this period in American history than at any time before or since. Public opinion could be focused, but it could not be invented. Whenever a politician's search for a hobby carried him beyond the unformed mood which was the substance from which he made success, he found himself slammed with great force into a wall of whose existence he had been unaware. The experience could destroy him.

Jeremiah Clemens evidently early developed a longing for acceptance. When, still a teen-ager, he delivered his first oration in a college debating society, he wrote an even younger friend, "Believe me, Clement, the applauses [*sic*] of a crowd are more than acceptable, let philosophers say what they will." Throughout his life, in fact, Clemens found applause completely intoxicating. Naturally he became a politician. In the legislature he alienated older members by his ruthless ambition and his sensitivity to insult. He arranged to have himself nominated for Congress, to replace an incumbent, by manipulation of the convention machinery; but the subterfuge was so coarse that he was forced to decline the race. In 1842, William L. Yancey, who was sitting in the assembly with Clemens, said of him, "Intellect and education sufficient to fit him for any station Mr. Clemens has—but he must sedulously cultivate a spirit of patience and curb his ardent—yea! fiery temperament."[55]

It was a warning which Clemens could not take. He ignored party discipline in order to bargain his way into the Senate in 1849. But in order to remain there, he had to find an issue with which to create a constituency. Like most Alabama politicians, he had been convinced by Taylor's election that southern rights was such a hobby. As soon as he entered Congress, he established himself as one of the most extreme southern spokesmen. He even repudiated the northern wing of the Democratic party as a tool of abolitionists, and he initially attacked the Compromise in unmeasured terms. But, as did many another, he discovered by the spring of 1850 that he had gone too far; public opinion was not supporting his intemperate position. When the vote on the Compromise measures came, he supported the Fugitive Slave Act and the Texas Boundary Act, and abstained on the rest.

When he returned to Huntsville, Clemens discovered that Unionism was even more popular than he had suspected. He therefore completed his conversion by endorsing, indeed embracing, the entire Compromise package. But he had overreacted. His new views were as extreme as his old ones had been, and he found no greater support. His colleague Senator King had cast the same votes on the Compromise bills, but King held to the moderate position which the votes implied, and used his influence to reorganize the Democratic party. Clemens in contrast accepted a position at the head of the abortive Unionist electoral slate. He was not returned to the Senate, of course. He became a Know-Nothing for a time. A few years later found him drinking heavily and demanding money in exchange for exerting what remained of his influence. In 1861 he went to the Secession Convention as a cooperationist, but when he discovered that immediate secession held a majority, he voted for the Ordinance of Secession. In 1862 he crossed into Federal lines and became a scalawag.[56]

55. Jeremiah Clemens to Clement Claiborne Clay, January 19, 1834, in Clay Papers, Duke University Library, Durham; Wetumpka *Argus*, March 23, 1842.

56. Bedsole's "Life of Clemens" does not do justice to its fascinating subject. For additional information, see Thomas J. Judge to Jefferson Franklin Jackson, March 15, March 19, 1855, in J. F. Jackson Papers; Jeremiah Clemens to Sam Houston, August 6, 1842, in Jeremiah Clemens Papers, Alabama Department of Archives and History, Montgomery; Susanna Withers Clay to Clement Claiborne Clay, February 1, 1834, Clement Comer Clay to Clement Claiborne Clay,

Clemens' case is more spectacular than most. He found himself slammed into the invisible barriers on both boundaries of the sectional issue, and he emerged from the ordeal a broken man. Probably he was hit so particularly hard because his exploitation of issues was extraordinarily calculating even by the standards of Jacksonian politics. Clemens set out to gratify his need for power in a coldly conscious way rather unusual for the time. Ordinarily, politicians possessed some degree of commitment to their issues, so that their own emotions protected them from the brutal reprisals which the system exacted from Clemens. Clemens had taken his positions from rational considerations; because he lacked true rapport with the moods he used, he was betrayed into extreme formulations which more sensitive politicians avoided instinctively. But precisely because he was thus exceptional, his career exemplifies starkly the fate which awaited the public man who, either because of excessive cynicism or because of unusual zealotry, transgressed the inherent limits of the political structure.

Most Alabama leaders read the signs better than did Clemens. Taylor's victory had been misinterpreted. During 1850, however, the radical oratory of the previous year was generally abandoned. By 1851 the real point of debate was which party was the more moderate. In fact, all along, the entire company of genuine southern rights men in the state hardly made a handful. And George Gayle appears to have been the only public man in Alabama who openly avowed a belief in immediate, separate state secession. There were just no votes in such positions.

There was a good deal of ranting during the Crisis of 1850 that the whole difficulty had been created by self-seeking politicians. The accusation is not without its measure of truth. But it is essential to note that just as political controversy fed the Crisis, so political controversy kept it from getting out of hand. The fire could not burn beyond the

February 4, 1840, Clement Claiborne Clay to Clement Comer Clay, August 4, 1841, and February 16, 1851, Clement Comer Clay to Clement Claiborne Clay, January 9, 1854, John D. Rather to Clement Claiborne Clay, July 29, 1856, all in Clay Papers; Jeremiah Clemens to George S. Houston, January 21, 1849, in Houston Papers; *House Journal*, Sess. of 1839–1840, pp. 74–75; Montgomery *Advertiser*, January 9, January 23, February 20, March 13, August 21, September 4, September 18, October 2, November 20, 1850, July 16, July 30, August 6, September 23, October 14, October 28, November 11, 1851, February 10, March 2, March 23, March 30, 1852.

limits of its fuel, the approbation of the electorate. It is not too much to say, therefore, that Alabama was saved from secession by the ambitions of her politicians. The wisdom of statesmen was not to be found in the state, but it was unnecessary. The operation of the political structure transformed the selfishly motivated actions of the politicians into a profound social conservatism which precluded the achievement of radical—or for that matter, of reactionary—goals through governmental institutions.

That statement, however, forces us to confront the fact that within a decade Alabama was to take, through her governmental institutions, one of the most radical actions which a polity can contemplate—revolution. The death of one of the political parties as a formal organization and the senility of the other is an inadequate explanation for the contradiction; for the logic of our discoveries about the events of 1850 would lead us to expect that secession could not have been accomplished without the elimination of the political structure itself. In the succeeding chapters we shall turn our attention to this problem. But before doing so, we have two remaining aspects of the Crisis of 1850 whose exploration will profit us. First of all, we should look at the sorts of arguments with which Democratic leaders sought to convince the masses of the necessity for assuming southern rights grounds, for the arguments of 1849 and 1850 are essentially identical to those of 1860. Secondly, we need to know more about the small band of genuine southern rights fanatics: who they were and how they viewed the unfolding events.

Southern Rights for Mass Consumption

A not inconsiderable portion of historians' misunderstanding of secession perhaps derives from a general failure to reflect seriously upon the social and political assumptions in the arguments offered in favor of that step. Numerous arguments of many different types were presented, by politicians, editors, theorists, and ordinary citizens. But the student who ponders them will come to see that almost all of them are, unconsciously, buttressing one or another aspect of a single, general case. The case is so logical and so internally consistent that it may almost be presented syllogistically. Its logic and consistency, however, were not dictated by one thinker, or even by a group of them, but by the society in which Alabamians lived. The skeleton of the case was formed of unquestioned social axioms, and the marrow of that skeleton was political reality.

At the beginning of the 1850s the arguments seemed to most people unconvincing; ten years later this situation had been altered. But the arguments themselves did not really change. The unfolding of events merely lent them more empirical weight. Thus, an analysis of the appeals made during the Crisis of 1850 will prepare us to understand the questions at issue in the coming decade's bitter contests. For this purpose, I have chosen a single important source, the newspaper which served as the state Democratic organ. I have analyzed and attempted to categorize every southern rights argument offered in its pages—from the editors, from letterwriters, from politicians' speeches, from the resolutions of public meetings, from reprinted articles—in short from every available provenance, beginning in the fall of 1849 and ending shortly after the final defeat of the Southern Rights party in August, 1851. The enterprise could simply have produced confusion, but it appears instead that the various positions arrange themselves quite naturally into a pattern—and a rather surprising one.

The case begins with portraits of what the South would be like without slavery. These portraits emphasize two complementary appeals—one to the race fears of the readers, the other to their sense of race superiority. The appeal to fears is typified by the following quotation.

Hemmed in on the North, West and Southwest by a chain of nonslaveholding States; fanaticism and power, hand in hand, preaching a crusade against her institutions; her post offices flooded with incendiary documents; her by-ways crowded with emissaries sowing the seeds of a servile war, in order to create a more plausible excuse for Congressional interference; the value of her property depreciated and her agricultural industry paralyzed, what would become of the people of the Southern States, when they would be forced at last to let loose among them, freed from the wholesome restraints of patriarchal authority, a population whose only principle of action has ever been animal appetite? With an idle, worthless, profligate set of free negroes prowling about our streets at night and haunting the woods during the day armed with whatever weapons they could lay their hands on, and way-laying every road through every swamp in the South, what would be our situation? The farmer, when his stock were all killed up, his corn house plundered, and perhaps his stable set on fire, would be forced to make a block house of his dwelling and sleep every night with his musket by his side. There would remain but one remedy for the evils thus inflicted upon our social system—a war of extermination against the whole negro race.

Another vision of the future was set in 1871.

The slave population will then be doubled in the few remaining slave States that are likely to hold on to that institution. Missouri, Kentucky, Maryland and Delaware, harrassed [sic] by the constant thefts of their slaves by citizens of the free States, will have sent them nearly all South, and will stand ready (some of them will have already done so) to abolish the institution in their limits. Many of the whites in the remaining slave States, being inconvenienced by this dense population of the negroes will sell out, being prevented by the free States from taking their slaves with them, and go themselves to free States. So will many others through fear and interest; and even the patriot Southerner, who is now branded as an "ultra and traitor" by the tories of the present day, tired of being abused and vilified, and disgusted with the pusalanimity [sic] and cowardice of his fellow-citizens of the South will, in many instances, take up his departure from a people that have shown so little willingness to defend their rights and honor. The negroes will become insupportable when they shall have doubled and trebled the white population South, with the sympathies of three-fourths of the whites in the United States against the institution. The sequel may be easily discerned. We have an illustration in point in St. Domingo. This is but an imperfect picture of the prospect before us. Gloomy, indeed—but is it not true? [57]

The two examples suffice to show the tone of these arguments. The sustaining vision of Jacksonian America was the prospect for future advancement. But the southern future held only horror. The prophecies would have their most profoundly depressing effect upon those citizens who had not yet arrived in the society, who counted upon America's continued march towards the sunlit uplands of tomorrow for the fulfillment of their personal dreams. And it is to be noted that the simple farmer, defending his corn house and his stable from the sneak attacks of alien guerrillas, is the hero of the descriptions. This point is even clearer in the arguments based upon appeals to race superiority.

The farmers were told that slavery "promotes equality among the

57. Montgomery *Advertiser*, November 21, 1849, February 12, 1851.

free by dispensing with grades and castes among them, and thereby preserves republican institutions." They were told:

The total abolition of slavery would affect more injuriously the condition of the poor white man in the slaveholding States than that of the rich slaveholder; for the slaveholder, having the means which attends upon the possession of slaves, would be able to maintain his *position*, whilst the poor man would have to doff that native, free-born and independent spirit which he now possesses, and which he prizes above all wealth, and would have to become virtually the slave (barring color) of the rich man. This would be one of the consequences of the abolition of negro slavery, and the poorest white man who walks, barefoot, our hills is wise enough to see it; and though he may only leave to his children the heritage of *freedom* and *poverty*, yet he is determined that neither they nor his children's children, to the latest generation, shall ever occupy, through their remissness of duty, the position of *servants*.

Future governor John Gill Shorter warned that "should the time ever arrive when four millions of slaves congregated in the South Atlantic and Gulf States were turned loose upon the country, there would then be a contest between the two races for supremacy; that while the rich would be able to leave a land thus cursed, the poor white man would be left in a most lamentable condition. He would, then, perhaps, instead of occupying the position of master, find his case reversed, and he reduced to the most abject and degrading servitude."

The editor of the *Advertiser*, as was his wont, cast the argument in somewhat more emotional terms. Speaking directly to nonslaveholders, he warned that abolition was to be accomplished by purchase, "so that in the first place you must be taxed to pay for the negroes of your wealthy neighbors." And he asked,

Is this fair? is it just? will you be willing to do it? But suppose all this settled, that they were all paid for! What is to become of them? Ah! Here is the rub. It is not contemplated to make any other disposition of them than to turn them loose among us. Well now, fellow-citizens, just suppose all the negroes of the country were on a *political* and *social* equality with us—that the present restraints of the master were removed. . . . In the first place, the wealthy slave owners, having received pay for their slaves in the bonds of the government drawing interest at six per cent (for which we have shown you must be taxed to pay) will leave a country where negroes are to be their *equals*, and seek a latitude where negroes are not allowed to go. This will then commence a contest for *political* and then social superiority. If the negroes out-number you, a war will have to be made on *them* by you; if you out-number the negroes and attempt, as you certainly will, to exclude them from political and social equality with you, they will commence the war upon you. Of all wars of which we have any knowledge, one of this character would be the most horrid and revolting—a civil war of castes and color between an inferior and superior race, where the one or the other would have to be *exterminated.* Need we attempt to picture to your minds the scenes to which it would give rise? Neither helpless infancy nor decrepid age, neither innocence nor virtue, the chastity of our wives or daughters, would be spared—our property plundered and destroyed, our homes rendered desolate—the country laid waste—poverty, distress and anarchy would rule supreme. Suppose the negroes exterminated; what would be your condition after such a struggle? Would it, could it be compared to your condition *now,* with the negroes as slaves under proper subjection, performing those low and menial offices for the rich, which our own *white blood* now do at the North?

But suppose the negroes should by accident succeed—as they may do by the aid of the abolitionists—is it possible to conceive of the degradation of the whites conquered by slaves! We will leave the contemplation of such a picture to your own imaginations.[58]

This particular discourse was directed explicitly at the poor farmer, but regardless of whether or not it was expressed, every one of these portraits of the future had the nonslaveholder principally in mind. It was always he who was driven from his home, plunged into the midst of an ocean of hostile, animal-like blacks, forced to fight to the death to retain his little plot of earth, threatened with becoming the menial of the wealthy. Secession was a political act and two-thirds of the electorate owned no slaves.

Not only would the abolition of slavery harm primarily the nonslaveholder, but it appeared that he was a major beneficiary of its existence. It kept the wages of working whites high, for it insured that they would never have to occupy the lowest rungs of the economic ladder. It gave the small farmer a ready market for his produce, because of the massive, local demand of the great plantations. But most importantly, it gave him a world in which he could govern his own life without the interference of society, or of social tumult. "In his social progress he encounters no mobs, no riots, no violent political excite-

58. Resolutions of the Montgomery Southern Rights Convention of March, 1852, *ibid.,* March 9, 1852; see also November 13, September 11, 1850, July 16, 1851.

ments, no communism, no agrarianism, no mormonism, no anti-masonism, no lawless leagues of rabble. In his labor he has to contend with no foreign pauperism, no home pauperism, no daily laborers going about begging but unable to obtain employment." [59]

The next step in the southern rights case was to link the exclusion of slavery from the territories with the forecast catastrophes. This relation was established by two arguments. In the first place, given the rapid rate of increase which the slave population showed, if slaves were limited to the South, the whites would soon find themselves a minority in a black sea. As in the case of emancipation, rich whites might flee, leaving the poor to deal with the increasingly restless blacks. Alternatively, the increasing number of Negroes could force the occupation of a greater and greater percentage of the arable land by plantations, forcing the nonslaveholders off their farms and driving them homeless into the world. On the other hand, the export of slaves to new areas and their employment in new pursuits would diminish overproduction of cotton, raise the price of the staple, and thus increase the small farmer's income. [60]

The second argument through which the territorial issue was connected to the interests of the electorate was even more revealing. The southern farmer—indeed, the American farmer—in the nineteenth century suffered from a sort of claustrophobia. He could not tolerate the prospect of being irrevocably condemned to his existing farm, of being shut out of the possibility of migration to a new life if events should ever require it. But his vision was not of migration to a new world and a new life-style; rather, he wanted the assurance that there was an accessible alternate community in which he could engage in fundamentally the same pursuits, but in circumstances which might produce greater success. Southern rights advocates constantly reminded him that the Yankee culture was very different from his own, and that if he allowed the territories to become re-creations of the northern states, he could thereafter migrate to them only at the cost of giving up his own egalitarian, democratic world for a socially stratified

59. Montgomery *Advertiser*, March 13, May 15, October 16, 1850; see also Second Inaugural Address of His Excellency Henry W. Collier, Montgomery *Advertiser*, December 23, 1851.
60. Mobile *Tribune*, quoted in Montgomery *Advertiser*, August 6, 1851; see also October 16, 1850, July 16, 1851.

society swept by the gales of class conflict and unbridled meliorist ferment. It is that condition which the writer quoted earlier was seeking to define with his long list of social ills and reformist movements. In the South, the farmer "lives quietly, and if he be industrious, comfortably"; his taxes were low, particularly because the government had few paupers to support; nor did he really compete with Negro labor, for he did not usually raise the staple crops.

Under this system of things all thrived and all were happy. From father to son, through a long succession of years, they progressed, and have gone on accumulating at a steady rate until, without apparently being aware of the fact, we, their posterity, have become a prosperous and wealthy people—not in the sense in which these terms are applied to England and the North—not by the concentration of capital in the hands of a few enterprising individuals, to whom the many are the mere "hewers of wood and drawers of water"—but by a general diffusion of wealth and happiness over the whole community.[61]

The fear of the antebellum reform movements—of the "communism, agrarianism, mormonism, anti-masonism and lawless leagues of rabble" which the earlier quotation deplored—reflects a deep-seated uneasiness which constitutes the next link in the southern rights case. Its advocates were frightened by the prospect that the sort of commotion observable elsewhere in the world would invade their own peaceful realm, and their apprehensions led them to see nascent danger in small circumstances. When Senator Clemens introduced into Congress a constitutional amendment for popular election of senators, the Mobile *Register* was concerned, despite its approval of the measure's object. "Let the instrument [the Constitution] pass under the hands of the political tinkers who are ever and anon thinking themselves wiser than its framers, and our habitual reverence for it as something sacred will be extinguished." When a writer ventured kind words about Aaron Burr, one editor lamented feelingly that it had now become the fashion to defend people formerly execrated. The heated debates in Congress dismayed observers; the absence of polite discourse in the halls of legislation seemed to many an omen of imminent social disintegration.[62]

One symptom of these forebodings of the future was a sudden

61. *Ibid.*, October 16, 1850, May 7, 1851; *cf.* July 23, 1851.
62. Quoted *ibid.*, January 23, 1850; see also April 3, April 24, 1850.

interest in recapturing the past. The Alabama Historical Society was organized in 1850, primarily by southern rights men. Albert J. Pickett published the first history of the state in 1851, and it received eager and laudatory attention from the press. The northern bias of history textbooks was a matter of long-standing concern in the state, but there was now a heightened desire for "the people of Alabama [to] show to the world that they do have a taste for something else besides the mere making of cotton bales and filling their pockets with 'filthy lucre.'"

It is full time that not only Alabama but the entire South should turn her attention to subjects of this kind [history]. Go to our colleges and seminaries, and even to the common school rooms, and we do not see a single volume, however small, the production of a Southern pen. The geographies and histories of our own native soil are written by foreigners, we may say—enemies of our institutions and laws, who give their own false colorings to their descriptions and narratives—calculated to mislead, if not [to be] of serious injury to the rising generation.[63]

The breach through which northern tumult was making its way into the quiet groves of the South was the sectional conflict, the first of the northern movements to pose any real threat to the fabric of southern society. And politicians were widely believed to exacerbate that conflict in order to secure their personal advancement. Thus the primary focus for the southern rights fear that the South might become as turbulent as the North was southern political leadership—the self-seeking placemen of these latter days. Politicians were coming to be seen as agitators and manipulators, and they were warned, "A storm is now brewing in the South that with the broom of destruction will sweep away those political tricksters who have too long duped her confidence."[64]

Governor Henry Collier, a moderate Democrat, believed that the sources of sectional rivalry were perfectly natural. "With the increase of our territory, and the diversity of the pursuits and habits of the people of the United States, there must be a corresponding conflict of interest." But a government wisely conducted should be able to re-

63. *Ibid.*, May 15, August 7, 1850; Marion *Review*, quoted *ibid.*, January 16, 1850. Cf. *Senate Journal*, Sess. of 1841–42, pp. 311–13. On the life of Pickett, see Frank L. Owsley, Jr., "Albert J. Pickett: Typical Southern Pioneer State Historian" (Ph.D. dissertation, University of Alabama, 1955).

64. Montgomery *Advertiser*, August 28, 1850.

strain those conflicts within acceptable limits. The country's problems, therefore, were solvable at the polls. "Let the political hucksters for high places and the suppliants for federal favors be repudiated, and the people rising in their strength practically maintain the right of self-government—the high boon we have received from our fathers." [65] By coupling this typically Jacksonian belief that the cure for social ills was correct political action with the Calhounite contention that the party competition for spoils was inherently corrupting, the new southern rights advocates were able to draw on two standard elements of Alabama's political tradition with which to support their increasingly strong conviction that every politician at all times, not merely non-Jacksonians or non-Calhounites, was a "huckster for high places." However rooted the elements of this argument were in the state's political tradition, though, this particular allegation was the most novel feature of the southern rights case—and the feature which the electorate was most reluctant to accept. We shall return to this problem later.

The various hints that the southern world too was changing created a profound sense of impending doom among the southern rights forces, a sense that an invisible sword of Damocles hung above them. This feeling sometimes led to startling outbursts. On one occasion, for instance, an editor wrote,

We feel quite sure that the North . . . will, sooner or later, carry, or attempt to carry, their ultimate designs upon the South into operation. Believing that it is to come, we say the sooner the better; we want the question settled one way or the other in our day, and not leave it to our children. If the South is to submit to the abolition of slavery, why in God's name let us know the result and be done with it. If, on the other hand, she is to resist it, let the acts of the North that are to produce resistance be done at once, and not keep us in this long lingering suspense, quarreling among ourselves instead of with the common enemy. [66]

Looking at the example of the North, then, these men felt uneasy at the ability of the South to maintain its unique social stability, and they sought actively to communicate their apprehensions. In the past, they liked to believe, the world had left the ordinary citizen alone; he

65. Second Inaugural Address of His Excellency Henry W. Collier, *ibid.*, December 23, 1851.
66. Montgomery *Advertiser*, September 30, 1851.

had been his own master, an autonomous unit; neither society nor other men had sought to dictate his course. But that day might be drawing to a close. Society, it appeared, was about to materialize on an Alabama farm, and its avatar would assuredly be mounted upon a storm. Could freedom survive the manifestation? With that question, we reach the core and motive force of the southern rights case.

So often that it became a sort of litany, southern rights advocates reiterated that freedom and equality were in imminent danger. Southerners had intimate experience with slavery, and it was their greatest dread. Now those with acute vision professed to see the very shackles being forged. There were two interlocking appeals, one to freedom and the ideal of individual autonomy, and one to equality and the alleged threat to manhood and self-respect. In either guise the argument touched the very meaning of the American experiment as the Jacksonian generations understood it. In any eventual contest, wrote an editor, "The issue . . . however painful the trial, cannot be doubtful. Sustained by the eternal principles of right and truth and justice, the people of the Southern States will be able, under the protection of Divine Providence, to pluck the principles of liberty and equality as recognized by the Federal Constitution from the destructive hand of fanatical and unprincipled ambition, preserve them unhurt amidst all the evils which threaten the pathway of the future, and present them untarnished to those who are capable of appreciating or worthy to enjoy them."

Congressman David Hubbard informed the voters:

It is clear that the power to dictate what sort of property the State may allow a citizen to own and work—whether oxen, horses or negroes; or what religion he may preach, teach or practice, on account of its morality, is alike despotic and tyrannical, whether such power is obtained by conquest in battle or by a majority vote and is equally galling and oppressive upon those whose consciences are made to conform to the standard of morality which the majority sets up; and was never surpassed by the British crown during the reign of her most absolute and despotic kings.

When a constituent expressed a willingness to accept emancipation with colonization if it would restore harmony to the Union, the congressman wrote him that

the white people in the Southern States had better exterminate both the negroes and their owners, who would turn them loose upon them, than allow any such scheme to be carried out, as you appear to be willing to adopt, rather than meet it as you ought. Because, the assumed power to put an end to slavery, or take the first steps towards that object, being a higher power than the Constitution has given Congress, is a violation of its provisions, and a destruction of liberty itself. It was constitutional liberty which our fathers fought to establish and *not* union! they *had* union with the mother country when they rebelled; they had *more* of it than they wanted, and the revolution was fought to get clear of such union as they then had, and to obtain liberty in its stead.

After they had gained liberty in battle, they established peaceable union, for strength to *protect* liberty. Now if the strength which union gives, is used for the purpose of *destroying* and not protecting liberty, we must get clear of such strength and keep liberty. This seems to me to be our plain duty.

Congressman Sampson Harris added a warning, "The peace that tyranny imposes can have no charms for a freeman. The measure of his rights, injustice may not limit. . . . Better, far better, a never-ending resistance to wrong, than the cold and joyless repose which awaits on conscious inferiority, and humbles the proud man's spirit to the lessons of obedience." Chancellor Wylie W. Mason noted the "constant tendencies of the Federal Government to upset the great predicate of our political system, viz: that all government rests upon the consent of the governed." And the Randolph County Democratic party pledged "to vanquish Federalism, Abolitionism and all other *isms* which tend to stifle the voice of free constitutional liberty and seek to overthrow a government founded in the wisdom, virtue and affections of the people." [67]

The southern rights advocates pictured southerners as a persecuted minority—indeed, "the most oppressed, insulted and plundered of all"—fighting valiantly for "the maintenance and perpetuation of those great principles of civil liberty transmitted to us by a glorious and venerated ancestry." They referred constantly, therefore, to two examples—the revolutionaries of 1776 and the contemporary European struggles against monarchy. The issue which southerners faced was "whether they are to be free or slaves—whether they are to be subjugated as Ireland and Hungary—whether they are to be partitioned as Poland, or erect themselves into an independent State"; and

67. *Ibid.*, June 5, February 6, May 1 (the attribution of this letter to Hubbard is inferred), August 28, 1850, August 6, December 23, 1851.

there could be but a single choice "as long as one drop of revolutionary blood courses our veins." The American tradition dictated rapport with the spirit of a seceding state, for Americans, who sympathized with all revolts of the downtrodden—Poland, Greece, France, Hungary, Ireland—and who indeed had lent concrete aid to snatch Texas "from the jaws of Mexican rule" and to aid Cuba "in throwing off Spanish tyranny," could never bear to see "a sister sovereign State, comparatively weak in numbers and means, overborne and crushed by the bayonets of the other thirty States!"[68]

Three events of this period—Lopez' invasion of Cuba, a bill introduced in Congress to invite to America Irishmen exiled for conspiring against British rule, and the struggle of Louis Kossuth—particularly stimulated southern rights support. A not inconsiderable number of Alabamians joined the Lopez expedition and "laid down fortune and lost their lives at the altar of liberty." The failure of Cubans to rally to Lopez' standard deeply shocked southerners; a typical comment read, "Cuba is not worthy of the priceless boon of freedom, it is true, and we hope that no brave American will ever again risk his life in her cause. But the noble example set by our countrymen in this struggle to free ignoble slaves will not be lost; other oppressed people will gather inspiration and courage from it." And history would praise those men "who left their own free and happy homes to give succor and freedom to a people they had been led to believe were struggling against unmitigated tyranny." Kossuth visited Alabama in the spring of 1852. He got no aid from the orthodox Democracy, but many fire-eaters, particularly in the Mobile, Montgomery, and Selma areas, were deeply impressed by his arguments. The first state southern rights convention of 1852, in fact, rejected American intervention in the anti-Hapsburg crusade by the relatively narrow margin of 22 to 32. These particular causes passed, but the general southern rights enthusiasm for movements of national liberation persisted throughout the coming decade.[69]

Even more important than the example of foreigners was the pre-

68. *Ibid.*, May 29, 1850, April 2, 1851, October 16, 1850, June 4, 1851.
69. *Ibid.*, September 3, September 10, 1851, March 9, 1852. See also July 30, August 13, August 27, September 3, September 16, September 30, October 7, October 28, 1851, January 27, April 13, 1852; Thaddeus Sanford to John Bragg, March 3, 1852, William R. Hallett to Bragg, April 3, 1852, in Bragg Papers.

cedent of the American Revolution. Southern rights advocates used that precedent both to inspire and to bludgeon. Wrote the radical southern rights man William F. Samford:

To this dirty competition[for office] the South, I fear, have ignominiously sold themselves, at the call of corrupt Southern aspirants, who care not what becomes of the principles of the Federal compact, or of the liberty of the multitude, provided they shall be able to succeed in their schemes of self-aggrandizement . . . Alas! how fallen are we below the lofty and dignified moral stature of our immortal ancestors. They, though few in numbers and unprovided, appealed to the God of battles and dedicated their lives to the preservation of a principle of English liberty. And is it possible that the descendants of such a race of men have forgotten that principle is the life blood of government?—that without it society could not exist—that it is the stronger cord that keeps the strong in awe—the standard of right—the aegis of the weak, the avenger of the innocent—the stay of the oppressor's hand—the light that has driven savage darkness from the abodes of men, and conducted worlds into an elysium of brotherly love, peace and harmony! He who deserts principle, deserts his own good, and is fit to be a slave.[70]

A Jefferson County meeting asserted that the South faced a "return to a colonial vassalage more galling than the one our fathers resisted." A Jackson County paper believed, "The same spirit of freedom and independence that impelled our Fathers to the separation from the British Government, will induce the liberty loving people of the Southern States to a separation" in the face of continued northern aggressions. The Huntsville *Democrat* said that the South's cause was "the cause of freedom, of constitutional liberty," and reminded all of "the Jeffersonian doctrine that 'Resistance to tyranny is obedience to God.'" A Fourth of July editorial from the Black Belt hailed the day "of our release from thraldom—from the insult, injury, tyranny and oppression of *power*" and proclaimed that in 1776 "the bloody ghost of anarchy, civil commotion" was held up to our ancestors as reason for compromise, but it "had no such terrors as to drive them from the assertion and maintenance of their rights. Why should we, the descendants of those people, suffer ourselves to be frightened by the same stories, from similar sources of the present day? Is it not more in consonance with the acts and determination of the patriots of the 4th of

70. Montgomery *Advertiser*, June 5, 1850.

July, 1776, that we their descendants should assert our rights, and if they are not awarded us, to fight for them if necessary?"[71]

The address of the first state southern rights convention of 1851, probably from the pen of Yancey, summed up the argument from liberty:

Like our fathers . . . we are driven to seek, not for a remedy for the past—that is hopeless—but for security for the future. . . . If we are not prepared for this, it seems to us that it has been in vain that the noble Declaration of Independence has been transmitted to us. If it is to be handed down to posterity but as a memento of an interesting event in history, only to be admired for its terse eloquence, vain indeed was the great example, vain the bonfires which have celebrated its anniversary, vain the teaching of the American youth to regard it as a duty incumbent upon them to perform its mighty truths.

But we do not shrink, nor can we believe that you will shrink from a line of duty prescribed and followed by Washington, Hancock and Adams, and the host of illustrious dead who made that declaration, and thus fearlessly appealed from the Tyrant to the God of Liberty. We may be stigmatized as rebels; but Washington was a rebel! LaFayette was a rebel, and so was Tell and so is Kossuth, rebels against abuse of power; and welcome to us be the appellation received in defence of our rights and liberties.

And he added his conception of what would happen if his opponents' policy of acquiescence in the Compromise settlement were adopted.

Free-soil State after free-soil State will come into the Union. The free-soil majority now in the Senate will increase with each accession. The free-soil majority in the House will continue to enlarge its gigantic proportions. The executive will be but the reflex of a dominant free-soil power in the government, while the South, with no hope of corresponding territorial expansion, will be struggling with the very plethora of slavery. Our public men, seduced from the thorny, self-denying path of duty, will be found struggling for place in the affections of some Northern President. And when time shall have ruthlessly produced these effects, and the sunny South has become the Ireland of the Union, the spirit of "acquiescence" may complacently claim them to be the fruits of her policy—a policy but occasionally and feebly disturbed by some Emmet whom the sufferings of our land may induce to attempt its rescue, and whose blood will quench the feeble fire of patriotism which his eloquence may serve to kindle in the bosoms of his abject "acquiescing" coun-

71. *Ibid.*, October 2, 1850, June 25, 1851; *Jackson County Democrat*, quoted *ibid.*, September 4, 1850; Huntsville *Democrat*, quoted *ibid.*, October 30, 1850.

trymen. . . . From such a class never yet has sprung a Washington, a Hancock, or a Patrick Henry.[72]

At least as important as the threat to liberty was the threat to equality. Southerners were being stripped of all self-respect by their treatment as second-class citizens. A Talladega County meeting resolved "that whenever an abolition majority in Congress, by aid of the interference of any officer of the Federal Government or by any other mode, shall deprive us of the inestimable right of *political equality*, and appropriate to themselves the vast territories of the United States (the common property of all the States)—it is then *their* Government, not ours. Then we shall be compelled to regard it as our enemy." Thaddeus Sanford concluded, "To resist such arrogant assumptions is but the ordinary impulse of manhood—to submit to them is voluntary degradation. An American freeman acknowledges no master but his God."

Former governor Arthur Bagby warned his audience in a speech,

You are to be degraded in the scale of social, moral and political existence, merely because you are the owners of property which you found in the pathway of your destiny, and much of which was put there to gratify the avarice and cupidity of those who now denounce you for holding it under the guarantees of the constitution. . . . There is not a term of reproach furnished by the vocabularies of Billingsgate or Grubb street, not daily applied to the Southern people by Northern presses and Northern people! . . . We are also pronounced unworthy to worship in the temple of the living God, because we are slaveholders. He mentioned these things not for the purpose of arousing the passions, but in order that his audience might see the extent of the injustice and the impositions inflicted upon us, and that we are not, as we are falsely charged to be, agitators without cause.

John Cochran maintained that the national government had clearly and consciously decided to halt the progress of the South because she "is not fit to keep pace with the North"; and he asked, "Now can the South submit to remain a party to a government which thus avows, both in words and deed, its purpose to be its ruin and degradation? I think not—I pray God that the South may tear herself from the power of the monster which does not conceal its purpose. . . . We feel that in

72. Montgomery *Advertiser*, March 26, 1851.

the confederacy we are degraded, and have now no remedy but secession." [73]

The emphasis upon equality led to frequent appeals to the memory of Andrew Jackson. "Gen. Jackson knew that this Government was formed on the great principle of equality, that it was a partnership of sovereign States, each equal to the other, and all entitled alike to a full share of its benefits, as all had alike to bear its burdens"; therefore, he could never have accepted "that under the Constitution Congress had the power to declare that a free citizen of Massachusetts was a better man and entitled to more privileges than a free citizen of Alabama." Of course, Jackson had opposed nullification, but southern rights men dismissed that point. "Gen. Jackson is the last man in the world that should be quoted by the submissionists to aggression and oppression; his whole life vindicates his character from such contamination—it is well known he bore to his grave the mark of a sword cut from a British officer because he would not clean his boots." Since southern rights advocates equated Unionism with self-abasement and slavish conduct, it naturally followed that Jackson's refusal to clean a British officer's boots placed the Old Hero in the southern rights camp. [74]

For the student who fails to realize the importance of the argument from equality, it must often seem that southern rights reasoning has, as in this instance, a peculiarly metaphorical character. But these are not metaphors. The society was structured so as to demand, and to appear to allow, the achievement of individual autonomy. Therefore, each man's self-respect was absolutely essential to his existence as a part of the social organism. Doubtless it is ironic that the antebellum world encouraged—indeed, was founded upon—a concept which in its very nature is socially disorganizing. The necessity for reconciling an antisocial ideal with the obvious imperative for communal cooperation induced the fascination with symbols which we have encountered so often in political propaganda. Observers focused their comments so intensely upon the symbolic issue or verbal formulation that the issue or formulation could pass beyond a mere hint at truth to the substance of truth in the minds of antebellum Americans. A metaphrastic render-

73. *Ibid.*, July 10, August 28, August 14, October 2, 1850.
74. *Ibid.*, June 25, June 11, 1851.

ing of the oratory of the period must miss the point, but just as the monster bank became the sum of evils, so the free-soil territory became the embodiment of humiliation.

We may thus understand what the southern rights forces meant when they called the Compromise of 1850 unconstitutional. Moderates like Senator King were puzzled by the charge. But William F. Samford pointed out that "despotism was always a sly, cunning, cowardly, quietly speaking bloody hypocrite. It never avows its designs. It is by stealthy encroachments that it labors to compromit and then destroy the rights of the people." One should not expect, therefore, that the bills introduced by the abolition conspiracy would directly violate the letter of the Constitution; their violation would be subtle. Any unjust act destructive of southern rights contravened the spirit of the compact, and should be considered void. "Unconstitutional" in these terms became more a moral judgment than a legal fact. In the same sense Congressman Hubbard could assert that it would be unconstitutional for Delaware, for instance, of her own accord to abolish slavery within her own borders, for by doing so she would reduce the remaining slaveholding states to a minority in the Senate, and thus violate the spirit of equality.[75]

The northern threat to southern self-respect could come in many guises. Its chief form was the free-soil movement. But cited with almost equal frequency by the press were personal insults to individual southerners who traveled to the north, and northern statements which indicated supercilious contempt for the South. Indeed, one beat meeting resolved that even if free-soil aggressions should cease, "the unwillingness of Northern men to sit around the same altars with Southern men—the denunciations of us by the press and people of the North—the false slanders circulated in their periodicals and reviews—the rending of churches for a theoretical sentiment, and then appropriating to their use what they sanctimoniously call the price of blood—have alienated the two sections of a common country, and would alone, at some future day, terminate in a dissolution of the union."[76]

Nevertheless, free-soil came to be seen as the primary symbol of second-class citizenship. It is true that in 1860 there were precisely two

75. *Ibid.*, November 20, 1850, July 16, August 13, 1851, May 22, 1850.
76. *Ibid.*, October 16, 1850; cf. *Jackson County Democrat*, quoted *ibid.*, October 2, 1850.

slaves in the entire territory of Kansas. But statistics are no measure of the validity of this appeal. Free-soil was of course the issue precisely because it involved obvious and demeaning governmental discrimination against the South. Northerners sometimes pointed out that it would exclude only slaveholders, not small farmers, from the territories. But the distinction was meaningless, for as we have seen, southern rights advocates countered effectively with the argument that southerners, devoted to individual autonomy, could never be happy in a society constituted on the northern model. Whatever the reality of society in the North, its stereotype was firmly fixed in southern myth. Therefore, "although a man may be poor and own no slaves, yet he has and feels an abiding interest in the institutions of his country, and . . . in the hour of trial he is the surest reliance for their defence and protection." [77] In southern society a man's worth was not simply assumed. Every citizen was prepared—was eager—to assert it in his every action, for it was the substance of his proudest claim: that he was a free man. The necessity for secession proceeded directly from that asseveration.

The southern rights case was complete. We may recapitulate it in deductive form. The essence of Jacksonian society was the worship of the idols Liberty and Equality. Southerners, because of their daily contact with genuine slavery, were even more fanatically devoted to the Jacksonian cult than were most Americans; they did not exclude human sacrifice in order to sustain it. Since absolute individual autonomy is antisocial, the society tended to use symbols with which to reaffirm to itself its professed ideals. But the ideals were consciously held, and any action which appeared to the citizenry to threaten individual autonomy was regarded as a challenge to democracy and a portent of thralldom.

Upon these assumptions, which Alabamians held without question or examination, was founded the portion of the southern rights case more susceptible of explicit expression. Insults to individual southerners, the division of the churches, and similar circumstances proved that northerners held their fellow citizens of the South in contempt. The goal of Yankee South-haters was domination of the general gov-

77. Montgomery *Advertiser*, June 4, 1851.

ernment. The adoption of a free-soil policy would follow immediately upon their gaining that control. Once free-soil was enacted, the South would be condemned to inferiority in the Union. Southerners would be imprisoned within existing southern boundaries, for to settle in the territories would be to abandon a truly democratic, truly free, truly American community for a community riven by social conflict, in which the many were directly dependent upon the few for their liveli-hood and in which genuine egalitarianism was therefore impossible. Given the rate of Negro population increase, confining southerners to the South meant trapping them to be drowned by a rising black tide. When the population imbalance became excessive, by perhaps 1870, the weak and rich would flee, leaving the yeomen to fight a race war or, alternatively, to accept equality with slaves. Equality with slaves destroyed the meaning of equality—the pride of manhood which flows from the knowledge of freedom. Now if the northern masses, under the guidance of their fanatical manipulators, were indeed com-mitted to free-soil, then their numbers would inevitably give them eventual mastery within the federal government. At that time only se-cession—escape from the tyrannical exercise of power which would follow—could preserve the substance of equality and freedom. But since free-soilism would ultimately become governmental policy, it was dangerous to tarry while the South was stealthily ensnared in the net of despotism. If southerners were to remain Americans, they must secede as soon as possible, while they were still able to do so.

Almost every argument offered by southern rights advocates was intended to buttress some aspect of this case. It is worth noting that a number of contentions unrelated to the case were also not in general use. There were surprisingly few assertions that slavery was beneficial to the slaves. Appeals to the substantial loss of capital investment, the diminution of the work force, and the disorganization of the planta-tion system of agriculture which emancipation would entail were rare. And far from pointing out the necessity of slavery if there was to be a wealthy planter class, the southern rights advocates went out of their way to picture small farmers as the vanguard of the secession crusade. Of one meeting we are told, "The yeomanry of the country was out in numbers equal to any previous meeting ever held in the county, and . . . 'they were all of one accord.' It was strictly a county meeting. The farmers were the principal speakers, and everyone present could easily discern that the present situation of the South and the aggressions of the North upon her constitutional rights had been deeply studied by our people, and that they are resolved no longer to submit to it." At another meeting, "The yeomanry made themselves felt, and were prepared for the adoption of far more decisive measures." Southern rights advocates "need not fear of meeting a hearty and unanimous response from the sturdy yeomanry of the hills and valleys of Alabama." And again, "Give us the honest yeomanry of the country forever—there are no free soilers or submissionists among them; Arnold's treason was detected and exposed by such men, and their honesty and patriotism was proof against the seductive influence of British gold. They are the same to this day. They can be relied on." [78]

The truth was, of course, as the election returns incontrovertibly demonstrated, that most of the Alabama electorate was Unionist. But the southern rights press repeatedly sought to place itself on the side of the masses for the same reason that it seldom bothered with arguments likely to convert the planters—who were equally Unionist in their sentiments. The entire thrust of the southern rights case was directed towards the people who mattered in Alabama politics, the small farmers. Secession was a political decision, to be accomplished through the governmental machinery, and political decisions were made by the voters. The Democrats knew how to win elections. Over many years they had perfected the techniques by which the fears of the citizenry were given concrete form. The politicians and the editors knew what to say and how to say it. The essential formulas had been refined in a thousand skirmishes with banks, internal improvement corporations, and other enemies of American liberty. The southern rights case was carefully crafted, and was as entirely persuasive as all its predecessors—right up to the final two steps in the chain of reasoning.

The reasons for secession were sufficient if, as the case asserted, the overwhelming majority of northerners was free-soilist. In that case, northern numbers would indeed give that section control of the federal government, and the chain of consequences which would result in southern degradation would be set in motion. But there remained substantial doubt that the greater part of northern voters really sym-

78. *Ibid.*, August 21, August 14, June 12, 1850.

pathized with free-soil, and as long as Yankee hostility was not an established fact, southerners would continue to pray that the world would simply leave them alone. It was therefore to the effort to demonstrate the northerners' enmity and scorn for the South that southern rights men devoted many of their sermons. Congressman Hubbard warned urgently that if southerners failed to demand an adjustment of the sectional crisis, "it will go far to justify the taunts made against them by their enemies: 'That they have become enervated and unfit for self-government on account and by reason of their peculiar institutions.' I know better—I know if you fail to act, it will be solely because you believe you are not in danger; but you will remember the fable that 'the wolf *did* come at last,' and if you now go on as heretofore, quarrelling about party schemes, he will find you off your guard and helpless."

Was the South in danger? Was it true, as asserted, "that there is a fixed determination on the part of a majority of the people in the free States to make the question of domestic slavery a controlling element in the politics of the country and in the action of the government"? It was the question of the hour. Former governor Bagby told an audience, "He had no expectation of success from the cooperation of our Northern friends, although he knew we had many in the Northern States. But they cannot sustain themselves: it is folly, therefore, to depend upon, for the preservation of our rights, those who cannot sustain themselves. They have become powerless. Year after year we see them going down amidst the roar of the tempest created by howling fanaticism and unprincipled ambition." The *Advertiser* went further. "That good faith and brotherly love at the North of which we now hear so much, exists only in the throats of the demagogues who want our money or our votes, and, with however much reluctance, we shall all soon be driven to the conclusion that not being able to preserve our equality in the Union, it is the solemn and imperative duty of the South to seek and maintain her independence out of it."[79]

The early demands of the abolitionists seemed absurd when first made, but most of them were by 1850 generally accepted in the North. If the past demonstrated anything, northern public opinion would be-

79. *Ibid.*, May 22, 1850, January 15, 1851, August 14, 1850, January 1, 1851.

come increasingly belligerent, increasingly radical. The abolitionists were winning. At least, the southern rights advocates begged, let us assume a posture which will force northern voters to declare themselves on free-soil; we may thus discover empirically whether the masses there are against us. William F. Samford wrote, "The Southern States, then, I think, are admonished by the considerations of honor, independence, present peace, future prosperity and glory, to take a position *now* that will fully test the temper and purpose of the Abolition States. If they be so resolute and fixed in their purpose of destroying the social organization of the Southern States as appears to be the fact, the latter will at once choose between abject submission with all the misery it will bring, and a separate existence with all its blessings."[80]

The Alabama electorate, however, could not be convinced to make the experiment. They merely watched apprehensively for signs that the southern rights men were right and the Unionists wrong about the sympathies of the ordinary northerner. Throughout the coming decade, evidence piled up. But the issue was not settled until the election of Lincoln. With that demonstration of northern opinion, the gap in southern rights reasoning was dramatically closed. Secession followed.

A final point is necessary. The careful reader will have observed a fundamental non sequitur in the southern rights case. If the great threat of free-soil was that it would trap southerners in the South amidst the rising tide of Negroes, how would secession remedy the predicament? Would not independence shut southerners out of the territories even more effectively than would the adoption of a free-soil policy by the federal government? When the point was raised, southern rights men had an answer. The property and the debts of the United States were acquired by Americans in common; when secession came, the South would have to pay its portion of the national debt and the North would have to give the South its proportionate share of the territories.[81] But the response clearly was a mere rationalization. There could be no assurance that the negotiations which would follow a peaceful secession would produce a mutually acceptable adjustment. If

80. *Ibid.*, August 7, July 3, 1850.
81. *Cf.*, however, *ibid.*, February 13, 1850, April 16, 1851. See also Eleanor Noyes Jackson to Mary Noyes, February 19, 1861, in Jackson Papers.

they did not, the only alternative would be war. Whether the South sought the requisite territory by gift or by seizure, a considerable element of chance was involved. If getting access to that territory was the primary southern goal, southerners had certainly not selected a means which gave obvious promise of being efficacious.

It is essential to note, however, that though this genuinely crucial link in the southern rights argument was, to say the least of it, weak, Unionists almost never mentioned the difficulty. The solution to this paradox is the identification of which element in the southern rights case was the primary source of its force. Despite all the discussion about the effects of free-soil upon southern slavery, the threat of Negro inundation was not the chief terror with which the case conjured; and the Unionists knew it. Unionists saw that answering the southern rights arguments with the assertion that secession would not give the territories to the South would be like answering the attacks on the bank by quoting from its balance sheet; it would miss the thrust of the appeal. The essence of the case was not what would happen to southerners when they were excluded from the territories but was the fact that they were to be excluded. That the exclusion would wreak ill in the economic and social environment of the South was mere lagniappe to the argument; the true ills would be wrought in the hearts of those debarred. Free-soil was an issue basically because it would represent an overtly discriminatory action by the common government.

The threat of second-class citizenship struck too near the vitals of the society for safe political discussion. If the Unionists got themselves identified as unconcerned about the preservation of equality, they could find themselves in the position of the members of the Broad River group who had failed to pronounce the shibboleths dictated by Israel Pickens—proscribed from participation in politics for all time to come. They did not venture to controvert the fundamental assumptions of the southern rights case. They contented themselves simply with maintaining that most northerners did not hate the South, that the North could thus be brought to compromise, and that compromise would restore calm to the republic and self-respect to all its citizens without the necessity for radical action. If the southern rights fears of discrimination should ever gain substance, however, Unionists agreed that immediate and harsh reciprocal action would be required.

Secession, then, was not really intended as a remedy for the consequences of free-soil, despite explicit statements to the contrary. It was to be revenge for the condemnation implied by the policy and the inequality inherent in it. Southerners were Americans and they wanted to be treated like Americans; we must never forget that they saw themselves as struggling to preserve the substance of the American dream. One editor wrote that if the sectional controversy were decided in favor of the South, "the people may continue free, united and happy, bearing steadily aloft the beacon-light of liberty, to conduct the wayfaring, the oppressed and downtrodden of other nations to the haven of freedom; but if decided the other way, the sun of liberty, as regulated by the eternal principles of justice, will have set in darkness, and the brighted hopes of man will be extinguished forever."[82]

The Fire-Eaters

However much the southern rights newspapers sought to make their movement appear an outpouring of popular sentiment, the truth is that it was the function of political leaders to focus the amorphous popular fears on some specific threat. Thus the politicians actively directed the time-tested mechanics of organizing public opinion. As future governor A. B. Moore recommended to another prominent Democrat, "I trust that public meetings throughout the state will be held for the purpose of enlightening the masses and causing them to understand and properly to appreciate the wrongs that have been done them by an unprincipled majority in congress. Before the common people will be prepared to resent insults and injuries in the proper spirit, they must be made to *know* and *feel* that they have been thus treated, and this can only be done by the press and public discussion."[83]

But there was a group of men in Alabama who were soon to repudiate such leaders. They went into the Crisis of 1850 deeply convinced of the necessity for strong action. They rallied to the political spokesmen who proclaimed defiance to Yankee aggression. And they watched with mounting dismay as the oratory of the spokesmen turned to compromise, as the political structure imposed its infrangible

82. Montgomery *Advertiser*, January 15, 1851.
83. A. B. Moore to Bolling Hall, November 15, 1850, in Hall Papers.

bounds on the debate, as concrete action was replaced by mere expressions of resentment, and eventually by acquiescence. Transformed in the flames of this controversy, they emerged from it as fire-eaters, southern rights men who looked on their cause as a crusade. Politics defiled the politician; the only leader fit to enjoin a crusade is a priest.

The southern rights case presented in the preceding section was argued by the candidates of the Southern Rights party and preached by the genuine southern rights men, but its substance did not vary. In the mouths of the latter expositors, however, two elements of the case received greater emphasis: the contention that the North and the South had developed different cultures was embroidered; and hostility to politics and politicians became the first article of the faith. As to the first point, a correspondent of the *Dallas Gazette* of Cahaba wrote that the sectional conflict was not mere factional strife. "It is the clamour of nations. It is the high-raised argument of many States sprung from the Pilgrim Race, mingling with that of other States sprung from the Virginia Race. And it is an argument that words may not—oh! cannot settle." He longed for the creation of an independent southern nation out of "all those kindred communities which have grown off from the Virginia stock, and in their progress Southward, have incorporated with and assimilated to them, and thus elevated the predominating races of Southern Europe. Commanding the Atlantic from the capes of the Chesapeake to the Land's End of Florida, and sweeping from that point around the magnificent expanse of the Western Mediterranean, this ample confederacy, stretching far into and across the curving continent, would look out upon the world of commerce from her hundred window-ports, and sit, like Ceres with her cornucopia, inviting all nations to inspect her treasures." He confessed, "[Abolitionist] fanaticism stimulated to the contemplation of this picture. The spirit of *American fraternity*, so long the predominating and master-sentiment of the Southern bosom, would never have called up this image of *separate nationality* if the Pilgrim Race had been true to public faith and to public honor." But whatever its source, the enmity between the two cultures had, he concluded, taken on a life of its own.[84]

84. Quoted in Montgomery *Advertiser*, December 25, 1850.

The differences between the regions were more often assumed than stated. But the principal charges seem to have been social conditions which left northerners prey to enthusiastic movements, and an intellectual tradition which encouraged zealotry in the pursuit of those movements. The northern social and intellectual milieu marked a profoundly sick society. This observation was the point of departure for an important distinction between the views of the Democrats and those of the fire-eaters. In the southern analysis, the North was at war with itself. The social condition which was primarily responsible for the numerous meliorist efforts in the region was the domination of its masses by "bankers, merchants, manufacturers and capitalists"; and the consequent search by the citizens for some mechanism through which the common man could recover his liberties, now so evidently lost. But northern oligarchs depended for their economic well-being on the South's contribution to international trade and national commerce. Southern secession would plunge the North into an extraordinarily severe depression. Thus a concerted southern threat of radical action might logically be expected to force the capitalists, whose control of northern politics usually lay dormant, to crush the fanatical anti-South movements and bring the region to the southern heel. The sickness of northern society might be made to play into southern hands.[85]

This line of reasoning was embraced by the moderate Southern Rights party establishment. The politicians argued that if the southern masses could be brought to support strong measures, the invocation of the measures would be unnecessary. If northerners actually believed that the South would secede, their economic interests would force them to yield to southern requirements. The case for secession was avowedly argued, therefore, in the belief that its acceptance would remedy the sectional difficulties.[86]

The fire-eaters rejected this notion. Secession was not a remedy for the past but a safeguard for the future, they said. The lack of true equality in the North might well be the source of the frustrations

85. *E.g., ibid.*, February 13, May 22, October 16, 1850.

86. On this point, note the *Advertiser's* rationale for praising George W. Gayle's radicalism: January 1, 1851. Of course, if the North failed to yield, the moderate Southern Rights men were perfectly prepared to secede. Northern intransigence would in effect establish the necessity for disunion. Indeed, to be successful, the experiment required exactly that sort of inflexible determination from all southerners.

which abolitionist fanaticism manipulated, but the fanaticism had proceeded too far. Capitalists would find themselves unable to check it. It had possessed the spirit of the people. Besides, the controversy had revealed northern society's hidden illnesses, and the inherent superiority of the southern way of life, so starkly that the fire-eaters no longer wanted union with the other region.[87]

There were thus three distinct positions on secession during the debates of 1850. The Unionists believed that the northern masses were at heart friendly to the South, that they were driven into the arms of abolitionists by resentment of southern rights bluster, but that if the South adopted a sweetly reasonable posture, the North would be happy to reach an accommodation. The Southern Rights politicians believed that a united southern threat of secession coupled with firm insistence upon a single set of demands would force the capitalists, who were in real control in the other region, to exact submission from northern voters. The politicians argued vigorously that most north-erners were abolitionists, but they clearly thought that more calculat-ing men held reins which were as yet slack, but were nonetheless strong. The fire-eaters believed that the general turmoil created by conditions in the North such as the concentration of wealth had taken political control from the economic powers and delivered it to half-crazed demagogues. Union thus tied the South like a Siamese twin to a socially leprous sibling. Naturally, therefore, the fire-eaters placed greater stress on cultural differences. It was one of the usual elements in the southern rights case, but for the fire-eaters it was a more than ordinarily consequential point. It raised secession above the level of intimidation to the status of a therapeutic amputation.

A corollary to this attitude was the fear expressed by a number,

87. The most convenient summaries of the fire-eaters' general attitudes are the Montgomery platforms of 1851 (*ibid.*, February 26, 1851) and of 1852 (*ibid.*, March 9, 1852), and the Montgomery Address of 1851 (*ibid.*, March 26 1851). The Montgomery Platform of 1852 bases its appeal squarely upon cultural differences, but as is so often the case, merely states that "the systems of civilization obtaining in the North and in the South have, through agitation, become antagonistic and at war with each other." Delineations of the points upon which the two cultures were supposed to differ are rare, and must be pieced together from numerous casual remarks. It was indignation at northern assumptions of superiority, rather than any clear sense of southern uniqueness, which was the true source of nationalistic arguments. Slavery was the only obvious dissimilarity, and fire-eaters therefore tended to attribute all good things in southern society to the influence of that institution.

though not by all, of the fire-eaters that southern society was being subverted from within by Yankee infiltration. Since slavery was the source of southern merit, and since slavery was a rural social pattern, naturally fire-eater suspicions were directed primarily towards urban phenomena.

There is a cancer in the very bosom of Southern society, corroding it at the vitals and which must ultimately destroy it, and with it our free institutions, unless it can be corrected. . . . Northern men with Northern feelings and prejudices and principles, the natural fruits of Northern education, habits and associations, occupy all the important departments of life. They occupy our pulpits—our seminaries of learning and to a great extent wield that mighty engine, the press. Indeed, there is scarcely a Southern city in the United States in which Northern men do not perform the larger portion of the business of life through all its relations and departments. . . . Cast your eyes at the public improvements in which, after the sleep of almost ages, we have engaged. They, too, have to be confided to Northern men, who swindle their employers and furnish free papers to their slaves. Am I not speaking the language of truth and soberness when I say that these people attempt to debauch our understandings and pick our pockets at the same time? These, with their Southern allies, are the elements of the new Union party now in the progress of formation.

There were resultant pleas for boycotts of anti–southern rights merchants and factors. Even the opinions of faculty members at the University of Alabama were drawn into the controversy, because of the enmity between the institution's southern rights president, Basil Manly, and its Unionist dean, F. A. P. Barnard.[88]

If the southern rights men feared northern influence in the cities, however, they were particularly concerned that their own membership was confined, for the most part, to the same areas. They were defending a society whose chief characteristic was slavery, but the slaveholders offered them little support. The natural concomitant of a fear of subversion is a belief that the threatened group remains apathetic. Thus the Mobile *Herald* bemoaned "one of the most astounding and hopeless features in Southern affairs." The region's lands and slaves were enormously valuable.

88. *Ibid.*, September 11, October 2, November 20, 1850, September 23, 1851. *Cf.* also the statement of Thomas S. Mays, *ibid.*, August 28, 1850.

Yet so indifferent are those who are mainly the proprietors of this immense treasure that to this day the whole control of our public opinion is left almost entirely to those who are only indirectly interested in its security and welfare. Whom does the security of Southern affairs proceed from? Whence comes the agitation which brings to us political health, equality and stability? Certainly not immediately, as a general fact, from the planter. He remains supine on his estates; or if he venture from them, he proceeds in search of pleasure, or something else foreign to the great end which should control his actions. He seems to have no more sensibility to the effect of national legislation than if he were a stranger to the country. A good deal of this doubtless is occasioned by his isolated condition—his remoteness from that stimulus to action which is usually found among dense populations. Public opinion mainly proceeds from our cities and towns, and we shall announce no heresy when we declare that it could not proceed from places less worthy of trust. Our [urban] citizens are not pure sources of political authority, and as long as they are implicitly confided in by the agricultural population we shall have no hope of an emancipation from the evils which at present environ of the South.[89]

The editor not only announced no heresy; he reiterated orthodoxy.

The trepidation at the twin dangers of infiltration and apathy left fire-eaters extraordinarily sensitive to small events, subject to paroxysm without warning. One such man attended a speech given by the Southern Rights Congressional candidate John Cochran, and there overheard an Alabamian of northern birth remark that Cochran should be hanged for his sentiments. It was enough to plunge the observer into a diatribe of considerable length and remarkable vehemence.

My countrymen, this is but the prelude of what awaits the South, "the degraded, starving" South . . . if we tamely submit to these indignities and aggressions of the North and Northern influence upon us from within and without our borders. . . . I call on the freemen of the South to meditate on these things and determine for themselves whether they will be free, or slaves to the North. . . . Your destiny depends on your action, whether you will submit to a social and political equality with the African race. . . . Estimate the ratio of their increase and you will find yourselves overwhelmed in a few years in their multitude. The Northern man can go to the uttermost ends of our country with all his earthly possessions, but Southern men are to be pent up and confined within the narrow limits assigned by the North to slave territory, "to die of dry rot" or any other catastrophe, [to which] circumstances thus imposed may subject them; and if the South, after appealing again and again, in

89. Quoted *ibid.*, January 15, 1851.

the spirit of brotherhood, to the North for the redress of these wrongs which no true Southern man justifies or excuses, without success, and we as freemen dare declare we will not submit longer, we are answered by being pointed to the halter by Northern men who come among us to execute a part of the Grand Scheme of emancipation by obtaining the control of our destiny, peaceably if we will submit, but if not by hanging us.

He concluded this philippic, "Our crusade is not against the Union; it is for liberty and equality, and we implore God we may find them in the Union, but whether to be found in or out of it, we go for 'liberty and equality.'"[90] The quotation contains a great many of the ordinary features of the southern rights case as we have discovered them; the essential point is that this highly articulated nightmare was triggered immediately by what was clearly an idle and innocuous comment. To men who believed that an alien culture sought their enslavement, such a happenstance could never be trivial; it was, instead, a clue.

The second point particularly emphasized in fire-eater oratory was the innate perfidy of political leadership. We have already noted the classic encounter between the Yanceyites and the Southern Rights party's candidate, Congressman Sampson W. Harris, in 1851. An analysis of Harris' letter to the Wetumpka *Guard* setting forth at great length his views on the sectional crisis, will reveal the substance of fire-eater objections. Harris called the Compromise "the foul record of our shame" and much else in the same vein. He expounded on the horrors awaiting southerners if they were shut out of the territories and pent up with the Negroes. But secession was not an appropriate remedy unless all southerners supported it, he said, for otherwise it would be socially divisive. "Discord pervades our ranks. We are at war among ourselves," he warned. "Any policy should be avoided at a crisis like the present which, by fomenting the spirit of party, may expose us to those dangerous extremes to which all parties become liable in the zeal of controversy. . . . I would make the people of the South a homogeneous community, identified in feeling and united in purpose; counselling in harmony, and acting together." As an alternative, he offered the development of southern manufactures as an "avowed principle of retaliation" which would appeal "to the cupidity of the

90. *Ibid.*, July 23, 1851.

North (the only bond that makes it prize the Union)," but more importantly, would serve "to unite the whole South and arouse it to a sense
of its danger."[91]

The Unionists called this letter the work of a fire-eater, but the
genuine southern rights men knew better. A few months earlier Harris
had spoken at Prattville. He dismissed commercial nonintercourse as
an "inefficient" form of response, and he "asserted the undoubted right
of a State to secede whenever she should see fit to adopt that remedy,"
but, "in reference to his precise position, he thought something ought
to be done. He confessed he could not tell what would be the best
course, but he would be the most ardent to support any plan of resistance that might be agreed on by the people of the State." In the letter,
Harris summarized his position succinctly: "The wisdom of any line of
policy depends much upon the measure of success which will probably
attend it." Yancey's Montgomery *Atlas* then commented, "In Congress, Maj. Harris has done well and, we believe, would do well
again. . . . [But] the battle has to be fought at our own doors—and we
recognize no more dangerous enemy to the true interests of Alabama
than such counsellors as the Hon. S. W. Harris."[92]

A correspondent who signed himself "Seceder" had earlier expounded the fire-eater view. "We, the people," he wrote, have no
"leaders who are not rather *followers* than guides." Politicians had
always to have a majority behind them.

Every argument they make tends towards [secession] and nothing else; they
tell us of insufferable wrongs, of aggression constantly increasing in boldness
and violence, of the futility of guaranties so often and constantly violated, of
the impossibility of avoiding wrong if we stay in the Union, and yet Secession!—they dare not say it, for fear that Messrs. A, B and C might become
alarmed, and so "they palter with us in a double sense." . . . Ah! my good
"leaders," who are not leaders, if you wish the truth to triumph, it is necessary
to speak the truth. . . . You can never make the people believe that which you,
their teachers and "leaders," are afraid to say you believe. . . . You want them
up to you, and to accomplish this you adopt the notable plan of going down
to them. . . . If we fail, I know our politic leader who delivered us over to
destruction by going down and encouraging, *in his way,* our friends below,

91. *Ibid.,* May 7, 1851 (a portion of the letter has been effaced by the disintegration of the
paper).
92. *Ibid.,* May 7, May 28, 1851, November 20, 1850; Montgomery *Atlas,* May 21, 1851.

will wash his hands, like Pilate, of the entire business, and not be discredited: if we succeed, mark me, he will be up in time to join in the shout of victory and claim the spoils of the vanquished.[93]

In this society, politicians were "teachers"—the agent who gave form to unformed fears. The masses were led into the way of truth by the oratory of the statesmen. But the process was always a two-pronged exploration; the politician sought both an effective symbol and a remedy which was generally acceptable. He did not in fact lead; he codified. Therefore the politician would not—could not—suggest an unpopularly radical action. Very early in the struggle of 1850, the genuine southern rights men were brought to understand this truth.

All over Alabama politicians joined Congressman Franklin W. Bowdon, who said that he was "in favor of immediate action, and of resistance of the most decided character," which when he was pressed, turned out to be for "the people to speak out against the aggressions of Congress in their primary meetings, and for the Legislatures of the oppressed States to remonstrate, and to pass laws of non-intervention [*sic*] until the North was brought to a sense of justice, and our liberties could remain undisturbed." Politicians agreed with Governor Collier that the people were not ready for making secession the issue. At least one Southern Rights legislator, a Whig, even publicly and abjectly confessed error, endorsed the Compromise, and became a Unionist.[94] From the perspective of the fire-eaters, these statements were the weapons with which the society's heroes were callously murdering the very electorate which had admired and elevated them. The politicians, for the sake of personal advancement, had consciously precluded the one policy which the politicians themselves believed to be the South's only hope—or so the fire-eaters thought. Thus, as the southern rights movement collapsed, the fire-eaters passed beyond despair to cold fury.

Some fire-eaters fell into the old Calhounite trap of attributing the politician's reluctance to assume radical positions—his lack of devotion to principle, they would have called it—to the everlasting scramble for spoils. Thomas S. Mays warned that once a southern man be-

93. Montgomery *Advertiser*, November 13, 1850.
94. *Ibid.*, October 23, 1850, April 16, 1851.

came an applicant for federal office, "he becomes a traitor to the South, bought with the hope of conciliating Northern favor." The Eufaula *Spirit* moaned that all of Alabama's congressmen soon deserted southern rights. "Their minds somehow or other are suddenly expanded by the air of the capital—and men who at home had some reputation for being pretty fair sectional men, as soon as they get in sight of the Presidential mansion and Treasury office are at once transformed into the most national beings in the world. . . . In the company of Senators, Foreign Ministers, English lords, Cabinet officers and Northern nabobs, [our representatives] forget their humble constituency at home who have confided to them the most important trusts." It added that "When Southern men *dare* not accept federal office without the permission of their own people, we may expect our rights to be protected." [95]

Most southern rights advocates came to believe, however, that the instinctive conservatism of the politicians grew out of the natural action of the party system. The address of the first state southern rights convention of 1851 proclaimed that the southern rights clubs were "composed of men who believed that the tendency of old party organizations has been to lead their members to avoid any decisive action on the great slavery question, and to wink at and acquiesce in aggressions on the South rather than endanger party success by opposition to them." Southern rights men "have not been blind to the mortifying fact that their aims and views have not met with that sympathy from the leaders and editors of the old parties, to which they were entitled. The rights endangered—the wrongs endured, it is true, are common. But men who have lived upon and are enjoying the honors and emoluments of party, are keenly sensitive to anything that will affect its organization, and interfere with well planned relations with their Northern allies."

This realization dictated that true fire-eaters cut themselves loose from the political structure and become a band of agitators. The address concluded:

The history of the great abolition party presents to us a lesson fruitful in wisdom. They were true to the aim they had in view. Regarding office and

95. *Ibid.*, September 18, 1850, February 12, 1851.

place as but means to advance their principles, they never made their principles square to such means. Consequently, from small beginnings and a position of disgust and contempt, they have risen to a position from which they command and control both the great parties of the country, and have most effectually given direction to the federal policy of this great confederacy. We have a purer, a nobler cause. It enlists the sympathies of every good man, of every enlightened patriot. We shall not be deterred by fear of defeat from its advocacy, but receiving new vigor from every fall, if such shall be our lot, shall rise again to do battle for the right.[96]

Former governor Arthur P. Bagby presented a response to such fire-eating sentiments which was typical of the politicians. Early in the crisis Bagby had sought to cooperate with the fire-eaters, and in June, 1851, he was still ready to call the Compromise "an intolerable and, in time, an insufferable evil." By that time, however, he was forced to add that the preservation of the Democratic party was an indispensable consideration. "Democratic principles, the Constitution and the Union must flourish and triumph together, or they must fall and perish together." A newspaper correspondent bitterly reported, "It has been avowed by some of these men [fire-eaters] that the democratic party and its leaders must be *put down*; and this would seem to be the *ultima thule* of the transactions of some men engaged in this controversy by the virulent manner in which some of [the Democrats'] prominent men are assailed, however true and sound they may be upon the Southern Question."[97]

The fire-eaters' hostility to the politician, and to the party structure which made him, was, more than any other aspect of the movement, its hallmark. But it was more; it was in a sense a repudiation of a quarter-century of the republic's political history. As late as 1848, Rush Elmore could write to Senator Lewis that the Alabama electorate was misinformed on the territorial question, that the people "entertain these opinions because they have not been able to get any information on the subject," and that it was Lewis' responsibility as senator to correct their errors.[98] The sentiment was natural. The Jacksonians had introduced a new conception of the government to Americans. It was

96. *Ibid.*, March 26, June 4, June 11, 1851. *Cf.* also the resolutions of the southern rights convention, *ibid.*, March 9, 1852.
97. *Ibid.*, June 4, June 11, 1851.
98. Rush Elmore to Dixon H. Lewis, March 2, 1848, in Lewis Papers, University of Texas Library.

neither the Jeffersonian vision—a minuscule organization whose sole domestic function was to restrain the citizens from injuring one another—nor the paternal state of modern times, cooperating with other vast institutions to create for the citizen a halcyon and antiseptic world. It was instead a sort of trade union of the electorate, a mechanism through which the masses, individually weak, could bring their collective weight to bear on menaces to the public welfare. It was not the potential enemy of the people, as in the Jeffersonian view, nor was it their wise guardian. It was rather the embodiment of their prejudices and their will, the tool with which they defended and enlarged their liberties. And the politician was the man who divined the current source of the threat.

Alabama was a particularly Jacksonian state, and its government was therefore particularly active in identifying and destroying the nightmares of the voters. For a generation the politician had been the society's superman, fighting a never-ending battle for truth, justice, and the American way. In a thousand quixotic jousts the politician had been the champion who had routed impending slavery and regained the elusive substance of equality for the common man. And now the fire-eaters asked the citizenry to believe that its paladin was its secret foe. The accusation was stupefying in its novelty. Everyone had known that there were evil politicians, of course, but the southern rights claim was that all politicians were rendered potential traitors by the demands of the party system. People could not be expected to alter their entire attitude towards government in an instant. The initial reaction to the charge was simple incredulity.

The remedy for unbelief is reiteration. Only dedicated agitation would break the electorate's dependence upon its political leadership to dictate the firmness of its response to the abolition threat. And so the fire-eaters joined William F. Samford in his plea for the faithful to "beware of the snare spread for our feet by the cunning spoilsmen. Have done with the old party shibboleths! Let every true Southern Rights man rend the last tie that binds him to party and resolve to fight for our firesides."[99]

Alabama politics was, as we have seen, intensely local in its struc-

99. Montgomery *Advertiser*, February 19, 1851.

ture. It should not surprise us, therefore, to discover that the fire-eaters were confined to a very few localities, and that each local group had its own approach to southern rights, shared among its members but clearly distinguished from that of each of the other groups. There were five centers of fire-eating sentiment. In order of radicalism, they were Cahaba, whose organ was the *Dallas Gazette*; Montgomery, whose organ was the *Atlas*; Eufaula, whose voice was the *Spirit of the South* (originally the *Democrat*); Mobile, whose views were expressed in the *Tribune*; and the upper Coosa Valley, centering on the towns of Jacksonville and Talladega, where the organs were the Talladega *Watchtower* and, to a lesser extent, the Jacksonville *Republican* and the Jacksonville *Sunny South*.We shall discuss each of these groups in turn, but a few initial generalizations are possible.

In the first place, an important point is emphasized by a glance at the population density map on page 240. It is at once apparent that the centers of southern rights views all lay in the most heavily populated areas. The fire-eater groups each centered about a town—ordinarily, a county seat—and each supported a press to elucidate its ideas. Neighboring rural counties sometimes contained individual southern rights men; but without an urban focus and a press to organize their opinions, they simply allied themselves with one of the coherent sects. Lowndes County, for instance, contained a substantial number of fire-eaters. It lay between two opinion centers, Cahaba and Montgomery, and its southern rights men appear to have divided accordingly, those in the neighborhood of Hayneville tending to ally with Montgomery and those around the village of Benton usually supporting the Cahabans. Perhaps trading patterns played a role in this schism, but on that point, evidence is lacking. It is clear, however, that the county never developed a position of its own, even though it contained a number of prominent exponents of the faith, including future Confederate congressman Cornelius Robinson, future supreme court justice George W. Stone, Edmund Harrison, Robert L. Scott, and James G. Gilchrist among others.[100] Southern Macon (modern Bullock) County seems to have been similarly divided between Montgomery on its west and Eufaula on its east.

100. On the position of Lowndes, see *ibid.*, October 2, October 9, October 16, 1850, February 12, February 26, April 23, May 21, June 18, December 16, 1851, March 9, 1852.

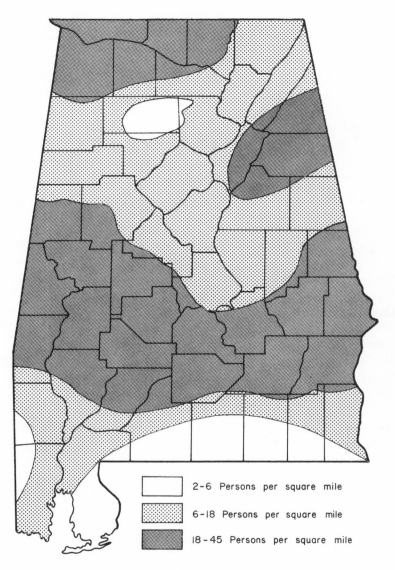

2-6 Persons per square mile

6-18 Persons per square mile

18-45 Persons per square mile

(After Dorman, Party Politics, p.215)

Population Density Map, 1850

A second generalization is probably a correlate of the fire-eaters' hostility to politicians. Few genuine southern rights men were prominent in politics previous to the Crisis of 1850. Of the 164 men who served as delegates to the state southern rights conventions of February, 1851, and of March, 1852, for instance, only 16 had previously served in the legislature. An additional 7 were elected subsequently. Still, only 23, or 14 percent, of the delegates ever achieved even this modicum of political importance.

Senator Clemens remarked that though "there are men among the Disunionists who would do honor to any station," many of them were men who "talk about character, who never had any of their own until they crawled into a Southern Rights Association and fancied that treason gave respectability to villainy."[101] The senator is not an unbiased source, but it appears that he hints at a truth. Many people who had not otherwise obtained influence were included in the number of the fire-eaters. They were not all persons without character. Some of the scions of the Broad River group, who were excluded from office for the sins of their ancestors, became fire-eaters. Percy and Leroy Pope Walker had earlier exercised some authority, but William Mathews Marks, James J. Gilmer, and Nicholas Meriwether, who participated actively in the Montgomery club, could never hope for high position, not least because of their ineradicable association in the public mind with great planter interests. Still, such men were not a substantial element among the southern rights disciples. Only 29 of the 164 southern rights delegates—less than 18 percent—owned fifty or more slaves in 1860. There is some evidence that a few young lawyers, too impatient for advancement to await the slow rewards of diligent service to the party, sought more rapid notoriety by joining the extremist element. It is possible that the modest, but still surprising number of fire-eaters who became scalawags during Reconstruction—Samuel F. Rice, Adam C. Felder, and Benjamin F. Saffold, for instance—represents this category.

But the ordinary fire-eater was neither wealthy nor ambitious nor politically prominent. He was simply an Alabamian, subject to the fears that had always been the substance of Alabama politics—that

101. *Ibid.*, September 23, 1851.

some alien and ungovernable force was preparing to destroy his liberty. The principal feature which distinguished him from his fellows seems to have been that he resided in a relatively urban area. There contact with the outside world was sufficiently extensive to make a threat from the abolitionists appear genuine. Previous threats had been close at hand—from the wealthy of the neighborhood, from local financial institutions; even the crusade against the Bank of the United States is of this type, since the bank had a branch at Mobile and since it issued a considerable portion of the currency with which the farmer purchased manufactured goods. The abolitionist specter was more remote. It did not impinge on the daily life of the ordinary citizen. The danger it presented was contingent upon the acceptance by a majority of the American electorate of a rationale not even argued in the Alabama citizen's hearing—or, indeed, in his entire region.

Thus, rather paradoxically, considerable intercourse with the North, and a knowledge of events there, was necessary before sectionalism could take firm root. The southern rights case clearly presupposed an awareness of trends in the rest of American society. Perhaps only in the urban centers were men sufficiently involved in national life to perceive a social movement in another section as being pregnant with consequences for their own. In that sense, the missing logical link in the southern rights case and the missing emotional element which alone would give fire-eaters victory at the polls were the same—convincing Alabamians that the northern populace was genuinely inimical to them. It was necessary to make the menace appear real and imminent. Only then would the politicians follow along in demanding radical action. But in 1850, the menace had taken definite form only in the minds of those men who both had contact with the North and had come to fear it.

Of course, this description is very far from the sort of characterization which would allow us to predict whether or not a given individual was likely to become a fire-eater. There are innumerable variables for which we have not accounted. Huntsville and Florence were urban centers in heavily populated areas, but they did not develop fire-eater congregations. Florence did not even have an important Southern Rights party effort. And in Huntsville the Southern Rights party consisted largely of the Clay family and its political dependents. The population concentrated in the Black Belt was largely black, and therefore excluded from politics; in the Coosa Valley it was overwhelmingly white. For our present purposes, however, the racial composition of the population is of relatively little importance, since whatever its hue, the population's density predisposed the area to a reliance upon the market economy. The most important caveat is that even in those towns in which fire-eaters were numerous, most citizens were not fire-eaters—and in fact, many citizens were Unionists. The foundation of the southern rights men's religion was dread of the future, and such anxiety must always remain a personal reaction.

The Cahaba group of fire-eaters included Joel E. Matthews, James H. Campbell, J. W. Brewer, Benjamin F. Saffold, and George J. S. Walker among its leaders, but without question its most famous—and most radical—member was George W. Gayle. Gayle alone among prominent Alabamians consistently and openly favored immediate, separate state secession. But his fellow Cahabans were only a half-step behind. Their public spokesman, Charles E. Haynes of the *Dallas Gazette*, had ranted that if the Compromise were passed, "let us have disunion—a secession of the slave States—a Southern republic—a division of the public property upon equitable terms—or the blood of our enemies." Though the Cahabans usually envisioned cooperative secession, they were certainly committed to effecting secession in some form. Even Haynes' position, though a bit more moderate than Gayle's, seemed ludicrous in more orthodox circles. The Montgomery *Advertiser* had responded to the *Gazette's* pronouncement by laughing, "That will do, Charlie, you may 'go head up.'"

Nevertheless, the Cahabans dreamed that they were the vanguard of a mighty host. Gayle wrote, "If secession brings on a conflict of arms, let it come! In that day there will be many a Kossuth in the field, animating the noble Southron." James H. Campbell asserted, "You may rest assured that the great body of the people are in advance of the politicians. Timid counsels find no favor even in *conservative Dallas*. Seven tenths of the people of this county are in favor of action, and I think I may add, immediate action. Rest assured that old party ties are here pretty well obliterated. A desperate struggle is made by a few to keep them up, to prevent the gathering storm, but it is all to no purpose." Of course such assessments were erroneous, but the Dallas

County men could never admit to themselves how far they stood in front of public opinion. They announced their categorical support of the extremist Montgomery Platform of 1851, pledging "that in our political intercourse we will know and teach no other doctrines, as we believe that these alone are right and proper." [102]

The career of George Gayle illustrates the fate which awaited these early radicals. When he entered politics, Gayle's future success seemed assured. A cousin of Governor John Gayle, he was also a relative, neighbor, and political and social confidant of Senator William R. King. As a young man, in 1830, he was elected assistant secretary of the state senate. In that position he got into a controversy with Senator James Abercrombie for having misquoted the senator in an anonymous letter to a newspaper, and showed his character by wailing that his was a battle of "the weak against the strong." He sat in the legislature in 1833 and 1834. In 1835, he ran unsuccessfully for a circuit judgeship, but thereafter was chosen judge of the Dallas County court, a position from which he resigned in 1837. He badly damaged his position with the Democratic party in 1839 when his maneuvering for a judgeship was blamed for the loss of the Mobile district congressional race to a Whig. Except for a single term in the legislature in 1845, he did not again hold elective office.

Meanwhile Gayle devoted himself to the destruction of Dixon H. Lewis and the elevation of Senator King, and quickly developed a reputation as an arch-Hunker. He had sought to have King returned to the Senate in 1845, and managed King's campaign in the epic battle with Lewis of 1847. The loss of that encounter evidently had a profound effect on Gayle, for by 1850 this man whose name was a synonym for the Hunker element in the Democratic party had broken with King and become a fire-eater, and an immediate secessionist at that. The transformation left Gayle, once a power with whom all reckoned, to be ridiculed as something of an elderly half-wit.

At the Democratic state convention of 1856, Gayle offered resolutions which, among other extremist propositions, endorsed secession if the North committed a single aggressive act during the following year, or if complete sectional peace was not restored at the end of that time.

102. *Ibid.*, January 1, 1851, June 5, August 28, 1850, March 19, 1851.

The reporter noted that "the reading of these resolutions caused considerable merriment." One delegate who fancied himself a wag proposed as a substitute that whenever a northerner abducted slaves, Alabama should arrest an equal number of free state citizens and imprison them until the slaves were returned. Much laughter ensued, and the reporter commented with high amusement, "Mr. Gayle was willing to vote for the amendment, provided he might be allowed to add as an amendment to the amendment, that the penalty for the second offense should be *hanging!*" In the late fifties Gayle began editing an absurdly radical newspaper which he called the Cahaba *Slaveholder*. In 1865, when President Lincoln was assassinated, George W. Gayle, hundreds of miles away in Alabama, was immediately arrested and imprisoned. He had firmly established his reputation as a lunatic.[103]

Like most of the fire-eaters, the Cahabans found themselves brought up short in 1851 by the politicians. James M. Calhoun, a nephew of the South Carolina senator, had been one of Alabama's leading exponents of southern rights theory since the days of the nullification controversy, and was naturally elected to the executive committee of the Cahaba Southern Rights Association. But the club's radicalism evidently soon put him off. In 1851 the county's southern rights men nominated a legislative ticket, headed by Calhoun for the Senate and including two men of similar credentials for the House. All three promptly declined, Calhoun writing that the nomination, which had been placed upon the Montgomery Platform, "imposed upon him restrictions and conditions which did not accord with his views and opinions." The *Dallas Gazette*, shocked and chastened, announced that henceforth it would cease commenting upon the differing positions of individual Southern Rights advocates. On that understanding, the three nominees reconsidered their refusals.

Thus, like their Montgomery brothers, many of the Cahaba fire-

---

103. *Senate Journal*, Sess. of 1830–31, pp. 120—23, 127, 151–52, 185–86; William R. Hallett to Arthur P. Bagby, undated [internally dated to spring, 1840], in Governors' Correspondence: Bagby, Alabama Department of Archives and History, Montgomery; Benjamin Fitzpatrick to Dixon H. Lewis, June 8, 1843, Lewis to Tandy W. Walker, September 23, 1847, M. C. Gallaway to Lewis, November 4, 1847, all in Lewis Papers, University of Texas Library; Montgomery *Advertiser*, January 16, 1856; Walter L. Fleming, "The Buford Expedition to Kansas," *Transactions of the Alabama Historical Society*, IV (1899–1903), 174, n. 16. Gayle had offered a reward for Lincoln's murder.

eaters patched together an alliance with the politicians for the last months of the 1851 campaign. But a number of the Cahabans were quite unhappy with the arrangement, and openly expressed their dissatisfaction. They stood ready to resume their independence as soon as circumstances permitted, and generally refused cooperation outside the county races. Indeed, they sought vigorously to obtain the nomination of a fire-eating gubernatorial candidate to oppose both the more moderate Southern Rights incumbent Henry W. Collier, and his Unionist opponent Benjamin Shields, a former congressman and United States minister to Venezuela.[104]

After the Cahabans, who stood for some form of cooperative secession, the next most radical group was in Montgomery. The usual spokesman for these men was William L. Yancey, but also prominent among them were Jefferson Noble, John Archer Elmore, Elmore's relative Judge Abraham Martin, Judge George Goldthwaite, Carnot Bellinger, James R. Dillard, and the old Nullifier Thomas S. Mays. As this list implies, the members of the Montgomery group were by and large men of greater prominence than was usual among the fire-eaters. Almost a fifth of the county's delegates to the southern rights conventions of February, 1851, and March, 1852, were at one time or another members of the legislature. And fully a fourth of them owned more than fifty slaves in 1860. In the fall of 1850 the Montgomery *Advertiser* reported that "some people are, or have been under the impression—pretendedly or not, we can't say—that most of this excitement and fuss rages alone about Montgomery." It would seem likely that this impression, to the extent that it gained currency, did so not because of the numbers of southern rights men in the area, but because of their respectability, which was such as to give a fair number of them reputations beyond the locality.

The Montgomerians stopped short of the Cahabans' advocacy of cooperative secession. They called instead for preparation for the disunion which would inevitably come at a future date. The address of the first state southern rights convention of 1851, probably written by Yancey, warned:

The causes of this [northern] hostility to our institutions are not transient or

104. Montgomery *Advertiser*, October 16, 1850, March 19, May 14, May 21, June 11, June 18, October 28, 1851.

light . . . they lie upon the oft-repeated idea so universally entertained at the North that slavery is a moral and political evil. That sentiment . . . is nearly co-extensive with the civilized world. . . . What folly, then, to suppose that the North is an exception to this rule, and that but a faction opposes us there! For more than a quarter of a century has that section pursued its darling object, the abolition of slavery in the United States. She has never taken a step backward in this matter. When obtaining one point, she has paused but to gather up her energies for the next assailment. . . . We would not now declare that Alabama should secede at any particular time, but simply that it is her duty to prepare for secession; and that if any other Southern State secedes, good faith to such State requires that we should sustain her by all means within our power and should likewise secede. . . . Let us put the State in a position to act promptly and efficiently with [the southern states] or any of them in any mode of resistance which may be adopted.

The Montgomerians felt, in other words, that northern aggressions would not—could not—cease, and would eventually drive some more radical southern state from the union. That event would provide the necessary lever with which to force Alabama to act. It is not difficult to guess on which state the Yanceyites pinned their hopes. At one meeting Yancey offered resolutions begging South Carolina to secede, and asserting that her failure to do so "will be the knell of all hope of resistance to federal oppression."[105]

A fascinating encounter between the Dallas extremists and the Montgomery group took place at the third state southern rights convention in March, 1852. Like contemporary European socialists, the fire-eaters were deeply concerned with the precise formulation of their positions. Historians not attuned to the differences which gave rise to these bitter doctrinal disputes have tended to ignore the conflicts altogether. But the southern rights men were convinced that what they were doing would determine whether or not their society would survive; the enterprise was of such magnitude that they devoted much of the following decade to what was, in the phrase of one fire-eater, a "resolutionary war."[106] It is beyond the scope of the present work to trace these internecine struggles in their enormous complexity. Lest that fact betray us into the insensitivity to the concerns of the southern rights forces which has characterized so many accounts, however,

105. *Ibid.*, October 16, 1850, March 26, May 28, 1851.
106. Edward C. Bullock to Clement Claiborne Clay, December 30, 1859, in Clay Papers.

perhaps we should glance at the 1852 collision. It may at least serve to convey the flavor of the subsequent difficulties.

The convention's resolutions committee, on which Yancey served, reported a platform which included a statement founded upon the Montgomery position on secession: "Resolved, that the people of this and of all the Southern States having decided against the policy of secession on account of the passage of the Compromise measures, the Southern Rights party of Alabama declines to urge that issue—its aim is to watch the future." The proposed formulation was attacked from two directions. William H. Northington of Autauga, who though ostensibly a fire-eater, appears in fact to have had close ties with the politicians in his county and to have used his influence within the southern rights movement to direct it toward actions acceptable to the established Democratic leadership,[107] moved to strike the phrase, "its aim is to watch the future." The result would be to leave an unequivocal pledge not to agitate for disunion as a response to the Compromise. The original draft, on the other hand, left the impression that such agitation was merely suspended temporarily. J. A. Strother of Dallas, meanwhile, proposed striking the entire resolution, with a view to inserting a more radical one. The dispute became so bitter that the convention adjourned for the evening.

The next morning Northington withdrew his motion. Yancey, seeking to save the original proposal, offered an addition to the committee's draft: "But believing those measures [the Compromise] to have originated in the design, and to be effectual for the purpose, of defrauding the South, we shall hold ourselves ready, at all proper times, to oppose them by all fair and constitutional means." The amendment was adopted, with the dissent of Dallas and Autauga from opposite ends of the fire-eater spectrum.

There was an important division within the Montgomerians' ranks, however, and it now surfaced. A powerful element in the Montgomery group was the remainder of Dixon Lewis' original followers who had left the Nullifiers for the Democrats in 1838 because of a disagreement over efforts to recharter the Bank of the United States. Even before Lewis' death, leadership of these men had passed

107. Leonidas Howard to Bolling Hall, June 7, 1853, William H. Northington to Hall, July 7, 1853, both in Hall Papers.

to Lewis' brother-in-law John Archer Elmore, a brother of South Carolina's Senator Franklin Elmore. Elmore was Yancey's law partner, but the association of Yancey and his immediate friends with Elmore's political faction was by no means longstanding; it dated only from the "Taylor Democrat" alliance of 1848. The Elmore clique were usually content to let the eloquent Yancey speak for all Montgomery fire-eaters, but the Elmoreites were in fact less committed than was Yancey to the notion that there was a certain inevitability about secession. They agreed that Alabama would be precipitated out of the Union by external events, but they believed that a good deal of effort at home would be required, also. Elmore, therefore, moved to amend Yancey's amendment by striking the words "constitutional means" and inserting "proper means not prohibited by the Constitution." When this division within the Montgomery delegation became apparent, such confusion ensued that eventually the entire original resolution together with Yancey's amendment was stricken out by unanimous consent.

J. A. Strother, one of the Dallas radicals, then proposed to fill the blank with a new resolution: "As the best means of preserving the organization of the Southern Rights party, that this meeting now proceed to nominate a candidate for President and one for Vice President of the United States." Most Montgomerians felt that the fire-eaters should pursue a form of agitation patterned on that used successfully by the abolitionists in the North, that is, holding themselves ready to deliver their votes to the traditional party which could be brought most nearly to adopt fire-eater positions. The Cahabans felt that the most effective form of agitation was the total rejection of both old parties and the formation of a separate, ideologically pure organization which would lead to conversion of the citizenry by example and moral force. The argument was to become a principal source of contention in the coming summer, but at this time the Dallas resolution provoked no enthusiasm, and was withdrawn.

The final stage of the encounter came when a delegate from Lowndes offered a compromise formulation. It was natural that Lowndes should be the source for the compromise, since the fire-eaters of the county were closely divided between pro-Cahaba and pro-Montgomery elements. Unfortunately, however, the Lowndes delegation was similarly divided. H. F. Lewis, a pro-Montgomery man, proposed the following wording: "Resolved, That we adhere to the conviction that the Compromise acts are unjust, unconstitutional, and dangerous to the South, and though we are constrained, in deference to the unanimous decision of the Southern States, not to urge secession on account of these measures, we avow our readiness at all times and upon all occasions to resist them by any means that may promise to be effectual." This proposal was a great deal stronger than the committee's original draft, even with Yancey's addendum. Indeed, its avowal of "any means that may promise to be effectual" went even beyond Elmore's "proper means not prohibited by the Constitution." It represented such a considerable concession to Dallas extremism that one might expect the Cahabans to have been satisfied, but they were not. One of the pro-Cahaba delegates from Lowndes, G. D. T. Moore, moved to strike the words "though we are constrained in deference to the unanimous decision of the Southern States not to urge secession on account of these measures." The pro-Cahaba element was a majority of the Lowndes delegates; that county thus joined Dallas in supporting Moore's motion. But they stood alone. Thereupon Lewis' wording was adopted, only Dallas dissenting. The final resolution, then, was more radical than the views of any of the delegations except those of Lowndes and Dallas, but was still not extreme enough for the Cahabans.[108] The sort of disputation exemplified by this encounter occupied a great many of the fire-eaters for the remainder of the fifties. It was symptomatic of the very real policy differences among the southern rights factions, and of the seriousness with which those differences were taken.

After Montgomery, the next most radical group was in Eufaula. The Barbour County fire-eaters were, however, unique in an important respect. Alone among the southern rights congregations, the Eufaulans were genuinely bipartisan, a survival from the campaign of 1848. When the Democratic politicians began agitating southern rights issues in 1849, Barbour was most likely the model that they had in mind of what would happen in Alabama politics as a result of their efforts. Barbour was a strongly Whig county, and such Democratic constituency as it had contained an unusually large percentage of Calhoun-

108. Montgomery *Advertiser*, March 9, 1852.

ites. The Democracy of the area, therefore, was easy prey for Whig propaganda about Taylor's nonpartisan candidacy, both because it resonated with the Calhoun dogma and because it offered the Democrats the unusual prospect of being on the winning side. Taylor swept the county by a margin of two to one. Taylor, however, was the last of the whiggish presidential candidates to carry Barbour. In 1852 it was one of the two counties in Alabama which supported the southern rights third-party campaign of George M. Troup.

When the Taylor tide receded, not all of the Whig fish in Barbour scrambled back into the familiar ocean. A group of Whigs, cast into union with the Democrats on a southern no-party basis, decided to retain the new allegiance. Their leader was an old Indian fighter and longtime legislator, Jefferson Buford, who was to gain fame as the commander of the Alabama expedition to Kansas a few years later. His chief lieutenant was his young law partner, future Confederate congressman and United States senator James L. Pugh. Buford's fear of the North was distinctly whiggish. He believed that the United States contained "two separate, dissimilar and hostile systems of civilization," the southern one assuming racial distinction but the northern "with its foundations reaching to communism and agrarianism." [109] The notion that the other region was guided by economic radicalism was unusual in the southern rights movement; the normal position was that an unjust social structure forced the populace there to embrace such philosophies.

The addition of this substantial element of Whiggery attracted to the emerging coalition some more regular Democrats who were particularly ambitious, such as John Cochran—whom the Calhounites had condemned as late as 1848 as "an old hunker of the first water, and a disciple of [former governor Arthur P.] Bagby." [110] In addition to Cochran, John Gill Shorter and his brother Eli S. Shorter fall into this category. But the bulk of the leadership of the new faction came from the Calhounites—Alpheus Baker, Sterling G. Cato, and his brother Lewis Llewellyn Cato, Paul Tucker Sayre, and Edward C. Bullock. All of these men were Eufaula attorneys; all were quite young; and all at

109. *Ibid.*, January 15, 1851. On Buford's desertion of the Whiggery, see his statement in *Alabama State Gazette* (Montgomery), July 21, 1849.
110. John A. Calhoun to Joseph W. Lesesne, February 19, 1848, in Lesesne Papers.

one time or another were editors of the county Democratic organ, which in recognition of the newly bipartisan nature of its subscription list, changed its name at this time from the *Democrat* to the *Spirit of the South*.

This three-cornered alliance became a permanent, and unique, feature of Barbour County politics. In terms of numbers, the Barbour returns in the presidential election of 1852 are a rough guide to the power of the new faction. Each of the major party candidates received about 300 votes, and Troup was given 571. The necessity to hold its disparate elements together gave rise to positions which have led some historians to regard the coalition as more radical than it was. The Eufaulans vigorously opposed the abandonment of a separate southern rights party organization and joined the Cahabans in their disinclination to endorse candidates nominated by either major party. They sought to emphasize the nonpolitical character of their movement in 1851 by nominating two candidates for the legislature who could claim no previous experience in politics. And they issued demands for firmer resistance to northern aggressions from their elected officials. Contemporaries, however, were well aware that these actions grew from the exigencies of an unnatural union. The Coffee County politician Gappa T. Yelverton assured a fellow Democratic leader in 1853, for instance, that John Cochran was at heart a party man who was prevented from supporting the party openly only by the peculiar situation of Barbour County politics.[111]

Far more important in determining the Eufaulans' actual position is their attitude towards secession. The Eufaula *Spirit* flatly rejected the Montgomery Platform of 1851, which contained a call for the state to put its house in order in preparation for eventual secession. The *Spirit* proclaimed, "Our rights are dearer to us than the Union—if either must be sacrificed, let the Union go." But it continued, "We do not believe that the 'last hope' of saving the Union and our rights is gone; on the contrary our opinion is stronger now than ever that the Union and our rights can be preserved." The faction's legislative ticket repudiated immediate secession.

111. Montgomery *Advertiser*, March 9, 1852; Gappa T. Yelverton to Bolling Hall, October 18, 1853, in Hall Papers.

Instead, the Eufaulans embraced long-term agitation to convert the entire electorate of Alabama to resistance. Unlike the Montgomerians, who expected their agitation merely to lay the groundwork to ease the state into secession in response to external events, the Eufaulans desired to await a genuine social consensus before positive action. They proposed, in short, to launch a crusade to convince the citizenry of the justice of the southern rights cause. Jefferson Buford condemned fire-eaters who demanded a direct response to the Yankee challenge. He warned:

There may be impatient spirits who think that secession is the only remedy, and must be applied now or never; they give up in despair because the country is [not] already ripe for extreme measures; the Georgia election utterly overwhelms them. To such I would say, if secession were permissible, yet it would not be desirable to begin and perfect the movement in a day, a month or a year; no great, valuable and lasting achievement was ever consummated without long and much toil and [tr]avail; the revolution of a day will go back in a day; we are no mercurial Frenchmen to deal in such transitory changes. It is best that we are not. With us it requires a long, very long time for new ideas to enter and imbue the public mind, and then they must, as it were, sink into our very bones and marrow and become a part of our being before they develope the fruit of action; the revolution required ten years' agitation to begin it, and the Declaration of Independence at last was hailed with little or no general enthusiasm. Instead of being cast down at the Georgia election, we should rejoice that it affords evidence that a third of her people are already beginning to wake up and to think. . . . Remember that we are struggling for existence; remember that no matter who are the visible combatants, this is but a war of supremacy between the two races among us; we must struggle or die; we must school our Southern impatience; we must organize, agitate, persevere, endure; if we cannot, we are unworthy of our rights, and cannot maintain, if we should win them.

Earlier John Cochran had expressed similar thoughts.

I do not think the Union will be dissolved immediately, but I believe, and rejoice in the belief, that at this moment there is amongst us here a leaven of disunion which by a more or less rapid but perfectly certain process will leaven the whole lump. . . . We have resolved to have no more to do with the North than we are forced to. We will not take their papers—buy their goods—and will tear ourselves away from them in every way possible. We will also do all we can to bring the government at Washington into disrepute amongst us—we hate it as the instrument of our degradation. We will further

discountenance Southern men who have contributed to our downfall by. . . .
persuading the South to submit.[112]

The general conversion which the Eufaulans desired would not be effected quickly, but they were prepared to wait. In the meantime, however, secession without a general demand for it would be a socially
dangerous step. Because they represented a one-issue coalition, and
because they believed in a conscious policy of agitation, they were as
radical as the most extreme fire-eater on the question of remaining
aloof from the regular parties. But on the mechanics and timing of
resistance, they were—at least for southern rights men—moderates.

The fire-eaters of Alabama's metropolis, Mobile, were quite distinctly commercial in outlook, and were therefore even more cautious
than the Eufaulans. Their mercantile viewpoint, moreover, was a principal source of their southern rights sentiments, and of their uniqueness as a southern rights group. The seeds of the Mobile position may
be clearly seen in an 1847 letter written by the Mobilians' most important leader, future Supreme Court justice John A. Campbell. He
lamented that the constant northern agitation of the slavery issue "has
impoverished our credit and it daily weakens our moral power. Our
states are fast losing their respectability. The tide of emigration flows
past them. They are carefully avoided. Our people look to the future
without confidence and our Slaves are emerging above their condition
not in intellect or moral culture but in feeling and temper." Chancellor
Joseph W. Lesesne placed the blame squarely on the colonial status of
the southern economy.

Our whole commerce except a small fraction is in the hands of Northern men.
Take Mobile as an example—7/8 of our Bank Stock is owned by Northern
men—as large a portion of the Insurance Stock of the Companies chartered
by our own Legislature; besides 7 or 8 foreign Companies who do their business by agencies. Half our real estate is owned by non-residents, of the same
section. Our wholesale and retail business—everything in short worth men-
tioning is in the hands of men who invest their profits at the North. The
commercial privileges extended by the Constitution has [sic] wholly deprived
us of a mercantile class—and thus deprives us (I think) of the most certain
means for the accumulation of wealth. Instead of the condition of Ireland
being that which we may *expect hereafter*, it is that which we now suffer. *This*

112. Eufaula *Spirit of the South*, quoted in Montgomery *Advertiser*, February 26, 1851;
Montgomery *Advertiser*, May 14, January 15, 1851, October 2, 1850.

*little town pays 2 millions annually for the reflected glories of the Union.*I speak advisedly and from figures. If a swarm of Locusts should every fourth year settle upon our fields of Corn, Cotton and rice and lay them waste, we should loose [*sic*] less than we do from the causes I have enumerated. . . . Financially we are more enslaved than our negroes.[113]

Between the Mobile southern rights men and the regular Democrats, there was much bad blood. The southern rights advocates deduced from their commercial concerns misgivings about the policies of the national Democracy. Campbell wrote, "The connexion of the Whig party with the Abolitionists has never disturbed me a great deal for the reason that . . . the tone of the party is derived from men of property and character, and they are in a measure held to respect property guaranteed by the constitution and laws of the country. The union of the democratic party with the abolitionists I have regarded as far more dangerous because they are held by few restraints and are ready to go farther lengths to carry their ends." Moreover, he held the Alabama party's leaders in contempt, concluding "that the Mountain democracy command the State and our politicians defer to their wishes. The whole of the talent of the democratic party in this State is with us but the county leaders are not. And our leaders are unwilling to combat. They succumb continually to those mountaineers." On the other hand, the boss of Mobile's regular Democracy, Thaddeus Sanford, bitterly called the southern rights men "a little band of factionists that in my soul I hope will go over to the Whigs."[114]

Despite the hostility between these groups, however, the Mobile fire-eaters were much more willing to endorse regular candidates than were the three Black Belt southern rights fraternities. There was among the Mobile fire-eaters a mildly southern rights element which, with a good deal of resignation and cynicism towards the political structure, nevertheless remained relatively loyal to the Democratic party. Included in this category were Campbell's law partner Daniel Chandler, Judge Edmund S. Dargan, Burwell Boykin, and the Mobile southern rights group's rising star Philip Phillips. Phillips, a young Jewish

---

113. John A. Campbell to John C. Calhoun, November 20, 1847, and Joseph W. Lesesne to Calhoun, September 12, 1847, in Jameson (ed.), *Correspondence of Calhoun,* 1144–45 and 1134–35.

114. John A. Campbell to Calhoun, November 20, December 20, 1847, *ibid.,* 1141, 1153; Thaddeus Sanford to John Bragg, March 13, 1852, in John Bragg Papers.

lawyer, was seeking to build a political career on a dual reputation as a moderate fire-eater and a strong proponent of state aid to railroads and other internal improvements, both relatively popular positions in the city and, given the sources of Mobile's southern rights sentiments, not at all irreconcilable.

Even though the expression "moderate fire-eater" may seem internally inconsistent, it actually identifies the position of the bulk of the Mobile group. One such man, H. B. Holcombe, explained his outlook this way:

My patience had been, I confess, exhausted with the confederacy, on the passage of the obnoxious, unjust and aggressive measures against our section by the 31st Congress. These measures appeared to my poor judgment the very *climax of outrage*, and I did not hesitate to denounce *all*, both *North* and *South*, who gave the slightest countenance to them. . . . But these acts have now passed into history and will be judged by posterity. We are a living, moving, acting generation, and must, nolens, volens, take our part in the great drama of life—social, moral, intellectual and political. A new era is now opened upon the country. All the old hacks of party have been unceremoniously cast into the past, and will I trust, if they are patriots, face into the ranks and yield a cordial, vigorous and efficient support to the nominees of the late Democratic Convention at Baltimore, Pierce and King, as I, a "fire-eater" and *almost* a *disunionist* will do.

Many Mobilians are best described by that unusual coupling of terms—a fire-eater and almost a disunionist. Theirs was a "living, moving, acting" environment—a commercial environment. Protracted brooding and unremitting agitation were not features of it. In 1852 most of the Mobile fire-eaters joined Holcombe in his eager endorsement of Pierce.[115]

A trifle more hesitant about such endorsements was a group including Campbell and Lesesne. This element had relatively close ties to John C. Calhoun—but not because they fully agreed with Calhounite ideology. Rather, their southern rights views forced them to reject Whig broad construction and their commercial outlook made them skeptical of the Democrats. Having thus condemned themselves to *tertium quid* status, they tended to identify with Calhoun as the most prominent national figure who had gotten himself into the same pre-

115. Daniel Chandler to John Bragg, April 26, 1852, H. B. Holcombe to Bragg, July 1, 1852, Burwell Boykin to Bragg, June 21, 1852, Chandler to Bragg, June 27, 1852, Thaddeus Sanford to Bragg, June –, 1852, all in Bragg Papers.

dicament. They admired him not so much because of his beliefs as because of his position as a political alien. If Calhounites at all, they were mercantile Calhounites. Their opinions differed little from the Chandler-Dargan-Phillips element except that their ties with Calhoun retarded their ability to cooperate with the regular party on occasion.

A final—and quite small—group among the Mobile southern rights men believed in the efficacy of a separate third-party organization. Percy Walker was the only prominent member of this faction. A rough indication of their strength is the Troup poll in Mobile in 1852—a total of 94 out of almost 2,600 votes cast.

Just as the Mobilians were overwhelmingly opposed to a separate organization, so they regarded secession as impolitic under the existing circumstances. They passed resolutions condemning the Montgomery Platform of 1851; present wrongs did not justify secession, they asserted, and separate state secession was not workable in any case. Southern rights men should devote themselves to persuading all southerners to united resistance at some future day, when resistance was really necessary; and in the meanwhile, should seek the adoption of programs "to consolidate [the southern states'] strength by a completion of their projected improvements, fastening the [southern] States together by hooks of steel: to establish manufactures and encourage home industry and employment of every kind: to build up a direct trade with foreign countries: to educate our children within our own borders: and to expend the large sums which Southern travel annually deposits at the North, to fructify and enrich our own section." This was precisely the program of "moderate resistance" being advocated at the time by the Southern Rights politicians—the program which fire-eaters in the Black Belt were deprecating in unmeasured terms.

With the Mobilians we have almost passed beyond the limits of the genuine southern rights movement. Perhaps the one element which identified the Mobile group with the fire-eaters was their acceptance of the belief that external events would eventually force secession. Campbell told the state southern rights convention of June, 1851, that he had never doubted that at a future date South Carolina would secede and thus force Alabama to act. He added that he had joined the Southern Rights Association for that reason alone. The Mobile resolutions in answer to the Montgomery Platform, while condemning the

policy of secession, had carefully emphasized that Alabama should resist the coercion of a seceded state. In a sense, therefore, the Mobile
position is a mild transmutation of the Yanceyite line, differentiated by
a large admixture of whiggish commercial concerns and a greater
willingness to cooperate with the Democratic party apparatus.[116]

The final southern rights congregation—the fire-eaters of the
upper Coosa valley—is the least radical group in the fellowship. In the
Black Belt it probably would have been classed with the Southern
Rights political establishment. But in the hill counties it was regarded
as a hotbed of extremist sentiment. The most prominent members of
the circle were Judge John J. Woodward and Chancellor Alexander
Bowie, both old South Carolinians and admirers of Senator Calhoun.
It also included some ambitious younger men, the most important of
whom were J. L. M. Curry and Samuel F. Rice. The Talladega-
Jacksonville faction was perhaps the one group of fire-eaters which
held to an ideology approximating Calhoun's. It was therefore distinctly moderate by southern rights standards. It sought new guarantees for the South within the Union, to be effected by bringing Yankees
to see the simple justice of the southern cause and the immorality of
abolitionist attacks upon it. It rejected parties because they divided
southerners along irrelevant lines and prevented the issuance of united
demands. But it was convinced that if such an ultimatum could ever be
promulgated, the North would cringe in the knowledge of its culpabil-
ity and acquiesce in southern exactions without necessitating secession. Thomas B. Woodward, a kinsman of the judge's, declared,

> If we desire to remain in the Union, which I take for granted, the Federal
> Constitution must be revived and vindicated. To do this, a moral power must
> be brought to bear upon the general mind of the abolition States that shall
> quell it into silence in reference to slavery; otherwise, a division of the terri-
> tory by the most unquestionable authority and in the most solemn form
> known to the proceedings of organized bodies of men [*i.e.*, the decision of the
> proposed new Constitutional Convention] will not secure the South against
> the mad, aggressive abolition spirit, or the scarcely less daring spirit of con-
> solidation. As they have overleaped the barriers of the solemn compact of
> union, so they would violate any compact in reference to the territory.

116. Montgomery *Advertiser*, April 2, June 18, 1851; see also August 28, October 16,
1850.

Not all of the upper Coosa group was wholly orthodox in its Calhounism. The Talladega *Watchtower* flirted with secession, and Samuel Rice was convinced that further northern incursions would force the South to choose between the Union and the Constitution. The younger members of the group were coming to embrace nationalistic sentiments in reference to their section. In the statement quoted in the preceding paragraph, Thomas B. Woodward also asserted,

A Southern Confederacy, on the principles of our glorious old Constitution, which has perished beneath the foul assaults of abolitionists and consolidationists combined, will place [southerners] in safety. It would embark them in a career of wealth, of power and glory. It could not be otherwise. Their institutions, their climate and soil, their great staples, and their geographical position, with the beautiful Pacific on the west, the deep Atlantic on the east, and the Gulf and a glorious field for expansion on the south, all together point to a pyramidal power to which they must reach, unrivalled in the history of the world!

On the other hand, the Jacksonville *Republican*, more moderate than the other Jacksonville newspaper, the *Sunny South*, declared that "a suspension of party divisions . . . is impossible; principles make parties; they cannot change, or be so easily forgotten." All three newspapers came, after the August elections of 1851, to support the effort to reorganize the Democratic party upon the old issues. Still, the Talladega-Benton faction came closer to a consistently Calhounite position than did any other.[117]

Calhoun's influence on the Alabama fire-eaters is worth a brief discussion. We have discerned his shadow in the background at the formation of each of the five genuine southern rights fraternities. But the conspiratorial mind may easily attach undue significance to this circumstance. In Dallas the old Nullifier James M. Calhoun had long been a dominant figure. In Eufaula James's brother John A. Calhoun exerted himself to control the Barbour Democracy during the late 1840s. In Montgomery Dixon H. Lewis and John Archer Elmore retained ties with the South Carolinians. In Mobile John A. Campbell and Joseph W. Lesesne were among the senator's correspondents. And in Talladega Judge Woodward and Chancellor Bowie were guided by

117. *Ibid.*, August 28, October 16, 1850, March 12, November 11, 1851.

early association with him. The essential point, however, is that in no case did he govern the fire-eaters; he was not their leader, but rather a sort of symbol. He was, they thought, defiantly a sectionalist, and for that attitude alone they, in common with many more moderate southerners, admired him. But admiration is not inspiration or control. The fire-eaters led their own lives.

In many cases, indeed, Calhoun's philosophy simply went over Alabamians' heads. His final speech to the Senate, containing hints of his proposals to restructure the government to accord with the principle of the concurrent majority, left his Alabama readers bewildered and amazed; it seemed, in fact, rather un-American. "The enunciation that the tendencies of our [democratic] government are towards absolutism, is startling in the extreme," the Montgomery *Advertiser* stammered in consternation, though it urged its readers to ponder the argument "and see if it can be altogether denied." Congressman Harris was certain that Calhoun's radical remedies were unnecessary; the South needed only the enforcement of the Constitution as the founding fathers had written it. But, he added, Calhoun had to be forgiven his eccentricities, for it was just his way of defending the South that all southerners loved. And, in the ultimate indignity, Harris transmuted Calhoun's beliefs into the only terms that made sense in Alabama—Jacksonian terms: Calhoun's "strong republican tendencies, therefore led him constantly to seek, not how a government could best get and maintain power, but rather, how liberty and equality, the great objects of government, could best be preserved to the people." [118]

There were Calhounites in Alabama up to 1848, but thereafter, for all practical purposes, there were not. Even the Talladegans soon abandoned the senator's ideology, as their leadership passed to younger members. The old Calhounites were often attracted to the fire-eater movements, but they were not its core. The events of the years 1848 to 1852 brought many new converts—dedicated young zealots no longer interested in the Calhounite vision of southern salvation within the Union, through the moral transformation of the American political structure. Such dreams were called up only in the Coosa valley in 1850, and were already being abandoned there. The

118. *Ibid.*, March 20, April 10, 1850.

new converts and the younger leaders were the prophets of a nascent faith. James M. Calhoun declined the Cahabans' nomination for the legislature because of their extremist stance. John A. Calhoun disappeared from Barbour politics. Campbell and Lesesne had always been only hyphenated Calhounites, and their commercial outlook was soon to evolve into the exuberant economic nationalism of Philip Phillips and Colin J. McRae.[119] Yancey was the spokesman in Montgomery. And Curry and Rice were preparing to succeed Woodward and Bowie in Talladega. The Calhounite *tertium quids* were a building block in the formation of the fire-eater movement, of course. But it did not join them; they joined it.

If the fire-eaters had passed beyond Calhounian notions by 1850, they clearly had not yet become uncompromising secessionists. The Cahabans would embrace secession if it came in the form of the cooperative action of all the southern states, accomplished through some such body as the Nashville convention. Needless to say, there was practically no possibility that so radical a policy could be adopted in that manner. The Montgomerians asked only that Alabama begin preparing for the inevitability that at some future date the state would have to consider secession. The Eufaulans thought that secession should be postponed until all citizens—or at least a number large enough to be considered a social consensus—had come to accept the necessity of political revolution. The Mobilians did not advocate secession under existing conditions, though they did espouse a program of economic resistance which would strengthen the state for the probability that events would demand the action in coming years. The Talladegans actually still were willing to accept a remedy within the Union—perhaps a constitutional amendment embodying an adjustment of the territorial question. And of course the Southern Rights politicians made even more moderate suggestions; for many of them, the answer was simply the election of a Democratic administration.

The fire-eaters had come a long way since 1844, when even so extreme a southern rights man as George Goldthwaite could write to a friend concerning the abolition movement, "Its horrors I look upon as

119. An extraordinary statement of the new spirit is Colin J. McRae to Thaddeus Sanford, August 22, 1857, in Colin J. McRae Papers, Alabama Department of Archives and History, Montgomery.

certain some day to fall upon us, but not probably in your lifetime or in mine." [120] But it remains a fact that the most extreme element among the fire-eaters, the Cahaba group, preached the very doctrine which the most decided conservatives urged in 1860. The only important leader advocating the policy which the majority of the electorate would adopt within ten years gained for himself thereby a reputation as a crank which he was never afterwards able to overcome. During the next decade, the entire center of Alabama political controversy shifted far to the left. The reasons for this startling transit will be the subject of our next chapter. But its sources are already visible.

The war between the Democrats and the fire-eaters passed through two rounds during the period presently under discussion. In the months leading up to the legislative elections of August, 1851, as we have seen, a widening breach between the groups threatened to become a formal schism, but it was papered over temporarily about six weeks before the voting. When the party was reorganized on the old issues during the following winter, a number of the more moderate fire-eaters—the Talladegans and a portion of the Mobilians—used the opportunity to return within the outer lines of the pale. An additional segment—including the bulk of the Mobilians—came in following the nomination of Pierce some six months later. But the hard core of the fire-eaters, most of them in the Black Belt, remained unconvinced.

The second round of the war was fought in the summer and fall of 1852. This round, unlike the first, was primarily a battle within the fire-eater camp. The Democratic establishment did seek to entice the southern rights men to Pierce's aid upon grounds of expediency: he could win, and at least he was a strict constructionist. But for the most part the Democrats were too confident of victory to bother with their disgruntled recusants. The principal source of dissension among southern rights advocates was an extraordinary one. Their state chairman, William L. Yancey, endorsed Pierce, and sought to persuade his fellow fire-eaters to do so as well.

The reason for Yancey's conduct appears to have been his conception of the correct way in which to carry on agitation. He had early come to believe that the mere fact of long-continued asseveration

---

120. George Goldthwaite to Joseph W. Lesesne, August 26, 1844, in Lesesne Papers.

would invariably produce profound social consequences. In 1840 he warned his Yankee countrymen of the abolitionists: "This fanaticism can alone be put down by the North. And we are seriously impressed that unless it is done, a separation of the Union must take place. . . . We are convinced that the reason and reflection of the Northern public is now against Abolition; we know she values the Union; we all cherish it. And we hope she will not remain in apathy until this fanaticism shall have mingled with her political relations to such a degree as to sway her public opinion and to direct her legislation." [121] The following decade seemed to him the working out of this prophecy. The abolitionists simply repeated the big lie often enough that it became "mingled with political relations," and thus swayed public opinion. He became convinced that if the technique could work for a lie, it could work for the neglected truth. He therefore desired fire-eaters to adopt abolitionist political tactics without change. The Liberty party had proved an ineffective device; the abolitionists had made political advances by remaining a self-conscious group but offering their support to the most tractable candidates of the major parties. Yancey wished southern rights men to pursue an identical course.

Pierce seemed to many fire-eaters a distinctly pro-southern choice. One of them wrote of the candidate, "He has been, through every change and crisis in our history since his appearance upon the stage of political life, a follower of Jefferson and a State Rights man; the firm friend and political admirer of Woodbury and Calhoun; the unpretending, modest but able, firm and consistent republican; the brave, patriotic and self-sacrificing soldier in our country's wars; and the self-poised and firmly balanced mind that has never yielded to the voice of faction nor the outcries of a wild, unchastened and demoniac fanaticism raging at his very doors." And he added in understandable bewilderment, "But my dear Sir, if he be so dear to the South, whence can he get support at the North and West to elect him?" [122] Such a view of Pierce obviously threatened the writer with disillusionment during the coming four years. But for the time being, it reconciled many a fire-eater to the Democratic party.

If the southern rights men were to influence the major parties, they

---

121. Wetumpka *Argus*, March 4, 1840.
122. H. B. Holcombe to John Bragg, July 1, 1852, in Bragg Papers.

must of course not only withhold their support from unacceptable nominees, but also fall in behind candidates favorable to their interests. Yancey joined the enthusiastic gentleman of the preceding paragraph in believing that Pierce's nomination had been a concession to the South, which must receive positive reinforcement in the form of an endorsement. But Yancey's was not the only perspective upon the situation. A considerable number of fire-eaters believed that intersectional parties were intrinsically emasculating, no matter what the views of their candidates might be. They, too, favored agitation, but they conceived of the process differently. Rather than guiding the major parties by reinforcement and deprivation—by awarding or denying the support of a clearly defined southern rights bloc, which was Yancey's interpretation of the abolitionists' tactics—Yancey's opponents desired to form a distinct third party, which would agitate by campaigning and would "influence" the major parties by throwing them out of office. They wanted to define a new organizing issue and to ride it to political dominance—certain that success would not temper their zeal, as it had that of the politicians.

These two alternative strategies came into collision at the state southern rights convention held in mid-July, 1852, to consider the nominations of Pierce and Scott. Yancey pled Pierce's case fervently. It soon became apparent, however, that he could not carry his point, and he hastily accepted a compromise. The delegates appointed a committee to address each candidate a formal set of questions on pending sectional issues. The convention then recessed to await the nominees' responses. Probably Yancey hoped that fate and organization would give him a majority at the convention's second session.

In mid-September the fire-eaters reassembled. Yancey again sought their acceptance of his type of agitation. Again, however, he found himself outvoted. The convention rejected Pierce's claims, nominated George M. Troup for president and John A. Quitman for vice-president, and selected a ticket of electors. Troup accepted, though with considerable reluctance, and the southern rights men launched a full-scale campaign. The Cahabans were, of course, in agreement with this decision; George W. Gayle was one of the Troup electors. The Eufaulans almost necessarily agreed, because the delicate bipartisan character of their coalition would admit only with difficulty of a different policy. And some of the Elmore faction among the Montgomerians also approved. Troup's vote was largely confined to these groups. He achieved significant totals only in Dallas (23 percent of the county's return), and Lowndes (40 percent), in which Cahaba authority was strong; Barbour (49 percent), and Henry (33 percent), which was in Eufaula's orbit; and Autauga (28 percent), where popular regard for Elmore was considerable. In the state at large, Troup received a trifle more than two thousand votes, or less than 5 percent of the total poll.[123]

On the other hand, Yancey's faction was at first no larger. His position had been in the minority at both conventions. That circumstance is explained in part, of course, by the fact that most of the Talladegans and Mobilians had reunited with the Democrats before the conventions were held. But by no means all of the fire-eaters who supported Pierce intended thereby to indicate an acceptance of Yancey's theory of agitation. Nevertheless, Yancey had succeeded in creating a reputation for himself as a steadfast champion of southern rights ideals who was willing to pursue their realization within the established party.[124] In the light of subsequent developments, many ambitious young men who believed southern rights an emerging issue came to think it politically advantageous to associate themselves with Yancey's apparently firm but reasonable attitudes; and his following thus began to amass prestige.

The dispute between the Yanceyites and the most extreme fire-eaters was never really resolved. No southern rights candidate was offered against Buchanan in 1856, but candidates continued to appear in state races. As late as 1859, the fire-eater William F. Samford challenged the Southern Rights Democratic incumbent, A. B. Moore, for governor.[125] Samford received more than 18,000 votes, or better than 27 percent of the return—still no majority, but a clear advance over

123. Montgomery *Advertiser*, July 7, July 21, July 28, September 1, September 22, October 13, October 20, October 27, November 3, November 10, 1852, April 13, 1853. Elmore practiced law in Montgomery, but his plantation lay just across the river from the city, in the part of Autauga which is today Elmore, named in honor of his father.

124. In the election Yancey announced that he would vote for Troup but that he would have voted for Pierce had there been any prospect of Scott's winning (*ibid.*, October 27, 1852).

125. As we shall see, however, sectional issues in this canvass were complicated by the question of state aid for railroads and by Whig maneuvers: see pp. 363–64 herein.

1852. He carried only two counties, however, one of which was his home county of Macon. This form of agitation, feeding on external events, was making slow progress. Meanwhile, the Yanceyite pattern was also yielding results. As the commander of an increasingly clearly defined and relatively deliverable bloc of votes, Yancey was elevated to an influential role within the Democratic party. In 1856 he was named a Buchanan elector, and by 1859 was in a position of sufficient strength to challenge the incumbent Benjamin Fitzpatrick for the United States Senate.

Neither Yancey nor Samford could claim success in 1859, but both were clearly more powerful than they had been in 1852. By disagreeing about the nature of agitation, the fire-eaters had accidentally hit upon a most effective form of agitation. They did not follow the precedent of the Liberty party, or the precedent of abolitionist work within the northern Whiggery. They followed both precedents simultaneously. This dual course had a devastating effect upon the regular Democratic leadership. The party could silence its tormentors neither by moving to the left nor by moving to the right. If it sought to placate the fire-eaters by yielding to Yancey, it still had to face his third-party confreres. But if it repudiated Yancey, it risked driving moderate southern rights men from the party. In any case, the issues would be constantly before the voters, harassing, indeed persecuting, the public mind. The Democratic party was beset from within and without; no matter what strategy it pursued, successful co-optation was impossible. The party, in its anguish, became thus the incubus which impregnated the body politic with secession, and with death.

Chapter V Fear and Favor

THE SOUTHERN dream of success was not complicated. When young Phillips Fitzpatrick came of age, his uncle offered him some advice.

Now as you are a young man and on your first legs and wishes [sic] to become rich and have a plenty of money and every other thing around you that heart could wish, this would be my plan to obtain it fairly, honestly and above board, is to get you a piece of good land and a healthy situation with plenty of good timber and water, with a good range or a range that will hardly ever give out, where a boat will come and cary [sic] off everything that you might have to ship off; and stick down upon it with some good woman for your wife (for without a good wife it is hard to get along), and raise every thing, and only wait for the woom [sic] of time to bring everything to bar [sic].

But the fields of Elysium were not without thorns. "My crop is sold and the money spent, and still I am in debt," reported former governor Joshua L. Martin. "What a glorious business planting is, for we always hope the next crop will bring us out. . . . This is horrid, but still it is my luck." The goddess who ruled this realm was not Ceres, but Fortuna. And the caprices of that fickle lady kept her subjects on tenterhooks—half fearful of the morrow, half longing for the dawn.[1]

The hope and anxiety which were an integral part of the farmer's daily round had been, as we have seen, the raw material of Alabama politics from earliest days. But the events of the 1850s intensified both the hopes and the anxieties enormously. The society was plunged into

1. A. Fitzpatrick to Phillips Fitzpatrick, August 20, 1849, in Benjamin Fitzpatrick Papers, Southern Historical Collection, University of North Carolina Library, Chapel Hill; Joshua Lanier Martin to John R. Mason, January 28, 1849, in George S. Houston Papers, Duke University Library, Durham.

an inner crisis which was a direct consequence of the ideals which the antebellum political order preached—and derivatively, therefore, of the most profound assumptions of the society itself. In the present chapter we shall turn first to the physical alterations in the community and the economy of the state during the decade. Thereafter we shall explore the impact of those alterations upon public opinion and political reality.

Economic Alterations

The principal element in the economic transformation of the fifties was the spectacular growth of railroads. The chart on page 269 contains a graphic representation of this phenomenon. In 1850 there was but one completed railroad in the state, the 44-mile line around the Muscle Shoals of the Tennessee River, which had been constructed in the prosperous thirties with the financial support of the Bank of Alabama at Decatur. At the end of the thirties the road was making some twenty thousand dollars a year, but the profits were apparently not sufficient to keep the railway in adequate repair. In 1845 the line was reported to be in ruinous condition, and at least by 1848 its locomotives had become so dangerous that the company abandoned steam power altogether in favor of horse-drawn trains. When the route was incorporated into the Memphis and Charleston Railroad in the middle fifties, the new owners found it necessary to relay the entire track.[2]

The only other railway in the state was the partially completed Montgomery and West Point, the construction of which had been suspended as a result of the Panic of 1837 when the road had constructed only thirty-two miles of its projected length. In the late forties the road resumed building, and by 1850 had finished an additional fifty-six miles. The entire road was opened in the spring of 1851. In 1855 a

2. *Senate Journal*, Sess. of 1839–40, pp. 308–321; Memorial of the Tuscumbia, Courtland and Decatur Railroad Company, Benjamin Sherrod president, to the Legislature of Alabama, undated [internally dated to 1838], in Governors' Correspondence: Bagby, Alabama Department of Archives and History, Montgomery; Hugh Lawson White Clay to Susanna Withers Clay, January 7, 1845, in Clay Papers, Duke University Library, Durham; William D. S. Cook to George S. Houston, December 26, 1848, in Houston Papers. From the outset the company had used horses as well as locomotives: Huntsville *Democrat*, July 23, 1834.

Railroad Construction, 1850–1860

Location of Railroads, 1861

spur was completed joining this line with Columbus, and thus with the Central of Georgia system. And the Atlanta and West Point, which met the northern terminus of the main road, was finished in 1854. Alabama's capital could boast in the last half of the decade of a double connection with Georgia's extensive rail network. The connection, however, was not a through one. The Montgomery and West Point was a standard gauge railroad, whereas every one of the Georgia lines—indeed, very nearly every railroad in the South—was laid at broad gauge.[3]

Beginning the decade, then, with two stretches of rail—the dilapidated and unprofitable Tuscumbia, Courtland and Decatur and the unfinished West Point—Alabama embarked on a period which saw the addition of 610 miles of track to her total, at a cost of more than $15.5 million. The most impressive actor in this episode is that distinctly prescient entrepreneur Charles T. Pollard, president of the West Point line. Almost alone among southerners, Pollard possessed a clear sense of the changes which the construction of railroads could wreak in economic geography. While others envisioned railroads as supplementary to steamboats and thus conceived of their lines as mere transfer points between two navigable waterways, Pollard dreamed of creating his own trade routes based not on the accidental course of rivers but on optimal patterns of distribution. The commercial crossroads of his system was to be his home town, Montgomery. Having completed the eastern links with the connections to Atlanta and Columbus, he set about organizing a southern road to join Montgomery with the Gulf ports of Pensacola and Mobile; a western route to join a projected road from Selma to the Mobile and Ohio at Meridian; and a northern line through the mineral belt to join the extension of the Louisville and Nashville, and the east-west Memphis and Charleston, at Decatur.

By the end of the antebellum period, Pollard had seen only the road to Pensacola completed. Construction on this link, financed in part with liberal loans from the profits of the West Point and with the proceeds from a 400,000-acre federal land grant, was begun in 1857

3. At considerable expense the West Point was relaid to broad gauge during Reconstruction, only to find itself compelled to return to its original standard gauge in the general adjustment of 1886. On the West Point in the fifties, see Montgomery *Advertiser*, April 17, 1850, April 30, August 6, 1851, May 19, 1852, July 20, 1853, December 13, 1854, April 11, 1855, April 16, 1856, April 15, 1857, July 14, 1858, April 20, May 4, 1859.

and reached its goal in the spring of 1861.[4] But planning on both the western link, styled the Western Railway of Alabama, and the northern link—the South and North Alabama Railroad—was far advanced at the outbreak of the war, and both were completed during Reconstruction. In anticipation of the construction of the South and North, the Tennessee and Alabama Central completed a link between Nashville and Decatur during the decade. And the Selma-Meridian road succeeded in opening thirty miles of its route, to the village of Woodville—or Uniontown, as it was later called.

Before concluding our summary of Alabama's railroad construction in the fifties by describing the four projects which were not undertaken at the instance of Pollard, we may pause to emphasize again the extraordinary influence which that remarkable collection of men, the Broad River group, has had in the state's history. Pollard was allied to the group by marriage; his father-in-law John B. Scott and the wealthy Broad River speculator Abner McGehee, a nephew of General Scott's, were the principal stockholders in Pollard's railroad. McGehee was an uncle of Francis Meriwether Gilmer, the president of the South and North Alabama Railroad and one of the earliest promoters of the development of the mineral resources to be found around the village of Elyton. The Elyton Land Company, the association which in 1871 founded the city of Birmingham, was backed initially to a considerable extent by Broad River capital. Thus the Broad River group may claim a major role in founding five important towns—Huntsville, Florence, Montgomery, Cahaba, and Birmingham—though of course the success of Cahaba did not equal that of the other four. The nature of antebellum politics was determined in great measure by the early struggles to wrest from the Broad River group the political dominance

4. The goal of Pollard's road was the Alabama-Florida border. The railway north to that point from Pensacola was constructed at the instance of Floridians during the same period. A spur to Mobile had built forty-nine miles of its route, to the Tensas River, by 1861, but the bridging of the swamps north of Mobile was not completed until 1872. The city of Montgomery agreed to purchase $500,000 of stock in the Pollard railroad, but the state legislature subsequently forbade this action. See *ibid.*, April 20, April 27, May 11, May 25, June 8, June 15, June 29, August 10, September 21, 1853, June 14, August 30, December 13, 1854, January 17, February 14, May 30, 1855, July 2, August 2, November 5, 1856, March 25, May 13, May 27, September 23, November 11, November 18, 1857, August 18, December 8, 1858, February 2, April 20, June 1, 1859.

it had gained through its association with William H. Crawford. And the course of Reconstruction politics in the state was influenced in no small degree by the scions of the same cousinry. Indeed, their financial speculations became an essential element in the partisan collisions of the postwar decade.[5]

Broad River capital came chiefly from agriculture, of course; very nearly all of these men were large slaveholders and extensive planters. But their investments were a great deal more diversified than those of most Alabama planters. In addition to their railroads, Broad River names are listed as incorporators of a telegraph line, a gas light concern, and an insurance company. The extensive Tallassee textile mills were owned by a Broad River partnership. At its sale under foreclosure in 1878, this enterprise boasted 238 looms and 18,272 spindles, in addition to a grist mill, a saw mill, a foundry, a machine shop, and 119 workers' houses.[6]

The economic development of the fifties is noteworthy, however, not because the Broad River group continued the active policy of investment which it had pursued even in the midst of depression. The decade is singular because other Alabamians began to seek outlets for their money in addition to the usual land and slaves. Thus, of the more than $17.5 million which had been spent upon railroads within the state by 1860, no more than $5.25 million represented the two Broad River railroads completed at that date. Another $2.5 million represented the Mobile Great Northern and the Tennessee and Alabama Central, built as we have seen in the expectation of linking with Broad River lines, and the Alabama and Mississippi Rivers Railroad—the Selma-Meridian link with which the Western Railway was intended to join. The approximately $10 million which remained was investment

5. Despite its faults, the best short summary of Reconstruction politics is still Horace M. Bond, *Negro Education in Alabama: A Study in Cotton and Steel* (New York: Atheneum, 1969; originally published, 1939), 35–72. The promoters of the South and North had early come to fear the competition of a southwest-northeast route (*e.g.*, *Senate Journal*, Sess. of 1859–60, pp. 23–25), and thereafter sought vigorously to forestall northern participation in the developing Birmingham trade.

6. *Acts of Alabama*, Sess. of 1847–48, pp. 37–40, 270–74; *Acts of Alabama*, Sess. of 1851–52, pp. 126–29; *Acts of Alabama*, Sess. of 1853–54, pp. 308–310; Notice of Sale under Foreclosure, a clipping dated September 16, 1878, in Houston Papers; *cf. Acts of Alabama*, Sess. of 1851–52, pp. 262–65.

in the four lines not connected with the rail system envisioned by Pollard: the Mobile and Ohio, the Mobile and Girard, the Alabama and Tennessee Rivers, and the Memphis and Charleston.

The history of the first three of these roads gives a hint of the fierce trade rivalries and the lust for commercial greatness which became so characteristic of the little southern towns in the 1850s. The Mobile and Girard was conceived by capitalists in the neighborhood of Columbus, Georgia, explicitly in order to circumvent Pollard's planned network, and thus to defeat Montgomery's ambition to become the marketing center for southeast Alabama.[7] Columbus was dependent on the Chattahoochee River trade for its livelihood. But it was clear that the impending completion of the Central of Georgia line to Columbus—which occurred in 1852—would create great changes in the marketing patterns of the area. Columbus merchants perceived that if they could link their city to Mobile by rail, thus creating a through line between the port and the Atlantic seaboard, they could capture a portion of Alabama's commerce, and stabilize the declining fortunes of their town.

The chief threat to Columbus' plan, however, was Montgomery, for a rail link between Montgomery and Mobile would equally as well serve to join the Gulf coast to the Atlantic seaboard, and would leave Columbus stranded at the far end of the Central of Georgia, cut off from the Alabama trading area. And the Montgomery route would require only some 170 miles of new track, whereas the Columbus link would take about 230 miles.

It might appear that Mobilians would have been neutral between these rivals, or even have leaned towards Montgomery. But in fact Mobile interests actively favored the Girard line. Montgomerians were not invited to the Mobile Internal Improvements Convention of 1851, and the resolutions of that gathering, in proposing a general program of railroad construction to be aided by the state, excluded Pollard's Alabama and Florida in favor of the Mobile and Girard. Indeed, Mobile was so hostile to the Montgomery project that Pollard and his associates were eventually compelled to select Pensacola as their road's objective.

7. Girard was the community on the Alabama bank of the Chattahoochee opposite Columbus. About 1890 it adopted the name Phenix City.

The reason for Mobile's conduct appears to have been the port's fear of the vigorous activity of Montgomery's merchants. At the end of 1847 Montgomerians succeeded in establishing a direct steamboat line between their city and New Orleans. Thereafter Montgomery merchants were able to stock their shelves without dependence upon Mobile intermediaries, with the effect of damaging Mobile's transshipment trade, and far more importantly, of diminishing the price of goods at Montgomery sufficiently to make the town an alternative trading center for planters of the upper Alabama valley. Thus while Columbus, situated on the Chattahoochee, posed no real threat to Mobile, Montgomery was rapidly becoming Mobile's principal inland competitor.

In order to finance the Girard, its Columbus backers counted heavily upon obtaining a federal land grant. One of the railroad's organizers, James Abercrombie, was elected to Congress in 1851, and there pressed vigorously for such assistance. Initially these efforts met with no success, but persistence finally obtained a 300,000-acre grant for the company in 1856. At the same time, however, the Girard's hated opponent, the Alabama and Florida, was given 400,000 acres. The Girard began laying track, but the Alabama and Florida could of course depend upon the financial backing of the West Point, and thus was able to outstrip its adversary in construction. In addition, Pollard had shrewdly outflanked the Girard in 1855 by building a spur line connecting Columbus to the West Point route at Opelika, further draining Columbus' trade and making risk capital even scarcer in the city.

No quarter was allowed in this bitter—and typical—struggle. Montgomerians were warned that "there is not a town of the least importance in the Southern country that is not stretching out its paws, in the shape of rail or plank roads, to take from its neighbor's storehouse and put into its own. Particularly is Montgomery liable to be thus pilfered—of course, it's legitimate, too. . . . We are far from complaining at the energy and industry displayed by these towns in endeavoring to extend their trade and influence by means of rail and plankroads; but . . . we can't be idle ourselves without danger of serious loss and injury to our growth and prosperity." The rewards of victory, however, would be great. "How our population will then increase—every branch of business enlarge and extend almost indefinitely—what life and activity daily exhibited in our streets! In this view, what visions of future greatness and prosperity appear. Rivals that have plotted our ruin will be overshadowed and become as pigmies."

By the end of the decade Montgomery had effectively won the competition with Columbus to become southeast Alabama's marketing center, and the Alabama and Florida had won the race to the Gulf. At the time of secession, the Girard had completed only fifty-seven miles of its road, to the little town of Union Springs. After the war, the company managed to push its track on to Troy, but there the enterprise collapsed.[8]

The route of another of the railways built in the fifties is a stark example of the intrusion of the old hostilities of Alabama politics into the new world of the 1850s. By 1849 the state had on hand some $500,000 in uncommitted proceeds of the two- and three-percent funds for internal improvement. Pollard set out to obtain a portion of this money for the proposed Montgomery-Decatur link in his system—a route which would connect the Alabama and Florida to the Tennessee and Alabama Central, when those roads were completed. In the legislative session of that year the Mobilians, jealous of Montgomery's growing influence, and the old Jacksonians who hated the Broad River group which Pollard represented, joined to oppose Pollard's efforts. As an alternative, they favored a projected railroad from Selma to Guntersville, via Montevallo, Talladega and Jacksonville. Playing on the fears and economic ignorance of the legislators, they claimed that there was no need to link the road to the developing national rail network, that steamboats would remain the chief form of transportation, and that what Alabama actually required was simply a rail portage between the state's northern and southern river systems. Pollard's logic was overwhelmed by resentment of his wealthy backers and

8. Montgomery *Advertiser*, March 9, 1852, June 15, 1853. See also November 14, 1849, July 30, August 6, August 20, October 7, October 14, October 21, November 4, 1851, April 13, 1852, May 18, May 25, June 1, June 22, June 29, July 13, July 20, July 27, August 3, August 10, 1853, July 26, 1854, January 10, January 17, February 7, February 14, 1855, September 9, 1857, July 21, 1858, February 2, 1859; Tuscumbia *North Alabamian*, December 31, 1847.

foreboding about the results of connecting the state to the nation. The assembly voted a $190,000 loan to the Selma line, aptly named the Alabama and Tennessee Rivers Railroad.

The Alabama and Tennessee Rivers could not, of course, secure the financial support which Pollard's road would have commanded. The state loan and a $50,000 purchase of stock by the city of Selma enabled the company to build a 55-mile stretch, to Montevallo, between 1851 and 1853. Construction halted there while the company sought additional money. Building began again during 1855, and the Coosa was bridged; but the bridge burned, and construction was again suspended. In 1858 the company tried again, and by 1861 had reached Jacksonville.

Throughout this period, however, the road was plagued by a shortage of funds, and spent much of its energy pleading with government to come to its rescue. In 1857 it even selected as its president a prominent politician, state senator Thomas A. Walker of Calhoun County, the better to prosecute these appeals. The company did manage to obtain a $200,000 loan from the legislature in 1856. But this act was one of the laws to which, as we shall see, Governor Winston refused to give effect. And, in connection with a general land grant to six Alabama railroads in the same year, Congress gave the Alabama and Tennessee Rivers 640,000 acres. But Winston refused to arrange for the transference of these lands, and the road did not in fact gain title to them until 1859. The Alabama and Tennessee Rivers was probably more successful than most corporate enterprises in the state in gaining public assistance. But despite the fact that it came closer than any other railroad to accommodating in its aims the demands of the social creed, the company's successes in seeking aid were not at all commensurate with the vigor of its efforts.

Long before the road reached Jacksonville in 1861, its stockholders had come to understand what Pollard had tried to tell them a decade earlier. They were stuck with 140 miles of track which wound tortuously up into the hills, and then just stopped. The company therefore abandoned to a most uncertain fate the Tennessee and Coosa Railroad, which was planning to build south from Guntersville to meet the Selma road, and determined to turn eastward to join the

Georgia rail system at Rome. This goal was effected in 1869. The Jacksonville-Guntersville gap was not finally closed until 1890.[9]

Though Mobile's enmity towards her inland rivals at Montgomery played an important role in the history both of the Mobile and Girard and of the Alabama and Tennessee Rivers, Mobilians afforded very little material support to either railroad. The explanation for this fact is that investment capital in Alabama's metropolis was almost entirely engrossed in the prosecution of one gigantic enterprise, the building of the Mobile and Ohio. This enormous undertaking, projected at 521 track miles, was intended to link the port with the southern terminus of the Illinois Central at Cairo, Illinois, and thus to provide a continuous rail line from the Great Lakes to the Gulf. Mobilians dreamed that with this railway they could cancel the advantage of New Orleans' river and replace their Louisiana adversary as the great entrepôt of the South. The M & O thus became a sort of obsession for them. And their dedication bore fruit. Though the prudent doubtless scoffed in 1850, by 1861 the M & O had placed no fewer than 483 miles of its route into operation. But only 63 of those miles lay within Alabama's borders. Thus throughout the 1850s Mobile's ambitions, concerns and, to a considerable extent, her financial resources were concentrated outside the state.[10]

Other than the M & O, there was only one railroad constructed in antebellum Alabama which was not either a part of Pollard's system, intended to link with Pollard's system, or built to outflank Pollard's

9. Montgomery *Advertiser*, January 9, 1850, March 26, September 23, November 4, 1851, February 3, February 10, March 16, April 27, May 11, 1852, February 16, April 6, 1853, November 29, 1854, June 23, 1858; *cf*. James F. Grant to Clement Claiborne Clay, July 19, 1854, Thomas A. Walker to Clement Claiborne Clay, July 19, 1854, in Clay Papers. It had been intended from the beginning that the final thirty-five miles would be the responsibility of the Tennessee and Coosa, but the two companies had planned to merge when their lines were joined. The Tennessee and Coosa had received a loan of some $54,400 from the state in 1856, initially promised by the act of 1845 which had provided for the West Point loan, and reconfirmed in 1854. The road was unable to claim an additional loan of perhaps $500,000 also offered by the 1854 act because of the restrictive construction of the law by Governor Winston. Moreover, it forfeited a land grant made by Congress in 1856 of 144,000 acres, apparently because it failed to commence building in time. It sunk more and more deeply into embarrassment, and in fact never completed the road, though eleven miles were finally opened in 1884. See Lewis Wyeth to John A. Winston, April 24, 1854, Marion A. Baldwin to Winston, August 14, 1854, Ezekiel D. Nickles to Winston, undated [Autumn, 1857], all in Governors' Correspondence: Winston; *cf*. *Acts of Alabama*, Sess. of 1844–45, pp. 39–41; *Acts of Alabama*, Sess. of 1853–54, pp. 280–82.

10. Montgomery *Advertiser*, March 2, May 11, 1852, May 18, May 25, 1853, March 7, 1855, April 22, 1857, April 13, 1859.

system—the Memphis and Charleston. This line joined Memphis to Chattanooga—and hence, by existing railways, to the Atlantic coast—via a route through the Tennessee Valley of Alabama which had been chosen in order to incorporate the old Tuscumbia, Courtland and Decatur track. The use of the Tuscumbia road did not, however, afford any really substantial savings to the Memphis. Its cost per mile—something more than $23,000—was about average for Alabama railroads.

The Memphis was highly unusual for the extent to which it was tied to prominent political leaders—including especially future governor Robert M. Patton, the wealthy Lauderdale merchant, planter, and financier; and former governor Clement Comer Clay and his powerful sons. Governor Clay, for instance, actually built a portion of the track, and he and his family lobbied actively for state aid and sought the assistance of out-of-state capitalists. In view of the Memphis' heavy involvement with politicians, it is worth emphasizing that the company did very poorly in obtaining governmental grants, either from the United States or from the state. In fact, probably no other railroad in antebellum Alabama was quite so consistently luckless in such activities.[11]

In 1850 Representative David C. Humphreys of Madison had told the legislature that the state's greatest need was a rail connection between north and south Alabama. It was as easy to get from Huntsville to New York as from Huntsville to Montgomery, he said. Men who believed north Alabama dependent on Mobile were mistaken. If the valley were not joined to the south, it would be better for the area to become a part of Tennessee. By 1860, the one railroad which had been building north had decided to turn eastward, and the heroic exertion of Tennessee Valley capital had chained the northern counties even more firmly than before to Tennessee trade patterns, centering on the

11. *Ibid.*, May 22, September 18, 1850, June 11, 1851, March 22, July 26, 1854, April 9, 1856, April 1, 1857, April 20, 1859; Clement Claiborne Clay to Hugh Lawson White Clay, May 28, 1852, Clement Claiborne Clay to Clement Comer Clay, December 27, 1849, November 23, 1855, all in Clay Papers. In addition to Governor Patton, the initial board of directors included the Huntsville secessionist George P. Beirne, future state senators William A. Austin of Jackson and J. C. Goodloe of Franklin—the latter of whom became a scalawag—and Robert Fearn, a kinsman of the delegate to the Provisional Confederate Congress. The road's first president was former Tennessee governor James C. Jones.

markets of Memphis and Chattanooga. This situation was destined to play a significant role in the secession crisis, for it predisposed the valley towards great caution in sustaining any actions which Tennessee seemed unlikely to countenance.[12]

The railroad revolution was largely completed in Alabama at the outbreak of the war. It had brought with it considerable economic change. Alabama was very far from industrialization in 1860, of course. She did have an annual industrial product of $10.5 million, more than double the figure for 1850. But almost all of this output was from light industry. Indeed, 40 percent of it came from just two sources—saw mills and grist mills. These two forms of enterprise accounted for 572 of the state's 1,459 manufacturing establishments, and employed 25 percent of its industrial work force of 7,900.

Still, there were signs to be noted. Grist mills, Alabama's most valuable industry, had been around for a long time. But saw mills—the state's second industry and largest industrial employer—were largely a product of the railroads. Before the tracks opened the state's vast and almost virgin timber stands to exploitation, there had been no practical way to get lumber to market in many areas. In addition, the growth of the lumber business was to some extent self-generating, for even in areas near rivers, in which lumber could have been put to use earlier, the forests were not generally thought of as natural resources until the profitability of the trade was made manifest. Thus, settlement in such counties as Clarke, Monroe, and Washington had been limited almost exclusively to the river bottom which bounded them; their interiors remained virtually unexplored. This situation explains the startling statistic that in 1850, of Alabama's 32,462,080 acres, 16,164,518—half the state—still remained unowned by anyone. In addition to lumber, forests, particularly in the southwestern section, were beginning to yield turpentine—some $650,000 worth a year by 1860.

The state's third most valuable industry was also a comparatively new one—the weaving of cotton cloth. There were fourteen textile

12. Montgomery *Advertiser*, February 6, 1850. On the general topic of antebellum railroads, there is much useful information in Thomas McAdory Owen, *History of Alabama and Dictionary of Alabama Biography* (4 vols.; Chicago: S. J. Clarke Publishing Co., 1921), I, 24–27, 505–12, II, 904–908, 972–75, 1011–18, 1067–69, 1162–78, 1339–40, 1395–98; *cf.* also *Census of 1860*, IV: Miscellaneous Statistics, 328–34.

mills in 1860, most of them in or near the Black Belt. They were turning out a product valued at more than $1,000,000 a year, up from only $380,000 in 1850. And they were Alabama's second largest industrial employer, with more than 1,300 hands, almost double the number ten years earlier. In addition, the state boasted some twenty foundries and machine shops, turning out goods worth about $800,000 a year. But such relatively heavy industry was most distinctly an exception to the rule. Moreover, it was generally directly dependent upon agriculture. The owner of one large foundry wrote of his booming business, "If we had more capital, we could employ fifty more workmen in our general business, chiefly in grist and saw mills for the planters." [13]

Though respectable by southern standards, Alabama's industry was pitifully small in comparison to the North's. Illinois' annual product was five times Alabama's, though the two had entered the Union as balance states and had pursued quite similar patterns of development. Indiana's product was four times as large, and that of the great northeastern states some twenty to thirty times. But the fact remains inescapable that during the 1850s Alabama's industry, though still based upon agriculture, had diversified greatly and was expanding rapidly, particularly along the lines of the railroads. The graph on page 282 shows the number of corporations chartered during the antebellum period. The enormous new interest in corporate activity in the last decade is readily apparent. At the time she seceded, the state had clearly reached the industrial takeoff point.

Two additional economic events will complete our portrait of the transformation of the fifties. The first is the re-creation of a banking system. The Bank of Alabama had been placed in liquidation in 1842 by the votes of those Democrats who opposed all banks as intrinsically corrupting, and of the Whigs, who wished to create a private banking

13. *Census of 1860*, III: Manufactures, 2–14; Montgomery *Advertiser*, March 5, June 4, June 11, July 23, October 21, November 4, November 11, November 18, December 9, 1851, May 18, 1853, January 24, 1855; *House Journal*, Sess. of 1849–50, pp. 219–22; Memorial of the Selma and Gulf Railroad to the Congress of the United States, February 6, 1838, in Governors' Correspondence: Bagby; William Alderson to John Bragg, February 17, 1852, in John Bragg Papers, Southern Historical Collection, University of North Carolina Library, Chapel Hill; John Gorman Barr to Clement Claiborne Clay, March 6, 1855, in Clay Papers. On the state's early smelters, see Ethel Armes, *The Story of Coal and Iron in Alabama* (Birmingham: Published Under the Auspices of the Chamber of Commerce, 1910), 27–103.

system in place of the public one. But the Democratic proponents of
public banking joined with the Democratic opponents of all banks to
defeat the private bank charters offered by the Whigs. Thus from 1842
to 1850 the state was without banks entirely, except for the small and
shaky Bank of Mobile whose charter, granted in 1818, could not con-
stitutionally be repealed. But throughout the forties the pressure for
some form of banking facilities grew.

The absence of banks did not give the state a wholly specie currency as the orthodox opponents of banks had hoped it would. The

Business Incorporations, 1818–1862

commercial demands of the community were simply too great to be carried on within the confines of so constricted a circulation. Rather, the absence of local notes attracted to Alabama the notes of banks in neighboring states—many of them of rather dubious reliability, accepted in Alabama largely out of necessity. Some out-of-state banks—most prominently Georgia's Bank of St. Mary's—established "agencies" in the state through which to place their notes in circulation.[14] Since these agencies were unrecognized in Alabama law, they were under no legal compulsion to redeem their notes in specie, though of course many did so anyway. But genuine anti-bank men took to referring to these bills as rag paper, and at the 1847 session of the legislature made a concerted effort to prohibit by law the circulation of "foreign" notes. The campaign was led by that peculiarly puritanical figure—Alabama's Soames Forsyte—future governor John A. Winston. The proposal failed of passage, however, since it was clear to cooler heads that any such move would severely damage the state's nascent economic recovery.

Of course commercial forces were as eager as any bitter anti-bank dogmatist to rid the state of non-local circulation—which naturally was received only at a discount. But it was absolutely essential that these notes be replaced by a sound local medium. In other words, it had become apparent to most Alabamians that the time had arrived when the state could no longer afford to dwell in a banking vacuum. This question became the great issue of the election of 1849. The Democrats feared that the renomination of the intransigent anti-bank governor, Reuben Chapman, would lead to general defeat of the party, so great had become the clamor for banks. They dumped the governor from the ticket in favor of the pro-bank state supreme court chief justice, Henry W. Collier, and as we have seen, pulled out a close victory—though the Whigs captured the Senate.

Despite their overwhelming defeat, however, the remnants of the anti-bank forces contested every inch of ground in the subsequent legislative session. The act to charter a second bank at Mobile, to be

14. *Bank of St. Mary's v. St. John, Powers and Co.*, 25 Ala. 566; Montgomery *Advertiser*, April 27, May 11, May 26, 1852, April 27, May 11, 1853. An accurate, though hostile, portrait of the financial condition of the Bank of Mobile is in the speech of Senator Mace T. P. Brindley, in the Montgomery *Advertiser*, February 20, 1850. In fairness, however, it should be noted that the bank had pursued a very conservative policy in the thirties—so much so that it drew opprobrium upon its head from the public at large for affording insufficient credit.

called the Southern Bank, was before the state Senate for six full days, amidst scenes of great bitterness. But in the end, not only was the Southern Bank chartered, but a free banking law was passed, allowing the formation of common law banking associations if United States securities were posted with the state treasurer to cover possible losses; and the required specie cover for the notes of the Bank of Mobile was reduced from one-half to one-third of the total circulation. Because the constitution forbade the legislature to create more than one bank at any one session, the new state banking system grew only slowly during the coming decade. But the passage of these three acts in 1850 broke the back of the anti-bank forces, and therefore new banks were chartered without especial difficulty.

A fundamental reason for the reversal of the political fortunes of the pro-bank men was that returning prosperity greatly increased the demand for an expanded circulating medium. But perhaps equally important was the fact that during the forties the advocates of banks learned to turn the anti-bank argument on its head. During the debate on the free banking bill, Senator James M. Beckett of Pickens, a convert from an anti-bank position, presented the new line of reasoning. Small farmers and, to a lesser extent, small planters longed to sell their crops at home, he said, if there were sufficient local capital to give them a good price. Otherwise, they were forced to sell in the distant and alien cities. The creation of large numbers of banks would afford the farmer the local market he desired. Only great planters would not be benefited. In addition, "by building up a sound and stable system of interior banks and . . . by the exertion of a monied [*sic*] power in the interior, [it would be possible] to protect the great farming and planting interest against a central monied [*sic*] power of extensive influence and with the dangerous ability, if uncontrolled and unchecked, to raise or depress at pleasure the price of our great staple." An extensive banking system, moreover, would open banking to all, precluding the grant of "exclusive privileges to favored companies or classes of men." [15]

The farmer's enemy, in short, was now not the bank, but merely the large bank. The assumption behind the argument, of course, was

15. Montgomery *Advertiser*, January 30, 1850; *cf. House Journal*, Sess. of 1849–50, pp. 204–205.

that every farmer, no matter how small his holdings, would grow for the market if he could. But as the prosperous fifties progressed, more and more the assumption gained substance. Selling one's crop provided money with which to buy "city goods," and in this booming decade, the baubles of the urban world glittered with all the brightness of fool's gold.

The map on page 286 points out the areas of the state which recorded during the decade the greatest increases in cotton production. Cotton, because it was the state's principal cash crop and because it is rather difficult to use for home consumption, is a very good index indeed to the extent to which farmers were producing for sale. As the reader will note, the Tennessee Valley posted negligible gains, and the Black Belt counties on the whole showed only moderate growth. But the small farm sections—the hill country, the Wiregrass and the southwest—demonstrate increases of phenomenal proportions. In four counties—Blount, Walker, and Winston in the north and Covington in the Wiregrass—the crop increased by more than 300 percent. It is doubtless unnecessary to state that by far the greater part of Alabama's cotton production continued to come from the plantation counties, and that the actual number of bales harvested in other areas remained, in several cases, modest. The pattern of a much more general involvement with the market economy in the state, including for the first time many small farm counties, is nonetheless an illuminating development. The extraordinarily heavy world demand for cotton and the relatively high cotton prices which characterized the fifties constitute the most important single factor in explaining the sudden availability of capital for investment during the decade. And the observation that, increasingly, such capital was being generated also in the small farm counties, goes far towards accounting for the unusual social tensions of these years.

By 1860 Alabama had created a rather extensive banking system. In 1850 there were but two banks in the state, the Bank of Mobile and the new Southern Bank, which commenced operation in October. Together they owned $2 million in specie, had $3.5 million in notes circulating, had deposits totaling $1.5 million and loans out to $4.5 million. By 1860 the state had eight banks. All eight held less than $2,750,000 in specie, hardly more than the two in 1850 had reported.

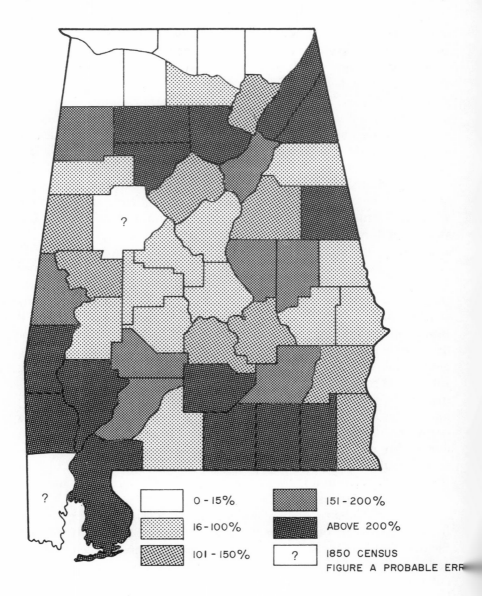

Percentage Increase in Cotton Production, 1850–1860

But, demonstrating the demands of prosperity, each of the other figures had far outstripped specie reserves. Circulation had more than doubled; specie cover fell from 56 percent to 37 percent. Loans almost trebled, to $13.5 million. And deposits more than trebled, to $4,800,000. This last was a particularly significant figure, since before 1860 few Alabamians would have trusted a bank to hold their money.

The geography of the second banking system was very different from that of the first. In the thirties there had been four banks at Mobile and three in north Alabama—at Huntsville, Decatur, and Tuscaloosa. The Black Belt had contained only one such institution, the branch at Montgomery. But in the coming decades the importance, both economic and political, of the Black Belt grew steadily, and the second banking system reflected the change. In 1860 there were but two banks in Mobile; however, there were five Black Belt banks— chartered banks in Selma, Montgomery, and Eufaula, and associations organized under the free banking law in Selma and Montgomery. North of the Belt there was only a single financial institution, at Huntsville. Thus capital, which had been excessively concentrated in the northern section precisely in the years during which the great planting empire of the Black Belt was being created, was now excessively concentrated in the southern section precisely in the years when interest in exploiting the mineral riches of the hills was reaching fever pitch. The former situation created what may have been an unhealthy reliance among south Alabamians upon the commercial and financial facilities of Mobile. The second situation, as the maps on pages 288 and 289 show, tended to concentrate the state's newly active investment in manufacturing in those counties with the least natural resources for the activity, while starving the counties whose industrial potential was boundless.[16]

16. *Census of 1860*, IV: Miscellaneous Statistics, 292. On the second banking system, see Montgomery *Advertiser*, November 28, 1849, January 23, January 30, February 6, April 17, May 29, October 16, 1850, March 5, 1851, October 6, 1852, March 30, September 28, 1853, March 29, July 12, November 15, December 6, December 13, 1854, February 7, March 14, March 21, September 5, November 14, 1855, October 21, October 28, November 4, November 18, December 2, December 9, December 30, 1857; Rufus H. Clements to Jefferson Franklin Jackson, June 30, 1847, in J. F. Jackson Papers, Alabama Department of Archives and History, Montgomery; Clement Claiborne Clay to Hugh Lawson White Clay, November 26, 1855, in Clay Papers; Daniel Sampson to John Bragg, June 28, 1852, in Bragg Papers; A. C. Matthews to George S. Houston, January 14, 1848, Edward A. O'Neal to Houston, January 15, 1848, Felix G.

Capital Invested in Manufacturing, 1860

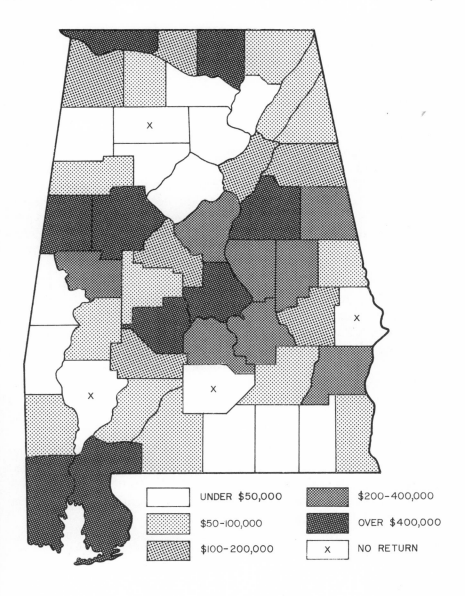

UNDER $50,000 $200-400,000

$50-100,000   OVER $400,000

$100-200,000   X   NO RETURN

Annual Value of Industrial Product, 1860

Despite the fact that the state's infant industry was strongest in the south, the final aspect of the economic miracle of the fifties which deserves emphasis is the realization of the possibilities hidden in the valleys of Alabama's stepchildren, the hill counties. The central figure in this event was a professor at the University of Alabama, Michael Tuomey. During the period of 1847–1857 Professor Tuomey undertook to map the geological structure of north Alabama. His initial findings, published in the Tuscaloosa newspapers, created great excitement. In 1848 he was appointed state geologist, and in 1850 the state published his preliminary report. The forces which were seeking state aid to a north Alabama-south Alabama railroad gave currency to the report's contents in order to prove the necessity for their venture. Professor Tuomey died in 1857, but a second and more detailed report was issued posthumously in 1858, and caused an equal stir. In addition the British geologist Sir Charles Lyell came to Alabama in 1846 and reported his more cursory observations.

These discoveries were the subject of much comment but of relatively little action. The absence of transportation facilities made any exploitation uneconomical. The completion of the Alabama and Tennessee Rivers Railroad to Montevallo in 1853, however, did allow the beginning of some coal mining in the Shelby area. William P. Browne, a former state representative from Mobile, opened a mine in that year, but the reluctance of owners to lease slaves for the dangerous work severely restricted his production. Still, by 1860 Shelby County was reporting more than $41,000 a year in coal production—virtually the entire output of the state.[17]

Upon the foundations of Tuomey's reports and Browne's slender success, vast dream castles were erected. Two railroads were organized to build lines through the mineral district. The South and North, one of the Pollard roads, would build north from Montgomery to join the

---

Norman to Houston, February 10, 1848, all in Houston Papers; A. B. Moore to William Knox, March 5, 1858, in Governors' Correspondence: A. B. Moore; *House Journal*, Sess. of 1849–50, pp. 25–26, 200–216, 397–400; *Senate Journal*, Sess. of 1859–60, pp. 13, 371–72.

17. An account of Browne's struggles is Virginia Knapp, "William Phineas Browne, Business Man and Pioneer Mine Operator of Alabama," *Alabama Review*, III (1950), 102–122, 193–99. See also *Census of 1860*, III: Manufactures, 10. On the Geological Survey, see Owen, *History and Dictionary*, I, 646–49; *cf.* Montgomery *Advertiser*, October 23, 1850, May 4, June 1, June 22, July 27, August 24, 1853, January 3, 1855; and Armes, *Coal and Iron in Alabama*, 40–103.

L & N extension at Decatur. The Northeast and Southwest would build northeast from the M & O line in Mississippi, through Tuscaloosa, to Chattanooga. Each road was intended primarily to open the Jones Valley area to capitalists. The two companies received substantial land grants from the United States in 1856, but neither was able to begin construction until after the war. Nevertheless, what the roads lacked in track during the fifties they supplied with propaganda as to the wealth awaiting their stockholders. In 1854 a somewhat frightened J. L. M. Curry reported from his home at Talladega, "Our country is all 'agog' with the mineral fever. Our people from the hills bring in pockets and saddle-bags full of rocks. . . . This speculating disposition so rife in the south is indicative of anything but the stability and discretion which ought to mark men's conduct." Still he added, "Our geological survey will undoubtedly prove Alabama to be rich in mineral resources, and future efforts may make them productive and profitable." [18] The lack of actual production thus is no index to the intense interest in the subject.

Society in Vertigo

The economic miracle of the 1850s—the railroad revolution, the re-creation of the banking system, the rapid expansion and diversification of the state's industry, and the preparations for the large-scale exploitation of the northern counties—had by no means ended Alabama's status as an overwhelmingly agricultural state. But it had proceeded far enough by the end of the decade to allow us a glimpse through the curtain of reality at an Alabama unscarred by civil war. The sweat of the slave glistens in the fiery belch of the open hearth furnace. The long coffle of black bondsmen moves sullenly, slowly into the waiting maw of the coal mine. And the screaming locomotives speed southward, bearing the wealth of industry away to the Black Belt as tribute to the planter-investors. These men control sufficient

18. J. L. M. Curry to Clement Claiborne Clay, July 11, 1854, in Clay Papers; cf. Montgomery *Advertiser*, July 5, 1854. On the two mineral belt railroads cf. Montgomery *Advertiser*, May 25, June 1, June 22, July 20, July 27, August 17, August 24, September 7, 1853, November 29, 1854, August 29, 1855, July 2, 1856, January 14, April 1, April 15, April 22, May 6, May 20, 1857, June 16, July 14, August 18, August 25, September 15, September 22, October 6, November 3, December 1, December 29, 1858, January 5, March 2, October 19, 1859.

and sufficiently heterogeneous sources of capital to prevent substantial penetration of their new enterprises by Yankee rivals. If alliances are effected, they are alliances of equals. The government becomes less and less the defender of the masses from the assaults of the few, more and more the tool of the social and economic elite. Indeed, the political and economic leadership tend to merge. All of these suggestions are mere extensions of trends clearly, unmistakably apparent in the fifties. And if we cannot mistake the trends, surely the Alabama farmer—a man to whom every evanescent movement was a precedent; who cast his auspices daily in the search for the Armageddon which could descend with any sunset—surely he would not miss the pattern being woven around him. Nor did he.

The world of the Alabama farmer was changing. The economic miracle did not arrive alone; social transformation accompanied it. The 1850s are marked by the rise in importance of the town. In the first place it appears that urban population was growing at a considerably faster rate than was the population at large. Both the census of 1850 and that of 1860 were inexcusably negligent in taking town populations. Nevertheless, seven cities appear in the schedules in both years—Florence, Huntsville, and Jacksonville in north Alabama, and Marion, Montgomery, Selma, and Mobile in the south.[19] While the total population increased by 25 percent in the decade, the population of these seven cities grew by more than 47 percent. Moreover, if we exclude Mobile, we find that the inland towns were growing even faster—by almost 56 percent. We note in addition that persons in occupational categories directly involved in agriculture declined from 75 percent of the adult white males in 1850 to 70 percent in 1860, while the total number in commercial, manufacturing, and professional activities rose from a fifth to a fourth of such males. The growth was apparent, and of about the same dimensions, in all three of the latter classifications. In 1860 about 6 percent of adult white males

19. The village of Kingston in Autauga County is also reported in both years, but I have found no independent evidence of the spectacular growth reported (from 186 in 1850 to 1,960 in 1860), and I believe the 1860 figure to be an error. I have therefore excluded these totals. In 1860 only the white population of Jacksonville is given, but I have adjusted for this fact by using the white figure for 1850 also. The Montgomery population reported in 1850 is an error, which was corrected in the *Compendium of the Census*. In order to determine which was the correct figure, I counted the original returns and found a population of 4,937, the total I have used.

were professionals, somewhat less than 9 percent were in commercial and mercantile jobs, and 10.5 percent were engaged in industrial or manufacturing pursuits.[20] The occupations reported in that year showed a considerable diversification over those of a decade earlier.

Not only were cities, and the jobs associated with them, beginning to emerge from extreme minority, but involvement with the trappings of urban life and values was coming to permeate the society. For instance, the number of public libraries increased from 4 to 361 in the decade, and the volumes they contained from 3,848 to 123,315. The number of newspapers, 10 at the close of the state's first decade and still only 28 in 1840, reached 60 in 1850 and 96 in 1860. Even more significantly, the number of copies printed annually, 2.5 million in 1850, nearly trebled to more than 7 million in 1860. The construction of the telegraph opened this new age. Its lines reached Alabama in 1848. Though the state's rather substantial number of illiterate adult whites increased a bit during the decade, the illiteracy rate per 1,000 of white population fell from about 80 to 72 in these years. Similarly, the proportion of the electorate which was illiterate fell from 14 percent to 12 percent.

The number of white children in school grew by 56 percent in the decade. In 1850 it represented 35.5 percent of the whites between the ages of five and twenty. In 1860 it was some 46 percent of this group. Since it was not usual in this period to leave a child in school as late as twenty, it would appear that fully half of the state's potential school population was actually in school by the end of the antebellum era. The number of schools, public and private, grew from some 750 in 1840 to about 1,300 in 1850, to 2,100 in 1860. It was the public schools which accounted for most of this growth; the number of public schools trebled, while private schools merely doubled. By 1860, 1,900 of the 2,100 schools were public. Total expenditures upon

20. These figures should be taken as suggestive only. Both the 1850 and the 1860 censuses contain the categories farmers, planters, overseers, and drivers, but the 1860 census introduces the new category farm laborers. I believe that farm laborers were counted as farmers in 1850. The category farmers and planters declined from 73 percent of adult white males in 1850 to 57 percent in 1860. There is some question about using adult white males as the base for figuring the percentages. While most of the persons for whom occupations were given were in that group, some clearly were not. At any rate, however, the proportions are roughly accurate. Of course, the classification of the various occupational categories was to some extent subjective.

schools increased by almost a third in the fifties. The state remained, of course, excessively reliant upon private schools. Although public schools were 90 percent of the total, they received less than 60 percent of educational expenditures. Nevertheless, public schools were beginning to receive a greater share of support during the decade. Financing of the public school system by taxes and other public money, chiefly the sixteenth section funds, grew by 360 percent. This enormous increase came primarily in response to the provisions of the Public Schools Act of 1854 and the Public Schools Amendments Act of 1856. The number of colleges in the state grew from two in 1840 and five in 1850 to seventeen in 1860. College income trebled in the fifties, though almost all of it continued to come from tuition charges.[21]

These statistics represent far more than random evidence of social modification. They reflect more than the state's increasing prosperity, though that indeed is to be seen in them. They form, rather, a pattern of changing emphases, changing values. Things which were earlier thought unimportant seemed now to be significant. Schools are an example. Throughout Alabama history it had usually been the social elite which had sought greater support for the public schools. Largely excluded from power, they blamed their inability to shape governmental programs on the ignorance of the masses, and worried that if republican forms were to survive the "pauper schools" must be strengthened and the "indigent funds" increased. As we have seen, it was a favorite tactic of the Democratic leadership to load the legislature's education committees with wealthy Whigs in order to increase the identification of the minority party in the public mind with the unpopular attitudes of the upper class reformers. Proponents of greater attention to the common schools made such statements as:

No people unless well informed are capable of self-government. The populace must learn to think for themselves, to know for themselves, to read for themselves, to investigate thoroughly for themselves; or demagogism will ruin this government. . . . Those who have never visited the poorer sections of the State know but little of the ignorance that prevails throughout the State. Let them examine the statistics of the State and see the number of persons who cannot

21. All of the statistics in the preceding paragraph were compiled from the various census reports. On the arrival of the telegraph, see A. C. Matthews to George S. Houston, April 2, 1848, J. J. Bell to Houston, April 24, 1848, both in Houston Papers, and Owen, *History and Dictionary*, II, 1306. *Cf.* Montgomery *Advertiser*, October 14, October 28, 1857.

read and write, and remember that a great number of those who can read seldom do, and consequently [are] no better citizens. . . . Let us not stop to consider whether it will be popular or unpopular—what the majority of demagogues (who would refuse to pay an honest debt, but would give liberally to any popular object, whether charitable or not), [would do]—but let us ask will it benefit mankind? is it just and right? is it my duty? If such a spirit would take hold of the legislators this coming winter in Montgomery, such a revolution for the benefit of mankind as would follow, the world has never before experienced.[22]

To most Alabamians, of course, these sentiments seemed unqualifiedly un-American, a betrayal of the principles of the democratic experiment. Persons not well informed are incapable of self-government! The masses of the state live in ignorance—and are not good citizens! Politicans should not stop to consider the popularity of their proposals! These were the teachings of aristocracy. On only one point would this writer have found support; all would have accepted his statement that if such a spirit seized the legislature, it would represent a revolution.

There had been a time when the populace could have safely ignored advocacy of this kind, except to laugh at it. But now the sentiments found support among a class in addition to the remnants of the Broad River group and men of their sort. The struggles to force through the legislature a second banking system and a program of assistance to railroads had been led by town dwellers. Theirs was a life of competition, each little village frantically clawing its way to dominance in some marketing area. Citizens of towns were constantly warned that the fate of their community depended on their activity in developing its resources. Each town therefore sought to outdo its neighbors.[23] In the urban struggle, banks and railroads were essential tools. The reluctance of the state government to make the accommodation demanded of it contributed powerfully to a growing sense in the cities—by no means irrational—that the state was not responsive to urban needs. Town dwellers came to blame the ignorance of a backwoods electorate for saddling Alabama with a government lacking what they conceived to be a soundly progressive spirit.

22. Junius W. Smith, in Montgomery *Advertiser*, October 21, 1851; *cf.* October 28, 1857.
23. *E.g.*, *ibid.*, May 14, 1851, March 9, 1852, April 27, June 1, June 15, June 22, June 29, July 27, August 10, 1853, July 2, 1856, March 16, 1859.

The increasing alienation of the towns interacted with a second element, the cynicism becoming widespread among politicians. We have encountered this peculiarly ironic development in our discussion of the fire-eaters.[24] As the years had passed, office seekers had become more and more consciously aware of how to obtain election by focusing popular uneasiness. As this process became conscious, it passed readily into a sort of exploitation which obscured the very real limits of political manipulation. It induced among officials a secret contempt for the voters and fed the emerging view that government's function was to benefit, rather than to represent, society. Voicing the spirit of the new age, the pro-bank Democrat Governor Collier told the legislature in 1849, "Among the paramount objects of government is the promotion of individual happiness by legal and appropriate means. The functions of legislation . . . reach not only to the protection of individual rights, but authorise the adoption of measures for the improvement of society." And he added, "Those States which are farthest advanced in prosperity have only attained their present condition by vast expenditures, for which they have realized far more than an equivalent. If we would overtake them in the race for human melioration, we must bear in mind that true economy will always justify an appropriation, if the money can be spared from other objects, when more than a full return is immediately made in public benefits."[25] Many politicians and town dwellers plunged willingly into the "race for human melioration," but most Alabamians had failed to hear the starting gun.

Despite the unpopularity of the townsman's whiggish views with the mass of the electorate, such urban notions had an important influence because the growing ability of politicians to manipulate the symbols of the social faith was, just at this time, beginning to create a marked change in the wealth and status of Alabama's political leaders. Indeed, no other event of the 1850s is more significant than this alteration. As we recall, the median slaveholding for legislators found in the 1830 census was nine, and for those found in the 1840 Census, 9.5.

24. See pp. 233–38 herein.
25. *House Journal*, Sess. of 1849–50, pp. 231, 234–35.

By 1849, this figure had reached 12.5, and in 1859 had soared to 17.[26]

As in 1840, the median slaveholding for Whig legislators in 1849 was nearly double that for Democrats—16 for Whigs and 8.5 for their opponents. The median for senators in 1849 was 16 and for representatives, 11. In 1859 the median for senators was 19.5, and for representatives, 14. Thus the chief growth in median slaveholding during the preceding two decades had been among members of the House.

The censuses of 1850 and 1860 include economic data in addition to the slaveholding statistics. In 1850 the census took the valuation of the real estate owned by each head of a family, and in 1860, the value of both his real and his personal property. The median value of real estate among the legislators of 1849 was $4,000. The figure for the House alone was the same, but for the Senate was $6,750. The median for Whig legislators was $5,500; for Democrats, $3,250.

In 1860 the median value of real estate holdings among the members for whom the statistic is available was $9,050, and the median personal property holding was $25,700. In the case of real estate, the median for the House was $7,000 and for the Senate, $19,000. The

26. The form of the manuscript returns for 1850 and 1860 makes it peculiarly difficult to determine median slaveholding figures for the legislatures of those years. In the censuses before 1850 free and slave populations were enumerated on the same sheet of paper. The name of the head of the household was entered in the left-hand column, and after it the number of residents in his household, white and black, in the appropriate columns. When, therefore, one finds no entry in the slave columns, one knows virtually to a certainty that the man in question owned no slaves. But in 1850 and 1860 slaveholdings were entered on a separate form, and non-slaveholders were omitted. Unfortunately, one cannot assume that the fact that a man is not listed in the slave schedule is proof that he was a non-slaveholder, for he may simply have been missed by the census taker. In fact, work with the earlier censuses instructs one that such omissions were quite common. Consequently, when the real and personal property holding figures and the occupation of an individual seem to make it unlikely that he was a non-slaveholder, I have counted him as missing. This precaution, though necessary, has resulted in the exclusion of sixteen legislators in 1849 and twenty-five in 1859, and may therefore have biased the median slaveholding figure upward somewhat.

In a recent work, *The People in Power: Courthouse and Statehouse in the Lower South, 1850–1860* (Knoxville:University of Tennessee Press, 1969), Ralph A. Wooster has failed to allow for the difficulty discussed in this note. He has simply counted all legislators whom he could not locate in the slave schedule as non-slaveholders. His percentages of legislators who were non-slaveholders are thus rendered highly suspect, and should probably be disregarded. For a graph of the distribution of legislative wealth at these sessions, see J. Mills Thornton III, "Politics and Power in a Slave Society: Alabama, 1806–1860" (Ph.D. dissertation, Yale University, 1974), 583–90.

personal property median for the House was $25,300, and for the
Senate was $31,180.

If we form scattergrams relating property values to slaveholdings,
we may thus develop boundaries in dollars for the four economic
classes for which we have already adopted slaveholding delimitations:
large planters, small planters, the middle class, and the lower middle
and lower group.[27] The class composition of the two assemblies produced by applying these indices may be expressed in tabular form:

Economic Groupings in Legislatures of 1849 and 1859

1849	*Slaveholding %*	*Real Estate %*
Poorest group	35.6	20.6
Middle class	28.8	33.6
Small planters	17.8	28.0
Large planters	17.8	17.8
(Total planters)	(35.6)	(45.8)

1859	*Slaveholding %*	*Real Estate %*	*Personal Property %*
Poorest group	31.2	21.9	30.2
Middle class	24.8	27.6	20.7
Small planters	21.1	21.0	23.6
Large planters	22.9	29.5	25.5
(Total planters)	(44.0)	(50.5)	(49.1)

Using these figures, we can complete our narrative of the shifting
weight of economic groupings over time within the legislature. As
we recall, in 1830 the middle class held half the seats; and the planters
and the poorer members each constituted a fourth of the body. Large
planters were less than 7 percent of the total. The middle class lost

27. See pp. 63–64 herein. The scattergrams produce the following bounds: in 1849 the
upper limit of real estate for the poorest group is $1,300; for the middle class, $5,000; and for the
small planters, $12,000. In 1859 the corresponding real estate values are $3,000, $10,000, and
$20,000. And the personal property values are $10,000, $27,500, and $55,000. Scattergrams for
the 1861 Secession Convention yield the same figures. It might be argued that the smaller
number of slaves, and the presumed fewer slaveholdings, early in the state's history would alter
the relation of numbers of slaves held to the social structure. What was a smaller holding in 1860,
it might be said, would have been larger, in relative terms, several decades earlier. But in fact, the
intrinsic requirements of plantation agriculture before the advent of mechanization insure a degree of objective inflexibility to the divisions used here, based as they are on numbers of laborers.

ground in the next decade, so that by 1840 each of the three social divisions had about a third of the members. Large planters were still only 10 percent of the whole. By the end of the coming decade, the strength of the non-planters' position had begun to erode a bit. The most marked growth was shown by large planters, who jumped from 10 percent to almost 18 percent of the legislators. The booming fifties were marked by the emergence of large planters into full political participation. At the end of the antebellum era, the four economic groups could each claim about a quarter of the seats.

In sum, then, both the small planters and the lower middle and lower classification completed the antebellum period with approximately the same percentage of legislators as they had possessed three decades earlier. But the large farmer middle class, which had been half the legislature in 1830, fell first to a third and then to a quarter of the membership. And the large planters, less than 7 percent of the total in 1830, held a fourth of the seats by 1860.

Another aspect of the assembly's changing complexion in the fifties was the increase in the number of attorneys in its ranks. As we have seen, in earlier years perhaps 70 percent to 80 percent of the members were connected with agriculture, while something like 15 percent of them were lawyers. But in the final decade, the proportion of farmers fell to about 60 percent and the number of attorneys rose to a quarter or more of the members. In 1849, 59 percent of the legislators were farmers and 26 percent were lawyers. In 1853, 58 percent of the assembly were connected with agriculture, and 52 percent were full-time farmers. Some 27.5 percent were lawyers. In 1859, 57.4 percent were full-time farmers, and 63.5 percent had some connection with agriculture. Again, 26 percent were attorneys.[28]

Increasingly in the fifties, as these figures suggest, assemblymen were coming to lack genuine empathy with the fears and aspirations of the ordinary voter; and their effort to give concrete form to his inchoate yearnings was often a brittle enterprise. Roll call votes in the legislature somewhat more frequently give evidence of the existence of divisions along economic lines. And the practice of relegating espe-

28. Wooster, *People in Power*, 123; *Acts of Alabama*, Sess. of 1853–54, Appendix, 385–88. See pp. 64–65 herein.

cially wealthy members to unimportant committees ceased.[29] The creation of a state-supported public school system is a product of the new political milieu.

At the beginning of the decade, Governor Collier had begun the agitation for greater support for common schools, declaring that they remained underdeveloped because "of the blighting apathy that pervades the community." He proposed as a first step the creation of the office of superintendent of education, an official whose duty it would be to gather accurate statistics on the condition of the schools. The legislature of 1849 refused even so limited a step, and the creation of a superintendency was again suggested at the session of 1851. The action, confided the chairman of the House education committee, was intended to be a part of "a plan . . . to make this the great question at the next state election . . . after the subject has been well agitated by the superintendent." The legislature rejected the bill a second time, but ordered a referendum in conjunction with the general elections of 1853 to determine whether the electorate would accept statewide consolidation of the various Sixteenth Section Funds. Consolidation was approved by 852 townships and rejected by 264 of them, but 456 townships failed to hold any election on the question at all. Nevertheless the issue was now sufficiently before the public so that ambitious politicians were beginning to seize upon it as a possible means to secure popular approval. Even a first-term legislator from a remote Wiregrass county had come to think public education "the great question of questions." The assembly session of 1853 established Alabama's public school system, and the session of 1855 completed the work by placing the funding of the enterprise upon a sound basis.[30]

In order to understand the significance of this achievement, we must understand the governance of the schools before the passage of the Public Schools Act. Prior to 1854, public schools were organized under an act of 1823. Each township had, of course, been given its

29. See pp. 87–91 herein. *Cf.* Thornton, "Politics and Power," 595–600.
30. *House Journal*, Sess. of 1849–50, p. 232; *Senate Journal*, Sess. of 1853–54, pp. 34–35, 132–33; *House Journal*, Sess. of 1853–54, pp. 303–312; Montgomery *Advertiser*, September 18, 1850, April 27, May 4, July 6, August 17, August 24, 1853, March 1, August 9, 1854; Charles P. Robinson to John Bragg, January 21, 1852, in Bragg Papers; Gappa T. Yelverton to Bolling Hall, September 9, 1853, George S. Walden to Hall, September 6, 1853, both in Bolling Hall Papers, Alabama Department of Archives and History, Montgomery.

sixteenth section in 1819 to support a school for the neighborhood. By the provisions of the act of 1823, authority over the sixteenth section schools was divided between two bodies. The township school commissioners, appointed by the county commission, administered the sixteenth section income; their responsibilities were limited largely to finance. The district school trustees, elected by the citizens of the area served by the school, ran the institution; they selected the texts, hired and fired the teachers, and made other educational decisions. Under this system the residents of the neighborhood had, for all practical purposes, absolute control over the school. All questions were settled within the township. The acts of 1854 and 1856 went far towards destroying this local autonomy. The offices of state and county superintendent of education were created and, particularly in the case of the latter, given great administrative discretion. The county superintendent, an elective official, could terminate any teacher's certification at will, and could issue absolute instructions for the conduct of the school. The management of the school income was in large measure transferred from the township to the county level, and the income of the various districts was equalized by the allotment of supplementary funds from the state when necessary. Each township was required to maintain a school.

Progress is in the eye of the beholder. The politicians' constant search for an issue with which to achieve office had combined with urban resentment of a government dominated by an alien outlook to give the state what it had never had, a centralized, state-supported public school system. But the point is that the state at large not only had not had such a system; it had not really wanted one. The politicians quickly discovered that the issue aroused no great enthusiasm. It was not the hobby they sought, and they dropped it. By 1859 the governor, while recommending increased funds for a variety of state programs, was telling the legislature that additional appropriations for the schools would be "inexpedient at this time." Indeed, there was even a movement to abolish the state and county superintendencies. It is true, of course, that some townships had not maintained a school only because their sixteenth section income had been insufficient to finance one. But in most cases the citizens had simply failed to accept the notion that schooling would significantly benefit their children.

Governor Collier had called this attitude a "blighting apathy," but it was in fact a policy decision. Governor Collier and men like him simply were incapable of appreciating—or even of recognizing—the values which underlay such a decision. These values were, however, still held by a majority of Alabamians, albeit a steadily diminishing one. And so, by mid-decade the state had a public school system, and almost no one in the government knew the price that had been paid in obtaining it.[31]

The schools are but one example of the general truth that the politicians' search for a hobby was now too often conducted without a genuine understanding of the assumptions upon which the political decisions of the populace were founded. Politicians therefore commenced, in seeking clues as to what might be popular causes, to look to newspapers, books, and other sources of opinion formation. But intellectual efforts tended to reflect the values of the booming urban environment and of the wider Victorian world. Thus the government, trying to please an obviously restless constituency, became more and more active. It is not that the causes which the politicians preached—public schools, an insane asylum, a hospital for the deaf and dumb, increased aid for the state university, reform of the judicial system, and other projects of a similar sort—met with hostility among the masses. Rather, they met with indifference. They could not move a people to whom they seemed unimportant. But the growing activity of the government could, and did, terrify a people steeped in the precepts of Jackson.

The enormous increase in state expenditures in this decade is too seldom emphasized. The graph on page 303 shows the total disbursements for each fiscal year from 1818 to the end of the period. Its pattern is obvious. Until 1848 expenditures remained distinctly modest—less than $200,000, except in a single instance. But in the fifties

---

31. *Acts of Alabama*, Sess. of 1822–23, pp. 73–78; *Acts of Alabama*, Sess. of 1853–54, pp. 8–18; *Acts of Alabama*, Sess. of 1855–56, pp. 33–48; *Senate Journal*, Sess. of 1859–60, pp. 16–18, 27–28. The session of 1859 in the end made only minor modifications in the school law: *Acts of Alabama*, Sess. of 1859–60, pp. 95–97. But for the hostility to the new school system, see Montgomery *Advertiser*, July 22, July 29, 1857. Incomprehension of the motives of the school system's opponents is particularly apparent in an article of reminiscence written in 1897 by the state's first superintendent of education: William F. Perry, "The Genesis of Public Education in Alabama," *Transactions of the Alabama Historical Society*, II (1897–98), 14–27, esp. 14–18.

the figures exploded upward, and by secession had reached the neighborhood of $1 million a year. Disbursements in 1860 were seven times those of 1849, and fifteen times those of 1847. But the disbursements for 1847 had been about the same as those for 1827. This spectacular growth is one of the most important events of late antebellum history.

County expenditures are more difficult to ascertain, since they must be compiled from the minutes of the various county commissions. A selection of such figures appears, however, to reveal the same pattern. Talladega, which was spending about $300 a year early in the thirties had reached $1,000 by the end of that decade. But growth in the forties was slow, and disbursements in 1847 were still only some $1,700. By 1860 the budget had topped $10,000, a sixfold increase. Expenditure by the whiggish Black Belt counties was always at a considerably higher level than in hill counties like Talladega. Montgomery

State Disbursements, 1817–1861

was already disbursing some $2,500 a year by 1829, and had reached $7,000 in the forties. But the figures jumped to $9,000 in 1850, $13,000 in 1854, almost $15,000 in 1856, and had topped $25,000 by 1858. A large part of the increase in many counties resulted from the permission, granted for the first time by the Public Schools Act of 1854, to levy a county school tax. But there were additional causes. Montgomery built a new courthouse early in the decade, and a new jail some years later. It also trebled its expenditure upon poor relief, to $1,500 a year. Talladega greatly increased its appropriations for building bridges in 1854, and launched a more extensive poor relief program in 1857. Each of these activities was relatively typical of the efforts undertaken by most of the newly active local governments.

Disbursements by cities and towns also increased in the fifties, but not by the spectacular leaps which state and counties recorded—primarily because town governments were already spending with comparative lavishness long before the final decade of the antebellum years. Alabama had few cities, but they were at all times in her history by far her most energetic jurisdictions. In 1829 Huntsville was already spending $1,300 a year. In 1843 the town disbursed $9,300, including $2,000 to finance the building of a city water system. Using 1850 population figures, the 1843 disbursement appears to be at least $3.27 per capita, or $6.24 per white resident. By 1850, the town of Montgomery was spending $6.33 per capita—$11.09 per free inhabitant—and this in a year when the state disbursed 61 cents per capita, or $1.10 per free inhabitant, and Montgomery County paid out 71 cents per capita, or $2.05 per free inhabitant. Expenditures of this magnitude—more than $6 per citizen in the early forties, and $11 per citizen at the end of that decade—would have been entirely impossible for any government other than one with an urban constituency.[32]

City budgets nevertheless rose even further in the fifties. Towns began wanting the trappings of their new status—waterworks, fire departments, gas light companies, public hospitals. All these and a number of other services came to be supplied in these years.[33]

32. Huntsville *Democrat*, December 25, 1829, December 14, 1843; Minutes of the Board of Aldermen of the City of Montgomery. *Cf.* Montgomery *Advertiser*, December 13, 1854, March 11, 1857.
33. Mobile, which alone among Alabama cities had experienced its greatest period of

Moreover, under the urging of the electorate, towns gave quite substantial aid to the railroads, whose completion promised such great commercial benefits. The assistance normally took the form of a purchase of stock. Selma invested $50,000 in the Alabama and Tennessee Rivers Railroad and Huntsville the same amount in the Memphis and Charleston. Mobilians levied a special property tax on themselves for the benefit of the M & O, producing some $300,000. And Montgomery voted $500,000 to the Alabama and Florida in 1853, and $300,000 to the South and North Alabama in 1860. In addition, the plank road fad of the early fifties received generous support. The undeserved popularity of the plank road seems to have resulted both from the fact that such roads were relatively inexpensive to build, and from the fact that they were made to appear more democratic than railways. Such an improvement would "give the people a road eminently suited to their wants as an agricultural people," because it "requires no costly machinery [*i.e.*, locomotives] to keep it in operation, but may be used by the ordinary vehicles of the country." [34] Many communities, particularly smaller ones such as Wetumpka and Cahaba but also larger towns like Montgomery, rushed to invest in these efforts. By mid-decade, however, their benefits had been recognized as largely chimerical.

Greatly increased governmental activity, the growing political power of the wealthy, a new attention to urban values, and a rapidly developing economy all would have caused uneasiness alone. But when the means for informing the masses of such developments had been greatly expanded—when newspapers were reaching more and more people, illiteracy was declining, libraries growing, and schools teaching novel and often alien notions to the children—and when an expanded credit system and a general transportation network were encouraging a much more general involvement in the market economy, it is no wonder that a society holding such beliefs as were current in antebellum Alabama would be plunged into cultural ver-

growth in the prosperous thirties, had obtained many of these urban amenities at that time. But the inland towns by and large had none of them before entering the boom of the final decade.

34. Montgomery *Advertiser*, December 9, 1851; *cf.* November 28, 1849, February 27, March 13, September 18, 1850, March 19, May 14, July 25, August 20, October 14, 1851.

tigo. Dazed, indecisive, frightened, Alabama's masses stumbled towards the final crisis.

A few statistics hint at the state of mind which was hidden beneath the booming prosperity. The suicide rate grew from 1.4 per 100,000 whites in 1850 to 4 per 100,000 in 1860. The murder rate grew from 2.6 per 100,000 whites to 6.7. Divorces grew markedly as well, as the graph on page 307 demonstrates. The biennial divorce rate per 100,000 whites was 11.6 in the prosperous years 1830–31, fell to 7.4 in depressed 1840–41, but soared with the return of prosperity—to 17.6 in 1850–51 and 22.1 in 1858–59. This evidence of social stress was a subject of concerned comment at the Secession Convention.[35]

We do not, however, need figures to tell us of the ferment which characterized the decade, for Alabamians left voluminous literary evidence of their perturbation. The evidence lacks a particular focus, of course; focusing anxieties was the traditional task of political leaders, but the new generation of politicians did not quite know what was expected of it. One of the elements at the core of the unformed public mood, though, was the thriving economy. Periods of success engendered agonizing tension in antebellum Alabama, for they were thought inevitably to cause depressions—a sort of natural retribution for extravagance. Indeed, Alabamians seem almost to have preferred depression, at least in the way that one would prefer penance to sin. The prosperity may have been pleasurable to the body, but the crash was good for the soul. Thus Governor Bagby informed the legislature in 1840 that calamities " should stimulate us to more vigorous habits of industry, frugality and economy," and to "the reflection that, although the hand of misfortune may for a season depress our energies and impair or diminish our abilities, it is most generally in periods of the

35. The 1850 census breaks suicides and murders down by race, but the 1860 census does not. I have adjusted for this fact by using the total figure in both cases, but the procedure unavoidably inflates the rates somewhat against a white base. The 1860 murder figure is a total of those deaths called "murders" and those called "homicides." It should be noted, as a general caveat, that the accuracy of the early census mortality schedules is distinctly open to question. Divorces were determined by counting the couples mentioned in the legislative acts on the subject. Since the legislature began meeting biennially in 1847, it was necessary to adjust earlier figures to this basis in order to make them comparable to later ones. The annual divorce rate would presumably be about half the figures given in 1850 and 1859. In 1830 it was 5.26 and in 1840, just over 2. See William R. Smith, *The History and Debates of the Convention of the People of Alabama, Begun and Held in the City of Montgomery on the Seventh Day of January, 1861* (Montgomery: White, Pfister and Co., 1861), 368–71.

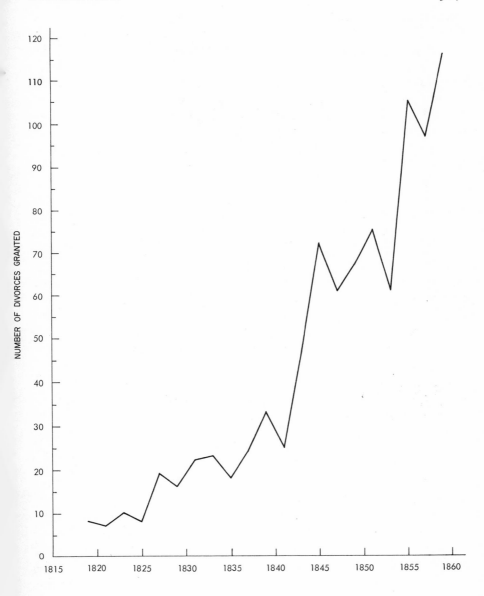

Divorces Granted, 1818–1859

darkest adversity that mankind have in the highest degree exhibited those great moral and intellectual qualities which assert and establish their high capacity for self government and entitle themselves, by the exhibition and practice of the cardinal virtues of temperance, moderation, firmness and patriotism to the admiration and gratitude of succeeding ages." And he insisted that "pecuniary embarrassments" were "almost necessarily and inseparably incident to a season of apparent prosperity and of actual exertion, speculation and enterprise."

In expressing these startling notions, the governor was merely giving voice to the common assumptions of the community. Moreover, it was generally believed that "seasons of speculation" were in large measure produced by inordinate governmental activity. Almost at the founding of the state, Senator Walker blamed the Panic of 1819 on his fellow members of Congress. " You yourselves were infected with the contagion of extravagance. The national coffers were overflowing, and you busied yourselves in devising new modes of expending your excessive wealth. You gave the tone; the people caught it and echoed it. Everywhere visions of magnificence occupied and heated the public mind." Similar charges were repeated throughout the state's history.[36]

It was against this background of belief—that governmental expenditure produced speculation, that speculation necessarily led to panic, that depression was judgment for the immorality of wealth— that Alabama entered the most prosperous decade in her history. At the very outset of the period, the orthodox political leaders had already begun chanting the warning of Cassandra. As the legislature debated re-creating a banking system, for instance, a hill county senator confessed grimly: "I know, sir, that my opposition to banks is rather out of time. A spirit of trading, speculating and banking pervades the whole country. When cotton was so low that it cost us as much to make it as it could be sold for, there was no use for banks. When nothing was made, speculation was not profitable. Now that cotton is up, we are asked to furnish banks to make money to buy it with." In addition to the long-standing fear of banks, the increasing industrialization added a new source of anxiety. "If we look to the most important and disastrous revulsions that have taken place in the

36. *Senate Journal*, Sess. of 1840–41, p. 8; *Senate Journal*, Sess. of 1841–42, p. 11; *Alabama Republican* (Huntsville), March 30, 1821.

commerce and business of the world," a writer admonished his fellow citizens, "we shall find that with few exceptions they have proceeded from the transfer and application of large amounts of capital from established to new and untried sources of investment and employment. If this is true as to other branches of employment, it will prove equally, perhaps more, so in relation to the great business of agriculture."

Such statements gnawed constantly at the back of Alabamians' minds. By mid-decade, a Huntsville lawyer commented with some desperation, "Money, money is the cry here from morning till night and if I were disposed to shave notes or lend at usurious rates of interest, I could almost double my means in twelve months. . . . There *must* be a crash and I *hope* it will not fall upon any of our blood." In such circumstances, when the break actually did come in 1857, its mildness was precisely the worst thing that could have happened to the state. Two banks—at Montgomery and at Selma—were forced to suspend specie payment for a few months, but because the cotton market largely resisted the downward pressures, few Alabamians were badly hurt, and by the end of the antebellum period, the boom had resumed at an even more feverish pace. The result of the panic, therefore, was to leave speculation undiminished, but to remind Alabamians, freshly and acutely, of the insubstantial nature of the paper prosperity all around them.[37]

In those counties which were just being incorporated into the market economy in these years, economic fluctuations seemed especially frightening, because the residents had had little previous personal experience with such difficulties. During one relatively mild period of instability, the senator from Henry, one of the Wiregrass counties, wrote the governor in consternation:

In relation to the pressure of the times, in consequence of the short crop and low price of cotton, the farmers in this part of the cuntry [sic] will be (the most of them) uterly [sic] ruined. I never have heard of such times in my life. The people is suing [each other] nearly man to man and . . . have been coming and requesting me to try and . . . se [sic] if there cannot be something done to prevent the people from being ruined. I now ask of you if such can be done

---

37. Montgomery *Advertiser*, February 20, 1850, April 23, 1851; Hugh Lawson White Clay to Virginia Tunstall Clay, January 2, 1855, in Clay Papers. Both suspended banks resumed payment in the summer of 1858: *Senate Journal*, Sess. of 1859–60, p. 13. *Cf.* Montgomery *Advertiser*, April 1, 1857.

and how it can be brought about and if you think the execution law can be stoped [*sic*] for awhile or a portion of the people's debts prolonged in some way.[38]

This plaintive cry is the voice of a section of the state facing an unfamiliar world—the world of commerce and contract.

A number of attitudes generally persisted from the political indoctrination of previous decades. There was a widespread apprehension that, as one old officeholder commented, "the influence of the [rail]roads already commenced, and those which yet remain on paper, I fear, will form a combination too strong for the integrity of the Legislature." One of the younger politicians realized that a traditional leader could "always command the vote of those who can't or don't read against any lawyer, townsman or state-rights man—each of whom is regarded as a suspicious character." Planters were told that they had "been too much in the habit heretofore of submitting their interest to the custody of those who do not produce, but speculate in, cotton"; and they took the criticism to heart. They began to offer schemes for controlling and manipulating their markets, and they sought greater efficiency through the adoption of scientific farming techniques. But they still feared and resented the newly cocksure residents of the towns. When the three cotton warehouses in Montgomery, early in the decade, announced that they would no longer repair poorly bound bales, the farmers of the area raged at this insolence. At a protest meeting, they acknowledged that more careful binding would bring them a better price, but they nevertheless furiously resolved that "we are opposed to the spirit of dictation" and "will reserve to ourselves the right of doing as we please." The squatters upon the public lands, who since the battles of the twenties had felt rather secure in their holdings, were horrified to find many of these small farms granted by Congress to the railroads during this period. One dispossessed settler denounced the action as "a monstrous wrong."[39]

38. James Searcy to John A. Winston, undated [probably winter, 1854–55], in Governors' Correspondence: Winston. *Cf.* Montgomery *Advertiser*, December 6, December 13, 1854, January 17, March 7, March 14, 1855.

39. John W. Bridges to Bolling Hall, October 5, 1853, Clement Claiborne Clay to Hall, September 30, 1853, in Hall Papers; Jacinth Jackson to Jefferson Franklin Jackson, January 17, 1852, in Jackson Papers; C. A. Bradford to John Bragg, July 20, 1852, Jessie M. Summers to Bragg, July 6, 1852, W. C. Dennis to Bragg, July 15, 1852, John A. Campbell to Bragg, January 3, 1853, all in Bragg Papers; *House Journal*, Sess. of 1849–50, pp. 33–35, 360–61; Montgomery

Even in the towns, there was uneasiness at the intensified spirit of materialism. A Mobilian who visited Montgomery in 1849 reported a "distinguishing trait more peculiar to this community than our own—the 'almighty dollar' is not worshipped with the same absorbing devotion; and the car of business is not driven recklessly over those who are unable to ride or get out of its track. Wealth is not so much the test of merit, and society is not divided to the same extent into cliques and upper and lower crust; though I learn this feeling prevails here, as perhaps everywhere even in republican America, to an improper degree."[40] The comment is beyond question not an accurate statement of conditions in Montgomery, but is rather an expression of the longing current in the state to believe that somewhere beyond the next hill, American ideals as Alabamians understood them were still practiced.

Finally, there was uncertainty about industrialization, and in some quarters even unblushing opposition to it. In 1850 the Senate's internal improvements committee reported that the state's mineral resources had attracted "much public attention," but confessed nevertheless that "the whole public mind and many private interests" were still "in their transition state in respect to this new class of industrial enterprises." The transit was a long and troubled one. A worried observer commented that agriculture had produced "a general diffusion of wealth and happiness over the whole community," but that "in the same proportion as we became a manufacturing, we should cease to be an agricultural people; because the capital required to build up these manufactories could be in no otherwise obtained than by diverting it from the planting interests of the country and turning it into this new channel of enterprise. And again, in the same ratio as we ceased to be an agricultural, we should cease to be a commercial people; for the simple reason that our commercial importance is based upon our agricultural products and is dependent upon them for its support and existence." This position was an extreme one, of course, and was not generally shared—but it was not without its audience.[41]

Advertiser, September 16, September 23, October 28, 1851, January 13, November 10, 1852, April 13, 1853, September 27, November 29, 1854, November 4, 1857, September 15, 1858.

40. Mobile *Tribune*, quoted in Montgomery *Advertiser*, October 31, 1849.

41. *Senate Journal*, Sess. of 1849–50, p. 379; Montgomery *Advertiser*, May 7, 1851; *cf.* also April 23, June 11, 1851.

In addition to the economic and social upheavals of the fifties, there were two other important sources of the unexampled tensions which mark the period—the new activism of state and local government, and northern agitation of the slavery question. To the former we have already adverted. In 1859 Governor Moore noted that in the preceding decade more laws had been passed "than perhaps ever were by any other State in the same number of years," and added a solemn warning: "We have too much legislation for the public good." This orthodox, if almost irrational, fear was reinforced by such revelations as those that opened the decade, of major defalcations by both the state treasurer, Samuel G. Frierson, and the state comptroller, Jefferson C. Van Dyke. But the fear was so deep-seated that it did not need tangential confirmation. The people had been told, "The essence of modern oppression is taxation. The measure of popular liberty may be found in the amount of money which is taken from the people to support the government: when the amount is increased beyond the requirements of a rigid economy, the government becomes profligate and oppressive." And taxes and expenditures were increasing rapidly.[42]

The people were reminded at every election, "The time will soon arrive when you will be called upon to signify who shall be the chief helmsman of the 'Ship of State'—whose voice and principles may seal the deeds which will forever alienate your rights." And they were enjoined, "Be jealous, therefore, of your constitutional rights; guard them with vigilance; permit not minions and traitors to wrest from you that priceless boon conferred upon you by your ancestors."[43] They knew that government could easily become the enemy of liberty, and that the function of the electorate was to restrain the always impending megalomania of its governors. The people were the only real guardians of their own liberties, and from the beginning the knowledge of this immense burden had tormented their minds. Now, as government pulled more and more strongly at increasingly frayed reins, the still faithful masses were thrown into mounting frenzy.

Fear of servile insurrection was present at the beginning of the

42. *Senate Journal,* Sess. of 1859–60, pp. 21–22; *Senate Journal,* Sess. of 1841–42, p. 93.
43. Resolutions of the Democracy of Randolph County, in Montgomery *Advertiser,* December 23, 1851.

decade—and for that matter, throughout the antebellum era—but it ordinarily remained at a comparatively low level. Indeed, it is probably better described as a nagging apprehension which had the potential for blossoming into genuine alarm in response to objective evidence, however slight. At no time was the state unprepared for the most startling abridgments of civil liberties if they appeared necessary for the preservation of the social order. During the Crisis of 1850, for instance, persons daring to utter allegedly emancipationist sentiments were driven from town by mobs in Auburn, Wetumpka, Troy, and Tuskegee, and vigilante committees were organized to suppress such sedition. Moreover, a Montgomery editor actually censured Wetumpkans in print for having merely expelled three supposed agitators, instead of "making a more delible [*sic*] mark of their displeasure upon these abolitionists. The ring-leader should have been hung as high as Haman, and the others should have been treated to a genteel coat of tar and feathers—first having received the 'cats' well laid on. We have great veneration for the laws of the land as a general thing, but when we see a man putting a torch to our dwelling and enacting means for the butchery of our wives and children, it is criminal to wait for the slow, uncertain process of the law." [44] It is essential, however, to note that Alabamians seldom expected slaves to act alone; if insurrection came, it would almost certainly come as a result of foreign instigation. And Alabamians remained rather confident that their harsh measures were sufficient to prevent the necessary spark from being struck. Therefore, until late in the fifties, the citizenry, though vigilant, was not unduly concerned.

After sectional hatreds were again inflamed by the encounters in Kansas, however, the notion that earlier precautions were inadequate to the new exigencies began to take root. The belief grew that northerners were steeling themselves to harsh aggressions; and it received what seemed to be confirmation in the Harper's Ferry raid. Thus, in the final year of the antebellum period, dread of stealthy abolitionist

44. Montgomery *Advertiser*, August 28, 1850; *cf.* July 31, September 4, December 25, 1850, January 15, February 19, July 23, August 20, September 16, 1851. *Cf.* also Huntsville *Democrat*, February 5, 1845, March 1, 1848; Montgomery *Advertiser*, September 21, 1853, October 24, 1855, August 27, 1856, September 23, 1857, January 19, 1859. Nor was approval of lynch law limited to race-related incidents: see Montgomery *Advertiser*, June 11, August 13, August 27, 1851.

infiltration mounted until it became a persistent, skittish suspicion. Governor Moore, vacationing in Talladega County in the summer of 1860, reported a typical flurry. "There is quite an excitement in the neighborhood of Fayetteville in regard to the slaves. A negro has made some disclosures which has [*sic*] alarmed the citizens. They yesterday purchased all the guns and pistols in Fayetteville, and have begged me [for state arms]. We have verbal confirmation that two men were taken up for conspiring with the slaves near Talladega (town) and that one of them had been hung [*sic*] and the other was to be tried yesterday. It seems that these occurrences are becoming common throughout the slaveholding states."[45] As was the case here, such episodes almost always turned on the dubious confessions of frightened slaves and rumors of events in other localities.

On the general subject, a caveat is in order. The anxiety at this period was probably not much more acute than was, for instance, the fear provoked by the mass mailing of abolitionist tracts to the South during 1835. Indeed, it may well not have exceeded greatly in its intensity the considerable trepidation which swept the state in 1882 in response to the events surrounding the Jack Turner affair.[46] We should note as well that the forebodings of 1860 had political overtones. The remnants of the state's Whiggery remained much calmer in the face of the supposed threat than did the orthodox Democrats. Very probably the circumstance is attributable in large measure to the fact that other sources of emotional stress had been at work in the minds of Democrats during the decade—events which had put Democrats off balance long before this particular threat had presented itself. The economic and social developments of the fifties had, of course, far less horrifying implications if viewed from the perspective of the Whig ideology. Such relative composure seemed wholly indefensible to more disquieted observers. After the description of the Talladega episode quoted above, Governor Moore proceeded to call old-line Whig leaders like Bell elec-

45. A. B. Moore to Watkins Phelan, August 30, 1860, in Governors' Correspondence: A. B. Moore. On these events, see *Alabama Reporter* (Talladega), August 30, September 13, September 20, September 27, October 4, October 11, 1860. *Cf.* Montgomery *Advertiser,* December 31, 1856, September 23, 1857.

46. See, *e.g.,* Huntsville *Southern Advocate,* August 4, August 11, August 18, August 25, September 1, December 1, 1835; William W. Rogers and Robert David Ward, *August Reckoning: Jack Turner and Racism in Post-Civil War Alabama* (Baton Rouge: Louisiana State University Press, 1973).

tor Joseph W. Taylor *"treasonable demagogues"* and added, "I have no patience with such men. If they continue, the people will stop them in their mad career." Failure to speak out strongly against efforts to foment bloody slaughter naturally appeared to anyone who believed in the reality of such efforts a treasonable omission, and one which could be explained only as a conscious decision to hide the truth from the electorate in order to gain political advantage.

But the various tensions of the fifties, when added together, did create more strain than had those of earlier decades, not only because the objective correlates of the tensions were more visible but also because the usual channel for the relief of mounting internal pressures in the society was closed off. When such pressures had become severe in earlier days, it had been the politicians who had dissipated them. Politicians gave the electorate an object upon which to focus attention, an explanation for the general uneasiness; and they launched a crusade against the new-found villain which caught people up in a sense that the society was working out its salvation with diligence. But the politicians of the new era were unable to locate any villains. They no longer attuned themselves to popular superstitions; they were too conscious of their role and they therefore undertook their search for villains intellectually instead of emotionally. And so the masses flailed about wildly—enlisted men seeking to fight a battle without officers to organize them. Since a political form for popular tensions was not forthcoming, the tensions necessarily revealed themselves in other ways. The decade is filled with such manifestations, both peaceful and violent. I have selected several as representative.

Benjamin W. Walker was a small planter from Macon County who had served a single term as a state representative at the session of 1849. In subsequent years he fell upon hard times and, in an effort to recoup his fortunes, conceived a rather desperate scheme to defraud the wealthy creditors of an estate of which he was an executor. Discovered in his plot, he was ordered by the chancery court to place the assets of the estate in the hands of a receiver. But Walker attempted to evade the order and in the spring of 1854, Chancellor James Clark had him arrested and imprisoned for contempt. An appeal to the state supreme court was unsuccessful, and November found Walker still languishing in jail, too poor to make bond. Thereupon his friends and neighbors organized themselves into a mob, stormed the jail, and freed the miscreant, who fled to Mississippi. Governor Winston sought his extradition, but the Mississippi courts refused because Walker had been imprisoned in connection with a civil rather than a criminal proceeding. When the press criticized the manner of Walker's release, the mob indignantly reconvened in a public meeting and adopted resolutions damning the chancellor's decision to jail Walker for contempt as "an act of oppression." [47]

The New Orleans and Ohio Telegraph Company completed its lines through northwest Alabama in 1848. In 1855 the governor's office received a frantic letter from the company's assistant superintendent in Marion County:

> With a heavy heart you will excuse me for what follows [sic]. The extraordinary superstition has got abroad here that the telegraph is in some way accountable for the dry spell we have had for the last summer and winter, and they have commenced tearing it down through this section. They say (I mean those who give any reason at all) say it sucks the lightning from the clouds, and the rain goes with it, and that it scatters the clouds. A great many through here are affected with that superstition. It appears to me a word from one whom all acknowledge to be a man of intelligence and a good Democrat to boot, would be of infinite service to us in this great peril and hazard of one of the wonders of the age. . . . They have torn down 7 or 8 miles at different times and the danger is imminent we will have to succomb [sic], when of course the telegraph through this state will be a dead letter. They threatened to tear down the jail should we arrest them, and I believe some of the reckless rascals would attempt it. [48]

It was the misfortune of Montgomery city alderman S. N. Brown to believe in the vigorous enforcement of the law. During the absence of Mayor Robert T. Davis in 1850, Brown became mayor pro tempore, and proceeded to apply town ordinances to the jot and tittle. The citizens were infuriated by the city's sudden intrusion into their lives. One September afternoon Brown's house was set afire and burned to

---

47. *Ex parte* Walker, 25 Ala. 81; Montgomery *Advertiser*, November 29, December 6, 1854, January 3, January 10, 1855. *Cf.* the similar case of Rufus Greene of Mobile: Montgomery *Advertiser*, January 8, July 16, July 23, 1851, September 1, 1858; Chison Root to John Bragg, April 18, 1852, in Bragg Papers.

48. A. E. Trabue to John A. Winston, March 9, 1855, in Governors' Correspondence: Winston.

the ground. No reward was offered for the incendiary. Alderman Brown was not reelected.[49]

Lawson Clay, a younger brother of the senator, found the practice of law in Huntsville unremunerative—his brother called it "a starving business"—and determined in 1854 to move to the west. As we have seen, when Alabamians went west, they were looking for areas which, though not yet fully settled, gave promise of becoming replications of Alabama. Naturally, therefore, their aspirations in the 1850s centered on Arkansas and Texas. Lawson reported early in his journey, "I am not mistaken in saying that we have passed more than 300 wagons since we left Alabama, all moving to Texas. I cannot tell how many buggies and on horseback we have overtaken. . . . In consequence of this general rush to that State, I am very much afraid we will be unable to get land upon such terms as we anticipated." His worst fears were justified when he arrived in Texas a month later. The area had no water and little wood. Moreover, "Notwithstanding these serious objections to the State, land is daily appreciating in consequence of the great influx of men, women and children, rich and poor, who have heard of the 'good country' and who, without first looking over it, have bundled up and removed thither—to be disappointed. Although I passed hundreds of mover[s] going to Texas, I also met quite a large number returning." [50]

The younger Bolling Hall, one of the leading political figures of Alabama, also longed to remove to Texas, and visited there in 1855. He, too, was disappointed. "Everything smacks strongly of frontier life and frontier manners and interests. . . . The difference is vast between the interests discussed here and those at home." But Hall could not shake the dream, and 1858 found him again considering the move. His son, Crenshaw, at the time a college student, was eager to join him, for the boy feared that Alabama was too thickly settled for her citizens to make a good living, especially so for a young lawyer just starting out.

49. Montgomery *Advertiser*, September 18, 1850.
50. Clement Claiborne Clay to Hugh Lawson White Clay, May 28, 1852, Clement Claiborne Clay to Virginia Tunstall Clay, July 11, 1852, Hugh Lawson White Clay to Susanna Withers Clay, November 8, 1854, Hugh Lawson White Clay to Clement Claiborne Clay, December 15, 1854, all in Clay Papers.

Longtime Montgomery postmaster Neil Blue moved to Texas at the beginning of the decade, but returned to Alabama in 1854.[51]

These three gentlemen were by no means unusual. There was considerable emigration in the fifties and much more longing to emigrate. Of all persons born in Alabama, 26 percent resided elsewhere in 1850. By 1860 the figure had risen to 30 percent. This growth represents 54,352 additional emigrants, an increase of some 65 percent over 1850. Nearly 43 percent of Alabamians living abroad dwelt in either Arkansas or Texas in 1860. The addition of persons who, like Blue, moved west but returned, and of those who, like Clay and Hall, wished to go but could find no adequate homes, would reveal considerable residential instability. Moreover, there was a not insubstantial movement within the state. Indeed, some counties such as newly created Choctaw actively sought immigrants. Readers were assured that there was no other section of Alabama "offering superior advantages to men of moderate means. . . . To those planters who are turning their thoughts on Texas and Arkansas, we say come this way and we will show you some fine settlements."[52] One of the most rapidly growing areas during the decade was the Wiregrass section in the southeast.

Religious revivals had long been a mechanism for the release of social tensions, and continued to be in the fifties. One moral crusade which was launched in the decade and rapidly gathered warriors was the temperance movement. With all the fervor which was to characterize their later, more successful forays, the prohibitionists campaigned for the reweaving of what seemed to them a rotting social fabric.[53] But pleas for moral reformation went on at the same time

51. Bolling Hall to Louisa Hall, February 16, 1855, Crenshaw Hall to Bolling Hall, July 2, 1858, James Mitchell to Bolling Hall, September 25, 1855, Bolling Hall to Louisa Hall, March 2, 1855, Green Wood to Bolling Hall, August 26, 1855, all in Hall Papers; William R. de V. King to Neil Blue, April 11, 1850, Neil Blue to Matthew P. Blue, March 12, 1854, both in M. P. Blue Papers, Alabama Department of Archives and History, Montgomery. *Cf.* Montgomery *Advertiser*, December 15, December 22, 1852.

52. *Choctaw County Reporter*, quoted in Montgomery *Advertiser*, May 1, 1850. *Cf.* Montgomery *Advertiser*, June 8, July 27, 1853, January 24, 1855.

53. Jefferson Franklin Jackson to Frederick J. Kingsbury, August 31, 1848, in Jackson Papers; H. Sample to Bolling Hall, June 28, 1853, Albert Elmore to Hall, July 19, 1853, J. N. Carpenter to Hall, October 1, 1853, David B. Smedley to Hall, November 30, 1853, John B. Brown to Hall, March 14, 1848, all in Hall Papers; *House Journal*, Sess. of 1859–60, p. 524;

as—and were in a curious way bound up with—the generally mounting fear of abolitionism which appears increasingly to have betrayed Alabamians into open callousness in the disciplining of their slaves. Mount Meigs was a wealthy and relatively cultured planting community east of Montgomery. On two occasions, in 1854 and in 1856, the citizens of Mount Meigs gathered to watch as an accused slave was burned alive. The spectators listened to the screams of the tortured victims with all the impassivity of Aztec priests, observing sacrifices to gods equally as bloody and as terrible as the Furies who ruled the heart of the South. There was no compunction; the oblation was demanded for the preservation of the society. Even Governor Winston, a man not given to sensitivity, was shocked by these proceedings. After the second occurrence, he ordered the solicitor of the circuit to seek indictments. But the solicitor sadly reported that he had presented the first episode to the grand jurors "and they scarcely paid any attention." The guilty citizens themselves passed resolutions which declared their willingness, "in ordinary cases of offence [*sic*] against the laws of the country, to submit them to legal investigation and [to] abide the decision of our Courts of justice," but which affirmed that "there are cases in which a more summary and exemplary mode of vengeance should be resorted to." They unblushingly recommended their course to other communities—and at least one adopted the precedent.[54]

Another aspect of the growing fear of slaves' enmity was the renewed movement in the decade to prohibit the importation of slaves into the state for sale. Such a prohibition had been enacted in 1827, repealed in 1829, reenacted in 1832 as a response to the Nat Turner insurrection in Virginia, but repealed a second time the following year. The matter continued to provoke occasional discussions, but was not seriously agitated again until the beginning of the final antebellum decade. In both 1849 and 1851, members from the plantation-dominated western Black Belt made a vigorous, though unsuccessful,

Montgomery *Advertiser*, October 13, December 8, December 15, 1852, January 5, April 20, June 1, June 22, July 20, July 27, August 3, 1853, March 29, June 7, July 12, 1854, January 24, June 6, 1855.

54. T. H. Croom to John A. Winston, December 12, 1855, Marion A. Baldwin to Winston, May 3, 1856, both in Governors' Correspondence: Winston; Montgomery *Advertiser*, September 20, 1854, January 21, 1857, February 23, 1859.

effort to gain legislative acceptance of the measure, arguing that it was necessary for the state's security.[55]

Towards the close of the decade, on the other hand, a number of politicians began to seek the reopening of the African slave trade. The idea engaged the fancy of several of the ambitious young adherents of the Yanceyite faction, and appears to have received some support in counties which were just moving into the market economy during these years. At the Secession Convention, Black Belt delegates and hill county members joined in denouncing this movement as highly impolitic; but two speakers ventured guarded approval for the proposal. Both men—Gappa T. Yelverton of the Wiregrass county of Coffee, and former congressman James F. Dowdell of the hill county of Chambers—placed their arguments upon the grounds that the resumption would strengthen the economic and social position of the small farmer. Yelverton denounced slaveholders "who have as many negroes as they want and are rich by the high price of their property" and therefore "urged that more and cheaper negroes and a new market might lessen their estates in value." He compared the reopening of the slave trade to the homestead policy. "We have vast amounts of wild lands which were unavailable while prices were high, for the poor could not purchase. But statesmen became liberal and reduced the price of these lands, by which millions have been enabled to secure homes for themselves and families." A similarly liberal policy towards slave prices would bring similar happy results, he implied.

Congressman Dowdell reminded his listeners that slavery "secures the equality of the white race, and upon its permanent establishment rests the hope of democratic liberty." He added,

I hope [the day] may never come at the South when safety to the institution of slavery shall require social or political inequality to be established among white people. No, sir; never let it come. . . . Let us keep the white race as they are here now and ought ever to be—free, equal and independent, socially and politically; recognize no subordinates but those whom God has made to be such—the children of Ham—and whose subordination to a superior race

55. *Acts of Alabama*, Sess. of 1826–27, pp. 44–45; *Acts of Alabama*, Sess. of 1828–29, p. 62: *Acts of Alabama*, Sess. of 1831–32, pp. 12–18; *Acts of Alabama*, Sess. of 1832–33, p. 5; Montgomery *Advertiser*, July 30, October 21, December 9, 1851, February 3, 1852; *Senate Journal*, Sess. of 1849–50, p. 100; *Senate Journal*, Sess. of 1851–52, pp. 53, 59, 254; *House Journal*, Sess. of 1851–52, pp. 362, 489. Cf. Huntsville *Democrat*, October 22, October 29, 1845.

secures their happiness, protection and moral elevation. A simple act of secession, then, will not stay the tide of immigration, and the influx of white laborers from the North will likely introduce the very evils which we have endeavored to avoid. How long it will be before the evil becomes serious, I cannot tell. But sooner or later it will be upon us unless the demand for labor at the South shall be supplied from some other source of a cheaper character, and consistent with our present labor system.[56]

It should be noted that the congressman here clearly implies that, at least as he understood it, secession was intended to halt the decline of social and political equality—to prevent the introduction of an economic system which would compel white men to depend for their livelihood upon other white men.

To summarize, then: the court system faltered under the weight of the public antipathy to power. American Luddites roamed the hills. Arson against the property of governmental officials went unpunished—and perhaps was secretly countenanced. Tens of thousands, voting with their feet, fled westward; and many more longed to follow. Rising suspicion bred increasingly public cruelty toward a helpless people. Unfamiliar anxieties produced novel and strident sentiments. These are not the internal conflicts which any society must face; these are the symptoms of a developing crisis—developing because the political process was unable to provide relief. We shall next glance at the politics of the fifties and then conclude the chapter with an analysis of the impact which the social crisis of the period had upon political relations.

Political Responses

For a brief time in mid-decade, it appeared that politics might after all be able to cope to some degree with the massive, and largely misapprehended, challenge which faced it. This momentary hope was provided by an extraordinary man, Governor John A. Winston. Winston came down from his native Tennessee Valley in 1835 to create a plan-

56. Smith, *Debates of the Convention of 1861*, pp. 232–33, 256, 258; *cf.* pp. 235–36. The complete debate on this matter is pp. 129, 164, 194–211, 228–65. On the controversy generally, see Montgomery *Advertiser*, November 26, 1856, May 20, August 26, September 2, September 30, October 14, 1857, January 27, March 24, December 29, 1858, January 5, January 12, January 19, January 26, June 22, 1859.

tation in the western Black Belt area which had just been ceded by the Choctaws and organized into the county of Sumter. In 1840 he was elected to the legislature. He did not seek reelection in 1841, but with that single exception, he was a member of every legislative session until he became governor in 1853. His accomplishment is the more remarkable because he was a Democrat; his colleagues from Sumter were sometimes all Whigs. Sitting in the legislature of 1843 with Winston was his friend and family physician Sidney S. Perry. Doctor Perry fell in love with Winston's second wife, whom Winston had married in 1842. Discovering their romance in June of 1847, Winston promptly murdered the doctor with a double-barreled shotgun. At the preliminary hearing, the county magistrates ruled the killing a justifiable homicide, and Winston was discharged. But the murder and the divorce from his wife which followed cast a cloud over Winston's later years. He slipped into an austere, bitter existence. In 1844 Winston had founded a cotton commission house in Mobile. After the murder it was Winston's habit to divide his time between his Mobile business and his Sumter plantation, with his winter months spent in Montgomery when the assembly was in session. He sought to fill his life by pursuing three different careers, but evidently a certain emptiness remained.

Winston became ever more cynical, manifested overt and unbending hostility to all who opposed him, developed a penchant for political manipulation, and abandoned true morality for a rather stiffly doctrinaire antagonism towards the mores and aspirations of the world. Winston hesitated to seek reelection to the Senate in 1849, for instance, but finally decided to run solely "to do the State some service in keeping back some upstart politicians who look to the next legislature to send them to the U.S. Senate. . . . I have no favors to ask, though some friends to punish. I think I can do it as well in the Senate as anywhere else." On another occasion he wrote, "I believe the law against carrying weapons, concealed or otherwise, a concession to sentimental hypocricy [*sic*] and stuff," and "a damn piece of nonsense." When, as governor, he undertook to pardon several convicts as part of a political deal, he instructed his clerk, "You will also enter at large, as private secretary, reasonable reasons that may confound any goon who will look into them. . . . [As to the nature of the reasons], you must exercise your ingenuity." In return for this connivance, Winston authorized the secretary to choose a notary public in Coosa County. These attitudes typified the man.[57]

It is not surprising, therefore, that a person of such hardened misanthropy would find himself without sympathy for the exuberant economic boosterism of the 1850s. Yet the division of the internal improvements advocates at the 1853 Democratic convention, sectional loyalties, and Winston's record as one of the principal engineers of the reorganization of the party the year before, gave him the nomination after seven ballots, and he thus became chief magistrate precisely at the moment when the campaign for state aid to railroad construction was reaching its climax. Winston was no orthodox opponent of state aid. He had been a prominent delegate to the Mobile Internal Improvements Convention of 1851, and his campaign statements on the subject in 1853 were moderate, leaving observers with the impression that he would support carefully guarded assistance.[58] During his first term he actually approved loans of $400,000 to the Mobile and Ohio and even more—though in a quite restrictive statute—to the Tennessee and Coosa. He was simply too dyspeptic a figure to accept a general program of aid. In addition, after he had begun his series of vetoes, the popular approbation which quickly manifested itself reinforced him in his course of conduct. He had, it seemed, accidentally stumbled upon a hobby.

The agitation for state assistance had begun with the new decade. Except for the loan to the West Point Railroad in 1845, the two percent and three percent funds, which by the act admitting Alabama to the Union were specifically reserved for financing internal improvements, had lain idle since the abortive efforts at clearing several rivers in the early thirties. The infant railroads eyed this money greedily. On

57. John A. Winston to Jefferson Franklin Jackson, May 3, 1849, in Jackson Papers; Winston to James H. Weaver, August 5, 1857, Winston to Weaver, May 4, 1857, both in Governors' Correspondence: Winston. On the murder of Perry, see Tuscumbia *North Alabamian*, June 18, 1847. On Winston's character generally, see, *e.g.*, Montgomery *Advertiser*, January 30, 1850, June 4, December 2, 1851, February 3, 1852; Winston to Jefferson Franklin Jackson, December 22, 1848, January 1, 1849, both in Jackson Papers; Winston to Matthew P. Blue, June 27, 1857, in Blue Papers; Winston to James H. Weaver, July 14, 1857, September 23, 1857, both in Governors' Correspondence: Winston; Sidney T. Douglas to A. B. Moore, January 26, 1858, Winston to Moore, January 27, 1858, both in Governors' Correspondence: A. B. Moore. Glenn N. Sisk, "John Anthony Winston: Alabama's Veto Governor" (M.A. thesis, University of Alabama, 1934), fails to do justice to its remarkable subject.

58. Montgomery *Advertiser*, June 11, 1851, April 6, May 11, May 18, June 8, 1853.

being elected speaker of the House in 1849, L. Pope Walker, one of the leading advocates of distributing it, painted a portrait which must have seemed nightmarish to the orthodox, of a state "with her railroads all gemmed with towns having about them the air and appearance of active, healthful life—a life of motion and of speed." And he added, "May we not, then, hope to feel at this session of the Legislature now just opening something of the liberalizing and expanding spirit of the age? of that spirit which animates to hopeful industry and excites to emulous enterprise the wonderful energies of our people, not only enlarging and extending with almost marvelous rapidity the geographical area of the country but harmonizing and assimilating its most remote sections by the benign influences of speedy intercourse and commercial relationship?"[59] The answer to Walker's question was a simple no; such assimilation was precisely what most Alabamians desired to avoid. It will probably not surprise the reader to learn that Walker was a converted Whig.

Despite their crushing defeats in the session of 1849, the internal improvements forces regrouped for an assault on the session of 1851. A large convention was called to meet in Mobile in early summer, and a lengthy address was approved proposing a general program of aid. Philip Phillips led the crusade. But the legislature again rejected all such proposals. The citizens of Mobile held a mass indignation meeting in protest.[60]

Four years of agitation were beginning to bear fruit, however, and the state-aid men had high hopes for the legislature of 1853. The search by ambitious politicians for a hobby brought those legislators in particular to the cause. When the session convened, a freshman member detected the division at once. He told his brother that "although the speaking talent, especially in the House, is in favour of the scheme, the bone and sinew, so to speak, are opposed to it."[61] On this attempt, loans to the M & O and to the Tennessee and Coosa were

59. *Ibid.*, November 21, 1849.
60. *Ibid.*, August 13, August 20, December 9, December 16, 1851, January 20, February 10, 1852.
61. Daniel J. Fox to John Fox, December 1, 1853, in John Fox Papers, Duke University Library, Durham.

passed and accepted by the governor. But Winston's known opposition to any general aid provisions and his quickly established propensity for vetoing bills with which he disagreed, contributed to the defeat of more ambitious proposals. Internal improvements thus became the dominant issue in the succeeding gubernatorial canvass.

During Winston's first term the opposition had reorganized itself into the Know-Nothing party.[62] The Know-Nothings were an unknown quantity in state politics, and it was widely believed that by playing upon the disaffection of pro-state-aid Democrats and upon the desire for intersectional reconciliation which the re-creation of a national conservative party promised, the new alliance might succeed in creating for itself an electoral majority. Discontent with Winston's railroad policies was particularly apparent among the more articulate element in the Tennessee Valley and the eastern hill counties, areas previously unshakably Democratic. The Memphis and Charleston, the Alabama and Tennessee Rivers, and the Tennessee and Coosa, all railroads which were aggressively seeking governmental assistance, were intended to pass through these counties. Partially as a result of the state aid issue, the Whiggery had made some gains in the hill counties in the legislative elections of 1853.

But the Know-Nothings were divided on how strongly to emphasize the internal improvements question. It would deliver some previously Democratic votes, but might also alienate rural voters in areas in which no railroads were planned. In January of 1855 the Know-Nothings held a state convention in Mobile, but their division prevented the selection of a gubernatorial nominee. In April one of the candidates for the nomination, Judge George D. Shortridge, formerly a state-aid Democrat, forced the issue by entering the race on his own motion. In June a second Know-Nothing convention accepted the *fait accompli*. For all his eagerness to enter the lists, however, Judge Shortridge soon found his issue much less popular than he had thought it to be. Governor Winston accepted—indeed, embraced—the challenge, and toured the state to deliver increasingly strident condemnations of his opponents' proposals to involve the government with the railroads.

62. See pp. 352–60 herein.

ALL DEMOCRATIC MEMBERS ANTI-RAILROAD

ALL DEMOCRATIC MEMBERS PRO-RAILROAD

DEMOCRATIC MEMBERS DIVIDED

NO DEMOCRATIC MEMBERS

Distribution of Democratic Legislators Voting on State Aid to Railroads, 1855

In early July Shortridge moderated his position on aid. By the end of the month he was attempting to ignore the question altogether. Winston and his party swept to an easy victory.[63]

Ironically, however, despite the Democratic triumph, Winston found himself faced with a hostile, pro-aid legislature. The Democrats in the Tennessee Valley and the eastern hill counties had been so frightened by the possibility that the Know-Nothings' internal improvements oratory would prove effective, and many of the party's leaders there had been so dazzled by the wealth which the projected railroads promised the areas, that the party had been induced to nominate state aid men for the assembly. Though the Know-Nothings carried some western Tennessee Valley counties, they were generally successful only in the usual Whig constituencies, the Black Belt and the southwest. But the Democrats' selection of pro-railroad candidates in so many north Alabama counties, when joined with the American victories elsewhere, gave the state-aid forces a legislative majority. In south Alabama, where the Whiggery had always been strong, the sudden advent of the Know-Nothings did not dismay the Democrats with the prospect of terminating a protracted hegemony. Nor were railroads nearly so necessary to the commercial exploitation of the region. Democrats in that region remained devoted to anti-corporate dogma. Indeed, a few Black Belt Know-Nothings—particularly in Sumter, Greene, and Macon—even adopted mildly anti-corporation positions, presumably in search of Democratic votes.

As the new assembly session opened, Winston frantically warned the legislators, in the classic formulations of his party's doctrine, "Experience already teaches us that any departure from the legitimate and simple purpose of government brings, as inevitably as a departure from physical and moral law, a speedy punishment. . . . The government cannot, without a violation of principle, take money from the people to lend to corporations, monopolies or individuals."[64] But his asseverations were without effect. Among other things the legislature

63. Montgomery *Advertiser*, November 15, November 29, 1854, January 17, January 24, January 31, February 7, February 28, March 14, March 28, April 4, April 25, May 23, May 30, June 13, June 20, July 4, July 18, July 24, August 22, 1855.

64. *Senate Journal*, Sess. of 1855–56, pp. 146, 148.

of 1855 renewed the M & O loan and offered substantial new loans to the Memphis and Charleston and the Alabama and Tennessee Rivers railroads.

Winston vetoed thirty-six bills during the session, but twenty-seven of his vetoes were overridden, sixteen of them granting corporate privileges. Nevertheless, he still proved able to outflank his opponents. In an effort to satisfy Winston's demand that any aid produce no increased taxation, the internal improvements forces had hit upon the scheme of loaning out the old Bank of Alabama notes, which had been accepted by the state in payment of taxes in order to retire them from circulation. At the request of the governor, Attorney General Marion A. Baldwin, though a political ally of Senator Fitzpatrick's, provided Winston with an excuse for refusing to execute the new laws: a legal opinion that such loans would in effect be an emission by the state of bills of credit, in violation of the federal Constitution. Thus, not a penny in aid left the treasury during Winston's second term. Moreover, Winston announced that the M & O had, through a technical omission, defaulted on its debt to the state, and that he therefore intended to sell the railroad's first mortgage security bonds to the public. The bonds were never actually sold, but the state courts eventually confirmed the governor's right to do so.[65]

Winston's maneuvers created a political convulsion. At last the masses had been given a cause in resonance with their emotions. Overnight "state aid" became a curse and Winston, rather incongruously, a heroic tribune. It was as if he had pressed some secret lever. At the beginning of Winston's tenure, office seekers were being advised to espouse aid to internal improvements projects. "There is enough in it to make the political fortunes of several members of Congress," one was told. Incumbents were attacked for opposing such efforts. By mid-decade prominent politicians were actively lobbying for aid at both the federal and the state level. And even legislators from remote

---

65. Montgomery *Advertiser*, February 14, 1855, January 16, January 23, March 26, April 9, June 25, July 23, July 30, November 19, November 26, 1856, May 20, 1857. *Cf.* Lewis Wyeth to John A. Winston, April 24, 1854, Marion A. Baldwin to Winston, August 14, 1854, February 29, 1856, May 3, 1856, John Archer Elmore to Winston, November 2, 1857, all in Governors' Correspondence: Winston.

areas expressed at least limited support for the proposals.[66] There were dissidents of course. One old representative feared that the schemes would deliver the state "into the merciless hands of speculators." Another legislator thought that they would "cripple and embarrass our energies for at least half a century to come." But these men were fighting a rear guard action.[67]

By the conclusion of Winston's term as governor, however, his position had swept the field. In 1853 the party's state organ had upbraided Alabamians for their suspicions of railroads: "There is too much distrust of companies. We are fully impressed with the importance of keeping a strict eye on monied [*sic*] corporations—of their liability to misappropriate funds, and also in loaning them money, to place proper restrictions around them; but still we should act upon correct information and not be led into foolish exactions." But in 1855 the same paper ranted,

It is an absolute imposition on the people to force them to furnish from the fruits of their self-denial the means of constructing works the benefit of which must conduce to swell the wealth of a few favored men banded together under the title of a company. Free government and high taxes are contradictory terms. . . . Corporations, when backed by wealth and supported by talent, are disposed to compass their objects by fair or foul means; in pursuance of this policy, they debauch the public morals, corrupt legislation, undermine the freedom of the press, and disarm opposition either by bribery or by strong and overawing denunciations. . . . The 'mania' for railroads is now at its culminating point. But a few years will suffice to produce a total revolution in the popular mind as regards the propriety of mixing the State up with a hundred ill digested and unneeded railways, and the public will then, if not till then, do justice to those who first resisted measures fraught with such perilous consequences.

66. Philip Phillips to John Bragg, February 8, 1852, Thaddeus Sanford to Bragg, March 13, 1852, both in Bragg Papers; Draft of a circular letter, spring, 1853, from Clement Claiborne Clay attacking Williamson R. W. Cobb, Clement Claiborne Clay to Clement Comer Clay, November 23, 1855, both in Clay Papers; Benjamin Fitzpatrick to John A. Winston, March 13, 1854, in Governors' Correspondence: Winston; John S. Kennedy to George S. Houston, January 17, 1854, in Houston Papers; Gappa T. Yelverton to Bolling Hall, September 9, 1853, David C. Humphreys to Hall, September 7, 1853, both in Hall Papers.
67. John W. Bridges to Bolling Hall, October 5, 1853, in Hall Papers; Daniel J. Fox to John Fox, December 1, 1853, in Fox Papers.

By 1857, the editor of this paper could pronounce opposition to state-aid Democratic party policy.[68]

For Winston's successor as governor in 1857, "All that seems to be required is that the nominee shall be anti-state aid," and a number of party leaders were excluded on that score. In the preconvention maneuvering, the leading contenders engaged in a contest to outdo each other in denouncing such assistance. Even the other party hesitated to nominate a candidate for Congress who was closely associated with the issue.[69] And as for Winston himself, he was the man of the hour. One of his adversaries, future governor Robert M. Patton, condemned his "mulish opposition to the Legislature," and claimed, "There is nothing more ridiculous than to talk about a Winston Policy, when this man never had sufficient intellect to originate an idea." But he admitted that, if given the opportunity, the electorate might demand Winston's elevation to the federal Senate. Another opponent, though asserting that the governor did not have the "talents, education, or intellect" to fill higher office, nevertheless added, "The popular masses admire his firmness as executive of the state, and would now sustain his anti State-aid Railroad policy by an overwhelming majority." And Winston's friends flatly declared him the most popular man in Alabama.[70]

Relying upon this celebrity, Winston launched a campaign to displace Senator Clay. As one observer noted, "It is true, with many of the members of the last Legislature, Governor Winston is very unpopular; but the next session will, I think, be composed of a new set of men, a majority of whom will, in all probability be elected as Winston men, without reference to the Senatorial election but as *anti-Rail road Winston men*. Then, if the election be brought before the next session and Governor Winston is a candidate, these members, without positive instructions to the contrary (which the people are loth [*sic*] to give) would vote for Winston." The analysis seemed persuasive, and

68. Montgomery *Advertiser*, June 29, 1853, February 14, 1855; Matthew P. Blue to Clement Claiborne Clay, April 10, 1857, in Clay Papers.

69. Gabriel B. DuVal to Clement Claiborne Clay, May 14, 1857, in Clay Papers; Wetumpka *Spectator*, May 28, 1857; Montgomery *Advertiser*, May 6, May 20, June 3, June 10, June 17, July 8, 1857; William F. Samford to Matthew P. Blue, April 8, 1857, in Blue Papers.

70. Robert M. Patton to Clement Claiborne Clay, June 5, 1857, J. M. Hudgins to Clay, May 11, 1857, Mace T. P. Brindley to Clay, June 19, 1857, all in Clay Papers.

Clay was badly frightened when the campaigning commenced in the spring. But at the beginning of June the state Democratic convention rejected an anti-state-aid platform on the grounds that it was a factional maneuver. And in July the senator reported jubilantly that Winston would do well to get any votes besides those of his cousin William O. Winston and his brother-in-law, future governor Robert B. Lindsay. In September Winston withdrew from the race "for various causes . . . amongst which is the want of much prospect of election."[71] The reader may well wonder what had happened. However, before we can comprehend this startling end to Winston's apparently well-founded ambitions, we must pause to explore the most important result of the social turmoil of the fifties.

We have already noted the rather sophomoric elitism which crept into the attitudes of younger Alabama politicians once they came consciously to understand the nature of the symbolic issue and how to manipulate it. The respect for the wrath of the masses—the knowledge that the tiger upon which they were mounted was more than a beast of burden—which had been implicit in the actions of earlier generations of leaders, had been replaced by a surreptitious cynicism. As important as was this development, however, an even more significant change was taking place in the attitude of the voters towards the politicians. The very foundation of the society was the belief that the political structure should be the sword of the masses in their struggle to forestall the slavery which nonpublic institutions sought constantly to impose. Politicians claimed to be the captains of the popular army. When the fire-eaters suggested at the beginning of the decade that these officers might be betraying the cause, the notion was met with disbelief, even consternation. But as the years passed, pressures mounted and the society's supermen floundered, unable to discover the key to the vague uneasiness they sensed. Among the electorate, doubts slowly became distrust.

The denunciations from the fire-eaters continued, in ever stronger language. William F. Samford railed that the party leaders were

71. J. M. Hudgins to Clement Claiborne Clay, May 11, 1857, George S. Walden to Clay, June 6, 1857, Clay to David Hubbard, July 8, 1857, all in Clay Papers; John A. Winston to James H. Weaver, September 23, 1857, in Governors' Correspondence: Winston; Montgomery *Advertiser*, January 16, 1856, March 25, April 1, April 15, April 29, May 13, June 3, June 10, June 17, July 1, July 15, August 5, September 23, October 14, October 21, November 18, 1857.

"tricksters. Power in the hands of a confident majority stagnates and creams over with green putridity like hard water. The oily and sleek gentry that know how to smile and fawn and simulate, are to have the spoils—men who are either too cowardly or selfish to encounter the foe in the day of danger." And he added angrily, "Let the 'wise men' beware! The cup of reckoning is brimfull and boiling over!" But such sentiments were coming to be widely shared. One of the pioneer settlers of the Tombigbee Valley was sickened by the new age. Early in the decade he confessed chagrin at the opposition which the Homestead Bill was encountering. "But has Congress become so sordid as to confine itself to a pecuniary view of this subject alone? I fear that there is less patriotizm [sic] in that body than formerly, that party strife has narrowed down the views of members, smothered their patriotizm [sic]: And if so, it has rendered them unfit for the honorable station they occupy." Then, as if in horror at the heresy into which he had been seduced, he cried, "I will not believe it!" A Huntsville priest and future bishop fretted that "in the policy of parties there is over-much trickery and management. Our destiny is, under God, in the hands of a very few; and how little do these few realize the responsibility" they bear.[72]

Towards the end of the fifties, these nascent attitudes began to find electoral expression. At a usual session of the legislature, as we have seen, about half of the members were new men. But of the 218 men who served in the sessions of 1857 and 1859, some 68 percent had never served in any assembly prior to 1857. This abrupt influx of novices into political prominence is the more significant when we recall that it came at the very end of the antebellum era, after forty years of political activity. It was in some part caused by north Alabama's repudiation in 1857 of the Democrats from the region who had opposed Winston at the preceding session, but that event by no means accounts for the phenomenon. Counties located in every section of the state give evidence of the tendency to turn against officeholders. Just a

72. George Strother Gaines to John Bragg, June 12, 1852, in Bragg Papers; The Reverend Henry C. Lay to Clement Claiborne Clay, November 23, 1855, in Clay Papers; William F. Samford to Matthew P. Blue, April 8, 1857, in Blue Papers. For other such statements by Samford, see Montgomery *Advertiser*, April 18, 1855, February 4, 1857, August 25, September 15, 1858, May 25, 1859.

fourth both of the pro-railroad Democrats and of the anti-railroad Democrats in the House of 1855 were returned in 1857. In north Alabama, the voters' hostility to state aid policies as frequently took the form of a restoration of older Jacksonians to favor as it did the elevation of new men. Instead, as the increasing acceptance of the fire-eaters' political analysis hints, the number of novices appears to be associated with a growth in importance of southern rights questions in state politics towards the end of the decade. In south Alabama, the Yanceyite faction challenged the traditional leadership for control of the Democratic party—with considerable success. And the adoption of southern rights as party doctrine had the unintended effect of facilitating the emergence of a coalition in north Alabama of younger, ambitious politicians and older Jacksonians, allied against the railroad element. The exploitation of southern rights villains enabled the coalition to hold the initiative which the events of the Winston administration had delivered to it.[73]

In both sections, the substance of these events is to be found in subtle generational misunderstandings. A glance at the views of one of the younger professionals who were coming to dominate politics during the fifties—and whose efforts had, by the end of that decade, so greatly exacerbated the voters' fears—will thus shed light upon the sources of the electorate's restlessness. Clement Claiborne Clay was the eldest son of the man who had headed the committee which drafted the state constitution, who had become the first chief justice, and who later had been both governor and senator. During the elder Clay's gubernatorial term, his son had acted as private secretary, and had subsequently served with some distinction in the assemblies of 1842, 1844, and 1845. After a term as judge of the Madison County court, he had been defeated in a race for Congress in 1853 by the legendary Williamson R. W. Cobb, a former itinerant peddler whose campaign practice it was to sing ditties to the crowds while accompanying himself on the banjo.

But Clay was able to turn the defeat to account; indeed, he actually rode it to the national Senate. Ever since the north Alabama unionist Democrats had united with the Whigs in 1851, the Democracy had

73. On these developments, see pp. 372–80 and 420–24 herein.

feared such an alliance on a permanent basis. As a result, unionism came to be regarded as a suspiciously anti-party belief, and southern rights—at least in mild form—became Democratic orthodoxy in all sections of the state. Because Cobb retained unionist views, Clay was able to picture Cobb's victory as a sign of Democratic weakness in the Tennessee Valley which, for its own welfare, the party needed to remedy. The proper remedy, he further argued, was the creation of a Democratic leader for the area whose eminence would lend weight to his efforts to inculcate regularity—and for this position he offered himself. He had been defeated, he wrote, "through a combination of Whigs and pseudo-Democrats, who falsely represented me as a Disunionist." His election to the Senate would be "a means of redeeming this vaunted stronghold of Democracy from the thraldom of Federalism [Whiggery]."

The Whigs have hitherto, and will continue to elect Cobb, until his power over the masses is broken. . . . Power and high place give dignity, might and importance to trifles. Cobb and [Senator Jeremiah] Clemens, as individuals, could not have misled the people, but as Congressmen, their voices are as potent with the masses as were the ancient oracles. To countervail and overcome that influence, revive the true principles of Democracy, and restore our party to its position, strength and purity, we should give to talent, energy and sound principle the vantage ground of high official station.

Failure to do so would deliver north Alabama to the Whigs through the Trojan horse of unionism.[74] This argument greatly impressed partisan Democrats and, only four months after having been defeated by Cobb, Clay found himself chosen to succeed Clemens.

The new senator's distinguished father was still alive, and of course sought to give the benefit of his experience to his son. The correspondence between these men presents an interesting example of the differing outlooks of the state's two generations of politicians. As we have seen, the elder Clay had succeeded in breaking his early identification with the Broad River group by strong advocacy of preemption rights in the purchase of public lands for squatters residing on them. Almost as soon as his son reached Washington, the old gentleman dispatched a letter urging a speech in favor of graduating federal land prices according to the quality of the land, at the very least. Indeed, he

74. Clement Claiborne Clay to Bolling Hall, September 30, 1853, in Hall Papers.

evidently advised his son to support the pending Homestead Bill. His son, however, called the proposal "contrary to the theory of our Government" and "against the spirit of the constitution and inexpedient." Moreover, he told his father that he intended to oppose pensions for veterans. "It is a corrupt and corrupting [system]; a tax on the many for the benefit of the few; anti-republican and opposed to the true spirit of the constitution." And he told the Senate with heavy sarcasm that such proposals would force "the Government" to "gather them [the beneficiaries] like puny fledglings beneath the sheltering wings of parental love . . . to help their toddling footsteps from the cradle to the grave." [75]

An admirer of the senator, young J. L. M. Curry, was, if possible, even more extreme on such questions. He wrote Clay in 1854,

You will allow me to say that I approve every word of your speech and regard it as an able and unanswerable exposition of the powers of Congress over the public lands. . . . The land question is a dangerous one. There are so many temptations to do wrong, so many inducements to corruption, so much pabulum for reckless demagogues, that unless the masses are indoctrinated with right principles and sound views, there will be a dangerous departure from original Jeffersonian simplicity and purity. The days of the Roman Republic, historians say, were numbered, when the people consented to receive corn from the public granaries. And our doom is sealed when the people are quartered on the Government and accustom themselves habitually to look to it for largesses and favors.

And he added, "I have some unusual views about man's individuality and the duty of government, but I will not tax you with them." [76] The extremes to which this budding ideologue pushed his views may have been unusual, but their spirit many younger politicians were coming to share. He expressed not the "purity" of "original Jeffersonianism," but the doctrines of the Victorian age.

The gulf which separated the assumptions of the Clays, father and son, and the even more explicit formulation of Curry, are symbolic of

75. Clement Comer Clay to Virginia Tunstall Clay, May 23, 1854, Clement Claiborne Clay to Clement Comer Clay, March 14, 1854, April 5, 1854, January 18, 1854, all in Clay Papers; *Congressional Globe*, 34th Cong., 3rd Sess., Vol. XXVI, 325 (speech of January 14, 1857). In this speech, Clay also opposed the pension distributions on the ground that the program would be elitist.

76. J. L. M. Curry to Clement Claiborne Clay, July 5, 1854, in Clay Papers.

a very real transformation in the role which Alabama politicians conceived for themselves. In our discussion of the legislature, we identified two sorts of popular reactions to the institution. The electorate responded favorably when the assembly acted to make each man independent of every other man, an autonomous unit. Thus efforts to destroy or cripple corporations or other privately controlled centers of power met with approval. But equally popular were efforts to make men economically independent—such as facilitating the purchase of public land or the seizure and distribution of Indian territories—and efforts to create alternative, communally controlled institutions, such as the Bank of Alabama. The electorate, on the other hand, responded unfavorably to all actions which seemed a potential threat to freedom. Thus any hint of collusion between government and private power centers was immediately condemned. Moreover, when an alternative institution failed to perform its functions adequately, as was the case with the state bank, corruption and evil intentions were generally assumed.

Everyone was aware that government itself could easily become oppressive if it ceased to obey the wishes of the electorate and involved itself with special interests. The signs that this calamity was in process, however, were well known and explicitly defined. They necessarily included an alliance between government and hostile power concentrations. The fire-eaters' message in the early fifties had been so startling, precisely because it had warned that these signs need not be present before the populace should take alarm; that public institutions were as innately corrupting as were private ones; that regardless of what the politicians told the people, politicians should in all cases be regarded with suspicion. This notion the electorate found hard to believe because at the time the warning was issued, political managers had for a considerable period been saying and doing the things that had always meant safety for the liberties of the masses. But beginning just at that moment, politicians started to take the sorts of actions which traditionally had signalized betrayal. They earnestly claimed to be friends of the people, of course, but their performance convinced many voters that the society's leaders had lost any clear conception of what a friend of the people actually was. The explanation of the fire-eaters for this phenomenon—that the leaders had been corrupted by the natural operation of the political structure—seemed more and more persuasive. As the decade progressed, one came frequently to hear the assertion that the "spirit of trickery and management," rather than the spirit of public service, lay at the heart of politics.

What an acquaintance with men like Curry and the junior Clay teaches us, however, is that the fire-eaters' doctrine, despite its widespread acceptance, was not really very accurate. The new generation of politicians did conceive of itself as friends of the people, as it claimed. It had simply developed a new notion of the sorts of actions such a friend should take. The new notion was an outgrowth of the standard Democratic belief that dependence was evil. In a sense, it did recapture an element of Jeffersonian teachings which had been neglected by Jacksonian theorists; for Jefferson's belief that government was a threat to individual freedom, though accepted by the Jacksonians, was far less important to them than their own belief that government was the proper tool for protecting individual freedom from the assaults of the private sector. But the new notion was not in fact Jeffersonian. It too strongly approved of the emerging urban and industrial world to merit that appellation. Its origins, as we have already hinted, are probably not to be sought in the American past at all, but in the contemporary intellectual milieu of the English-speaking world—a milieu which was just then producing Charles Darwin's theories of nature, Henry Thomas Buckle's impressions of history, and Herbert Spencer's assertions about society. We must never forget that the late antebellum South was inescapably, and rather aggressively, a part of the Victorian community of letters.

The novice politicians applauded efforts to foster economic growth and social enlightenment—to bring the South, as they saw it, into the modern world. They countenanced public schools, the streamlining of the court system, and other such "progressive" reforms. But their devotion to the doctrines of laissez-faire made them hostile to governmental involvement in the economy, except in unusual circumstances. On the question of state aid to railroad construction, there was something of a generational difference even within this younger group. Those men who had already gained a measure of prominence before 1855—including both Clay and Curry—tended to regard the building of railroads as enough of a special case to warrant assistance. Men who gained office in the midst of the political up-heaval engineered by Winston in 1857, found themselves convinced to the contrary. But both elements of the group agreed that, as a general rule, government aid to the populace would undermine its self-reliance, and should therefore be avoided.

We have previously discussed the covert elitism of these young men. Their economic doctrines reflect the attitude. At base, their posi-tion amounted to the contention that, even though citizens might de-sire the assistance of their government, the government must withhold it. The citizens did not fully realize the harm which receiving such assistance would do them. The essence of true leadership was to con-test, even to the sacrifice of all popularity, the erroneous opinions of the masses—to save the people from themselves. It need hardly be said that, in the eyes of Jacksonians, opinions of this character passed be-yond mere heresy, to approach consummate paganism.

Many of these young men, especially in south Alabama, allowed their ambitions to carry them into alliance with Yancey, whose star seemed to be rising in the latter years of the decade. The conjunction was a natural one. The southern rights movement tended to be cen-tered, as we have seen, in relatively urban areas. It preached liberation from outmoded doctrines and a degrading sectional dependency. And it offered a vehicle for rapid advancement. Yancey's theory of agitation emphasized the necessity to take control of the Democratic party. The young laissez-faire ideologues—usually attorneys and town dwellers—became the backbone of his campaign to do so. And during the Buchanan administration, the campaign carried numbers of them to positions of considerable eminence.[77]

This second generation of Alabama politicians was, however, out of sympathy not only with its predecessor but also with its constitu-ency. Most Democrats continued to favor, not laissez-faire, but posi-tive governmental intervention in support and defense of the common

---

77. In a work published after the completion of the present study—*The Secessionist Im-pulse: Alabama and Mississippi in 1860* (Princeton: Princeton University Press, 1974)—William L. Barney presents much new evidence to establish the relative youth and upward mobility of the Yanceyites (61–76). While my interpretation of some other points differs from Professor Barney's, I strongly agree with his emphasis on the importance of age and ambition in explaining political alignments in 1860.

man. And the Whigs continued to long for a government which would act energetically to develop the economy. The doctrines of the dawning age contained no cure for the frustrations of either group.

We are faced, then, with a profoundly somber irony. Three factors—the electorate's fear and disorientation, the older, radical fire-eaters' dogmatic hostility to politics, and the faith and actions of the young Yanceyites—were all converging, from different directions, towards a single result: a new and volatile suspicion of established political institutions, a combustible doubt fed by all sorts of independent factors. The voters could no longer rest in the assurance that their leaders had identified the enemy and were planning its destruction. Indeed, the politicians suddenly found themselves in imminent danger of being transmuted in the public imagination from champions into insidious foes.

This observation allows us to return to an explanation of Governor Winston's puzzling defeat by young Senator Clay in 1857. Clay was not an especially strong figure. He had won his first term, as we have seen, more as a tactical maneuver in the partisan wars than because of any great enthusiasm for his own personal qualities. The 1857 encounter was only his second effort for statewide office. Winston, on the other hand, was enormously popular, and he was riding the crest of the most important issue in state politics. The justification offered by most legislators for preferring Clay is direct enough. William A. Musgrove, a former representative from Marion County, wrote, "There is not a man in the State that I esteem more hily [*sic*] than I do Governor Winston. He is certainly intitled to the confidence and esteem of every Democrat for the bold and fearless manner with which he has conducted the affairs of State. But I think to elect him to the U.S. Senate would be placing the rong [*sic*] man in the rong [*sic*] place at this time." Senator Mace T. P. Brindley of Blount told Clay that "the people appreciate your zeal, honesty and ability to serve the state at this critical moment, and would not be willing to see you ousted by anyone." Another observer noted that Winston's popularity had "reference to a *policy of purely local* and *State* interest." In other words, it was argued that the exigencies of the sectional crisis demanded that Alabama place a talented advocate in the Senate rather than a pragmatic politician, even a popular one.[78] But of course this observation does not solve the puzzle, for the argument involves a value judgment—the belief that the southern rights issue was more important than the state aid issue—and we must inquire why the legislators were led to choose as they did. Sectional hatred had indeed been somewhat exacerbated by 1857, but another circumstance causes us to look for an additional motive in the general acceptance of the line of reasoning.

A Wiregrass writer noted that "the [Know-Nothing] opposition hates Winston" and "the Democrats who have been in the Legislature do not like him much. They think him too head strong in his veto power." John T. Heflin, one of the most prominent politicians in Randolph County, noted that, whereas Winston was popular with the masses, not one of the leaders in his section was for the governor. And longtime Jefferson County senator Moses Kelly wrote that, despite Winston's strength, all the party leaders in Jefferson favored Clay.[79] These men seem to be stating aspects of a general truth: the electorate was overwhelmingly for Winston but almost every politician in the state was against him. What could have caused such an extraordinary division?

Formulated in this way, the question readily yields its answer. The real villains in the melodrama which Winston's policies had staged were not the railroads but the politicians. The implication of Winston's vetoes was that the legislators had yielded the welfare of the state to the needs of corporations. Ambitious politicians could not afford to go further with the state aid issue than popular sentiment demanded, for to lend it importance was to declare themselves untrustworthy. The difficulty would have faced legislators not involved in the passage of the acts of 1855, as well as those men who were chargeable with direct complicity; for once the precedent was fixed, any effort to develop the

78. William A. Musgrove to Clement Claiborne Clay, June 15, 1857, Mace T. P. Brindley to Clay, June 19, 1857, Burwell T. Pope to Clay, July 1, 1857, Alphonzo A. Sterritt to Clay, June 12, 1857, James W. Davis to Clay, June 15, 1857, all in Clay Papers. Winston also made enemies by his course in the gubernatorial contest: see Crawford M. Jackson to Clement Claiborne Clay, June 12, 1857, Thomas A. Walker to Clay, June 28, 1857, both in Clay Papers; William F. Samford to Matthew P. Blue, July 14, 1857, in Blue Papers.

79. John L. Hays to Clement Claiborne Clay, June 1, 1857, John T. Heflin to Clay, June 6, 1857, Moses Kelly to Clay, June 11, 1857, all in Clay Papers.

economy would fall under its ban. Only a return to the ostentatious attacks upon economic institutions which had characterized earlier decades would satisfy its demands, and that course would violate the most cherished views of the new politicians, large numbers of whom were gaining office at this time—in some cases, ironically, by using Winston's issues. The session of 1857 repealed the aid laws of the previous meeting, an action which public opinion absolutely compelled. But the session of 1859, the last legislature of the antebellum period, enacted a general system of railroad aid far more extensive than anything dreamed of four years earlier—though the statute passed amidst cries that "its ultimate effect will be to deliver over the government of the State to the control of a combination of corporations."[80]

If ever a man was the victim of malevolent fates, it was John A. Winston. He had discovered a hobby which could have carried him to a position in Alabama politics unrivaled since the days of Israel Pickens. But the nature of the issue precluded its acceptance by the political structure. The second generation of politicians was no longer content to represent and to focus; it desired to create and to lead. Winston was returned to the brooding solitude of his Sumter plantation, and his issue was left to incubate in the minds of a frightened populace.

It is perhaps not unreasonable to suppose that, if the events of Winston's administration had resulted in the explosive political crusade which would have taken form in earlier decades, the mounting tensions of the fifties, by thus finding a political outlet, could have been to some extent diminished. But politics had been caught in the act of trying to divorce itself from such functions. Therefore, the final result of the episode was to strengthen immeasurably the citizenry's sense that its liberty was imperiled, and at the same time to assist in elevating to prominence the element in the society which most insistently claimed both to know the precise nature of the danger and to be able to deal with it. The electorate desperately needed a crusade. The politi-

---

80. *Senate Journal*, Sess. of 1859–60, pp. 341–42. *Cf. House Journal*, Sess. of 1859–60, pp. 391–92, 516–18; *Acts of Alabama*, Sess. of 1859–60, pp. 31–34, 35–36, 54–61, 110–11, 292–93.

cians needed some cause with which to regain public confidence. The old ideologies had failed to produce one. The new ideology had left its adherents with only one serviceable villain to offer. Secession had received its cue.

Chapter VI Secession

THE MAP on page 344 reveals the principal obstacle to an accurate conception of secession in Alabama. Those counties shown in white elected to the Secession Convention delegates pledged to vote for immediate separate state secession. Counties in gray rejected such candidates. The pattern is abundantly clear: south Alabama was for immediate secession and north Alabama was not. However straightforward this statement may be, though, it is subject to misinterpretation. First of all, the geographical division is between north Alabama and south Alabama. It is not between plantation counties and small farm counties; if it were, the Tennessee Valley and the Black Belt on the one hand would be grouped against the hill counties and the Wiregrass in the southeast, on the other. And similar groupings would appear if the division represented black majority counties against white majority counties. Nor is the division along Whig-Democrat lines; in that case, the Black Belt and perhaps a border county or two would stand alone against the rest of the state. Nor is the division urban or thickly populated against rural or thinly populated, nor relatively industrialized against solidly agricultural counties. Growth for the market is not the determinant; the Tennessee Valley had grown for the market long before statehood, whereas the Wiregrass was only tentatively entering the market economy at this period. In short, the map does not show any simple division along lines of interest, social organization, or institutional ties. Indeed, in order to explain the division, we must discover factors which would cut across all of these lines and tie quite diverse groups together in strictly sectional alliances.

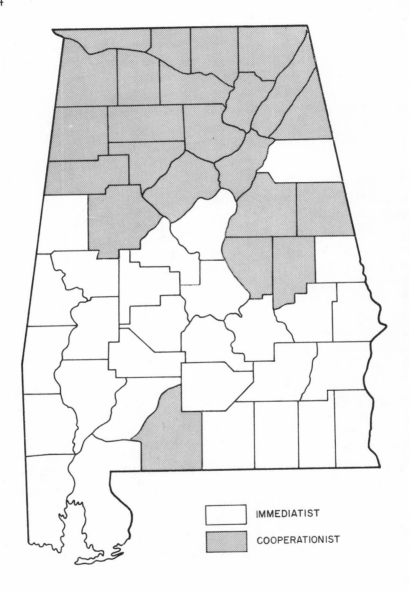

Election of Delegates to the Secession Convention

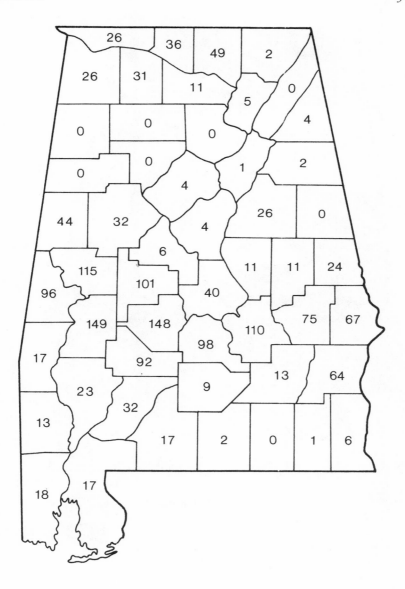

Number of Owners of Fifty or More Slaves, 1860

UNDER $1,000,000 $3-5,000,000

$1-2,000,000   OVER $5,000,000

$2-3,000,000

Cash Value of Farms, 1860

In the second place, a vote against separate state secession was not a vote for continued union. It was in virtually every case a vote for cooperative southern secession. The cooperationists went out of their way to repudiate charges that they were unionists. There were divisions in their camp, of course. Some cooperationists wanted a list of extreme southern rights demands presented to Congress as an ultimatum, with secession to follow if the demands were rejected. Other cooperationists had no patience with further efforts to gain southern rights in the Union, but wanted assurances that a varying number of other southern states—usually five or seven—would join Alabama in a new nation. Their primary fear was simply that an independent republic of Alabama would not be economically viable. But all cooperationists were united in agreeing that the election of Lincoln could not and should not be tolerated. Their doubts were directed specifically at the wisdom of immediate separate state secession as a particular policy decision.

These two observations would seem uncomplicated enough. Failure to emphasize them, however, has led students too often to halt their analyses at precisely the point at which careful inquiry would have been most profitable. The enigma of Alabama's secession remains, in consequence, unsolved—indeed, almost unexamined.[1] It will be the purpose of the present chapter to describe how the state came to make a fundamental commitment to communal action as a mechanism for achieving salvation, and secondly to explain why, granted that such a commitment had been made, the delegates to the Secession Convention were divided.

1. The standard presentations are Clarence P. Denman, *The Secession Movement in Alabama* (Montgomery: Alabama State Department of Archives and History, 1933) and Lewy Dorman, *Party Politics in Alabama From 1850 Through 1860* (Wetumpka: Wetumpka Printing Co., 1935). Also advancing implicit theories of secession are Theodore H. Jack, *Sectionalism and Party Politics in Alabama, 1819–1842* (Menasha, Wis.: George Banta Publishing Co., 1919) and Walter L. Fleming, *Civil War and Reconstruction in Alabama* (New York: Columbia University Press, 1905). Two works from the previous century grapple with the problem primarily in political terms: John Witherspoon Dubose, *The Life and Times of William Lowndes Yancey: A History of Political Parties in the United States from 1834 to 1864, Especially as to the Origin of the Confederate States* (2 vols.; New York: Peter Smith, 1942; originally published, 1892) and Joseph Hodgson, *The Cradle of the Confederacy; or, the Times of Troup, Quitman, and Yancey: A Sketch of Southwestern Politics from the Formation of the Federal Government to A.D. 1861* (Mobile: Register Publishing Office, 1876).

The Whiggery in Crisis

At the end of the campaign of 1857, one Democratic editor pontificated, "In our country there is great danger of overlooking the scope and aim of politics; every higher consideration is too often merged in mere party antagonisms . . . and the gravest questions which affect the fortunes of the Republic are treated with a levity as ill-timed as it is culpable." [2] The editor would doubtless not have considered himself subject to the danger; he actually meant to charge the opposition with cynical manipulation of worsening sectional relations in the search for office. But his observation perhaps has greater force than he knew. Because winning elections was so large a part of what politics was about, the events of the developing crisis in the fifties were persistently, if unconsciously refracted through the lenses of factional hostility. The feeling generated by political and personal rivalries simply ran too high to admit of any other situation. We are not dealing here with cynicism so much as with something more tragic—a limited view, limited by the silent and virtually unnoticed, but wholly invincible operation of the institutional structure of the society.

As late as 1848, southern rights issues were not really an ordinary part of the political dialogue in Alabama. They came up, and in increasingly strident terms, at each presidential election, but they did not figure significantly in the electoral encounters at the state and local levels. The parties were too deeply involved in debating other issues which seemed of more immediate concern to the voters, and over which the parties were more clearly divided—questions of economic and social power. Even the introduction of southern rights into the presidential campaigns was ordinarily simply an effort to steal a portion of the opposition's constituency by convincing it that there was a reason in that particular election for southerners to disregard the real and continuing sources of party division and to unite as southerners.

The presidential campaigns of 1848, 1852, and 1856, however, turned almost entirely upon southern rights issues, and gradually accustomed the parties to hurling the epithet of traitor at one another. Moreover, after the campaign of 1844, which had also included fre-

2. Montgomery *Advertiser*, August 19, 1857.

quent references to southern rights, the state's attention had returned to other subjects. But southern rights dominated nearly the whole quadrennium from 1848 to 1852, both in congressional and in legislative canvasses, and compelled a far-reaching, if temporary reorganization of the state's parties.[3] Of course, it is true that the same thing did not happen after the elections of 1852 and 1856. From the introduction of the Kansas-Nebraska bill in 1854 to the passage of the Kansas conference bill of 1858, the sectional duel in that sad territory was the principal issue in federal elections. Yet as we have just seen, it was during precisely the same period that state politics was being shaken to its foundations by the altogether unrelated questions of governmental loans to railroads. Nevertheless, it is not too much to say that the central event of the fifties is the end of the exclusive association of southern rights disputes with the presidential canvass and their integration into the general politics of the state. In the next two sections we shall examine in turn the two relatively independent proceedings whose interplay in great part created this lamentable circumstance: the tireless Whig search for an electoral majority; and the dispute between the right and left wings of the fire-eaters as to the efficacy of cooperation with the Democrats.

Perhaps the most important point about the course of the Whiggery after its rather reluctant reorganization in the summer of 1852 may be made at the outset. Despite the clear identification with Unionism which the Whig politicians had acquired during the Crisis of 1850, at no time did they ever abandon their efforts to portray themselves as the South's true defenders. The Democratic party was, they said, a coalition of northern crypto-abolitionists and southern crypto-disunionists, held together only by a common desire for office from which stealthily to effect their unholy designs. In the first part of the decade, their own party—the Whiggery in 1852, 1853, and early 1854; the American party in late 1854, 1855, and 1856—was, as they saw it, a union of all sound conservative men to suppress the agitation of the radicals, both abolitionist and disunionist; to end all discussion of slavery; and thus to restore the South to a full and secure partnership in national life. In 1857, 1858, and 1859, after they had for all

3. See Chapter IV, herein. The banking issue dominated the legislative elections of 1849, however.

practical purposes ceased to belong to a national party, they proclaimed that, because they were emancipated from the necessity to compromise in order to placate northern allies, they alone could fully sustain southern rights. But throughout the decade their efforts to place themselves on the right side of the southern question—and the Democrats on the wrong side—were indefatigable.[4]

These Whig exertions, when coupled with the concern about the encounters in Kansas, led politicians into an increasingly aggressive dogmatism on the rather abstruse subject of the place of territories in the American constitutional order. It quickly became necessary that they seek to outdo each other in the certitude with which they affirmed debatable legal theories—thus tending to leave with the electorate the notion that the North, for the sake of sectional advantage, was seeking to strip southerners of rights and privileges unquestionably theirs. The North, simply because it possessed a majority, had determined to rely upon the law of the jungle and to seize by force what justice denied it.

There had been no particular demand in the Alabama press for the extension of popular sovereignty to the Louisiana Purchase territories, until the introduction of the Kansas-Nebraska bill. Thereafter most Whigs continued to regard the action as an unnecessary disturbance of a sleeping dog, and warned that the bill would aid the free-soil movement by writing into the statute books the erroneous doctrine that a territory had the power to prohibit slavery. The Democrats rallied to their president, announced that the bill was proof of his determination to reestablish southern equality, and claimed that it allowed the prohibition of slavery only when the territory became a state because a provision forbade any action inconsistent with the Constitution and abolition by Congress was, of course, unconstitutional. Democrats noted that the effect of the bill was simply to extend to additional territories the determination of the Compromise of 1850 as to New Mexico and Utah.

Neither party, however, seems to have had any sense that the new

4. *E.g.*, Montgomery *Advertiser*, August 4, August 11, 1852, January 26, March 23, September 21, 1853, March 22, May 24, 1854, May 9, June 13, June 20, June 27, July 4, July 24, July 31, September 19, 1855, February 13, February 27, 1856, June 24, July 15, July 22, August 12, August 19, 1857, July 21, November 10, 1858, April 13, April 27, May 4, May 25, June 22, 1859.

law might produce a test of sectional wills. Reports of efforts in New England to organize parties of emigrants to Kansas were received with good humor. The intrinsic strength of slavery would become apparent in any free and open competition; northerners who saw slavery in operation would be converted; the "natural laws of immigration" were on the side of southern settlers. In July of 1854, J. L. M. Curry told Senator Clay, "It is difficult for us to comprehend or credit the excitement that is said to prevail in the North on account of the Nebraska question." In Alabama, he said, the subject was "seldom alluded to, in private or public." During the fall and winter, various newspapers published correspondence from visitors to the territory, informing the public that the area was well suited to hemp plantations, and warning that if Kansas did not permit slavery, Missouri would be left in an exposed position, surrounded on three sides by free states. But despite a growing belief that Kansas was a prize worth having, even as late as January of 1855 an editor could write that, thanks to the wisdom of Congress in eliminating politics from the decision, the status of Kansas would be settled by the inflexible and impartial decrees of the cosmic order; and that the victory of slavery appeared, therefore, certain. His assumption that a laissez-faire policy would necessarily favor the South explains many future attitudes. "Interest is wiser than any Legislature. Trade and enterprise can best take care of themselves—and especially in a matter where all sections of the Union have equal rights, it is nothing less than downright robbery and fraud to use any intervention to prejudice one class and patronize another."[5]

By the spring of 1855, the tone of comments on Kansas had changed. Observers now claimed that northern emigrant aid societies were distorting the operation of the laws of immigration. April found the editor who had been so confident in January now proclaiming the North's goal to be the *"conquest of Kansas from the South,"* and asserting grimly, "It is ours by nature, by legislation, by the will of the people in a Territorial capacity, and it *must* be ours by the State Constitution."[6] This sudden bellicosity marked the abandonment of the

5. J. L. M. Curry to Clement Claiborne Clay, July 5, 1854, in Clay Papers, Duke University Library, Durham; Montgomery *Advertiser*, January 17, 1855; *cf.* March 22, April 12, May 24, May 31, June 14, July 26, November 8, November 22, November 29, December 13, 1854.

6. Montgomery *Advertiser*, April 25, 1855; see also March 14, March 21, March 28, April 18, May 9, May 16, May 30, 1855.

previous year's willingness to leave Kansas to the workings of nature—an abandonment which was to take tangible form in the autumn and winter in Jefferson Buford's movement to organize an expedition to the territory.[7] The change may be partially explained, of
course, as a reaction to events in Kansas itself. Alabamians were
greatly irritated by what they took to be a northern determination not
to give popular sovereignty a chance to work. But there is another
explanation, of at least equal importance, which is not nearly so obvious. The course of the Kansas controversy in Alabama was profoundly
influenced by the birth of the American party.

Know-Nothing lodges made their first appearance in Alabama in
the summer of 1854. The famed humorist Johnson J. Hooper moved
to the capital from his home in Chambers County and founded a state
organ for the new movement, the Montgomery *Mail*.[8] In succeeding
months, the bulk of the Whiggery and not a few Democrats rushed
to embrace the "Order of the Star Spangled Banner." Winfield Scott
had received only 34 percent of the state's vote in 1852; many prominent Whigs including Congressmen Alexander White and James
Abercrombie—and Johnson J. Hooper—had refused on southern
rights grounds to support him. Moreover, the Whiggery's gubernatorial effort had been grossly mishandled in 1853; the regular nominee,
Richard Wilde Walker, had withdrawn in mid-campaign and the party's leadership had been unable to agree on a successor. Winston, the
Democratic candidate, took 64 percent of the poll against three opponents.[9] But the party was not dead by any means. Whigs captured 40
percent of the seats in the 1853 legislature. And 30 percent of the
Whigs in the lower house were from the hill counties, a fact which
resulted in part from the growing enthusiasm among some elements of
the hill-county electorate for state assistance to the railroads which
would open their isolated region to the world of commerce. It was
certainly not unreasonable for Whigs to believe, therefore, that the

7. *Ibid.*, November 7, 1855; *cf.* August 4, August 15, August 29, November 21, 1855,
January 21, 1857.
8. *Ibid.*, March 29, April 19, June 21, June 28, July 26, 1854.
9. *Ibid.*, March 2, March 9, March 16, April 13, April 20, May 4, May 11, May 19, May
26, July 7, July 14, July 21, August 18, August 25, September 1, September 8, October 27, 1852;
March 16, March 23, May 18, June 8, June 22, June 29, July 6, July 13, July 27, August 3, 1853;
Alabama Journal (Montgomery), June 3, 1853.

addition of those Democratic converts to their ranks which the Know-Nothing movement seemed to promise, might raise them to a statewide majority.

Know-Nothingism also gave promise of solving the Whiggery's growing problem with southern rights. There was deep resentment within the party for what the Whigs regarded as their betrayal by the Union Democrats during the legislative session of 1851. The Whigs had completely committed themselves to the Compromise of 1850, which they portrayed as a promise by the North to leave the South alone in future. But they were fully aware that their electoral success depended upon their ability to maintain a clear distinction in the public mind between their own description of the Compromise and the cowardly submissionist sentiments which their opponents attributed to them. The desertion of the Union Democrats in the winter of 1851–52 made the distinction much more difficult to maintain, for it virtually compelled them, against their will, to resume their alliance with northern politicians who, under pressure from Free-soil forces, were dissociating themselves from the Compromise and from the commitment which Alabama Whigs claimed that it represented. The nomination of Scott, who refused an unequivocal endorsement of the Compromise, over Millard Fillmore, who had no such hesitation, made the Whig position particularly awkward.[10] The fact that the general received just a third of Alabama's vote indicates that possibly a quarter of the Whigs' usual voting strength deserted his candidacy.

Nor did the problem disappear with the end of the presidential campaign. In the following spring, when the party began to organize for the coming gubernatorial election, Johnson J. Hooper's southern rights Whig *Chambers Tribune* reported sadly "that the unfortunate attempt to bolster up the late Presidential nomination and force a candidate notoriously unsound upon the party, has resulted in loss of confidence among those who believe that the conservatism of Southern Whiggery should extend to and embrace the institution of slavery. . . . The people will say, 'The Whigs may be the party of progress; they may, more than the Democrats, incline to such a course of policy as will develop our resources and stimulate our industry; they may be

10. Montgomery *Advertiser*, July 21, November 17, December 22, 1852, June 22, 1853.

against filibustering; but if they are willing to take Scotts and Sewards for Presidents, we cannot and will not assist them to power.'" And, Hooper added, the people were correct to hold such views.[11] Thus, at least by 1853 there were real differences within the party over whether the preservation of its catholicity was worth the price. The results of the disagreement were clearly visible in the bitter intraparty collisions which marked the congressional elections of that year, particularly in the Mobile and Montgomery districts.[12]

It is not difficult, therefore, to understand why the Whig leadership should have regarded the advent of Know-Nothingism as a gift from heaven. The new party promised the restoration of the Unionist coalition which had given Whigs such a smashing victory three years before. It would emancipate them from bearing a party name which was acquiring a popular association with northern Free-soilers. It would restore them to membership in a national conservative alliance which was dedicated to the permanent suppression of all sectional recrimination, and the acceptance of full southern partnership in an all-American crusade—the very formulation which had been so successful in 1851. It would permit recovering the support of many Union Democrats, who would be impressed by the possibilities of such a movement for reemphasizing the common nationality of the two sections; moreover, the return could be carried off gracefully, as cooperation with the movement would not require membership in the party of Henry Clay. If the Order gave prospect of winning, it might readily draw to itself a further accretion of ambitious Democratic politicians, since their conversion would not of necessity make them appear ideologically inconsistent. This factor was additionally important because it would allow the Whigs to exploit what—on the basis of their gains in the hill counties in the legislative elections of 1853—they took to be an emerging enthusiasm in north Alabama for state aid to railroads. They could seek votes for internal improvement without immediately running afoul of the deep prejudice in the area against the Whig label. Finally, the Whigs even believed that they could turn to account the issue of restricting citizenship with which Know-

11. Quoted *ibid.*, March 23, 1853.
12. *Ibid.*, April 6, April 20, May 4, May 18, July 6, July 13, July 20, August 17, August 24, 1853.

Nothingism was saddled. By claiming that much of the electoral support for Free-soil came from immigrants, they sought to make alteration of the naturalization laws appear to be another effort to eliminate
antislavery agitation.

It is quite easy to understand why Whigs rushed to embrace the
Know-Nothing cause. It is also quite easy to understand why the
Democratic leadership was so frightened of the development. Between
the summer of 1854 and the spring of 1855 the Order grew apace.
Fortunately for the Democrats, there were no elections during this
period. The legislature of 1853 had helped matters a bit by enacting a
vicious gerrymander of the state's congressional districts which, it was
believed, left only one potentially Whig constituency. But if the
Know-Nothings could gain any substantial number of Democratic
converts, this calculation would of course come to nought. And it appeared that the Know-Nothings were succeeding in doing so. A Democratic editor who wished to emphasize the power of Whigs within the
new party, for instance, was nevertheless compelled to estimate that a
third of the delegates to the Know-Nothing state convention in the
summer of 1855 were former Democrats.[13] Moreover, as they had
done in 1851, the Whigs handled their new allies carefully, elevated
them to positions of leadership and, when the time came, nominated
them to office. Three of the Know-Nothings' five congressional candidates in 1855 were former Democrats, as too was their gubernatorial
nominee.

The Know-Nothing threat to the Democratic party's long
hegemony in Alabama, then, seemed very real in the spring of 1855, as
the parties began to prepare for the August general elections. And it is
for that reason, perhaps, more than any other, that the Democratic
press at that precise moment suddenly blossomed with aggressive concern for the situation in Kansas. Governor Winston's policies during
his first term had virtually insured that the issue of state aid to railroad
construction would dominate the campaign for state offices; and
Democratic politicians, particularly in north Alabama, were as yet unconvinced that opposition to such aid was the popular side of the question. The obvious remedy was an effort to outflank the Know-

13. *Ibid.*, June 20, 1855.

Nothings by attacking the principal source of their party's growing strength—the profound hope that it could suppress the sectional conflict. The Democrats began to use the congressional races to emphasize an alleged connection between Know-Nothingism and the Kansas question, praying that they could thus halt, and if possible eventually reverse, the flow of desertions to their opponents.

In attempting to connect the Order with Kansas, the Democrats developed a clever case. It began, of course, with the declaration that Know-Nothingism was "a new development of the aristocratic element of our society; that element can always be detected in any political organization which affects to treat the people as *children* to be deceived and humored, instead of as *brothers and equals in political rights.*" Elitism underlay the Order's secrecy and its assumption of superiority over immigrants. In that sense, there was no difference at all between the Know-Nothings and the nascent Black Republicans. "It is true, their avowed objects differ; but it is by the assertion of the same fundamental idea that they exist. It is that it is consistent with the Constitution of the country, with the theory of our institutions and the principles of civil liberty, to confer privileges upon one class of citizens and deny them to another . . . that the establishment of privileged classes, an *inequality* of rights, is consistent with republican institutions. . . . One wishes to create a privileged class of Yankees; the other, of native Americans."[14]

Once having established that the social attitudes of abolitionists and Know-Nothings were identically hostile to the egalitarian foundations upon which the existing constitutional structure rested, Democrats moved easily to clinch their argument. The two primary results of the Know-Nothing agitation were obvious to everyone except perhaps to the movement's blind partisans. In the North, Know-Nothing opposition to sound, prosouthern Democrats had on countless occasions permitted Republican victories which would otherwise have been impossible. And in the South, the presence of the Order had prevented the region from presenting a united front to the enemy. As the Mobile *Register* put it, "While our firesides, our lives and property are threatened by a powerful and infuriated enemy thundering at our

14. *Ibid.*, July 26, 1854, August 27, 1856.

gates, we are called upon to abandon the sure defences of our walls and fall to squabbling about the naturalization laws."[15] Of course, many of the Know-Nothings, particularly in the South, were honest men. But could the crusade's practical consequences really have been unintended? It seemed unlikely.

Black Republicanism and Know-Nothingism both sought the same un-American, antidemocratic goals. The efforts of the latter party invariably aided the former. The conclusion was inescapable. The Know-Nothings were dupes of—and many of their northern leaders were conscious allies of—the aristocratic forces which since the days of Alexander Hamilton had endeavored to shackle the South, undermine liberty, and erect the rule of wealth on the ruins of sectional and personal equality. Northerners, one observer wrote, not satisfied "with abolishing black slavery among themselves and instituting white slaves in their place," now wished to extend the same class tyranny to southerners—through abolitionism—and more, to dictate what southerners could eat and drink—through temperance—and how they could worship God—through Know-Nothingism.[16] It was all part of a single conspiracy to enslave and degrade the region's freemen.

The date of the Know-Nothing party's birth was thus no accident. "The Order as a political organization originated in, and derived its chief strength from, the *sectional strife* growing out of the discussion of the Nebraska bill before Congress." Moreover, "They originated in the anti-slavery States. . . . We, among others, regarded it as a new move of the enemies of the South from the first." Indeed, "How can the fearful aspect of the political horizon in the Free States but compel suspicion that all is not right—that a stronger element pervades Northern society than hostility to foreigners and Catholics?—an element which, controlling the powerful machinery of the Know-Nothings, is surely mounting towards a position of defiance to the South." In fact, northern Know-Nothings were "rather openly committed and pledged to agitate and push the South to the wall in regard to slavery extension, the Nebraska bill, the admission of Kansas as a Slave State, and on the Fugitive Slave law." Why did they attack

15. Quoted *ibid.*, February 27, 1856; see also February 21, March 21, April 11, April 18, May 9, June 20, September 5, September 12, 1855, July 23, 1856.
16. *Ibid.*, June 13, 1855; see also July 24, November 28, 1855.

Catholics and foreigners? Despite the assertions of southern Know-Nothings to the contrary, the reason was that in the North, Catholics and immigrants voted solidly Democratic and thus sustained the pro-administration forces. And, rather as an afterthought, the Democratic case sometimes appended the explicit charge that southern Know-Nothing politicians, to subserve an unscrupulous ambition, had secretly assured their northern allies that they would accept the restoration of the Missouri Compromise line, once the party had succeeded in electing a president. Both the Republicans and the Know-Nothings, then, wished to make Kansas a free state—the former by denying her admission until she drafted an antislavery constitution; the latter by reenacting the Compromise line.[17]

One might argue—and correctly, no doubt—that this entire case depended for its acceptance upon the existence of a certain measure of paranoia in the minds of its audience. But it is essential to note that there was nothing novel about this paranoia. The threat lurking outside the society's walls was the same threat which had waited there since the days of Jackson; the essence of the fear was the prospect of enslavement by the monster aristocracy. The sectional guise in which the monster now appeared represented a relatively recent change of costume, to be sure. But the assumptions which lent force to the notion that Know-Nothingism and abolitionism were leagued to destroy American freedoms were the very assumptions which had made Nicholas Biddle appear to be the heir of George III.

In any case, during the summer of 1855 the argument began to take effect. A number of prominent men who had joined the Order in the previous fall—including John T. Morgan, Robert C. Brickell, Chancellor Wylie W. Mason, and Nicholas Davis, Jr.—announced their withdrawal from it, and they were joined by many lesser known apostates.[18] In August, the Know-Nothings elected only two congressmen—both former Democrats, and one an incumbent. Their gubernatorial nominee received just 42 percent of the vote. And in the legislature, the new party held on to 39 percent of the seats, barely equaling the Whigs' showing of two years earlier.

17. *Ibid.*, July 18, February 21, April 25, June 20, November 14, 1855, September 3, October 1, 1856.
18. *Ibid.*, July 18, July 24, 1855.

For once, the Democrats were sufficiently conciliatory to encourage the continuation of the Know-Nothing defections. When the new legislature convened, they elected Richard Wilde Walker, a Whig who had refused to join the Know-Nothings, but whose brother Percy Walker was one of the state's two Know-Nothing congressmen, as Speaker of the House. They agreed to caucus jointly with the anti-Know-Nothing Whigs in order to fill the numerous offices subject to legislative election. And when the state Democratic convention met in January, 1856, it formally changed the party's name to the "Democratic and Anti-Know-Nothing Party." Hooper derisively dubbed them the "Democratic McWhigs." In the spring, the Know-Nothings were further hurt by two other developments. Their national convention adopted a platform which many in Alabama regarded as unsound on southern rights questions. And the massive outpouring of public support for Winston's vetoes of the measures passed by the preceding legislature for state aid to railroad construction proved to them that their state issue was much less popular than they had believed.

As a result of these three circumstances, in the late spring and summer of 1856 the conversions from the Know-Nothing cause became a flood. George D. Shortridge, the party's gubernatorial candidate the year before, refused to support Fillmore. And a host of other Know-Nothings or former Whigs went even further, to a public endorsement of James Buchanan. Included in this number were Congressman Percy Walker—who was hanged in effigy for the action—Arthur F. Hopkins, John J. Ormond, and Benjamin F. Porter, three of the Whiggery's founders; future governors Robert M. Patton and Rufus W. Cobb; Robert H. Smith, Luke Pryor, Alexander White, Isham W. Garrott, John W. Lapsley, William B. Martin, and Tristram B. Bethea. Almost all of these men gave the danger to southern rights as the principal reason for their decision.[19]

Fillmore managed to carry just eight of Alabama's fifty-two counties; he received 38 percent of the state's vote, only a bit better than the poll accorded the much less popular Winfield Scott in 1852. The desertions continued, and were crowned in the following April by the stun-

19. *Ibid.*, September 19, October 3, October 17, October 24, November 21, 1855, January 16, March 26, July 2, July 16, July 23, July 30, August 20, August 27, September 3, October 1, October 22, November 5, 1856; *Macon Republican* (Tuskegee), January 31, 1856.

ning announcement that the state's most famous Whig, Henry W. Hilliard, had become a Democrat, on the ground, he said, that all southerners must unite against the Republican menace. The Know-Nothings, now thoroughly demoralized, staggered towards a disastrous defeat in the August general elections. In a desperate effort to regain the support of all non-Jacksonians, the party adopted the name "American and Whig," but the maneuver was completely unsuccessful. No gubernatorial candidate could be found, and the Democrat A. B. Moore thus ran unopposed. The Know-Nothings lost every congressional race. And in the legislature the Opposition, which had held about 40 percent of the seats in both 1853 and 1855, fell to a mere 16 percent of the House and 18 percent of the Senate. Not since the twenties had the Democrats commanded such enormous majorities.[20]

Know-Nothing leaders were, however, presented with a bright spot, albeit a small one, in the returns. In the Montgomery congressional district, the American nominee, Thomas J. Judge, had lost to his opponent by only 86 votes, out of almost 13,000 cast. To have come so close to victory in the midst of the general party debacle was a considerable feat. Political managers sought eagerly for the secret of Judge's strength. Nor did they have to search far. In 1853, Congressman James Abercrombie had achieved reelection by accepting the support of left fire-eaters, who felt that rewarding Abercrombie for his refusal to support Scott in the previous year would contribute to the destruction of the intersectional party system. The reapportionment of the district had led Abercrombie to retire in 1855, but the American nominee to succeed him, Thomas Hill Watts, had learned from Abercrombie's tactic and had run a strong, though losing, race in part by exploiting southern rights issues. And so in 1857, Judge, Watts' law partner, had determined to pull out all stops, employing a southern rights appeal almost exclusively. He attacked the Yanceyite incumbent, James F. Dowdell, relentlessly for Dowdell's refusal to repudiate a Democratic administration which was pursuing allegedly free-soilist policies in Kansas. He frequently linked Dowdell's name with that of the traitorous Robert J. Walker. Dowdell, injured by the charges, re-

20. Montgomery *Advertiser*, February 27, March 4, April 8, April 15, April 22, April 29, May 6, May 13, June 17, July 22, August 5, 1857.

plied that as a member of a national party he was better able to defend the South in Congress than Judge, from within a tiny minority faction, would be. But Judge fell upon this assertion with the greatest gusto, adopting the left fire-eater argument that the very structure of a national party compelled the compromise of radical positions, and adding that precisely because his own party was now wholly southern, he would come under no such pressure.[21]

Hooper had long charged that the Democratic party was more interested in winning presidential elections than in defending the South. During the autumn of 1857, as the protracted Kansas agony mounted towards its crisis, Hooper, Watts, and Judge in the eastern Black Belt and Stephen F. Hale in the western Black Belt used the evidence of Judge's success to lead much of the dazed Opposition into an extreme, intransigent southern rights posture. Party leaders commenced an open courting of the left fire-eaters, demanding congressional acceptance of the Lecompton Constitution, and warning that Democrats in Washington would find some way to compromise the issue. Partially to combat this offensive, the overwhelmingly Democratic state legislature passed resolutions at its winter session ordering the governor to summon a secession convention in the event that Congress rejected Lecompton.

In this situation, the enactment at the beginning of May, 1858, of the Kansas conference bill, requiring a new referendum in the embattled territory—passed with the unanimous support of Alabama's entirely Democratic congressional delegation—considerably strengthened the Opposition's hand. The resultant rallying of the state party to the acceptance of the solution was virtually a textbook illustration of the warnings which the Opposition and the left fire-eaters had been issuing. Towards the end of March, for instance, the Montgomery *Advertiser* had roundly denounced anyone who "could stoop to the miserable acts of the compromiser. How harshly does the word grate upon the Southern ear. With what unctuous sweetness does it roll from the lips of aspirants for federal position." The editor had reminded

21. *Ibid.*, April 20, April 27, May 4, May 18, July 13, July 20, August 3, August 10, August 17, 1853, May 9, June 13, July 24, July 31, 1855, June 17, June 24, July 1, July 8, July 15, July 22, August 5, August 12, 1857.

Alabamians of "the degradation under which the compromise of '20 kept us grovelling for 30 years," and had warned them against permitting another such surrender. He had more than once reiterated these admonitions during the following month. And in mid-May, after the conference bill had become law, he had damned it as "a miserable time-serving subterfuge," and had concluded that the state's congressmen "merit our contempt far more than our gratitude." Nor did the editor conceal the principal reason for his dismay; he feared that the Democrats would now have difficulty in repelling the Opposition's attacks. "Who can foretell the direful consequence which may ensue to our party when the people of the South shall have demanded at our hands a reckoning for this shameless betrayal of Southern Rights by Southern Representatives?"

But at the end of May, the *Advertiser* suddenly discovered that, in the passage of the bill, "Our representatives were taken unawares by the Douglas wire-workers. . . .We have heretofore declared, and we again declare, that the South has been betrayed by her representatives in Washington. But it was by the Southern Congressional aspirants for the Presidency, by those who prefer Democratic harmony to Democratic principles, who seduced the true Southern Democracy into voting for the bill under the cry of party union. . . . And so, while we censure the measure, we cannot join in the outcry against those who voted for it from Alabama, it may be reluctantly, certainly without time allowed them for deliberation." And by the beginning of June, the editor was actually praising the state's congressmen because "they saw [that] the issue was a bad one to make before the people and they dared, like brave men and true, to avert that issue and postpone it, even at the risk of their own political fortunes." Thus, within a three-week period Alabama's Democratic organ had, for all practical purposes, publicly reversed its position on the acceptance of the conference bill, in an effort to save the seats of the state's Democratic representatives. Thereafter, despite vehement protests from the radicals, Governor Moore announced that Kansas had not really been denied admission, and that no secession convention was therefore warranted.[22]

22. *Ibid.*, March 24, May 12, May 26, June 2, 1858. See also August 19, September 2,

The conference bill question dominated state politics through the rest of 1858 and 1859 because, as we shall shortly see, the Democracy was internally divided between Yanceyite forces who condemned the bill while tending to absolve the representatives who had voted for it, and supporters of Senator Fitzpatrick who regarded the bill as something of a southern victory. The emerging alliance of the Opposition and the left fire-eaters denounced both the bill and the representatives. Because of the force of the Opposition's arguments and because of the Democratic feud, it appeared by the spring of 1859 that the Know-Nothings might elect congressmen in the Montgomery and Eufaula districts, and possibly also in the Mobile district. In the former two districts, alarmed Democratic leaders decided that they had no alternative but to force the incumbent Yanceyite members—James F. Dowdell and Eli S. Shorter—off the ticket, solely because of their vote in favor of the conference bill. Dowdell and Shorter were replaced as the Democratic candidates by two uncontaminated Yanceyites, David Clopton and James L. Pugh. In the Mobile district, Representative James A. Stallworth was renominated and drew an anti–conference bill fire-eater, F. B. Shepard, into the field against him.

The August general elections dashed all Opposition hopes. The dumping of Dowdell and Shorter was sufficient to emasculate the Opposition's issue in the party's two strongest districts. Pugh was a former Whig and the Know-Nothings therefore refused to oppose him; he swamped the left fire-eater, J. E. Sappington, who did make the effort. In the Montgomery district, Judge tried again, but lost by a wider margin than he had two years before. And Shepard's violent oratory earned him only 37 percent of the vote against Stallworth. In the gubernatorial race the Opposition endorsed the eccentric fire-eater William F. Samford, who attacked Governor Moore for having refused to summon a secession convention in response to the conference bill and for failing to declare himself against all forms of state aid to corporations, under any circumstances. Samford's own inflexible opposition to state aid considerably tempered Know-Nothing enthusiasm for him, and he received less than 28 percent of the poll;

September 16, 1857, January 13, January 20, January 27, February 17, February 24, March 3, March 17, March 31, April 7, April 14, April 21, April 28, May 5, 1858, June 22, 1859.

most of his support was confined to southeastern Alabama. In the legislative elections, the Opposition was unable to improve on its dismal showing of 1857.[23]

The extreme southern rights tactic adopted at the urging of Johnson J. Hooper and his associates was a failure. Many Opposition leaders, particularly in the western Black Belt, had been unhappy with the strategy in any case.[24] In the presidential election of 1860, therefore, most of the party returned to a version of the rationale which they had used early in the decade, modified to make it acceptably consistent with party pronouncements of the preceding two years. John Bell would be able to silence all intersectional bickering, to restore a sense of national community—and thus to gain from a friendly North positive federal protection for slavery in the territories. Hooper, Judge, and their closest allies, however, followed their issue into a formal endorsement of Breckinridge.

The ceaseless Whig search for a statewide majority was not over, of course. As we shall see, the crisis of the union gave the Whiggish remnant—still perhaps as much as a third of the electorate—renewed hopes of outflanking its rivals. But another phase of the search had ended. And yet, though the Opposition's flirtation with southern rights extremism between 1857 and 1859 appears at first glance to have had only a limited impact on the state's politics, it in fact constitutes an essential element in the coming of secession. The Whiggery's "no-party" maneuver in 1848 and 1849 played an important role in giving form to the Crisis of 1850. The Whiggery's Unionist maneuver of 1851 left unionism a suspiciously heterodox sentiment in the eyes of Democratic partisans. The Whiggery's Know-Nothing maneuver at mid-decade contributed to the adoption by the state's Democratic leadership of a very hard line on the Kansas question. And the Whiggery's "Southern Rights Opposition" maneuver in the late fifties drew left fire-eaters away from the support of the Yanceyites, and thus forced William L. Yancey toward the actions which would produce the sectional collision at the Charleston Democratic convention. Before we

23. *Ibid.*, June 2, June 30, July 7, July 14, July 21, July 28, August 4, August 11, August 18, September 8, October 6, October 20, 1858, January 26, March 16, March 23, March 30, April 13, April 20, April 27, May 4, May 11, May 18, May 25, June 1, June 8, June 15, June 22, June 29, July 6, July 20, September 21, 1859.
24. *Ibid.*, May 5, 1858, January 26, April 6, May 4, 1859.

can understand this event, however, we must retrace our steps, and glance at developments within the fire-eater movement during the decade.

The Fire-Eaters in Crisis

When last we examined the fire-eaters, we left the sect dedicated to forcing the South into a posture of resistance, but in disagreement as to the most effective method for achieving such a result. Leadership in the movement was passing to a group of younger ideologues who could join J. L. M. Curry in viewing one congressional contest, involving Curry's friend Samuel F. Rice, in the following enthusiastic terms: "Rice is, you know, a South Carolina Nullifier—one of the Chivalry, a true Representative of the Young Democracy, and utterly opposed to every species of old Hunkerism. It will be a decided victory for progressive democracy over conservatism—of Calhounism over Bentonism and Van Burenism."[25] Such men, who consciously identified themselves as radicals and who thought of the southern rights cause as a repudiation of the conservatism of the past, were as we have seen usually residents of relatively heavily populated and market-oriented communities. As towns increasingly became centers of opinion formation in the fifties, this view of the nature of American political conflict began to receive respectful attention. In the minds of many voters, the ill-informed rural masses clinging to their faith in the Union came to seem old-fashioned, out of touch with the spirit of the age. Youthful fire-eaters, using the terminology of the Young America movement, with which they at first associated themselves, began referring to their political opponents as "the old fogies." William F. Samford described the proper course as one of deliberately "antagonizing the *fogies* and *tricksters*" and "inviting a Union of all true *Southern* men—*anti-State Aid* men."

A secondary element among the fire-eaters was the remaining Calhounites. They viewed the developing crisis in terms similar to those of an old Montgomery Nullifier, Thomas Williams. "The trammels of party bind down" most southern politicians, he lamented:

25. J. L. M. Curry to Dixon H. Lewis, June 13, 1845, in Dixon H. Lewis Papers, University of Texas Library. As it happened, however, Rice lost to Felix G. McConnell.

Although they see the right and know the wrong yet they open not their mouths but with, as they suppose, the strong side. . . . If the people of the South from the beginning had had men of talents and firmness *demanding our rights* and absolutely and resolutely refusing submission to wrong, great as was our minority, our rights demonstrated (which talents would do), the dominant party clearly seeing these rights and unmistakingly knowing our firmness and determination for their preservation, our case today as a people would be very far different from what it is. . . . For my own part I have but a faint, very faint hope for this union. We have yielded so much and so long and so constantly, that the North *confidently* expects other and further yieldings—and if I am not mistaken, on this expectation the North will again act, forgetting that "the last pound will break the camel's back." And if so, the fault will be in part ours, because we did not at first do our duty to ourselves.

These embittered old men were not the leaders of the fire-eater movement, but the condemnation of politics which was the essence of the Calhounite analysis left an indelible impression on the ideology of the group as a whole. Samford's term for the politicians—"tricksters"—was the usual one among his confreres.[26]

The movement during the fifties received converts in response to the arguments of both of these basic elements in the coalition. Recent statistical studies have hinted at a broad tendency for young men in their twenties to ally themselves with the southern rights forces in 1860.[27] And many older citizens agreed with elderly businessman George Strother Gaines in asking themselves,

Is it not to the demoralizing influence of party spirit which the good people of the United States have permitted [*sic*] to controul the elections, that we are

26. William F. Samford to Matthew P. Blue, December 31, 1856, in M. P. Blue Papers, Alabama Department of Archives and History, Montgomery; Thomas Williams to Clement Claiborne Clay, December 5, 1859, in Clay Papers. *Cf.* Montgomery *Advertiser*, January 19, July 20, 1853, December 20, 1854, September 16, 1857, January 27, February 17, March 17, May 26, June 16, 1858, March 23, 1859.

27. Kit Carson Carter, Jr., "A Critical Analysis of the Basis of Party Alignment in Lowndes County, Alabama, 1836–1860" (M.A. thesis, University of Alabama, 1961), 45–46; Frank M. Lowrey, "A Critical Analysis of the Relation Between Selected Factors and Party Affiliation in Montgomery County, Alabama, 1840–1860" (M.A. thesis, University of Alabama, 1964), 49. But *cf.* Mary Jane Pickens, "A Critical Analysis of the Basis of Party Alignment in Autauga County, Alabama, 1836–1860" (M.A. thesis, University of Alabama, 1963), 25, 43. An element in this tendency was the decline of the Whig party, which naturally turned the ambitious to the ranks of the Democracy. Support for Stephen A. Douglas was still practical for the ambitious in Autauga in 1860, however, because of the strength of the Regency there. An important segment of the Regency, including John J. Seibels, was for Douglas. A new study, William L. Barney, *The Secessionist Impulse: Alabama and Mississippi in 1860* (Princeton: Princeton University Press, 1974), esp. 50–100, emphasizes the relative youth of Breckinridge's campaigners.

indebted for the existing controversy between the northern and southern States, threatening the dissolution of the Federal Government? There is nothing else that could have blinded and besotted our keen sighted northern bretherin [*sic*], than this mischeivous [*sic*] demon. . . . Blind and besotted they must be to beleive [*sic*] it their duty to meddle in our domestic affairs, to keep up a cowardly agitation for years to the injury of the very class they pretend to favor [the slaves].[28]

But during most of the fifties the growth of fire-eater numbers was by no means impressive. The principal reason for this lack of progress was the continued faith of most Alabamians that the political process could produce an acceptable adjustment of the nation's difficulties. In the letter just quoted, Gaines also affirmed, almost mystically,

I do not dispair [*sic*]; for, although the hot party agitations which has [*sic*] for years past stirred up and floated into Congress some of the very drugs [*sic*] of society, too light and too filthy to comprehend any duty save that of obedience to party leaders, there is too much good sense in the people to suffer this state of things to exist much longer. . . . I am a firm beleiver [*sic*] in the ability of the people to govern themselves—in the stability of this good government of ours—and in the waking up of the people, although stupified for a time by a party press, party stump orators, and cheated out of their votes by party machinary [*sic*].

From the inauguration of Pierce until well into the Buchanan administration, it appeared to many moderate southerners that the federal government was at least pursuing a neutral path in the sectional dispute. And some, usually Democratic politicians, even claimed to detect a benevolent neutrality. Governor Moore reported later that he, in company with many others, had believed that the Kansas-Nebraska Act and the subsequent Dred Scott decision heralded a new era of sectional peace based on firm guarantees for the South. But by the end of 1859 he was willing to admit that he had been wrong.[29]

Confirmed southern rights men such as Mobile's Burwell Boykin were much more pessimistic, but their passive mood of watchful waiting at this period was no less a contribution to the general hope.

28. George Strother Gaines to A. W. Dillard, August 8, 1857, in George S. Gaines Papers, Alabama Department of Archives and History, Montgomery.

29. Second Inaugural Address of His Excellency A. B. Moore, December, 1859 (Typescript in Governors' Correspondence: A. B. Moore, Alabama Department of Archives and History, Montgomery); *cf.* Montgomery *Advertiser*, March 16, April 27, May 4, 1853, May 9, July 18, 1855.

"Pierce stood up manfully for the South, and in doing so, like other Northern men, sacrificed himself—and thus will it always be," he observed sadly. "We are under the ban of proscription, and to defend our Constitutional rights is to entail political national ostracism. It seems to me no man can be President but for one term who will perform his sworn duty. . . . If the past casts its shadow before, the future is pregnant with ill omens." But still he added, "If any hope remains to us, I think it alone is to be found in the Democratic party and its principles. But there is no use in speculating about these matters either in or out of Congress. We shall see what we shall see."[30] The fact that men of Boykin's stripe still had hope in the Democratic party and were willing to eschew predictions of impending doom boded well for sectional peace.

In 1856 two prominent fire-eaters, William L. Yancey and L. Pope Walker, had served as state electors-at-large on Buchanan's ticket, and Yancey had even been proposed for Buchanan's cabinet—though he declined since such a post would leave him "crippled for future usefulness if ever we shall be forced to act against Mr. Buchanan, which God forefend!"[31] Indeed, some fire-eaters had become so attached to Buchanan's cause that they had difficulty thinking ill of him even after he had become trapped in the quicksand of Kansas. In July of 1857 William F. Samford affirmed in a hurried note, "My impression of Kansas *imbroglio* daily being verified. I do not doubt the fidelity of the National Administration—that Kansas will come in a *Slave State*, to which result it will soon be apparent that [Robert J.] Walker has so essentially contributed that it could not have been without his *ambidextrous diplomacy*."[32] But by October of 1858 Samford had entirely altered his position. Buchanan's, he declared bitterly, "does not come up to my idea of a Southern Rights Administration, and I am grievously disappointed in it."[33] In the intervening months, of course,

30. Burwell Boykin to Clement Claiborne Clay, undated [internally dated to summer, 1856], in Clay Papers.

31. William L. Yancey to Clement Claiborne Clay, February 15, 1857, in Clay Papers; cf. Montgomery *Advertiser*, December 3, 1856, January 7, January 14, 1857, January 27, 1858.

32. William F. Samford to Matthew P. Blue, July 14, 1857, in Blue Papers; cf. Montgomery *Advertiser*, February 6, May 7, June 25, August 13, 1856, February 18, April 15, July 8, July 15, July 22, August 5, August 12, August 26, September 2, October 7, October 28, 1857.

33. William F. Samford to Clement Claiborne Clay, October 20, 1858, in Clay Papers; cf.

Buchanan had backed away from his support for the Lecompton Constitution and had accepted the Kansas conference bill. But it appears from the remainder of Samford's letter that the sources of his disillusionment lay deeper. His attitude is worth examining.

"Indefinite ideas of Southern advantage to result from Mr. Buchanan's election had preoccupied the Southern mind before its [the administration's] inauguration," Samford stated. "Kansas, Cuba, South America—all loomed up as inviting Southern expansion, outlet and development. The *dream* has been sadly dissipated; the galling *reality* is too recent and current for the South to listen to the miserable party mongering and party expediencies of the Cabinet and the Washington *Union*." Buchanan's compromising course had become untenable. "We cannot accept the issues of this Administration and make the battle of 1860 upon them. . . . Depend on it, *defeat*—disastrous—ruinous, awaits us if we make this Administration the standard and watchword of the Democracy!" And so Samford had been pushed into an extreme formulation. "You know my politics," he told his correspondent. "You know I have from the beginning opposed 'Lecomptonism straight' [that is, an unqualified acceptance of the constitution, including the slavery article] as a Southern issue, that I am opposed to Kansas [as an issue] *under any circumstances*, that I care not a fig about the 'Conference Bill,' [but instead] want open, plain issues with the Black Republicans, without any nonsense about 'Squatter Sovereignty' among them."[34]

As Samford implies, the process which was going on here was in essence an effort to recapture a dream. At the time of the 1852 election, perhaps a majority of genuine fire-eaters accepted the policy of noncooperation with either political party. At least two thousand Alabamians expressed their approval of this position by voting for Troup. But Pierce received a consistently favorable press in southern rights quarters, and substantial numbers of fire-eaters thus became convinced of the efficacy of Yancey's policy of infiltration within the

---

Montgomery *Advertiser*, January 27, February 3, February 10, February 17, March 10, July 28, August 25, 1858.

34. William F. Samford to Clement Claiborne Clay, October 20, 1858, in Clay Papers; *cf.* Montgomery *Advertiser*, July 21, September 1, September 15, October 20, October 27, 1858, June 1, 1859.

Democratic party to compel it to conform to southern standards. Though Pierce's favorable actions predisposed fire-eaters to think well of Yancey's notion of agitation, however, the high tide of conversion to his faith was not reached until the campaign of 1856.

The general conversion did not result from enthusiasm for Buchanan by any means. Most southern rights men would have preferred Pierce. A Black Belt editor confided, "We regret that Pierce has been thrown overboard, for we know that the cause of it has been his devotion to the rights of the states, the south included. . . . We will support Buchanan of course, cheerfully, but he cannot command that enthusiasm which the name of Frank Pierce would have done." Young Senator Clay observed to his father that the ticket chosen was the strongest one possible, but he added grimly that "it does not suit me or any Southern Rights man I have seen who spoke to me confidentially." Another term for Pierce would have seen strict construction victorious "and the Government fixed on the old republican tack." Buchanan's advocacy of protection and economic activism, however, would inhibit the pursuit of limited government; and because of that deficiency, "With our present nominees, the issue will not be fairly fought with Abolition and our triumph will be incomplete." Indeed, Buchanan's views might even increase the South's isolation. "The Atlantic states of the South and the Gulf states except Louisiana will be the only faithful representatives of the strict construction faith, and will curse Buchanan as bitterly as the North now abuses Pierce. The Democratic party will sever on the tariff and internal improvements, unless the more absorbing interests of slavery keep them together."[35]

It was not Buchanan but what was happening to the Democratic party in Alabama that was the source of the fire-eaters' new loyalty to the party. Yancey's command of a relatively cohesive and deliverable bloc of votes had already made him a respected leader in the party. About this time, however, the party gained support from quite another source. As we have seen, a not inconsiderable portion of the Whiggery, increasingly unhappy with the Know-Nothing party, embraced the rival sect.[36] Pope Walker, a former Whig and an advocate of aid to

35. Zacharias L. Nabers to Clement Claiborne Clay, June 11, 1856, Clement Claiborne Clay to Clement Comer Clay, June 7, 1856, in Clay Papers.

36. See pp. 358–60 herein. Cf. also William B. Figures to Clement Claiborne Clay, un-

internal improvements as well as a southern rights man, was selected to join Yancey as elector-at-large in an effort to consolidate the party's hold over both of its new accessions. From the point of view of the Yanceyites, the Whig addition was not especially welcome, for it made the party more difficult to control in the interests of southern rights. Their position had been expressed succinctly four years before by Philip Phillips: "I think the only danger to the Democratic party now is that it will become too much of an omnibus in this State. We have nothing to fear from either the Union or Whig party or both combined; from their friendship and adherence, much."[37]

But of course, as the party became an omnibus, the other school of fire-eaters would fear it less and less. They desired a general social conversion, outside of the partisan structure. If the whole society, regardless of its policy differences, came to be encompassed within the Democratic party, then internal Democratic politics would become the equivalent of statewide politics. The control of the party and the conversion of the society would now be virtually the same thing. If everyone were in the same party, then the essence of party corruption—the sacrifice of principle in order to win voters away from the opposition—would be eliminated. At least, so it seemed to them at first blush. Doubtless with residual misgivings, they entered the party and lent their support to what they apparently mistook as an emerging southern rights consensus.

As Samford said, these fire-eaters were moved to dream great dreams in 1856 and 1857. They had always thought that if internecine political war could be eliminated in the South, the resultant southern united front would deliver dominance to the region. And now the goal seemed in their grasp. They prepared to press the Buchanan administration hard for the realization of their long-suppressed desires. But it took no more than a year of the new president's tenure for the separatist fire-eaters to learn some important political truths—truths particularly painful because they reaffirmed elements of the fire-eaters' own dogma which they had ignored in the flush of excitement. Even a

---

dated [internally dated to summer, 1856], Gabriel B. DuVal to Clay, May 14, 1857, in Clay Papers.

37. Philip Phillips to John Bragg, February 8, 1852, in John Bragg Papers, Southern Historical Collection, University of North Carolina Library, Chapel Hill.

united South could not control the government without northern aid, which could be had only by defeating the Republicans. And many southern politicians were eager to contribute to that effort. Senator Fitzpatrick played a role in effecting the adoption of the conference bill, and endorsed it enthusiastically. Opposition orators in Alabama, pointing to the bill, warned stridently that the mere existence of a political party, no matter how broad the base of its membership, was sufficient to prevent the assumption of unalloyed southern rights grounds. In the summer and fall of 1858 Whig charges compelled many fire-eaters to take a long look at their actions of the preceding two years: they discovered to their horror and disgust that they had allowed themselves to be seduced. Samford had correctly described their reaction: "The *dream* has been sadly dissipated; the galling *reality* is too recent and current for the South to listen to the miserable party mongering and party expediencies" of the politicians. Thus, after its brief infatuation with the universal Democracy, the separatist wing of the fire-eaters began pulling back to the political isolationism which had been its initial policy—at the same time casting some flirtatious glances towards the rather involuntarily isolated Oppositionists.

The disenchantment with participation in the Democratic party on the part of many fire-eater purists left the Yanceyite wing of the movement in particular disarray, and their effort to deal with the situation represents the next step on the road to Charleston. Ever since his struggle to obtain a fire-eater endorsement of Pierce in 1852, Yancey's influence with the Democrats had been growing. His pronouncements on slavery in the territories, which had seemed so extreme in 1848, had received substantial acceptance by the Supreme Court in the Dred Scott decision. His early attacks on Senator Douglas and popular sovereignty began to look like party orthodoxy after Douglas had broken with Buchanan and been disciplined by the party's Senate caucus. His venomous denunciations of the Know-Nothings as tools of abolitionism reinforced the party line on that point. In September of 1855, Yancey publicly announced the renewal of his Democratic vows, and his selection as a presidential elector in 1856 certified the prodigal's reinstatement. Of course many in the party still had no high opinion of him. A delegate to the 1856 convention wrote, "Both the electors for the state at large (Yancey and Walker) are as distasteful to me as they are to a large majority of the Democracy of Alabama, but at a time when expediency rather than acceptability was the controlling power with the nominating convention, they were obliged to cast about for those men whose speaking powers alone would be most effectual in persuading the masses. Neither of the gentlemen referred to are [*sic*] popular now, never have been and never will be." He therefore concluded confidently that the electorship was not of sufficient importance to "subserve the aims of a daring ambition."[38] But the influx of substantial numbers of new Yancey supporters into the party just at the time when Yancey's canvassing for the national ticket made him seem to be an accepted party leader raised him to new heights of influence.

During 1856 and 1857 it appeared that Yancey's notions of the proper way to conduct agitation had gained dominance in the movement. But the reconsiderations of 1858 dashed Yancey's aspirations for gaining control of the party. As his power base began to disintegrate, Yancey came to see that he needed some victory which would blunt the Opposition's antiparty arguments, by proving that he did indeed have the ability to bend the Democracy to his will. Only thus could he halt the southern rights desertions. His first goal was to induce the 1859 legislature to elect him to replace Senator Fitzpatrick.

Yancey seized on Fitzpatrick's unqualified support for the Kansas conference bill as the principal issue on which to contest the senator's seat. Yancey may well have been the author of a series of newspaper letters immediately after the passage of the bill, attacking it vigorously as a surrender to northern aggressions.[39] At any rate, in the months leading up to the election of the new assembly in August, 1859, he repeatedly questioned the extent of Fitzpatrick's devotion to southern rights. The charges puzzled Fitzpatrick himself. Ever since his term as governor from 1841 to 1845, Fitzpatrick had been an acknowledged leader of the south Alabama Democracy. His political machine, the so-called Montgomery Regency, had been formed during the effort to elect his brother-in-law Dixon Lewis to the Senate over William R.

38. James E. Peebles to Clement Claiborne Clay, March 11, 1856, in Clay Papers; *cf.* Montgomery *Advertiser*, January 26, July 6, 1853, July 4, July 11, July 18, September 5, September 12, September 26, 1855, January 16, 1856.
39. J. Withers Clay to Clement Claiborne Clay, May 8, 1858, in Clay Papers; *cf.* "Southron" in Montgomery *Advertiser*, May 5, June 16, 1858.

King. It included such prominent members of the Southern Rights political establishment as Crawford M. Jackson, Bolling Hall, John J. Seibels, and Albert Elmore. Of course, Fitzpatrick had never hesitated to say of himself, "You know very well, however, that I have always been a caucus and a party man."[40] But as we have seen, there was no conflict in the minds of south Alabama partisans between devotion to the Democratic party and commitment to Southern Rights. They argued with considerable justice that suppression of any political debate upon the slavery question had been a fundamental tenet of their party since its birth. The notion that Whiggery and abolition were somehow linked had been Democratic dogma at least since the Van Buren-Harrison race of 1840, and Whig domination of the Unionist alliance of 1851 had reinforced the notion that Southern Rights beliefs were essential to party regularity. It was this fact which Yancey expected to manipulate to give himself acceptance by the party. His argument to the Democracy's rank and file was at base an assertion that Fitzpatrick's views were not regular—that is, were sufficiently ill-defined that they could play into the hands of the Opposition.

In making the case, Yancey collided with a different notion of Southern Rights common among the partisans. From Yancey's perspective, southern rights were a group of privileges to which the region was entitled in order to assure it equality in the national arena. But the Democrats had always maintained that the fundamental southern right was the right to be left alone. One view was positive and assertive; the other negative and passive. Thus Fitzpatrick could easily consider the conference bill a triumph, the latest in a happy series. "The election of Mr. Buchanan to the Presidency, and the consequent defeat of the conspiracy against the peace of the Union, and the evident satisfaction that the event diffused through the land afforded a clear indication that conservative men were in a large majority in the United States," he wrote. Moreover, recent "decisions of the Congress, of the President and of the Supreme Court of the United States—sustained as they were by the people—placed the Southern States upon a proud eminence. They proved that, in this long existing and dangerous controversy, the Southern States had been occupying

40. Benjamin Fitzpatrick to Bolling Hall, October 5, 1853, in Bolling Hall Papers, Alabama Department of Archives and History, Montgomery.

the surest foundations of constitutional right. The contest had been commenced by others; their position had been all the time a defensive one." He could now hail with joy the dawn of "the era of the complete restoration of the Southern States to equality in the Union." In this light, the conference bill represented a disastrous defeat "to those who have been the apostles of strife, confusion and disorder—to those who have made profit from the morbid and diseased condition of the public mind." It was a measure tending "to mitigate the irritation, discontent and heartburnings which for nearly a generation has [*sic*] disturbed our country. I believe that at this time we have a better prospect for peace than we have enjoyed for many years, and that the Kansas bill will be an element of peace."[41]

These sentiments Fitzpatrick intended as an avowal of his devotion to Southern Rights—and, more, an assertion that he had essentially forwarded the effort to protect them. But Yancey sought to paint Fitzpatrick's position as a weak acceptance of compromise in order to preserve party harmony. Perhaps partially to aid in delineating his differences with the senator Yancey took up the issue of reopening the African slave trade, an action which Fitzpatrick flatly opposed. Yancey did not explicitly advocate reopening the trade, however; his argument was of another sort. While the Constitution forbade the Congress from prohibiting the slave trade before 1808, it of course did not require that Congress prohibit it thereafter. Yancey called for the repeal of all federal laws on the subject, which would have had the effect of allowing each state to decide for itself whether to forbid the importation. As to whether, in that case, he would urge Alabama to permit the trade Yancey made no statement. The thrust of his case was against federal legislation branding slavery by implication as immoral, but was not in favor of the trade. Reopening was a policy question, to be decided on the basis of whether the supply of slaves was sufficient in a given area.[42]

The implication of this argument for Yancey's disagreement with

41. Statement of the Honorable Benjamin Fitzpatrick Upon the Kansas Conference Bill, May, 1858 (MS in Benjamin Fitzpatrick Papers, Southern Historical Collection, University of North Carolina Library, Chapel Hill).

42. A convenient statement of Yancey's careful and rather equivocal position on the slave trade question is his speech to the Secession Convention on the subject: William R. Smith, *The History and Debates of the Convention of the People of Alabama, Begun and Held in the City of Montgomery on the Seventh Day of January, 1861* (Montgomery: White, Pfister and Co., 1861),

Fitzpatrick is clear. It pointed up Yancey's contention that attitudes which marked slavery as reprehensible and the South as an inferior partner infected every aspect of the nation's dealings with the persecuted section. Equality was not to be achieved, as the senator appeared to believe, merely by halting aggressions from the North and guaranteeing the South's right to enter the territories. The process would require a total reformation of fundamental assumptions and power relationships throughout the political structure of the republic—including the repeal or modification of statutes dating back to the administration of Jefferson, and beyond. But Fitzpatrick apparently never understood the meaning of Yancey's parables. He had always been a Southern Rights advocate, he affirmed in bewilderment. He could think of but one explanation for the attacks being made upon him: his true position must have been misrepresented.[43]

To Yancey's charges that Fitzpatrick's devotion to the southern rights portion of Democratic party dogma was questionable, Fitzpatrick's friends replied that Yancey secretly desired to destroy the Democratic party from within. This allegation Yancey denied. Far from seeking the party's destruction, he sought to use it as the primary mechanism for the achievement of full southern equality. Thus it was fundamentally upon the question of the future of the Democratic party that the contest went to the legislature, after a debate which had been a central feature of Alabama politics for almost two years.[44] The result of the balloting represented a partial defeat for Yancey, but contained elements which left his supporters optimistic for the future.

Fitzpatrick entered the legislature stronger than Yancey, but a

---

237–52. But Yancey made repeated attempts in the late fifties to explain his position: see Montgomery *Advertiser*, June 2, 1858, June 22, June 29, August 31, 1859.

43. Benjamin Fitzpatrick to Clement Claiborne Clay, August 30, 1859, in Clay Papers.

44. In the acrimonious encounter Fitzpatrick's organ was the Montgomery *Confederation*, edited by his friend John J. Seibels, and Yancey's champion was the Montgomery *Advertiser*, edited by George H. Shorter and his assistants William A. Beene, Yancey's cousin, and Samuel G. Reid, a young protégé of the orator's who had been a delegate to the Lecompton constitutional convention in Kansas and who became a scalawag during Reconstruction. See Montgomery *Advertiser*, January 27, February 3, March 3, March 10, March 24, April 7, April 14, June 2, June 9, June 30, July 14, July 21, August 4, August 11, August 18, September 15, October 6, October 20, November 3, November 24, December 8, 1858, June 29, July 6, July 13, August 10, August 17, August 31, October 19, November 2, November 9, November 30, December 7, 1859. An interesting sidelight on the canvass is provided in three letters from Bolling Hall III, a student at the University of Alabama: Bolling Hall III to Bolling Hall, February 24, March 13, 1858, Bolling Hall III to Mary Louisa Hall, May 9, 1858, all in Hall Papers.

small bloc of members committed to former governor Winston represented the balance of power. Yancey had at first been convinced that he could stop Fitzpatrick in the early ballots and gradually wear away the senator's support subsequently, so as to emerge the victor. Therefore his supporters had joined Fitzpatrick's in announcing publicly that they favored bringing on the election at that session. But when the assembly convened, a nose count convinced Yancey that he could not win, and his supporters began to seek some way consistently to oppose the resolution ordering the contest. In the House, fidelity to public statements forced most Yanceyites, much against their better judgment, to accept an election. But the resolution was defeated in the Senate by a vote of 18 to 14, thanks to a clever tactical maneuver from the devious brain of Senator Edward C. Bullock of Barbour County, one of Yancey's floor leaders. Bullock chuckled, "Fitzpatrick was there with Seibels and other retainers to see the concurrence. A more melancholy looking set of old fogies never darkened a Senate Chamber."[45]

We can, of course, never know if Fitzpatrick would have won, had the election been held. In his letter Bullock offered a comment on that question. "Governor Fitzpatrick counted on 70 votes on the third ballot, but I am certain that his calculations were not all correct, and my own impression is that there would have been many ballotings but no choice. . . . I think Governor Fitzpatrick would have started off with about 58, Yancey with about 50 and Winston with 22." But there was certainly a possibility that the senator could have triumphed. As Bullock candidly admitted, "Winston's friends with the balance of power were too uncertain to hazard the result in their hands. There is more affinity between Winston's and Fitzpatrick's positions than between either of them and Yancey." And in addition, Fitzpatrick's reelection would have made him a strong candidate for vice-president, thus affording Winston the possibility of an earlier vacancy.

The senator's political strength, then, is most certainly not to be dismissed. And yet the Yanceyites emerged from the encounter not greatly disturbed by their loss. A glance at the Senate vote refusing to bring on the election reveals why. Fitzpatrick, as we have noted, was a recognized leader of the south Alabama Democracy. Indeed, the north

45. Edward C. Bullock to Clement Claiborne Clay, December 30, 1859, in Clay Papers—a fascinating inside account of the episode.

Alabama Democrats, whose revolt had led to the elevation of Jeremiah Clemens in 1849, had refused to support Fitzpatrick in that election precisely because Fitzpatrick was so closely associated with south Alabama interests. On page 379 is a map showing the home counties of the senators who were supporting Fitzpatrick. It is clear that his support was confined almost entirely to north Alabama—indeed, exclusively so except for the Wiregrass county of Butler and the two relatively urban counties of Montgomery and Mobile. The backbone of his strength was in the eastern hill counties.

This circumstance was more than extraordinary. It represented a moral victory for Yancey. The dispute between the two men had turned upon the future of the Democratic party. Clearly Yancey had succeeded in convincing many politicians in Fitzpatrick's own wing of the party that the senator was not a sound representative of the faith. Moreover, by confining Fitzpatrick's support to a section whose regularity had been suspect ever since it had cooperated with the Whigs a decade earlier, Yancey identified Fitzpatrick even more thoroughly with rather dubious associates. And in addition, it appears that Yancey was making progress towards isolating his rival from the political novices in the assembly. At any rate, of the ten senators who had never served in the legislature before 1857, only two supported Fitzpatrick. The median age of Fitzpatrick's senatorial adherents was forty-seven and of his opponents, thirty-seven.

The rise of the Yanceyites involved an alteration in notions about the proper role of the party in the society. During most of Alabama history, as we have seen, the party was regarded as a sort of nurturing mother from which the politician graduated to influence and to which he owed gratitude and loyalty. But increasingly for all politicians, as it had always been for a few exceptional leaders, the party came to seem a mere tool for effecting policy objectives. The society was in crisis; its salvation was not to be achieved by an alliance for patronage, but only by an ideological union, forged in a common dedication to the enactment of a program of solutions. The acceptance of this change, of course, depended upon the acknowledgment that the society was indeed in crisis. Yancey preached this doctrine incessantly, but he could not claim primary credit for the growing belief in it. Far more important in that process was the action of malevolent fate in coupling the

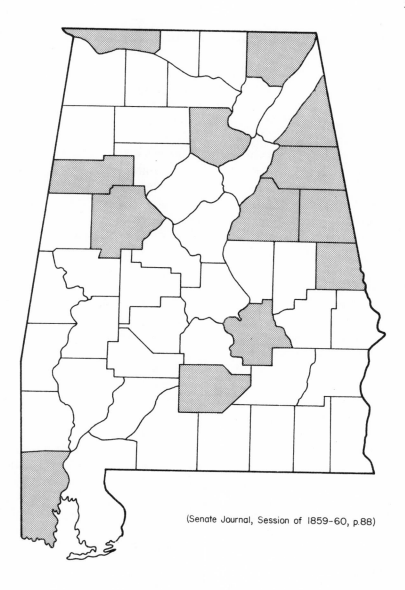

(Senate Journal, Session of 1859-60, p.88)

Home Counties of Senators Supporting Fitzpatrick, 1859

objective reality of supercilious northern denunciations with the foreboding, disorientation, and longing for direction which permeated the electorate and of which the sensitive politician was constantly aware. Equally significant was the increasing contact of the state with the outside world, which made a threat from faraway regions suddenly appear credible. The reiteration by the fire-eaters that the abolitionists posed a genuine danger did have the effect of causing the public mind to look in that quarter, rather than in some other, for the force which sought to enslave them this time. But Yancey's real achievement was in offering the redirection of the Democratic party—the elimination of the corrupt competition for spoils and the institution of a clear ideological orientation and commitment—as the proper mechanism for deliverance from the impending doom.

The vote refusing to bring on the senatorial election in 1859 was a most favorable index of the progress which Yancey's notion had made towards general acceptance. When the House had voted to hold the election, one of Yancey's few north Alabama supporters, former congressman David Hubbard, had filed an angry protest. He stated that "the probability is that if an election be now made, the result may show that a mistake was made" because, he asserted, "the whole South is in a transition state. New issues are now just emerging from the womb of events, and no main presciner [*sic*] can divine the political status two years hence," when the new senator's term would begin. He concluded with the solemn warning that "if the man now elected should happen to misrepresent the state, how fearful will be the accountability of those who bring such calamity on the country." Whatever we may think of the calamitous implications of refusing William L. Yancey a seat in the Senate, we may at least agree that a genuine transition—in response to events, and in response to the strident interpretation of those events offered by the agitators—was indeed taking place. The Yanceyites emerged from this episode confirmed in their long-standing belief that "future developments must strengthen and could not weaken the Southern Rights wing of the party."[46]

There was, however, one audience observing the balloting which too often goes unnoted. The Yanceyites believed that they had good

46. *House Journal*, Sess. of 1859–1860, p. 109; Edward C. Bullock to Clement Claiborne Clay, December 30, 1859, in Clay Papers.

reason for confidence. Fitzpatrick found himself delivered to a new constituency, and the circumstance could not but trouble the Montgomery Regency. But the most important group had no real part in the battle. The left fire-eaters—the group that, after its flirtation with the universal Democracy of 1857, had been led by national developments and by fervid admonitions from the Whigs to commence withdrawing into uncorrupted isolation—remained unconvinced. One of the circumstances which had made Yancey's effort to displace Fitzpatrick necessary was the steady erosion of Yancey's constituency within the party. Yancey had hoped to demonstrate by a decisive victory that he had the power to make the party conform to his ideology, rather than, as the left fire-eaters thought inevitable, finding himself assimilated into the vague generalization which was the heart of political alliance. But he had effected no such irrefutable demonstration. The case for intraparty agitation would have to be proven beyond cavil to convince men whose persistent skepticism of it had only recently been reinforced by their revulsion at their own partisan activities. The striking alteration in factional allegiance which the actual vote represented was quite apparent to Yancey's supporters. But the left fire-eaters, predisposed as they were to doubt, saw only the fact that Yancey had lost.

As the presidential election year of 1860 commenced, therefore, Yancey found himself in a curious position. He was stronger with the politicians than he had ever been before. But a substantial and important section of the constituency which had raised him to that eminence remained dubious of his tactics, and was deserting his standard. The arguments of the Hooperites had not helped the Opposition, but they had had their effect upon the southern rights radicals. It was clear to Yancey that he could not maintain his position in the party indefinitely if it became apparent that many fire-eaters would not support the use of the party as a weapon with which to achieve their goals. The Yanceyite politicians had been convinced that allowing Yancey to remake the party as a tool of sectional struggle would unite the society behind the Democratic party. If they could not thereby gain support, there was really no reason for political leaders to deliver their party into Yancey's hands. But at the same time, convincing the left fire-eaters to rally to the party depended upon convincing the politicians to surrender the party to Yancey. Unless some action was taken, the situation gave promise of deteriorating into a classic and insoluble paradox. The desertion of his purist allies, therefore, was in many ways the principal obstacle Yancey faced to the realization of his great vision.

Yancey's Crisis

Fortunately, the fact that 1860 was a presidential election year presented the possibility of effectively dealing with Yancey's problem. He hit upon a course of action modeled on that of his political mentor Dixon H. Lewis in 1848. As we recall, in order to defeat King in 1847, Lewis had been forced to make explicit pledges to desert Calhoun and accept Hunker control of the Democracy. He had, however, sought to outflank the Hunkers and regain his ideological freedom through the stratagem of the Alabama Platform. If his candidate for president, Levi Woodbury, were nominated at the national convention with the united support of the Alabama delegation—which the Alabama Platform in effect bound the delegation to give—then Lewis could consistently return to a southern rights stand, while proclaiming loudly that he was merely conforming to both the national and the state party line. The plan failed on both levels: Woodbury proved unable to get the national nomination, and the Alabama delegation ignored the Alabama Platform. But Lewis' young lieutenant William L. Yancey absorbed the lessons of the effort.[47]

Yancey believed that the Charleston convention would provide him with a mechanism both for gaining control of the Alabama party and for convincing the doubters among the fire-eaters of the efficacy of his course. He wished to induce the national party to adopt a more explicit avowal of the principle of positive protection of slavery in the territories than the Cincinnati formula of 1856 had been. And he wished the selection of a candidate who would be willing to endorse such a platform. He did not expect a fully southern rights platform. He had accepted the Cincinnati statement four years earlier, and was ready to negotiate phraseology this time. Nor did he expect the nomi-

47. Lewis' strategy is explained in detail in Ralph B. Draughon, Jr., "William Lowndes Yancey: From Unionist to Secessionist, 1814–1852" (Ph.D. dissertation, University of North Carolina, 1968), 177–203, esp. 190–95.

nation of a man fully acceptable to him. He, and many other fire-eaters, had determined, as a compromise, to support Henry A. Wise, whose career in Virginia had marked him as an advocate of suffrage extension and an enemy of the Tidewater planters, and whose career on the national scene had left him free of the taint of "Lecomptonism," which weakened supporters of Buchanan in the eyes of many northern voters.[48] Yancey, in short, did not go to Charleston with the purpose of disrupting the American Democracy. He went with the purpose of nudging the party a bit further along the road to an open acceptance of southern equality.

Some noticeable movement by the national party—even if it were only a modest advance—would help Yancey enormously in Alabama, however. The antiparty fire-eaters would be deeply impressed. They might demand of Yancey total victory before the Alabama legislature—which after all had two years earlier virtually unanimously demanded disunion if Kansas were admitted under a constitution other than Lecompton—but being sane men, they would not expect the immediate conversion of the entire national party. Indeed, their actual expectation was that Yancey, by virtue of the clarity of his position, would find himself unable to influence the national Democracy at all. Therefore if he returned with a relatively acceptable platform and a not unacceptable candidate, the left fire-eaters would look on it as rather a minor miracle. It would lend strong support to the argument of the Yanceyites—that a firm demand from southern delegates who knew exactly what they wanted would lead to the immediate acquiescence of the convention, in order to avoid alienating southern voters.

The victory would influence local Democratic politicians as well. The sanction thus given positive protection would make heterodoxy on this issue almost impossible. But more, given the natural tendency of political oratory towards simplification—seeking the level of the slogan—Democratic ideology would receive a powerful impetus in the direction of an extremist formulation in line with Yancey's own views. And the victory itself would bring even more ambitious younger politicians into Yancey's camp, since it would strengthen the impression that Yancey was an emerging leader, alliance with whom could

48. J. Withers Clay to Clement Claiborne Clay, March 30, 1860, in Clay Papers; *cf.* William F. Samford to Clement Claiborne Clay, October 20, 1858.

prove quite profitable. At one blow, then, success at Charleston would hasten the conversion of the Democratic party into a mechanism for achieving full southern equality, would halt—and possibly even reverse—the desertion of the left fire-eaters from the party, and would fortify Yancey's control over the younger politicians. It could reignite the dreams of 1856.

While this line of reasoning is not at all irrational, it does perhaps rest upon an irrational presumption—the notion that the national party would grant any halfway reasonable southern demand if the demand came from a determined and united South. Yancey did indeed hold that presumption. It was, moreover, the essence of his difference with the purists among the fire-eaters. Their conception of the demands of the American political system was harsher, more hopeless but—I may confess to the belief—also more realistic than was Yancey's fevered faith. We are not at liberty, though, to dismiss the fundamental axiom upon which Yancey operated, for we would thereby strip his actions of the internal logic which they otherwise possess. However much Yancey's program may appear to have been doomed from the outset, it is nevertheless true that Yancey sincerely expected the Democratic mountain to yield at least a few inches if he but put his shoulder firmly to it—and thus to reveal ground upon which the Alabama party could rally to his principles. The experiment had not worked for Lewis in 1848. It was to give Yancey a success very different from that which he expected.

Of course, whatever program Yancey pursued, the Montgomery Regency felt compelled to oppose. The county conventions to choose delegates to the state gathering began in mid-November, just as the Fitzpatrick-Yancey duel was reaching the voting stage. The state convention met in mid-January, while politicians were still anxiously seeking signs of the future in the encounter's inconclusive result. It was clear that if Fitzpatrick hoped to win the second round, before the assembly of 1861, he would have to regain a position of leadership within the south Alabama Democracy. Thus the state convention almost inevitably became an extension of the senatorial contest.

Both Yancey and Fitzpatrick apparently controlled about 150 votes at the convention, with perhaps most of the remaining 150 or so votes in the hands of Winston men.[49] The first day's session was a wild affair. Yancey's forces offered Henry D. Smith of Lauderdale, one of Yancey's few north Alabama supporters, for convention president, and the Fitzpatrick men sought the office for Michael J. Bulger of Tallapoosa, one of the few young followers of the Montgomery Regency. The Gainesville *Independent*, Winston's hometown newspaper, announced, "We are grieved and mortified at the disorderly scenes that marked the organization of the convention. . . . The whole cause of the tumult and disorder is to be found in the angry contest between the friends of Messrs. Yancey and Fitzpatrick," it stated, adding, "We are sorry to see men of sense and judgment stooping to become the thick and thin partizans of these gentlemen, and helping to sow discord in the Democratic ranks by their injudicious and destructive course. The true policy is to look upon men as subordinate to principles, and to teach ambitious and aspiring men that they cannot ruin the party to secure their own personal aggrandizement."[50] But Winston's forces, under his political lieutenant Alexander B. Clitherall of Pickens, were no less well organized, and proved a decisive factor in the convention's actions.

The conflict over the convention presidency was compromised by choosing Francis Strother Lyon who, because of his service as commissioner to supervise the liquidation of the Bank of Alabama, had been elevated to the status of a nonpartisan institution. The next difficulty was a bitter credentials contest from Mobile. In 1859 the purist fire-eaters, as we have seen, had offered candidates against two regular southern rights Democrats, Pugh and Stallworth, in congressional races. Both regular nominees had won handily, but F. B. Shepard's race

---

49. *Proceedings of the Democratic State Convention Held in the City of Montgomery Commencing Wednesday, January 11, 1860* (Montgomery: Advertiser Book and Job Steam Press Print, 1860; pamphlet in J. L. M. Curry Pamphlet Collection, Alabama Department of Archives and History, Montgomery, Vol. XXVII, No. 36), 20, 21, 30. The first two roll calls I take to isolate the Yanceyites, and the last the supporters of Fitzpatrick. The number of votes controlled by the various factions is not the same thing as the number of delegates which each had present, as votes were apportioned among the counties on the basis of Buchanan's poll in 1856, and then divided among each county's delegates.

50. Gainesville *Independent*, January 21, 1860. On the fight over the choice of a presiding officer, see Sutton S. Scott, "Recollections of the Alabama Democratic State Convention of 1860," *Transactions of the Alabama Historical Society*, IV (1899–1903), 318–20.

against Stallworth had carried over into local politics in Mobile. Shepard's supporters had nominated a slate of legislative candidates headed by Henry F. Drummond to oppose the official candidates. When the county convention to elect delegates to the state convention subsequently met, this dissident group seized control and chose a southern rights delegation, including both Shepard and Drummond. Later a meeting of regulars selected a group to contest the seats of the fire-eaters.

The regular delegation argued that the Shepard men had demonstrated themselves not to be Democrats by having opposed the ticket. But the credentials committee was dominated by Yanceyites who, of course, were desperately eager to encourage the purists to become active in party affairs. In its report, therefore, the committee argued "that the door of the Democratic party should be always kept open for those who may desire to join the party; those who admit the principles of the Democratic party, and in good faith attend and participate in a Democratic meeting should be considered and treated as Democrats."[51] It reported in favor of the Shepard group.

When the contest reached the floor of the convention, Winston's leader A. B. Clitherall moved to table the report and seat the regulars. The motion was carried, presumably by a union of Winston and Fitzpatrick men, 295 to 155. The vote proved that if these two groups would work together, they could control the meeting. But of course it was not Winston's aim to strengthen Fitzpatrick. The senator was as much Winston's rival as was Yancey. Winston needed to pursue a course which would distinguish his position from that of both his opponents. He hoped, as the weakest of the three major contenders, to establish himself as an acceptable compromise figure in the eyes of the two other factions. He therefore wished to picture himself as a champion both of party regularity and of southern rights. His presses followed the pattern we have already seen in the Gainesville *Independent*, attacking both Yancey and Fitzpatrick for placing more importance upon settling their personal score than upon preserving the integrity of the Democracy as an institution. His forces thus sought to differentiate themselves from Yancey's by rejecting the claims of the

51. *Proceedings of the Democratic State Convention,* 19.

untrustworthy Shepard delegation. But to have continued cooperation with Fitzpatrick's supporters would have been to deliver control of the party to the senator, something Winston most certainly did not wish to do. Ever since he had left the governorship at the end of 1857, Winston had been making southern rights speeches. His state aid issue had given him considerable popularity, but had not availed against Senator Clay's southern rights issue. Therefore Winston had set out to gain for himself southern rights credentials at least the equivalent of the junior Clay's. The proper moment for Winston's forces to separate themselves from Fitzpatrick's and to establish the supposed affinity of Winston's and Yancey's views came when the convention took up the report of the platform committee.

The factions had been maneuvering to control the composition of the platform from the first day. A motion to have the president appoint the committee was tabled. An effort by Clitherall to postpone writing a platform and appointing presidential electors until after the Charleston convention, and a lengthy statement of southern rights principles offered by a Yanceyite, Robert G. Scott of Monroe, were both sent to the unchosen committee, as were three equally controversial formulations from other factions. Finally the convention voted to have the delegates from each of the seven congressional districts caucus and elect two members to the committee.[52]

It was in the election of these fourteen men that the Yanceyites scored their great triumph of the convention. The committee as it emerged had at least seven Yanceyite members, and the remainder men who could be influenced by the strength and clarity of the Yanceyites' views. The resultant platform was fully a statement of Yancey's position. It reaffirmed the Cincinnati platform, but also endorsed the positive protection planks of the Alabama platforms of 1848 and 1856— in the composition of which Yancey had played a large role. It went on to restate the principles of positive protection and to assert that the Dred Scott decision supported them. Finally, it imposed the unit rule on Alabama's delegates to Charleston, and instructed them "to insist that said Convention shall adopt a platform of principles recognizing distinctly the rights of the South as asserted in the foregoing resolu-

52. *Ibid.*, 7, 9–11, 22–26.

tions; and if the said National Convention shall refuse to adopt, in substance, the propositions embraced in the preceding resolutions prior to nominating candidates, our Delegates to said Convention are hereby positively instructed to withdraw therefrom."

Crawford M. Jackson, one of the Regency's most important figures, who was, as it happened, only six weeks away from his sudden death, led the effort of the Fitzpatrick forces to delete these instructions to the national convention delegates. Jackson sought instead to have the resolution provide that, if the convention failed to endorse positive protection, "our delegates are instructed to co-operate with those from the other slaveholding States by pursuing such course as sound policy, duty to their section and patriotism may suggest"—an "instruction" which was, of course, meaningless. Jackson's motion gave the Winston men the opportunity they desired to distinguish their position from Fitzpatrick's. They joined their opponents on the earlier credentials roll call in voting to table Jackson's substitute, 277 to 153.

The strategy of the Winston forces in this encounter had evidently been preconcerted, and it is possible that they had not expected the platform committee to report quite so strong a statement of the Yanceyite position. At any rate there are hints of some last-minute confusion in the Winston camp. During the voting upon the platform, A. B. Clitherall asked, but failed to obtain, a reconsideration of the vote rejecting Jackson's alternative resolution. And a month after the convention, after time for reflection, the Gainesville *Independent* reluctantly admitted,

The Platform is unwise, impolitic and absolutely suicidal. It is obviously the progeny of some disunionist *per se*, and one link of the intended project for "precipitating the Southern States into a revolution."

[The delegates] are sent to Charleston gagged, manacled and hampered. . . . That the Alabama delegation will have to withdraw, we consider indisputable. There is small ground to hope that the demand for a new plank in the national platform will be conceded. . . . While we have an abstract right to congressional protection, the assertion of the right ought to be determined by a fair comparison of its advantages and disadvantages. If no practical good is to result from it, it is foolish and wicked to stake the union and safety of the South on the assertion of the right.

Though Winston may have been coming to the realization that his strategy had been less successful at Montgomery than he would have wished, he nevertheless did not abandon the strategy. His maneuvers at Charleston were directed towards the delineation of the same medial position.[53]

Before turning to the Alabamians at Charleston, we should perhaps consider the *Independent*'s charge that the state platform was "obviously the progeny of some disunionist *per se.*" Yancey had indeed proclaimed in 1858 his desire to "precipitate the cotton States into a revolution." As the senatorial election of 1859 approached, he ceased making such statements openly. But, whether he stated it or not, disunion had been Yancey's most cherished dream for the preceding decade. Nor did the fire-eaters hesitate to confess, at least privately, that many of their actions were intended to facilitate secession. When the legislature was considering mandating a convention in case a Republican were to win the presidency, for instance, Edward C. Bullock confessed himself disgusted with such ploys, "but we can't get out of the Union without a convention, and nobody could call that but the legislature. It seemed an inevitable necessity if we are to go out on the election of a Black Republican President."

To understand such assertions correctly, however, we must remember two points. First, Yancey had since 1850 believed that if the South were ever to secede, it would do so in response to some direct action by the North. He and his associates viewed their role as one of constantly insuring that the southern states were ready to respond to any such action quickly, before tempers could cool and the political mechanism could compromise away the issue. Such had been Yancey's advice to the Cahaba Southern Rights Association in 1851, and it had remained his guiding principle in succeeding years. Thus, Bullock desired Alabama to be prepared for Lincoln's election, but it was perfectly possible that the event might never materialize. Two years before, the legislature had issued a flat threat of secession if Kansas were admitted under a constitution other than Lecompton. At that time Bullock had reported enthusiastically that the action had been supported with "perfect unanimity in the General Assembly. The Resolutions were the work of a joint committee of both Houses, representing every section and every phase of Alabama politics, and certainly to all ap-

---

53. *Ibid.*, 27–34; Gainesville *Independent*, February 11, 1860.

pearances not only their heads but their hearts were thoroughly enlisted." However well prepared the fire-eaters had been, though, their hopes had gone aglimmering because the Congress had refused to supply the necessary external act. There was no real reason to believe that they would be able to do better this year.

This observation leads us to the second caveat about the fire-eaters' attitude. Though they might pray for some sudden gratuitous aid, they did not genuinely look for it at any given moment. Many opportunities had presented themselves during the preceding decade for demonstrating in irrefutable terms that the sections were social antipodes, that history had declared their differences irreconcilable. But on each such occasion the political process had intervened to compromise or conceal the points at issue. From bitter experience, therefore, the fire-eaters had lost much of their sense that the final crisis was imminent. Again Senator Bullock's words provide us with a portrait of the fire-eaters' mood. "The contest for Speaker [of the national House] is looked to with intense interest," he wrote to a friend in Washington.

The universal feeling is one of hope that there will be no election and that the Government will thus demonstrate itself to be a failure and find an end. It is the concurrent testimony of all men that the disunion sentiment never was half so deep. Everybody would be relieved to hear that some sudden collision and bloodshed in the House had precipitated the catastrophe. The Gordian Knot which had successfully resisted ten thousand ingenious efforts to untie it, yielded to a single blow of the sword. It may be that an accident will dissolve the hateful tie that wisdom and patriotism have labored in vain to sever.[54]

This notion that the political structure of the republic was a vast Gordian knot, endlessly, almost supernaturally capable of repelling the plans laid against it, had virtually permeated the fire-eater faction. They stood ready to capitalize on the arrival of any Alexander—even so unlikely an Alexander as a gangly lawyer from Springfield, Illinois. But in their hearts they feared that the stars had not yet foretold the birth of such a leader. Thus Yancey was far from expecting that he would be able to destroy the Democracy in 1860, or even from desiring to do so. He was ready for secession whenever events delivered it. But unless the fates were extraordinarily kind, he expected that he

54. Edward C. Bullock to Clement Claiborne Clay, December 30, 1859, Bullock to Clay, March 9, 1858, both in Clay Papers.

would have to arrange many more demonstrations of his contention that southern inequality was an inherent feature of the American nation. It would aid him in doing so if the Democracy would commit itself to the achievement of southern equality; then southerners could observe how long northerners would adhere to it. And the affirmation of the principle of positive protection would represent a first small step towards such a commitment. Yancey was seeking precisely what he claimed: not to destroy the party but to remake it into a tool for effecting southern rights proposals.

In that limited sense, at least, the *Independent*'s assertion that the state platform was the "progeny of some disunionist *per se*" is rather misleading. Yancey was certainly a disunionist, of course, and he no doubt regarded the resolutions as marking progress towards that goal. But he would not have shared the *Independent*'s confident declaration, "That the Alabama delegation will have to withdraw [from the convention], we consider indisputable." The precise wording of the resolution of instruction is essential to this point. The delegates were required to withdraw if the convention failed to approve positive protection "in substance." The standard left considerable room for negotiation, particularly when we recall that in 1856 Yancey had brought himself to regard the Cincinnati Platform as an endorsement of positive protection. Of course, the fact that his interpretation of that document had by no means been universally shared, made him desire more explicit language in its successor. Still, Yancey did not think himself quite so "gagged, manacled and hampered" as the *Independent* thought. Rather, he expected through firm insistence coupled with moderate private concession, to return with a formulation which would impress the fire-eaters on his left.

The state platform was, then, not an effort to achieve disunion at once—something that in Yanceyite doctrine could only come by the action of adventitious events—but was an effort to prepare the citizenry for disunion in the future. The 1858 letter to which the *Independent* had alluded, in fact, had actually been an explicit statement of Yancey's rather special form of party loyalty, as we have come to understand it.

If the Democracy were overthrown, it would result in giving place to a greater and hungrier swarm of flies. The remedy of the South is not in such a process.

It is in a diligent organization of her true men for prompt resistance to the next aggression. It must come, in the nature of things. No national party can save us; no sectional party can do it. But if we could do as our fathers did, organize Committees of Safety all over the cotton States (and it is only in them [the cotton states] that we can hope for an effective movement), we shall fire the Southern heart—instruct the Southern mind—give courage to each other, and at the proper moment, by one organized, concerted action, we can precipitate the cotton States into a revolution.[55]

Yancey's plans for the Charleston convention were thrown awry by his old antagonist from the convention of 1848, John A. Winston. The majority of the platform committee reported clarifications of the Cincinnati Platform which were acceptable to Yancey, but it quickly became apparent that the supporters of Senator Douglas were determined to reject the report. Yancey already regarded the majority report as something of a compromise. Still, his attitude was not at all adamant. Even on Sunday night, after the convention had substituted the minority platform, Yancey, we are told, met with Richard Taylor, the future general, Senators Slidell, Bayard, and Bright, and perhaps other leaders, evidently to work out a compromise. In order for these negotiations to succeed, however, it was necessary that the Alabama delegation not withdraw from the convention on Monday, as they were expected to do. Once the delegation had withdrawn, of course, Yancey would have thereby been committed publicly, and a subsequent quiet compromise would become impossible. It could be too easily made to appear a surrender. Therefore Yancey, the story continues, undertook early on Monday to persuade his colleagues to remain in their seats, at least for the time being.

Winston's strategy turned upon painting Yancey as dangerously disloyal to the party. Even though he opposed the instructions in the state platform, the former governor was consequently determined "to force those who had brought the trouble from Alabama to stand by their work." If Winston could compel the delegation to bolt, the event would have the dual effect of making Yancey appear to have disrupted the Democracy, and of portraying Winston as a calm leader whose devotion to southern rights and faithful obedience to party instruc-

55. William L. Yancey to James S. Slaughter, June 15, 1858, quoted in Dubose, *Yancey*, I, 376; see also Yancey's speeches urging the organization of the League of United Southerners, in Montgomery *Advertiser*, July 21, July 28, 1858.

tions had obliged him to acquiesce in the demands of a crisis forced upon him by his reckless opponent. Winston and his supporters in the delegation therefore are said to have insisted that Alabama withdraw. Winston's actions thereafter are consistent with this tactic. He walked out of the convention of bolters a few days later on the grounds that, by adopting the original convention's majority report on platform, the southern delegates—without the excuse, now, of a necessity to compromise—had failed to state the full and unqualified southern case, and thus revealed themselves to be no true advocates of southern rights. Returning to Alabama, he made speeches at Montgomery and Mobile, charging Yancey with having pursued in Charleston a calculated and malignant scheme to destroy the party and force the election of a Republican. Very probably Winston intended by this seemingly contradictory course to emphasize again his complementary contentions that he was, as Democratic orthodoxy required, devoted equally to southern rights and to party regularity—and further that his opponents had not managed, as had he, to unite these principles effectively.

An additional group of dedicated partisans of Senator Douglas in the delegation apparently cooperated with Winston's supporters, under the impression that the withdrawal of the southerners would make it easier for Douglas to obtain the necessary two-thirds vote. At this point in the proceedings, the Douglas camp believed that the rule required two-thirds of the delegates present and voting for a nomination, and in fact protested vehemently when the president, Caleb Cushing, decided that they were obliged to obtain two-thirds of the whole number. It is unclear whether or not the Alabamians who followed Winston's example in proclaiming an unalterable intention to withdraw constituted a majority of the delegation. But it was not really requisite that they be so many. If any substantial bloc, including in their ranks one of Yancey's principal rivals for party leadership, did bolt, Yancy could not remain. To do so would have destroyed forever his credibility with the already dubious left fire-eaters. He would have marked himself in their eyes as a man corrupted into the betrayal of his convictions by the blandishments of power. The competition in which Yancey was so deeply involved, to gain control of the Alabama Democracy, therefore, compelled the defeat of Yancey's first effort to build an acceptable platform—a platform which he needed precisely in order to further his struggle to control the Alabama Democracy.[56]

After the bolt, Yancey's guiding principle was to achieve southern Democratic unity since, according to his theory of agitation, the northern wing of the party would immediately yield to any firm southern demand rather than risk the loss of southern votes. He favored a southern presidential nomination—first by the convention of bolters at Charleston, and later by the Richmond convention—under the impression that the other Democratic convention would thereupon endorse whomever the southerners chose. The tactic would, he told the state convention in early June, "meet and crush out one of the great evils of the day—a belief in the minds of the people of the North at large and of the national Democracy in the North, that the South is not in earnest. . . . It would bring the whole country to face the principle upon which such nomination would be based, and to give an honest solution of the difficulties surrounding us." Moreover, it would "address itself to the fears and selfishness" of the politicians, who placed victory and patronage above principle.

But because it was necessary that whatever action the South took be a united one if the national party were to be forced to acquiesce, Yancey never at any time insisted on his preference for a separate nomination. At Charleston he readily yielded to the contrary advice of the "timid and perhaps wise men in our councils." And when Mississippi and Louisiana determined to accredit their delegates to both Richmond and Baltimore, it was Yancey who personally induced the Alabama convention—over the determined opposition of the radicals from the eastern Black Belt—to follow the same course. The particular

56. The sources for this story are not beyond impeachment. It rests fundamentally on an account in Richard Taylor's memoirs, *Destruction and Reconstruction: Personal Experiences of the Late War* (New York: D. Appleton and Co., 1879), 11–12, embroidered a bit in Dubose, *Yancey*, II, 466–67, 472–75, and in Glenn N. Sisk, "John Anthony Winston: Alabama's Veto Governor" (M.A. thesis, University of Alabama, 1934), 43–48. Austin L. Venable added some additional evidence in support of its validity in his "The Conflict Between the Douglas and Yancey Forces in the Charleston Convention," *Journal of Southern History*, VIII (1942), 226–41, from which comes the contention that Douglas' search for a two-thirds majority played a role in the episode. The story's appearance in Dubose also lends it strength, since Yancey's younger brother Benjamin collaborated closely with Dubose in the preparation of the biography. See also Winston's speech in Huntsville *Southern Advocate*, September 19, 1860, and Yancey's speech at Memphis on August 14, 1860, in Montgomery *Advertiser*, Extra (bound after September 19, 1860). In the last analysis, however, I am led to accept the account because it seems to me so completely consistent with what I believe to have been the strategies of both Yancey and Winston throughout 1859 and 1860.

strategy was of secondary importance; his real aim, he told the convention, was "to preserve the unity of the Cotton States, in order to force and thus preserve a unity of the National Democratic party upon principle."[57]

Yancey left for Maryland in considerable confidence. He believed that he could already detect the beginnings of the surrender by the northern Democrats which he had predicted.[58] But the Yanceyites' seats were contested by a group of the orator's opponents, led by the voice of the Regency, John J. Seibels, and one of the state's most prominent supporters of Douglas, John Forsyth. There is very little doubt that Yancey's was the true delegation. It had been chosen by a convention regularly summoned by the state executive committee in compliance with the resolutions of the January gathering. The Seibels-Forsyth group was the product of a self-constituted body with no legitimate standing.

The contesting delegates did not make much of an effort to establish the legality of their claims, though they did assert that since the state executive committee had been appointed after the January convention had adjourned, it was therefore improperly constituted and could not summon a new meeting. The true case for the contestants, however, rested upon the fact that they were for the most part Douglas supporters, and that they would make no trouble about the platform. The bulk of their statement to the convention was an attack upon Yancey, whom they pictured as a man consciously endeavoring to destroy the party and thus produce secession. On this point Yancey was peculiarly vulnerable. He found it virtually impossible to explain to persons outside the fire-eater movement how he could be a disunionist and yet not really a disunionist—that he expected an inevitable northern aggression, on the basis of which he expected to force secession, but that in the meantime, he genuinely sought the preservation and reform of the Democratic party. Not only did he fail to convince many northern Democrats of what they could only regard as a trivial and almost meaningless distinction; he also failed to satisfy politicians

57. Greenville *South Alabamian*, June 16, 1860; William L. Yancey to Clement Claiborne Clay, May 4, 1860, in Clay Papers.
58. See the statement of the Yanceyite Alabama delegation to the Baltimore Convention, quoted in Dubose, *Yancey*, II, 477–78.

from his own state who were not attuned to the fine gradations in the fire-eaters' doctrinal disputes. Thus Seibels and Forsyth were no doubt sincere in regarding Yancey's actions as a part of a secessionist conspiracy. These fears and Senator Douglas' ambitions led the convention to reject the Yancey delegation in deference to the highly questionable credentials of its rival.

The decision was so clearly dictated by the exigencies of the political situation rather than by the evidence of the case that it shocked not only many southerners but also a great number of anti-Douglas northerners. It is too seldom emphasized that the Baltimore convention's decisions in the Alabama and Louisiana contests led to the withdrawal of a considerable number of northeastern delegates, including among others the convention's president Caleb Cushing. These men had believed along with Yancey that the demonstrated sensitivity of the southerners upon the platform, coupled with the evident willingness of Yancey to reach an accommodation, would lead the Douglas forces to adopt a somewhat more tractable position. But in the credentials votes the Douglas delegates offered only intransigence, founded presumably in an insuperable distrust of Yancey's motives. It is of course entirely possible that, had the Yancey delegates been seated, the convention could have failed to produce an acceptable platform, in which case the Alabamians might well have staged their second withdrawal. However, it would have so advanced Yancey's political interests to be able to claim that he had coerced concessions—even moderate ones—from the national party, that one may be forgiven for thinking it likely that a serviceable formulation would have emerged. Yancey would thereby have won a great victory for his theory of agitation. Whether Douglas' presidential hopes could have survived in the process is an open question. The motives which led Douglas' managers to reject Yancey—and thus also the effort to save the party as a national institution which his seating would have permitted—we may certainly regard with sympathy. But neither the senator nor his managers may escape their considerable immediate responsibility for the final disruption which resulted.

The seating of the Seibels-Forsyth delegation must have struck the Yanceyites with the force of a bolt of lightning. The action was inconsistent with Yancey's most fundamental assumption about the nature of the party. When politicians were faced with a determined group which had a clear idea of what it wanted and a substantial bloc of votes at its command, in theory the politicians always surrendered. This notion had been formed on the basis of experiences with the state party. There areas of disagreement, though enormously important, were seldom so broad as to preclude yielding, even if reluctantly. But when this form of agitation was transferred to the national level, the gulf separating the contending factions widened proportionately. The northwesterners argued with conviction that if they accepted Yancey's phraseology they would destroy their own state parties. Of course it would profit them little to gain the votes which Yancey offered if they would thereby lose a corresponding number of votes at home. Yancey was consequently deprived of the leverage upon which his success depended. He had always believed that the sections were very far apart. Now he had discovered in a most forceful way that the process of separation had proceeded even further than he had imagined—so far that it had artificially supplied at least some politicians with a physical feature which they congenitally lacked, the backbone.

This discovery left Yancey even more favorably disposed to the candidacy of Vice-President Breckinridge. The orator had long maintained that the South's only hope of achieving equality within the Union was to commit the Democratic party to that goal, and then to have northern Democrats retain their loyalty to the party. He did not believe that the northern Democracy was in fact prepared to accept true southern equality, of course. He believed rather that if the party ever made such a commitment, northern Democrats would renounce their allegiance. He therefore deduced that the South had no hope of achieving equality in the Union. But he held these beliefs without their having been conclusively tested. If circumstances should ever produce an empirical trial of northern sentiment, and if, contrary to his expectations, he found the northern Democracy generally favorable to the principles of southern equality, he would then be compelled to admit that the South had a substantial basis for attempting again to make her northern marriage work. Yancey's discovery at Baltimore that the assertion of southern equality, even to the modest extent that it had proceeded thus far, had driven the politicians of the Northwest completely to suppress their natural inclination to compromise, reinforced all of his doubts about the northern Democracy and led him to think that the moment was opportune to verify his hypothesis. Since Breckinridge's candidacy would have a somewhat southern cast to it, Yancey hoped that it would largely settle the question of how many northerners were genuinely favorable to the South's rights. If Breckinridge's poll in the North were small, Yancey would offer the figures as a demonstration of just how precarious was the South's position in the Union.

It is essential to note, however, that Yancey never ceased to wish that he might be pleasantly surprised at the election's result. He reacted to charges that his support of the vice-president was part of a design to compel disunion with startled surprise and indignation. The allegation was, he said, "an infamous calumny."[59] His surprise is understandable. From his perspective, the vote for Breckinridge was not only not a vote for disunion, but was the final test of whether or not union was possible. Nor was Yancey, by his own omissions, tending to bias the results of his experiment against the Union. On the contrary, he undertook an exhausting tour of the northern states in behalf of the vice-president's claims. He spent much of the fall of 1860 on this tour, speaking daily and sometimes twice or three times a day, until his voice and his health were badly strained; he did not finally return to Montgomery until election eve. The tour was a triumph. He spoke to large crowds in New York, Boston, Rochester, Cincinnati, and many lesser northern cities, and drew admiring remarks even from the Republican press. When the vote was taken, Yancey could rest assured that he had done all he was able for Breckinridge.

The Voters in Crisis

At the Secession Convention some months later, Yancey told the delegates, "The people have had this question of secession before them for a long time and have maturely considered it in two late elections, namely: those for Electors of President, and for delegates to this body. The issue was as distinctly made in one as in the other, and in both

59. William L. Yancey to Beverley Matthews, August 6, 1860, in William L. Yancey Papers, Alabama Department of Archives and History, Montgomery.

they decided the issue in favor of secession." [60] It is a misinterpretation of this remark, however, to believe that Yancey was here conceding that Breckinridge's candidacy had been a stalking horse for secession. To understand Yancey's contention properly, we must leave the rotund orator on his northern tour and return to glance at the canvass in Alabama.

Lincoln offered no electoral ticket in the state, but the virtues of each of the other three candidates found their vigorous expositors, both on the stump and in the press. Douglas could claim, among others, three of the state's most important newspapers, Forsyth's Mobile *Register*, Seibels' Montgomery *Confederation*, and William B. Figures' Huntsville *Southern Advocate*, traditionally a Whig organ. In addition, Governor Winston's faction generally rallied to the Little Giant. Bell received the backing of most of the former Whig leaders, prominently including Henry W. Hilliard—who offered his support despite the fact that he had become a Democrat in 1857 and had been a member of the Alabama delegation which had unseated the Yanceyites at the Baltimore Douglas convention—Thomas Hill Watts, Ripley Davis, and James H. Clanton. Breckinridge received the endorsement not merely of the Yanceyites but of most Democratic papers and politicians. We are told that fifty-five papers supported the vice-president, sixteen urged the cause of Bell, and thirteen were for Douglas. [61] Moreover, the vice-president's forces had two rather surprising sources of strength. Though a portion of the Regency backed Douglas, Senator Fitzpatrick and his closest associates, including Bolling Hall, grudgingly endorsed Breckinridge. And the Breckinridge camp also received the support of Johnson J. Hooper and the most consistent advocates of the Whiggery's extremist southern rights tactic.

The Hooperites in the Montgomery area held a convention at the beginning of July, and Watts sought to convince them to accept Bell. When he failed, he and those delegates sympathetic to him walked out. But Hooper's cohorts were not at first very happy about coalescing with the Constitutional Democracy. They were convinced that if Douglas should win, the Breckinridge men would troop tamely back

---

60. Smith, *Debates of the Convention of 1861*, 140.
61. Sisk, "Winston," 48.

into the national party. Hooper, Judge, and their allies of course desired to see a permanent wedge driven between the two Democratic
factions, as a step towards the formation of a sectional southern rights
party which would continue agitation into future years. In the late
summer, however, these Whigs accepted integration into the Breckinridge campaign machinery. They really had nowhere else to go.[62]

Senator Fitzpatrick's choices were similarly restricted. He bitterly
lamented that, "The great Democratic party, almost the last ligament
that bound the Union together . . . has been rent asunder by this Territorial question which has been so unfortunately and needlessly
forced upon it." But however deplorable he might believe this situation, he had to face it as a fact. "Having to make a choice between [the
candidates], I shall support that one who most nearly approaches my
principles, and promises equality of rights to all the country."[63] Southern rights had long since become party orthodoxy, of course, and
Fitzpatrick was firmly on record in favor of positive protection. When
he was forced to choose between two good Democrats, one of whom
accepted positive protection and one of whom explicitly rejected it, he
actually had only one possibility unless he was willing to make his
earlier position seem insincere.

But Fitzpatrick could and did rail at the turn of events which had
put him in this predicament. To have any hope of salvaging his political influence, Fitzpatrick had now to stand up to the beliefs he had
claimed to hold, by endorsing Breckinridge. Yet when the bulk of the
party establishment, including Fitzpatrick, wheeled into line behind
the vice-president, it thereby unavoidably elevated Yancey to the status
of party spokesman, and enormously aided Yancey's campaign to displace Fitzpatrick at the head of the state's Democracy. Fitzpatrick
seemed to be following the party line only reluctantly, while Yancey
seemed to be its most prominent and vigorous exponent. Moreover,
Yancey's northern tour placed him almost beyond criticism; he became
a popular hero. Unflinchingly bearding the arrogant Yankees in their
foul lair, uncompromisingly hurling the justice of the southern cause in

62. Charles W. Bell, "Montgomery and the Presidential Election of 1860" (M.A. thesis,
University of Alabama, 1967), 74–79; Greenville *South Alabamian*, June 23, July 7, July 14,
1860.

63. Montgomery *Confederation*, August 8, 1860; cf. Montgomery *Mail*, July 26, 1860
(both clippings in the Benjamin Fitzpatrick Papers).

the faces of his self-righteous opponents, Yancey became in the fall of 1860 a sort of oratorical Preston Brooks—the voice of an aggrieved section, saying to the North what all southerners longed to say. When Yancey, returning to Montgomery at the beginning of November, passed through New Orleans, he was greeted by a wildly enthusiastic crowd reported as twenty thousand, chanting his name. When he reached his home, fully half the citizenry of the little town turned out to meet him; bands played and bonfires were lighted in the streets.[64] Clearly the events surrounding Breckinridge's candidacy had given Yancey a boost towards political leadership in Alabama.

Faced with these events, Fitzpatrick and politicians like him quite naturally came to the rueful conclusion that Yancey must have planned it all—that he was a master tactician who had maneuvered the conservative forces into an inescapable cul-de-sac. In fact, however, Yancey's mind was very possibly the least tactical in its orientation of any of his contemporaries. Such strategy as he employed derived almost wholly from an unshakable faith that history was on his side, so that he could afford to wait, coupled with a dogged devotion to his own only partially correct reading of how the abolitionists had come to have influence with the major parties—by working within the party machinery, guiding prospective candidates to a correct position through awarding or withholding the support of a coherent bloc of votes. Of course Yancey had long desired to force the conservatives into the position of having to live up to their oratorical pronouncements, for he felt that their words would then be revealed as sounding brass. But when the conservatives actually were placed in the trap, Yancey was no more responsible for the turn of events than were they. In the unfolding drama, the role of each actor was essential to the denouement.

Having thus defined the opposing forces in the campaign, we may turn to the canvass itself. The principal issue in the election at the national level was the extension of slavery into the western territories. But in Alabama that question was never very clearly posed, because all three parties agreed that southerners should have the right to take their hard-earned possessions with them when they moved to a new home.

64. Montgomery *Advertiser*, November 7, November 14, 1860.

Southerners, like other Americans, wished to create on the frontier a democratic and egalitarian society, in which no man need be dependent on another man for his welfare. They also, quite inconsistently, desired a mobile society, in which settlers could hope to accumulate property, and thus to achieve the status of those men whom they had envied in the older states. For southerners, however, both the acknowledged ideals of democracy and equality, and the more covert dream of status, were bound up with slavery.

Senator Douglas' followers embraced popular sovereignty precisely on the grounds that, given the condition of the country, popular sovereignty was the only practical method by which new slave states might be created. Campaigners both for the vice-president and for Senator Bell replied that slavery, like any other form of property, could not exist without protection from lawless elements in the community. If the federal government was willing to suppress cattle rustling on the frontier, for instance, but was not willing to suppress the stealing of slaves there, it would clearly have favored owners of one sort of property over owners of another—and by implication, have pronounced southerners to be second-class citizens.

Bell's partisans were not any the less strident than were Breckinridge's in demanding positive protection. The Bell state convention, held in Selma in late June, adopted a platform so militant that a Breckinridge paper called it an effort to "appropriate Democratic thunder." But the paper quickly added that since neither Bell nor Everett would endorse the Selma resolutions, "they of course mean simply nothing."[65] In sum, then, the only question in relation to the extension of slavery which was canvassed in Alabama was which of the three parties was the most realistic advocate of the position.

The actual issue of the election in the state was secession, and on it the parties were genuinely divided. At first glance the division is obscured by a "red herring" formulation of the question. The Bell and the Douglas men spent much of the campaign expounding upon the allegation that the Breckinridge leadership was engaged in a conspiracy to force secession on the state—a charge which the Breckinridge men denied with shrill indignation and at interminable length. But

65. Greenville *South Alabamian*, July 7, 1860. The platform is in the *Pickens Republican* (Carrollton), July 12, 1860.

through the smoke of this debate, there quickly appeared a real difference. The Breckinridge speakers repeatedly proclaimed that, though existing wrongs were not adequate to justify secession, the election of Lincoln would be sufficient cause. Over and over they challenged Bell and Douglas spokesmen on this point. And just as often Bell and Douglas men refused to admit it.

Douglas campaigners stated that if northerners were all Republicans, the contention might be true. But as long as millions of voters in the section were for Douglas, they said, then the elevation of a Republican would be the fault not of northern enmity, but of southern extremists' maneuvers. Bell speakers tried frantically to avoid the issue, using the stock response that they would abide by the will of the voters if the question ever arose. But when pressed, Bell men generally confessed the personal belief that the mere victory of Lincoln, without any accompanying overtly hostile act, would not justify withdrawal.[66]

Subsequent events—Lincoln's startlingly large margin of election in the northern states, and the triumph of immediatism in December—allowed those Douglas and Bell men who wished to do so easily to reconcile their earlier positions with a later acceptance of secession. But during the canvass the difference between the clear and uncomplicated statements of the Breckinridge men on the issue and the hesitant and negative replies of the Bell and Douglas supporters was unmistakable.[67] And upon this confrontation, fundamentally, the election went to the voters. It was to this fact that Yancey was referring when he called the contest a referendum on secession. He meant that, since a vote for Breckinridge was presumably a vote in support of the posi-

66. *E.g.*, Montgomery *Advertiser*, June 27, August 22, August 29, September 5, September 12, September 19, September 26, October 3, October 10, October 17, 1860; Greenville *South Alabamian*, November 17, 1860; *Alabama Reporter* (Talladega), August 30, October 4, October 25, 1860; Greenville *Southern Messenger*, July 18, October 17, 1860; Huntsville *Southern Advocate*, September 19, October 3, October 17, October 24, November 7, 1860; *Pickens Republican* (Carrollton), August 30, September 6, September 27, 1860.

67. Durward Long, "Political Parties and Propaganda in Alabama in the Presidential Election of 1860," *Alabama Historical Quarterly*, XXV (1963), 120–35, appears, however, to have mistaken it. It is true, of course, that individual campaigners sometimes differed from the mass of their confreres on this question. Bell supporter Thomas H. Watts, for instance—in an effort to remain consistent with his public statements made before his break with the Hooperites—did proclaim the election of Lincoln a sufficient cause for secession. But we must not miss the forest for the trees. The fact remains that there are very few exceptions to the generalizations offered in the text.

tions taken by Breckinridge's proponents, therefore the vice-president's poll represented, not a vote for disunion *per se* but an affirmation that the victory of a Republican was grounds for the adoption of such a course.

We should note a caveat to Yancey's contention. To some indeterminate extent, the Breckinridge total may have represented simple party loyalty. The vice-president did, after all, command the backing of most of the state's established Democratic leaders, and the fact could hardly have been without its impact on the party's rank and file. But the presence of Douglas in the canvass tempers the force of this observation considerably. Douglas' organization included a number of very prominent Democrats. Moreover, as we shall discover, the Little Giant actually received quite significant support in some of the state's most heavily Democratic counties. We may thus reasonably assume that there was no strong force repelling straight-ticket regulars from the senator. If, therefore, such voters rejected the position assumed by the Breckinridge campaigners, they did possess a real alternative short of Whiggery.

Even allowing for the factor of party loyalty, however, there is a very good reason for viewing the poll in precisely Yancey's light: the opposition did so and, on the basis of the November balloting, decided in the campaign for delegates to the Secession Convention not to deny the existence of a sufficient cause for disunion. Breckinridge had received 54 percent of the total, beating both of his opponents together by no less than 7,200 votes. Moreover, Breckinridge appears to have defeated Douglas within the Democracy by almost three to one.[68]

As soon as this result became known, the Montgomery *Post*, the state's leading organ for Bell's cause, declared that, though the method of secession—whether by cooperative or separate state action—was still open, the election of Lincoln had settled the necessity for some form of secession. It was true, the *Post* said, that in the late campaign, "Personal feeling, flowing out of party feeling, has been engendered; but now that safety and security to Southern rights and institutions

68. This figure was determined by accepting as roughly accurate Governor Moore's estimate of the number of Whigs who would vote for Breckinridge (Andrew B. Moore to E. Young Fair, October 3, 1860, in E. Young Fair Papers, Alabama Department of Archives and History, Montgomery) and therefore deducting 10,000 from the vice-president's total.

seems to exist [only] in the formation of a Government suited to the necessities of the Southern people, we should consent at once to lay aside previous party predilections and personal animosity, and as brethren prompted by patriotic motives, prepare to maintain the rights and institutions of our section."

And at the same time, the Montgomery *Confederation*, voice of the conservative Democracy, commented, "The issue—though we regretted it—was made this summer that the election of Lincoln was a good cause for secession. The Black Republicans knew this. They were told so by our friends [Douglas supporters] who were battling throughout the North for the rights of our section. The issue, we may say again, has been made and we must stand up to it. We shall and must resist Lincoln." [69] Throughout the weeks leading up to the election of the Secession Convention on Christmas Eve, as we shall show in due course, the cooperationists maintained this attitude. The question, they said, was the mechanism to be used, rather than the goals to be sought.

There is, however, one other objection—in addition to the argument of party loyalty—which might be raised to the belief that the Breckinridge poll represented agreement that Lincoln's election would justify withdrawal. It might be argued that the issue had been prejudged by the legislature when, a year earlier, it had passed resolutions which ordered the summoning of a secession convention in exactly that eventuality; and that many voters might therefore have regarded the matter as already settled. There are two answers to such an argument.

In the first place, even though the resolutions were passed unanimously in the Senate, and with only two negative votes in the House, they did not in fact express the judgment of the legislature upon the adequacy of a Republican's election as a cause for disunion. In fact, the moderates in the legislature regarded the resolutions as something of a victory for their cause. When the resolutions were first offered, the moderates were prepared to oppose them. As it happened, however, the legislature of South Carolina had made a formal request that each

69. Montgomery *Post*, November 14, 1860; Montgomery *Confederation*, quoted in Durward Long, "Unanimity and Disloyalty in Secessionist Alabama," *Civil War History*, XI (1965), 261.

of the other slave states appoint delegates to a southern consultative assembly; and Governor Moore, a moderate Southern Rights man who had spent most of his term attempting to avoid the issue, had fallen under intense pressure from the fire-eaters to recommend that Alabama accede to the proposal. The governor, terrified at the thought of taking so unequivocal a stand, hit upon the pending secession convention resolutions as a device for postponing decisive action on South Carolina's request.

He transmitted the request to the legislature along with a message declaring that South Carolina desired the southern assembly in order to consult upon "secession from the Union," and adding, "To call a convention with this view at this time is in my opinion, premature." Instead, he urged the adoption of the resolutions for the contingent summoning of a state secession convention, for then, "if [a Republican victory] does not occur, there will be no necessity for a convention." The fire-eaters apparently evinced a willingness to accept this compromise; the opponents of the resolutions therefore withdrew their objections and the resolutions passed. Moore then happily employed this action, in a letter to Governor Gist of South Carolina, as a plausible excuse for his decision to disregard South Carolina's proposal.[70]

It might appear with hindsight that the moderates had by this ploy only put off for a few brief months the day when they would have to take a stand. But hindsight, particularly when applied to the months just before some great event, may often be misleading. We find it hard to accept that people could have been ignorant of the approaching cataclysm. But the republic had muddled through crisis after crisis during the preceding decade, and many observers thought that the danger in 1860 was no more imminent than before. At the beginning of that fateful year, it was still possible that the Charleston convention would find an acceptable formula for the platform and choose an inoffensive personality for president—in which case observers generally felt that

---

70. *House Journal*, Sess. of 1859–60, pp. 230–31, 474; *Senate Journal*, Sess. of 1859–1860, p. 127; Edward C. Bullock to Clement Claiborne Clay, December 30, 1859, in Clay Papers; Andrew B. Moore to William H. Gist, April 2, 1860, in Governors' Correspondence: A. B. Moore. The two dissenters on the passage of the resolutions were Whigs A. Q. Bradley of Perry and Newton L. Whitfield of Tuscaloosa. It seems reasonable that the excitement which followed John Brown's raid also may have contributed to the passage of the resolutions: see the speech of Jeremiah Clemens, in Montgomery *Post*, September 5, 1860.

the Democracy would be returned to power. This outcome was expected by politicians from Fitzpatrick to Yancey.

Moore and his allies in the legislature, therefore, seem to have believed that by providing for a secession convention if a Republican were elected, they had disposed of the agitation for another four years. They had successfully avoided both appearing less than fully committed to southern rights and declaring for disunion—either of which

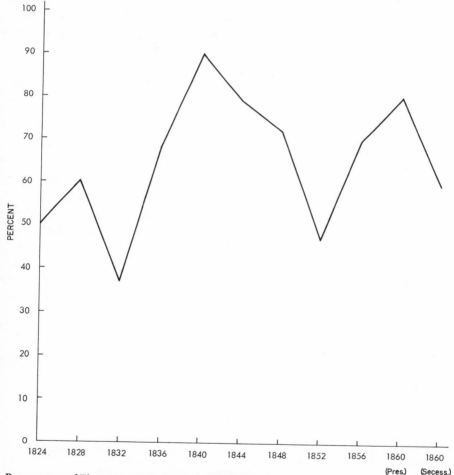

Percentages of Electorate Voting in Presidential Elections, 1824–1860, and in Secession Convention Election

positions would cost votes. Moreover, most fire-eaters rather ruefully agreed that the moderates had executed an adroit maneuver.

The second answer to the contention that the legislature's secession convention resolutions had prejudged the question of withdrawal should Lincoln win turns on the behavior of the voters themselves. Throughout the state's history, the turnout at elections seems to have had a rather direct relation to the importance which the citizens attached to the question being decided. The graph on page 407 shows that the turnout percentage in November, when many voters evidently thought that they were in some sense determining the value of the Union, soared to an enormous 80 percent, a figure exceeded only by the 90 percent turnout achieved in 1840. But in December the percentage fell back to a more normal level—higher than the 1852 turnout but less than that of 1856. Of course, turnout rates normally decline in nonpresidential elections. And much of the decline in this case is attributable to south Alabama, where the November results had led most politicians to abandon opposition to immediatism.[71] But the special circumstances of the December election—including that mass conversion of south Alabama politicians—may well suggest the existence of an additional factor: a feeling in the electorate that the question posed in December was not so far-reaching as that presented in November; that it turned simply upon the mechanics by which the November verdict was to be implemented. The returns from the December canvass, then, really give us only the slightest hint of the opinions of the citizenry on the propriety of the act of secession itself. The alternative of inaction was not offered the voters; the single question which the rival candidates presented was the form which the state's response should take. If, therefore, we wish to know which Alabamians had concluded by 1860 that the election of a Republican would justify resistance, we in fact have only the Breckinridge poll to offer us a substantial clue. The presidential election was certainly no clear referendum on the issue, but it was much more nearly so than was the election for delegates to the convention.

71. Turnout declined precipitously in immediatist counties, from nearly 82 percent to 51 percent. But the decline in cooperationist counties was much more modest, from about 77 percent to about 70 percent. Indeed, four cooperationist counties—Blount, Jefferson, Walker, and Winston—actually had a larger poll in December than in November.

The maps on pages 410, 411, and 412 attempt to identify the areas of strongest support for each of the three presidential candidates by noting those counties in which the candidate received an unusually large percentage of the vote. Bell received a bit less than 31 percent of the vote statewide. By indicating the counties in which he got more than 40 percent, we discover that the basis of his strength was in the non–Black Belt Whig areas—counties bordering the Black Belt on the east, southeast, and northwest, and a number of the southwestern counties whose residents were particularly under the spell of the commercial leaders in Mobile. The counties shown in lighter gray on the map are those in which Bell's percentage was greater than his statewide average, but less than 40 percent. A number of these counties, including those in the lower Tennessee Valley, were thus reflecting about their usual Whig poll. But the Black Belt presents an interesting exception. The belt counties were of course consistently, if fairly closely, Whig. Obviously many of their committed Whig residents did not deviate from this usual allegiance. But the diminution in the ordinary Whig presidential poll throughout much of the belt points to a substantial defection at the heart of Whiggery, even as its satellites were demonstrating that in national elections they maintained an undiminished loyalty. As we have seen, during the summer the Hooperites had entered into alliance with the Breckinridge forces. Whereas this effort seems to have carried along relatively few of the Whig faithful outside the Black Belt, in the belt itself it appears that as much as a quarter to a third of the party's past adherents deserted Bell—a figure which represents some three or four thousand voters.

Douglas received only a trifle more than 15 percent of the poll. If we identify the counties in which he took 30 percent or more of the total, an obvious pattern emerges. He achieved a respectable showing in Mobile, under the whip of the *Register*, and in Autauga and Coosa, where the Seibels wing of the Regency was able to deliver a bloc of votes. But except for these two areas, Douglas' strength was confined to a group of counties in north central Alabama. The group includes a number of the commercial and planting counties of the Tennessee Valley, but it also includes several of the hill counties whose population was composed almost entirely of nonslaveholding small farmers. This latter class, we have traditionally been led to believe, was strongly

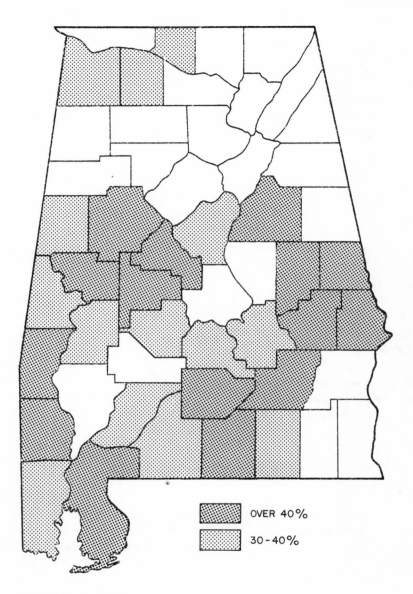

OVER 40%

30-40%

Counties Voting Heavily for John Bell, 1860

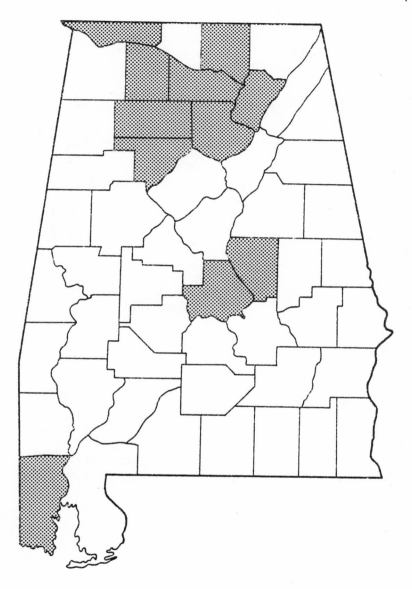

Counties More than 30 Percent for Stephen A. Douglas, 1860

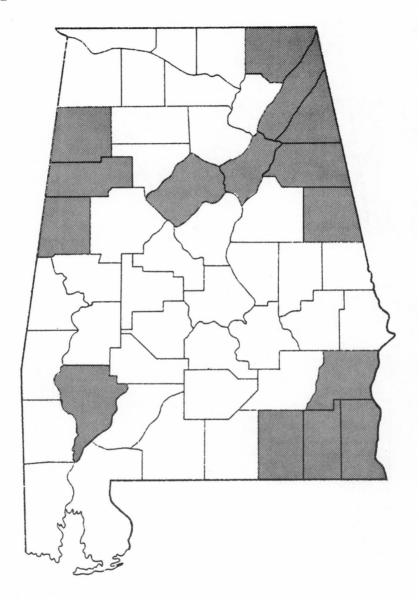

Counties More than 65 Percent for John C. Breckinridge, 1860

unionist in sentiment; and it appears at first blush that the Douglas vote in this area is a confirmation of the tradition. But as we have already remarked, it is possible, and instructive, to view the returns in another light. Rather than confirming the widespread unionism of small farmers, the poll instead offers proof that farmers who were genuinely unionist in outlook could and would sustain Douglas—that there were no real restraints to inhibit voters who agreed with the Little Giant from expressing that approbation with ballots. Since we know that Douglas did in fact do well in some of the hill counties, we may with increased confidence assume that a substantial Breckinridge vote in other hill counties represented authentic support for the vice-president's faction.

Breckinridge received almost exactly 54 percent of the statewide total. If we mark the counties in which he received 65 percent or more of the poll, swamping his two opponents, a clear and startling sectionalism shows itself. Whereas Douglas had been strong in the central hill counties, Breckinridge took the eastern and western counties of that area; his support was greatest in those counties and in the Wiregrass section in the southeast. Thus the vice-president achieved his broadest appeal in distinctly small farm communities. In only three of the fifteen landslide counties—Barbour, Clarke, and Pickens—were slaves a substantial percentage of the population, though a fourth, Henry, was in the process of becoming a plantation area in this period. In the remaining eleven counties which voted most heavily for the Constitutional Democracy, slaves were only some 15 percent of the inhabitants.

These communities were the very ones which were most distressed by the transformations of the fifties, and were most desperately in search of a villain against whom to direct their formless terror and rage. It was here that the supercilious assumptions of superiority by Yankees were most hated and the northern threat to imprison the South in permanent inequality was most feared. The vote in these counties was far more than a mere affirmation of long-established party loyalty. It was, by and large, what both Yancey and his opponents thought it was—an acceptance of the position of Breckinridge's canvassers that the election of Lincoln would be intolerable. And the acceptance of this notion was most forcefully expressed not in those areas which would have the most to lose, in a material sense, from emancipation. The threat was neither primarily material nor was its substance emancipation, except in the long run. The abomination with which the Republicans menaced the South was not freedom, but slavery. So, at least, the orators proclaimed, and in those terrified marginal communities clinging forlornly to the tattered symbols of their independence, so it was believed. Indeed, the danger had long been anticipated; only its source had been in doubt. Thus most of the hill counties and the Wiregrass voted overwhelmingly for Breckinridge, while the commercial and plantation regions complacently gave much of their vote to his opponents—to Douglas in the Tennessee Valley and to Bell in the south. Only the desertion of several thousand southern rights Whigs in the Black Belt warned that anxiety there was beginning to spread beyond the ranks of the fire-eaters.[72]

If, as it appears, approval of resistance to the election of Lincoln was at least as general in small farming as in plantation counties, we must explain what happened in the election of delegates to the convention. We have already noted briefly one of the things which did not happen: north Alabama did not repudiate secession by voting for cooperationists. The cooperationists were not a whit less belligerent than were the immediatists in their attacks on the Republicans.

Senator Fitzpatrick, perhaps the most prominent advocate of the cooperationist position, complained bitterly that "the halls of Congress have rung with the denunciations and invectives heaped on the South, and slavery has been held up as 'the sum of all villainies.'" "The political parties of the country have," he lamented, "been strangled" by the slavery agitation. He proceeded to damn in uncompromising terms "the purely sectional candidates of the Black Republican Party and the revolutionary dogmas advanced by that party in utter disregard of the constitutional rights of the Slaveholding States."

---

72. Durward Long, "Economics and Politics in the 1860 Presidential Elections in Alabama," *Alabama Historical Quarterly*, XXVII (1965), 43–58, attempts to correlate Douglas' strength with growth of crops other than cotton for the market, but the argument does not persuade me. Barney, *The Secessionist Impulse*, 75–76, 98–99, claims that Breckinridge's campaigners in the hill counties were considerably wealthier than Douglas' were, but his evidence on the point is quite thin. At any rate, for our present purposes the central question is not who offered the Breckinridge appeal, but what portion of the state's citizenry was most likely to find it persuasive.

This party heeded not the warning from the South that the election of men professing [such] principles would endanger the Union. . . . What stronger or more conclusive proofs does the South require to satisfy them that Lincoln and Hamlin, when clothed with the powers and resources of the government, will carry out the principles of the party that have elected them? . . . We cannot shut our eyes to the fact that we have attained a most alarming and dangerous crisis. For one, I think it is time this question of slavery should be finally settled. If we cannot live in peace as a nation, let us separate and each section provide for itself.

These sentiments were typical of cooperationist pronouncements during the coming campaign. Nor do they seem to have been feigned. For years northern aspersions upon southern morality—attitudes which had even been elevated to the statute books with the passage of the various state personal liberty laws—had infuriated southerners across the entire political spectrum. The result of the November election had, in very much the same way, struck almost every citizen as a consummate, mortifying indignity. This reaction has its roots in the profound social commitment to the democratic faith.

The Republican standard-bearer was a shadowy figure in the South at best; indeed, a rural Black Belt newspaper informed its readers that the Chicago convention had nominated for president one Gabriel Lincoln. But the absence of a party in the region to advance Lincoln's claims allowed him to sink even further into the background once the canvass had actually begun. He was, in fact, a man whom one could easily forget in the heat of the debates among the partisans of the three "real" candidates. Of course the question of whether or not Lincoln's election would justify secession did keep his name before the public. The discussion of that question, however, had a rather abstract quality about it. It was difficult to believe that a person so uninvolved in the campaign could win. Thus when the votes were counted, it appeared that an individual who had not in reality been subject to the decision of the electorate had somehow been chosen.

Senator Fitzpatrick raged, "The Black Republicans, flushed with a confident belief that they possessed the power within themselves of electing a President and Vice-President, determined to nominate two men of their own section; nor did they present for the Presidency a statesman of enlarged views whose mind had been trained and enlightened by a long service in the public councils. . . . On the contrary, his public career has been very short, leaving no evidence of greatness or statesmanship behind him." And the editor of a Bell newspaper was equally incensed. The Republicans had not received a single southern vote; their candidates "are purely sectional, and if these facts were accompanied by no other circumstances calculated to irritate and exasperate the States thus designedly shut out from a just and fair participation in the Executive Magistracy of the nation, they could not fail to excite jealousy and discontent among [the southern] people." Lincoln was a tyrant, for he would rule the region without the consent of the governed. Alabamians felt themselves stripped of the most fundamental right of American citizens.[73]

On the first day of the Secession Convention, therefore, the cooperationists could without any discomfiture join the immediatists in the unanimous adoption of a rather intransigent resolution. This document, a compromise draft passed only after discussion and revision, declared that Lincoln had been elected "upon the avowed principle that the Constitution of the United States does not recognize property in slaves and that the Government should prevent its extension into the common Territories of the United States and that the power of the Government should be so exercised that slavery, in time, should be exterminated"; and it concluded that "the State of Alabama cannot and will not submit to the Administration of Lincoln . . . upon the principles referred to in the preamble." Of course, this last clause would permit persons unsure about the necessity for secession to argue that the state should wait for an overt act which would prove that Lincoln did indeed intend to act on the principles which he had advocated. But one cannot lightly dismiss the fact that the resolution passed 98-0, the only cooperationist doubts coming in the form of two abstentions, by Michael J. Bulger and Allen Kimball, both of Tallapoosa.

And when the Ordinance of Secession had been passed, thirty-three of the cooperationists who declined to sign it issued an address to

73. Benjamin Fitzpatrick to Tilman Leek *et al.*, November 15, 1860 (clipping from Benjamin Fitzpatrick Papers, Alabama Department of Archives and History, Montgomery); *Pickens Republican* (Carrollton), May 31, 1860; Greenville *Southern Messenger*, November 21, 1860.

explain the refusal. Their statement represents a last, careful effort to define their precise position:

Designing persons have misrepresented, and will continue to misconstrue, their refusal to participate in a mere form of attestation, into opposition and hostility to a solemn act of the State. This act is binding on all citizens alike, and none are more ready than the undersigned to yield a cheerful obedience to the will of their State, to which they owe their first and paramount allegiance. . . . If, therefore, the enemies of the State derive comfort from the refusal of the undersigned to sign the Ordinance, the fault will lie with those who misrepresent their motives or impugn their patriotism and loyalty to their State.

In fact, the statement emphasized, they opposed only independent state action: "Not only comity, but the interest of all concerned, and none more than Alabama, dictated the policy of respectfully consulting with all the States whose identity of interest makes their ultimate destiny inseparable from ours." In such cooperation would lie the possibility of presenting "a united strength, a moral power and a national dignity," and of "establishing a new Confederacy of all the States engaged in a common cause before finally severing all connection with the Federal Government, and thus avoiding to the individual States the burdens and dangers of an independent and separate national existence, placing the formation of a new Confederacy beyond the risks and hazards to which it would be subjected by the conflicting interests and views of disunited States, each acting for itself without concert one with another; and leaving no interregnum during which men's minds could be unsettled and all material interests jeoparded by the uncertainties of the future."

With these words the cooperationists presented a succinct and accurate summary of the position which they had argued before the voters during November and December. It is perhaps appropriate, in that light, to add a brief comment on the effect upon the canvass of the secession of South Carolina. South Carolina adopted her ordinance on December 20, and Alabamians voted on December 24. We may doubt that the intervening three days allowed sufficient time for the action to make a significant impact on the public mind in Alabama. But to the extent that it did, it appears to have redounded as much to the benefit of the cooperationists as to the benefit of the immediatists; for cooperationists could hold it up as a horrible example of exactly the sort of separate state decision against which they were campaigning—a blind leap into a doubtful future.[74]

But if the cooperationists claimed to disagree with the immediatists merely over the structure of resistance, rather than over the necessity for it, why was the election so bitterly contested and the electorate so closely divided? What produced the peculiar sectional alliances apparent in the voting? There are two lines of explanation, one for the northern part of the state, and one for the southern. In the south, the key to the result is the course of the Opposition leadership. As we have seen, massive American losses in the elections of 1857 had caused the party's strategists to acquiesce in the adoption of an extreme southern rights position. Its campaigners alleged that Democrats were compromising vital sectional interests in order to appease the northern wing of their party. But the Opposition had failed to reap any new electoral dividends from this effort in the elections of 1859. Thus the willingness which northern conservative Whigs evinced in early 1860 to join in an anti-Republican alliance had led most of the Alabama Opposition to assume a somewhat moderate posture, and eventually to accept the nomination of John Bell.

The November returns, however, presented the minority party with a new disappointment. At each of its changes of tactics after 1848, the Whiggery seems to have left some portion of its constituency behind it, wedded to the deserted position. In 1860, those members who had become most firmly committed to the southern rights rationale of the preceding two years had joined Hooper in a formal endorsement of Breckinridge. And the results of the voting disclosed, as we have noted, that perhaps a quarter to a third of the usual Whig strength in the Black Belt had followed this Hooperite defection. Now the Opposition, despite its poor showing in 1857 and 1859, was by no means a hopelessly weak party. Even in its darkest days, it had never failed to receive considerably more than a fourth of the statewide poll, and in 1860 it controlled perhaps 35 percent of the vote in those counties which were carried by immediatists. But it simply could not afford

74. Smith, *Debates of the Convention of 1861*, 24–25, 30, 445–47, 105–106.

to ignore desertions of such a magnitude within the Black Belt. The belt was the party's last reliable bastion; half of the Oppositionists who had managed to gain election to the state House in 1859 represented belt counties. The presidential returns made it appear that the Democrats, using Yancey's issues, might be about to rob the Opposition of a substantial part of its remaining strength there, and thus deprive the already seriously debilitated party of any access to the public platform which only office could provide. The fact that Bell's candidacy had failed to hold the faithful in the Black Belt in line, Opposition leaders could only take as a word to the wise.

It became apparent, therefore, that the party's public spokesmen very much needed to resume their aggressive stand on southern rights. Of course it would profit the Opposition nothing to regain the allegiance of the deserters if the party thus alienated those of its members who had been enthusiastic supporters of John Bell. But that possibility seemed remote. No matter how far Opposition politicians moved towards emulating Yancey, the bulk of their party would presumably still find a Whig alternative more palatable than a Democratic one. Moreover, despite the southern rights strategy's failure to produce gains in 1859, Oppositionists continued to hope that, under the proper conditions, it might even result in splitting the south Alabama Democrats from their north Alabama allies, and thus in opening the way for the Opposition to arrange a coalition with the Yanceyites. The Whiggery, its captains dreamed, could thereby emerge from the ordeal of the Buchanan years with a statewide majority, founded upon the elements which they had sought unsuccessfully to weld in the wake of the Taylor "no-party" campaign of 1848. At the very least, the party would again consolidate its usual support.

In direct response to the presidential returns, then, many Black Belt Whig politicians who had been zealously urging the claims of Bell and the glorious union only weeks before, in mid-November underwent a new conversion and announced support for Yancey's position of immediate secession. The immediatists in the belt thereupon put forward coalition tickets such as Montgomery's—Yancey and Thomas Hill Watts—and the even more remarkable one in Dallas, which linked William S. Phillips, a wealthy Whig planter and grandson of the Huntsville Bank president Leroy Pope, with John T. Morgan, a young

Democratic attorney and self-educated son of a hill-county squatter. The Opposition leaders probably did not expect the masses of their party to follow them in this latest metamorphosis; at any rate, the masses did not do so. Black Belt supporters of Bell, on the whole, voted cooperationist when such candidates offered themselves, or simply abstained.[75] But it was not important that the leaders carry their party with them in the December election. The positions to be filled were of temporary and limited authority, and the success or failure of the immediatist tickets was no essential factor in the Whig leadership's strategy. The point was to stake out clear public ground in support of the Yanceyite version of southern rights. Thereafter, in the elections for offices which really mattered, the orthodox Whigs would rally to the standard rather than support a Democrat, and the southern rights Whigs would be able consistently to do the same, since to follow their party inclinations would no longer seem a betrayal of their section. In addition, in a statewide election, if the Democratic nominee were, for instance, a Fitzpatrick man, many Yanceyites might support a Whig candidate as well, for his course in December would have made him appear a more devoted advocate of southern rights than his opponent. The Whig shepherds, therefore, left their flocks safe in the partisan fold to go in search of the lambs who had strayed. The flocks were left temporarily without any superintendence, but the shepherds fully intended to return to claim their own. Meanwhile, however, the maneuver left much of south Alabama essentially without any organized opposition to immediate secession. Most of the Democrats in that section had been in awe of Yancey's influence since the senatorial campaign of the previous year. With virtually all prominent politicians of both parties advocating the policy, then, its opponents were reduced to floundering confusion and went down to defeat in every county except Conecuh, which they won by twenty-seven votes.

In north Alabama positions in the December canvass were equally influenced by the exigencies of political rivalry. The primary factor there, however, was the competition for ascendancy in the Democratic party. As we have seen, the nomination of Breckinridge and the sup-

75. A case made convincingly by Thomas B. Alexander and Peggy J. Duckworth in their "Alabama Black Belt Whigs During Secession: A New Viewpoint," *Alabama Review*, XVII (1964), 181–97.

port for him which circumstances had coerced from the bulk of the party establishment had enormously increased Yancey's standing in the state. Fitzpatrick had already lost control of the politics of his own region, as the result of the Senate contest the previous winter had demonstrated. But the landslide victory of Breckinridge in much of north Alabama, coupled with Yancey's sudden emergence as a respected spokesman for the slave states in the sectional dialogue, portended a coming deposition of the senator and of the politicians who had allied themselves with him. Of course such politicians could simply desert Fitzpatrick for Yancey, but to do so would be to deliver mastery of the party to the south Alabama faction. It might save north Alabama politicians their own offices, but it would deprive them of any substantial access to the dispensation of patronage. If the north Alabamians could salvage Fitzpatrick's hopes, he would of course direct rewards towards them. If Yancey won, he had a coterie of south Alabamians already in place about him who would receive prior consideration.

The north Alabama faction's predicament seemed, however, not at all irremediable. The key to victory in 1851, as they remembered it, had been the formulation of a program which seemed to join firmness with moderation—to make no concessions of southern rights, but to avoid radical action which could compel unnecessary conflict. Cooperative secession appeared to offer the same qualities. Conservative leaders quickly espoused it—Fitzpatrick in the middle of November—and by early December, tickets were being nominated in its behalf. In the succeeding canvass, as we have seen, cooperationist orators spent most of their time embroidering the difficulties Alabama would face as an independent republic.[76]

The real point of such an appeal was to raise doubts in the popular mind about the extent to which immediate secession was a carefully considered response to the threat. Its opponents wished to make it appear a hasty, radical proposal, generated by emotion and replete with concealed pitfalls. They sought to paint themselves, on the other hand, as calm and deliberate statesmen, long familiar with public affairs, unlike the novice Yanceyites. Their proposal was intended to

76. E.g., Thomas J. Butler to Andrew B. Moore, December 25, 1860, in Governors' Correspondence: A. B. Moore.

seem no less firm in its defense of the South, but a more rational and carefully matured reaction. In short, they planned to outflank Yancey with precisely the same tactic through which he had been foiled a decade earlier—by isolating him in the occupation of untenably radical ground.

The immediatists were able to secure a greater part of the vote in the north than were the cooperationists in the south. The immediatists carried their 29 counties by an aggregate majority of nearly 18,000, but the cooperationists took their 23 counties by an aggregate majority of only 9,600. A principal reason for this differential is that, whereas almost no important politician was left to oppose immediate secession in south Alabama once most Whig leaders deserted the cause, in north Alabama there were some politicians who had nothing to fear from Yancey's rise and therefore embraced his movement. Most prominent among these men were Senator Clay and Congressman Curry, both of whom had admirers in the south and were certain to have the ear of Yancey's associates. Another group, typified by L. Pope Walker, had usually encountered difficulty in gaining high office because their combination of whiggish and southern rights views, which would have been acceptable further south, deprived them of a strong local power base. Such men had nothing to lose and everything to gain by the overthrow of the Democratic establishment of the region. Former Bell supporters in the Tennessee Valley, who were not immediately threatened by the southern rights Whig desertion that had so frightened their Black Belt brethren, by and large supported the cooperationists; and the faction therefore nominated fusion tickets—and indeed a few all-Whig tickets—in that area. But the campaign in north Alabama became in considerable measure a contest between the outs and ins of the section's Democracy for control of local patronage and political influence.

We have already explored the process by which the fire-eaters had induced the Democrats to preach southern rights with increasing fervor during the fifties, and the forces which had left north Alabamians increasingly convinced of the southern rights analysis.[77] But of course it does not follow that the decade saw any growth in north Alabam-

77. See pp. 233–38, 291–306, 331–42 herein.

ians' affection for the fire-eaters themselves. Southern rights had entered north Alabama through the speeches of the area's Democratic politicians and officeholders. Early in the Winston administration, as the state entered a period of booming prosperity, many north Alabamians had been temporarily dazzled by the prospect of using railroads to enable their isolated region to participate fully in the market economy, and this infatuation had undermined the influence of the area's traditional political leadership. We have noted that nearly a third of the Whigs in the House of 1853 were from the hill counties. This concrete evidence, together with the untested potential of the Know-Nothing movement, had caused a considerable number of the young Democrats in the section to follow Clay, Curry, and Walker into advocacy of state aid for railroad construction. But the voters' approval of Winston's intransigence in the elections of 1857, followed in the fall by the Panic of 1857, which made Winston's policies appear sagacious, had driven all those politicians who could do so to scramble back towards the accustomed Jacksonian position. A sort of generational division emerged among the younger Democrats, as those men who had not held important office before 1857 suddenly discovered the virtues of the statesmen whom, as they claimed, blindly ambitious youths had been shouldering aside at mid-decade.

But the electorate's restlessness with the inability of its old spokesmen to locate an appropriate villain upon whom to blame the tensions induced by social change still continued unabated, and would surely have rendered the restoration a brief one had not the events of the Buchanan years provided a plausible villain just at this moment. As we have seen, party orthodoxy had begun to require elderly Jacksonians, in common with all Democrats, to denounce the northern free-soil menace. Perhaps a bit to their surprise, the Jacksonians found that the new crusade worked with the voters. The traditional north Alabama leaders therefore began eagerly seeking to identify themselves with Senator Fitzpatrick, the symbol of the south Alabama Southern Rights party establishment. The situation is replete with irony. The same crusade which permitted the young and aggressive Yanceyites to supersede the more established politicians—including Fitzpatrick's Regency—in south Alabama, enabled the old Jacksonians to inject a new vigor into their enfeebled north Alabama hegemony. While Yanceyites in the south were not especially troubled by the 1857 watershed, in the north it tended to create an unusual alliance between the Democracy's eldest and its very youngest politicians, against that area's emerging Yanceyites. And, even though Yancey's allies in both sections held very similar economic notions, circumstance had emphasized in north Alabama their earlier belief that railroad construction was deserving of an exception from their general hostility to governmental paternalism, and hence had allowed their opponents to paint them as men entertaining rather whiggish opinions.

Thus, though the triumph of Breckinridge had been proof that north Alabamians had indeed accepted the Democrats' new monster, the result had not by any means represented an endorsement of the Yanceyite faction. Most north Alabamians continued to think of such men as Clay and Pope Walker as dubious figures, harboring somewhat heterodox notions of urban origin. Of course, if traditional leaders had advocated a policy of submission, not a few voters might reluctantly have supported the immediatists. But such a difficult choice was unnecessary. A vote for the cooperationists was, these voters were told and believed, a vote for firm but moderate resistance under the command of sound Southern Rights politicians; while a vote for the immediatists came to seem a vote for hot-headed action under the erratic command of inexperienced zealots. The cooperationists carried every county in north Alabama except Calhoun.

The prospective fortunes of the state's various political factions, then, was the determining force in creating the strange sectional alignment of the Secession Convention vote—in grouping on the one side the wealthy commercial and plantation region of the Tennessee Valley and the poor, sparsely settled, small-farm area of the hill counties, and on the other side the wealthy Black Belt with the poor, small-farm Wiregrass. With most elections we have no trouble admitting the truth that maneuver for political advantage may play an essential role. However, the widely accepted notion that when Alabamians went to the polls on Christmas Eve they were deciding the profound question of war or peace serves to inhibit our acceptance of such an explanation in this case. At so critical a juncture, the politician could hardly conduct business as usual. But this analysis in fact conceives the vote in terms subtly, yet nonetheless genuinely different from those accepted by contemporaries.

Throughout November and December the politicians assumed that the presidential election had already settled the question which later observers have thought them in the process of arguing during these months. Thus for Alabamians at the time the Christmas Eve election seemed to involve not the event of secession but who would control the secession movement and the seceded state. The fact that factional maneuver dominated the canvass, then, is not to be seen as callous cynicism in the midst of a dangerous emergency, but rather as a rational effort to adjust successfully to the exigencies of changing issues. Once we correctly understand the nature of the election as contemporaries perceived it, we are no longer troubled that the principal explanatory factor in the formation of the sectional alliances apparent in the voting is not some great source of social or economic conflict, some force which reaches to the foundations of antebellum society, but is simply an attempt by the Whigs to keep Yancey from stealing a portion of their constituency, and by the conservative Democrats to keep Yancey from stealing the party machinery—is, in other words, a reaction by older politicians to the political muscle of a younger one, as demonstrated in the November results.

A final point on this subject is necessary. Just as we often think of the Christmas Eve election as decisive of a great question, so we tend to believe that politicians must have expected secession to inaugurate a new political era. In fact, of course, they had no such anticipation. They did not know what the future would hold, but they certainly never doubted that the structure of governmental institutions would remain the same, that the fundamental political alliances would go on, that campaigners would continue to appeal to voters in the same terms, that the wise statesman would tend to the mending of his fences with sedulous zeal. The requirements of politics were unchanging. Even in the midst of the suspense generated by the sectional crisis, therefore, politicians expected to reap the benefits of their actions. New friendships formed or old ones reinforced would not fail to be useful. The continuity of Alabama's political life was assumed on all hands, and the actors in the drama behaved accordingly. Fitzpatrick and Yancey were, for instance, no less expected to be rivals for the Senate before the next legislature merely because the senate in question might not be that of the United States.

Getting Around the Crisis

Since both the north Alabama cooperationists and the south Alabama immediatists were coalitions formed for mutual advantage, we would like to be able to make further distinctions among the delegates. The ordinary statement that the Secession Convention included fifty-three immediatists and forty-seven cooperationists tells us relatively little except that the Democratic factions from the two sections were as nearly equiponderant as ever, and that as usual the Whigs were the balance of power. Nor are economic data very helpful. The median slaveholding and real and personal property values in the convention were virtually identical to the corresponding figures for the legislature of 1859. Moreover, the four economic classes could each claim about a quarter of the delegates, as of the legislators. The immediatists were, on the whole, a great deal wealthier than were the cooperationists, but that fact is of course a function of the sectional nature of the two alliances.

There is, however, one quite significant statistical difference between the convention and the assembly. In the legislature, persons connected with agriculture constituted 63.5 percent of the members, and attorneys were 26 percent. In the convention, the proportion of farmers fell precipitously to 43 percent, and lawyers advanced to 37 percent. Moreover, cooperationists held small majorities both among delegates who were farmers and among delegates who were neither farmers nor lawyers; but attorneys were overwhelmingly immediatist—by a margin of two to one. This striking circumstance is almost certainly a reflection of the full emergence of the Yanceyite faction within the Democracy during the presidential campaign. Many—indeed, perhaps most—of the young and ambitious advocates of laissez-faire policies in government and industrialization in the economy, who constituted the mainstay of Yancey's political organization, were attorneys. In that connection, it is worth noting that those lawyers in the convention whom I would classify as Yanceyites, had an average age three years younger than the average of immediatists as a group, and nearly five years younger than the average of the cooperationists.

A close analysis of the proceedings of the convention can allow us to distinguish with at least rough accuracy two other sorts of divisions within the convention. We can discover, as to the cooperationists, to how many their recommendation of cooperative secession was simply an effort to find some reasonable alternative to Yancey's separate state secession, and to how many it represented a covert attempt to delay or even to foil the act. And we can determine what percentage of the delegates was whiggish in its outlook, and what percentage opposed governmental activism.

It is, within limits, possible to arrange the forty-seven cooperationists along a scale in accordance with their views of the nature and purpose of concerted southern action. Of all the cooperationists, by far the closest to the immediatist position was future Confederate congressman John P. Ralls of Cherokee. Indeed, some historians have classified him with the south Alabamians, since he voted against them only in favoring the submission of the Ordinance of Secession to a popular referendum. In fact, however, he was not really an immediatist. His conditions for cooperative action had simply been fulfilled by South Carolina's secession and the pending but clear decisions of Mississippi and Florida. There could now be no fear that Alabama would find herself out alone, and Ralls thus considered the question of the canvass settled by events.[78]

Next to Ralls, who believed that cooperative secession had already been accomplished, is a group of seven men who would have preferred more formal cooperation, but were willing to vote for the ordinance on its final passage. This band included Jeremiah Clemens of Madison, whose conversion may well have been a result of his burning political ambition, and the three-member delegations from Talladega and Coosa, whose decision presumably turned on the specific form in which the issue had been stated in their counties during the preceding month. An additional four delegates—the two delegates from Lawrence, David P. Lewis and James S. Clarke, William S. Earnest of Jefferson, and John W. Inzer of Saint Clair—refused to vote for the

78. Smith, *Debates of the Convention of 1861*, 105–106.

ordinance but agreed to sign it later, thus parting company with most
of their faction. These twelve men may be considered somewhat more
amenable to the Yanceyite policy of separate state withdrawal than
were most cooperationists. Though convinced of the wisdom of
cooperative secession, they evidently felt—to the extent, at any rate,
that we may generalize about the motivations of the group—that the
achievement of secession in some form was more important than the
mechanism by which it was achieved.

Thirty-three cooperationists refused to sign the ordinance after it
had been engrossed. This group issued the address which was quoted
earlier, asserting a genuine and unshaken commitment to the rationale
for preconcerted southern action, but avowing their desire to support
the state's decision now that it was a fact. Six of the thirty-three
delegates who signed this address, however, indicated by a vote a
somewhat more unionist stand. One cooperationist member, J. P.
Timberlake of Jackson, offered an amendment to the pending Secession Ordinance declaring that Alabama was resuming the powers she
had delegated to the United States only in order "to form a Provisional
Government and a Southern Confederacy upon the basis of the Constitution of the United States of America, with such of the slaveholding
States as will join in forming the same." The amendment would have
had the effect not only of binding Alabama to surrender her independence as soon as possible but also of limiting severely the modifications
which she could permit in the new Confederate constitution. Many
cooperationists nourished lingering fears that the radicals desired substantial changes in that document.

The immediatists refused to support Timberlake's proposal because, said Yancey,

For us to vote for this amendment as now worded is to ask us to declare a
motive for secession which was never entertained by its friends. The advocates
of secession placed their actions upon far higher grounds. They believed that
the rights and liberties of the people of Alabama were assailed and endangered by the Northern majorities who control a majority of the States and
who are about to control the legislation of the Union. Believing this, secession,
or withdrawal of the State from under the power of that hostile majority, was
advocated purely for the purpose—for the purpose alone—of protecting and
preserving the endangered rights of the people of this sovereign State—even
though not another State should follow our example. Though this was the

sole purpose of secession, yet we all believed that other States would secede, and in that event it was our hope that they would join us in forming a new Confederacy upon old-fashioned Republican principles.[79]

Only one immediatist—Benjamin H. Baker of Russell—voted for the Timberlake amendment. But ten cooperationists voted against it. Three of these men, Clarke and Lewis of Lawrence and Ralls of Cherokee, had demonstrated at least moderate leanings towards the immediatist position, and may have accepted Yancey's reasoning on this question. But the remaining seven, six of whom were signers of the cooperationist address—Lang C. Allen of Marion, Nicholas Davis, Jr., of Madison, John Green of Conecuh, Henry C. Jones of Lauderdale, Thomas J. McClellan of Limestone, and Richard J. Wood of Randolph—evidently opposed the amendment because they were unwilling to place Alabama under a formal obligation to enter a new nation. They perhaps retained the hope that the state's secession might shock the North to its senses and bring from the Congress an offer of acceptable guarantees for southern rights. In that case, they probably were prepared to urge reconstruction of the Union. But Timberlake's proposal would require the state to seek the formation of a southern confederacy, and thus inhibit any such reconstructionist movement.

Two cooperationists remain unmentioned—C. Christopher Sheets of Winston and R. S. Watkins of Franklin—and these men must be accounted the closest thing to unionists that the Alabama convention contained. Both not only voted against the ordinance and refused to sign it, but also refused to sign the cooperationist address, which explained this action as a mere difference over mechanics. In addition, though Watkins supported the Timberlake amendment, Sheets was one of the ten cooperationists who voted against it. But both men had favored the first day's resolution refusing to accept an emancipationist national administration. Watkins, a maverick Whig, told the delegates that, though he would support the action of the Convention, he was not at all reconciled to it.[80] Sheets, a Democrat from the county in the state which was the most overwhelmingly opposed to the immediatists, made no statement for the record, but his actions mark him as, of all the members, the most hostile to secession.

79. *Ibid.*, 90–92.
80. *Ibid.*, 101–102.

    In sum, then, twelve of the forty-seven cooperationists had strong
secessionist leanings—eight of them sufficiently strong to lead them to
vote for the ordinance in the end. Twenty-seven of the forty-seven
cooperationists were evidently genuinely committed to the virtues of
that particular mechanism, either because it held out some hope of
producing an acceptable adjustment of the crisis, in the form of congressional acceptance of a southern ultimatum, or because it included
guarantees against Alabama's finding herself out of the Union
alone—or most probably, because of both reasons. Seven of the forty-
seven were at least somewhat reconstructionist in sentiment—that is,
they gave evidence of willingness to seize gratefully upon compromise
initiatives from Washington if the initiatives were forthcoming. Finally, one of the forty-seven cooperationists—one of the one hundred
delegates—displayed some sign of holding moderately unionist views.
The convention contained no unconditional unionists.

    Our second question was the extent to which the delegates shared
a whiggish outlook. There are two ways to approach this problem—
through a determination of formal party membership, and through a
study of voting behavior. I have been able to determine—at least probably—the party affiliation of thirty-seven of the forty-seven
cooperationists and forty-four of the fifty-three immediatists. Thirteen
of the immediatists—or about 30 percent—were Whigs or Know-
Nothings. Sixteen of the cooperationists—or some 43 percent—were
in the same category. The latter percentage, however, may be somewhat overstated, because the ten cooperationists of unknown party
affiliation were, with a single exception, from the hill counties, and
most of them were therefore likely Democrats. But we may with at
least relative assurance say that about a third of the immediatists and
about two-fifths of the cooperationists were Whigs. In each case most
of the Whigs were in the convention because of their presence on fusion tickets.

    Two sets of roll calls give us additional information on the subject.
Moreover, they throw into clear relief issues which, though central to
the life of the society and therefore hotly debated at the convention,
are far too often simply ignored in accounts of the period. After adopting the Ordinance of Secession, the delegates proceeded to write
Alabama's second constitution. For the most part they modified the

constitution of 1819 only where it was essential in order to recognize the new situation. Some changes which are primarily of technical significance were adopted: the legislature returned to annual sessions, but each session was limited to thirty days; the provision that each county be given at least one member in the House regardless of its population was eliminated, thus according counties with large white populations increased representation; courts were granted the power to issue divorce decrees, which had previously required a legislative act; the creation of new counties was made more difficult; and the provisions requiring the humane treatment of slaves were worded more vaguely, though they were not necessarily thereby weakened. Emancipation was forbidden, thus codifying the social consensus on the subject which had emerged since 1819. The legislature retained its right to prohibit the importation of slaves for sale. In addition to these alterations, however, the constitution of 1861 contained several enormously important new sections, adopted as direct consequences of the great struggles over economic questions which had dominated the preceding decade. The second constitution represents nothing less than an effort to turn back the tide which had set in the fifties towards governmental collaboration with corporate wealth.

The new organic law forbade the chartering of banks except by a two-thirds vote of each house of the legislature. It required the same majority in order to sanction the suspension of specie payment by a bank, and required that if the sanction were not granted the bank's charter was thus automatically forfeited. It prohibited the state from borrowing money and from endorsing the bonds or debts of corporations; and from loaning any corporation or person any money, credit, or thing, without the approval of two-thirds of each house. It forbade special laws for the benefit of persons or corporations if there was a general law on the subject or if the relief sought could be granted by the courts. It precluded the granting of the right of eminent domain to persons or corporations, though it permitted empowering corporations to lease—but not take ownership of—rights of way. Finally, it denied government any power to delegate the levying of taxes to any individual or corporation; or to levy taxes for the benefit of a citizen or corporation unless every person so taxed gave his individual consent. Taken together, these provisions imply an almost unmitigated censure of the activities of the state—and of many counties and cities, for that matter—under Collier, Winston, and A. B. Moore; and constitute, in a sense, the final triumph of Winston's issues, which were now shorn of any exclusive association with Winston and elevated to the level of social orthodoxy.

Adoption of these various prohibitions was accompanied by debates of considerable acrimony. The provisions were a compromise formulation between the positions of the old Jacksonians, generally cooperationist, who longed for a governmental crusade against industrialization and would have made the prohibitions absolute and the somewhat younger Yanceyite devotees of governmentally enforced individualism, who however favored industrialization and desired to give the state some flexibility to aid the development, in especially deserving cases. These two groups, then, provided the affirmative votes on the new sections. The opposition consisted of Whigs from both factions and a few whiggish Democrats, mostly from south Alabama—the heart of the coalition which ever since 1849 had been pushing the state towards a policy of assistance to private enterprise.

The roll calls on this question, therefore, cut across the lines established in the votes on the Ordinance of Secession and provide us with an indication of the relative weight of whiggish views in each group. It appears that among the delegates at large, about 65 percent displayed anti-corporation tendencies, and 35 percent favored governmental intervention in the economy. Among cooperationists, some 70 percent were in the former group and 30 percent in the latter. Among immediatists, whiggish notions had greater strength, though still in the minority by 60 percent to 40 percent.[81]

81. An analysis of twelve roll calls directly related to economic questions, supplemented by an additional twelve on issues with overtones of class division, produced the following results. Seven immediatists were fully pro-corporation and another eight moderately so. Eleven immediatists were fully anti-corporation and nine others moderately so. The votes of five immediatists display no discernible pattern, and six immediatists were absent from so many roll calls that I can venture no statement on their views. Finally, seven immediatists were often absent, but participated sufficiently so that I can tentatively identify leanings; five of these men seem to be anti-corporation and two pro-corporation. I thus arrive at a total of twenty-five anti-corporation and seventeen pro-corporation immediatists.

Five cooperationists were fully pro-corporation and another six moderately so. Fifteen were fully anti-corporation and nine others moderately so. Three displayed no tendency, and five were too often absent for any statement. Four men—three anti-corporation and one pro-corpora-

The existence of these divisions, Yancey's political opponents quickly perceived, would make it possible to defeat him if they could bring together cooperationists who distrusted the orator's extreme southern rights views, and immediatists who rejected economic radicalism and feared that such policies would attend the rise of the Yanceyites to political supremacy in the state. They were able to do so, however, only rarely during the convention. On the issues surrounding secession, the remarkable south Alabama alliance of whiggish and Yanceyite members managed to hang together. On economic questions, sectional alignments were replaced by more usual blocs, which cast the whiggish members into minority. Nevertheless, on one highly significant occasion—the election of delegates to the Provisional Confederate Congress—an anti-Yancey coalition was formed.

Yancey had profoundly wished to be chosen to the congress, but he received only 38 votes from his colleagues, implying that more than a fourth of the immediatists deserted his cause. A friend reported that he was "greatly mortified at his defeat." His biographer tells us that the election filled Yancey with foreboding that it would be viewed in retrospect as "a first false step." And the Montgomery *Confederation*, voice of those elements in the old Regency which were most hostile to Yancey, exhibited signs of euphoria at the results: "It is beyond dispute [now] that there is a large majority of the Convention who are not in favor of the rash plans and precipitate measures of the defeated [Yanceyites]. . . . Were it a time now for us to laugh and be merry, we should certainly do so over the downfall" of the radicals.[82]

A part of Yancey's mortification very likely derived from the identity of the man who defeated him. Robert H. Smith, a Whig railroad attorney from Mobile who had formerly represented Sumter County in the legislature, had headed the Mobile cooperationist ticket which had been vanquished at the Christmas Eve election. To have been passed over for a cooperationist rejected by the voters less than a month before could only have seemed to Yancey an arrant indignity.

---

tion—evince probable attitudes. In sum, therefore, I find twenty-seven anti-corporation and twelve pro-corporation cooperationists.

82. John Bragg to Colin J. McRea, January 21, 1861, Colin J. McRea Papers, Alabama Department of Archives and History, Montgomery; Dubose, *Yancey*, II, 571; Montgomery *Confederation*, January 20, 1861.

But the real importance of this encounter—and the principal source, doubtless, of Yancey's foreboding—is the nature of the immediatist defection from Yancey's candidacy. Since the congressmen were selected by secret ballot, one cannot identify precisely which immediatists refused to vote for the orator. A glance at the results of the other elections in this series, however, renders it virtually certain that the deserters were those members of the immediatist alliance who were Whigs.

The anti-Yancey Democrats among the cooperationists sought throughout the process of choosing the delegates to wean away the whiggish, non-Yanceyite element among the immediatists. The Whig immediatists of course could not regularly afford to vote for opponents of separate state secession, since to do so would call into question the devotion to southern rights which they had gone to such lengths to establish. Moreover, there was nothing in the ideological position of a Jacksonian to attract a Whig. If, therefore, the conservative Democrats wished to halt the rise of the Yanceyites, they would have to support Whig votaries of pro-business activism, preferably with southern rights sympathies.

The exigencies of dividing the immediatists thus induced the anti-Yancey Democrats to accept perhaps the most economically conservative delegation, and certainly the most heavily Whig delegation, which Alabama had ever sent to any official assemblage. Only three of the nine men were practicing Democrats. Two of the delegates were actually closely associated with the Broad River group: Richard Wilde Walker was a son of former senator John W. Walker and a grandson of Leroy Pope; Thomas Fearn, an elderly Huntsville physician, had been a political ally of the group and had served as a presidential elector on the slate pledged to William H. Crawford in 1824.

From the Montgomery district all three of the nominees—William P. Chilton, Samuel F. Rice, and Thomas J. Judge—were southern rights Whigs, though Rice was a relatively recent convert to the Opposition. Chilton, the victor, was the most restrained in his southern rights opinions and the most unwavering in his adherence to Whig dogma of the group. From the Tuscaloosa district, Stephen F. Hale, a southern rights Whig and country lawyer, defeated both Newton L. Whitfield, a cooperationist Whig and president of the Northeast and

Southwest Alabama Railroad and Isham W. Garrott, a former Whig who had become a secessionist and Breckinridge Democrat. From the Mobile district, the Mobile factor and railroad speculator Colin J. McRae was selected over future senator Edmund W. Pettus, a first cousin and associate of former governor Winston. McRae, though one of the three Democratic delegates, was nevertheless chosen most probably because his economic sentiments were much more obviously whiggish than were his opponent's. From the Florence district, future scalawag governor David P. Lewis, a moderate cooperationist favorable toward business interests, who was at this time relatively unknown in state politics, achieved election when a prominent champion of aid to railroads, Oppositionist Luke Pryor, deadlocked with a strong opponent of such aid, Democrat John E. Moore.

The only two genuine Yanceyites in the delegation, Congressman J. L. M. Curry and future governor John Gill Shorter, were both chosen under special circumstances. Shorter, a right fire-eater, won a classic encounter with an uncompromising left fire-eater, Lewis Llewellyn Cato. Shorter was thus ironically made to appear the more temperate of the two aspirants.

The north Alabama Jacksonians—perhaps hoping that, since they were voting for so many whiggish candidates, the immediatist Whigs would accept a Jacksonian in return—nominated a hill-county Douglas Democrat with strong doubts about secession, future scalawag governor William H. Smith, to oppose Congressman Curry. Curry held the modish economic views of the younger Yanceyites: though he desired industrial development, he generally tended to resist governmental assistance to the process, on the grounds that such policies undermined self-reliance. Curry had in fact been a proponent of state aid to railroad construction in 1855, but from the perspective of an orthodox Whig, Curry's doctrines seemed only slightly more satisfactory than Smith's.

In such a contest, there was nothing to encourage the Whig desertions which defeated the Yanceyites on the other roll calls. Consequently, in this encounter, alone among the nine, immediatist-cooperationist lines apparently held. Curry won, 52–47. But the fact that the change of only three votes would have elected Smith shows once again just how extraordinary this set of ballots had been. Indeed, it is difficult to suppress astonishment at the realization that the Secession Convention came within three votes of sending to represent the state in the Provisional Confederate Congress both of the men who were later to serve as the only Black Republican governors in Alabama history.

There thus was good reason for Yancey's having regarded the appointment of these individuals as a "first false step." Even the fact that six of the nine were southern rights advocates was not likely to give him much comfort, since four of the six had defeated candidates still more firmly committed to the southern rights creed than were they. And three of the delegates had been vigorous foes of immediate secession. But the true significance of the elections was in their abundant demonstration of the power of party affiliation and economic attitudes to determine the delegates' voting behavior.

In that sense, the drafting of a constitution emphatically intended to limit the state's connections with corporate enterprise and the selection of a congressional delegation overwhelmingly friendly to governmental cooperation with business are aspects of the same reality. The actual divisions in the convention, as in the society, were not between immediatists and cooperationists. The convention included whiggish members, who believed that the path to freedom lay through energetic intervention by the political structure to assist the growth of commerce and industry; Jacksonians, who thought that the essence of the struggle for freedom was the destruction of any institution which had the power to coerce obedience from the citizenry; and younger politicians—the group which constituted the backbone of the Yanceyite faction and which shared many of its ideas with the emerging school of laissez-faire radicals in England—who accepted the need for industrialization, but felt that real freedom required that government involve itself in the economy and in the society as infrequently as possible.

When the Jacksonians, in an effort to halt the rise of the Yanceyites, voted for Whigs, they thus produced an activist congressional delegation. But when later the issue of the proper role of the state in economic affairs arose, the Yanceyites joined the Jacksonians in placing restrictions on that role. The delegates' maneuvers in both of these proceedings reflect the existence of deeper concerns—among the members and among their constituents. For in Alabama there was always only one question which really mattered: how to maintain one's freedom. The genuine factions in the convention were ideological groupings determined by convictions upon this all-important subject. We may surmise that Yancey, as he observed the convention's roll calls, came to realize that the victory of disunion had represented, not any thorough-going acceptance of his theoretical positions, but merely an acquiescence in the substance of his warnings, that northern actions threatened to deprive southerners of full citizenship; and that the knowledge of the limits of his triumph was the fundamental cause of his forebodings.

In the much more limited terms of immediate political success, however, Yancey's fears proved unjustified. Except in the single instance of the elections for members of the Provisional Confederate Congress, no anti-Yancey coalition was able to sustain itself during the early years of the war. The primary reason for this failure was the enormous popularity which secession proved to have with the electorate, once the act had been consummated.

The notion has rather wide currency that the hill counties remained bitterly opposed to the new order of things. In fact, however, the evidence in support of the contention is unconvincing. The evidence dates either from the campaign in the previous December, when doubts about the policy had indeed been freely expressed, or from 1863 and thereafter, when battlefield reverses and the operation of the hated Conscription Act had begun to challenge the people's loyalty; or if the evidence is temporally relevant, it usually proceeds from local family and factional rivalries. Since the government was as yet only precariously established, some unscrupulous persons appear to have hoped that denouncing a neighbor's beliefs as unpatriotic would advance their own interests. Such men presumably wished new officials to rely on one local faction in preference to another.[83]

A correct understanding of north Alabama sentiment, however, is essential to an explanation of the outcome of the state elections in

83. This question has been the subject of a relatively recent debate: Hugh C. Bailey, "Disloyalty in Early Confederate Alabama," *Journal of Southern History*, XXIII (1957), 522–28; Hugh C. Bailey, "Disaffection in the Alabama Hill Country, 1861," *Civil War History*, IV (1958), 183–93; Long, "Unanimity and Disloyalty in Secessionist Alabama." As to the points at issue, I find myself in complete agreement with Professor Long.

August of 1861. One need not deny that there were hill-county farmers who agreed with a Winston County resident in doubting that any real solidarity existed between slaveholders and non-slaveholders. He warned his son that the young man would be asked to "go to fight for [the planters'] infurnal negroes, and after you do there fighting, you may kiss there hine parts for o [all] they care."[84] It is important to note, however, that the son who received this admonition was a zealous Confederate. Just as few north Alabamians failed to vote for Breckinridge, few doubted that Lincoln's policies meant degradation for all southerners alike. Of course they were not eager to kiss the hind parts of Black Belters, but kissing the hind parts of Yankees seemed a more pressing osculation.

Former senator Clemens concluded that at the time of the presidential elections, one-fourth of the people of Alabama had been secessionists; that by the election for delegates to the convention, secessionists had advanced to a majority of the voters; but that by the beginning of February, at which time he wrote, nine-tenths of the populace "sustain the action of the convention and before the 4th of March [Lincoln's inauguration] there will not be one man in a thousand to raise his voice against it. Of this there cannot be a shadow of a doubt." Already in mid-January Robert M. Patton, a strongly anti-secession Tennessee Valley Whig and future Reconstruction governor, stated his belief that the citizens of his section would stand by the ordinance. Towards the end of February, former congressman David Hubbard reported, "The secession movement is not popular here [in Lawrence County] with Union savers, but the Ambitious who expect to be known throughout the state are not only becoming reconciled but are preparing their followers to be reconciled, and will support the measure as soon as they can do so."

In January a Huntsville meeting rejected the pleas of the secessionists by a margin of four to one. In early March the same question was argued before the same community by the same cast of characters and the secessionist effort was sustained by at least three to one. By the end of March a Black Belt legislator confidently asserted, "Don't let Reconstruction or anything of that sort disturb your dreams. There is

84. Quoted in Bailey, "Disloyalty," 525.

no danger of it under heaven. The people would not go back if you would let them make the terms. The Separation is 'final, complete and perpetual.'" In the summer, future governor George S. Houston made a tour through Walker and Winston, the supposed heart of the disaffection. Houston, for the preceding twenty years the congressman from the district including those counties and an uncompromising Jacksonian, had remained a unionist even after Lincoln's election. His assessment of the situation thus carries particular weight. He wrote Governor Moore:

I found the people very anxious to hear speeches in relation to the present condition of the country. They attended the appointments in very large numbers, much larger than I have ever known before in those counties, and listened to the addresses with the greatest attention and interest. A good deal of ill feeling had been engendered between the parties, growing out of old political divisions, and harsh epithets were quite common towards each other; but I found no organization or the trace of one indicating a purpose of hostility to the Confederate Government, and I am very confident those people entertain no such purpose. The most of them were reluctant to give up the old Union and while some of them express regrets upon that subject now, they at the same time avow a determination to stand by the South, and have impressed me with the truth of their expressed purposes.[85]

All of these statements find strong corroboration in the August election returns. Senator Joshua P. Coman of Limestone, who had been a cooperationist anti-corporation delegate in the Secession Convention, arrived for the legislative session with the hope that factional strength in the new assembly would be at least roughly comparable to that in the earlier body. He began active consultations looking towards the creation of a conservative coalition to prevent Yancey's elevation to the Confederate Senate. Very soon, however, he was forced to despair. He wrote a political associate,

No conservative man can possibly live in this Sea of Secession. He can't touch bottom no where. The whole thing is straight and dead out against all who

85. Quoted in Vergil L. Bedsole, "The Life of Jeremiah Clemens" (M.A. thesis, University of Alabama, 1934), 112; Ellen Noyes Jackson to Sarah Noyes, January 12, 1861, in J. F. Jackson Papers, Alabama Department of Archives and History, Montgomery; Hugh Lawson White Clay to Clement Claiborne Clay, January 11, 1861, Edward D. Tracy to Clay, March 6, 1861, Thomas E. Irby to Clay, March 30, 1861, David Clopton to Clay, December 13, 1860, all in Clay Papers; David Hubbard to Andrew B. Moore, February 23, 1861, George S. Houston to Moore, August 27, 1861, both in Governors' Correspondence: A. B. Moore.

stand in that connection. In the State Convention of last January, there was an element of hostility among the secessionists to Yancy [*sic*], which combining with the Cooperatives was able to defeat him for the Provisional Congress. I have looked for the same element of hostility among his side in this Legislature, but I see none. That element has been crushed out in South Alabama and Yancy comes before this body with South Alabama unanimous for him. How is it in North Alabama? The conservatives in the August elections did not even hold their own, but lost on every field. In the State Convention, North Alabama was a unit against him; in this Legislature he makes a very respectable divide in the votes of that section.

Coman reported bitterly, "The Secessionists from North Alabama all . . . seemed to be feverishly anxious to place themselves *rectus in cura*—right on the goose—unmistakeably [*sic*] free from any and all sympathy past, present and prospective with Conservatism or Unionism. . . . These men are more our enemies than any down here." The cooperationist faction, he said, "has been crushed out, and there is scarcely a greasy spot left of us." An anti-Yancey candidate for the Senate would not merely be beaten, but would "have his posteriors so ricked and mauled that he is bound to pass *bloody urine* for six months thereafter." Coman concluded with the acid observation, "Mr. Yancy . . . advised the secessionists to act inside of the Democratic Party, watching for a time to disrupt, fire the Southern heart and then precipitate into a revolution. This is now I believe the only and best course for the Conservatives."[86]

These remarks correctly convey how completely the Yanceyites triumphed in August. The gambits of both the south Alabama Whigs and the north Alabama conservative Democrats backfired upon them. These groups brought out for governor the Montgomery Whig Thomas Hill Watts, who had supported John Bell but had thereafter become an immediatist. Watts carried twenty-three of the state's fifty-two counties, but only seven of them were in north Alabama. Most of his remaining counties were traditionally Whig, but he lost eleven south Alabama counties, seven of them normally Whig and four of them in the Black Belt. The margin of victory for his opponent, the Eufaula fire-eater John Gill Shorter, thus rather resembled the support for Breckinridge a year earlier: hill-county farmers and southern rights

86. Joshua P. Coman to George S. Houston, November 6, 1861, in George S. Houston Papers, Duke University Library, Durham.

Whig deserters. Shorter won by a majority of nearly 10,000. Fitzpatrick sought a Senate seat. In the previous assembly he had at least battled Yancey to a draw, but now Yancey's power was so great that Fitzpatrick was compelled to abandon the effort, and Yancey was chosen unanimously. By the end of 1861 Yancey was as thoroughly the master of state politics as ever Israel Pickens had been.

Pickens died a decade before the failure of the bank allowed a challenge to the hegemony of the issue which he had created. Yancey's dominance had been erected upon an even more unstable foundation—Confederate success. Yancey died on July 28, 1863, a mere fortnight before his allies suffered a defeat as devastating as their victory two years earlier had been decisive. He may well have lived long enough to recognize his failure. Watts beat the incumbent Shorter for governor ignominiously; Shorter carried only four counties and received fewer than 10,000 votes. Watts thus became the first Whig ever to win a statewide election in Alabama. The death of Yancey and the expiration of Clay's short term gave the new legislature the opportunity to fill both Senate seats. A coalition similar to that which had emerged in the convention sent two Whigs to Richmond—the wealthy Tuscaloosa industrialist Robert Jemison and, after an epic battle of twenty ballots, the scion of the Broad River Richard Wilde Walker. In the first Confederate Congress, only two of Alabama's eleven members—William P. Chilton and Thomas J. Foster—were Whigs. But in the second congress, five of the eleven were Whigs.[87]

The growing influence of politicians favorable to economic activism was a marked feature of state politics in the early fifties, but towards the end of the decade they had begun to encounter opposition, as a result both of Governor Winston's actions and of the rise of the young laissez-faire ideologues who were the backbone of Yancey's support within the Democracy. During the early Confederate period, the tide seemed to turn against whiggish views, and the group fell almost completely from power. In reality, however, secession had only

---

87. Two men who were members of both congresses—James L. Pugh and William Russell Smith—were Democrats but had formerly been Whigs. Pugh had severed his ties with the Whiggery when he became a part of the Eufaula bipartisan radical group in 1849, later served as a Buchanan elector, and was sent to the U.S. House as a Democrat. Smith became a Democrat in 1843, during the Clay-Tyler dispute, and remained one, though in 1855 he had run for reelection to Congress on the Know-Nothing ticket.

briefly stemmed the flood. Confederate reverses and the extreme hard-
ships into which Yanceyite policies had led the state produced a revulsion against the new rulers. Indeed, the revulsion was so strong that it
even permitted persons whose affiliation with Whiggery was open and
formal, to achieve electoral success—something that the earlier experiment with a whiggish program had never done. The alliance of
Whigs and north Alabama Democrats which gained power in 1863
continued into Reconstruction. The politics of that decade is largely
the story of north Alabamians' oscillation between the two parties in
search of a congenial home. But the uneasy alliance calling itself the
Democratic and Conservative party that emerged from Reconstruction
proved a Trojan horse through which the old Jacksonians were finally
and irrevocably betrayed. At the end of the century, forced into increasing alienation by the social and economic attitudes now dominant in the party, those citizens who still remembered the antebellum
tradition undertook one last crusade to recapture the state government—and the dream to which that government had once given form.
The leader of the poignantly anachronistic Populist Revolt, Commissioner of Agriculture Reuben F. Kolb, was a nephew of the Eufaula
fire-eater and Yanceyite governor John Gill Shorter.

Scorpio Rising

In the preceding brief summary of the events surrounding secession, I have sought to demonstrate that the act of disunion can
be—and should be—understood in terms of the rival ambitions and
ideologies of the state's several political factions. I must emphasize,
however, that I do not take this analysis to be an explanation of the
reasons for the adoption of secession, but rather of the process by
which the policy came to achieve adoption. That is to say, secession as
an answer to the sectional crisis was a response whose roots lay deep
in the society, a decision which is political only in the sense that politics
always forms a pale reflection of the conflicts and concerns of the society. But secession as a specific act was accomplished through the political mechanism; therefore, there must necessarily be a level on which
the ordinance—like any other piece of legislation, however broad its
social significance—should be conceived in political terms, as the out-

come of political activity. It has been the aim of the present chapter to explore that particular level. Any attempt to isolate this chapter from the earlier ones I would regard, however, as a profound error, for one would thereby isolate politics from the social and institutional context in which it is practiced. That I may guard against such a misreading of my purpose, it would perhaps be useful to conclude by recapitulating the Alabama context as we have discovered it.

Alabamians were a people preoccupied with slavery. Their fathers had bequeathed them democracy, unquestioning faith in the capacity of the individual to shape his own life, and an overwhelming conviction that such activity was indispensable to self-respect. Their fathers had also bequeathed them property in man and consequently had placed always before them the reality of freedom lost, the horror of dependence. American politics in the Jacksonian Age turned almost wholly on the discovery and elimination of all sources of coercive dependence. Independence, indeed, was the element which linked freedom and equality: one became free, in the antebellum understanding of the term, only when one's life was one's own; and such a state could be achieved only when one had no superiors who were able to limit one's autonomy. Individual autonomy could be limited either by institutions or by other individuals. In either case, the dependence ordinarily was thought to result from economic relationships, though it might, rarely, have other sources. To permit the preservation of such relationships could have but one inevitable result: dependence of any sort by one citizen upon another destroyed equality of citizenship and therefore the social foundation of democracy and the freedom which only democracy could engender. It resulted, in short, in slavery. The government was the citizen's sword in his constant, desperate struggle to ward off reduction to fawning subhumanity.

Government could act to destroy slavery in either of two ways. In Whig ideology, it sought to develop the economy and thus to raise the citizen's income—to provide him with the competence which would deliver him from the enslavement of economic inequities. In Jacksonian ideology, it became the union of the electorate, bringing the vengeance of the community to bear on the selfish few who pursued their own aggrandizement at the expense of others. But all politicians campaigned by promising the voters emancipation from the shackles of inequality. In the depressed 1820s and 1840s Alabamians were particularly enthusiastic in support of attacks on private concentrations of power, whereas in the more prosperous thirties and fifties—particularly in the latter decade—they tended to look with hope to economic expansion. Probably, however, most Alabamians at all times held simultaneously tenets of each of the two great political faiths, merely adjusting the balance of the mixture in response to changing circumstances. Thus even in the booming fifties there remained an extremely important residue of Jacksonian doubt.

The institutional structure created by the constitution of 1819 and the political tradition formed in the struggles surrounding the dissolution of the Huntsville Bank and the creation of the Bank of Alabama both placed enormous emphasis on direct governmental response to the popular will. Like the wind's will, however, the will of the populace made strong and potentially destructive, but not easily defined demands. It always assumed that enslavement was imminent, and it always demanded protection from subservience; but discovering the source of the danger and the proper remedy to be applied was the task of the aspiring politician. His success in his occupation was determined by his skill in focusing electoral discontent on some plausible enemy.

The surface of the political planet, beneath its cloud cover of democracy, was therefore swept constantly by gales of extraordinary fury. Yet these storms were as nothing compared to the force of the seething volcanic terror which lay at the planet's core. The world was formed around two irreconcilable facts—the existence of society and the ideological necessity for individual autonomy. Northern states were faced with this competition, too, but southern states faced it in a peculiarly immediate form. Individual autonomy was the line which separated the free from the slave. To abandon self-government was to abandon the substance of liberty—to slip screaming down towards the bestial black mass which formed the sum of all hatred and fear. Southerners, then, were condemned to attack constantly, and almost at random, institutions. Institutions could never be wholly eliminated because they are the fabric of society. But southerners could never acquiesce in the existence of institutions because institutions became so easily symbols of the society's most profound anxiety, the loss of freedom. And the very functioning of the political mechanism continually exacerbated the anxiety, continually preached that each man's liberty was under attack and that its preservation depended upon his decisions at the polls. The citizen was made to feel that his fate rested in his own hands—and it was an awful awareness.

The final decade added additional unstable elements to an already volatile brew. Politicians, who until the fifties had done a good job of divining the nature of public discontent and providing release through political action, became increasingly divorced from their constituents. They had come to understand consciously that electoral success depended upon the exploitation of popular fear through the manipulation of symbolic issues; and with that understanding came cynicism and contempt for the masses. But conscious exploitation failed. The earlier politicians had been guided by a genuine rapport with the popular mind. The new generation, lacking an intuitive sense of what would strike fire in the voter's breast, merely floundered. Only the fire-eaters preached a true crusade against a concrete enemy.

Alabamians were slow to accept the fire-eaters' devils. Before the 1850s Alabama was an isolated state. The North seemed exceedingly remote, and danger from that quarter was simply not credible—particularly since northerners continued to elect careful and conservative men. But the state's rapid economic development and a concomitant enormous increase in governmental activity produced three conditions which tended to challenge the previous incredulity. First, a greater percentage of the populace, distributed more generally through the state, was drawn into the market economy. As such ties with the outside world took on importance in the lives of ordinary citizens, Alabamians came more fully to appreciate the extent to which they were bound in a national net of complex interrelationships. In addition, a more effective educational effort, more numerous libraries and newspapers, and immensely improved means of transportation and communication all undermined the state's protective parochialism.

Second, the Jacksonian heritage induced a general uneasiness in the presence of a booming economy. The constant anticipation of a crash and the deep doubts about the moral implications of prosperity would have taken their toll alone. But their effects were considerably magnified by the almost unalloyed terror with which many voters regarded the sudden expansion of government, at both state and local levels. Unprecedented rates of expenditure and the inauguration of novel projects were among the clues which a generation had been taught presaged oppression and eventual despotism. These rather un-formed fears were pushed into the danger zone by the inability of the political structure to deal with them. Many younger politicians failed to understand the sources of the anxiety and were unable to provide any outlet for the pressure. Indeed, they suppressed, because it was a threat to their own positions, the one political movement—Winston's—which gave promise of involving the electorate. Conditions, therefore, left many Alabamians ripe for a crusade which would seek to focus the misgivings so widespread in the society upon a specific villain.

Finally, slavery in the territories, the specific issue through which Alabamians were introduced to the fire-eaters' villains, carried within it elements which resonated with many of the aspirations and assumptions of the populace. In 1847 Daniel Pratt, the great industrialist, wrote a long and plaintive letter in which he detailed the difficulties to which the agrarian attitudes of the state subjected him.

I feel myself to be a permanent Citizen of this State. Nearly all I have is here and here I expect it to remain. Consequently I do feel a deep interest in our state affairs. . . . And I further believe that if a majority of both parties were situated as I am (that is, so they could not pull up stakes at any time when they chose and be off) that they would act and manage very different from what they now do. The great eval in our State is that persons janerally do not consider themselves settled [and] consequently do not take nor feel that inter-est in the future prosperity of our State they otherways would.[88]

Pratt had seen to the heart of the society. Alabamians were as fear-ful of permanent residence, of putting down roots, as they were of dependence. In fact, permanency seemed a form of dependence. If one became locked into a particular place and station, one lost in some measure the capacity to shape one's own destiny. External forces be-came powerful in determining the course of one's life, and powerful external forces are by definition limits upon individual autonomy. The entire government of the state was carried on as if it were a temporary expedient, an ad hoc arrangement permitted to interfere briefly and

88. Daniel Pratt to Dixon H. Lewis, September 21, 1847, in Lewis Papers, University of Texas Library.

gingerly in the lives of the citizens solely in order to guard their right to live undisturbed. In the fifties, just as the government was becoming more and more active, the society more and more organized, the influence of the outside world more and more apparent, just as the populace was developing a rather desperate sense that it had been trapped on flypaper, at that moment the free-soil agitation undertook to close off the farmer's escape route into the territories. It was of no comfort to the non-slaveholding farmer that he would be able to move to a territory if he were willing to desert a slave society. Almost all Alabamians believed that northern society was a society of dependence—and it was dependence, in the form of organization and permanency, which immigrants to the territories would be seeking to escape. If slavery were the bulwark of individualism and equality, if the absence of slavery dictated the existence of an economy which placed one citizen's livelihood at the mercy of a fellow citizen's whim, then the enactment of free-soil legislation would present the yeomen with two unacceptable alternatives: they could move out of the South, and thus sacrifice true liberty and equality at once for the mere forms of the faith, or they could remain where they were and wait for a slower sacrifice, as commercial and elitist attitudes gradually reduced the masses to thralldom.

It is no wonder, then, that Alabamians easily made an association between the agitation to bar "the South" from the territories and the increasing organization of their own community. Fire-eaters had no difficulty in convincing many voters that the villains upon whom the electorate should focus its fear, unrest, and hatred were northern anti-slavery men. This focus was at least as reasonable as had been the focus upon the Monster Bank in an earlier such episode. But the territorial issue did not derive its force only from the terror of being shut in, as refracted through the alterations in the state's economy and society and the new insensitivity of the state's government. These were the factors which brought the threat to liberty into play, but other factors made the threat to equality an element supportive of the crusade as well.

The nature of the quest for office in Alabama made class resentments and envy standard parts of political oratory. Each person was expected to affirm and defend his equality constantly, and politics was a principal dueling ground upon which to carry out this process. If any significant element of the populace allowed itself to be treated as second-class citizens, it thereby opened to the government a path to despotism, and went far towards destroying the line which separated free from slave. Northern actions seemed to many southerners to demand exactly this sort of sacrifice of their equality. Particularly insulting and denigrating were the personal liberty laws which had been passed by numbers of northern states in order to nullify the Fugitive Slave Act of 1850. Historians have perhaps underestimated these laws as a cause of secession. In the debates of the Alabama convention before the adoption of the ordinance, only the election of Lincoln was cited so often as reason for the action, and these two were the only substantial grievances regularly mentioned. The convention's Committee of Thirteen, which wrote the ordinance, said, for instance, "The wide-spread dissatisfaction of the people of this State which has finally induced them to dissolve the Union styled the United States of America, has been with the conduct of the people and Legislatures of the Northern States setting at naught one of the plainest provisions of the Federal Compact, and with other dangerous misinterpretations of that instrument, leading them [Alabamians] to believe that the Northern people design by their numerical majority, acting through the forms of government, ultimately to destroy many of our most valuable rights."[89] The laws seemed to prove that the Constitution, no matter how explicit, was no protection to the South, because southerners were a weak minority. The laws represented a contemptuous flaunting of the fact that the North had the numerical power to disregard a statute gained by the South at the cost of considerable and humiliating concessions—and so gained even though the statute in question was beyond dispute the South's right in the first place. Viewed in this light, the personal liberty laws became intolerable affirmations of southern inferiority—a derisive scoff at southern pretensions to equal partnership as Americans. It was in the grip of such emotions that southern rights forces adopted as their motto, "Equality in the Union or Independence Out of It."

89. Smith, *Debates of the Convention of 1861*, 131.

The committee's statement also points to the most important sense in which equality was at issue in the sectional controversy. The committee feared that the personal liberty laws were a precedent for using "the forms of government. . . . to destroy many of our most valuable rights." There can be little doubt as to which valuable right they thought most threatened; the committee very probably had reference to enforced emancipation. The fear was general in Alabama that the Republicans intended, at least eventually, to adopt such a policy for the South. And emancipation would rob equality of the substance which made equality worth having: the pride and self-assurance that flow from a sense of one's political and social worth. Who would attribute dignity to, and seek to maintain, a position to which even a Negro could aspire? An equality with former slaves, far from generating pride, would be a source of shame—would become itself a form of slavery for whites.

In all of these ways and many others, fire-eaters were able to make their crusade for secession a crusade for the only two things that really mattered in Alabama—liberty and equality. In that form, it fell readily into an old and essential place in the structure of the society, as the functional element relating political action to social needs. Once the secession movement had succeeded in taking on this role for an important element of the electorate, the political mechanism dictated an almost certain outcome. It has been the purpose of the present chapter to show the relentless, horribly logical meshing of gears within that mechanism during the final months of peace. But the machine could not have begun its grinding until all the precedent elements had been established. Thus the nature of the interaction between the political and social structures before 1850 was essential; and equally so were the events of the fifties which knocked the structure off balance and forced it to attempt to regain its equilibrium by embracing a potentially destructive cause. The election of Lincoln at that critical juncture swept away the contentions that had become the final refuges of conservative politicians in pleading for moderation. It provided proof that the bisectional character of the Democratic party alliance could no longer guarantee the South's safety on a tolerable basis. And it proved that the majority of northerners were hostile to the establishment of genuine sectional equality. These now incontestable facts compelled the political structure to give substance to the crusade it had recently and rather hesitantly accepted.

In 1859 one frightened citizen wrote to a newspaper that the prolonged existence of the political party as an institution had conditioned southerners "to follow in slavish obsequiousness its demagogical dicta" and to "pay it such abject fealty as to become oblivious to the identity of our interests, our cause and our enemy who stands as a solid phalanx against us." The writer begged southerners to break "loose from its [party's] trappings and its collars (fit habiliments for unreasoning creatures only)." Otherwise, the South was "destined to remain tributary and subservient to her imperious and exacting master, the Abolition North"; and southerners were condemned "to crouch and cower Spaniel-like at the heels of the loathsome monster." Moreover, the writer added that the emancipation must come quickly because "We are moving [as] rapidly to increasing weakness, as our enemy is to accumulating strength and power." [90]

There are at least three points which we should note about this exhortation. In the first place, its force derives almost wholly from its repeated invocation of the image of slavery. Second, its fear that partisan competition, by perpetuating social divisions, would inhibit resistance to northern exaction, was largely misplaced. Devoted membership in a national party did impose some limits on a politician's radicalism and incline him towards the acceptance of compromise in order to insure a common effort in presidential campaigns. But a search for southern unity would, from similar considerations, have compelled a similar abandonment of advanced ideological positions. Actually, southern social division was not the enemy of the southern rights crusade, but its chief ally. The writer would have been correct if he had declared that the existence of rival political factions, actively seeking to give concrete form to the electorate's deepest apprehensions, had in the past been the heart of the mechanism through which mounting social pressures had been relieved. But the irony of the changes which overtook Alabamians in the fifties is that, under the impulse of the new political and social circumstances of that decade, partisan

90. Montgomery *Advertiser*, April 13, 1859.

competition—the very substance of the levees which had constrained and channeled the citizenry's seething fear in earlier days—became an indispensable element in bringing the state to perceive events through the eyes of the extremists.

Perhaps, however, the most important observation which the letter provokes turns on its assertion that the South was rapidly becoming weaker during this period. Observers often issued such warnings. But as a matter of fact, the region in these years was booming: its economy was experiencing the most startling growth; its people were caught up in unexampled prosperity; risk capital was abundant and was actively seeking new areas of investment. The commencement of hostilities found the South stronger than she had ever been before, incomparably better prepared for modern warfare than she had been even ten years earlier. The point, of course, is that such standards of strength were virtually irrelevant to the definition of the sectional crisis, as Alabamians understood it. To a generation which had been reared in the shadow of the Battle of New Orleans, to a people who believed that the spirit of the American democrat would surely prevail against mere arms, the degree of freedom and equality enjoyed by the citizen seemed the true source and measure of might, rather than railroads and cannon. And the belief had increasing currency in the South that southerners were becoming—had become, as it seemed after the elections of 1860—a minority group powerless to influence the government through political action, and therefore by definition weak.

An awareness of the profoundly disquieting implications which such an impression would have had for men of that time, coupled with a realization of the unprecedented relationship which developed between government and corporations in the fifties, prepares us at this point to move a step beyond the contention that political considerations underlay the formation of the cooperationist and immediatist factions. From the rather abstract, but nonetheless instructive perspective of social ideology, the factions can be seen to have been separated by something more than rival ambitions. The events of the preceding decade which had so shaken the society had generated a new notion of how one might force politics to respond to one's needs, and the factions in the Secession Convention were arguing in essence about the accuracy of that notion. The cooperationist position resisted the full implications of the lessons of the new age, while the immediatist argument rested firmly upon those lessons. A speech by Delegate John Potter of Cherokee County makes this point clearer. "Our grievances should be redressed," he told the convention. "This is what we all desire, and only differ in regard to the proper method to be adopted. For one, I have not been able to see that secession is the best mode, and therefore I cannot adopt it. . . . It cannot be denied that our rights and interests have been disregarded and set at nought by many of our sister States. But can we come up to the full measure of duty and secure all to which we are entitled by the act of secession? I think not." Whether to gain access to the territories, to preserve slavery, or to vindicate offended honor, he said, withdrawal was simply inexpedient. He would not oppose the action if it gave any promise of achieving these ends. But it did not.[91]

The fundamental assumption of Potter's argument is revealed in the first sentence of the quotation: "Our grievances must be redressed," he had said. An immediatist would have said, "We must redress our grievances"; or more probably, "We must secure our rights from invasion." The immediatists no longer thought of redress as something for which one need petition. Secession was an act of self-performed redress. Andrew P. Calhoun, a son of the South Carolina senator but for twenty years a planter in Marengo County, described the moment of his native state's secession in such terms. "At this point, the accumulated aggressions of the third of a century fell like shackles at her feet, and free, disinthralled, regenerated, she stood before her devoted people like the genius of Liberty, beckoning them on to the performance of their duty. The argument closes here so far as Federal aggressions in South Carolina are concerned."[92]

Social grievances may be eliminated in two places—at the source, where the wrong originates, and at the outlet, where it is received. Eliminating a grievance at the source requires a recognition by the group that one of its segments is wronging another segment and a resultant collective action to destroy the channels through which the wrong occurs. Such action, because it must be collective, is governmental, and therefore political. The discovery of its potential was

91. Smith, *Debates of the Convention of 1861*, 107–108.
92. *Ibid.*, 32.

the central event of the Jacksonian era. The ordinary citizen found that he could use the collective will of the society—the government—to protect himself from his more powerful neighbors. But he could do so only if he organized politically to convince the society of the validity of his grievance. This discovery was so powerful that it fascinated America for the next two decades. In the fifties, however, the limits of its usefulness were more and more exposed by the examples, with which the decade was replete, of actions by segments of society which defeated—or even dictated to—the collective will. The agitation by railroads for governmental aid, the establishment of public schools, and many other such developments seemed to most Alabamians to fall into the category of collective capitulation to pressure groups. The government was now less the voice of society in disciplining interests than it was merely the mechanism through which interests dealt with the majority.

Alabamians were frightened of these incidents, and yet irresistably fascinated by the new potentialities of associative action by minorities, which appeared to them almost as great as at an earlier period the potentialities of actions by the collective society had seemed. Those older men who remained true to the Jacksonian vision continued to believe that this new form of behavior was somehow immoral, because undemocratic. Action gained legitimacy, they thought, only when it could claim the general sanction of the society. And so throughout the decade of increasing sectional tensions, they continued to try to convince northerners of the justice of the southern case and the depth of southern commitment to it. For these men redress still implied forcing the source of the wrong to correct its misbehavior. Potter's speech stands in this tradition. And of course within this framework Potter's argument was entirely correct; secession was by no means the most effective mode of gaining northern acquiescence in southern aims. But immediatists no longer desired northern acquiescence. They believed now that they could work out their own salvation by their own actions. Potter's line of reasoning thus became not an error but a museum piece.

Most Alabamians consistently rejected the kind of pressure group activity so common in the fifties, but its example imperceptibly infiltrated their minds and became a part—though not an entirely conscious part—of their assumptions about the world. The personal liberty laws seemed so important to them in part because such laws demonstrated that minority pressure groups could defeat the will of the majority in this realm as well as in the economic sphere. Under the guidance of events, immediatists came to see that, in seeking redress for their grievances, they were not, as a minority, limited to plea, expostulation, and threat, precisely because they did not have to be a majority in order to work their will. They did not have to wait for the government to suppress the wrong directed at them. They themselves could render hostile forces powerless simply by removing themselves from harm's way. It was this liberating gospel which the immediatists struggled to convey to the cooperationists: that secession was an efficient remedy not because it would effect historic southern goals, but because it would make the goals irrelevant.

Yancey told the delegates,

Some gentlemen seem to think that in dissolving the Union, we hazard the "rich inheritance" bequeathed to us. For one I make a distinction between our liberties and the powers which have been delegated to secure them. Those liberties have never been alienated—are inalienable. . . . The course we are about to adopt makes no war on our liberties—nor indeed upon our institutions—nor upon the Federal Constitution. It is but a dismissal of the agent that first abuses our institutions with a view to destroy our rights, and then turns the very powers we delegated to him for our protection against us for our injury. These powers were originally possessed by the people of the sovereign States, and when the common agent abuses them, it seems to me but the dictate of common sense as well as an act of self-preservation that the States should withdraw and resume them. . . . We propose to do as the Israelites did of old under Divine direction—to withdraw our people from under the power that oppresses them and in doing so, like them to take with us the Ark of the Covenant of our liberties.[93]

The oratory which surrounded the new gospel was not new. It was so reminiscent of Calhoun and of Jefferson that it inhibited Alabamians at the time, and has inhibited students since, from grasping just how original a message it carried. But the fire of the dawning age burned beneath these cadenced sentences, and provided the force which drove the populace to an acceptance of the immediatist cause. The differences between the factions at the convention, then, were more than

93. *Ibid.*, 115–16.

political. They reflected also two competing conceptions of the moral use of power: collective versus associative action; working to create a majority versus striking as a minority for a minority interest.

One final point remains to be noted: that such an explanation of secession reduces the role of long-standing fire-eaters—the men who had been committed to a radical southern rights position as early as 1850—to relatively limited significance. Indeed, a genuinely startling number of radicals from 1850 were cooperationists in 1860. A partial listing of such men would at least include John A. Campbell, his brother-in-law George Goldthwaite, Benjamin F. Saffold, Adam C. Felder, Henry Churchill Semple, and even Charles E. Haynes of the Cahaba *Gazette*. Perhaps the source of this conversion lies in the fact that these men, generally young outsiders in 1850, had by 1860 been more thoroughly incorporated into party power. Those southern rights men who remained true to the cause became increasingly hostile to politics and tended more and more to hold aloof from such activity; this group I have designated left fire-eaters. They were important in that their very existence served to insure that Yancey and the right fire-eaters would not too far abandon principle in pursuit of party control. They constantly reminded the Yanceyites that political power was only a means to the end of southern rights. But beyond this limited function, it was not the old and bitter left fire-eaters but the young and visionary right fire-eaters who were the mainstay of the crusade which the political structure took up at the end of the decade.

This younger group, whose members commonly began winning important office only during the Buchanan administration, attached itself to Yancey's leadership, though its ideology was not precisely coincident with his. The dogmatic individualism which was so important to many right fire-eaters was somewhat less important to Yancey, but their ambitions and his theory of agitation both required activity within the Democracy rather than purity outside it. When the advocacy of southern rights brought them electoral success, the young men were bound even closer to Yancey, a process which resulted by the end of the decade in the creation of the identifiable and powerful Yanceyite faction. It was the existence of this group which accounted for the large number of attorneys in the Secession Convention. Thereafter political circumstance, for reasons which we have already discovered, virtually dictated a general adherence by more experienced politicians to the crusade which the Yanceyites were preaching. In these accelerating events the aspirations of the new fire-eaters, rather than the perseverance of the older ones, showed the way. And in that particular sense, the real leaders of this, as of every great political movement in antebellum Alabama, were not the politicians at all, but the voters.

There is a famous passage from Caesar which I have always thought rather symbolic of the events of southern secession. During the invasion of Britain, the Roman fleet was standing off the Dover coast, prevented from approaching too near the shore by high seas. The soldiers—unable to tell the depth of the water, weighted down with armor, and faced with a hostile army drawn up in the surf— hesitated to jump from the ships. "Atque nostris militibus cunctantibus, maxime propter altitudinem maris," Caesar tells us, "qui X legionis aquilam ferebat, obtestatus deos, ut ea res legioni feliciter eveniret, 'Desilite,' inquit, 'commilitones, nisi vultis aquilam hostibus prodere. Ego certe meum rei publicae atque imperatori officium praestitero.' Hoc cum voce magna dixisset, se ex nave proiecit atque in hostes aquilam ferre coepit. Tum nostri cohortati inter se ne tantum dedecus admitteretur, universi ex nave desiluerunt." [94]

In this little allegory, the role of the standard bearer is taken by South Carolina among the southern states, and by the fire-eaters within each state. I would hope, though, that my parable might make another point. However important the action of the standard bearer may have been to the outcome, it would clearly be absurd to explain the episode only—or even primarily—in terms of the motives which created the standard bearer's loyalty to the republic and his leader. Rather the principal factor surely must have been the values of the other soldiers, which gave the standard bearer's action its power. What magic there was in the title by which he addressed them! *Commilitones*, he called them—fellow soldiers. The real dynamic of the

94. Gaius Julius Caesar, *Commentaries on the Gallic War*, Bk. IV, 25. The passage might be rendered: "While our soldiers were delaying, because of the enormous height of the seas, the man who carried the standard of the tenth legion, having called on the gods to grant that his legion might bear its part successfully, shouted, 'Jump, fellow soldiers, unless you wish our standard surrendered to the foe; for I shall certainly perform my duty to the Republic and her general.' After he had thus proclaimed his intentions, he threw himself from the ship and began to carry the ensign towards the ranks of the enemy. Then our cohorts shouted to each other that they could not permit so great a disgrace to their standard, and leaped from the ship as one man."

situation was that they all, the bold and the hesitant, were bound together by a common sense of membership in a mutual enterprise. When one man acted, they could not regard his action from the standpoint of spectators. He was an intrinsic part of the group, and his action was an extension of their own.

An analysis of secession which argues that the fire-eaters' manipulations produced the event, or that South Carolina's decision forced the issue, leaves unexamined the most important element—the support, ranging from acquiescence to enthusiasm, of nearly the entire electorate of the Lower South. At any time during these years, the voters could have halted the movement towards secession. Alabamians could have rejected secession as late as Christmas Eve of 1860. But when Christmas Day dawned, the Rubicon had been crossed—with Yancey mounted pompously astride the lead horse, perhaps, but with few deserters from the army at his back.

The decision was taken because the voters wanted it taken. They believed it necessary. The process by which they had come to this belief does not feature, it is true, much edifying debate upon the true implications of the points at issue. But Jacksonian politics had never generated much discussion of that character. Instead, the process, with all its imperfections, was the same process by which political decisions had been made since the days of Israel Pickens. The only real difference was that the light of past experience, reflected from the new circumstances, made them seem so frightening that the populace, in its terror, was moved to exceed the inherent bounds which the political structure had always imposed upon previous crises. Until events moved beyond this "fail-safe point," however, it was quite difficult to tell the crisis of the Union from its predecessors in Alabama—the Huntsville Bank controversy; the struggle to gain remission of a portion of the public land debt and to gain preemption rights for squatters; the crisis over the removal of the Creeks; the failure and dissolution of the Bank of Alabama; the Crisis of 1850; the opposition to state financing of internal improvements; and the thousand other crusades launched in the name of popular liberty and social equality. The last crusade produced an extreme decision because the threat to freedom which it sought to repel seemed more substantial and more horrible than had the earlier ones. But when the leaders of the crusade leaped from the ship, the masses followed because this crusade was a common enterprise, fought not for some alien cause but for the preservation of each individual soldier's most valued possession, the thing which made him a man. He sought, therefore, to save the essence of America as he understood it.

I may confess, in conclusion, that it is my notion that the institutional and intellectual structure which effectively impelled Alabamians into secession was operative, *mutatis mutandis*, in most of the other southern states as well. To demonstrate such a contention would, of course, take us much beyond the limits of the present study. I must leave that journey for another time and, possibly, another voyager. But at the level of simple assertion, I am entirely prepared to go still further, to maintain that the Alabama pattern holds important implications even for the strength of the free-soil movement in the North.

The Jacksonian era was a national, not merely a southern episode. While condemnations to slavery might have had more frightening reality for southerners, even the rather metaphorical northern form of the threat had sufficient strength to move northern voters to repeated political activity. And in the North as in the South, one important element in the decline of liberty as citizens perceived it was the feeling of being locked into a structure, imprisoned without any path of escape in an area of increasing social immobility. Like southern politicians, their northern brethren also sensed these ill-formed fears and sought to give them focus, thus relating political action to social need. The creation of such a crusade was no less in the North than in the South the path to office and power. And so in the 1850s northern politicians came increasingly to warn—not without some measure of accuracy—that the federal government had fallen into the hands of southerners, who were seeking to use their control to effect the extension of slavery to all the territories, and that if the effort were successful northern emigrants to the territories would be compelled to abandon the open and egalitarian society which they had known for a stratified, aristocratic one. The territories thus not only would cease to be a possible alternative to older areas, but moreover would become a positive threat to the sphere of freedom which existed, hemming it in and gradually reducing it to minority status in the Union. The free-soil argument on these points was the veritable mirror image of the southern rights case. Nor was it so by accident, but because it was offered in response to the demands of a nearly identical political climate.

Probably northern society was not in quite so extreme a period of internal stress as was that of the Lower South at the time these issues became prominent; and the North's reaction to the warnings was consequently not quite so extreme. The free-soil question had great political power, of course. But it is difficult to believe that the northern states would have rebelled had Breckinridge won the election, even though some northerners might have advocated the step. Despite this essential difference in the force of the issue—which is to some extent the measure of the real difference between the two sections—it remains true enough that the political path to the victory of Lincoln and the political path to secession are parallel roads.

It is strange how often poets seem to know intuitively things about the past which historians discover only after the most arduous labor. I do not wish to be thought disloyal to Clio. She is surely the most beautiful of those sisters. It is just that it takes so much work to earn her favor. At any rate, Robert Penn Warren has written a poem which, in the way of poems, contains a considerable truth. It is cast in the form of the reflections of a young Union officer—recently graduated from Harvard and even more recently killed—upon the place of his Confederate foe within the eternal order.

"I didn't mind dying—it wasn't that at all.
It behooves a man to prove manhood by dying for Right.
If you die for Right that fact is your dearest requital,
But you find it disturbing when others die who
               simply haven't the right.

Why should they die with that obscene insouciance?
They seem to insult the principle of your own death.
. . . .
I tried to slay without rancor, and often succeeded.
I tried to keep the heart pure, though hand took stain.
But they made it so hard for me, the way they proceeded
To parody with their own dying that Death which
               only Right should sustain.
. . . .
         And I was dead, too.

Dead, and had died for the Right, as I had a right to,
And glad to be dead, and hold my residence
Beyond life's awful illogic, and the world's stew,
Where people who haven't the right just die,

with ghastly impertinence." [95]

It must have been that way. Young men in that war must have been puzzled at the extraordinary tenacity of the opposing army; at the willingness of the opposing soldiers to lay down their lives for so poor a cause. It was almost as if the enemy were sustained by Right—but of course it could not be.

The final irony of the Civil War was that the armies which met on the Peninsula, where Patrick Henry had once delivered his orations; near Shiloh Church, where earnest evangelists had proclaimed the might of truth; at Chickamauga, where the tiny patches of farm clung without surrender to the sides of the eroded hills; and before Atlanta, where the railroads crossed—these armies were composed of Americans, with all the conceits of Americans. No American—and surely no southern American—ever needed to be reminded that the loss of freedom is slavery.

We must not wonder, then, that the people of Alabama greeted with such joy the sentence of suicide which they had just passed upon themselves. A cooperationist delegate from Tuscaloosa described the scene in the convention just after the passage of the ordinance:

When the doors [of the convention hall] were thrown open, the lobby and galleries were filled to suffocation in a moment. The ladies were there in crowds, with visible eagerness to participate in the exciting scenes. With them, the love songs of yesterday had swelled into the political hosannas of to-day.

Simultaneously with the entrance of the multitude, a magnificent Flag was unfurled in the centre of the Hall, so large as to reach nearly across the ample chamber! Gentlemen mounted upon tables and desks, held up the floating end, the better thus to be able to display its figures. The cheering was now deafening for some moments. It seemed really that there would be no end to the raptures that had taken possession of the company. . . . Amid the wild enthusiasm that had taken as well possession of the hall as of the streets and the city, the Convention adjourned.

95. Robert Penn Warren, "Harvard '61: Battle Fatigue," in *Selected Poems New and Old,* 1923–1966 (New York: Random House, 1966), 130–31.

The roar of cannon was heard at intervals during the remainder of this eventful day. The new flag of Alabama displayed its virgin features from the windows and towers of the surrounding houses; and the finest orators of the State, in harangues of congratulation, commanded until a late hour in the night the attention of shouting multitudes.[96]

The antebellum world celebrated its death. And somewhere—brooding, perhaps, in that region of the mind to which we condemn ideas which have become axioms—somewhere, Andrew Jackson understood.

96. Smith, *Debates of the Convention of 1861*, 119, 122. See also James F. Dowdell to William F. Samford, January 11, 1861, in George Petrie Papers, Auburn University Library, Auburn.

Appendix 1 House Votes Indicating Party Divisions

Session of 1839	Yea	Nay
To postpone indefinitely a bill to reorganize the banking system and charter a joint stock bank	54D, 7W, 4? 90%, 26%	6D, 20W 10%, 74%
To table a resolution authorizing the state banks to suspend specie payment	45D, 7W 75%, 24%	15D, 22W, 4? 25%, 76%
To conduct an inquiry into the expediency of guaranteeing wives a separate income from their separate estates	23D, 22W, 2? 42%, 81%	32D, 5W, 3? 58%, 19%
To pass a bill "for the benefit of settlers on the public lands"	29D, 9W, 2? 60%, 38%	19D, 15W, 3? 40%, 63%
To extend debts due the state bank and provide for issuing postnotes	32D, 19W, 3? 55%, 70%	26D, 8W, 2? 45%, 30%
To amend the act abolishing imprisonment for debt	23D, 8W, 1? 52%, 36%	21D, 14W, 3? 48%, 64%
To postpone a bill to improve the Muscle Shoals	27D, 25W, 3? 46%, 83%	32D, 5W, 1? 54%, 17%
To postpone a bill to assist works of internal improvement	34D, 7W, 3? 74%, 37%	12D, 12W, 2? 26%, 63%
To reconsider above vote	15D, 14W, 2? 30%, 56%	35D, 11W, 3? 70%, 44%
To table a bill to incorporate a railroad	28D, 10W, 2? 67%, 50%	14D, 10W 33%, 50%
To postpone indefinitely a bill more effectually to restrain the sale of liquor	35D, 17W, 2? 58%, 68%	25D, 8W, 2? 42%, 32%

Session of 1840		
To conduct an inquiry into the expediency of purchasing two-fifths of the stock of a private Mobile bank	12D, 30W 24%, 71%	37D, 12W 76%, 29%

	Yea	*Nay*
To agree that biennial legislative sessions would be inexpedient	23D, 22W 46%, 65%	27D, 12W 54%, 35%
To elect U.S. congressmen on a general ticket (at large)	45D, 1W 98%, 2%	1D, 41W 2%, 98%
To put a new roof on the capitol	15D, 17W 48%, 74%	16D, 6W 52%, 26%
To table a resolution forbidding any further improvement of the Black Warrior above Tuscaloosa	23D, 4W 62%, 16%	14D, 21W, 1? 38%, 84%
To appropriate not more than $4,000 to erect a state arsenal	27D, 16W 77%, 53%	8D, 14W, 1? 23%, 47%

Session of 1841

	Yea	*Nay*
To postpone a bill relating to dower rights	29D, 16W 69%, 44%	13D, 20W 31%, 56%
To postpone indefinitely a bill to permit the governor to nominate state bank directors	24D, 38W 48%, 97%	26D, 1W 52%, 3%
To take up a bill placing in liquidation the Bank of Alabama at Decatur	21W 81%	43D, 5W 100%, 19%
To create a third chancery district	16D, 21W 55%, 72%	13D, 8W 45%, 28%
To grant squatters on the state's public lands preemption rights, and to distribute the the proceeds of land sales	36D, 1W 100%, 4%	25W 96%
To table a bill to resume levying taxes	26D, 34W 51%, 81%	25D, 8W 49%, 19%
To repeal the General Ticket Law	21D, 36W 41%, 97%	30D, 1W 59%, 3%
To postpone a bill to put a new roof on the capitol	35D, 25W 66%, 57%	18D, 19W 34%, 43%

Session of 1849

	Yea	*Nay*
To postpone a bill to change the name of a county named for Thomas Hart Benton	43D, 7W 83%, 18%	9D, 31W 17%, 82%
To table a bill to prohibit the taxation of "labor or industry"	40D, 12W 85%, 33%	7D, 24W 15%, 67%
To table an amendment declaring any adult white male competent to practice law or medicine	42D, 19W 84%, 51%	8D, 18W 16%, 49%
To postpone resolutions repealing white population as the basis for congressional districting	48D, 8W 96%, 24%	2D, 25W 4%, 76%

	Yea	Nay
To table an amendment to replace the poll tax on slaves with an *ad valorem* tax on slaves	23D, 25W 50%, 78%	23D, 7W 50%, 22% (all 23 Democrats from white counties)
To allow Florence Bridge Co. to issue bank notes	10D, 24W 21%, 83%	37D, 5W 79%, 17%
To loan state funds to two railroads	25D, 27W 52%, 71%	23D, 11W 48%, 29%
To tax income of officers of corporations and of public officials	30D, 13W 64%, 42%	17D, 18W 36%, 58%
To have tax assessors elected by people	26D, 13W 57%, 35%	20D, 24W 43%, 65%
To make each stockholder of a bank individually liable for the total debts of the bank	32D 58%	23D, 40W 42%, 100%
To incorporate a new joint stock bank	24D, 40W 44%, 95%	30D, 2W 56%, 5%
To reduce the sales tax (1)	24D, 24W 48%, 63%	26D, 14W 52%, 37%
To increase the sales tax (2)	33D, 15W 73%, 39%	12D, 23W 27%, 61%
To increase the sales tax (3)	28D, 12W 64%, 32%	16D, 25W 36%, 68%
To increase the sales tax (4)	39D, 18W 74%, 46%	14D, 21W 26%, 54%
To unite duties of county judge and county clerk in a new office, probate judge	33D, 14W 67%, 39%	16D, 22W 33%, 61%
To table a proposal to repeal an act guaranteeing separate estates to married women	18D, 30W 38%, 77%	29D, 9W 62%, 23%
To repeal an act prohibiting out-of-state banks from doing business in Alabama	13D, 25W 31%, 78%	29D, 7W 69%, 22%
To permit free banking after the deposit of U.S. securities with the state treasurer	15D, 29W 37%, 85%	26D, 5W 63%, 15%

Appendix 2 House Votes Indicating Economic Divisions

MEDIAN SLAVEHOLDING

Session of 1829	Yea	Nay
To postpone indefinitely a bill to prohibit judges from charging juries	7	10½
To exempt a spouse's estate from execution for the other spouse's debts	13	6
To consolidate the offices of state treasurer and president of the state bank	8	11
To apportion state bank loans among counties by taxes paid instead of population	13	7

(The five members who opposed establishing a state board of internal improvement had a median holding of only 2; but the 13 members who opposed abolishing the board in 1830 had a median holding of only 5.)

Session of 1830		
To repeal the poll tax on white persons	7	14
Gabriel Moore vs. John McKinley for U.S. Senator	13 (Moore)	5 (McKinley)
To establish a separate state supreme court	4½	10
To permit the American Colonization Society to hold a state convention in the capitol	6	14½
Three votes involving the improvement of the Coosa River	10	6½
	9	7½
	10	7
To complete the building of the capitol	6	14
To postpone indefinitely a bill to admit indigent students to the University of Alabama free	9	7½

(The seven members who voted against resolutions nominating Andrew Jackson for a second term and commending the Maysville Road Bill veto, had a median holding of 20.)

Session of 1831	*Yea*	*Nay*
To exempt Indians from taxation	11	8½
To establish a separate state supreme court	7	11
Resolutions constituting the legislature as a caucus to nominate a slate of presidential electors	10½	7
To charter a joint stock bank	11	5½
To prohibit the sale of liquor to workmen on the Muscle Shoals Canal	6½	10
To print marginalia in English for Latin phrases used in statutes	11	4
To endorse the Maysville Road Bill veto and the refusal to use force against Governor Troup and the Georgians	14½	7
To state that President Jackson did not seek to coerce South Carolina by force	13½	7
To allow certain persons without special training to practice medicine	7	11
To table resolutions opposing the Bank of the United States	10	7
To invoke cloture on the debate on the anti-Bank of the U.S. resolutions	7	10½

(The fifteen members who voted against the bill to extend Alabama's jurisdiction over the Indian territory had a median holding of only 4.)

Session of 1839

To table a petition to abolish the sale of liquor	44D, 18W, 3?	12D, 10W, 2?
	7½	12
Democrats:	7½	10½
Whigs:	11	16
To table a second petition to abolish the sale of liquor	24D, 9W, 1?	23D, 13W, 2?
	13	6½
Democrats:	7	8
Whigs:	23	7
To postpone indefinitely a bill to "promote the cause of education"	29D, 10W, 2?	21D, 11W, 2?
	7	15
Democrats:	6½	16
Whigs:	14	18½

	Yea	Nay
To postpone indefinitely a bill to reorganize the state banking system, and to charter a joint stock bank	54D, 7W, 4? 7	6D, 20W 14½
To postpone (and thus kill) a bill to assist works of internal improvement	34D, 7W, 3? 5	12D, 12W, 2? 16
Democrats:	5	20
Whigs:	8	14
To reconsider preceding vote	15D, 14W, 2? 16	35D, 11W, 3? 6
Democrats:	18	6
Whigs:	19½	8
To table a bill to incorporate a railroad	28D, 10W, 2? 7	14D, 10W 11
Democrats:	7	8
Whigs:	10	14

Session of 1840

	Yea	Nay
To purchase two fifths of the stock of a private Mobile bank	12D, 30W 14	37D, 12W 8
Democrats:	9	7
Whigs:	14½	39
To agree that biennial sessions of the legislature would be inexpedient	23D, 22W 11	27D, 12W 7
Democrats:	9	5
Whigs:	12½	15½
To elect U.S. congressmen on a general ticket (at large)	45D, 1W 7	41W, 1D 14½
To put a new roof on the capitol	15D, 17W 9½	16D, 6W 6½
Democrats:	8	7
Whigs:	11½	5

Session of 1841

	Yea	Nay
To repeal the General Ticket Law	21D, 36W 12½	30D, 1W 7
Democrats:	14	7
To postpone indefinitely a bill in relation to dower rights	29D, 16W 11	13D, 20W 9
Democrats:	9	6½
Whigs:	12	11
To postpone indefinitely a bill to improve the Alabama River	30D, 19W, 1? 8	22D, 24W 13
Democrats:	7½	13½
Whigs:	11	12

	Yea	Nay
To postpone indefinitely a bill to permit the governor to nominate state bank directors (at the time elected by the legislature)	24D, 38W 8	26D, 1W 10
Democrats:	2	11
To reconsider passage of a bill to give broad powers to the committee investigating corruption in the state banks	20D, 15W 8	27D, 28W 11
Democrats:	3	7½
Whigs:	17½	12
To create a third chancery district	16D, 21W 12½	13D, 8W 9
Democrats:	12	5½
Whigs:	13	14½
To grant preemption rights to squatters on the state's public lands, and to distribute the proceeds of the land sales	36D, 1W 6½	25W 14
To table a bill to resume the levying of taxes	26D, 34W 8½	25D, 8W 11
Democrats:	1	13½
Whigs:	12	7

MEDIAN SLAVEHOLDING AND REAL PROPERTY VALUE

Session of 1849	Yea	Nay
To postpone indefinitely a resolution to reduce the pay of legislators	21D, 23W 4½	23D, 13W 11
	3,000	5,000
Democrats:	4	8
	1,500	3,500
Whigs:	14	17
	4,250	9,650
To table an amendment to facilitate damage suits against railroads	18D, 11W 9	12D, 11W 12
	2,500	4,250
Democrats:	4	8
	1,300	4,000
Whigs:	15	14
	7,550	4,250
To postpone indefinitely a bill to prohibit killing of deer in Barbour County at certain seasons	26D, 18W 11	17D, 14W 8
	3,000	3,200
Democrats:	2½	9½
	1,800	2,400
Whigs:	16	3
	3,800	3,700

	Yea	Nay
To reduce the sales tax (first vote)	24D, 24W	26D, 14W
	14	6
	5,000	3,200
Democrats:	14	3
	3,500	1,475
Whigs:	14	17
	6,400	3,800
To tax the income of officers of corporations and of public officials	30D, 13W	17D, 18W
	7	21
	3,000	7,000
Democrats:	4	20
	2,250	4,750
Whigs:	14	32
	3,450	9,300
To have tax assessors elected by people	26D, 13W	20D, 24W
	10	13
	2,000	4,500
Democrats:	5½	10½
	1,800	4,250
Whigs:	15	13
	3,400	5,500
To make each stockholder of a bank liable individually for the total debts of the bank	32D	23D, 40W
	4	17
	1,800	4,500
Democrats:	4	12
	1,800	3,000
To reduce the tax on slave children	23D, 19W	23D, 19W
	21	12
	3,250	4,250
Democrats:	18½	4
	2,000	2,400
Whigs:	21	16½
	4,250	10,000
To increase the sales tax (second vote)	33D, 15W	12D, 23W
	11	14
	3,250	5,750
Democrats:	5	22
	3,000	4,000
Whigs:	17	10
	3,750	6,250
To increase the sales tax (third vote)	28D, 12W	16D, 25W
	9½	14
	3,000	5,750

	Yea	Nay
Democrats:	5	21
	2,150	3,000
Whigs:	25½	14
	3,500	9,650
To increase the sales tax (fourth vote)	39D, 18W	14D, 21W
	10½	11
	3,000	5,500
Democrats:	4	17
	1,800	5,000
Whigs:	22	9
	3,500	6,250
To unite duties of county judge and county clerk in a new office, probate judge	33D, 14W	16D, 22W
	4	21
	3,000	6,500
Democrats:	4	18½
	1,800	3,000
Whigs:	11½	21
	3,700	9,300
To table a proposal to repeal an act guaranteeing separate estates to married women	18D, 30W	29D, 9W
	15½	6
	4,750	2,000
Democrats:	12½	6
	4,750	1,800
Whigs:	17	11
	4,900	4,250

MEDIAN SLAVEHOLDING, REAL ESTATE AND PERSONAL PROPERTY VALUE

Session of 1859	Yea	Nay
To prohibit the sale of liquor in a specified community	20	9
	10,000	3,500
	30,000	10,000
To table an amendment opposed to appointing a salaried chaplain for the House	20	12
	9,525	3,950
	30,000	15,000
To add five members to the judiciary committee who were not lawyers	25	9
	12,000	4,150
	33,000	18,750
To grant an extension of time to the Mobile and Ohio to repay its debt to the state	14	17
	13,500	4,000
	30,250	17,022
A resolution expressing appreciation to northerners who are favorable to the South	12	34
	5,500	13,500
	15,000	29,435

	Yea	Nay
To loan state funds to aid the construction of railroads	7½ 6,950 17,925	19 6,400 25,800
To improve the harbor of Mobile	13 12,000 26,400	15 4,000 17,625
To allow residents near any church or school to prohibit by vote the sale of liquor	9 5,000 19,000	18½ 10,000 29,545
To establish an insane asylum	26 15,000 30,000	5 3,000 10,000
To equip the militia for the threatening sectional conflict	27 15,000 32,500	5 3,000 12,000
To establish a military system at the University of Alabama, and to fund it	16 15,000 30,000	9 3,000 10,000
To loan state funds to aid two railroads	23 15,000 30,000	12 4,500 15,000
To prohibit the immigration of free Negroes into Alabama	7½ 4,000 11,179	17 12,000 30,000
To postpone (and thus kill) a bill to prohibit the circulation of out-of-state bank bills of less than five dollars	9½ 3,975 15,000	23 15,000 30,125
To postpone (and thus kill) a bill to acquire a governor's mansion	13 5,500 16.850	14 12,000 30,000
To table a bill to regulate the conduct of elections	9 4,500 15,925	25 12,000 22,500

Ratio of Legislative Roll Calls to Votes Indicating Economic Divisions

	A *Total Important Roll Calls**	B *Total Roll Calls Analyzed†*	C *Total Votes Indicating Economic Divisions*	D *Ratio of C to B*
SESSION				
1829	38	12	4	33.3%
1830	28	15	7	46.7
1831	29	15	11	73.3
Totals	95	42	22	52.4%
1839	37	15	7	46.7%
1840	30	10	4	40.0
1841	36	10	8	80.0
Totals	103	35	19	54.3%
1849	80	29	10	34.5%
1859	53	22	16	72.7%

* Excludes procedural votes, elections to local or state office, votes on local or trivial bills, and votes precedent to a final vote.

† Excludes, among others, roll calls in which the result was not sufficiently equiponderant to make the median a useful summary statistic.

Bibliographical Note

A VOLUMINOUS catalog of the works dealing with the Jacksonian movement and with the origins of the Civil War—the two general areas to which the present study is related—would be a tedious exercise and, on the whole, not a very useful one. An interesting study of the historiography of the Civil War is Thomas J. Pressly, *Americans Interpret Their Civil War* (Princeton: Princeton University Press, 1954). A thorough bibliography, which includes more recent investigations, is appended to James G. Randall and David Donald, *The Civil War and Reconstruction* (2nd ed.; Lexington, Massachusetts: D. C. Heath and Co., 1969). Alfred A. Cave, *Jacksonian Democracy and the Historians* (Gainesville: University of Florida Press, 1964), is a full-scale treatment of the historiography of the earlier decades. Edward Pessen, *Jacksonian America: Society, Personality, and Politics* (Homewood, Illinois: Dorsey Press, 1969), includes a most useful bibliography. For studies dealing more specifically with the South, uniformly serviceable bibliographies are contained in Thomas P. Abernethy, *The South in the New Nation, 1789–1819* (Baton Rouge: Louisiana State University Press, 1961), Charles S. Sydnor, *The Development of Southern Sectionalism, 1819–1848,* (Baton Rouge: Louisiana State University Press, 1948), and Avery O. Craven, *The Growth of Southern Nationalism, 1848–1861* (Baton Rouge: Louisiana State University Press, 1953), Vols. IV, V, and VI, respectively, of Wendell Holmes Stephenson and E. Merton Coulter, eds., *A History of the South* (10 vols.; Baton Rouge: Louisiana State University Press, 1948—).

One instructive way to approach the Jacksonian South is through biographies of southern politicians. Charles M. Wiltse, *John C. Calhoun* (3 vols.; Indianapolis: Bobbs-Merrill Co., 1944, 1949, 1951), studies a figure whose importance has often been overestimated. Charles G. Sellers, *James K. Polk* (2 vols. to date; Princeton: Princeton University Press, 1957, 1966), studies a somewhat more typical leader. But designating any politician as typical of the region that produced Andrew Jackson and Henry Clay, Sam Houston and John Tyler, Benjamin F. Perry and Albert Gallatin Brown, Judah P. Benjamin and Alexander H. Stephens, Andrew Johnson and Jefferson Davis, is of course an exercise in absurdity. Provocative biographies of all ten of these gentlemen—and of scores of other equally significant and equally diverse characters—are available. Clement Eaton, *The Mind of the Old South* (Rev. ed.; Baton Rouge: Louisiana State University Press, 1967), is at least successful in communicating a sense of the complexity of the civilization.

Few scholars, if pressed, would question the assertion that an essential element of the Jacksonian movement—and of its Whig foil—was southern. Nevertheless, one would hardly gather this truth from most standard works. In addition to Pessen's, important statements include Arthur M. Schlesinger, Jr., *The Age of Jackson* (Boston: Little, Brown and Co., 1945); Lee Benson, *The Concept of Jacksonian Democracy: New York as a Test Case* (Princeton: Princeton University Press, 1961); Marvin Meyers, *The Jacksonian Persuasion: Politics and Belief* (Stanford: Stanford University Press, 1957), a particularly salutary work; John William Ward, *Andrew Jackson, Symbol for an Age* (New York: Oxford University Press, 1955); Leonard D. White, *The Jacksonians: A Study of Administrative History, 1829–1861* (New York: Macmillan, 1954); Joseph Dorfman, *The Economic Mind in American Civilization, 1606–1865* (New York: Viking Press, 1946), Vol. II; and Richard Hofstadter, *The American Political Tradition and the Men Who Made It* (New York: Alfred A. Knopf, 1948), Chap. 3. Most of these works—and the list could be multiplied to many titles—tend at least by implication to deny the South any real role of influence in the movement. Joseph L. Blau, ed., *Social Theories of Jacksonian Democracy: Representative Writings of the Period 1825–1850* (Indianapolis: Bobbs-Merrill Co., 1954), is a useful collection of sources which manages to incorporate the sentiments of precisely two southerners— President Andrew Jackson and Vice-President Richard M. Johnson.

Thomas P. Abernethy, *From Frontier to Plantation in Tennessee: A Study in Frontier Democracy* (Chapel Hill: University of North Carolina Press, 1932), and his "Andrew Jackson and the Rise of Southwestern Democracy," *American Historical Review*, XXXIII (October, 1927), 64–77, imply a disjunction between Democratic theory and the practice of southern Jacksonians. Bray Hammond, *Banks and Politics in America from the Revolution to the Civil War* (Princeton: Princeton University Press, 1957), is sure-footed amidst technicalities but lacks genuine empathy for the economic ideologies of the age. Hammond's emphasis upon commercial rivalries in the Northeast makes both sides in the Bank War seem to be eager capitalists. But James Roger Sharp, *The Jacksonians Versus the Banks: Politics in the States after the Panic of 1837* (New York: Columbia University Press, 1970), shows that Democrats in other sections were a great deal more radical. Fletcher M. Green, *Constitutional Development in the South Atlantic States, 1776–1860: A Study in the Evolution of Democracy* (Chapel Hill: University of North Carolina Press, 1930), and his "Democracy in the Old South," *Journal of*

Southern History, XII (February, 1946), 3–23, and Chilton Williamson, *American Suffrage from Property to Democracy, 1760–1860* (Princeton: Princeton University Press, 1960), tend to confuse statute with practice. Richard McCormick, *The Second American Party System: Party Formation in the Jacksonian Era* (Chapel Hill: University of North Carolina Press, 1966), tends to confuse formal institutions with substance. Edwin A. Miles, "The Jacksonian Era," in Arthur S. Link and Rembert W. Patrick, eds., *Writing Southern History: Essays in Historiography in Honor of Fletcher M. Green* (Baton Rouge: Louisiana State University Press, 1965), pp.125–46, is a thorough and informative survey of the various southern state studies of the Democratic and the Whig parties. Richard H. Brown, in "The Missouri Crisis, Slavery and the Politics of Jacksonianism," *South Atlantic Quarterly,* LXV (Winter, 1966), 55–72, emphasizes the South's role in the Democratic party, but seems to feel that in doing so he is somehow convicting the Jacksonians of a guilt by association.

Better than any of the modern works is Alexis de Tocqueville, *Democracy in America* (2 vols.; New York: Schocken Books, 1961; originally published in 1835, 1840). It should be read in conjunction with his *Journey to America,* trans. George Lawrence, ed. J. P. Mayer (Garden City, New York: Doubleday, 1971), a translation of the young tourist's notebooks; and with George Wilson Pierson, *Tocqueville and Beaumont in America* (New York: Oxford University Press, 1938).

Studies of the Whiggery are a bit less chary than are those of the Democracy of acknowledging southern participation—perhaps because in the end the Whigs, unlike the Democrats, freed themselves from the entangling alliance. The standard general works, both emphasizing southern Whiggery's ostensible elitism, are E. Malcolm Carroll, *Origins of the Whig Party* (Durham: Duke University Press, 1925), and Arthur C. Cole, *The Whig Party in the South* (Washington: Reprint of the Prize Essays of the American Historical Association for 1912, 1913). On the party's ideology, an interesting essay in Glyndon Van Deusen, "Some Aspects of Whig Thought and Theory in the Jacksonian Period," *American Historical Review,* LXIII (January, 1958), 305–322. A perceptive examination of the social foundations of the party in the South is Charles G. Sellers, "Who Were the Southern Whigs?" *American Historical Review,* LIX (January, 1954), 335–46. And a number of the state studies mentioned in the Miles article cited above are instructive. Nevertheless, the general difficulty which historians have had in integrating the South into the politics of the period carries over to the minority party.

I am inclined to the belief that this difficulty stems from a failure to appreciate the real demands of the southern political structure. A particularly bald example of the phenomenon is Stanley M. Elkins and Eric McKitrick, "A Meaning for Turner's Frontier," *Political Science Quarterly,* LXIX (September, December, 1954), 321–53, 565–602, which offers a convincing explanation for the origins of a political style which, however, may never have existed. Sydnor's *Southern Sectionalism*, cited above, and Ulrich B. Phillips, *American Negro Slavery: A Survey of the Supply, Employment and Control of Negro Labor as Determined by the Plantation Regime* (Baton Rouge: Louisiana State University Press, 1966; originally published in 1918), and his *Life and Labor in the Old South* (Boston: Little, Brown and Co., 1929), also attribute much to this supposed style. The most uncompromising recent statement of its implications, however, is Eugene D. Genovese, *The Political Economy of Slavery: Studies in the Economy and Society of the Slave South* (New York: Pantheon Books, 1965), and his *The World the Slaveholders Made: Two Essays in Interpretation* (New York: Pantheon Books, 1969). An instructive counterpoint on this theme may be formed by contrasting Charles S. Sydnor, *A Gentleman of the Old Natchez Region: Benjamin L. C. Wailes* (Durham: Duke University Press, 1938), with Mack B. Swearingen, *The Early Life of George Poindexter: A Story of the First Southwest* (Chicago: University of Chicago, 1934).

Efforts to recapture the reality of southern politics, therefore, must turn on efforts to recapture the reality of southern society. Avery O. Craven, in his *Southern Nationalism*, cited above, and in *The Coming of the Civil War* (New York: Charles Scribner's Sons, 1942), made a few gentle efforts along this line (e.g., *Nationalism*, 157–63). Frank L. Owsley, *Plain Folk of the Old South* (Baton Rouge: Louisiana State University Press, 1949), launched a frontal attack on earlier interpretations, but Fabien Linden demonstrated that Owsley's statistics were by no means finely honed, in "Economic Democracy in the Slave South," *Journal of Negro History*, XXXI (April, 1946), 140–89. David Donald, "Died of Democracy," in David Donald, ed., *Why the North Won the Civil War* (Baton Rouge: Louisiana State University Press, 1960), 79–90, is concerned with inflexible libertarianism in the Confederacy, particularly in the southern armies; and his "An Excess of Democracy: The American Civil War and the Social Process," included in his *Lincoln Reconsidered: Essays on the Civil War Era* (rev. ed.; New York: Vintage Books, 1961), 209–235, attempts to emphasize the common devotion to individualism of all the republic's regions in the antebellum years. But both imply a portrait of the late Jacksonian South which is in many respects congruent with my own notions. William R. Taylor, *Cavalier and Yankee: The Old South and the American National Character* (New York: George Braziller, Inc., 1961), explores the social origins of the myth of the South, but makes only a limited attempt to establish that the perceptions with which it deals were inaccurate. Thomas P. Govan, "Was the Old South Different?" *Journal of Southern History*, XXI (November, 1955), 447–55, and a most suggestive new study, Otto H. Olsen, "Historians and the Extent of Slave Ownership in the Southern United States," *Civil War History*, XVIII (June, 1972), 101–116, both deal with the problem more directly. Edmund Wilson, *Patriotic*

Gore: Studies in the Literature of the American Civil War (New York: Oxford University Press, 1962), is an informative effort. C. Vann Woodward, *Tom Watson, Agrarian Rebel* (New York: Macmillan, 1938), is an exploration of the relation between antebellum and postbellum political leadership, whose full implications for the antebellum period have been too often ignored.

The debate between these alternative general lines of interpretation has, over the decades, tended to become increasingly barren—primarily, I think, because the participants have so seldom distinguished between social structure and social ideology. Just as the Revolutionary generation in the South fervently preached a Lockean gospel to a Burkean world, so their grandsons proclaimed Jacksonian dogma in the midst of plantations. The two resultant rebellions were not so unlike as some have supposed. A recent essay by Gavin Wright, "'Economic Democracy' and the Concentration of Agricultural Wealth in the Cotton South, 1850–1860," *Agricultural History*, XLIV (January, 1970), 63–93, undertakes to demonstrate that the distribution of wealth was more sharply skewed in the rural Southeast than in the rural Ohio Valley states. Of course, for the antebellum southerner, the crucial comparison would have been between the rural Southeast and the urban Northeast; and Professor Wright hints that, as southerners believed, the advantage in that comparison would lie with the former section. But for the purposes of the present study the entire exercise is really beside the point. Whatever the structure of wealth distribution in the society, the electorate and the government it selected responded, in both sentiment and action, primarily to the social ideology. The definition of southern reality, then, must begin with an understanding of the southern perception of reality. Such an understanding acts to dissolve the sterility of earlier debates as to the character of the region: whether agrarian democracy or planter-dominated hierarchy. And as a result, the true relation of southern politicians to the political issues which divided Jacksonian America may begin to emerge. Somewhat similar comments have quite recently been offered by George M. Frederickson, in his review article "Two Southern Historians [Fletcher M. Green and David M. Potter]," *American Historical Review*, LXXV (June, 1970), 1387–92, and his *The Black Image in the White Mind: The Debate on Afro-American Character and Destiny, 1817–1914* (New York: Harper and Row, 1971).

I may add that, as aids to a correct understanding of the southern political self-image, historians have too much neglected the southern humorists, particularly Augustus B. Longstreet, *Georgia Scenes, Characters, Incidents, Etc., In the First Half Century of the Republic, by a Native Georgian* (New York: Sagamore Press, 1957; originally published in 1835); Johnson J. Hooper, *Adventures of Captain Simon Suggs, Late of the Tallapoosa Volunteers* (Chapel Hill: University of North Carolina Press, 1969; originally published in 1845), and Joseph Glover Baldwin, *The Flush Times of Alabama and Mississippi: A Series of Sketches* (Athens: University of Georgia Press, 1966; originally published in 1853). The laughter through tears which their world wrenched from each of these writers is an enlightening insight into the attitudes which the social elite actually held towards the society which some claim they controlled. Also instructive in this regard is Daniel R. Hundley, *Social Relations in Our Southern States* (New York: H. B. Price, 1860).

These comments will, no doubt, make clear why I can regard so few accounts of the sectional crisis as satisfactory. Roy Franklin Nichols, *The Disruption of American Democracy* (New York: Macmillan, 1948), properly places the events in a political setting. David M. Potter, *Lincoln and His Party in the Secession Crisis* (New Haven: Yale University Press, 1942), tends to obscure the fact that what was moderation in one region was often extremism in another; every Alabamian would have dismissed as utterly absurd the notion that Lincoln was a unionist. In an informative new work, *Free Soil, Free Labor, Free Men: The Ideology of the Republican Party Before the Civil War* (New York: Oxford University Press, 1970), Eric Foner describes an ideology which is very nearly a mirror image of southern views at the time. Ollinger Crenshaw, *The Slave States in the Presidential Election of 1860* (Baltimore: Johns Hopkins Press, 1945), deals adequately with its subject. And Ralph A. Wooster, *The Secession Conventions of the South* (Princeton: Princeton University Press, 1962), adds some new statistical information, though without deducing any special point from the figures. Jesse T. Carpenter, *The South As a Conscious Minority, 1789–1861: A Study in Political Thought* (New York: New York University Press, 1930), remains a challenging study. And of course Allan Nevins, *The Ordeal of the Union* (8 vols., New York: Charles Scribner's Sons, 1947, 1950, 1959, 1960, 1971), is an awe-inspiring achievement. Nevertheless, I cannot refrain from concluding these citations with the general thought that, as to this subject, *plus ultra*.

INDEX